Armies of Sand

KENNETH M.
POLLACK

Armies of Sand

The Past, Present, and Future

of Arab Military Effectiveness

OXFORD
UNIVERSITY PRESS

OXFORD
UNIVERSITY PRESS

Oxford University Press is a department of the University of Oxford. It furthers the University's objective of excellence in research, scholarship, and education by publishing worldwide. Oxford is a registered trade mark of Oxford University Press in the UK and certain other countries.

Published in the United States of America by Oxford University Press
198 Madison Avenue, New York, NY 10016, United States of America.

First issued as an Oxford University Press paperback, 2020

Library of Congress Cataloging-in-Publication Data
Names: Pollack, Kenneth M. (Kenneth Michael), 1966– author.
Title: Armies of sand : the past, present, and future of Arab
military effectiveness / Kenneth M. Pollack.
Description: New York, NY, United States of America :
Oxford University Press, 2019. | Includes bibliographical references.
Identifiers: LCCN 2018012932 | ISBN 9780190906962 (hard cover) |
ISBN 9780197524640 (paperback) | ISBN 9780190906986 (epub)
Subjects: LCSH: Arab countries—Armed Forces—History. |
Military art and science—Arab countries—History. |
Military art and science—Soviet Union—History. |
Arab countries—Military policy. | Economic development—Arab countries.
Classification: LCC UA854.P654 2019 | DDC 355.00917/492709045—dc23
LC record available at https://lccn.loc.gov/2018012932

9 8 7 6 5 4 3 2 1

Printed by Sheridan in the United States of America

For my remarkable professors,
Paul Bracken, Paul Kennedy, and the late Brad Westerfield

In gratitude for their wisdom and guidance

CONTENTS

WHAT'S WRONG WITH the Arab armies? Why do they lose so many wars that by all rights they should win? And why is it that when they do win, their victories tend to be so modest, if not outright pyrrhic? Why have the Arabs lost to Israel time and again? Why did it take Iraq eight long years to defeat an Iran wracked by revolution and cut off from the rest of the world? Why was that same Iraqi army then crushed effortlessly by the US-led Coalition in the Persian Gulf War of 1991? How on earth did the Libyans manage to lose to Chad in 1987? Chad! And the Libyans weren't just beaten, they were routed. Why did the Iraqi army collapse under ISIS attack in 2014? And why was it so hard for Iraq to drive ISIS out of their country despite massive American air power and the assistance of 62 other countries?

Those are the questions at the heart of this book.

It's a critical issue for the Middle East and for the United States. The puzzling weakness of the Arab armed forces has driven the military balance in the Middle East since the Second World War. Every other aspect of the international relations of the region rests on this balance. The smart Arab leaders learned over time that military solutions just weren't a viable option for them in their dealings with other countries. Conventional force was effectively removed from their foreign policy toolkits.

In some ways, that has been good for the United States. It has meant that the existence of Israel—our principal ally in the Middle East since the early 1970s—has been assured. The Arabs just don't have a realistic military option against the Jewish state. It also allowed us to win a spectacular and virtually bloodless victory over Saddam Husayn in the Persian Gulf War and to prevent many other regional wars with only a small military presence.

But it has been problematic in other ways. Saddam is only one example of an Arab leader who did not understand the weakness of his armies and so embarked on wars that he had no business fighting. That may be fine when it is one of our enemies. The problem is when it is one of our allies, like the Saudis, who in 2015 plunged into the Yemeni Civil War in a way they never should have because they lacked the capacity to win it quickly or decisively.

Since the late 1970s, the United States has been trying to build up various Arab armies because the stronger they are, the more likely they can deter threats against themselves, and the less likely it is that the United States would have to fight on their behalf. So we have been trying to strengthen the Egyptian, Jordanian, Moroccan, Saudi, Emirati, Qatari, Bahraini, Kuwaiti, Omani, and Iraqi armed forces. Yet, as the Saudi debacle in Yemen in 2015 and the collapse of the Iraqi security forces under ISIS attack in 2014 have demonstrated, their weaknesses have typically defied our efforts to strengthen them. And when they fail, we find ourselves forced to intervene to shore them up or fight their wars for them.

Of course, there are some Arab militaries that have demonstrated a better ability to fight. The problem is that today these are the biggest troublemakers in the region. Hizballah, ISIS, al-Qa'ida, Jabhat Fatah ash-Sham (the former Nusra Front), and a variety of other vicious, Islamist militias—both Shi'a and Sunni—have proven more able in battle than most of the armed forces of the Arab states. That too is a big problem for the United States since all of these groups see the United States as one of their primary enemies and all of them are actively fighting American allies. Understanding why these non-state militaries have proven more effective than the state armies we have been trying so hard to improve is more than just an intriguing mystery, it is a vital national interest.

My hope is that this book will help answer all of these questions. More than that, I hope that it will provide some sense of the changes going on in the Middle East, because they are profound and they could transform the long-standing balance of power over the next several decades.

Finally, I hope that this book will shed more light on the broader question of how different societies generate military power and why some countries are so much more powerful than others, often in ways that seem to defy simple tallies of population and resources. The history of the world has been shaped by military outcomes that defied predictions based on simple material assumptions about what constituted military strength. The reality is that wars are far more often decided by the abilities of the combatants and that, in turn, is typically an outgrowth of the societies themselves. So to really understand the sources of military power, we often need to understand the societal factors that drive them. Doing so for the Arabs during the modern era is the goal of this book.

ACKNOWLEDGMENTS

I N MANY WAYS I have been writing this book for nearly 30 years. When I was a young military analyst at CIA, right after I had written the first draft of the post-mortem on the Iraqi armed forces during the Persian Gulf War, I had to clear on a report written by one of my colleagues on the Syrian military. In reading through it, I was struck by how the Syrians had all of the same problems with military effectiveness that had hobbled the Iraqis during the Iran-Iraq and Gulf wars. I began to wonder why that was. Because of their similarly dictatorial systems? Because they were both Arab countries? Because they had some degree of Soviet tutoring (although the Iraqis had *far* less than the Syrians)? Ever since, throughout my career, I kept pursuing the answer to that question. On all of my many trips to the Middle East and especially when talking to American, British, Australian, French, German, and other military personnel who were training or fighting alongside Arab armed forces, I kept gathering data, even as I shared my preliminary findings and insights with them in return for the stories of their experiences. This book is the culmination of that long journey.

A work of such time and effort could only have come about with the help of many people. I want to begin by thanking my friends Daniel Byman, Brent Sterling, and Steven Ward. They get pride of place not only for providing me with a king's ransom of thoughtful commentary, counsel, and insight, but for doing so on multiple drafts over many years. Even a book of this length could barely encompass all of their terrific suggestions and sage warnings. Of equal importance, all of them provided much-needed encouragement at moments when the weight of this effort bore me down. Like all lives, mine has had its ups and downs, but their friendship has been a constant joy throughout.

I also need to single out Barry Posen and Stephen Van Evera for their roles. The idea for this book may have come at CIA, but it did not take material form until my graduate work at MIT. The first draft of this book was my doctoral thesis, and any value that it may have had was largely due to the labors of Barry and Steve, who were, respectively, the chairman and first member of my thesis committee. Barry Posen and Stephen Van Evera are two of the finest minds and finest men I know. Their teaching was invaluable. Their standards of scholarship daunting. And their criticisms devastating. It is hard for me to convey how important their guidance was in the shaping of this book, except to say that if you learn anything from it, it is because of the two of them.

Next comes the hardest paragraph of all to write. This is the paragraph where I need to thank everyone else who read part or all of one of my drafts and provided me feedback, comments, and criticism. It is hard because each of these people gave so generously of their scant time and vast experience that they each deserve many words of praise and gratitude for their contributions. However, there are so many of them that to do justice to each would require a second volume. I hope that you—and they—understand how important their help was to me in the completion of this book. So let me just say that during the many iterations of this project I had the great good fortune to be able to call on some of the best minds in many fields to help me: Andrew Bacevich, Ali Banuazizi, Amatzia Baram, Joe Bernard, Stephen Biddle, Joe Cutler, Tom Donnelly, Michael Eisenstadt, Eugene Gholz, Shadi Hamid, John Lynn, Hank Malcom, Ian Merritt, Ben Miller, Stephanie Neuman, Bruce Pease, Ed Pendleton, Charles Perkins, Daryl Press, Bruce Riedel, Bilal Saab, John Spacapan, Lt. General Bernard Trainor, and the late Myron Wiener. I would also like to thank two anonymous reviewers for Oxford University Press, who likewise provided a wealth of smart comments that greatly improved this work.

I was also fortunate to have had the help of an amazing cabal of research assistants and interns, many of whom have gone on to remarkable careers of their own—doubtless a function of their assistance with this project. Kevin Ball, Edward Bottomley, Ayatalla El Khatib, Eytan Fisch, Jonathan Lincoln, Isabelle Mahnke, Ian Merritt, Dafna Hochman Rand, Lauren Rossman, John Spacapan, and Jennifer Williams were all sensational. They deserve only praise for their roles in the crafting of this book. I know exactly why each of them is a star.

I spent 15 of the years I was working on this book at the Brookings Institution. I want to thank Strobe Talbott, Jim Steinberg, Carlos Pascual, Bruce Jones, and Martin Indyk, my bosses during that time. I also want to thank Laura Mooney and Sarah Chilton of the Brookings library. Librarians are too often taken for granted, especially in an age where so much is now available at the press of a button. But Laura and Sarah are both great research librarians, keepers of great knowledge, an art that may soon be lost. They still practice that art with skill, and they were immensely helpful to me and my platoon of researchers.

In 2017, I moved to the American Enterprise Institute. A journey of about 100 feet, but much farther intellectually. It was an ideal move, and I want to thank Arthur Brooks, David Gerson, and Danielle Pletka for welcoming me and running such a superb organization. As every author knows, the hardest part of any book is the endgame. I could not have asked for a better place or better people to work with than AEI to get this book across the finish line.

The writing of this book was supported by a generous grant from the Smith Richardson Foundation. It was also supported by the friendship, encouragement, and wisdom of Allan Song, Marin Strmecki, and Nadia Schadlow. They have my deepest gratitude for all of it.

Over the years, I may have conducted as many as a thousand interviews for this book, formal and informal. Only a handful of those interviewed agreed to allow me to quote them on the record. Those who did have been quoted by name in the text or the notes. Unfortunately, however, the vast majority agreed to do so only on condition of anonymity because they were serving US, Israeli, European, Australian, German, Egyptian, Jordanian, Iraqi, Saudi, Emirati, Bahraini, and Turkish military officers or intelligence analysts whose governments would not have approved of their making statements on the record. In other cases they were retired Iraqi, Egyptian, or Jordanian military officers who nevertheless felt it impolitic to have themselves quoted. All those who consented to be interviewed have my deepest thanks. They made this book a far richer work than it otherwise might have been.

David McBride at Oxford has been an absolute pleasure to work with as my editor on this book. He has a light, deft touch that left the book very much in my voice, but pointed out any number of critical course corrections. He has also guided the book adroitly through the labyrinth of academic publishing. I am thrilled with Caroline McDonnell's cover design and she also has my thanks. I think you will agree with me that the maps in this book were a key ingredient, and George Chakvetadze has my thanks and admiration for their accuracy, clarity, and elegance. Brooke Smith was a careful, meticulous copy-editor who saved this book from death by a thousand typos. Liz Davey, the production manager; Erin Meehan, the marketer; and Sarah Russo, the head of publicity for OUP, were all great and made the entire process painless and easy—which as other authors know, is about the highest praise I can offer for the laborious process of publishing and selling a book. Finally, Claire Sibley and Emily Mackenzie were just outstanding at making all of the trains run on time and helping me to get done everything that Oxford needed from me.

A considerable amount of the historical material in this book, particularly in the Introduction and Chapters 3, 6, 7, 11, 12, and 22 are adapted from *Arabs at War: Military Effectiveness, 1948–1991* by Kenneth M. Pollack by permission of the University of Nebraska Press. Copyright 2002 by the University of Nebraska Press.

An early manuscript version of this work was reviewed by both the Central Intelligence Agency and the Defense Intelligence Agency prior to publication to ensure that it contained no classified material. Neither agency altered the text in any way. Nothing in its contents should be seen as asserting or implying US government authentication of my factual points or endorsement of my opinions. Moreover, I would like to thank Ben Bonk, Bruce Pease, Jack Duggan, Winston Wiley, and Phil Ferguson for helping to guide it through the laborious prepublication review process with the minimum of pain.

Finally, I cannot end without thanking the people who matter to me most. My wife, Andrea, my son, Aidan, and my parents, Ann and Peter. They stuck with me through all of this, even if Aidan came a bit late to the party. They have my most profound thanks for putting up with the long hours researching and writing, the countless trips to the Middle East, and the overflowing shelves of books on a hundred wars and a dozen academic disciplines. More than that, they have my unfailing love.

Armies of Sand

The Six-Day War and the Mystery
of Arab Military Ineffectiveness

I N JUNE OF 1967, most of the world thought Israel was a goner. That included most of the population of the State of Israel itself. Another Arab-
Israeli war was brewing, and this time it looked like the Jewish state was
finished. The Arab governments, their military commands, and their people
were ecstatic, anticipating the destruction of Israel.[1] Many Israelis feared another Holocaust. The government braced itself to suffer terrible casualties and
ordered 10,000 coffins prepared for the dead.[2] Israel's prime minister, Levi
Eshkol, told a reporter that in the event of war, he feared that Israeli "Blood
would run like water."[3]

The Arab coalition threatening Israel had every material advantage.
Altogether, the main Arab combatants—Egypt, Jordan, and Syria—would
deploy roughly 275,000 men against Israel with about 1,800 tanks, 2,000
armored personnel carriers (APCs), and 1,700 artillery pieces. For its part, the
Israel Defense Forces (IDF) would field about 130,000 troops with roughly
1,000 tanks, 450 APCs, and maybe 500 artillery pieces. In the air, the Israeli
Air Force (IAF) had 207 combat aircraft, against 716 Egyptian, Jordanian,
Syrian, and Iraqi warplanes.[4]

A range of other factors also seemed to be on the side of the Arabs. In
every category of weaponry, Arab equipment was at least as good as Israel's if
not better. For instance, although the IAF had 72 advanced Mirage IIIs, the
rest of its planes were older French models while the Arab air forces boasted

305 Soviet MiG-21s and British Hawker Hunters, both of which were rough equivalents of the Mirage. Israel would be forced to fight on three fronts. At least a third of the Egyptian soldiers deployed to Sinai for the war were veterans of Cairo's military campaigns in Yemen. To top it all off, all of the Arab armies would start the war dug-in behind heavily fortified positions in difficult terrain. Israel's defeat and then destruction seemed like a foregone conclusion based on these "objective" measures.

But there were deeper truths known to a small number of people, particularly the leadership of Israel's armed forces. They knew that Israeli intelligence had penetrated to the highest echelons of the Arab militaries, and this access had brought them a wealth of information. From this, Israel had developed a remarkable profile of the Arab armed forces, their capabilities, deployment, operating procedures, and leadership. The IDF high command also knew that their own forces had become highly proficient in modern mechanized and air warfare, but that Arab doctrine was random and honored more in the breach than the observance. Moreover, training in the Arab armies was pathetic and their leadership poor. Israel's generals had also used their intelligence advantage to devise a brilliant war plan that they expected would allow the Jewish state not just to survive, but to win.[5]

The Israeli Air Strikes

In the early hours of June 5, 1967, the IAF put its well-rehearsed plans into motion, launching a massive air strike that caught the Egyptians by surprise and crippled the Egyptian Air Force (EAF).[6] For three hours, every 10 minutes, 10 flights of four Israeli aircraft attacked airfields and other installations throughout Egypt. During the course of the morning, the Israelis struck 18 of Egypt's airbases, cratering runways, blowing up aircraft, and destroying support facilities. The EAF lost 298 of its 420 combat aircraft, and at least 100 of its 350 combat pilots.[7]

As if that weren't bad enough, Cairo's air force commanders tried to cover up the disaster. These were all highly political officers, some of them jumped up from low ranks to the highest echelons because they had participated in the Free Officer's coup of 1952 that brought Gamal 'Abd al-Nasser to power. They were not about to admit to anyone, even Nasser, that the mighty air force they had built had been lost in a single morning. So they lied, telling Nasser that they had won a great victory: They had destroyed three-quarters of the Israeli air force and Egyptian planes were now pounding Israel's airbases.[8]

When the Syrians heard of the incredible victory the EAF had won, they wanted in on the action. Damascus launched a handful of its own aircraft to join the fray. The Syrian planes arrived over Israel while the IAF was finishing off the Egyptians and so faced no opposition. Yet there was no particular purpose or strategy to their attacks. In the words of a former IAF officer, "they sent a duo here and a trio there in a disorganized fashion, somewhat hysterically and with no real preparation."[9] They did no damage to any military targets, but provoked the IAF to retaliate by striking Syrian airbases as they had the Egyptians. Syrian aircraft were lined up neatly on the tarmac of each airfield, making them easy prey for the Israelis, who destroyed about half the Syrian Air Force including all but four of its MiG-21s. The Syrians also lost four MiG-17s in air-to-air combat with the Israelis, while the IAF lost only one older Mystere.

Israel didn't want to go to war with Jordan in 1967, and tried as late as the morning of June 5th to convince King Hussein to remain on the sidelines. However, the king had reluctantly agreed to support Nasser and so rejected the Israeli entreaties. Like the Syrians, upon hearing the Egyptian reports that the IAF had been annihilated, Amman dispatched its own small air force to attack Israel. They too did poorly, causing only light damage. Nevertheless, this raid, coupled with Jordanian shelling of Israeli cities and a ground attack on Israeli positions in Jerusalem, was enough to convince the Israeli government that Jordan would not sit this war out. At about 1300 hours, while the Jordanian planes were being refueled and rearmed for their next mission, eight Israeli planes struck, destroying 16 of Jordan's 22 Hawker Hunters and badly damaging another four. Another two Hunters were late returning from Israel and were shot down by Israeli Mirages as they came in to land.

The final act of the day for the Israeli Air Force was dealing with the Iraqis. At about 1400 hours, two Iraqi Tu-16 bombers tried to bomb Israel, but could not locate either Ramat David airbase or the city of Tel Aviv, and so dropped their ordnance on Israeli farmland. An hour later, Israel responded. Eight planes flew 500 miles across the Syrian desert and attacked Iraq's al-Walid (H-3) airbase near ar-Rutbah, the westernmost Iraqi airfield. In this raid, and a subsequent strike on June 6, the Israelis destroyed 10 Iraqi aircraft on the ground. In addition, on both days, Iraqi fighters rose to meet the attackers, allowing the IAF to shoot down 21 Iraqi aircraft while losing only 3 of their own.

The Egyptian Front

The terrain of Sinai makes east-west movement difficult, effectively channeling an attacking army into three or four well-known corridors. The Egyptians deployed all seven of their divisions and another eight independent brigades along these routes in a Soviet-style defense-in-depth to block an Israeli offensive. Three infantry divisions and a mechanized division—reinforced by three attached armored brigades and extra artillery—held the forward line of fortifications. Farther west, Cairo deployed its operational reserves, two armored divisions, and a motorized infantry division in position to reinforce the forward infantry divisions or counterattack the main Israeli penetration when it was identified.[10]

On June 5, while the Israeli Air Force was pounding Egypt's airbases, the Israeli army hit the Egyptian forces in Sinai with 11 brigades: six armored, one infantry, one mechanized infantry, and three paratroop. Most of these were grouped into three divisional task forces, or *ugdot* (sing. *ugdah*) in Hebrew. Beginning at 0800 hours, the three Israeli *ugdot* smashed through the first line of Egyptian infantry divisions in their fortified positions. Farthest north, an *ugdah* under Brigadier Israel Tal drove straight into the formidable Egyptian defenses at Khan Yunis and Rafah, punching through the Egyptian lines in a few hours. While its paratrooper brigade turned north to clear the Gaza strip, its two armored brigades turned west and fought their way through the narrow and heavily defended Jiradi defile. The Egyptians resisted fiercely but not effectively, and the Israelis won quickly and with relatively minor losses. By the end of the first day, Tal's vanguard had broken through and was racing westward toward the Canal.

In central Sinai, another *ugdah* under Brigadier Ariel Sharon moved forward into attack positions during the day on June 5th, and that night executed a complex series of enveloping maneuvers that overcame Egypt's formidable, Soviet-devised defenses at Abu Ageilah and Umm Qatef. Sharon's infantry rolled up the Egyptian trench lines from the flank, his paratroopers made a heliborne descent on the Egyptian artillery batteries, and one of his tank battalions outflanked the entire Egyptian position and smashed both an Egyptian armored battalion and an armored brigade in a series of tank battles during the night. Meanwhile, the lead armored brigade of Brigadier Avraham Yoffe's *ugdah* had pushed through the sand dunes between Rafah and Abu Ageilah, overwhelmed the Egyptian defenses at B'ir Lafhan, and during the night of June 5/6 had taken position where it could block an Egyptian move into the flank of either Tal's *ugdah* to the north or Sharon's to the south.

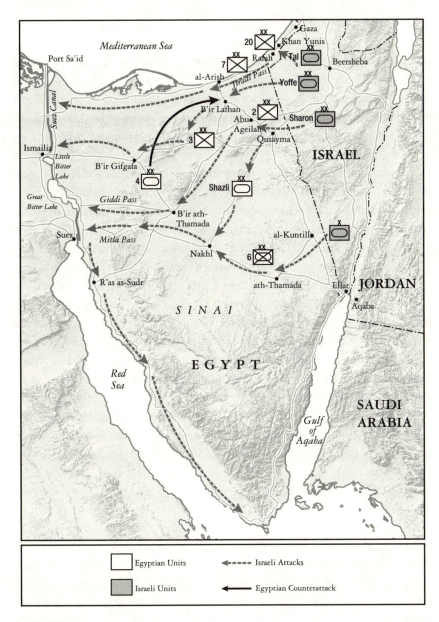

Mediterranean Sea

Port Sa'id

Gaza
Khan Yunis
20
Raḥfl
7
al-Arish
Jiradi Pass
Beersheba
Tal
Yoffe
B'ir Lafhan
2
Abu
Ageilah
Sharon
3
Qusayma
ISRAEL
Suez Canal
Ismailia
Little
Bitter
Lake
B'ir Gigafa
4
Shazli
Great
Bitter
Lake
Giddi Pass
B'ir ath-
Thamada
Mitla Pass
al-Kuntilla
Suez
Nakhl
6
R'as as-Sudr
ath-Thamada
Ellat
JORDAN
Aqaba
S I N A I
E G Y P T
Red
Sea
SAUDI
ARABIA
Gulf
of
Aqaba

☐ Egyptian Units	◄-----	Israeli Attacks
▦ Israeli Units	◄———	Egyptian Counterattack

MAP 1 The Sinai Front in the Six-Day War

Thus, by the end of the first day of the war, and with minimal direct assistance from the Israeli air force, Israel's ground forces had busted through the toughest part of the Egyptian defenses. In every case, they did so remarkably easily, taking only a few hours and suffering very modest casualties compared to what comparable armies had suffered assaulting similar defenses in World War II and Korea. Part of that can be attributed to Israeli tactical skill, which was superlative. However, at least an equal part stemmed from Egyptian tactical incompetence.

In battle after battle, Egypt's field commanders demonstrated almost none of the skills needed to prevail in mechanized maneuver warfare. Egyptian soldiers fought hard enough—and their units typically maintained their cohesion—while the Israelis were attempting to breach their fortified lines. But as soon as the Israelis had broken into their positions, let alone after they had broken *through*, Egyptian tactical formations became helpless. Time and again, Egyptian tactical commanders simply failed to react to Israeli penetrations or flanking attacks. They would not counterattack, they would not refuse a flank, they would not reorient their defenses to meet the new direction of the Israeli assault, they would not even withdraw from a position that had been compromised by Israeli maneuver. As a result, all across the front, once Israeli forces had penetrated an Egyptian defensive line, it was merely a matter of rolling up the rest of the line from the flank.

Similarly, it was the rare occasion when Egyptian reserves moved to reinforce or counterattack an Israeli assault. There were only a handful of latecoming, slow-moving counterattacks by Egyptian armored reserves, and these were clumsy frontal assaults into the teeth of the Israeli attack. In the vast majority of instances, however, the Israelis moved so fast and the Egyptians so slowly (or not at all) that Israeli mechanized forces caught the Egyptian reserves still in their staging areas, and crushed them effortlessly. The Egyptian mechanized forces performed worst of all in these fights because their junior officers seemed to have no understanding of combined arms cooperation, their formations could not maneuver, their armor acted like movable pillboxes rather than mobile tanks, their infantry did not seem to know either how to take out Israeli tanks or how to guard their own against Israeli infantry, their artillery was incapable of shifting fire to keep pace with the Israeli maneuvers, and their tank crews were dismal marksmen who rarely, if ever, moved to get flank or rear shots against the agile Israelis.

If Egypt's tactical commanders were badly outfought by the Israelis, their senior leadership was psychologically paralyzed by the speed and extent of the unfolding catastrophe. Egypt's high command was largely manned by cronies of Marshal 'Amr, the commander-in-chief of the Egyptian armed forces.

These men were chosen more for their loyalty to 'Amr than any innate ability. Although initially euphoric at the chance for what they believed would be an easy victory over the despised Jews, they were then shocked that the IAF had been able to obliterate their own air force in one fell swoop. They were further stunned at the ability of Israeli armored columns to punch through their fortified lines in Sinai so quickly and then pulverize their tactical reserves with such ease.

Egyptian junior officers in Sinai contributed to that shock by thoroughly misleading their superiors. At first, Egypt's frontline commanders refused to admit that they were being defeated and instead sent glowing reports up the chain of command that they were crushing the Israelis. By midday on June 5, this misinformation left the Egyptian high command believing that its army was *advancing* into Israel itself, prompting Cairo to beg King Hussein of Jordan to launch his own offensive out of the West Bank in the fantastical belief that their armies could link up and cut Israel in half. Later, when it became impossible to hide the scope of the defeat, Egyptian junior officers reversed themselves and began claiming that they were being overwhelmed by enormous Israeli forces far greater than their own. 'Amr himself apparently suffered a nervous breakdown of sorts (or a drug- or alcohol-induced stupor) on the first day, overwhelmed by the defeat of his army.[11] The result was chaos in the Egyptian chain of command, and paralysis in Sinai as none of Cairo's field commanders—from the division commanders on down—would take the initiative to act without explicit orders from the high command.

With the Arab air forces all but obliterated, the IAF was able to devote most of its assets to attacks on the Arab armies starting on June 6th. Because of Israel's geographic vulnerability to Jordanian forces and respect for the reputation of Amman's army, IDF units on the West Bank had first call for air support. Of the ground-attack sorties Israel flew against Egypt, the vast majority were interdiction missions against rear echelon targets. The IAF essentially began by hitting targets in the Canal Zone and, as these were eliminated, slowly worked their way eastward, back toward the advancing Israeli ground forces.[12]

Of course, a number of Israeli fighters were still required for counter-air missions. Although the Syrian and Jordanian air forces were removed from the fray after June 5, the remnants of the EAF fought on, mustering 150 attack sorties during the war. These strikes did little damage, but they still occupied a fair number of IAF fighters over the next several days. The Israelis prevailed easily in these air-to-air engagements as well. Few Egyptian pilots could really take advantage of the capabilities of their aircraft, fewer still seemed proficient at air-to-air tactics, and almost none could act and react as quickly as the IAF fighter jocks. Altogether, the IAF shot down 42 Egyptian aircraft for the loss of only 6 of their own.

On the ground on the second day of the war, the Israeli army effectively finished off the Egyptian army. During the night of June 5/6, Cairo had collected its senses long enough to order two brigades of the elite 4th Armored Division to counterattack either Sharon's or Tal's *ugdot*. At B'ir Lafhan, these brigades were caught by two tank battalions from Yoffie's *ugdah*, which destroyed them in another churning tank battle with help from the IAF.[13]

The defeat of the 4th Armored Division at B'ir Lafhan appears to have been the last straw for Marshal 'Amr. With his theater reserve (and the best unit in the Egyptian Army) defeated by a much smaller Israeli force, 'Amr conceded that he could not hold Sinai. In the afternoon of June 6, he ordered a general retreat back to the Suez. He did not bother to inform his theater or front commanders to allow them to develop a plan for an orderly withdrawal, but instead called up division staffs directly and ordered them back to the Canal immediately, setting off a mad rush westward. Later that evening, several professional General Staff officers persuaded 'Amr that the situation was not irretrievable and convinced him to amend the original withdrawal order, but by then the damage had been done and the retreat was irreversible.

The Egyptian withdrawal turned into a rout almost from the start. Many senior field commanders simply jumped in their staff cars and fled, often without issuing any orders to their subordinates as to how to conduct the withdrawal. In most of these cases, no one stepped forward to fill the leadership void with the result that some units began to fall apart immediately. Taking a cue from their superiors, some Egyptian junior officers also decided that it was every man for himself and set out on their own, abandoning the soldiers under their command. Other large formations stuck together despite the desertion of their senior officers, but without direction from the GHQ, most Egyptian units proved incapable of any action except uncoordinated flight. Only a few tried to stand and fight to cover the Army's retreat or even deployed rearguards to cover their own withdrawal.

Compounding Egyptian problems, the Israelis were now in their element. The IAF bombed command and control facilities and movement chokepoints, and flew constant road reconnaissance sorties, strafing Egyptian columns as they fled for the Canal. Having broken through the initial fortified lines of the Egyptian army and penetrated into its operational depth, Israeli armor now had room to run and cause havoc. The Israelis quickly developed an exploitation strategy by which they sent armored columns deep into central Sinai to cut the Mitla, Giddi, and B'ir Gifgafah passes before most of the Egyptian army could get through them. Most Egyptian units, including two intact

Egyptian heavy divisions, were cut off by Israeli armor at the passes and then destroyed by Israeli air and ground forces. In many cases, even this was unnecessary as large numbers of Egyptians abandoned their vehicles and attempted to make it out on foot when they saw the passes were blocked.

Some Egyptian units tried to fight their way past what were initially very small Israeli blocking forces at the various passes, but without much success. For example, for most of the day on June 7th there were only nine Israeli tanks (four of them without any fuel) holding the Mitla pass against the bulk of three Egyptian *divisions* trying to escape to the Canal. Given this absurd force imbalance, it would be an understatement to say that the Egyptians fought poorly. At the Mitla and elsewhere, the Egyptians mostly did not maneuver or counterattack at all but just kept pressing forward, occasionally trying to drive the Israelis off with inaccurate tank fire. In those rare instances when the Egyptians launched a determined attack against an Israeli blocking force, in every case it was a clumsy, slow-moving frontal assault that the Israelis had little trouble dispatching with a few deft maneuvers and deadly long-range gunnery. Moreover, the Egyptian attacks were conducted only with armor—no effort was made to have infantry engage what were often unsupported Israeli tanks and hit them with antitank weapons. Similarly, the Egyptians directed very little artillery fire against the Israeli blocking forces, and the few barrages they did conduct were inaccurate and caused almost no damage.

With Israeli armor blocking the passes, beginning late on June 7, the Israeli Air Force increasingly directed its ground attack sorties against the masses of Egyptian vehicles bottled up in central Sinai. Between these constant air strikes and the destruction of the few remaining cohesive Egyptian units by the Israeli ground forces at the passes, the Egyptian army dissolved. Units began to surrender en masse, while large numbers of other Egyptian soldiers abandoned their equipment and set out across the desert on their own. Most either died or were picked up by Israeli forces days later.

The Jordanian Front

The Jordanians had done an even better job than the Egyptians in deploying their forces to repel an Israeli invasion of the West Bank. They correctly deduced that the IDF would conduct two major thrusts—one against Jerusalem and the other southward along the Janin-Nablus axis—coupled with a "defensive" attack around Qalqilyah/Tulkarm to push the Jordanians back from the Israeli population centers along the coast. The Jordanians marshaled nine brigades (seven infantry and two armored) and several independent battalions for the war. Amman deployed five of the infantry brigades in Jerusalem and along the borders with Israel. Another infantry brigade and the elite 60th Armored Brigade were bivouacked in the Jordan Valley near Jericho where they were to move forward to support Jerusalem. Similarly, an infantry brigade and the elite 40th Armored Brigade were held back near the Damiyah Bridge to support Janin and parry the expected Israeli thrust toward Nablus. Finally two armored battalions were deployed forward to provide support for the front-line infantry, one near Janin and the other near Hebron.

This deployment scheme concentrated division-sized forces in the two main Israeli breakthrough sectors: Jerusalem and Janin. For this reason, and because the Jordanians had had 19 years to fortify their lines in the superb defensive terrain of the West Bank, Amman was confident that it could hold the West Bank against an Israeli offensive for two to three weeks. Moreover, the Jordanians intended to use their concentration around Jerusalem to take most or all of the Jewish half of the city, which they could use as a bargaining chip to be traded for any Israeli gains elsewhere.

Despite Amman's prescience in forecasting the Israeli battle plan, the IDF made short work of the Jordanian army. The Israelis deployed eight brigades (one armored, two mechanized, and five infantry) against the West Bank. Brigadier Uzi Narkiss, in charge of Israel's Central Command facing Jordan, launched a three-brigade *ugdah* from the Galilee south toward Janin and Nablus, used two other infantry brigades to seize the Jordanian stronghold at Latrun and push the Jordanians back from the coastal plain between Qalqilyah and Tulkarm, and employed another three-brigade *ugdah* to conduct a double-envelopment of Jerusalem—exactly as Amman expected.

Yet, as in Sinai, on June 5th and 6th, Israeli ground forces cracked the Jordanian front-line infantry positions and then defeated Amman's armored reserves with relative ease. During the morning of June 5th, Jordanian forces attacked the neutral UN compound at Government House to secure their southern flank. The Israelis correctly read this as the opening move in a larger Jordanian attack on Jerusalem, which prompted the IDF to shelve its hopes that Amman would stay out of the war and reluctantly launch its own offensive against the West Bank. An Israeli Infantry Brigade checked and then counterattacked the Jordanian forces in southern Jerusalem, clearing the formidable Jordanian fortifications there with minimal losses. During the night of June 5/6, the IDF also attacked Ammunition Hill in the Shaykh Jarrah area north of the Old City. This was the most heavily fortified part of the entire Jordanian line, and Amman had a reinforced battalion entrenched there, supported by artillery and mortars. That night, the Israelis mounted a frontal assault into the Jordanian lines with a paratrooper brigade and a company of

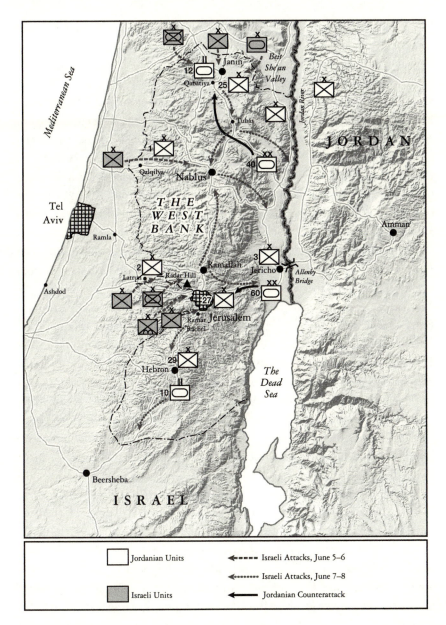

MAP 2 The Jordanian Front in the Six-Day War

Map legend:
- Jordanian Units
- Israeli Units
- Israeli Attacks, June 5–6
- Israeli Attacks, June 7–8
- Jordanian Counterattack

Sherman tanks. Although the attack was hastily planned and poorly executed, the Israeli paratroopers overpowered the Jordanian defenders in a few hours of fierce combat. The Israelis took probably their heaviest losses of the war in this fight (50 dead and 150 wounded), but they quickly regrouped and pushed on to envelop the Old City from the north that morning.

Other Israeli units moved to secure the northern shoulder of the Jerusalem corridor. An Israeli infantry brigade overpowered the Jordanian 2nd Infantry Brigade defending the stronghold at Latrun, which dominated the western end of the corridor. Closer in to Jerusalem, the Israeli 10th Mechanized Brigade assaulted up the slopes of Radar Hill and the escarpment marking the corridor's northern boundary. Although several Jordanian battalions were entrenched in this outstanding defensive terrain—and the Israeli attack should have been suicidal—Jordanian resistance was so inept that the Israelis punched through their lines with ease in just a matter of hours. With the Jordanian infantry in full retreat, the Israelis turned east and marched on Tel al-Ful, a key height commanding both the northern approaches to Jerusalem and the southern approaches to Ramallah.

In northern Samaria, the key contest was the battle for Janin. The Israelis attacked south from the Galilee with three brigades (one armored, one mechanized infantry, and one infantry) in a complex pincer movement. The mechanized brigade busted through the Jordanian 12th Armored Battalion to envelop Janin from the west, while the Israeli infantry brigade completed the encirclement from the northeast. Meanwhile, the IDF armored brigade bypassed Janin altogether and headed south to seize Nablus in central Samaria. The next morning (June 6) the Israelis smashed the Jordanian 25th Infantry Brigade entrenched in Janin. Meanwhile, an Israeli infantry brigade attacking from the coastal plain drove back Jordan's 1st Infantry Brigade, which collapsed under minimal pressure, leaving Tulkarm, Qalqilyah, and the borders of the West Bank open to the IDF.

The most remarkable aspect of all of these battles on the West Bank is how closely they mirrored the fighting in Sinai. Accounts of the two campaigns read like virtual carbon copies of one another. Despite the reputation of Jordanian forces—and their better performance in 1948, discussed later in this book—they fought just like the Egyptians. Jordanian forces often stoutly defended their fixed positions, and they were generally better marksmen than Cairo's troops. But like the Egyptians, the Jordanians refused to counterattack, shift their forces, or reorient their defenses to meet Israeli penetrations or flanking attacks. The Jordanian units themselves simply did not maneuver, they could not shift their artillery fire, and their tanks either rumbled forward in slow, clumsy frontal assaults or sat in place till they were picked off by Israeli armor or infantry that could stalk them as if they were fixed bunkers. Jordanian units showed effectively no capacity to integrate the different combat arms into combined arms teams, and their commanders were also prone to exaggerate and even lie to their superiors about their situation to cover up their mistakes and defeats. As in the Sinai, the Israelis found that they simply needed to turn or penetrate a Jordanian defensive line, and then it was just a matter of rolling it up from the flank. It was frightening work in the hills of the West Bank and narrow streets of Jerusalem, but it was straightforward, even simple.

For its part, the Jordanian high command was just as stunned by the destruction of their air force as the Egyptians, but it was not paralyzed like 'Amr and his generals, and Amman began shifting reserves to reinforce threatened sectors. Late on June 5, the Jordanians moved additional infantry to shore up the defenses of Jerusalem, and ordered the main body of the 60th Armored Brigade to Tel al-Ful to block the Israeli 10th Mechanized Brigade. Meanwhile, Amman ordered its 40th Armored Brigade to counterattack the Israeli penetration at Janin.

In part because of air strikes, but mostly because of the superiority of Israeli ground forces, these smart Jordanian countermoves failed to stop the tide of the advancing Israeli army. The Jordanian 60th Armored Brigade was trounced by a much smaller and worse-armed force of Israeli tanks and mechanized infantry as it attempted to reinforce the Jordanian positions in Jerusalem. In northern Samaria, the 40th Armored Brigade—with one of the finest field commanders any modern Arab army would ever produce in Brigadier Rakan al-Jazi—counterattacked the Israeli forces at Janin around mid-morning on June 6th. Al-Jazi's Patton tanks mauled an Israeli reconnaissance company and a battalion of refurbished World War II–era Shermans at Qabatiyah crossroads south of the town before falling back to a good defensive position blocking the Israeli advance. At dawn the next morning (June 7), however, the Israelis launched a set-piece assault preceded by a brief, fierce air and artillery bombardment. One Israeli combined-arms team pinned the Jordanians while another swept around its flank, forcing the Jordanians to fall back to the south. Once the Jordanian tanks were out in the open, they became vulnerable to Israeli armor and air strikes. The brigade suffered heavy casualties and slowly disintegrated as it tried to retreat.

In Jerusalem, the IDF was still working to cut off the Old City. In southern Jerusalem, Israeli infantry launched a clumsy frontal assault that still smashed the entrenched Jordanian defenders in their second and third lines of defense. From there, the Israelis turned northwest and hit Mt. Zion from the rear, causing a Jordanian brigade to collapse and flee. The IDF's northern pincer made similar progress. After taking Tel al-Ful, the Israeli 10th Mechanized Brigade had dispatched a battalion task force to capture Ramallah, and then sent another east to join the envelopment of Jerusalem. This allowed the IDF to move a combined force of paratroopers and Sherman tanks to take the Augusta-Victoria ridge east of the city and complete its encirclement late on June 6.

Thus, by the morning of June 8th the West Bank was lost. The Jordanian Air Force lay in ruins. Frontline Jordanian forces defending heavily fortified positions had been routed at Latrun, Tulkarm, Qalqilyah, Janin, Ammunition Hill, Shaykh Jarrah, Mivtar Hill, Abu Tor, and Mt. Zion while Jordan's armored reserves had been broken at Tel al-Ful, the Dotan Valley, the Janin-Tubas road, and eventually Qabatiyah. There were few reserves left to the Jordanian high command, and Israeli air power was making a coordinated defense of the West Bank impossible. At noon, the king ordered a withdrawal of all his forces from the West Bank. Amman's army streamed down to the Jordan river bridges with Israeli units close on their heels.

The Syrian Front

Unlike the Egyptians and Jordanians, the Syrians were kept in suspense for four days. After the destruction of much of the Syrian Air Force on the 5th, Damascus launched a halfhearted attack on the Israeli kibbutzim in the exposed "finger" of Galilee. The attack was clumsy and slow, and was stopped by the kibbutzniks themselves. Thereafter, the Syrians were largely content to trade artillery rounds with Israeli forces while the IDF made short work of Syria's Egyptian and Jordanian allies. In addition, the IAF began to work over Syrian defenses on the Golan in preparation for the Israeli ground assault, flying roughly 100 ground-attack sorties against Syria on June 6 and 7, and 225 sorties against Syria on June 8.[14] In that time, the Israelis kept only a single *ugdah* of one armored and two infantry brigades to watch the Syrians, while the rest of the army fought in Sinai and the West Bank.

Nevertheless, when the Israelis finally attacked the Golan, the odds still did not seem terribly favorable. Damascus deployed 12 of its 16 brigades on the Golan—including both of its armored brigades and its lone mechanized brigade—in three brigade groups. In addition to the size and weaponry of these forces, the Syrians also had the advantage of extremely formidable natural positions and extensive fortifications. The Golan is a forbidding obstacle to assault, especially from the west, where it climbs sharply from the Huleh Valley in an escarpment rising 1,000–2,000 feet to the crest in many places. With the help of their Soviet advisers, the Syrians had developed a

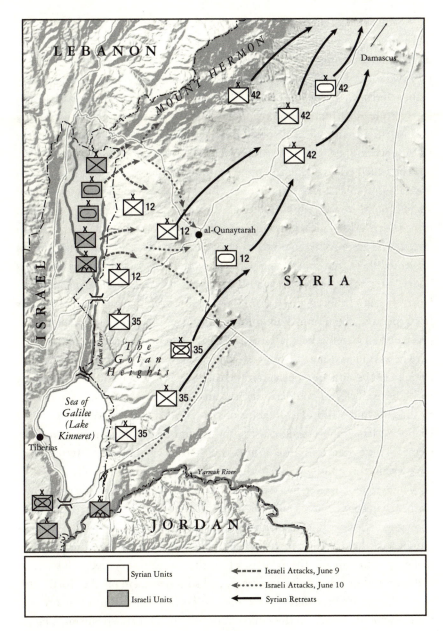

☐ Syrian Units	◄----- Israeli Attacks, June 9
▣ Israeli Units	◄······ Israeli Attacks, June 10
	◄——— Syrian Retreats

MAP 3 The Golan Front in the Six-Day War

sophisticated series of fortified positions throughout the depth of the Golan. The Syrians and Soviets had identified most of the key avenues of advance and had carefully sited defensive positions to block and trap an Israeli attack along any of them.

Against the Syrians on the Golan, Israel mustered a smaller force than it had against Egypt or Jordan. The Israelis attacked with seven brigades (two armored, one mechanized infantry, two paratrooper, and two infantry) grouped into two *ugdot*. Four of these had fought in Sinai or the West Bank and were rushed north with little rest or refit. One advantage the IDF possessed was that by the time of their attack on the Golan, the IAF was free to participate fully against the Syrians, all of its other missions having been completed. Despite its busy week, the IAF could still muster over 150 serviceable combat aircraft.

The Israeli offensive began on the morning of June 9, 1967, with a tremendous air assault. The IAF directed its full might against the Syrians, flying 299 air-to-ground sorties, while IDF engineers cleared paths through the Syrian minefields.[15] Although the air strikes caused few casualties among the Syrian forces, who were well protected in their deep bunkers, it pinned them and prevented them from interfering with the work of the Israeli sappers. At 1000 hours, after their air strikes had shifted eastward, the Israeli armor and infantry began climbing the Golan. The main Israeli attack came in the far north because the terrain was so forbidding here that the Syrians thought it precluded an Israeli attack, and so had left it more lightly defended.

The assault was not the most elegant breaching operation ever conducted. Because of the difficulty of the terrain, the Israelis lost large numbers of tanks and other vehicles to boulders, ditches, and loose gravel, which caused tanks to slide down the hillsides. In addition, the limited road network in the area channeled Israeli movement, causing traffic jams and confusion whenever lead elements hit Syrian resistance or terrain obstacles. Finally, several Israeli units took wrong turns and got lost in the winding paths of the Golan.

The Syrians, however, failed to take advantage of any of these Israeli miscues. Rather than counterattacking the vulnerable Israeli columns as they stumbled through the forward defenses, the Syrians sat in their positions. Syrian units fought back hard whenever the Israelis came into their fields of fire, but they made no effort to hit the Israelis while they were disoriented, constricted, and confused during the initial assault and so throw them off the Golan altogether. Syrian artillery units proved useless. Their batteries could only fire preplanned fire missions into the Huleh Valley (far behind the advancing Israelis) and would not adjust their fire to hit the Israeli forces climbing the escarpment and penetrating their front lines.

This pattern held true at every level of the Syrian hierarchy. The company, battalion, and brigade commanders manning the forward defensive positions failed to order counterattacks against the Israelis as they breached the Syrian lines. This greatly eased the burden on the Israelis, because it meant that all they needed to do was silence the defenders immediately in front of them and then clear away minefields and earthworks. At a higher level, the reserves of the Syrian brigade group in the north—an armored brigade and an infantry brigade—failed to counterattack or even move up to support their forward infantry brigades when the Israelis successfully breached the forward defense lines. At a higher level still, the Syrian General Staff would not release the 42nd Brigade Group from GHQ reserve to counterattack or reinforce the forward Syrian lines when the Israeli penetration in the northern sector began to unhinge the entire defensive system on the Golan.

The passivity of the Syrians gave the IDF a crucial grace period, which they used to get their assault back on track. Demonstrating the improvisational abilities the IDF has always nurtured, Israeli units simply kept moving forward, finding new paths east and unplanned routes to outflank and overpower Syrian defensive positions. By the end of the day, they had worked their way along a number of routes to the east, at which point they began pushing southward in a wide flanking maneuver designed to envelop the entire Golan.

At this point, the campaign had effectively been decided. Although there were plenty of Syrian units still manning formidable defensive positions in the southern and central Golan, the entire northern quarter of the plateau was in Israeli hands, and it was simply a matter of time before the IDF pushed south, rolled up the Syrian lines from their flank or rear, and cut off the entire Syrian army on the Golan. Because the Syrians would not counterattack or reorient their defenses, there was no real chance that they could stop the Israelis. Indeed, rather than even try, the Syrian General Staff responded by pulling most of the 42nd Brigade Group back to Damascus during the night of June 9/10 to guard against an Israeli attack on the capital. Syria's military leadership appears to have been in a state of chaos, and left the rest of the army on the Golan to their own devices.

The IDF offensive resumed early in the morning of June 10. Israeli armor and infantry task forces made their way south and east, seizing crucial road junctions and clearing important defensive positions, mostly from the rear. Throughout the Golan, the Syrians fought back bravely, but because they continued to remain immobile in their bunkers it was only a matter of time before each Syrian position was reduced by the Israelis.

Then, at 0845 on June 10, Syria's government-controlled radio announced the fall of al-Qunaytarah to the Israelis.[16] Israeli units were still several kilometers from the town and were mystified by the announcement. Most of the Syrian units on the Golan were not as clear about the situation and took this report to mean they were trapped. The result was the general collapse of the Syrian Army. Some units remained in place and continued to defend their fortifications because they had not been ordered to do otherwise. These units had to be mopped up by Israeli forces in difficult hand-to-hand fights. However, the bulk of what was left of the Syrian Army ran. In a number of cases, Syrian officers simply jumped into their staff cars and fled, abandoning their troops, who were forced to make their way out on their own as best they could. Because al-Qunaytarah had not fallen to the Israelis, some Syrian units in the central and southern sectors were able to escape in relatively good shape, while others dropped their weapons and fled pell-mell. By the end of June 10, the Syrian Army had deserted the plateau, and the Israelis had accepted a UN-brokered ceasefire.

Explaining Arab Defeat in the Six-Day War

When the dust finally cleared on June 10th, Israel had won one of the greatest victories in modern military history and the Arab armies had suffered one of its most shocking defeats. Altogether, about 20,000 Arab soldiers were killed and another 5,000 captured. Against this, Israel suffered 776 dead.[17] Far from being driven into the sea, the Israelis had conquered the Sinai, the West Bank, and the Golan Heights. The IDF had also demonstrated a mastery of modern air and mechanized warfare that ironically, but intentionally, rivaled the Wehrmacht at its height.

As impressed as observers were by Israeli prowess, they were just as aston-ished by Arab failings. Most perplexing of all was how uniform the problems seemed to be across the Arab armed forces. All of their air forces floundered in air-to-air combat and performed just as poorly in air-to-ground missions. All of them had proven tactically inept: their ground forces would not ma-neuver, would not counterattack, and would not shift or reorient themselves. They would not do anything except sit in their fortifications and fight back against Israeli frontal assaults—which were never more than fixing attacks or penetrations undertaken only when no flanking options were available. Arab junior officers demonstrated virtually no initiative, no aggressiveness, and no ability to devise creative ad hoc solutions to unexpected problems. They had no understanding of combined arms operations. Egyptian and Syrian (but not Jordanian) senior officers were largely clueless political appointees who mostly panicked when their front-line forces began to fall apart, and then abandoned their troops when their personal safety was at risk. All three Arab armies experienced crippling problems with information: they collected almost no intelligence on the Israelis, their tactical forces did not bother to patrol, senior commanders withheld important information to keep their subordinates in line, and their subordinates lied about what was happening to them, such that their entire chains of command fought in a thick fog of misinformation and duplicity. Even at the most basic level, few Arab soldiers could take full advantage of what was often superior weaponry to whatever the Israelis brought to the fight.

The mystery of Arab military problems only deepened with time. Arab performance in the 1973 October War was uneven at best and mostly poor, and in 1982 the Israelis won another crushing victory over the Syrians in Lebanon. Meanwhile, in their 1980 invasion of Iran, the Iraqis turned in a performance that rivaled Arab experiences in the Six-Day War for ineptitude. They would eventually go on to eke out a meager victory over an isolated and exhausted Iran in 1988, only to be crushed by the US-led Coalition during the Persian Gulf War two years later. The Saudis and Egyptians both participated in that conflict too, but did nothing to impress. Finally, the Libyans took Arab military fortunes to new lows with their losses to Tanzania in Uganda in 1979 and to Chad in 1987.

After the 2003 invasion of Iraq (yet another lopsided victory over a hapless Arab military), the United States took it upon itself to rebuild the Iraqi armed forces, only to come face-to-face with the weaknesses it had benefited from for the past 12 years. This time around, the Americans were trying to overcome those problems, and found it daunting. American officers devised their own explanations for Arab military weakness and debated how to train a new Iraqi military in light of the officers' conflicting theories of what those problems were.

Both the extent of these problems and their curious consistency across the Arab armies have sparked endless conjecture. Various theories have emerged to explain these patterns of behavior. Some experts and many Western military officers blamed Arab reliance on Soviet-style doctrine and military methods for their repeated lackluster performances.[18] Others, including many political scientists, argue that it was the product of poor civil-military relations and the excessive politicization of Arab militaries resulting from the constant coups— and coup-proofing—endemic to the Arab states.[19] Still other academics and military officers assumed that the weakness of Arab armed forces was a result of economic factors, particularly the chronic underdevelopment of the Arab states throughout the post–World War II era.[20] Finally, casual observers and active participants in the various Middle East wars have frequently commented that Arab military operations are inhibited by patterns of behavior derived from Arab culture.[21]

Although numerous observers have written books, articles, and papers arguing for one explanation or another, no one has ever looked at all of them collectively to try to deduce which are wrong and which right; whether these recurrent patterns of Arab military ineffectiveness[22] could be traced back to just one overarching source, or a combination of some or all.[23] Despite the persistence and continued salience of Arab military ineffectiveness, all of these different theories about what is going wrong continue to percolate, with real-world impact on the security and stability of the Middle East. Yet no one has ever tried to sift through them and figure out which ones hold water, and which are just hogwash.

That is the purpose of this book. In the chapters that follow, I am going to look at each of these different explanations to try to assess the extent that each suggested source—Soviet doctrine, politicization, underdevelopment, and cultural patterns of behavior—was responsible for the problems experienced by Arab militaries since 1945.

Plan of Attack

To do that I have organized the book into four Parts, each of which looks at one of these alternative explanations. In each Part, I describe the explanation in greater detail—what does it mean to say that politicization or Arab culture caused these problems in Arab military effectiveness? That lets me lay out whether the actual experiences of the Arab armed forces in combat conformed to how these explanations suggest they would. I am also going to ask whether the Arab armed forces even experienced the problems as described by the different alternative explanations. So for instance, if the problems that the Arabs have been experiencing were the result of their reliance on Soviet doctrine, they should have the same weaknesses (and strengths) as the Soviet armed forces.

I am also going to look at a number of important instances where an Arab state became more or less susceptible to one of the proposed underlying causes. So at different times, Arab states increased or decreased the political controls on their militaries, and those shifts should have led to corresponding changes in their combat performance if politicization was the source of their problems. Finally, I compare the performance of the Arab militaries to the armed forces of other, non-Arab states that experienced the same root source phenomenon to see if they had the same problems in battle as the Arabs. So, for instance, I look at the combat performance of the North Korean and Cuban militaries, both of which relied heavily on Soviet military doctrine and methods, to see if they had the same problems as the Arabs. If they did, that's powerful evidence that the Soviet system was at least part of the problem, if not the whole problem. If they didn't, then that tends to discredit the notion that the Soviets were to blame.

Finally, I am going to look at the exceptions to the rule. Not every Arab military stunk. Some did notably better than others, whether the Jordanians in 1948, the Egyptians in 1973, the Iraqis in 1988, Hizballah in 2006, or ISIS/Da'ish in 2014. These are critically important. For any explanation to be worthwhile, these outliers need to be exceptions that prove the rule, rather than exceptions that it just can't explain.

Covering Modern Arab Military History

One of the biggest challenges in writing this book was deciding what to do with the military history that lies at the heart of the analysis. In the end, it's all about the history. It is only by sifting through the experiences of the various Arab militaries in combat—both broadly and in specific circumstances—that we can discern the sources of Arab military ineffectiveness. The problem is that there is so much modern Arab military history to consider.

I cannot possibly present all of that history, country-by-country or war-by-war in chronological order in this book and still have the space to discuss the sources of Arab military problems. That would require a book thicker than the US tax code. I'm particularly cognizant of that extensive record because the first book I ever wrote, *Arabs at War: Military Effectiveness, 1948–1991*, was a military history of six of the Arab states (Egypt, Jordan, Iraq, Libya, Saudi Arabia, and Syria) up through the Gulf War, and it clocked in at a svelte 717 pages. I can't possibly make a reader wade through all of that, plus however many more pages would be needed to cover the wars since 1991, *and then* discuss the sources of the problems. What's more, one of the best ways to understand the sources of Arab military performance is to compare it to the performance of a number of non-Arab militaries, which means discussing the relevant aspects of their military experience as well. That's just too much history for any one book.

My solution to this problem has been to present summary descriptions of key conflicts or events in Arab military history as needed to illustrate the various points under consideration. In some instances, I will just mention something that happened to one or several Arab militaries with only a brief description. In other places, I provide a somewhat more detailed account, such as the overview in this Introduction of Egyptian, Jordanian, and Syrian military performance during the Six-Day War. I have tried to make sure that the reader gets a good summary of all of the crucial moments in modern Arab military history because they are critical to understanding the sources of their problems, but I have not provided these summaries in a straight chronological fashion. Instead, I have brought them in to the story where they are most relevant to illustrate particular points.

So I am going to do my best to make sure that this book tells you everything you need to know about the Arab-Israeli Wars, the Iran-Iraq War, the Persian Gulf War, the Libyan invasions of Chad, and the most important civil wars that have convulsed the region since 2003. But I'm not going to detail every Middle Eastern war fought since 1945, and those I do discuss, I am going to present where I think each is most needed to illustrate specific points related to the sources of Arab military ineffectiveness.

CHAPTER I | # Patterns of Arab Military Performance

T O UNDERSTAND THE sources of the problems of the modern Arab militaries, it is important to understand the problems themselves. You can't just say that the Arab armed forces were terrible and leave it at that. They have not been bad at all things at all times. There are some operations that the Arab militaries have consistently and uniformly performed badly. But there are other things that they have just as steadily done well, and still other aspects of military operations where there is no particular pattern either from army to army or from war to war. Consequently, it is critical to understand what it is that the Arab armed forces have done poorly—and consistently poorly—to understand why.

The rest of this chapter presents a summary of the major patterns of Arab military effectiveness since 1945.[1] So we are all on the same page, I consider the Arab world to be Morocco, Algeria, Tunisia, Libya, Egypt, North Sudan, the Palestinians, Jordan, Syria, Iraq, Kuwait, Saudi Arabia, Bahrain, Qatar, the United Arab Emirates (UAE), Oman, and Yemen. It is the performance of their militaries in combat since 1945 that I want to explore in this book, and whose broad patterns of military effectiveness I present below.

Of course, there have been exceptions to even the hardest rules of modern Arab military effectiveness, exceptions that I have *not* presented in this chapter. In many ways, these exceptions are the most interesting and important cases to explain. For that reason, I address these exceptions directly throughout the book. So if, as you read through my description of the patterns below, you think of exceptions to my conclusions, please bear with me and have confidence that I will discuss them later on. I spend quite a bit of space on these exceptions because they are so important.

As a final caveat, the summary below does not constitute an assessment of the Arab armed forces in every aspect of military operations since 1945. That would require too much text and is unnecessary. Instead, I have focused only on those aspects of military operations that were particularly problematic for the modern Arab militaries (and for pretty much all of them) or aspects of military performance that are important to one or more of the rationales that people have offered to explain the underachievement of Arab armed forces since World War II.

Tactical Leadership

Without question, the greatest, most consistent and most persistent problem of Arab armed forces in battle since 1945 has been the poor performance of their junior officers. From war to war and country to country, Arab tactical commanders regularly failed to demonstrate initiative, flexibility, creativity, independence of thought, an understanding of combined arms integration, or an appreciation for the benefits of maneuver in battle. These failings resulted in a dearth of aggressiveness, responsiveness, speed, movement, intelligence gathering, and adaptability in Arab tactical formations that proved crippling in every war they fought. The summary of combat operations during the Six-Day War provides one example of this phenomenon and how it crippled all three of the Arab armies that fought in 1967. So too will every other description of Arab military operations throughout this book.

In war after war, Arab junior officers were generally unimaginative and passive, making it nearly impossible for the formations under their command to engage effectively in maneuver warfare, meeting engagements, ad hoc operations, or other forms of combat in which authority devolved upon the local commanders on the spot. Arab militaries found it difficult to adapt quickly to unforeseen events and were rarely able to improvise tactical solutions to unexpected problems. Arab formations generally could not maintain a rapid pace of operations. On the defensive, Arab units rarely shifted forces to meet the enemy's thrust or counterattacked to seal or smash an enemy penetration. On those occasions when they tried, it was often the case that they would only do so when ordered to by senior commanders, they moved too slowly, and by the time they acted the decisive moment had passed. The recurrent pattern among Arab armies has been that once an enemy broke through their lines and was threatening to roll them up from the flank, the Arab units would fight tenaciously from their existing positions but could not or would not shift to form a new line to prevent their adversary from reducing their positions in detail. On the offensive, Arab forces usually attacked straight ahead with little or no thought given to potential threats or opportunities waiting elsewhere on the battlefield.

Arab tactical units were repeatedly defeated by enemy forces of equal or smaller size because the Arab units clung to doctrine or orders from above that were applied rigidly even when they had clearly been overtaken by events, and refused to act in response to the vicissitudes of combat. All too often, Arab units remained passive for lack of orders, even when action might have staved off defeat. In addition, Arab militaries consistently centralized decision-making at the highest levels of command. This helped create a vicious cycle in which Arab senior officers were unwilling to delegate command authority to their subordinates because they believed their subordinates would be unable to properly exercise that authority. Whenever Arab junior officers did have command delegated to them—either on purpose or, more often, because of the chaos of battle—they performed so poorly that it confirmed their superiors in the belief that command shouldn't be delegated to tactical commanders.

Arab tactical units rarely attempted to gain an advantage over an adversary by actively maneuvering on the battlefield. Consistently, Arab combat units on the defensive stayed in their prepared positions and relied on firepower to defeat an attacker. When attacking, Arab armies likewise tended to rely on firepower and mass, employing either frontal assaults to simply overwhelm a defender or stand-off bombardments in which they attempted to obliterate enemy defenses by calling in massive fire support before advancing. In particular, Arab armies employed their armored forces either like battering-rams or mobile, direct-fire artillery, and rarely attempted to maneuver against an opponent for flank or rear shots. Similarly, Arab artillery units generally were only able to conduct pre-planned fire missions and proved incapable of rapidly and accurately shifting fire, conducting counter-battery missions, concentrating fire from geographically separate batteries, or providing on-call fire support in a timely or accurate fashion. As a result of these problems, whenever Arab forces became involved in fluid battles—and were most in need of fire support because of their difficulties fighting such battles—their artillery was incapable of delivering.

Arab armies typically displayed poor combined arms coordination. Arab junior officers generally had little understanding of how to integrate the various combat arms even if they did recognize the need for them to operate in unison. Too often, Arab armor charged into battle without infantry support. Likewise, Arab mechanized infantry frequently did not dismount to engage enemy infantry and eliminate antitank units—even in difficult terrain or when they knew they were opposed by dug-in infantry with antitank weapons—but remained buttoned up in their armored personnel carriers. Arab artillery simply could not support maneuver units in battle beyond their initial preparatory barrages. Combat engineers and other specialized support troops were often an afterthought, and only rarely integrated into the scheme of an Arab attack. Finally, as limited as combined arms coordination among Arab ground forces was, it was that much worse between Arab ground and air forces, who invariably fought their own separate wars because they could not fight together.

Arab air forces experienced identical problems to those of their counterparts in the ground forces. In all kinds of missions, most Arab pilots proved to be rigid, unaggressive, unimaginative flyers who could only employ simplistic tactics. They had poor situational awareness, and if they did react to circumstances, they usually did so too slowly to make a difference. Arab fighter pilots mostly demonstrated poor dogfighting skills and fared badly in air-to-air engagements. Arab air force units frequently were defeated by smaller, but more competent adversaries. Even against mediocre opponents, Arab air forces were only able to prevail in aerial combat when they enjoyed a heavy advantage in numbers. Arab pilots often could not react to unexpected moves by their adversaries and instead kept doing what they had been doing even after it became clear that their adversary was moments from converting the kill. Arab pilots were heavily reliant on ground-controlled intercept guidance and many could not function without it.

The performance of Arab air forces in air-to-ground missions was as bad or worse than their performance in air-to-air combat. At the most basic level, Arab air strikes rarely put ordnance on targets. They were often inadequately reconnoitered, haphazardly planned, simplistic, and dangerous. Arab pilots showed little ability to make last-minute adjustments to bring their weapons on target, and had great difficulty adapting to unforeseen developments. Arab pilots also generally did not employ independent judgment as to the value of different targets, striking only those they were ordered to while leaving higher-value targets untouched. Arab close air support missions achieved little, taking too long to approve, plan, and execute to be of benefit; remaining under the control of the air force high command rather than the local ground commander who was best positioned to know what and where to direct the air strike; and failing to do much damage to the targets they did attack.

Information Management and Intelligence

All of the Arab militaries suffered from problems with the flow of information all along their chains of command. A tendency to compartmentalize information was in evidence in all of the Arab militaries, to a greater or lesser extent. Arab officers often saw knowledge as a form of power, allowing them to enforce their authority over their subordinates and gain leverage over their peers. Consequently, knowledge was often hoarded, and key information frequently was not conveyed to those most in need of it.

It has been the history of Arab armed forces that personnel throughout the military consistently exaggerated and even falsified reporting to higher echelons. Simultaneously, superior officers routinely withheld information about operations from their subordinates. These reinforcing tendencies meant that Arab militaries routinely operated in a thick fog of ignorance and half-truths. The lying and obfuscation that enveloped the Egyptian armed forces during the Six-Day War is simply the most famous example of this persistent problem. Lower echelons sent inaccurate reports to higher echelons, who then made plans based on this misinformation. Since the higher echelons rarely provided all available information to lower formations, many units had to execute operations with little knowledge of the enemy, the terrain, or the larger mission. The lower echelons then either had to try to execute the operation—which may have been suicidal because of the limited and inaccurate information available to the planners—or lie and report that they did perform it when they had not.

At tactical levels, Arab armies did uniformly poorly because junior officers rarely patrolled their defensive sectors or their routes of advance. Indeed, on a stunning number of occasions, Arab tactical commanders even failed to deploy security screens/observation posts/listening posts in front of their night laagers or defensive lines. Arab commanders at platoon through brigade level generally relied on information passed down from higher levels rather than attempting to find out for themselves what was over the next hill.

The paucity of reliable information flowing upward from tactical forces was only one liability for Arab strategic intelligence. Arab air forces flew inadequate—and often misdirected—reconnaissance missions, and Arab intelligence services produced little in terms of human reporting. Numerous Arab generals must be faulted for failing to appreciate the importance of proper intelligence. In most cases, little was collected because little was requested by the senior planners and operators.

Indeed, intelligence was another, related problem of Arab militaries. Arab intelligence services too often made little effort to collect information on their adversaries, even unclassified information that could be gathered from press reports and military literature. Analysis was frequently skewed or superficial and distribution of intelligence was badly inadequate, to some extent because of the compartmentalization of information, both formal and informal. At times, intelligence collected by Arab military forces and intelligence services was distorted at the highest levels to conform to the preconceived notions of the regime. Consequently, Arab armies often went into battle with little understanding of the order of battle, organization, infrastructure, plans, or tactical doctrine of their enemy.

Technical Skills and Weapons Handling

The soldiers and officers of Arab armed forces experienced persistent and debilitating difficulties employing modern war machines in pursuit of military operations. Arab armed forces required long periods of time to learn to employ new weapons and other equipment. In many cases, they required longer to absorb new technology than other Third World militaries. With only a few exceptions, Arab armies and air forces were unable to take full advantage of the equipment at their disposal. They rarely were able to employ the more advanced capabilities of their weapons, and often used sophisticated weapons in unsophisticated fashions.

Even when their equipment should have given them a commanding advantage over an adversary, they frequently found themselves beaten in the very area of military operations in which their equipment was so dominant. A particularly harmful aspect of this problem was that Arab fire discipline and marksmanship was often poor, and they were frequently outshot by their opponents. Consequently, even when the Arabs had a significant advantage in the range, accuracy, or power of their guns and missiles, they often lost artillery, armor, rifle, and aircraft duels. For instance, in the 1990–1991 Persian Gulf War, many Iraqi Republican Guard batteries employed the G-5 or GHN-45 howitzer, probably the finest artillery piece in the world at the time. Although the G-5 had greater range, precision, and firepower than any of the Coalition howitzers, Republican Guard batteries lost every counter-battery duel they engaged in with US batteries employing the M109 howitzer.

The general dearth of technical skills among Arab military personnel also limited the number of sophisticated weapons systems that Arab armed forces could effectively field. The best example of this was the poor pilot-to-aircraft ratio of all of the Arab air forces, which limited the number of aircraft that they could muster at any given time. Arab air forces were rarely able to sustain even a 1:1 pilot-to-aircraft ratio, and there were numerous examples of worse ratios. For instance, the Egyptian Air Force in 1956 had only 30 pilots for its 120 MiGs, a 1:4 ratio. Libya had only 25 trained pilots for its 110 Mirages in 1973, and four years later had only 150 pilots for the 550 aircraft in its air force. Indeed, after the 1967 Six-Day War, the Egyptians essentially accepted that it was impossible for them to train more than about 30 pilots a year, despite a population of 30 million people.[2] These problems were not confined to Arab air forces either: the Libyans were never able to train crews for more than about a third of the tanks in their arsenal, while the Syrians had trained crews for only two-thirds of their armored vehicles before civil war broke out in 2012.

The result of these problems has been that Arab armies and air forces with advanced, even state-of-the-art equipment were often defeated by adversaries possessing less advanced, even primitive weapons, because the Arab armies got so little out of their equipment. The defeat of heavily armed Libyan forces first by the Tanzanians in Uganda in 1979 and then by the Chadians in 1986–1987 are good examples of this problem, but there were many others.

After many of their wars, Arab apologists have frequently blamed their defeat on foreign intervention. There certainly has been considerable foreign intervention in some Middle Eastern wars, and at times that intervention has been very important—such as the Anglo-French invasion of the Canal Zone during the 1956 Suez-Sinai War. That said, this phenomenon has been exaggerated, often badly. One aspect of it touches on military effectiveness. That is the claim that Arab armies have consistently lost because their adversaries have always had superior Western technology. First, as I noted in the Introduction and as other cases in this book will make clear, the Arab militaries often had better weapons than their foes. Second, even where their adversaries did possess significantly better weapons (Israel versus Syria in 1982, the United States versus Iraq in 1991), the gap in weapons quality was almost irrelevant because of how poorly Arab soldiers and airmen employed them. In many instances, their employment was so bad that it did not matter whether the weapons were better or worse than those of the foe; used that badly, they were going to lose.

Strategic Leadership

In contrast to tactical leadership, information management, and technical skills, the strategic leadership of Arab armed forces has varied widely since the Second World War. Some of the generals commanding Arab armies and air forces have proven completely incompetent, at times to the ruin of the forces under their authority. But not all Arab generals have been inept political hacks, and even some of the political appointees have turned out to be first-rate generals—such as Jordan's Zaid Bin Shakir, Syria's Ali Aslan, and Iraq's Husayn Rashid Muhammad at-Tikriti.[3] Yet neither did modern Arab states produce a string of brilliant generals to rival twentieth-century Germany, nor any military geniuses of the caliber of Napoleon, Marlboro, Saladin, or Alexander. Overall, Arab generalship fluctuated and their fortunes, to some extent, fluctuated with it.

It is certainly true that in some Middle East wars, Arab militaries have been led by incompetent senior commanders who bear much of the responsibility for defeat. The incompetence and corruption of Iraq's senior officers was one of the most important reasons—if not the single most important reason—for the collapse of the Iraqi Army in the face of the Da'ish assault in June 2014. In an earlier war, Baghdad's generals planned and directed their invasion of Iran in 1980 about as poorly as possible. Iraqi senior commanders directing the war against the Kurds in the early 1960s, and to some extent against Israel in 1973, also turned in performances that were mediocre at best. Libyan direction of its air and air defense (and naval) forces against the United States in the 1980s was comical to anyone but the soldiers, airmen, and sailors who died as a result of their amateurishness. Finally, Cairo's direction of the Egyptian defense of Sinai during the Six-Day War was flat-out abysmal.

In other wars, Arab generals performed reasonably well, not necessarily paving the way to victory single-handed, but also not damning their armies to defeat. Egyptian generalship in Palestine in 1948 was fine, occasionally better and occasionally worse, but mostly doing an adequate job. Likewise, by the late 1960s, Baghdad had figured out a strategy to beat the Kurds in their long-running secessionist struggle, and the Iraqi high command put together a number of competent operations that probably could have resulted in victory if the tactical forces at their disposal had been more competent. Syria's high command did a decent job in 1982 against Israel, and the Syrian loss cannot really be laid at their feet. Libyan generalship in Chad was mostly adequate, especially in the early years. Tripoli's commanders sometimes displayed more and sometimes less deftness with the third-rate forces at their disposal, but they generally got the job done. The Egyptian high command did all that was asked of them in the Sinai-Suez conflict of 1956, and most of their strategic moves were eminently sensible. Likewise, Amman's direction of the defense of the West Bank in 1967 was also reasonably good, and even those moves that ultimately proved harmful were based on creditable strategic thinking.

Finally, in some of their wars, Arab armies have been led by very competent senior commanders, but these generals were able to achieve only very modest results because they were hamstrung by the poor performance of the armies under their command. Indeed, in these cases, it has been the limited abilities of Arab tactical forces that have hindered the achievements of their generals, and not vice versa. Egyptian generalship in the October War and Iraqi generalship against Iran in 1987–1988 (and to a slightly lesser extent in the Gulf War) probably deserve the highest praise. Hizballah and Da'ish's senior leaders deserve nothing but respect for their masterful handling of the 2006 war against Israel and 2014 invasion of Iraq, respectively. Jordan's generals did an excellent job conducting the campaign against the PLO after the initial false start of Black September in 1970. In addition, US military personnel have frequently expressed a high degree of respect for many of the Emirati senior officers they have worked and fought with since 2011. The extensive American experience in Iraq since 2003 has provided a wealth of insight into the Iraqi officer corps, and US personnel can point to Iraqi generals who range from superb leaders to utter incompetents, and everything in-between.

In short, Arab generals have run the gamut, and no consistent pattern of competence or incompetence can be found in their military history since 1948.

Arab military planning largely paralleled these trends. When the senior commanders knew their business, they put together capable staffs who planned and directed operations in a competent fashion. The Egyptian military staff that planned the October War and the Iraqi military staff that planned its war-winning offensives against Iran in 1988—and the subsequent invasion of Kuwait in 1990—stand out as particularly able. Not surprisingly, these staffs came together under some of the most skilled generals to ever lead modern Arab militaries. And some of those Iraqi staff officers eventually went on to serve as the chief planners for ISIS, responsible for its terrifying run of conquests in Syria and Iraq in 2013–2015. In contrast, the Egyptian staff responsible for preparing for the Six-Day War and the Iraqi staff that "planned" the 1980–1982 invasion of Iran were utterly incompetent and amateurish, contributing to the rout of both armies. Not surprisingly, in both of those instances, these staffs were headed by some of the worst generals to ever don an Arab military uniform.

Unit Cohesion

No ironclad pattern of unit cohesion emerges from the history of the Arab armies since 1948 either. Instead, the cohesiveness of Arab units has varied to a considerable degree not only from war to war and army to army, but even within armies during the same war. There often was no way to tell beforehand which Arab formations would flee at the first shot, which would fight to the death, and which would fall somewhere in between. Nor was it always obvious after the fact why some units had fought and others had run. In 1956, a battalion of Egyptian infantry at Qusaymah collapsed when first attacked by the Israelis, while the other two battalions of its brigade fought like lions to hold nearby Abu Ageilah under repeated assaults by larger Israeli forces.

Nevertheless, although the evidence is not entirely consistent, on the whole, the unit cohesion of Arab armies has more often been good than bad, and on many occasions it was outstanding. The most prevalent pattern has been for Arab tactical formations to remain cohesive and combat effective even when placed in dire situations in which it would have been reasonable to expect the forces of any army to dissolve. Hizballah's tenacious defense of South Lebanon against the IDF in 2006; the stand of the Iraqi Republican Guard during Operation Desert Storm in 1991; the repeated attacks by Iraqi armor against more competent Israeli defenders during the October War of 1973; the Egyptian defense of Abu Ageilah and Umm Qatef in 1956, and again in 1967; the Jordanian defenders of Ammunition Hill and many other positions around Jerusalem in 1967; the tenacious Syrian defense of the Bekaa Valley in 1982; and the determination of Libyan units to hang on in the Tibesti region of northern Chad in 1987, all attest to superb cohesion by Arab formations under extremely adverse conditions. Likewise, while they are slightly different situations, the ability of Houthi forces to mount repeated offensives against the Yemeni government since 2010, their ability to hang on in the face of a far better armed and supplied Saudi-Emirati counteroffensive after 2015, and the stubborn Da'ish defense of various Iraqi and Syrian cities from Ramadi to Raqqa in 2015–2017 attest to similarly impressive cohesiveness.

There have been instances of Arab units disintegrating under fairly light pressure. The Egyptians at Qusaymah in 1956, the Libyans at Lukuya in Uganda in 1979, the Jordanians in Hebron in 1967, and the Iraqi forces that dissolved in the face of the Da'ish attack in June 2014 all come to mind. While these cannot be written off as mere exceptions to the rule, it is nonetheless the case that this pattern has been considerably less prevalent than instances of Arab units holding up well (or even superbly) in difficult situations.

Arab forces tended to fall apart in large numbers and without repeated pummeling most frequently when they were ordered to conduct a general retreat and were faced with aggressive pursuit by their attackers. Many of the worst routs suffered by Arab forces took place in these situations, including Egyptian forces in Sinai in 1956 and 1967, Jordanian forces on the West Bank in 1967, Syrian forces on the Golan in 1967, Libyan forces in northern Chad in 1987, and Iraqi forces in Iran in 1981–1982. All of these armies only began to collapse after they had begun to retreat and their escape routes were unexpectedly threatened or cut. In contrast, when Arab units were allowed to retreat without much pressure from an attacking force, and therefore were able to move slowly and deliberately, they tended to remain cohesive. The retreat of Syrian forces up the Bekaa Valley in June 1982 and of Jordanian forces being attacked by the Syrians in the Vale of Ramtha in 1970 were both occasions when an attacking force did not aggressively pursue a retreating Arab army and the retreating army was able to fall back in reasonably good order. These patterns strongly suggest that it required the psychological blow of defeat and retreat, coupled with the tremendous tactical difficulties Arab armed forces regularly experienced when attempting to quickly improvise unplanned combat operations, to cause large-scale loss of cohesiveness in Arab armies.

Consequently, one cannot blame poor unit cohesion for the consistent underachievement of Arab armed forces. In fact, quite the contrary has been true: unit cohesion was probably more a strength of Arab armies than a weakness.

Logistics and Maintenance

The sustainment of Arab forces in battle presented another mixed picture, but in a different way. On the one hand, most Arab militaries performed quite well in terms of formal logistical tasks such as the provisioning and movement of combat units and supplies, especially for the first several decades after World War II. On the other hand, Arab armed forces uniformly experienced severe difficulties in terms of maintenance and repair of military equipment. This disjuncture is odd since there is overlap in the skills and mindset needed for both, and maintenance is typically considered an aspect of logistics.

Other than maintenance, logistics was generally a strength of most Arab armies, at least during the twentieth century. By and large, Arab armies and air forces did not suffer in combat because they lacked ammunition, food, water, fuel, lubricants, medical supplies, repair tools, spare parts, or other combat consumables. Arab quartermasters generally did at least an adequate job of assuring that their combat formations got the provisions they needed to do the job. Similarly, it was mostly the case that Arab armed forces did not suffer from inadequate lift. Arab supply and transportation units performed very competently at moving large combat formations and their necessary support and supplies.

Nevertheless, there was considerable variance across the cases. The Egyptian, Libyan, and Iraqi armed forces *before the fall of Saddam* performed well in most aspects of logistical operations. Their forces were never hindered by inadequate or incompetent logistical support, and in a number of wars, their combat service support performed brilliantly. The deployment and provisioning of as many as 70,000 Egyptian troops in Yemen over five years in the 1960s was no mean feat, while the logistical requirements of Egypt's massive assault across Suez to start the October War in 1973 were truly daunting—and the fact that Egyptian forces suffered only very minor problems in this operation has to be considered a very impressive achievement. The Libyan armed forces did remarkably well moving and sustaining brigade, division, and larger formations in Uganda and Chad, thousands of miles from the main Libyan military support infrastructure along the Mediterranean.

The Iraqi case highlights some of the perplexities of this pattern of behavior. Despite the rigidity, over-centralization, and lack of imagination that characterized much of the pre-2003 Iraqi military, Baghdad's quartermasters demonstrated surprising flexibility manipulating their hodgepodge logistical system. They performed extremely well moving and maintaining a reinforced corps in combat with the Israelis in southwest Syria in 1973, and meeting all the sustainment needs of a million-man army fighting Iran for eight years. Even in the Persian Gulf War, not only were Iraqi logistics more than adequate to sustain a very rapid advance over 150 kilometers to conquer Kuwait, but prior to the start of the Coalition air campaign, Baghdad had relatively little difficulty moving and sustaining an army of over half-a-million men in the difficult logistical conditions of Kuwait and southwestern Iraq.[4]

There were some Arab services that experienced significant logistical problems. The Syrian armed forces consistently suffered from supply deficiencies. Syria's war effort in 1948 was hampered by inadequate provisions, which forced Damascus to decide which of its two thrusts into Israel would get the provisions to keep fighting and which would have to dig-in and wait. The Syrian invasion of Lebanon in 1976 was constantly hamstrung by a logistical system that could not keep pace with its combat forces, even though its combat forces were moving at a snail's pace. Similarly, some Syrian units in Lebanon in 1982 were hampered by inadequate supplies. To a certain extent, these Syrian problems can be attributed to the failure of Syrian personnel to understand their Soviet-style "push" logistical system. To a lesser extent, they can also be tied to the endemic graft that had infected the Syrian Army in Lebanon. But the Syrian forces that invaded in 1976 had not had the opportunity to wade into Lebanese graft, nor did the Syrian Army of 1948 employ a Soviet-style system. Consequently, these explanations can only be taken so far.

Since the American invasion of Iraq, Baghdad's rebuilt armed forces have experienced crippling problems with logistics that run contrary to their pre-2003 successes. It is hard to know exactly what is going on here. Part of it is undoubtedly the corruption that plagues the Iraqi government and armed forces. It is hard to keep troops fed, armed, and otherwise supplied when funds frequently go missing, along with the ammunition, medical supplies, food, vehicles, and even uniforms they are meant to buy. It all makes keeping track of what the army has or where it is being delivered very hard, and ensuring that everyone has what he needs harder still.[5] However, another part of the problem can be attributed to the American-directed shift from a paper tracking system to a computerized system that many Iraqis hate and few seem to know how to use. Finally, like many of the Gulf Arab states, the post-Saddam Iraqis have had to bring in Western contractors to handle the most sophisticated Western weapons, such as their M1 tanks and F-16 fighters, which have proven too advanced for their own personnel to sustain.

In fact, most of the Arab air forces—even those of countries that enjoyed good logistical support in other areas—suffered from significant logistical problems. The Egyptian, Iraqi, Libyan, and Syrian air forces all had low sortie rates throughout their history. It took long periods of time for their ground crews to service aircraft for flight operations. Overall, the sortie rates for these air forces averaged less than one per day per aircraft. At times, armorers sent these aircraft off with the wrong ordnance for the missions they were to perform. This has been a frequent complaint about the Saudi air campaign against Yemen since 2015. Of course, some blame for this must also be accorded to Arab air force planners, who may have specified the wrong type of ordinance in their orders, or Arab unit commanders, who may not have checked to see that the planes were armed with the munitions called for in the mission orders. Aircraft frequently were not checked out properly and sent off with problems that forced them to abort.

A considerable part of the inability of Arab air forces to sustain even average sortie rates has to do with the shoddy maintenance practices found in all of the Arab militaries, albeit to a lesser extent in Jordan. Most of the Arab armed forces had a poor track record of keeping their weapons, vehicles, and other equipment up and running. Most Arab soldiers and officers showed little appreciation for the need to attend to their equipment, with the result that units generally had operational readiness (O/R) rates of only 50–67 percent. O/R rates greater than 70–80 percent were rare among Arab units, while rates as low as 25–30 percent were not. Combat units had too few personnel capable of repair work, requiring them to perform even the most minor repairs at large central depots. In addition, the personnel manning these repair depots were often foreigners.

Morale

The morale of Arab armies fluctuated from war to war and army to army. There have been wars in which Arab soldiers and officers had little inclination to fight right from the start. The Iraqi armed forces were less than thrilled with the idea of fighting the United States well before Operation Desert Storm commenced in 1991, and they had even less interest the second time around in 2003. The Egyptian armed forces at the start of the Egyptian-Israeli War of Attrition were still badly demoralized from their defeat during the Six-Day War. To a certain extent, Egyptian soldiers were frustrated, apathetic, and disaffected even before the Six-Day War, in part because of the weeks spent wandering around Sinai while 'Amr and Nasser decided whether they were going to fight Israel, and in part because of the neglect of Egyptian enlisted personnel shown by their officers. Even still, morale was generally reported as high among Egyptian troops by the time the war began on June 5, 1967.[6]

Moreover, there have been other wars in which the Arab armies were totally committed to their cause. For instance, Egyptian and Syrian forces were highly motivated for the October War, and all of the Arab armies were enthusiastic about going into Palestine in 1948 to claim what they believed rightfully belonged to the Arabs, just as Libyan troops were motivated to fight for the Aouzou strip in northern Chad because they believed it was Libyan territory that had been taken from them. In more recent times, Hizballah, Da'ish, and Yemeni Houthi troops went to war with very high morale.

In addition, there were any number of instances in which Arab morale declined precipitously during the course of a war in response to a bad turn in the fighting. Many Egyptians went to Yemen in the 1960s believing they were fighting with their Arab brothers for Arab unity, only to lose heart when they were forced to endure years of fruitless counterinsurgency against an enemy army also composed of brother Arabs. When Da'ish first swept into Iraq in 2014, the zeal of its fighters was one of its most important weapons. However, by late 2016, a steady stream of crushing defeats at the hands of the US-led Coalition had doused the fire in the bellies of most of their fighters. As a result, in places such as Fallujah and East Mosul, some Da'ish units offered meek resistance and others broke upon contact. It was a far cry from the juggernaut they seemed at first.

What emerges from the history is that when Arab armies have had poor morale it has hurt them, and when they have had high morale it has helped them, *but not by that much*. Egyptian forces in October 1973 were nearly in a frenzy when their offensive finally started, and that motivation was an element in their success on October 6–10. However, Egyptian morale was equally high just days later—actually even higher given the stunning victories they had achieved the previous week—yet on October 14 many of the best units in the Egyptian Army put in a remarkably inept performance against the IDF despite their tremendous enthusiasm. Likewise, the determination of Syrian troops to retake the Golan in 1973 had little impact on their actual combat effectiveness, which remained miserable. Syrian forces were highly motivated for the war, but very bad at fighting. Ultimately, the fact that they did not fight well was far more important to the course of the war than the fact that they fought so hard.

As a final note, officer-enlisted problems do not appear to have been as bothersome to the Arabs as was once widely believed. Problems between officers and their men have their greatest impact on morale, discipline, and unit cohesion. Yet Arab armies that suffered from officer-enlisted problems did not always suffer from morale, discipline, or unit cohesion problems. Moreover, even in those cases where both were present, it was not always the case that the one was the product of the other. For example, for 20 years before the Six-Day War, Syrian officers had paid little attention to their men, considering the preparation of their units for combat irrelevant to their professional ambitions. Many of them fled when they realized the Israelis had flanked the entire Syrian defensive system. However, Syrian tactical formations showed no lack of commitment, discipline, or cohesiveness. Although there were some Syrian units that melted away even before Israeli forces came near them, far more stayed in place and fought hard even when their positions were hopeless and their officers had abandoned them. This is not to suggest that poor officer-enlisted relations were not harmful, only that the harm appears to have been less than has often been claimed. Like poor morale more generally, Arab armies have suffered from having poor officer-enlisted relations at times, but have not suffered excessively from it. It never proved the difference between victory or defeat.

Training

With regard to the training of Arab armies, there are two issues that require discussion because they are important to some of the explanations I assess in the book. First is the extent to which Arab militaries spent their time preparing to fight other armies and air forces as opposed to concentrating on preserving internal security. This is important because militaries that are principally focused on internal security—and train exclusively for that mission—can't really be expected to do well when they are then thrown into a war against a foreign power. The second is how seriously the Arab armed forces took the task of preparing for war. Was their training lax and haphazard, or was it conscientious and deliberate (even if it may have been misguided)?

The first matter goes to the explanation offered by some Middle East experts (discussed in Chapter 5) that the Arabs did poorly in battle because their armies mostly concentrated on internal security matters, prepared little for conventional military operations, and so performed poorly because they were being asked to undertake a mission they were never intended to conduct. The second speaks to the claim of others that Arab problems in combat stem from the fact that their forces simply did not train diligently or "seriously" for any kinds of military operations, against external or internal foes.

In both cases, the historical evidence is mixed. At some points, in some armies, training was lackadaisical and largely neglected. For instance, until the Gulf War, the Royal Saudi Land Forces never made training a major consideration, and what training they did was infrequent and perfunctory. They fell back into that pattern after Desert Storm, with the result that Saudi ground forces have fared poorly in combat with Yemen's Houthis since 2015. In other cases, Arab militaries trained little because their officers were more interested in maneuvering for political position and were not rewarded for preparing troops for battle. The Syrian army suffered from these sorts of distractions throughout the 1950s and 1960s, as did the Iraqi armed forces after the departure of US troops in 2011, with the result that the Iraqis stopped training almost entirely.

However, other Arab militaries were extremely diligent about training and exercises. While their training was not always terribly effective, it was rigorous and constant. After 1986, Iraq's Republican Guards trained constantly in mechanized, combined arms operations. Likewise, the incredible rigor of Egyptian training between 1967 and 1973 is attested to by the fact that the Egyptian armed forces practiced the entire assault across the Suez Canal 35 times, and individual units rehearsed their specific roles hundreds, if not thousands of times. Even the Syrian military made a conscious effort to be diligent about training for war after Hafiz al-Assad took power in 1971 and began to prepare his forces for an offensive against Israel.

Nevertheless, a clear pattern does emerge from Arab military history regarding the training of Arab armed forces that contradicts both claims regarding the role of training on the military fortunes of the Arabs since 1945. Virtually all of the Arab armed forces other than Jordan largely neglected proper training at first, and what little training they did was mainly directed at internal security duties. But as the years passed, a number of them became increasingly diligent and serious about preparation for war with foreign foes.

For the Egyptians and Syrians, defeat in the War of Israeli Independence was a rude awakening, resulting in the overthrow of their governments and a determination to rebuild Arab military power to be able to defeat Israel. For the Iraqis it was repeated defeats by the Kurds and Israel, coupled with the growing threat from Iran. By the 1970s and 1980s many of the Arab militaries had become very professional in their devotion to rigorous and frequent training for conventional military operations against foreign armies. That was particularly true for the Egyptians, Syrians, Iraqis, and Jordanians. The same can be said for the Emirati military in the early twenty-first century.

However, these shifts in the emphasis and focus of Arab training produced only very modest improvements in Arab military performance. The same problems continued to haunt Arab militaries regardless of the extent to which they concentrated on external, vice internal, security operations and no matter how diligent they have been about training and exercises.

There were two exceptions to this rule. First was the Jordanians who conducted rigorous training right from the start because of the tutelage of the British officers who had led the Arab Legion. Similarly, even though one of its responsibilities was suppressing tribal dissent against King Abdullah's rule, the British made sure that the Legion constantly trained for conventional operations against foreign armies. For this reason, Jordanian training deteriorated after 1956, when the British officers were forced out, unlike many other Arab armies whose attention to training increased over time.

The other exception was the Libyans, whose training practices remained moribund from the start and never really improved before the country was swept up in civil war in 2011. Prior to that watershed, Libyan formations had been fixated on internal security concerns, with the exception of the late 1980s when the war in Chad forced Tripoli to focus its training practices more on conventional operations. Similarly, the rampant politicization of the Libyan military meant that the training of Libyan formations often was neglected by their officers who had little reason to care whether their units were battle-ready.

These patterns strongly indicate that diligent training for conventional war against external adversaries was not one of the more important problems that have hindered Arab militaries in combat. The fact that the most powerful Arab states learned to concentrate their militaries on training for conventional war, and that their militaries trained diligently for these wars, but that these labors produced such modest results, indicates that the emphasis and rigor of their training were not the primary problems. The two exceptions lend further support to this conclusion. The Jordanians in 1948 did not suffer from these problems to the same extent as the other Arab states (including at other times) and they did enjoy better military effectiveness than the other Arab states at that time. Likewise, the Libyans never improved their training practices and clearly performed even worse than the other Arab armed forces in battle.

Still, what is most noteworthy is just how relative these distinctions were. The Jordanians were generally better than other Arab militaries in most categories of effectiveness, especially in 1948, but not by much. Likewise, the Libyans were worse than the rest, but again not by much. If we compare the Jordanian army of 1967, the Iraqi army of the late 1980s and early 1990s, and the Libyan army of the 1980s, there are definitely differences: The Jordanians were better than the Iraqis, who were better than the Libyans. However, the Jordanians were still a mediocre military. The Libyans were incompetent, but not that much more incompetent than the Iraqis. Perhaps of greatest importance, all three forces demonstrated the same crippling problems in the areas of tactical leadership, air operations, information management, and technical skills. These problems remained constants for Arab armies no matter how hard they trained. Indeed, even when Arab armies trained specifically to overcome these problems—as the Iraqis did in the 1980s and again under American tutelage after 2003 and 2014—they had almost no success. Clearly then, something else was at work among Arab armies and air forces beyond simply inadequate training.

Bravery and Cowardice

Arab military history demonstrates that of all the problems experienced by the Arabs in combat since 1945, a pervasive cowardice has *not* been among them. It puts the lie to the slanders of those who have dismissed the Arabs as cowardly soldiers. Of course, one can point to any number of incidents in which individual Arab soldiers, officers, or even entire units behaved in a less than valorous manner.

However, this is true for every army. Even the Japanese Army of World War II had its share of cowards. The key questions are how widespread was such behavior, was it more prevalent than courageous performances, and how much did acts of cowardice affect Arab fortunes? On each count, the historical evidence demonstrates that Arab armies performed creditably, if not meritoriously. There are countless anecdotal accounts of Arab soldiers and officers sacrificing their own safety for their comrades or their mission, and the opponents of the Arabs generally credited them with staunch (albeit not necessarily skillful) resistance.

On the offensive, Arab forces routinely charged into murderous fire and kept up their attacks even when mauled by their adversaries. This pattern was evinced by the Iraqis against the Israelis in southwest Syria in 1973, by the Syrians on the Golan in 1973, by the Syrian Air Force over Lebanon in 1982, by the Libyans at Aouzou in 1987, and by the Saudis at the Battle of Khafji in 1991. Whatever we may think of Da'ish, no one can say that their fighters were not tremendously brave throughout the 2014–2015 offensives.

On the defensive, Arab units often fought ferociously from their positions, even long after they had been outflanked, bypassed, or otherwise neutralized. Jordanian defenders on the West Bank in 1967 and at al-Karamah in 1968; Libyan forces in northern Chad in 1987; Egyptian forces in the Fallujah pocket in 1948, at the Mitlah pass and Abu Ageilah in 1956, at Rafah, Khan Yunis, Abu Ageilah, Umm Qatef, and the Jiradi Pass in 1967, and at the Chinese Farm and Ismailia in 1973; Iraqi forces at al-Basrah in 1982 and again in 1987; as well as Syrian forces on the Golan in 1967, and in Lebanon in 1982, all demonstrated tremendous courage in standing their ground and fighting hard in extremely difficult situations.

Arab rearguards, when they were employed, usually fought hardest of all, sacrificing themselves to see that the rest of their armies escape safely. Egyptian forces at Jebel Libni and B'ir Gifgafah in the Sinai in 1967, and the stand of the Iraqi Republican Guard against the US VII Corps in 1991 attest to the willingness of Arab rearguards to do their duty even when it meant their destruction. Indeed, what is truly noteworthy about Iraqi performance in the Gulf War is not that 200,000–400,000 deserted or surrendered to coalition ground forces, but that after 39 days of constant air attack, the destruction of their logistical distribution network, their lack of commitment to the cause, and their clear inferiority to Coalition forces, another 100,000–200,000 Iraqi troops actually stood their ground.

On to the Explanations

Now that we are all on the same sheet of music regarding how the Arab militaries performed throughout the post-1945 era, we can begin to explore the question of why. In the next four Parts of this book, I consider the four principal arguments that have been offered to explain the consistently poor performance of Arab arms: reliance on Soviet doctrine, politicization, underdevelopment, and cultural patterns. For each, I lay out the explanation itself, ask if the Arab armed forces performed the way each explanation claims, look at a number of specific examples from Arab military history that shed light on the question, and then compare Arab military performance to that of other, non-Arab militaries known to have suffered from that problem to see if the Arab armed forces performed in a similar fashion. All of this together will help us find some answers.

TABLE 1.1 Summary of Patterns

Area of Operations	Good or Bad?	Pattern of Behavior
Tactical Leadership	↓	Consistently poor. Junior officers passive, unimaginative, will not take advantage of opportunities or act to solve problems, will not maneuver or counterattack, do not understand combined arms operations.
Strategic Leadership	↕	Uneven. At times, poor strategists, planning is absent or haphazard, react foolishly or not at all to the course of battle. At other times, very good strategists, careful planners, react well to combat developments. At still other times, middling—neither great nor terrible.
Tactical Information Management	↓	Consistently poor: do not patrol or collect information, do not disseminate it when they have it, do not act on it when they hear it. Obfuscate, exaggerate, or downright lie to cover mistakes.
Strategic Information Management	↕	Uneven. Typically varies in correlation with strategic leadership. Varying from excellent—which typically requires reliance on strategic collection systems and/or external sources to avoid the problems at tactical levels—to just as abysmal as tactical mishandling of information.
Technical Skills and Weapons Handling	↓	Consistently poor. Personnel take long periods of time to learn how to use new equipment, rarely are able to take full advantage of the capabilities of their weapons.
Unit Cohesion	↕	Uneven. Tends to vary toward the extremes: either extremely good unit cohesion in which formations will hang together under severe circumstances that would break those of other countries, or extremely poor in which units crack under very light pressure.

TABLE 1.1 Continued

Area of Operations	Good or Bad?	Pattern of Behavior
Logistics	⇧	Generally simple but effective. Rare to find poor logistical performances and frequently find extraordinarily good capabilities.
Maintenance	⬇	Consistently poor. No real understanding on the part of personnel for the need for preventive maintenance. Very little is performed. Repairs typically require depot-level servicing, often performed by foreigners.
Morale	⬌	No clear pattern. Often very good.
Training	⬍	Uneven. At times, trained hard and well for operations. In other circumstances, training was nonexistent. At other times and place, they trained but not hard or particularly well.
Bravery	⇧	Generally very good.
Tactical Air Operations	⬇	Consistently poor. Air Forces were equally bad at air-to-air and air-to-ground operations. Performance of individual pilots, 2- and 4-ship formations, and squadrons was very poor.
Strategic Air Operations	⬍	Uneven. Often, strategic direction—including planning, weaponeering, sortie allocation, etc.—also poor. On other occasions, reasonably good, especially in light of the limits of their subordinates. Better performances often correlated with poor generalship and poor strategic information management.

| Soviet Doctrine

| The Soviet Way of War

THE FIRST EXPLANATION for modern Arab military ineffectiveness I am going to look at is the idea that it's all the Soviets' fault.[1] This is an idea that has been around for decades and still hangs around in some corners, including in the US military, where some have not quite shed their longtime fixation with the Red Army. But they're not the only ones. Egyptian authors such as Anwar Abdel-Malek and Mahmud Hussein have argued that from the late 1950s onward, "reliance on Russian weapons systems and the tactics which such systems necessarily implied" hindered Egyptian military operations.[2] These claims have been echoed by some Western commentators. For instance, one British scholar writes that "Arab disadvantages were heightened by the application of Russian introduced tactical models that were ill-suited for the fluid situation created by Israeli deep penetration tactics."[3]

That the Russians have worked with Arab militaries for many decades is indisputable. Soviet involvement with Middle Eastern armed forces dates back to the early days of the Cold War. In 1955, Egypt bought a raft of modern weapons from the Soviet Union, which used Czechoslovakia as a cutout for the sale. The so-called Czech arms deal was a major augmentation of Egyptian strength that allowed Cairo to skirt the arms embargo Britain, France, and the United States had imposed on Israel and the Arab states to dampen further conflict between them.[4] Egypt's success in obtaining the arms it desired on easy terms prompted other Arab states to follow suit. By 1970, Syria, Yemen, Iraq, and Libya had all concluded similar agreements with the USSR.

Of course, weapons were not the only thing Moscow provided. In many cases, Arab states received Soviet advice and training as well. Some Arab countries reorganized their armed forces along Soviet lines. Soviet advisers provided training in weapons use and combat operations to a number of Arab militaries, and numerous Arab officers took courses at military schools in the USSR. So between 1955 and the collapse of the USSR in 1991, the Soviets played a major role in the development of many Arab armies.

Determining whether the Russians are to blame for the poor performance of Arab militaries since World War II requires understanding how the Soviets fought. And how they *really* fought, as opposed to the caricatures of Soviet military methods often portrayed in Cold War diatribes. If you aren't familiar with the Soviet military system, you can't understand whether it is responsible for the problems that have plagued Arab armies since 1945. That means spending a little time getting to know the Soviet way of war. After all, that is what they taught anyone who wanted their help, including the Arab armed forces. So this chapter provides an overview of how the Soviets approached military operations, which is what they passed on to the Arab militaries as best they could.[5]

The Operational Level and Soviet Command and Control

Any discussion of Soviet military methods should begin with its emphasis on the operational level of warfare. The operational level refers to the conduct of military forces in a single campaign or theater. It is the level of military action between tactics (actions within a single battle) and strategy (the broad military conduct of a war), and generally involves the employment of army groups ("fronts" in Soviet terminology), armies, and occasionally corps or divisions. Whether by choice or necessity, the Soviets concluded that victory in war depended on winning at the operational level. Battles could be won or lost, but win the larger campaigns and victory in the war itself was assured. Or so they believed. The Soviets also concluded the opposite was true: if you lost the campaign, what did it matter how many battles you may have won along the way? Consequently, Soviet military thinkers and practitioners consciously and consistently sought to maximize their ability to prevail at the operational level even at the expense of other considerations.

The most important and far-reaching effect of this focus was the difference in command and control the Soviets created between their tactical formations and their operational (and strategic) formations. Essentially, the Soviets believed that to maximize their ability to prevail they had to ensure that operational level commanders had the maximum latitude to make decisions and the maximum ability to call on military assets.

This emphasis led the Soviets to circumscribe the decision-making of tactical commanders. For an operational-level commander in the Red Army, there was only one requirement: win the campaign however you could. For tactical commanders, there were far greater constraints to ensure that they acted in a manner consistent with what their superiors expected, making them predictable and reducing the likelihood that they would do something that might create an unanticipated problem for the higher-ups. It was generally the case that the Soviets expected their senior officers to be aggressive, innovative, flexible, and decisive. They expected the same from their junior officers *but* within carefully delineated parameters. The great Soviet military expert, John Erickson, once pointed out this duality, remarking that "In many respects, Soviet performance was a paradox: centralization and inflexibility giving way to improvisation and rapid adaptability, doggedness to deftness, the unimaginative and the stolid to boldness and even dash."[6]

For Soviet junior officers, NCOs, and enlisted personnel, this approach meant a training system that was quite rigid and consciously sought to restrict their independence and initiative. In the words of Christopher Donnelly, writing in the heyday of the Cold War, "It became important that the subordinate formation and unit commanders followed set orders, implementing them by means of a number of established alternative drills. The commander, therefore, did not make a plan, but a 'decision,' that is, he decided from a choice of alternatives upon one 'variant,' amended it according to local circumstances, and implemented it."[7]

There is a very important codicil to the points above: Soviet junior officers were *not* trained to be automatons, bereft of all judgment and mindlessly implementing the detailed plans of their superiors. Not at all. Instead, they typically had a short menu of acceptable ways to execute a mission, but the tactical commander on the spot still made that decision and had several options from that menu for any situation. These options were called "battle drills" by the Soviets, set plays to be used in different circumstances the way that a football team has one set of plays it might use for 1st and 10, and a different set for 3rd and short.

Nevertheless, the local commander was also expected to adapt these generic plans to the specific circumstances at hand. Soviet tactical commanders were expected both to choose an appropriate battle drill and then modify it as needed for the circumstances of the moment: the size and disposition of the enemy, the terrain, the weather, the friendly forces present, the availability of fire support, etc. It was never the case that the Soviets wanted their tactical commanders to merely implement battle drills by rote.

Of course, this effort to limit tactical decision-making to various preset approaches could produce a fair degree of stiffness among Soviet tactical formations, especially those with inexperienced commanders unsure of how to adapt the battle drills to the circumstances of the moment. These would often overcheck their decisions with higher headquarters to be on the safe side. In 1987, the Mujahidin leader Abdul Haq would crow that, "in Afghanistan, you need quick decisions and still Russian officers cannot decide for themselves without going back to their higher commands."[8]

The flip side, however, was also true. When the Soviets had seasoned tactical commanders, their way of war could be devastating: flexible, creative, adaptive, fast-paced, and adept at decisive maneuver. Indeed, throughout his insightful two-volume history of mechanized warfare on the Eastern Front in World War II, Robert Forczyk demonstrates that a key variable in the course of that conflict was the lack of training and experience of Soviet tactical commanders early on. It was these failings—and the incompetence of too many of Russia's operational leaders, the traumatized survivors of Stalin's purges—that enabled Germany's stunning early victories, not any inherent flaw in the Soviet system. That system performed brilliantly once Moscow had developed a new cast of superb operational commanders who could rely on a large number of experienced junior officers to execute their orders.[9]

The constraints on tactical decision-making also extended to the Soviet air forces, although Western military experts have often exaggerated the extent to which they were inflexible, dogmatic, and tactically inefficient. In particular, Soviet pilots were trained to rely on ground-controlled intercept (GCI), personnel who would direct the pilots into battle and in some ways, in battle.[10] However, here as well, there were limits. Soviet pilots were taught how to dogfight and how to fight on their own, both because Moscow recognized that NATO would try to jam the GCI feed in a war, and because in the chaos of an aerial dogfight, survival often requires the kind of split-second decisions that GCI cannot provide.

According to Alexander Zuyev, a Soviet MiG-29 pilot who defected to Turkey in 1990, by the mid-to-late 1980s (when many Arab air forces still relied on Soviet advice, guidance, and practices), Soviet fighter doctrine had become far more flexible than many Western experts understood. Zuyev's description both of the training practices of his unit as well as their expected operations in wartime suggest that Soviet fighters would not have been dependent on GCI and could have been expected to show imagination and aggressiveness in combat.[11]

Indeed, beginning in the late 1970s and early 1980s, Soviet military theorists apparently began to recognize that future battles would likely demand more decentralized authority, and thus the traditional Soviet predilection for obedient tactical commanders could be a handicap. This thinking was reinforced by the Soviet experience in Afghanistan, where the Soviets were forced to rely on small, independent forces to combat the Mujahidin—a pattern that taxed the Soviet command and control system. Zuyev's comments indicate that by the late 1980s, the Soviets had taken these lessons to heart and were attempting to introduce appropriate changes into their forces. His description of improvements in Soviet fighter doctrine has been echoed by other reports since the collapse of the Soviet Union and, by accounts of Russian air operations in Chechnya, Georgia, and Syria—although these conflicts all occurred well after the heyday of Soviet influence on Arab militaries.[12]

Not surprisingly, the Soviet emphasis on operational freedom at the expense of tactical flexibility typically produced inefficient, poor, or—when coupled with inadequate training—disastrously bad Soviet tactical performances. The skill of Soviet operational level commanders varied widely from the brilliance of a Konstantin Rokossovsky to the utter incompetence of a Semyon Budenny. But the best Soviet generals were those who learned how to win regardless of the competence of the tactical forces they commanded. For example, in 1939 at Khalkin Gol, General Georgi Zhukov triumphed because of a superb operational plan, material superiority over the Japanese, and lengthy time to plan and prepare his moves, but largely *despite* the limited capabilities of the units under his command.[13] Likewise, against Germany, a major factor in the dramatic reversal in Soviet fortunes was the remarkable improvement in Soviet generalship over the course of the war.

While it is true that even late into the war the Soviets often prevailed over the Germans through sheer weight of numbers rather than tactical skill, this ultimately bears testimony to the formidable talents of Soviet operational leadership, which frequently succeeded in outmaneuvering the Germans and concentrating enormous force against the Wehrmacht's weak points.[14] Where German generals might have relied on the skill of their tactical formations, their Soviet counterparts learned to be just as good using masses of men and machines to compensate for lesser tactical prowess. Soviet commanders were trained to make up for tactical "imperfections" with "ruthlessness and brutality," and a willingness to accept high casualty figures in the course of operations.[15] By the end of the war, Soviet ground-air campaigns were more powerful and deft than any the Germans had ever mounted, featuring devastating speed and maneuver, despite the fact that their subordinate formations were still no match for properly trained German units in tactical engagements.

The German generals would continue to boast that their troops still "won" many of the firefights and even battles, but it was the Russian generals who won the campaigns, and then the war.

The Best Defense Is a Good Offense

The Soviet system stressed offensive operations. Even before the Second World War, evolving Soviet ideas about modern warfare developed by officers such as Marshal Mikhail Tukhachevsky emphasized the need to seize the initiative by going on the offensive. The experience of World War II reinforced this predilection as the Soviets learned that leaving the initiative to the Germans could be extremely dangerous. Only by going on the attack themselves were the Soviets able to dictate the course of operations to the Germans, destroy the Wehrmacht, retake their land, and win the war.[16]

This approach was borne out by the constant stress on offensive operations in Soviet training. For example, the Soviet General Staff Academy taught that "the offensive constitutes the principal form of strategic actions of the armed forces," and "defense is considered a forced form of military action. Defense is assumed only when forces and means are not sufficient to attack or when gaining time may be necessary in order to concentrate forces and provide favorable conditions for the initiation of a decisive offensive operation."[17] Indeed, so great was the Soviet stress on offensive operations that commanders were taught to try to launch an immediate counteroffensive in response to an enemy offensive: "A first-echelon front should be ready to initiate the offensive in situations requiring repelling the enemy in a meeting engagement or enemy attack, destroying opposing enemy groupings, and ensuring the development of the operation in great depth with a high rate of advance."[18]

Soviet offensives relied on a combination of factors for success. The first was surprise. The Soviets made surprising their adversary a crucial characteristic of their operations.[19] To this end, the Soviets developed a formidable capability for camouflage, concealment, and deception (maskirovka).[20] Closely related to the Soviet obsession with maskirovka and obtaining surprise was a constant attention to reconnaissance and intelligence gathering.[21] As a result, Soviet senior leaders tended to do a pretty good job with the information battle, putting to good use the various intelligence assets available at national, theater, front, and army levels and constantly prodding subordinates to reconnoiter their sector of the front.[22] One Cold War expert on the Soviet military wrote that "The importance that Soviet military science attaches to reconnaissance cannot be overstated. In some World War II campaigns, for example, twenty-five to thirty percent of all aerial sorties were for reconnaissance purposes."[23]

The Soviets also taught that a successful offensive required a fast operational tempo (OPTEMPO). A high OPTEMPO allowed the attacker to keep the defender on his heels, forcing him to respond to the attacker's blows before his forces were ready. According to Benjamin Miller, the Soviets recognized a key interaction among offensive operations, surprise, and a high OPTEMPO. As Miller describes it, the Soviets taught that surprise was best exploited by offensive operations to keep the initiative and force the adversary to react to your actions, and a rapid pace of operations was crucial to magnify the effects of surprise and prevent the defender from regrouping sufficiently to put up strong resistance.[24] Thus Soviet forces were trained to penetrate the enemy's front and push quickly into its depth, bypassing areas of resistance to maintain the momentum of the attack.[25]

Another aspect of Soviet military practice that can be traced back to Tukhachevsky and the interwar Soviet military theorists is the importance of deep offensive thrusts. Soviet strategy for offensive operations was to penetrate as far (and as fast) into the enemy's operational depth as was possible. In John Hemsley's words, the Soviet "accent is on deep armored thrusts through to strategic objectives rather than seizing and holding ground at a tactical level."[26] During some of the Soviet offensives in 1944 and 1945, the Red Army drove as far as 200 kilometers into German rear areas before they brought the offensive to a halt to regroup for the next attack.[27]

Other Key Aspects of the Soviet Model

Soviet doctrine also emphasizes reliance on maneuver to concentrate overwhelming mass at the decisive point of the front (the *schwerpunkt*, as the Germans termed it) and to employ flanking attacks and encirclement to destroy enemy forces with the minimum necessary force.[28] During the Second World War, Soviet commanders displayed a remarkable talent for both. Even during the disastrous summer of 1941, the Germans were amazed at how Soviet generals constantly worked the flanks of German penetrations with counterattacks. In 1943–1945, Soviet generals were regularly able to concentrate sufficient forces to have 10:1, 20:1, or even greater superiority over the Germans in tanks, artillery pieces, and men at the *schwerpunkt* of the attack— and so more than compensate for the usual German advantage in tactical skill. Likewise, Soviet offensives consisted of constantly interlocking inner and outer encirclements of German forces.[29] After World War II, the Soviets began to integrate airborne and helicopter units into their operations to conduct vertical envelopments of enemy forces.[30] Indeed, in Afghanistan, the Soviets became adept at inserting elite *Spetsnaz* and airborne units to block the exits from a valley before sending mechanized forces into it to destroy any Mujahidin operating there. The Mujahidin described these as the most effective Soviet operations they had to face.[31]

Perhaps more than any other modern military except the Germans, the Soviet armed forces emphasized combined arms operations as the key to success in modern combat.[32] The Soviets were among the first to understand the need to integrate armor, infantry, artillery, engineers, air power, and other supporting elements into combined arms teams.[33] The Soviet system stressed this integration at all levels of the chain of command.

Although the effectiveness of Soviet (and now Russian) forces has varied over time, this stress on integrating their forces into combined arms teams has remained a constant. In the early years of the Second World War, Soviet commanders struggled to implement combined arms, and paid a devastating price at the hands of the Germans who had thoroughly mastered it. But as the war churned on, Soviet formations became increasingly adept at it, and this was one of the keys to their eventual victory. Even when they lacked the ideal equipment, the Soviets usually found a way to improvise and achieve the same results—like having infantry ride into battle on the backs of tanks when not enough motor transport was available.[34] In his encirclement of the German forces in the Korsun-Shevchenkovsky bulge in January 1944, General Ivan Konev of the 2nd Byelorussian Front stripped much of the armor from the 5th Guards Tank Army to ensure that the 53rd Army had adequate armored support to break through the German defenses. While this diminished the striking power of his exploitation force, Konev concluded that without a proper combined arms mix, the 53rd Army would not be able to break through at all, making exploitation a moot point.[35]

Similarly, the Soviets invaded Afghanistan with extremely well-integrated combined arms teams. Of course, the forces they brought were designed for high intensity combat on the North German plain and were entirely inappropriate for counterinsurgency operations in the mountains of Afghanistan. Nevertheless, by 1984, the Soviets had dramatically transformed their army in Afghanistan, forging a (for them) new type of combined arms team that relied on mechanized forces equipped with lighter weapons (for example, wheeled BTRs instead of tracked BMPs), airmobile elite infantry units (*Spetsnaz* and airborne troops), light artillery units, engineers, and helicopter gunship support. This mix worked quite well. So well that the United States and UK eventually felt obliged to provide the Mujahidin with advanced surface-to-air missiles (Stinger and Blowpipe) and antitank guided missiles (Milan), which then allowed the Mujahidin to inflict heavy casualties on the Soviets and eventually force them to withdraw.[36]

Because of the dominance of the ground forces in Soviet military strategy, air power was relegated to missions in support of the army and was directly subordinated to the higher-echelon ground commanders. Nevertheless, the Soviets recognized the need for air superiority over the battlefield, primarily because their experience in World War II taught them that the side with mastery of the skies can greatly inhibit the ground operations of its adversary. Consequently, the Soviets wanted to make sure that they had command of the air and their opponent did not. For this reason, counter-air missions had a high priority in the Soviet Air Force. The Soviet General Staff academy taught that "For successful initiation and conduct of strategic operations using conventional weapons, gaining air superiority is of particular significance."[37] In addition, the Soviets stressed air missions in direct support of ground forces such as reconnaissance, close-air support (CAS), and battlefield air interdiction (BAI). The Soviets did not buy into Western "airpower" theory, and so they paid little heed to strategic bombing or deep interdiction missions—except to aid deep ground penetrations.[38]

Soviet logistics were generally characterized as unsophisticated but effective.[39] The Soviets developed a "push" logistics system in which higher formations regularly sent supplies forward to subordinate formations without specific requests from the front-line units. While this method was wasteful, it was the best guarantee that the advancing armored units would not have to stop and wait for supplies.[40] The Soviets stressed the replacement of combat units rather than their reconstitution in place. Thus Soviet units were often referred to as "disposable," because they were tailored to participate in high intensity combat operations for only a few days, at which point the entire formation would be pulled off line and reconstituted in toto. For example, John Erickson observes that the Soviets expected a Motorized Rifle Division (MRD) to be engaged in combat for five days at which point it would be combat ineffective and withdrawn from the fray.[41] Similarly, Steven Canby has remarked that Soviet "combat divisions and even armies can be used like drill tips on a high-speed drill—ground down and replaced until penetration occurs."[42] This practice also helped to ensure the maximum rate of advance for attacking Soviet forces because it meant that units did not have to stop for refit: there were always fresh units ready to take the place of those burnt out by combat.[43]

The combination of the Soviet focus on high-speed armored offensives, and their general tendency to replace units in combat rather than reconstituting them, meant that while maintenance was expected to be high among Soviet combat formations to ensure that the fewest number of weapons were off-line because of mechanical problems, repair skills were not a major concern because the Soviets generally expected to replace combat losses rather than repair them. In addition, to obviate the need for proper maintenance, Soviet units kept their combat equipment in storage and practiced either with small portions of that equipment or with older models of the same weapons. This kept the latest equipment in pristine condition, ready for use when war came. As a result, the best Soviet units showed high standards of maintenance but had little organic repair and recovery capabilities.[44] These were instead concentrated at higher echelons (army- and, especially, front-level) that could be employed to completely reconstitute a unit after it had been ground down in combat.[45]

The Theory of the Case

If the problems that Arab militaries faced in wars since 1945 were a product of their reliance on Soviet military methods, then there are three things that we should find in the history of their combat experiences during that time. First, the Arab armies should fight like the Soviet armies and have problems where the Soviets had problems. Second, those Arab armies that did not rely on Soviet methods—and there were more than a few—should fight a lot better than those that did. For the same reason, those Arab armed forces that adopted Soviet methods at some point should have experienced a noticeable decline in their military effectiveness when they did so, whereas those who jettisoned their Soviet doctrine for something else should have experienced an equally noticeable improvement in their military competence. And finally, if the problem was Soviet military doctrine, then other countries that relied on those practices should have fought like the Arabs and experienced the same problems they did.

Given the patterns of combat performance of Arab armed forces described in Chapter 1 and the summary of Soviet military methods presented in this chapter, you may already be dubious that the latter was responsible for the former. I agree with you. Nevertheless, I think it important to look deeper at the performance of Arab militaries relying on the Soviet system, and at non-Arab militaries that did the same. There are two reasons for this. First, there are a lot of people who have argued that Arab problems stem from Soviet practices, and it is important to take this claim seriously and not dismiss it out of hand. Second, doing so allows me to bring in a number of important historical episodes that are not just important for assessing the role of Soviet doctrine, but also for the other proposed explanations: economics, politics, and culture.

So in the next chapter, I am going to try to address the first two of the three predictions above, namely "did the Arab armed forces fight like the Soviet armies, and did their problems get worse when they adopted Soviet doctrine—or improve when they dropped it?" Then in the chapter after that, I will look at some non-Arab militaries that also used Soviet military doctrine to see whether they had experiences similar to the Arabs.

CHAPTER 3 | Arab Militaries
and Soviet Doctrine

NOT ALL ARAB armies have relied on Soviet military systems. Table 3.1 lists 48 different instances when an Arab military fought in a Middle Eastern conflict since 1945. Of these 48 cases, Arab militaries relied on Soviet practices *to any extent* in only 25—barely half. In only 14 cases did an Arab military rely *heavily* on Soviet doctrine and methods, and in another 6 cases the Arab armed forces in question did employ Soviet techniques to a significant degree, but not necessarily more than another doctrine—whether it was Western or indigenous.

There have been other Arab militaries that had some Soviet influence, but in these instances, Soviet practices were so slight that they cannot be held responsible for the military's performance, good or bad. For example, in 1956 the Egyptian army had only just come under Moscow's tutelage, and the various Soviet-style training programs were only just getting underway. Thus, in the 1956 Sinai-Suez War the Egyptian Army was still largely reliant on its original, British doctrine. Likewise, beginning in the late 1950s and 1960s, the Iraqis received considerable military assistance from the Soviets, but the Iraqis never really adopted Soviet methods except in certain discrete areas, such as logistics and air defense. Even at the time of the 1973 October War, when Soviet influence in Iraq was greatest, Iraqi doctrine was overwhelmingly British, with some French and indigenous elements.[1]

This list of Arab experiences in battle since World War II presents the first big problem for the claim that it was Soviet military practices that doomed

TABLE 3.1 Arab Military Reliance on Soviet Military Practices

Arab Military—Conflict	Extent of Its Reliance on Soviet Methods
Algeria – Sand War, 1963	None
Algeria – Algerian Civil War, 1991–2002	High
Egypt – Israeli War of Independence, 1948	None
Egypt – Sinai Suez War, 1956	Low
Egypt – Yemeni Civil War, 1962–1967	Medium
Egypt – Six-Day War, 1967	Medium
Egypt – War of Attrition, 1967–1970	High
Egypt – October War, 1973	High
Egypt – Border War with Libya, 1977	Medium
Egypt – Persian Gulf War, 1990–1991	None
Hizballah – Conflict with Israel, 1985–2000	None
Hizballah – Second Lebanon War, 2006	None
Hizballah – Syrian Civil War, 2012–Present	None
Houthis – Yemeni Civil War, 2010–Present	None
Iraq – Israeli War of Independence, 1948	None
Iraq – First Kurdish War, 1961–1970	Low
Iraq – October War, 1973	Low
Iraq – Second Kurdish War, 1974–1975	Low
Iraq – Iran-Iraq War, 1980–1988	Medium
Iraq – Persian Gulf War, 1990–1991	Medium
Iraq – Iraqi Civil War, 2003–2009	None
Iraq – Iraqi Civil War, 2014–2017	None
ISIS – Syrian Civil War, 2012–Present	None
ISIS – Iraqi Civil War, 2014–2017	None
Jordan – Israeli War of Independence, 1948	None
Jordan – Six-Day War, 1967	None
Jordan – Black September, 1970–1971	None
Jordan – October War, 1973	None
Lebanon – Israeli War of Independence, 1948	None
Libya – Border War with Egypt, 1977	High
Libya – Uganda-Tanzania War, 1978–1979	High
Libya – Chadian-Libyan War, 1978–1987	High
Libya – Libyan Civil War, 2011	High
Morocco – Sand War, 1963	None
Oman – Dhofar Rebellion, 1962–1976	None
North Yemen – Yemeni Civil War, 1994	High

(*continued*)

TABLE 3.1 Continued

Arab Military—Conflict	Extent of Its Reliance on Soviet Methods
Saudi Arabia – Persian Gulf War, 1990–1991	None
Saudi Arabia – Yemeni Civil War, 2015–????	None
South Yemen – Yemeni Civil War, 1994	High
Syria – Israeli War of Independence, 1948	None
Syria – Six-Day War, 1967	Medium
Syria – Black September, 1970–1971	High
Syria – October War, 1973	High
Syria – Lebanese Civil War, 1976–1991	High
Syria – Israeli Invasion of Lebanon, 1982	High
Syria – Syrian Civil War, 2012–Present	High
UAE – Yemeni Civil War, 2015–Present	None
Yemen – Yemeni Civil War, 2015–Present	Low

Key:

High—Soviet methods played a very significant role in the armed forces' operational doctrine during the particular war.

Medium—Soviet methods shaped the armed forces' operational doctrine during the particular war to some extent, but did not predominate over indigenous or Western practices.

Minimal—Soviet methods played only a very marginal role in the armed forces' operational doctrine during the particular war.

None—Nation did not rely on Soviet-style military system at all during the particular war.

Arab armed forces. Simply put, Arab armed forces performed poorly—and performed poorly in virtually identical fashion—regardless of whether they relied on Soviet practices. If anything, a number of Arab armed forces actually showed *improvement* in certain areas of military effectiveness after adopting Soviet methods. Let me illustrate by digging into a few of the cases listed above.

Egypt, Jordan, and Syria in the Six-Day War

Let's start by going back to the history of Arab military fortunes in the Six-Day War presented in the Introduction. All three of the principal Arab armed forces that fought that war—the Egyptians, Jordanians, and Syrians—lost catastrophically, and an important element in each of their defeats were the severe failings of their own forces. In particular, all three experienced remarkably similar problems with poor and inflexible tactical leadership, a consequent inability to wage maneuver warfare either offensively or defensively, poor combined arms integration, appalling mismanagement of information, miserable air-to-air combat skills, negligible air-to-ground capabilities, minimal weapons handling skills, and poor maintenance practices. It's not just that they all had the same problems, it's that they experienced the same problems in almost exactly the same fashion, to the point where Israeli, Western, and even some of their own accounts of the fighting on each front read like plagiarized versions of one another.

Here is the problem for those who would blame this on the Russians: these forces did not all rely on Soviet practices. Egypt and Syria were still adopting Soviet doctrine and tactics. Their equipment was heavily Soviet by this point, as was their organization, but neither had adopted Soviet practices lock, stock, and barrel. To some extent, that's because neither the Egyptian nor the Syrian military trained and practiced enough to have fully internalized the new doctrine. Many officers continued to do certain things in the old, Western fashion that the Egyptians and Syrians had inherited from their former British and French colonial masters—or in the even older Ottoman manner.

On the other hand, Jordanian equipment, organization, doctrine, and everything else were wholly British. Although Amman had purged its seconded British officers and trainers in 1956, it had retained all of the old practices and traditions. Despite this severe disjuncture in British versus Soviet doctrine, Jordanian military performance in 1967 was little better than that of the Egyptians or Syrians—and considerably worse on a unit-for-unit basis than the Arab Legion's performance in 1948 (a topic I address later in this book). The Jordanian forces evinced all of the same problems as the Egyptians and Syrians and lost the entire West Bank in 72 hours while inflicting only slightly heavier casualties on the Israelis.

Of course, there were some differences. In particular, the Egyptians and Syrians also suffered from horrendous strategic leadership. Although Jordan's top leaders bought Egypt's lie about having defeated Israel and launched a counteroffensive into the Negev, thereafter, Jordanian generalship was quite creditable. Likewise, the Israelis singled out Jordan's Hawker Hunter pilots as having been notably more formidable than either Cairo's or Damascus's MiGs. In some battles, the Israelis felt that the Jordanians were decent marksmen (meaning they were pretty good at handling their weapons), but in plenty of others they proved to be terrible shots.

At the most obvious level, this history is a big knock against the claim that Soviet practices were responsible for poor Arab military performance. The British-reliant Jordanians were just as bad—and bad in the same ways—as the more Soviet-reliant Egyptians and Syrians. That strongly suggests that it wasn't the Soviet practices that were hurting the Egyptians and Syrians but something else. The fact that Jordanian generalship was better than Egyptian or Syrian generalship is another problem given the Soviet emphasis on operational-level competence and freedom of maneuver. That should argue for better generals than junior officers. Finally, the superior performance of Jordan's fighter pilots does suggest that the Soviet air-warfare system, which relies more heavily on ground-controlled intercept direction, may be part of the problem in this area. But that is a narrow segment of warfare, and only one of many areas in which Arab armed forces have had crippling problems time and again.

Egypt, 1973–1991

Having looked at three different Arab militaries that relied on different doctrines at the same time in the same war, let's change gears and look at one Arab military over time from one war to another. Egypt's reliance on Soviet doctrine changed dramatically over the decades following World War II, and if its problem was that doctrine, its military fortunes—or at least its patterns of military performance—should mirror its reliance on Soviet methods.

Broadly speaking, the Egyptian Army built up during World War II under the British protectorate employed British equipment, organization, and doctrine to the extent it had any. It was this army that fought and lost against Israel in 1948. Beginning with the Czech arms deal in 1955, the Egyptians slowly shed their British practices for Soviet, although this was a slow transition, in part because of the lack of professionalism in the officer corps and in part because Nasser was a fierce anti-communist and wary of turning his army over to the Russians in any way. However, after repeated humiliations in Yemen in the 1960s, in the Six-Day War of 1967, and again at the hands of the Israeli Air Force in the War of Attrition of 1969–1970, Nasser felt it essential to improve the combat performance of his armed forces and believed that a greater Soviet presence and a greater reliance on Soviet practices were necessary to do so. Sadat was equally suspicious of the Russians, but he needed a military victory over Israel to advance his ambitious diplomatic, political, and economic agenda, and so he continued Nasser's push for the Egyptian armed forces to embrace Soviet practices and the more serious and coherent approach to war-fighting they entailed.

By the October War, Egypt had adopted a great deal of Soviet tactics and doctrine. Although Egypt was not wholly reliant on Soviet practices, the Soviet method formed the basis of its approach to combat operations both on the ground and in the air.[2] In particular, Egyptian armor, air defense, and air-to-air tactics were heavily modeled on those of the Soviets. Thus, Egypt enjoyed its greatest military success ever, in the opening days of the 1973 October War, when its reliance on Soviet doctrine was greatest. That's another problem for the claim that reliance on Soviet methods hurt Arab military effectiveness. Yet during the war as a whole, overall Egyptian performance was uneven, and no better than in past wars in many key areas. (I discuss Egypt's experiences in the October War in greater detail in Chapter 6.)

The Gulf War 1990–1991. After the October War, Sadat would use Egypt's limited military achievements in masterful diplomatic fashion. He signed a peace treaty with Israel and won back the Sinai Peninsula doing so. Of equal importance, he severed Egypt's 20-year alliance with the USSR for a new one with the United States that included massive economic and military assistance.

So starting in 1978, the Egyptian armed forces began purchasing large quantities of American weaponry and procuring American assistance in reorganizing and reforming their armed forces. Eventually, the United States became Egypt's primary security benefactor and undertook a complete over-haul of the Egyptian armed forces. Large numbers of US military advisers were sent to Egypt to provide weapons instruction and operational training, and Egyptian officers began attending US training courses in droves. By the mid-1980s the Egyptian military had largely abandoned the Soviet practices they had acquired between 1955 and 1973.

Egypt's role as America's principal Arab ally in the region was put to the test when Saddam Husayn invaded Kuwait in 1990. Egyptian president Husni Mubarak committed his military both to the defense of Saudi Arabia (Operation DESERT SHIELD) and the offensive to liberate Kuwait and crush the Iraqi armed forces (Operation DESERT STORM). It was the first combat test for the Egyptian armed forces since they had exchanged Soviet methods for American.

Egyptian participation in the Gulf War was limited, but still significant. Egypt sent the second-largest Arab contingent to the war, and one of the largest contingents overall. Cairo dispatched two divisions—the 3rd Mechanized and 4th Armored—as well as the 20th commando regiment (brigade), an airborne brigade, and supporting units. All of these formations had been converted to American equipment and doctrine and were specifically sent because they

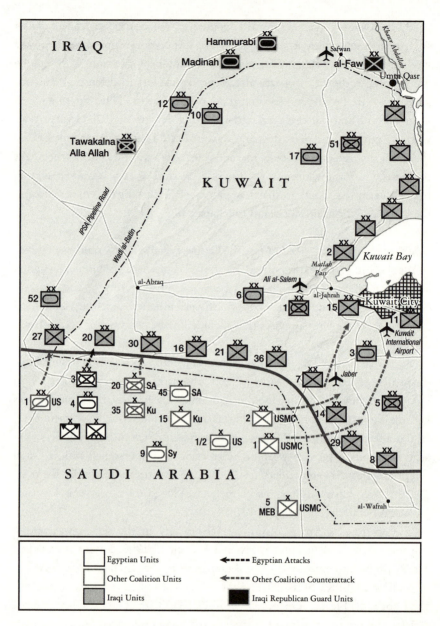

MAP 4 Egyptian Operations during the Gulf War

were considered the best in the Egyptian army. All told, the Egyptian force consisted of over 40,000 troops and about 400 tanks.[3]

The Egyptians were made the centerpiece of the Joint Forces Command-North (JFC-N), one of two major Arab formations in Desert Storm. In addition to the Egyptians, the JFC-N included two Saudi heavy brigades, two Kuwaiti brigades, a Syrian armored division, and a Syrian commando brigade. Nevertheless, the Egyptians were considered the heart of the JFC-N not only because they had the largest force, but because US military planners expected them to be the most capable and reliable. There was great uncertainty as to whether the Syrians would participate in the offensive at all, and because their Soviet equipment was virtually identical to that of the Iraqis, they were kept in reserve to avoid friendly-fire problems. The Saudis and Kuwaitis on the other hand were simply not judged to be serious combat units by the US personnel assigned to them.

Thus, it was decided that the Egyptian 3rd Mechanized Division would spearhead the attack, the 4th Armored Division would serve as an exploitation force, the Kuwaiti and Saudi units would conduct supporting attacks on the Egyptians' right flank, and the Syrians would serve as a corps reserve to be called on only if the other units encountered serious problems. Although US military planners had more confidence in the Egyptians than other Arab contingents of the multinational force, this was entirely relative. In fact, US Central Command (CENTCOM) held the US 1st Cavalry (Armored) Division in theater reserve behind the JFC-N so a heavy US force would be available to rescue them if they ran into trouble.[4]

The JFC-N was assigned the sector between the US Marine Corps' I Marine Expeditionary Force (I MEF) and the US Army's VII Corps. The I MEF was the primary diversionary force, tasked with attacking into the "heel" of southeastern Kuwait to draw Iraqi attention and reserves from the main Coalition effort. The US VII Corps would be the main effort of the Coalition offensive and would attack into southern Iraq west of Kuwait and then turn east to crush the Iraqi Republican Guard. The JFC-N, sandwiched between these two powerful American forces, was given western Kuwait as its operational sector and assigned the task of penetrating into Kuwait itself and then turning east to cut off an Iraqi retreat from southeastern Kuwait by seizing the main al-Basrah/al-Jahrah highway, along which Iraqi forces in southern Kuwait had to travel to escape. An important aspect of the JFC-N's mission was to protect the flanks of the two American forces from a counterattack by Iraqi armor deployed in central Kuwait.

The JFC-N attack was originally slated to kick-off at first light on the second day of the ground war, February 25, 1991. However, the I MEF offensive into southeastern Kuwait went so well that the CENTCOM commander, General Norman Schwarzkopf, decided to advance the timing of both the US VII Corps attack and the JFC-N attack. Of all the various units that were affected by this decision, only the Egyptian commander of the JFC-N said that he could not comply. Schwarzkopf did his best to persuade, cajole, and even threaten the Egyptians to get them to move up the start time, but they simply refused. Eventually, Schwarzkopf had to have Cairo order the Egyptian commander to advance the start time of his attack, but even then the Egyptians were not able to attack until 1500 hours, well after what CENTCOM had wanted.[5]

When the Egyptians finally did get moving, they advanced at a glacial pace against almost no Iraqi resistance. The Egyptians attacked into the sectors of the Iraqi 20th and 30th Infantry Divisions, both of which had been heavily depleted by desertions during the six-week Coalition air campaign. In addition, these units had been repeatedly worked over by Coalition strike aircraft, especially A-10 attack planes, which had destroyed most of their supporting armor and artillery. The US deputy theater commander, General Calvin Waller, remarked that "what the Egyptians are facing, two sick prostitutes could handle."[6] The Egyptians' mission for the first day was to breach the Iraqi defensive lines and seize the al-Abraq barracks about 20 miles into Kuwait. However, when the Egyptians reached the flame trenches the Iraqis had dug in front of their defensive lines, the Iraqis lit the trenches and the Egyptians stopped. The Egyptians apparently had not thought through the problem of how to extinguish or cross lit flame trenches, despite having known about them for months beforehand. Rather than improvise a solution on the spot, they just sat and waited for the fires to burn out, which took 10 hours. By the end of the first day, the Egyptians had not even crossed the flame trench, let alone breached the main Iraqi defense lines.

On the second day, the Iraqi units in front of the Egyptians began deserting en masse, a process that accelerated when Baghdad announced a general retreat from Kuwait later that day. The Egyptians resumed their attack at 0700 that morning, led by the 3rd Mechanized Division. Because of the disintegration/retreat of the Iraqi forces, the Egyptians encountered almost no resistance penetrating the Iraqi defensive lines. Egyptian artillery lay down a massive barrage to cover the advance, but this did little damage because the Egyptians insisted on firing on locations that US intelligence revealed the Iraqis had already abandoned. But because these targets were in the Egyptian artillery fire plan, the Egyptian commanders insisted on hitting them no matter what.

Soon after getting underway, the 3rd Mechanized Division came under desultory fire from a couple of Iraqi artillery batteries. A US liaison officer later reported, "At no time did [the Iraqi artillery fire] ever jeopardize the attack," but the Egyptians again halted.[7] They requested US air support, but bad weather prevented this. When their American advisors suggested the Egyptians silence the Iraqis with counter-battery fire, the Egyptian leadership refused: their artillery had exceeded its ammunition expenditure allocation for the breaching operation and would not allocate any additional rounds to silence the Iraqi artillery. So the Egyptians decided to stop and simply wait until the Iraqis stopped firing, which took until 1000.

When the Egyptians finally got going again, the few remaining Iraqi infantry manning the front-line defenses mostly either fled or surrendered. Nevertheless, the Egyptians moved painfully slowly in breaching the essentially undefended Iraqi lines. As late as 1300, the Egyptians still had not finished their breaching operations, causing great distress among CENTCOM personnel who wanted the Egyptians to move quicker to cut off the Iraqi retreat from southern Kuwait. The Egyptians kept inching forward and would not speed up their movements to try to catch the Iraqi forces as they fled. Eventually, CENTCOM became so concerned about the gap opening up between the rapidly advancing Marines and the floundering Egyptians that they reoriented several American units to cover the I MEF flank.

By the morning of the third day of the ground war, the Egyptians still had not taken their first day's objective of al-Abraq, and so CENTCOM ordered them to forget al-Abraq and instead turn east and move to al-Jahrah immediately. Once again, the Egyptian command refused to deviate from their plan unless they received a formal order from the Coalition political leadership. When confirmation of the CENTCOM orders finally arrived, the Egyptians swung part of their force east to creep toward al-Jahrah, but CENTCOM found it necessary to give this task instead to an American unit because the Egyptians were moving so slowly.

Meanwhile, it had been decided that both Arab commands would enter Kuwait City together as a show of Arab solidarity. By February 26, the Iraqis had abandoned Kuwait City, and other Arab forces that had come up from Saudi Arabia were sitting south of the city waiting to make a triumphal entry, but the JFC-N was nowhere near Kuwait City. Ultimately, selected units of the JFC-N were simply road marched to Kuwait City to join the parade, while the rest of the JFC-N plodded on. However, the Egyptian commander again objected. He had no specific orders to send units to enter Kuwait City, and he refused to comply until Schwarzkopf reached Mubarak himself and had Mubarak order the Egyptian commander to do so. By the end of the war, the Egyptians had somehow taken nearly a hundred casualties and had nothing to show for the effort.[8]

Egyptian Military Effectiveness since 1973. The Gulf War revealed what US military personnel had privately admitted for years: that despite 13 years of American aid, advice, and training, Egyptian military effectiveness had improved little, if any, since the Arab-Israeli wars. If anything, it had *declined*. In particular, while numerous Westerners who have had contact with the Egyptian military claim that many of Cairo's generals are quite competent, tactical leadership remains abysmal.

Egyptian junior officers still tend to show little innovation and initiative in combat. The halting movement of Egyptian units during the Gulf War, their unwillingness to adapt to opportunities presented by the course of battle, and their inability to solve unforeseen tactical problems were indistinguishable from the problems Egyptian units suffered in 1948–1973. Egyptian combat operations in the Gulf War and in training exercises since have been set-piece operations on both the offensive and defensive. According to one US military officer very familiar with the Egyptian military, "The Egyptians would make the simple complicated; something had to be done the way it was always done because they were so inflexible."[9] Over-centralization remains the rule throughout the Egyptian armed forces. One Western military officer observed that "There are few observable signs of real change in the centralized command and control system in either the Army or the Air Force," despite constant US efforts to encourage the Egyptians to decentralize authority.[10] Virtually all decisions must be made by a general officer, and it is nearly impossible to reverse a decision, even when it is no longer applicable because of changed circumstances—such as the insistence on executing every pre-planned artillery fire mission during Desert Storm, even against Iraqi positions known to be deserted. At times, initiative among junior officers is purposely suppressed by senior officers, but more often than not, tactical commanders display zero willingness or ability to act aggressively whenever they are delegated decision-making authority. One US military officer who has trained and advised the Egyptian armed forces remarked that "the lower you get in the chain of command the less initiative and creativity you see," while a civilian DoD official who has worked with the Egyptian military stated simply that "there is no initiative at all" among lower echelons of the Egyptian armed forces.[11]

Egyptian forces continue to show little understanding of combined arms operations. In most exercises, there is a complete separation of the combat arms, and there is little effort to teach their proper integration. Even the most sensationalist Israeli analyses of the Egyptian military have conceded that rather than improving their ability to integrate air and ground forces, the Egyptians have regressed since the Arab-Israeli wars.[12] According to US military officers and DoD officials familiar with the Egyptian military, training rarely takes place above the battalion level, and infantry, armor, and artillery almost never train together. These same officials unanimously aver that

Egyptian infantrymen have little or no understanding of armor operations, and vice versa.[13]

American personnel suggest that part of this problem may be related to a persistent inability or unwillingness to integrate details into a coherent whole. For example, one US official remarked that tasks are kept so discrete that Egyptian personnel rarely see how they relate to the functioning of an entire machine or unit: "This guy does not *repair* tanks, he puts *this part* onto a tank and that's all he knows how to do."[14] Similarly, Egyptian training focuses on set-piece operations with little emphasis on maneuver to gain an advantage over an opponent. This tendency was displayed in the Gulf War when Egyptian armor formations stumbled forward in frontal assaults, rather than attempting to outflank or envelop Iraqi defensive positions.

As they learned in 1973, Egyptian operations are scripted in minute detail, even for routine training missions, and no deviation is allowed from these scripts. One US military officer quipped that "Egyptian exercises are totally canned: they aren't for training, they're for show."[15] Another US officer remarked that "The Egyptians put an inordinate effort into tremendously detailed planning, and if the situation changes, don't expect the plan to change: they're sticking with the plan."[16] The efforts of American advisers and training personnel to convince the Egyptians to improvise operations, or to issue only broad guidelines and allow subordinates to fill in the details, regularly fall on deaf ears. Even the operations and training flights of the elite F-16 squadrons are completely scripted. As one US DoD official observed, "They know where to turn, and where to pretend to fire munitions, and who is going to win" before a training flight even begins.[17] Moreover, the Egyptian pilots would get extremely upset when someone did something he was not supposed to do. For this reason, there apparently is widespread dislike of joint training exercises with US forces because the Americans constantly and deliberately improvise rather than sticking to the agreed-upon script. As another example, the Egyptians were very impressed with US all-arms coordination, maneuver warfare, and the ability of US forces to carry the battle throughout the depth of the enemy's defense during the Gulf War. However, after the war, the Egyptians argued that the best way for them to emulate the Americans was with a highly detailed operational plan that determined objectives, assigned routes to the forces, allocated all air missions beforehand, and detailed the administrative and logistical support at all levels. In other words, they were willing to accept US AirLand Battle doctrine, but only if it was conducted in a rigid, scripted Egyptian fashion.

Manipulation of information throughout the chain of command also remains a major problem. During Operation Desert Storm, and despite the presence of US military personnel and journalists with their units, the Egyptians still consistently reported fierce battles even though they actually encountered almost no resistance at all.[18] United States' military personnel assigned as liaison to the Egyptian corps reported a pronounced "lack of inter-staff coordination and information sharing within the Egyptian corps staff."[19] Egyptian forces continue to suffer from fabricated reporting— sometimes even directed by commanders to hide problems from higher echelons. United States' military officers and DoD officials report that most senior Egyptian military commanders have little idea what is going on in their subordinate commands because they are constantly misled. These same personnel also report that compartmentalization in Egypt is so severe that before even the most minor decisions can be taken all officers with knowledge bearing on the issue must be brought together because no one has sufficient knowledge of the entire situation to make an appropriate decision on his own.[20]

Maintenance continues to be another source of problems for the Egyptians. United States' personnel unanimously observe that Egyptian mechanics daily do a remarkable job patching up the simpler and more rugged pieces of machinery to make them work well enough to serve their function. However, they have little capacity to handle more sophisticated machinery or more complicated tasks, nor do most Egyptian military personnel understand the functioning of their equipment well enough to fix and maintain it properly. For example, Egypt required a large US presence for many years after receiving the F-4E Phantom II. In the mid-1980s, the Egyptians decided that they could handle the F-4s on their own and canceled the US maintenance contracts for these aircraft. The Phantom squadrons quickly became nonoperational because the Egyptians rarely performed preventive maintenance and could not make proper repairs. Consequently, Cairo had to reverse itself and even then, they still had to have depot-level maintenance performed in the United States.[21] They encountered similar problems when they began receiving the F-16 later that decade.

The Egyptian Air Force has received the most extensive support from US advisers, it has the most advanced US equipment, and large numbers of EAF pilots have US training, yet it remains moribund. According to US DoD personnel, well into the 1990s, virtually none of Egypt's pilots used the avionics on their US-built aircraft—even the F-16 pilots. If the radar was even on while they were in the air (which wasn't always the case) the pilots would rely on visual sighting and ignore the radar. Fortunately for them, because their exercises were always scripted, there was no reason to use the radar or other avionics: every pilot knew exactly where everyone else would be, how they would maneuver, and who would win.[22] As one US military official put it, "They fly our planes and use our tactics, but you'd never know it."[23] Some US military personnel suspected that Cairo chose not to send any air units to participate in the Gulf War for fear they would do poorly in combat and embarrass Mubarak, a former EAF general.

Overall, the changes since 1973 have had little impact on Egyptian military effectiveness. Despite abandoning the Soviet model of operations and adopting the American one, Egyptian forces have continued to manifest the same patterns of strengths and weaknesses they displayed at the height of their reliance on the Soviets. Perhaps more accurately, one US military officer intimately familiar with the Egyptian military argues that "All the Soviets ever did was bring 'science' to what the Egyptians like to do anyway."[24] Indeed, Egyptian military effectiveness has resisted change to a remarkable degree throughout the period since 1948, regardless of whether they employed British, Soviet, or American doctrine. Clearly then, Soviet practices cannot be held culpable for Egyptian military failings during this period either.

Whose Soviet System?

There is another set of evidence that bears on this question, and that's what the Soviets themselves thought of their Arab charges. You probably won't be surprised to learn that the Russian advisors and trainers who worked with the Arabs had little positive to say about what their Arab students did with their battle-honed doctrine. Overall, Soviet personnel seem to have found their experiences training Arab armies and air forces as frustrating as American, British, and other Western officers entrusted with the same tasks. The Soviets generally felt that the Arabs did not understand the core concepts of their doctrine and, to the extent that they attempted to execute it at all, did so in ways that the Soviets never intended. In particular, the Soviets consistently complained that the Arab militaries were far too rigid, inflexible, scripted, lacking in improvisation and good information management, and incapable of maneuvering as Soviet formations would have.

Egypt, 1973. A great example of the Soviet experience with Arab armies comes from Egyptian armor training for the 1973 October War. As I noted above, in the run-up to the October War, the Egyptians adopted Soviet tactics to a greater extent than ever before. At that time, Soviet doctrine was to have the commander of a tank platoon designate a single target, at which the entire platoon (three tanks including the commander's) would then fire until it was destroyed, at which point the commander would designate a new target. The Soviets calculated that, given the gunnery skills of their crews, it normally would take three salvoes from the platoon (nine shots) to kill an enemy tank. Rather than seeing this as a general guide for planning, the Egyptians turned it into a hard-and-fast rule and taught all of their tank platoons to fire three salvoes at the designated target and then move on to another target. Egyptian tank gunnery turned out to be considerably poorer than Soviet marksmanship, and as a result, during the October War, it was often the case that none of the shots fired in the three salvoes of an Egyptian tank platoon hit the Israeli tank they had targeted. Nevertheless, because the Egyptians had been taught to fire three salvoes and then move on, they would shift their fire to the next target even though they had not actually destroyed the first one. In this way, the Egyptians drove their Russian advisors to distraction trying to convince them not to take their guidelines as unbreakable laws. It was also one of many reasons that the Egyptians lost so many tank duels to the Israelis.[25]

Their Soviet advisors had similar problems with Egypt's air defense forces. One former Soviet advisor interviewed by a Russian military publication after the collapse of the USSR, stated that

> The Egyptians . . . had no confidence in the Soviet hardware, which they often said was inferior. But it was by no means the Soviet equipment that was to blame for their defeats, it was rather the low training standard of their missile crews. For example, they would promptly vacate their work states upon firing a missile, and it never occurred to them that a missile needed to be guided in flight. The Soviet advisors with the Egyptian battalions could not do much and they often perished with the poorly trained crews. For you to compare, our battalion took 32 minutes to take up a new position, and an Egyptian one required 3 to 4 hours.[26]

Syria, 1973. Another example comes from the Syrians in the October War. The Syrian military of 1973 and its campaign plan for the October War were as close as any Arab military ever came to replicating the Soviet system, or at least trying to. The Syrian military was organized like the Red Army. Its plan of attack against the thinly held Israeli defenses on the Golan Heights was a textbook Soviet-style armored breakthrough operation. It was led by a lead echelon of three (partially mechanized) infantry divisions backed by a second echelon of two armored divisions that were to exploit the breakthroughs created by the first echelon and penetrate into the IDF's operational depth on the Golan. The campaign plan was heavily shaped by Syria's Soviet advisors, complete with Soviet-style phase lines.

The most critical thing about the plan was the importance of capturing the three bridges across the Jordan River, which controlled all access between Israel and the Golan. Taking those three bridges would effectively cut the Golan off from Israel and put Syria in the best position either to shift to the defensive and hold the Golan, or else continue the attack into Israel proper. Consequently, all sources—Syrian and Soviet—are clear that taking those bridges were the ultimate objective of the first phase of the Syrian campaign plan, and that the phase lines were set with pauses only *after* they were taken.

Yet that's not at all what happened. On October 7, the second day of the war, Syrian forces broke through the Israeli defenses in the southern Golan, and by afternoon, four Syrian armored and mechanized brigades were racing along the roads of the southern Golan toward those bridges with virtually nothing in front of them. They could have taken the bridges with ease. They *should have* taken the bridges with ease. But they didn't.

Farthest south, one of the brigades was stopped by an under-strength battalion of Israeli Super Shermans. In a sharp firefight, the Israelis knocked out 17 T-55s for the loss of only four Shermans, causing the Syrians to retire for the night, rather than pushing through the Israelis to the river even though it was still only late afternoon. This action took place so far south that Jordanian officers (along with Brigadier Syed 'Ali El-Edroos, an observer from the Pakistani Army) were able to watch the battle from Jordanian territory and were astounded that so large a Syrian armored force would hunker down for the night early rather than force their way through the much smaller defending force to achieve their crucial objective.[27]

Farther to the north, the Syrian 47th Armored Brigade with over 100 tanks was charging toward the Arik Bridge when it ran into a company (14 tanks) of Israeli Centurions and, in a brief firefight, lost 35 tanks while destroying only 3 Centurions. This bloody nose prompted the 47th Brigade's commander to pull in his horns and go into laager for the night. Also pressing toward the Arik bridge, the Syrian 2nd Mechanized Brigade blundered into a column of IDF infantry reservists heading east to join the fight, completely unaware that the Syrians had penetrated so far west. Although the Syrians quickly dispersed the Israelis with little damage to themselves, for some reason, this skirmish led the Syrian brigade commander to order his men into night laager as well. This despite the fact that there was at least an hour of daylight left, the Syrians had superior night-fighting gear, and the brigade had encountered few other Israelis for the last few miles. Finally, the Syrian 91st Armored Brigade made excellent progress along the route to the B'nat Ya'acov bridge, encountering no Israelis until the middle of the afternoon when they overran four Israeli self-propelled guns. Later, around 1700 hours, the brigade vanguard encountered a handful of Golani Brigade infantry who put up only desultory fire and were easily broken up by the Syrian tanks. However, in response to this clash with Israeli infantry, the 91st Brigade commander inexplicably stopped rather than pressing on. At that point, the 91st Armored Brigade—with virtually its entire complement of 95 T-62s intact—was only three miles (a 10-minute drive) from the B'nat Ya'acov bridge, which was defended by nothing but a platoon of Israeli infantry.

Syria's Soviet advisors were incredulous that the Syrian brigades would halt without taking the bridges when they were so close, they faced so little Israeli resistance, and the bridges were the key to the entire war.[28] This was entirely contrary to the most basic tenets of Soviet doctrine (and common sense). The very next day, Israel used those bridges to begin shifting reserve armor formations to the Golan, which first pushed back, then encircled, and then destroyed all of these Syrian brigades, enabling Israel to mount its own counteroffensive that brought them to the gates of Damascus.

The Iraqi Air Force, 1980–1991. Iraqi Air Force doctrine prior to the fall of Saddam was a strange amalgam of Western (mostly French and British) tactics tied to Soviet-style GCI. During the Iran-Iraq War, Iraqi fighters were regularly defeated by the Iranians. While neither side scored many kills, most went to the Iranians, and a principal reason that so few kills were converted was that the Iraqis generally avoided engaging Iranian fighters for fear of being shot down. Only toward the end of the war, when Iraq was able to engineer dogfights in which their elite Mirage F-1s had advantages of 3:1 or 4:1 over an Iranian Air Force badly depleted by sanctions and the loss of their pre-revolution American patron would the Iraqis actively seek air-to-air combat. Iraqi pilots rarely displayed any aggressiveness, imagination, improvisation, or flexibility in dogfights despite the emphasis on these skills in Western air-to-air combat doctrine. Moreover, Iraqi pilots demonstrated little ability to fly, let alone fight, without GCI direction. Indeed, to a far greater degree than the Soviets ever imagined, Iraqi air-to-air engagements were directed from the ground.

In 1991, *Komsomolskaya Pravda* printed an interview with a Soviet MiG pilot who had trained the Iraqi Air Force in Iraq and who complained that the Iraqis were incapable of demonstrating the aggressiveness, flexibility, and improvisational abilities required by the Soviet air system. He noted that Iraqi training exercises were jokes: canned operations in which everything was scripted, including which planes were going to employ which maneuvers; when, who was going to shoot whom; and who would win.[29] His comments were identical to the complaints of the American pilots training the EAF in the 1990s and 2000s.

Not surprisingly, when the United States jammed Iraq's air command and control network during the Persian Gulf War, Iraqi fighters displayed a complete lack of situational awareness and basic flying skills. Once deprived of GCI guidance, Iraqi pilots were sitting ducks: incapable of dogfighting or even fleeing effectively, they showed no aggressiveness, imagination, or capacity for independent action. As the US Air Force's *Gulf War Air Power Study* concluded:

> The consistent and overriding pattern evident in debriefs of engagements by Coalition pilots was the evident lack of situational awareness by their Iraqi adversaries. Accustomed to relying heavily on direction from controllers on the ground, Iraqi interceptor pilots showed little capacity to adjust to dynamic engagements or to exercise much initiative. Those shot down during Desert Storm generally did not react to radar lock-on by Coalition fighters and, for the most part, performed little effective maneuvering, either offensive or defensive; time and again, the principal defensive reaction by Iraqi pilots subjected to attack by Coalition fighters was to descend to low altitude in the apparent belief that the pulse-Doppler radars of Coalition fighters could not lock onto them there.[30]

As a result, Iraq lost 36 aircraft to just 1 Coalition fighter shot down, and many of the Iraqi pilots were killed not by Coalition missiles or gunfire but because *they flew into the ground*. Whatever the limitations introduced by Soviet reliance on GCI, Russian pilots typically flew and fought infinitely better than the Iraqis, and the Iraqis' inability to fly, fight, or even think without GCI goes far beyond anything that the Soviet system ever entailed. These are not problems that can be laid at Moscow's doorstep.

Syria, 2012–2016. Finally, just to include a more recent example, it seems that the Syrians continue to frustrate their Soviet (now Russian) allies even though they claim to be implementing the same doctrine. In September 2016, a former Russian Army colonel, Mikhail Khodarenok, wrote a scathing critique of the Syrian Army's performance during the Syrian civil war based on the reports of Russian military personnel in Syria. His commentary was published by the Kremlin-controlled news website Gazeta.ru. Among the many charges he leveled against Bashar al-Asad's armed forces were that

> At the start of the civil war, the government troops enjoyed a quantitative advantage in everything, especially aviation, tanks and artillery.

Assad could reasonably hope for a swift success in fighting irregular armed groups of the rebels. However, the Syrian Civil War and the fight against islamists [*sic*] have once again confirmed that a numeric and technical advantage is not enough to achieve victory. Even good theoretical knowledge of the leadership does not play a decisive role. In order to win a military conflict, just like in old times, one needs a strong spirit, an unyielding will for victory, trust in oneself and one's troops, decisiveness, bravery, inventiveness, flexibility and an ability to lead others. All this lacks [*sic*] severely in Assad's army.[31]

Once again, Russian military officers were bewildered by the rigidity, dogmatism, and passivity of an Arab army, in this case the Syrian military that still nominally clings to Soviet doctrine. Clearly it is not the doctrine itself that is creating these problems. Instead, it is the Arab armed forces injecting these problems into Soviet military methods, just as they have with British, French, and American practices.

The Arabs and the Soviets

As you can probably imagine, there are a lot of other examples beyond these that make the same point. It is hard to comb through the modern military history of the Arabs and find strong evidence for the belief that the Soviet system was responsible for the underwhelming performance of Arab arms since 1945. No more than half of the Arab militaries ever adopted Soviet practices at all, and only a handful adopted it to any significant degree. Even then, the Soviets felt that the Arabs had not adopted those practices properly, and they tore their hair out at the unwillingness of the Arabs to take their methods to heart and implement them as Moscow intended and as the Red Army practiced. Yet all of the Arab militaries more or less suffered from the same set of problems in combat, regardless of whether they claimed to rely on Soviet methods. All of this should make us skeptical that the Russians really were to blame for the failure of Arab armed forces to punch at their weight.

CHAPTER 4 | North Korea, Cuba, and Soviet Doctrine

B EFORE WE CAN come to a conclusion about the impact of Soviet methods on Arab military performance, there is another set of evidence we should look at. That's how other Third World militaries performed when they employed the Soviet model of military operations. If the Soviet system is really the problem, then other armed forces should have had the same problems as the Arabs.

So in this chapter I am going to look at how two non-Arab countries that relied on Soviet military doctrine fared in combat. To make this comparison most useful, it's important to look at non-Arab militaries that relied heavily on Soviet methods, and I chose two that did so to an even greater extent than the Arabs did. I also wanted to look at non-Arab militaries that fought in roughly the same time frame with essentially the same Soviet equipment so that it would be clear that those factors weren't influencing the outcomes.

Ultimately, I settled on the North Korean armed forces and their performance in the Korean War in 1950–1953 and the Cuban armed forces and their performance in both Angola in 1975–1988 and Ethiopia in 1978. These two militaries were heavily reliant on Soviet doctrine, equipment, and advisory assistance. In fact, they were so steeped in the Soviet tradition that the Russians often used them as stand-ins or adjuncts to their own forces when they wanted to help out an ally somewhere else in the Third World but hoped to limit their own commitment. The Cubans and North Koreans also faced some very tough opponents—the Americans in Korea and the South Africans in Angola—which helps to illustrate that their successes were not merely the result of fighting weak adversaries.

North Korea, 1950–1953

By the time that North Korea invaded the South on June 25, 1950, it was well prepared for the war to follow. By then, North Korea's military—the Korean People's Army (KPA)—had 135,000 troops, 230 T-34/85 tanks, 200 artillery pieces, and an air force with 200 Yak-9 fighters and Il-10 attack aircraft. All of its weaponry was of Soviet origin.[1] The army was organized along Soviet lines and trained in Soviet doctrine.[2] In fact, the last Russian combat troops had only withdrawn from Korea months before and Soviet advisors had remained behind.[3] In the run-up to the invasion, Moscow sent a new team of advisors, many of them highly accomplished veterans of the Second World War, who drew up the North Korean invasion plan.[4] Moreover, as many as half of the KPA's troops had fought in the Chinese Civil War.[5] Consequently, the Russian planners expected the KPA to advance at a rate of 15–20 kilometers per day and finish off the South in less than a month.[6]

South Korea and its American protectors were thoroughly unprepared. The South had only 98,000 men under arms. Although an American advisory mission had remained behind in Korea, it had not had the same success as the Russians across the 38th Parallel. Much of the Republic of Korea (ROK) Army was preoccupied with counterinsurgency and suppressing political dissent. In the wake of the massive American postwar demobilization, there was little Western support forthcoming for the ROK, which had no tanks and relatively few antitank weapons at the time of the invasion. Its air force had barely 20 planes, none of them dedicated combat aircraft.[7] And while there were 4 US divisions in Japan, they were all on occupation duty. They were under-strength, underequipped, and had only recently begun to train again for combat operations.[8] As a final nail in the coffin, the size and scope of the North's invasion caught General MacArthur's headquarters in Tokyo and, to a lesser extent, the South Korean high command in Seoul by surprise.[9]

Even taking into account all of these advantages, the KPA invasion was still impressive and reflected considerable military skill.[10] The North Korean divisions moved swiftly, employing deft maneuver to gobble up large chunks of terrain and South Korean formations. Within three days, the Northern forces had overrun Seoul, and by June 30th, the ROK Army had been reduced to barely 20,000 men still effective. The United States quickly dispatched a light battalion task force ("Task Force Smith") from Japan, but it was

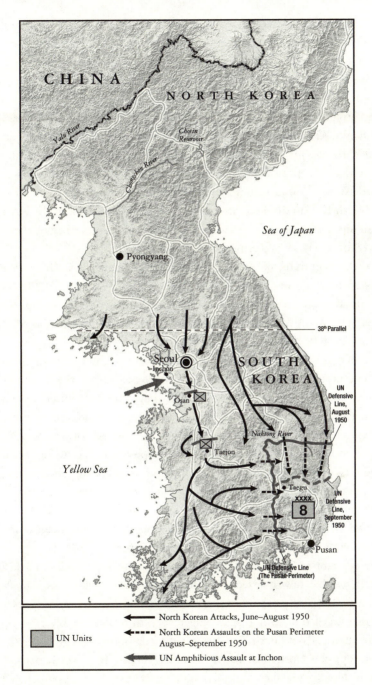

CHINA

NORTH KOREA

Yalu River

Chosin
Reservoir

Ch'ongch'on River

Sea of Japan

● Pyongyang

38th Parallel

Seoul ◎
Inchon

SOUTH
KOREA

UN
Defensive
Line,
August
1950

Osan ⊠

Naktong River

Taejon ●

Yellow Sea

⊠

Taegu ●

XXXX
8

UN
Defensive
Line,
September
1950

Pusan ●

UN Defensive Line
(The Pusan Perimeter)

	North Korean Attacks, June–August 1950
UN Units	North Korean Assaults on the Pusan Perimeter August–September 1950
	UN Amphibious Assault at Inchon

MAP 5 The North Korean Offensive, 1950

overrun by two KPA regiments on July 5 at Osan. As more American forces were deployed to Korea, the KPA made short work of them too, successfully enveloping one force at the Kum River and another at Taejon. In both instances, North Korean units fixed the Americans with strong frontal assaults and then flanked their positions. In Allen Millet's description, "The Communist soldiers flowed around the infantry companies, taking and inflicting casualties. From both flanks KPA infantry fixed and thinned bits and pieces of the [American units]."[11] By late July, the remnants of the ROK Army were fleeing back to an enclave that American and other Western forces, now under the auspices of a United Nations military command, were trying to establish in the far south. Two North Korean divisions attempted to turn the left flank of the UN's line by attempting to pivot around Taegu, and almost did so before they were blocked by newly arrived American formations.[12]

By the beginning of August, the KPA had penned the UN and ROK forces up in what was known as the Pusan Perimeter. There, 70,000 North Koreans attempted to crush a UN/ROK force that had already reached 92,000 troops (and would continue to grow to 180,000 during the course of the battle). The KPA lost that fight decisively, but not for lack of trying or any dearth of capability. The North identified four possible breakthrough sectors and concentrated forces against them to try to overstretch the defenders and achieve successful penetrations. Although they were now forced to conduct frontal assaults, the KPA did so skillfully, integrating armor, infantry, combat engineers, and artillery to effect breakthroughs in several sectors. Having done so, KPA mechanized formations quickly attempted to penetrate into the depth of the UN positions and roll up the flanks of neighboring formations. They failed, but they failed because they could not overcome the numbers and fire-power (particularly the air power) of the burgeoning UN force, led by an able commander in Lt. General Walton Walker, who used the advantage of interior lines to blunt each North Korean penetration in turn.[13]

By September 1950, the KPA had shot its bolt. It had failed to dislodge a UN force that now boasted 225,000 men and over 500 tanks. The North had only 40 operational tanks, and while it had largely replaced its man-power losses, it did so by dispatching raw recruits and forcibly conscripting tens of thousands of South Koreans to substitute for the roughly 60,000 vet-eran troops the North lost in the summer battles. It is worth noting that the UN forces had taken a similar number of casualties despite their huge advantages in manpower and firepower, again illustrating the quality of their North Korean foes.[14]

Moreover, UN forces had considerable difficulty breaking through the North Korean lines when they launched their own counteroffensive in

September in conjunction with the Inchon landing that cut the supply lines of virtually the entire KPA. The North Koreans fought hard, gave ground only grudgingly, and counterattacked aggressively and often. Even after the further, devastating losses the KPA suffered from Inchon and the breakout from the Pusan Perimeter, UN forces still faced a grueling fight against the dregs of the KPA as they pushed into North Korea itself. When the Chinese entered the war in December 1950, their massive forces largely subsumed the remnants of the KPA, but the North Koreans had effectively crushed their southern counterpart and given the Americans a run for their money.[15]

North Korean Military Effectiveness. Overall, the KPA performed well in its invasion of South Korea, and even in subsequent military operations after the US landing at Inchon had reversed their initial gains.[16] North Korean strategic leadership was quite good, although the invasion plan was largely the work of Soviet combat veterans. KPA generals reacted well to unexpected developments, such as the appearance of ever-larger American units. They kept their forces moving and found ways to overcome ROK and American blocking positions without slowing the advance appreciably. They also devised a creditable plan for cracking the Pusan Perimeter. While it failed, it is hard to lay that failure at the feet of the KPA senior leadership or their plan. Moreover, in combat, many North Korean generals performed skillfully, especially after command resubordinations in early July placed more experienced senior officers in charge of KPA corps and divisions than had been the case in the initial drive to overrun Seoul.[17]

Still, the North's generals did make several crucial mistakes that probably meant the difference between victory and defeat. In particular, Pyongyang showed the embryonic American intervention and the leftovers of the ROK Army more respect than they probably deserved in late July 1950. Thus, they opted to try to outflank the US and ROK forces as they fell back to the Pusan Perimeter, rather than simply overrunning them. The US and ROK forces were probably still too weak to withstand a deliberate KPA frontal assault, whereas developing the operational maneuver around Taegu gave the Americans and South Koreans the time to regroup and dig-in elsewhere along the perimeter. While understandable, this ultimately proved to be a fatal error.

At tactical levels, North Korean forces were quite formidable. North Korean tactical commanders always tried to seize and maintain the initiative. They patrolled aggressively and regularly, seeking out unit boundaries in particular, and their operational security and use of camouflage, concealment, and deception (CC&D) were also very good.[18] As a result, they rarely missed an opportunity to exploit a mistake by their opponents. They were flexible and responded well to the vicissitudes of combat. They maneuvered constantly, to the point that US units *expected* to be outflanked in combat with the KPA. In particular, within weeks of the start of battle, the KPA had learned to "fix American and ROK units with limited frontal attacks, then conduct deep envelopments with sharp, penetrating attacks that bypassed strongpoints."[19] They kept up a very quick pace of operations and tried hard not to give a beaten enemy any time to regroup and reform his lines. They handled their tanks adequately—not great—but they were good at concentrating armor to break through a defensive sector then sending the armored formations ahead at top speed to overrun rear areas and encircle front-line forces while infantry formations were left to reduce the trapped enemy pockets. In the words of one American officer surprised by North Korean prowess, "Instead of charging wildly into battle, they employed a base of fire, double envelopment, fire blocks on withdrawal routes, and skilled infiltrations."[20]

On the defensive, North Korean tactical forces were very active, luring UN forces into fire sacks, counterattacking aggressively, shifting reserves to meet each new UN thrust, and suddenly sweeping around the UN's flank to try to cut off a penetration at the shoulders.[21] Ultimately, in the breakout from the Pusan Perimeter, the KPA was just overwhelmed by American (and South Korean) manpower, firepower, air power, and logistical weight. As the UN forces crossed the 38th Parallel and pushed into North Korea proper, these advantages grew as the UN increasingly faced green KPA formations, hastily mobilized and sent into battle without adequate training or weaponry. These still fought hard against the invaders, but they fared far worse than the formations that mounted the invasion.

North Korean operations demonstrated a reasonable degree of combined arms cooperation that improved over time. KPA tanks, infantry, artillery, and engineers were all used in conjunction and at times coordinated their operations very well—especially later in the campaign—with each arm aiding and covering the vulnerabilities of the other.[22] At times, KPA armor would charge off on its own, especially early on when the ROK Army had almost nothing to counter KPA tanks. But this problem receded as the United States brought tanks and other antitank weapons into the fight that made it more and more dangerous for the T-34s and SU-76s to act independently. North Korean artillery was quite good, and conducted sophisticated fire schemes in support of both offensive and defensive operations.[23] Millett specifically notes that the KPA's artillery was particularly effective *because of* its reliance on Soviet methods.[24]

North Korea's ultimate loss in 1950 had little to do with its own military effectiveness. There were really only two areas in which the North Koreans contributed to their own defeat: logistics and air defenses. The North Koreans had a tiny air force and meager amounts of ground-based air defenses, with the result that the United States quickly established air superiority and began hammering their supply lines. North Korean fighter pilots were forced to contend with American veterans of World War II, in many cases flying more advanced jets than North Korea's propeller-driven fighters.[25] The KPA's logistical structure may have been inadequate even absent US air attacks, but in the face of the American air effort, it slowly crumbled. By the time of the decisive battles around the Pusan Perimeter in mid-August, KPA tanks literally began running out of gas in the midst of combat.[26]

The other reasons for North Korea's defeat were unrelated to KPA combat effectiveness and include (1) Pyongyang's operational blunder choosing to flank the UN forces rather than overrun them, (2) the tremendous increase in US military strength and firepower on the peninsula, (3) severe losses among North Korea's veteran soldiers and their replacement with raw recruits and South Korean conscripts, and (4) the intelligence coup of the war, when American intelligence broke several of North Korea's most important military codes and so gained advance knowledge of KPA operations.[27] Indeed, the United States finally broke through the KPA lines around Pusan only by using its intelligence advantage to find out where the North Koreans intended to attack and then concentrating enormous firepower in that sector to annihilate the KPA assault force. In this way, the United States gradually wore down KPA combat strength to the point where the North Koreans lacked the forces to maintain a contiguous line opposite the Americans. Otherwise, the North Koreans often gave US and ROK units fits in battle.

North Korea and the Soviet Military Method. Relying on the Soviet military system—its organization, doctrine, and tactics—certainly did not hurt the North Koreans. Of greatest importance for our purposes, they performed far better than the Arab armed forces. Overall, the North Koreans were a formidable adversary who conducted quite creditable offensive and defensive operations. The KPA repeatedly demonstrated its comfort and competence with mechanized maneuver warfare and suffered none of the problems with tactical flexibility, aggressiveness, creativity, and information management that have bedeviled Arab militaries. It is worth noting that North Korean pilots and tank crews were often less capable than their American counterparts, and this may be related to the Soviet model's de-emphasis of tactical skill in favor of operational skill. However, in the areas that were the critical limiting factors of Arab warfare, the North Koreans conversely performed very well.

If anything, North Korea seems to have benefited from the Soviet system. The Soviets taught aggressive, offensive warfare, the constant use of maneuver and combined arms at all levels, concentration in narrow breakthrough sectors followed by rapid exploitation of success, and a highly active defense featuring relentless counterattacks. This was exactly how the KPA fought during its period of primacy during the Korean War. It is also why the North Koreans came so close to victory in August 1950, and proved to be such a difficult opponent in September and October. It is also the polar opposite of how Arab armed forces fought time and again in the modern era. Far from hindering North Korea's war-making, Pyongyang's reliance on a Soviet method of operations served it well, and absent the massive American intervention, almost certainly would have enabled a total victory over the South.

Cuban Military Effectiveness, 1975–1988

After the 1959 revolution, Fidel Castro turned to Moscow for aid and assistance of all kinds. One key aspect of Russian support for the new Cuban communist state was to provide weapons, training, and all other forms of military aid, all of which the Cuban armed forces readily embraced. Cuban officers and pilots received extensive instruction from Soviet advisers, and many underwent training in the USSR. Cuban forces strictly employed Soviet tactics and doctrine in all types of conventional military operations. As a result, the Cuban military relied heavily on a Soviet-style of operations, as much as the North Koreans in the 1950s, and to a greater extent than any of the Arab states.[28]

Angola, 1975–1976. By late 1975, the Angolan revolution was in trouble. The communist Popular Movement for the Liberation of Angola (MPLA) had seized the capital of Luanda after the Portuguese pulled out earlier in the year, but by autumn, they faced multiple challenges. In the south, South Africa had invaded Angola from Namibia in support of the National Union for the Total Independence of Angola (UNITA). In the east, the National Front for the Liberation of Angola (FNLA) was mounting its own offensive from Zaire bolstered by Portuguese special forces, Zairian regulars, and Western mercenaries. Finally, in the north, the secessionist Front for the Liberation of the Enclave of Cabinda (FLEC) was fighting the MPLA for control of Cabinda province, also with Zaire's backing. In July, the Cubans sent 50 weapons specialists to aid the MPLA's army, the People's Armed Forces of Liberation of Angola (FAPLA), then added 480 combat advisors and trainers in September.

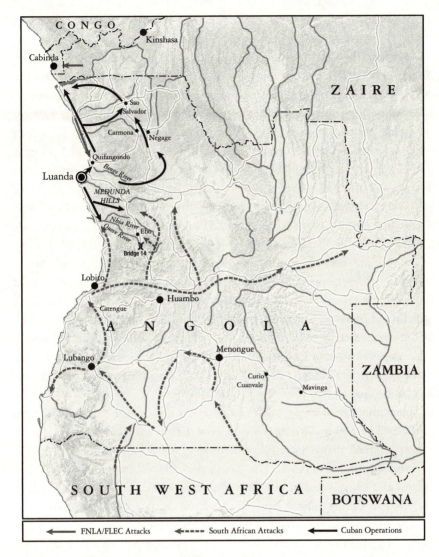

| FNLA/FLEC Attacks | South African Attacks | Cuban Operations |

MAP 6 Cuban Operations in Angola, 1975–1976

But in October, the South African Defense Force (SADF) launched its invasion of Angola (Operation SAVANNAH) and made rapid gains. One prong of the SADF's offensive drove 3,100 kilometers in 33 days, defeated FAPLA forces in several dozen engagements, and was only a few hundred kilometers south of Luanda by early November.[29]

So, on November 4, Castro acceded to an Angolan request and sent 36,000 Cuban combat troops and 300 tanks to Angola to save the MPLA regime. A huge airlift (eventually with Soviet aid but initially all Cuban) began pouring Cuban forces into the country, and by the second half of November, 4,000 Cuban soldiers were fighting on all fronts.[30]

By then, the Cuban advisors had already taken control of the war effort. In late October, the Cubans put together a plan to defend Luanda against the SADF/UNITA force threatening the capital from the south.[31] At Catengue on November 2, a Cuban-led FAPLA battalion (with 50 Cuban advisors fighting alongside them) surprised an SADF/UNITA task force, which the South African commander commented provided the "best organized and heaviest FAPLA opposition to date."[32] But the South Africans were still the better army, and the Cuban/FAPLA force was eventually beaten and sent reeling.

Nevertheless, Cuban intervention turned the tide of the Angolan Civil War. On November 10, 1,000 Cuban and FAPLA troops backed by Cuban BM-21 multiple-rocket launchers (MRLs) met a combined force of 2,000 FNLA, 1,200 Zairians, and 120 Portuguese Mercenaries with armored cars and South African artillery support at Quifangondo on the Bengo River. The Cubans turned back several crossing efforts by the FNLA and their allies and then lured them into a prepared kill zone where the BM-21s hammered them. The battle stopped the FNLA offensive cold.[33] From November 10 to November 14, other Cuban and FAPLA units defeated in succession four converging offensives by the FLEC and Zaire against Cabinda, nailing down Luanda's control of its disconnected province.[34]

Inevitably, the fighting in the south against the South Africans was the hardest. The South Africans had adopted Israeli military doctrine, Israeli officers trained many South African troops, and a large number of SADF officers had studied in Israel.[35] The South Africans had learned well, and they moved and maneuvered in ways that must have made their mentors proud.

The first Cuban combat units arrived at the Queve River (about two hours' march time from Luanda) on November 13. They threw a screening force across the river to hold back the SADF and then blew all three bridges, which gave them time to bring up additional forces and build a formidable defensive line along the river.[36] The SADF shifted its primary axis of advance eastward, and attempted to flank the Cuban/FAPLA line by crossing the Nhia River. But on November 23rd, Cuban forces caught the SADF's vanguard in an ambush at Ebo, and destroyed 60 percent of the South African armored vehicles. The South Africans would have their revenge in December, when another SADF formation smashed an inexperienced Cuban/FAPLA force of about brigade size in the Battle of Bridge 14. Still, the Cubans responded quickly, dispatching armor and motorized infantry reserves, which established a new defense line that the South Africans did not relish having to breach based on their recent experiences with the Cubans.[37]

In January 1976, the Cubans and FAPLA went on the offensive in a series of Cuban-designed and -led offensives. They launched multiple attacks against the South African and UNITA positions in the Medunda hills south of Luanda. In ferocious fighting, Cuban infantry backed by the fearsome BM-21s pushed the SADF and UNITA out of these positions. This defeat convinced Pretoria that its bid to install a friendly government in Luanda had failed, and so the SADF pulled back to Namibia.

The Cubans quickly recognized that the South African withdrawal created an opportunity to smash UNITA and they sent armored columns south as fast as they could. These forces repeatedly demonstrated good combined arms, good use of tactical maneuver, a good ability to improvise solutions to tactical problems, and excellent speed of advance overall. The offensive covered 400 miles in a little over three weeks and crippled UNITA's conventional military capability, forcing it to make the painful decision to revert back to guerrilla operations.[38]

With the South Africans and UNITA tamed, the Cubans and Angolans turned back north to deal with the FNLA and their Zairian allies. This too was a highly impressive campaign led by a Cuban commander, Brigadier Víctor Schueg Colás. FAPLA units built around Cuban armored formations launched a sudden offensive that overran the main FNLA air bases at Negage and Camabatela and a day later the FNLA's "capital" at Carmona. They then developed a pincer attack that captured the FNLA's last major base at Sao Salvador. In addition to these tactical maneuvers, the entire campaign was a wide, operational-level envelopment of the FNLA defensive network, looping around broadly to the east, driving north, and then heading west to outflank the extensive FNLA defensive positions up the West African coast. So complete was the Cuban/FAPLA victory that the FNLA was never again able to pose a significant threat to the MPLA regime.[39] By the end of March 1976, thanks largely to the Cubans, Angola was back in MPLA hands, the FNLA had been virtually destroyed, and UNITA was so badly battered that it took several years before it could even take up the fight again as a guerrilla force.[40]

Ethiopia, 1977–1978. The Cubans barely had time to enjoy their victory in southern Africa before they were pulled northeast. In 1974, the pro-Western emperor of Ethiopia, Haile Selassie, was toppled by a Marxist revolution. But the revolution threw Ethiopia into a state of semi-chaos with multiple insurgencies attempting to bring down the Derg, the revolutionary leadership in Addis Ababa. Inevitably, the countries of the Soviet bloc welcomed the new Marxist regime—all but one that is. The Marxist government of

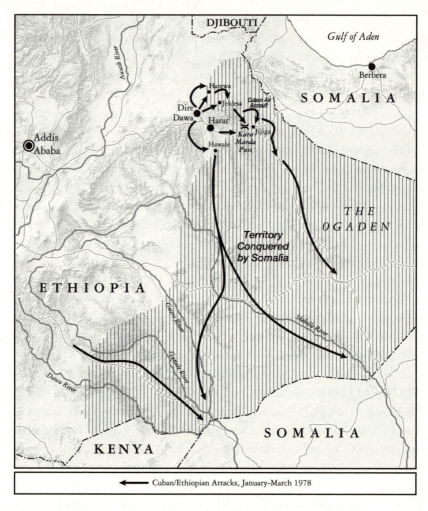

MAP 7 Cuban Operations in Ethiopia, 1977–1978

neighboring Somalia invaded Ethiopia in July 1977, believing that revolution and civil war had so weakened the Ethiopian military that Somalia could regain the disputed Ogaden region.

The Somali armed forces in 1977 were among the best-armed and most capable in sub-Saharan Africa, having themselves benefited from years of diligent Soviet mentorship. Mogadishu's army boasted 35,000 troops with 250 tanks, 300 armored personnel carriers, and 66 aircraft including 40 MiG-21s. At Russian urging, the Somalis had largely motorized their infantry, enabling them to wage the kind of high-speed, maneuver war the Soviets preached. The Somalis also benefited from extensive intelligence on Ethiopian military positions and readiness provided by Somali guerrillas that Mogadishu had supported in the Ogaden for over a year.[41]

Meanwhile, the US-trained Ethiopian military was in shambles from the revolution. On paper, Ethiopia had more men under arms (47,000), but fewer arms: no more than 100 tanks, about 100 APCs, no SAMs, and only about 36 aircraft (mostly F-5s and F-86s). The usual revolutionary purges had killed or ousted large numbers of officers, who were replaced by more junior men who lacked the experience or training of their predecessors. As the great historian of the Ogaden War, Gebru Tareke, has written, "the new government in Addis Ababa was beset by murderous power struggles at the center and multiple revolts on the periphery. . . . Insurgents had captured most of Eritrea, while Afar, Oromo, and Tigrayan rebels were causing havoc in their respective areas and beyond."[42] As a further complication, the United States had cut off arms sales and other military support after the revolution.[43] The other superpower also added to Ethiopia's woes: the Soviets (who still had large numbers of advisors in Somalia) assured their new Ethiopian comrades that Mogadishu would not invade, convincing Addis to leave few forces in the Ogaden.[44]

To the chagrin of their Soviet allies, the Somalis invaded on July 13, 1977. It was the highly mobile Somalis who first displayed their mastery of Soviet military operations and put it to excellent effect. Somali armor and mechanized formations, employing Soviet tactics and doctrine, smashed the meager Ethiopian forces garrisoning the Ogaden. The Somali units exhibited good combined arms, and they used speed and maneuver to hit Ethiopian positions from multiple directions and so quickly overcame Ethiopian resistance. By early August, the Somalis had penetrated 700 kilometers into Ethiopia and seized 350,000 square kilometers.[45]

The fighting got harder after that. The Somalis had conquered mostly open desert and now found themselves pushing into the more mountainous terrain of central Ethiopia to try to take the main population centers of the Ogaden. In mid-August, they assaulted the town of Dire Dawa, but their mechanized forces were stopped cold by aggressive Ethiopian counterattacks and a punishing air campaign from the Ethiopian air force, which had largely won air superiority thanks to its superior (Western) tactics and American-made AIM-9 Sidewinder missiles.[46]

The Somalis did better at Jijiga in early September. The fighting was vicious and control of the town changed hands several times, but in the end the Somalis concentrated their armor behind massive support from their artillery and MRLs and broke through the Ethiopian lines to not only take the town but overrun the strategically vital Kara Marda Pass beyond it. The Somalis then launched a pincer attack against the City of Harar, the fall of which would have solidified Somali control over all of eastern Ethiopia.[47]

The battle for Harar would rage for four months, during which time the Somali government of Siad Barre broke its treaty with the USSR and tossed out all of its Soviet advisors. Siad Barre appears to have hoped that the Americans would step in to replace the Russians—and would be far more generous with their aid because they would not share Moscow's divided loyalties between the two warring Marxist regimes. This combination of factors convinced both the Soviets and the Cubans that they had to act decisively to buck up the Ethiopian revolution and ensure that it was not undermined by the loss of so much territory. So in the late fall of 1977,[48] Ethiopia began to receive Soviet military equipment, Cuban combat troops, and a large contingent of Soviet advisors—many of them former advisors to Somalia who went directly from Mogadishu to Addis Ababa, bringing with them a wealth of knowledge about the Somali military. By January, 3,000 Cuban combat troops were operating with the Ethiopians. A month later the force had grown to 18,000, complete with T-62 tanks, and General Arnaldo Ochoa Sánchez, who had commanded the final Cuban campaign in Angola in 1975–1976.[49]

The Cubans first saw battle in late January, when the Somalis launched one last assault to take Harar, another pincer move to surround the city before reducing its defenses. This time they ran into the new Ethiopian 11th Division, built around the hard core of a Cuban armored brigade. The defenders blocked both Somali prongs and held them in place for several days, which allowed the Ethiopian Air Force to work them over. Then, on January 23, a pair of Cuban armored brigades led a counterattack that outmaneuvered and routed the Somali forces, inflicting the worst losses the Somalis had ever taken in a single action since the start of the war.[50]

In February, the Ethiopians and Cubans launched a broad counteroffensive to expel the Somalis altogether. The operation was conducted by a half-dozen Ethiopian divisions, each built around one or more Cuban armored brigades that served as both the division's offensive spearhead and operational reserve. On February 1, they launched a diversionary attack against Hawale, south of Dire Dawa, using artillery and a fixing attack by the Ethiopian 9th Division to convince the Somalis that the attack would come from one direction while Cuban armor and artillery outflanked their lines at Harewa to the north and rolled them up from the rear. At Jeldsea, barely a week later, they repeated the same performance.

The Cubans and Ethiopians then employed the same approach at an operational level, sending the Ethiopian 10th Division and the Cuban 102nd Armored Brigade to outflank the Kara Marda Pass altogether, while another

Ethiopian division with another Cuban armored brigade pushed into the pass itself, again routing the Somali defenders. Freeing the Kara Marda Pass enabled an assault to retake Jijiga, where the Somalis counterattacked fiercely with armor and artillery of their own. The Cubans deftly parried each of these Somali thrusts, then employed a vertical envelopment, using Mi-8 helicopters to airlift a Cuban battalion behind the Somali lines. Jijiga was retaken and the Somalis lost roughly 150 tanks and almost 3,000 of their 6,000 troops.[51]

Thereafter, the Ethiopian and Cuban forces routed the demoralized, scattered, and undersupplied Somali forces holding the southern Ogaden. In a series of rapid encircling maneuvers, Cuban mechanized brigades again led Ethiopian formations in obliterating the remaining Somali forces. When Somalia committed its strategic reserve (a mechanized brigade task force) Cuban pilots flying Ethiopia's new MiGs and Sukhois busted up the Somali columns and sent them fleeing across the border. By the end of March 1978 the Ogaden was back in Ethiopian hands while the Somalis had suffered 8,000 dead and lost over 200 tanks and 25–30 combat aircraft.[52]

Back to Angola, 1976–1986. Whatever one may think of Fidel Castro, he repeatedly proved himself a canny general. After his troops saved the Angolan revolution he hoped to bring most of them home. He recognized (before either the Angolan communists or the Soviets) that Angola's war against UNITA had now degenerated into a counterinsurgency (COIN), and he wanted no part of it. He began withdrawing his forces but had only removed about 2,000 when he was forced to stop.[53] Victory (albeit temporary) in the civil war provoked vicious infighting among the MPLA leaders, along with a decision to support Namibian insurgents of the South West African People's Organisation (SWAPO) against the South African occupation. Pretoria responded with regular preemptive raids into Angola to prevent SWAPO from launching operations of its own. The first came at Cassinga in May 1978, and led to a brief firefight between a Cuban mechanized reserve that counterattacked the SADF force as it cleaned out a SWAPO base. The Cubans (fighting with nothing but old T-34s and BTR-152s) got the worst of it, but the battle convinced Castro that if he withdrew significant numbers of troops, the South Africans would have their way in Angola, and that would jeopardize the political hold of the MPLA in Luanda.[54]

So the Cubans stayed. But they left the COIN war to the Angolans and instead focused on protecting the regime from a South African invasion. This left southern Africa a battleground among the alphabet soup of FAPLA, SWAPO, UNITA, and the SADF, with Cuban units only occasionally becoming involved. Over the next 10 years, South African forces mounted incursions into

Angola over a dozen times, and in May 1981, the SADF took over the southern part of Angola's Cunene province—both as a forward base to operate against SWAPO and a buffer zone to block SWAPO operations into Namibia.[55]

In December 1985, with the war dragging on, the Soviets upgraded their advisory mission in Luanda and took control of the fight. They sent a senior Soviet general along with roughly 1,000 field grade officers—many of them veterans of Afghanistan—to serve as advisors, and charged them with bringing Angola's debilitating war to an end. Despite their Afghan experience, the Russians believed that large-scale conventional operations to destroy the UNITA bases in southern Angola were the only way to end the insurgency.[56] The Cubans knew better and argued against this strategy, but in 1986 Moscow got its way. With Soviet advisors attached down to company level, an army of 20,000 FAPLA troops with 150 tanks and a number of Mi-24 Hind attack helicopters, plus 7,000 SWAPO guerrillas, launched a massive offensive against UNITA. But UNITA was now being armed with American Stingers and TOWs, and a 3,000-man SADF force came to its aid. Not surprisingly, the offensive was a complete failure and the FAPLA troops were given a drubbing. Still, the Russian generals clung to their strategy.[57]

Cuito Cuanavale, 1987–1988. The next time, the Soviet generals amassed a somewhat smaller, but better armed and trained force to succeed where the previous year's offensive had failed. They concentrated 10,000 FAPLA troops with 150 T-55 and T-62 tanks, several dozen Mi-24s, as well as a large artillery park made up of D-30 and long-range M-46 guns.[58] The offensive would be launched from the FAPLA base at Cuito Cuanavale, a town at the confluence of the eponymous Cuito and Cuanavale rivers. Four FAPLA brigades with 6,000 troops and 80 tanks would lead the attack by mounting a double envelopment of UNITA/SADF positions along the Lomba River west of the UNITA staging base at Mavinga. Once those forces were eliminated, the FAPLA brigades would turn east and overrun Mavinga from the flank, before developing a second-stage offensive against UNITA's capital farther south at Jamba.[59]

Once again, the offensive was a disaster. The attack kicked off in mid-August 1987, but the Angolans used the same tactics and even the same routes of march as they had the prior year. Although initial UNITA resistance was relatively light, the Lomba River line was held by a South African force 3,000 strong with 30 Olifant (modified Centurion) tanks, dozens of Ratel armored fighting vehicles, and several batteries of deadly G-5 howitzers.[60] FAPLA units had poor unit cohesion and erratic command and control—with orders to attack followed by long stretches without any orders at all. Moreover, the South Africans performed extremely well, darting around the heavy bush such that

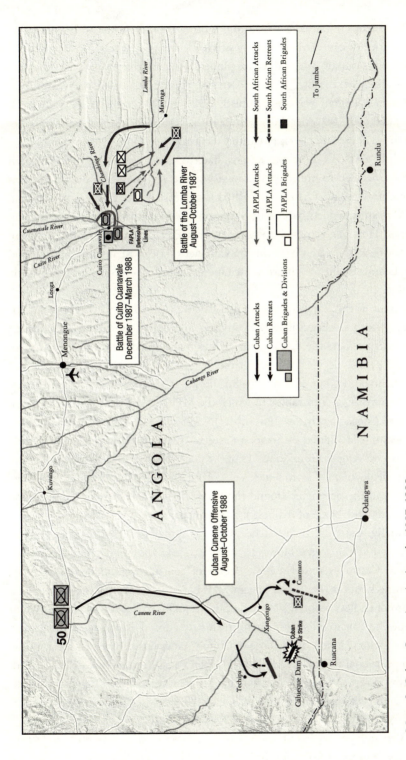

MAP 8 Cuban Operations in Angola, 1987–1988

FAPLA's Russian tanks really could not bring their firepower to bear, whereas the South African artillery was positively lethal. On several occasions when SADF guns caught Angolan troops pinned along the river banks, their fire was devastating. By the first week of October, the FAPLA offensive was broken, with two of its four brigades crippled, 2,000–3,000 casualties, as many as 60 tanks and over 100 other AFVs lost, and the remainder of the assault force demoralized and beaten back to Cuito Cuanavale.[61]

With FAPLA's best formations battered and retreating helter-skelter, Pretoria decided to press its advantage. At the very least, the South Africans wanted to clear all FAPLA and allied forces east of the Cuito River, leaving UNITA an expanded base of operations and new pathways into the Angolan interior. However, some sources suggest that Pretoria envisioned taking Cuito Cuanavale as the gateway to the big Cuban air base at Menongue, and beyond it to Luanda itself, to achieve what Operation SAVANNAH had failed to do in 1975.

Defeat at the Battle of the Lomba River again panicked the MPLA leadership, which sidelined its Soviet advisors and appealed directly to Cuba for aid. Castro reluctantly agreed, but having made the decision to recommit to Angola he also decided that this time, he needed not only to halt the South African invasion, but to force the SADF out of Angola altogether and create the diplomatic circumstances in which the MPLA could deal with UNITA on its own. Consequently, on November 15, 1987, Castro ordered a massive air- and sealift—facilitated by Soviet air assets—that rapidly increased the Cuban presence in Angola from about 15,000 to over 50,000 in early 1988. As part of this deployment, Castro sent his elite 50th Division, the formation that normally held the perimeter around the American military base at Guantanamo Bay, along with some of his best fighter squadrons.[62]

Finally, Castro also dispatched General Arnaldo Ochoa Sánchez to take command at the scene. However, demonstrating the importance of this operation, Castro exercised a high degree of control over operations directly, spending hours at the Cuban general staff headquarters in Havana, receiving a stream of endless reports, situation updates, and force laydowns from a swarm of aides he sent to Angola to perform this function. Ultimately, it was Castro himself who planned the defense of Cuito Cuanavale and ordered many of the key operational moves of FAPLA and Cuban forces during the battle.[63] Indeed, Castro's direct exercise of command infuriated Ochoa, leading Castro to increasingly sideline him in favor of General Leopoldo Cintra Frías (known as "Polo").[64]

Although he may have been 6,000 miles away, Castro's generalship at Cuito Cuanavale proved critical. He ordered that all of the FAPLA brigades pull back to a narrow, triangular bridgehead on the east side of the Cuito River, literally where the bridge crosses into Cuito Cuanavale on the west bank. The position was protected by tributary rivers and heavy bush to both the north and south. Castro had Cuban engineers build extensive trenches and minefields in depth around the perimeter of what was called the Tumpo bridgehead. He deployed five FAPLA brigades in a tight, two-tiered defense within the bridgehead, each brigade paired with a battalion or company of Cuban regulars to stiffen their spines. He dug-in another FAPLA brigade on the west bank to hold the Cuito bridge along with a Cuban armored brigade as an operational reserve for the whole force, and placed four battalions of Cuban artillery and MRLs on high ground on the west bank where they could range the entire battlefield and even use direct fire across the river if the South Africans got that close.[65]

Between February 14 and March 23, 1988, the SADF mounted at least four deliberate attacks against the Tumpo bridgehead.[66] Each was a ferocious struggle, the SADF mustering a mechanized force of 2,000–3,000 men, with roughly 30 tanks, and several dozen Ratels and other armored vehicles backed by a dozen or more artillery pieces including the outstanding G-5s and G-6s. Typically, several thousand UNITA fighters also participated, although South African accounts often ignore their role altogether. In some of the early battles, the South Africans made progress against the outer line of Cuban-backed FAPLA positions, prompting Castro to decide in early February—against Ochoa's advice and prompting his replacement by Polo—to pull all of his units back to the west bank except the FAPLA 25th Brigade and a task force organized around the Cuban 3rd Tank Battalion. He ordered Cuban and FAPLA sappers to build additional bunkers, trenches, antitank obstacles, and minefields, and concentrated all of the Cuban and Angolan artillery directly behind these positions, along with additional Cuban tanks in hull-down positions along the west bank of the river.[67]

Castro's moves ultimately won the battle. In each subsequent attack, the SADF would spend hours trying to punch through a forward defensive line, all the while under heavy fire, only to find the forward trenches abandoned—a tactic the Germans had first pioneered. When the South Africans attempted to push forward, they would then (repeatedly) blunder into skillfully laid secondary minefields and defensive lines, where they would get hammered even harder by Cuban artillery and armor, and then would typically find themselves counterattacked by Cuban armor leading to harrowing firefights. "The fighting was chaotic, and the Cuban tanks impressed the Olifant commanders with their aggressive (and often suicidal) sallies into the midst of the South African squadron in search of targets."[68] In addition, Cuban MiGs won air superiority over the battlefield and constantly harassed South African units, greatly impeding their movements and silencing the G-5 and G-6 artillery pieces that previously had dominated the fighting. Although SADF losses were typically much lighter than Cuban and FAPLA casualties in each of these battles, UNITA lost heavily, and ultimately, the South Africans simply could not withstand Cuban firepower while simultaneously trying to clear the thick defenses and fend off determined Cuban armored counterattacks. The SADF's attacks on the Cuito Cuanavale defenses in February and March began to cost them painfully without accomplishing any of their goals. Pretoria could not afford to continue the fruitless assaults, and so it ordered the SADF to fall back to Namibia.[69]

Then Castro went on the offensive. He understood that humiliating the SADF at Cuito Cuanavale wasn't enough to achieve the political settlement he wanted. He needed to threaten Pretoria's buffer zone in Cunene Province. To do so he mounted what is now called his "Western Offensive." He dispatched the elite 50th Division, his 40th Armored Brigade (with T-62 tanks), air defense radars, additional anti-aircraft artillery and 150 SA-8 launchers to Cunene, along with two of his best MiG-23 squadrons. Eventually, the Cuban forces in Cunene would amount to two full divisions, over 200 tanks, and hundreds of SA-2/3/6/8/9 launchers all netted together with MiGs, AAA, and radars in a daunting integrated air defense system (IADS).[70]

Then, at the end of June, the Cubans launched a two-pronged offensive, with one force advancing from Xangongo to capture Cuamoto and the second moving from Techipa to Calueque. The first, western Cuban column ran into a South African blocking position, and although the Cubans gave better than they received, the force still pulled back. The second, eastern Cuban column, however, caught a South African force in an ambush on June 27 and began to hammer the SADF in a fierce fight. The SADF sent up a force of Olifants to rescue the situation but the Cubans counterattacked with a battalion of T-55s in a flanking maneuver that forced the South Africans to withdraw all the way back to Namibia, harassed by Cuban MiGs the whole way. That same day, Cuban MiGs struck the Calueque dam and hydroelectric plant, which was critical to powering South African–controlled Namibia. The attack was extremely accurate and effective, severely damaging the bridge and nearby sluicegates, as well as the power plant, engine rooms, and an important freshwater pipeline. The Cuban mechanized forces then began patrolling aggressively and in force preparatory to resuming their ground advance—which Pretoria worried would not only drive the last South Africans from Angola, but would press on into Namibia. Between their heavy casualties (by South African standards), the humiliating loss of territory, and the fear of the war shifting to Namibia, the South African government decided finally to negotiate an end to the war.[71]

Patterns of Cuban Military Effectiveness. During their various campaigns in Africa between 1975 and 1988 Cuban forces consistently performed well in most aspects of combat operations, although they did perform poorly in some. Not only did the Cubans perform notably better than Arab armies overall, there was little overlap between the Cuban patterns of performance and Arab patterns.

Of greatest importance, Cuban tactical leadership was generally quite good.[72] Cuban commanders from brigade-level down were flexible and creative in their approach to combat situations.[73] They were very aggressive and rarely could be faulted for failing to seize the initiative or take advantage of opportunities arising in the chaos of battle. The South Africans felt that Cuban mechanized formations were aggressive to the point of being almost suicidal. Cuban tactical units made excellent use of tactical maneuver. They repeatedly confounded SADF units with flanking counterattacks in the battles at Cuito Cuanavale, Cuamato, and Techipa in 1988. In the Ogaden, the Cubans made superb use of maneuver, regularly outflanking and enveloping the defending Somali forces. The pace of operations and dramatic victories won by Cuban forces in these fluid maneuver battles was only possible because Cuban tactical commanders were willing to improvise and take the initiative when opportunities presented themselves.

Cuban forces demonstrated superb cooperation both within units and among units (and armed services). Cuban formations of all sizes generally evinced thorough integration of all combat elements into effective combined arms teams. In Ethiopia and again in Angola, Cuban armor, mechanized infantry, infantry, engineers, helicopters, and fixed-wing aircraft worked extremely well together. In Angola in particular, the thick vegetation of the bush made it essential for dismounted infantry to work together with armor to take advantage of the strengths and cover the weaknesses of each arm. Cuban units also did a good job working together and supporting each other in combat. In particular, the success of the large-scale Cuban maneuvers in all of their wars were possible only because of the ability of geographically distant Cuban units to coordinate their actions in pursuit of broader objectives. Finally, the Cuban Air Force (DAAFAR) did a good job supporting Cuban ground forces. This was especially evident in Angola in 1987–1988 when ubiquitous Cuban close air support and battlefield air interdiction missions made it difficult for SADF units to maneuver or artillery to provide fire support.[74]

Individually, the performance of the various Cuban combat arms was more mixed, but never poor. Cuban tankers were mediocre marksmen but consistently attempted to "stalk" South African armor in the bush of Angola and otherwise maneuvered to gain advantageous positions over their adversaries.

Likewise, Cuban antitank teams relentlessly hunted SADF tanks, forcing the South African armored units to fall back several times or risk heavy losses. Cuban artillery units were accurate and could shift fire well. Although often outdueled by South Africa's outstanding G-5s and G-6s, in 1987–1988 when Cuban MiGs eventually shut down the SADF artillery units, Cuban M-46, D-30, and (especially) BM-21 batteries displayed an impressive ability to chase South African formations around the battlefield and quickly shift fire to cover the operations of their own maneuver units.

Cuban tactical commanders also paid excellent attention to reconnaissance and other forms of intelligence gathering. Throughout the campaigns at Cuito Cuanavale and Cunene in 1988, Cuban units relied on constant patrolling to deprive SADF units of the element of surprise, on rapid counterattacks by mobile reserves, and on aggressive maneuvers against the SADF's flanks to halt and ultimately drive back the South Africans.

The ultimate success of all three major Cuban military campaigns derived from these tactical skills. After their third attack on Cuban positions in the Tumpo bridgehead failed on February 29, 1988, one of the South African task force commanders famously explained their defeat by remarking that "the enemy is strong and clever."[75] Even the South African author Helmoed-Römer Heitman grudgingly said of the Cuban-FAPLA units defending Cuito Cuanavale that they had "once again demonstrated their ability to conduct an effective and imaginative defence, and competent control of their artillery."[76]

When the Cubans were allowed to command, their strategic leadership was also very good. In the Ogaden War—and disastrously at the Battle of the Lomba River—Soviet generals were ultimately in charge.[77] However, in Angola, both during Operation CARLOTA in 1975–1976, and again at Cuito Cuanavale and Cunene in 1987–1988, the Cubans ran things the way they wanted. In particular, Fidel Castro proved to be a gifted commander, contributing considerably to CARLOTA and saving the day at Cuito Cuanavale.[78] Leopold Scholtz has written the best account of the fighting in Angola from the South African perspective, and he grudgingly concluded about Castro that "Whatever one may think of his politics, he was a very good tactician and strategist."[79]

In the air war, DAAFAR performed well in both ground-to-air and air-to-air operations. Cuban MiGs and SAMs quickly established air superiority over Ethiopia in 1978 and Angola in 1987–1988. There were only a handful of air-to-air engagements between Cuban and South African pilots, and they tote up to a draw in numeric terms. In these very limited engagements, South African pilots nonetheless concluded that their Cuban counterparts were very "aggressive and clever," and concede that they lost several of the handful of engagements that took place.[80] And this despite the fact that the Cubans flew according to Soviet doctrine and so were somewhat reliant on GCI.[81]

While South African accounts swear up and down that they were not afraid of the Cuban air force, the bottom line is unmistakable: between the MiGs; the heavy, integrated SAM network; and the long distances that SAAF fighters had to fly, they effectively ceded the skies to DAAFAR. The South Africans were so worried by Cuban air power in 1987–1988 that they restructured their operations to mitigate DAAFAR's impact on the fighting. They tried to mount their various assaults on the Cuito Cuanavale defenses in periods of bad weather when the Cubans could not fly. Worse still, the SAAF itself was reduced to toss-bombing* to avoid the Cuban fighters and SAMs.[82] This method of air strike is so inaccurate that it effectively prevented the SAAF from conducting either CAS or dynamic interdiction missions, and limited South African pilots to deliberate strikes against Cuban/Angolan positions. It really meant that the SAAF just could not target Cuban/FAPLA tactical forces.

The Cuban record in air-to-ground operations was more mixed. The accuracy of Cuban air strikes varied. As in most air forces, Cuban pilots did better when attacking stationary targets—such as the Calueque dam—and ground forces deployed in open terrain—as in the Ogaden—but did not fare as well against ground forces moving quickly or in heavy vegetation, such as the thick Angolan bush. Nevertheless, even against the South Africans in Angola, Cuban air-to-ground operations were paralyzing. The SADF constantly had to invent schemes to divert or confuse the Cuban MiGs to allow them to conduct ground operations without interference, but these ploys rarely worked. Ultimately, an important factor that prompted the South Africans to call off their attack on Cuito Cuanavale was that Cuban aircraft began to pound South African supply lines and bases, threatening the SADF's logistical lifeline.[83] The Cuban MiGs effectively suppressed the deadly South African G-5 and G-6 artillery pieces, even though they never destroyed a single gun. Although

---

* When a plane "toss bombs" it flies very low to its target to avoid detection by enemy air defenses. Then, as far from the target as possible, the plane suddenly climbs (which makes it more likely to be detected by enemy radar) and releases its (unguided) weapons during this sudden ascent. The plane then turns and drops back down to the deck and screams back to its base and safety. Meanwhile, its bombs, having been "thrown" from the plane while it was climbing, follow a ballistic trajectory that allows them to cover a considerable distance before striking the ground. This allows the plane to make its escape long before it gets close to the target, thereby minimizing its exposure to enemy air defenses and maximizing its chances of survival. The problem is that toss-bombing is very inaccurate, relying on a pilot to release while flying at high speed, while still far from the target, and while ascending (which means flying away from the target on the ground, as opposed to the preferred approach of flying toward the target). It is not a precision method of bombing, and it is useless for striking small moving targets such as tanks or trucks, although it can work when striking large stationary targets such as airfields.

Heitman maintains that Cuban and Angolan MiGs did little actual damage, he acknowledges that "What they did achieve was to hamper South African operations quite considerably. It would not be going too far to say that on several occasions it was only the timely arrival of [Cuban] MiGs over a battlefield that prevented the complete destruction of a FAPLA brigade."[84]

Cuban unit cohesion was good but not great. In Angola in 1975 the first real impact of Cuban forces was to stiffen FAPLA resolve and demonstrate to the South Africans that Angola would not be a walkover. FAPLA units regularly disintegrated under any real pressure from either the SADF or the FNLA; however, while the first small Cuban contingents were repeatedly outflanked and forced to retreat, they never broke and ran. Moreover, in all three campaigns, there are no recorded instances of Cuban units falling apart under pressure, even in the bleakest moments along the Queve River in 1975, at Harar in 1977, or at Cuito Cuanavale in 1988. By and large, Cuban mechanized formations fought exceptionally hard, taking risks to carry out their missions that earned the respect of the South Africans. At other times and in other places, Cuban units preferred to give up a position and retreat rather than sacrifice themselves defending it.[85] This is not necessarily an indictment of Cuban courage, and may well reflect the perceptiveness, initiative, and quick-thinking of Cuban junior officers who recognized when a position was untenable and preferred to pull their troops out rather than have them needlessly killed or captured.

Cuban forces also did reasonably well at logistics. Cuban units never suffered from a lack of supplies, even when conducting fast-paced operations over great distances, such as in Ethiopia, or in extremely difficult terrain, as in Angola.[86] Lt. General Bernard Trainor, who observed Cuban operations in Angola in 1987–1988 as a war correspondent, commented that Cuban logistics operations were very impressive, and in some ways even rivaled US logistical feats during the Persian Gulf War. In particular, Trainor noted that Cuban quartermasters reflected the aggressiveness and daring of their operational counterparts by establishing forward supply points to facilitate their rapid mechanized advances.[87] In addition, the Cubans demonstrated real imagination and determination in moving forces over long distances when the need arose. The redeployments to Angola in 1975, Ethiopia in 1977, and southeastern Angola in 1987 were quite remarkable, moving tens of thousands of Cuban troops and their equipment over thousands of miles in very short periods of time. Although the Soviets often provided help for these redeployments, the initial deployment to Angola was a wholly Cuban enterprise, and Havana pressed into service warships, merchant ships, fishing boats, and an assortment of private craft as well as ancient Bristol Britannia transport aircraft, which had to land to refuel three times to make the trip across the Atlantic.[88]

Maintenance and repair appears to have been a particular strength of Cuban forces. In the 1970s when Cuba had only small numbers of heavy weapons, Havana made a major effort to keep this equipment operational and so imposed high maintenance standards on its troops. These standards continued to hold even into the late 1980s after the Cuban arsenal had expanded considerably. In 1979, the US Defense Intelligence Agency concluded that Cuban forces were fully capable of all major repair and overhaul on all but their most sophisticated equipment, such as the latest Soviet electronic warfare gear.[89] At least two additional pieces of evidence suggest the Cubans were quite good in this area. First, in 1987–1988, Cuban and Angolan MiGs, which were maintained and repaired by Cuban technicians, flew tremendous numbers of sorties. Heitman remarks that the MiGs were "constantly in the air," and Scholtz states that the Cubans flew 1,283 sorties in about 60 days in January–March 1987 at Cuito Cuanavale (or roughly a sortie per day per aircraft).[90] This level of sustained activity in combat in the inhospitable environment of the Angolan bush suggests an impressive repair and maintenance capability. Second, Cuban technicians and technical advisers were employed by numerous Third World allies of the USSR, including many of the Arab states. In particular, before the 1973 October War, the Syrians found themselves incapable of maintaining some of their new Soviet hardware, such as T-62 tanks, and so Cuban technicians were brought in to man the Syrian repair and maintenance depots. Clearly then, Cuban technicians were at least considered significantly more capable than Arab technicians.[91]

Of course, Cuban forces were hardly perfect. They had areas of weakness too. Cuban soldiers and weapon crews do not seem to have been terribly good shots. In Angola in 1987–1988, this failing was particularly evident as Cuban units fired tremendous amounts of ordnance at close ranges and often into the flanks or rear of SADF units and yet scored few hits. In part this can be excused by the difficult terrain, and in part by the inferior equipment of the Cubans, but ultimately these are only partial explanations. It is still the case that South African units regularly outshot Cuban units, even when the Cubans had gained an advantage through maneuver or positioning.[92]

As a final note, the South Africans themselves came away with a healthy respect for their Cuban enemies—a respect that no Arab army has ever earned from either ally or adversary. Leopold Scholtz conceded that "Tactically, the Cuban and South African armies measured up well against each other. The Cubans were surprisingly aggressive and at times even rash, although the battle-hardened SADF probably had the edge because of its superior doctrine, experience and training."[93] Likewise, South African combat veteran Ross Mardon told another author that the SADF was "definitely by far outgunned, out-maneuvered, out-fought, out-tacticed [*sic*], out-everything you want to say," by the Cubans at Cuito Cuanavale.[94]

Conclusions: Non-Arab Armies and the Soviet Military System

This comparison of North Korean and Cuban combat performance pretty much puts the nail in the coffin of the theory that Soviet military doctrine is to blame for the poor showing of Arab militaries since 1945. Although both the North Koreans and Cubans relied heavily on Soviet military methods— far more heavily than any of the Arab militaries at any time—they fought markedly better than the Arabs. In particular, they did well in those aspects of military effectiveness that were most troublesome for the Arabs: tactical leadership, flexibility, maneuver, combined arms, battlefield intelligence, information management, maintenance, and air operations.

At the most basic level, they just did not fight like the Arabs. Neither the Cubans, the North Koreans, nor the Soviets in World War II suffered from the same problems that consistently hampered Arab war-making. All of them demonstrated a good-to-great ability to conduct mechanized maneuver warfare. All of them demonstrated a strong commitment to and understanding of combined arms operations. All of them devoted proper attention to reconnaissance and intelligence. All of them were able to mount and sustain sophisticated air campaigns—although all of them performed less well than many of their opponents in terms of individual pilot skills. In this last area, the Soviet de-emphasis of tactical skill may have played a role, especially given the better performance of Western-trained pilots from South Africa, South Korea, and even Ethiopia. The same may have been true for armored operations, where all of these armies handled armor well in terms of doctrine and tactics (and in ways that Arab armies never demonstrated) but their individual tank crews were typically less skillful than their Western-trained opponents, whether it was North Koreans versus Americans or Cubans versus South Africans. (Still, Soviet-trained Somalis were far better tankers than the American-trained Ethiopians.)

Taken together, this chapter and the last show that there was little difference in the battlefield performance of the Egyptian, Jordanian, and Syrian militaries in 1967, despite the wide variance in their reliance on Soviet doctrine. Similarly, there was very little change (and certainly no improvement) in Egyptian military effectiveness between 1973 and the present, despite Cairo's shift away from a Soviet-style system to an American system. However, there was a considerable difference between the performance of Arab forces (even those ostensibly relying on Soviet military doctrine) and the performance of the North Korean and Cuban militaries that also relied on Soviet military methods.

For the most part, the difference was not in *how* operations were conducted, but how *well* those operations were conducted. North Korean and Cuban forces seemed to rely on the same tactics and doctrine as the Syrians and Egyptians in the Six-Day and October Wars, but the Cubans and North Koreans were just much better at executing them. In other words, the evidence is about as conclusive as it can get that Arab military weakness was not a product of their reliance on Soviet military doctrine. Indeed, as Yaacov Ro'i and Dima Adamsky put it, "The problem [for the Arabs] was less one of adherence to Soviet methods than of application of those methods in a rigid, mechanical manner that was not intended by their authors."[95]

This should not be terribly surprising since the Soviet military system was actually a very effective approach to warfare. While there were certain aspects of it that struck Germans and Americans as foolish or even "wrong"— specifically the de-emphasis on tactical flexibility so as to maximize operational flexibility—it is a system that nevertheless worked, and worked extremely well during the Second World War. When it failed, in the early days of the war, it failed primarily because it was being implemented by largely untrained officers at lower levels and too many incompetents at higher levels, because its combined arms doctrine was immature, and because the Russians were fighting the most terrifyingly competent military of the twentieth century.

If anything, reliance on Soviet methods was probably *helpful* to the Arab militaries.[96] The Soviets found effective (if sometimes crude) solutions to many of the problems resulting from their own societal issues—issues that mimicked challenges for the Arabs.[97] In particular, the Soviet system was designed to win despite poor tactical performance. How much of that was because the Soviets knew that their populace would not produce large numbers of gifted soldiers, NCOs and junior officers, and how much a result of their obsession with prevailing at the operational level of war is impossible to know. It may well be a proverbial chicken-and-egg problem in which the Soviets made a virtue out of necessity. But by devising a system meant to win *despite* limited tactical abilities, the Soviet system was tailor-made for the Arabs and probably helped them to avoid their Achilles heel to some extent. So we can't blame the Russians for Arab defeats, and we may just have to give them some of the credit for Arab successes, limited as they were.

PART II | Politicization

CHAPTER 5 | Politicization

T HERE IS AN inherent tension between civilian and military leaders. It is rare when both see issues identically, especially in war. Civilian leaders often see nonmilitary goals that are of equal or greater importance in their minds to purely military objectives. Military leaders often focus on the logic of military strategy (how do I defeat/destroy my enemy?), sometimes without regard for political questions (how do I establish an enduring peace, or satisfy a critical ally or domestic constituency?).

At bottom, it is generally the case that civilian officials and military officers just think differently and approach problems differently, reflecting the very different formative experiences they encountered over the course of their careers. Typically, it takes a soldier turned statesman or an unusually perspicacious civil servant to bridge the gap. And there are never enough of either of those. It is why I tend to believe that there really is no such thing as good civil-military relations, just different versions of bad. However, the differences are important, and they can range in severity from just "the usual grousing" to open hostility.

When civil-military relations are particularly bad, we tend to speak of a "politicized" military. By that we mean that civil-military relations have gotten to the point where there are major malfunctions in the relationship between the civilian and military chains of command. Politicization speaks to a breakdown in the efficient functioning of the armed forces in its military role, the discrete functioning of the political process in governing the armed forces, or both at the same time.[1]

That said, not all politicization is alike. Civil-military relations can break down in at least three different ways, and the differences are as important as the similarities. The first and best-known variant is what I refer to as "praetorianism." The term has been around for a long time, and derives from the oldest scholarly conception of politicization. It speaks to excessive military influence in politics, including when the armed forces seize power and govern the country outright as a military dictatorship. The name derives from Imperial Rome's Praetorian Guard, which protected the emperor himself, and beginning with Claudius, usurped the power to choose or depose the emperor.[2]

The second variant of politicization is what I call "commissarism." Commissarism refers to excessive political involvement in military affairs to ensure that the military is loyal to the government and obeys civilian orders. This may sound like ordinary civilian control of the military—a key element of how civil-military relations are supposed to work—but commissarism refers to this process taken to its illogical extreme, when it becomes destructive.[3] When the government fears the military, believing that the generals intend to disobey or overthrow the government, the civilian leadership may impose controls on the military that can be deleterious both to civil-military relations and to military operations. The name derives from the political commissars that the Soviets implanted throughout the Red Army after the Russian Revolution to ensure its subservience to the Communist Party and prevent it from overthrowing them. In this way, commissarism is the opposite of praetorianism, since one of the main rationales for regimes to employ commissarism (excessive government control of the military) is to prevent praetorianism (the military taking over the government).

I refer to the third variant of politicization by the somewhat awkward term "palace guardism." In some instances, the primary (or even only) function of a country's armed forces may be to protect the regime from *internal* threats: coups, revolutions, terrorists, insurgents, rioters, assassins, you name it. In these cases, the military is, in effect, nothing more than a palace guard. This means that the military really isn't intended to fight foreign foes and typically receives little to no training or equipment to handle the external security mission. If praetorianism is bad for a military because it means that the military is involved in politics in a way it shouldn't be, and commissarism is bad because it means that politics intrudes on the military in ways that it shouldn't, palace guardism is bad for a military because it means that it is focused on enemies that shouldn't be its primary—let alone its only—concern. The danger, of course, is that if a palace-guard military is forced to fight a foreign army, it may do really badly because it was not trained, armed, or otherwise prepared for that conflict.

The three variants of politicization are closely related. So much so that they often blend into one another. A famous Middle East scholar, J. C. Hurewitz, highlighted the interplay among the three forms when he wrote that "Each time an army overthrows or tries to overthrow a Middle East monarchy, all the surviving monarchs take a deep breath and a close look at their own armies and tighten screening procedures for officer loyalty."[4] In other words, fear of praetorianism breeds commissarism, even among palace-guard militaries that have no other function than to maintain the autocrat in power. Insecure leaders employ commissarism to prevent a praetorian coup, sometimes going so far as to turn their military into nothing more than a palace guard, but once a military dictator has taken power in praetorian fashion he then imposes commissarist controls so that no one can do to him what he just did to his predecessor. Some experts have even argued that it is the palace-guard origins of most Arab militaries that made both commissarism and praetorianism endemic to the region even after the armies had relinquished their roles as dedicated palace guards.[5]

Because civil-military relations in the Arab world have tended to range from bad to horrendous throughout the post–World War II era, exhibiting all three flavors of politicization, a number of people have argued that this is the cause of the underperformance of Arab militaries during that same period. It is undeniable that politicization does have an impact on militaries, although that impact is not uniform and has been exaggerated as frequently as it has been overlooked.[6] This chapter and the following three dig into this issue to assess how much the weakness of Arab armed forces can be traced back to politicization in all its forms.

Praetorianism

Experts on militaries and civil-military relations have been talking about praetorianism for a long time.[7] The most extreme form of this variant of politicization is a coup d'état that results in a military dictatorship. However, the military need not actually take over the running of the government to be considered praetorian. It might intervene only to overturn the current regime and then step aside to allow another civilian government to take power. At an even more subtle level, the military can simply threaten such actions so as to influence government policy.

Right after World War II, there was a lot of praetorianism in the Middle East. Military takeovers were so common to the region that many Arabs, as well as many Western social scientists, considered military rule to be "the natural course" in the area.[8] There were at least 30 military coups, successful and unsuccessful, in the six Arab states of Egypt, Iraq, Jordan, Syria, Sudan, and Yemen between 1949 and 1966 alone.[9] In 1958, Iraqi military officers overthrew King Faysal II, ushering in a decade of seemingly constant military coups and countercoups as various groups and personalities within the armed forces vied for power. From that point until Saddam Husayn's final consolidation of power in 1979, depending on your criteria, there were as many as 19 coup attempts in Iraq.[10] Similarly between 1949 and Hafiz al-Assad's takeover in 1971 there were as many as 15 different coup attempts in Syria.[11] Although the Jordanian and Saudi monarchies reigned throughout this period, both had to survive a number of unsuccessful military coups. Indeed, virtually every Arab country has experienced several successful and/or unsuccessful military coup attempts since the Second World War. Ultimately, the primary manifestation of politicization of Arab militaries before about 1970 was praetorian interference in governance by the military. During this time, commissarism was largely a secondary problem, a byproduct of this ubiquitous praetorianism as military dictators attempted to prevent their subordinates from taking power as they had done so themselves.

Praetorianism and Military Effectiveness. Praetorianism can have a considerable impact on military effectiveness, but it tends to exert that influence by two primary means.[12] First, praetorianism breeds distrust and suspicion within the military. Those who plotted and executed the coup will be resented by those who were excluded from the plot, and those excluded were probably left out because the plotters did not trust them to begin with. Once in power, the generals and admirals become responsible for making decisions on highly contentious political issues, such as raising and allocating revenues. Corruption goes hand in hand with praetorianism as military officers will suddenly have the opportunity and authority to enrich themselves, and once having taken the illegal act of seizing power, why not get rich too? The scramble for money and power often creates severe divisions within the leadership and so breeds factionalism within the chain of command. The factionalism and dissension can impair cohesiveness within, and coordination among, units or services. In extreme cases, it can lead to intra- and interservice violence, troops questioning or disobeying orders, and officers executing operations in combat with an eye toward political ramifications rather than military objectives. Moreover, military officers may aspire to political power and may well employ Machiavellian methods in pursuit of this goal, all to the detriment of trust among the officer corps generally.

The second general problem created for military effectiveness by praetorianism is that it can distract military officers from the practice of purely military skills. The intrusion of the military into civilian politics typically means the intrusion of politics into all aspects of military affairs, including promotions, where generals and admirals often try to promote subordinates loyal to them to advance their political interests, rather than those with military skills. At the highest levels, the dictator and his top aides are likely to have a full plate just dealing with the constant demands of running the government. Managing the governmental bureaucracy and making political decisions is a full-time job, and even the most energetic generals will find it hard, if not impossible to attend to all the demands of governance and simultaneously meet the needs of the military by formulating strategies, directing planning (or combat operations), allocating resources, and monitoring the training of the forces. Something's got to give, and typically it is the military tasks that get crowded out by the political demands.

In a similar fashion, praetorian officers tend to put less time and effort into the training of their units and the honing of their military skills. In some cases, this is because officers may be interested primarily in political power, and what is required to achieve it is rarely what contributes to military effectiveness. Alternatively, many officers will pay little attention to their professional tasks because of the absence of attention from the top levels of the hierarchy.

There are several important secondary effects of these problems. Training can fall by the wayside because officers no longer believe that their units need to perform well for them to advance in rank. Loyalty and politicking become more important, and the officers may spend more time on that than on the military preparatory tasks that ought to be their primary concerns. The mistrust and competition among services or branches of services bred by rivalry among their leaders vying for political power can lead to difficult combined arms or joint operations. Officers may see knowledge as power and so choose to hoard information as a way of aggrandizing their own power within the system, meaning that the people who need critical information for battle may not have it. And taken altogether the general emphasis on politics at the expense of military skills, plus the ripple effects this creates, can be demoralizing for troops and junior officers and can erode unit cohesion. Indeed, praetorian militaries often have fragile morale, prone to crack from relatively minor setbacks because troops and their commanders alike know that their superiors are distracted and often achieved their positions by playing politics, not by learning how to wage war.

Commissarism

In contrast to praetorianism, the recognition of commissarism as a distinct manifestation of politicization is a more recent development.[13] It is the same phenomenon that Jim Quinlivan of RAND has dubbed "coup-proofing."[14] It refers to heavy-handed efforts on the part of the regime to ensure the loyalty and obedience of the military. The regime seeks to make sure that the military will execute its orders and, more important, that the military won't try to oust the regime.

Commissarism generally takes the form of debilitating civilian control over the armed forces, including micromanagement of training and operations and loyalty-based screening procedures for promotion. Commissarist regimes typically worry about generals cultivating the loyalty of their troops, so they will frequently and arbitrarily rotate commands, leave loyalists in place for long periods of time, and generally pay close attention to command assignments. Another typical feature of commissarism is sudden purges of the officer corps to remove those suspected of disloyalty. Also, commissarism almost invariably includes efforts to "pack" the military—particularly the senior leadership—with family members, political allies, friends, and ethnic or religious groups considered especially loyal to the despot.

Commissarism in the Middle East. Extensive and often draconian measures to ensure the loyalty and responsiveness of the military to the regime have been widespread in the Middle East, particularly between the 1970s and the early 2000s. The Iraqi military under Saddam, the Syrian armed forces under the Asads, and the Libyan military under Muammar Qadhafi were notorious for their high degrees of commissarism.[15] In the 1970s and early 1980s, Saddam took commissarism to its extreme, conducting fearsome purges, only promoting generals of proven loyalty to himself, establishing multiple intelligence agencies to watch his own military (and one another), and even going so far as to deliberately imitate the Soviet political commissar system by attaching Baathist "political officers" to military units. In Syria before the 1973 October War, Hafiz al-Asad could identify only five generals he trusted to command divisions, so he only created five divisional commands—even though his army was so big it really needed twice that many. Likewise, Qadhafi was so fearful of his generals that he defended his strongholds in Chad in the late 1980s with battalions drawn from different brigades that were left under the command of the headquarters of their original parent units, some of which were not even deployed to Chad.

Even lesser autocracies often manifest commissarist traits. When Nasser finally gained control of Egypt he immediately packed the high command of the armed forces with fellow coup participants from the Free Officers Movement. In one of many extreme moves, he promoted his friend 'Abd al-Hakim 'Amr from the rank of major to major general and made him commander-in-chief of the Egyptian armed forces.[16] The Saudi military also goes to considerable lengths to ensure that its troops cannot mount a coup. The primary function of the Saudi Arabian National Guard (SANG) is to protect the regime, and to ensure its loyalty, the SANG is recruited entirely from Najdi tribes loyal to the House of Sa'ud.[17]

As part of the commissarist controls, many Middle Eastern armed forces have favored one or more ethnic, tribal, or religious groups over others in the military. In some cases, entire ethnic/tribal/religious groups have been discriminated against or excluded altogether from certain units or branches of the military. Jordanian Bedouin and Circassians dominate the combat arms of the Jordanian military while the majority Palestinians are relegated to supporting functions even though the Palestinians are the most urbanized, best educated, and most technically skilled in the populace.[18] Sunni Arabs dominated the Iraqi officer corps, the Republican Guard, the Air Force, and other key units under Saddam, while Shi'a Arabs were relegated to line infantry formations.[19] Not surprisingly, after Saddam's fall and especially after the departure of US troops from Iraq in 2011, the Shi'a prime minister Nuri al-Maliki pushed many Sunnis out of the Iraqi officer corps and replaced them with loyal Shi'a. Members of the Asads' Alawi sect filled most key command slots and dominated the Syrian Air Force and regime protection units.[20] Not surprisingly, these were the formations that remained loyal and fought for the regime when the 2011 revolution devolved into civil war in 2012.

Ultimately, the dictators who took power between 1967 and 1973 proved so successful in packing their officer corps, micromanaging training and operations, and otherwise distorting the military hierarchy that they effectively neutralized the military as a political force. In effect, commissarism defeated praetorianism. Indeed, by the turn of the twenty-first century, commissarism in the Arab world (and Iran) had proven so successful, that the militaries were no longer seen as the greatest threats to the regimes. Instead, popular revolts by the people as a whole or some key segment of it—an ethnic, religious, or tribal group—displaced military coups as the regimes' first obsession. As a result, many Middle Eastern militaries were pushed back into the palace-guard model as their primary responsibility became guarding against these internal threats. It is worth noting that, even after the Arab Spring revolts in 2011 when states were crumbling across the region, there was only one true coup in the Arab world: in Egypt in 2013.

The Effects of Commissarism on Military Effectiveness. Commissarism can have a significant impact on military performance. Commissarist regimes tend to intervene excessively in a range of military activities to ensure that the armed forces are doing exactly what the regime wants and nothing else, in both peace and war. Thus, commissarist militaries impose a high degree of centralization of authority and unwillingness to delegate authority to (less-politically reliable) lower levels of command. This is one of the defining features of a commissarist military. The commissarist regime fears an independent military because this freedom allows for the possibility that the military will turn on the regime. So the regime places its most trusted personnel in the top command slots of the armed forces and then drastically centralizes all authority to ensure that all important decisions are made by those trusted personnel.

The perverse complement to the over-centralization characteristic of commissarist militaries is that they often have bad generals. The problem is that commissarist regimes fear the most senior officers the most (since these can potentially command the most troops to move against the regime if they choose to do so). Consequently, commissarist regimes generally seek to put their most trusted people into the top military command slots, favoring loyalty over competence. They often grow suspicious of victorious generals—whose prestige and ability could give them a greater ability to seize power—and may even sack them because of their success. In the most extreme cases, a commissarist regime might even deliberately place incompetents in the top military slots to ensure that they can defeat any coup should they face one, although this is actually quite rare. The impact is that the military operations of commissarist militaries are often poorly planned and led.

It gets even more complicated than this—and why none of us would want to be a general in a commissarist military. Balanced against the potential hazards of success are the even greater risks of failure.[21] Commissarist regimes are uncomfortable with victorious generals, but they are terrified of military defeat. Failure in war can provoke unhappy elements in the society to move against the regime that led them to defeat. The military itself will often be humiliated and infuriated by defeat, and if they blame the regime—often for placing such commissarist shackles on them—their anger can move then to burst their bonds and rid themselves of the regime. Defeat tends to make the regime look weak and vulnerable in general, potentially encouraging other would-be rivals to move against a defeated regime. Thus, illegitimate autocracies inevitably fear that losing a war will provoke coup attempts and revolutions.

That fear has proven very well grounded historically, especially in the Middle East, where military defeat has triggered a staggering number of coups and revolts against the government. From Syria in 1949 and 1967, to Egypt in 1952 and again in 1970, to Iraq in 1963 and again in 1991, to Libya time and again in the 1980s, defeat in war has often been a trigger for successful and unsuccessful bids to overturn Middle Eastern regimes. Moreover, commissarist regimes sometimes suspect that a setback in battle may be the result of disloyalty on the part of the commander who purposely "threw" the battle to make the regime look weak. Either way, they have a bad habit of sacking or shooting unsuccessful commanders, "pour encourager les autres" (to encourage the others) as Voltaire put it.

Consequently, officers in a commissarist military have every incentive to perform well, not just for the normal reasons of personal ambition and patriotism, but because failure can be a mortal sin. While Westerners tend to emphasize (and exaggerate) the perils of succeeding in a commissarist military, the truth is that failing tends to be far more hazardous to one's career and life expectancy. Soviet and German generals throughout the Second World War were acutely aware of the dangers of failing Stalin or Hitler, and these were far more powerful incentives than any fear they might have had that if they succeeded too much it would arouse the dictators' suspicion. The same was true of Iraqi officers under Saddam, Syrian officers under Hafiz al-Asad, and Libyan officers under Qadhafi.[22] Historically, generals serving paranoid dictators are far more likely to get sacked or shot for losing than for winning. For that reason, commanders in commissarist militaries often fight *very* aggressively, attack hard, counterattack whenever possible, and feel the need to take action lest inaction be seen as treachery.

Modern military aircraft are extremely expensive pieces of equipment costing tens or now even hundreds of millions of dollars. Military aircraft are also powerful weapons systems. And once a pilot has taken off from his airfield, it is hard for his commanders on the ground to control his actions. If the pilot does not obey, the most the commander can do is try to shoot him down—or scare him into doing what he is told. For all of these reasons, commissarist regimes also tend to stress loyalty over flying skills in pilot selection, which can potentially impair air operations.

The fear of being punished for failure can also affect the information flows of commissarist militaries, although this tends to be only one part of the problem. Personnel in commissarist militaries have an important incentive to lie, exaggerate, and shift blame to cover their mistakes. A great, recently discovered example of this comes from the Battle of Kursk in 1943, where intrepid historians have now demonstrated that the common perception of a vast battle involving thousands of tanks—and equivalent losses on both sides—is just plain wrong. The climactic battle at Prokhorovka on the southern front of the Kursk battle was fought by several hundred Soviet tanks against about a third as many German tanks, and the Germans won an overwhelming victory, destroying as many as 15 Soviet tanks for every one they lost. However, General Nikolai Vatutin, the Red Army's front commander, was terrified that if he told Moscow the truth about what had happened, Stalin would sack or execute him. So instead, he invented the story of the massive clash of armor and claimed devastating losses on *both* sides. After all, Vatutin's losses seemed much less disastrous if he claimed that a much larger Soviet force had been engaged (and so those destroyed represented a lesser percentage), and if he had destroyed a comparable number of German tanks.[23]

Along similar lines, a constant of brutal dictatorial regimes is that their advisers tend to tell them what they want to hear. Because no one wants to be the bearer of bad news, there is a powerful tendency for intelligence services to politicize their analysis along the lines of the preordained beliefs of the leadership. The incentives for personnel in a politicized military to falsify, conceal, and exaggerate to cover mistakes also contribute to the confused picture of the battle the leadership is likely to receive. Moreover, because analysis tends to be based on what the regime wants to hear, and no one wants to unearth unwanted truths, there is often little incentive to conduct comprehensive, aggressive intelligence collection operations.[24] All this said, it is worth noting that recent evidence from Saddam's Iraq gathered by US personnel after the 2003 invasion demonstrate a surprising willingness on the part of many of Saddam's senior subordinates to level with him—and even challenge his beliefs—about critical questions of war and peace.[25] Consequently, we should recognize that there are limits to this tendency as well.

The last effect of commissarism on military operations that is worth noting is the cumulative impact of all of the other problems on morale and unit cohesion. Virtually every aspect of a commissarist system works to undermine the morale of the military. Let's start with the fact that the soldiers and officers typically know that they are not trusted by the regime. Then there is the fact that the unique skills the military prizes above all else—the skills of war-fighting—are not necessarily valued by the regime, and may not be made criteria for determining senior promotions and command assignments. Then there is the effort of the regime to prevent officers from developing bonds between themselves and their troops. Consequently, too many soldiers and officers may suspect that their leaders are less capable than they are because their superiors may very well have gotten to their positions through loyalty to the regime rather than demonstrated ability. Ultimately, soldiers and officers may fear that the high command is made up of men who are more loyal to the leader than competent. All of that is really bad for morale.

In parallel, commissarism often creates problems with unit cohesion stemming from the officer-enlisted frictions, frequent rotations of commanding officers, and potential lack of confidence of soldiers and officers in their leaders. In commissarist militaries there is normally a pervasive atmosphere of mistrust and deception created by the presence of regime informers and the powerful incentives to lie and shift blame for mistakes. That is all really bad for unit cohesion.

Of course, there can be countervailing forces even in commissarist militaries. Let's go back to the granddaddy of all commissarist militaries, the Red Army in World War II. Early in the war after the German attack on the USSR, Soviet morale was abysmal, and unit cohesion was uneven, and often terrible. Many factors went into that, including surprise, but widespread dislike of the Stalinist regime and its methods of military control was also an important element. As the war went on, however, both unit cohesion and morale improved, for a complex set of reasons. Part of it was Stalin's terror: NKVD formations routinely followed the Red Army divisions into battle to machine gun any who tried to desert (or even just retreat). However, another part of it was the genuine patriotism and fear for their families that the German war of extermination inspired and that Stalin learned to cultivate. Moreover, Stalin also allowed for a major depoliticization of the Soviet armed forces, promoting the best commanders regardless of other considerations, curtailing the power of the political commissars, being more flexible about retreats, all of which loosened the political shackles on the Red Army and played a role in their improved combat performance. The more that Soviet soldiers and officers felt respected and trusted, the more they won, and the more they won the more that the esprit of the force grew in a benevolent cycle.[26] In short, commissarist controls can be highly destructive of morale and unit cohesion, but they can be counterbalanced by other forces and their impact can abate quickly when they are reined in.

Palace Guardism

Technically speaking, palace guards are military forces charged with protecting the person of the ruler and preventing the overthrow of the regime by other elements from within the society. When people refer to a "palace-guard military" in the modern world, what they typically mean is a military whose primary role is to protect the regime from internal threats such as coups, revolutions, insurgencies, and assassinations. The important point is that such a military is really not expected to conduct combat operations against the armed forces of a foreign power.

The reason this phenomenon is important to Arab military ineffectiveness is that some have argued that Arab armies have performed poorly in combat since 1945 because they are nothing more than palace guards that were never meant to fight other organized armed forces, and therefore it is not surprising that they haven't fared well in combat. As one respected scholar put it to me, Arab militaries "are not expected to engage in full-scale warfare and are therefore not trained to improvise, innovate, etc. When they get into 'real' wars— for example, Iraq-Iran or even [the Six-Day War]—it is by mistake and with predictably dismal consequences."[27]

In essence, this version of politicization posits that the political leadership has redirected the armed forces from their ostensible purpose (defending the nation from foreign threats or attacking foreign countries) to the domestic political purpose of defending the regime (and particularly the paramount leader) from internal rivals. In some cases, the military may have a secondary mission of fighting foreign armies, but this is only a distant second: one so unimportant that the military spends little or no time preparing to fight conventional battles, and it is this lack of preparation that is claimed to cause the consistently poor showing of Arab armed forces in combat since 1945. In other words, this explanation contends that the problem is that Arab soldiers and officers are not trained to fight properly, that it is the absence of such training that leads to poor performance in combat, and that if the Arabs ever did bother to train their armies to fight "real" wars, they would do fine.

Palace Guardism in the Middle East. There is an historical logic to this explanation. Virtually all the Arab armed forces began life focused on internal security. Most were created by the European powers during the late nineteenth and early twentieth centuries, occasionally built on whatever could be salvaged from the wreckage of the Ottoman Empire. Although some Arab militaries were created initially to help the imperial forces defend the colony (or Mandatory state) against an external threat, most turned their attention toward internal threats to the regime. For instance, the British created the Iraqi army shortly after World War I to help British regulars guard against a threatened Turkish invasion, but this danger quickly abated and the army shifted to internal security issues, leaving external security to the British. In Libya, Syria, Lebanon, Algeria, Morocco, and Egypt as well, the armed forces were likewise preoccupied with internal security duties at first.

That said, there is also a problem with this explanation that needs to be raised right at the start. The problem is that, over time, many of the Arab armed forces—and all the most important ones, those whose combat performance we are most interested in—shed their palace-guard roles and their focus on internal security. In the 1960s, 1970s, and 1980s, they committed wholeheartedly to preparing and conducting conventional warfare against external adversaries. In many cases, the original internal security role of the military became a tertiary mission.

The Egyptian armed forces furnish a good example of this shift. Prior to 1948, the Egyptian military functioned largely as a true palace guard, responsible mostly for protecting the king and his retainers. External security was largely an afterthought. Consequently, and consistent with the claims of this explanation, when the Egyptian army was committed to battle against Israel in 1948 it was ignominiously defeated. But this beating prompted the cabal of the Free Officers to overthrow the monarchy, and one of their primary motives was to rebuild the army as a "real" fighting force to avenge the disaster of 1948. Beginning in the mid-1950s the army was gradually relieved of its internal security duties and slowly but deliberately retrained to wage conventional warfare against foreign opponents. This trend reached its apogee between 1967 and 1973 when the last vestiges of responsibility for the protection of the regime were removed and the military focused exclusively on fighting Israel.[28] Similar shifts in the priorities of the military from internal to external threats occurred in Iraq after the 1967 Six-Day War and the 1968 Ba'thist coup, in Syria after the Six-Day War and Assad's 1971 coup, and in Libya after the 1978 invasion of Chad.

Middle Eastern states accomplished this transition in part by creating dedicated internal security forces. That solved both the problems associated with "palace guardism"—the military does not have to worry about defending the regime from internal threats—as well as those associated with praetorianism, because the regime then has another force that can protect it against military coups. For instance, in 1955, after an attempted military coup, the Saudis created the Saudi Arabian National Guard to handle the internal security role and protect the royal family from the army. After the Six-Day War, Nasser created the Republican Guard (sometimes called the Presidential Guard) to serve the same function. In Iraq, this role was originally played by an Iraqi Republican Guard, but during the Iran-Iraq war, Baghdad eventually found it necessary to turn the Guard into a "true" military force that became more focused on external security operations. As a result, the regime then split off a small part of the Guard, which it named the Special Republican Guard, to perform the function formerly entrusted to the Republican Guard.

In some other Middle East states, internal security was never the only concern of the military. For example, it is unclear to what extent the Jordanian military ever really fit the palace-guard model, because the external security mission was always an important concern of Jordan's armed forces, and its importance compared to the internal security mission has varied over time.

The Combat Effectiveness of Palace-Guard Militaries. Modern combat is no place for amateurs. Armed forces that have been created solely for the purpose of guarding the regime against internal threats should not be expected to fare well when asked to fight other organized militaries. The mechanization of armies, the development of air forces, as well as the tremendous advances in communications, engineering, and intelligence gathering, have all revolutionized warfare over the past century. It is one thing to line up a bunch of artillery pieces to blow up a rebellious village, or to roll tanks through the streets to overawe dissidents; it is quite another to use the same equipment against a well-armed and equally mobile opponent. For instance, effective combined arms operations require the proper integration of the whole range of military specialties, which in turn requires good training and constant practice for success. Maneuvering mechanized ground forces on the battlefield requires a thorough understanding of how armored forces move and fight, and the ability to take advantage of both the mobility and firepower of those forces. Militaries that don't practice these skills regularly get rusty fast, and those who have never practiced them at all typically get slaughtered.

But militaries charged only with keeping the peace and defending the regime against internal threats often get lazy. Because it generally doesn't take much skill or effort to keep the civilian populace in line or to defeat a coup or even a popular revolt, palace-guard militaries usually see little reason to overexert themselves training. Consequently, many palace-guard militaries neglect training altogether, whether it is directed toward internal security operations or conventional operations against a foreign army.

Relegating a military to palace-guard status can also have an impact on leadership. The single most important criterion for any member of a palace guard is that he must be willing to fight and die to defend the ruler/regime against other members of the society. So unswerving loyalty to the despot has to be the overriding criteria for membership and command in the palace guard. In effect, this may be considered an area in which commissarism and palace guardism overlap or even merge together as aspects of politicization.

There are two complications to note regarding palace guards, however. First, palace guards tend to be smaller than militaries designed to fight other militaries. Secrecy is the key ingredient of a successful coup and, if secrecy can be achieved, it requires very little military force to overthrow a government. As a result, to protect secrecy most military coups involve fairly small bodies of troops.[29] Thus, a palace guard does not require much military force to defeat a coup attempt. Similarly, popular rebellions are typically not well-armed, and therefore can be defeated by a smaller but better-armed force. Historically, what matters in the face of popular unrest is whether the soldiers are willing to shoot civilian protesters; if they are, even small numbers of troops can do the job.[30] If they won't shoot, it doesn't matter how big the army is.

Second, many palace guards, especially in the Middle East, are manned by personnel with preexisting bonds of loyalty to the despot. The military will draw heavily on men from a particular area, ethnic group, or religion who see the ruler either as "one of them," or else as their protector against some other rival area, ethnic group, or religion within the country. This is how Bashar al-Asad survived the Syrian popular revolt in 2011 and turned it into a civil war. He called on his fellow Alawis who manned a variety of regime-protection units within the Syrian army—in effect a palace guard within a larger military—and convinced them that the revolution was an effort by Syrian Sunnis to overthrow the Alawi-led regime, with potentially disastrous consequences for their whole community.

The effect of these two tendencies is to diminish the likelihood of incompetence within a palace-guard military. Because palace-guard militaries are normally fairly small there are fewer officer slots, and so it is more likely that the regime will be able to find suitable candidates to fill those slots who are *both* loyal and competent. This task is further eased by the reliance on certain groups that are fiercely loyal to the despot. As long as the regime recruits from these loyal elements, it can concentrate on promoting qualified personnel from within these groups. Consequently, Hafiz al-Asad found a number of quite competent Alawis to serve as his top commanders, just as Saddam Husayn found a number of well-qualified Sunni Arabs from tribes loyal to him to serve as Iraq's top commanders.

Finally, like the other flavors of politicization, being a palace-guard military typically has an important impact on morale. In some cases, a palace-guard military ordered to fight a foreign army may recognize beforehand that it is being thrown into a lethal situation for which it is unprepared, and so will suffer from poor morale even before the battle has been joined. Those too naïve or deluded to see this ahead of time are likely to discover it quickly in combat. Palace-guard militaries committed to conventional warfare are likely to suffer heavy casualties and may be overwhelmed by the terror of battle, for which their training and experiences in internal security operations will not have prepared them. These two factors alone can shatter morale.

On the other hand, we shouldn't get too carried away with the problems that being a palace-guard military creates. At first glance one might expect palace guardism to produce over-centralization, a dearth of innovation and initiative, poor intelligence operations, and poor unit cohesion, but there is no reason that it should. For example, there is no reason that palace-guard militaries should not approach problems creatively and innovatively. The best palace guards would be those who did act aggressively and creatively to eliminate internal security problems before they became significant threats. Just because a palace guard's training focuses on internal security missions, there is no reason that training cannot encourage aggressive, improvisational behavior. In the abstract, all that matters is protecting the regime, and palace guards should be prepared to accomplish that mission any way they can.

A Top-Down Problem

There is one last, critical aspect of politicization that needs discussing. That is the tendency for politicization to be a top-down problem, particularly the commissarist and praetorian varieties. I am going to discuss this in some detail because many academics have failed to recognize this phenomenon and so have exaggerated and distorted the impact of politicization. It also turns out to be important in understanding what politicization has and has not meant for Arab military effectiveness over the years.

Very simply, politicization tends to have the greatest impact on the highest levels of command with diminishing impact at lower ranks. This is because political leaders are most concerned with the loyalty and obedience of senior commanders whose rank, experience, and status make it more likely they could organize a move against the ruler. The more senior the officer, the greater his (or her) ability and legal authority to lead large numbers of troops, either to organize them for a coup or to prevent other elements of the military from stopping one. Generals are far more dangerous to an illegitimate regime than colonels, who are more dangerous than majors, and so on down the chain of command.

It is extremely difficult to mount a successful coup without the participation of high-ranking officers. Even coups organized by more junior officers typically feel it necessary to secure the cooperation of a senior officer because only they have the prestige and recognition to gain the loyalty of the rest of the army, and hopefully the populace as well. Thus, Egypt's Free Officers needed General Mohamed Naguib, the Iraqi Ba'thists needed Generals Hasan al-Bakr and Hardan al-Tikriti, the Syrian Ba'thists needed

Amin al-Hafiz, and the various Yemeni officer cadres were forced to throw in their lot with General Sallal. If the military takes over the government (praetorianism) it is the senior leaders who typically have to devote the most energy to running it, and they also experience the most important rifts as a result of it.

The greater impact of politicization at the top of the chain of command is also a function of size: senior military positions are easier to politicize since there are relatively few of them. Conversely, despite the best efforts of authoritarian regimes, it is virtually impossible to ensure the loyalty of every major, captain, or lieutenant because there are so many of them, and so few have been in a position to show their political stripes. By way of example, in 2016 the United States' armed forces had 208,037 officers in the lower six grades (through colonel or Navy captain), but only 886 generals and admirals.[31] Also, the much smaller threat posed by junior officers typically makes even the most paranoid regimes willing to tolerate junior officers with more competence than loyalty. An excellent example of this was Saddam Husayn's willingness during the Iran-Iraq War to recall to active duty many junior officers previously dismissed for suspected disloyalty. He did not extend the same amnesty to senior officers.[32]

Empirical evidence regarding the behavior of politicized militaries overwhelmingly supports this point. For example, during the purges of the Soviet military in the 1930s, the higher ranks suffered proportionately greater losses than the lower ranks. Of five marshals of the Soviet Union only Stalin's two old cronies, Budenny and Voroshilov, survived. Of 80 members of the 1934 Military Soviet, 75 were purged (94 percent) by 1938. All 11 Deputy Commissars for Defense were eliminated (100 percent), as well as every military district commander (100 percent). Thirteen of 15 army commanders (87 percent), 57 out of 85 corps commanders (67 percent), 110 out of 195 divisional commanders (56 percent), and 220 out of 406 brigade commanders (54 percent) were also purged by 1938.[33]

Clearly, even in this most outrageous of purges, the axe fell most heavily on the highest echelons of the officer corps with lighter and lighter blows further down the chain of command. Yet this is the norm with military purges, whether in commissarist systems like Stalin's or praetorian systems. For instance, in Nigeria, the two coups of 1967 triggered purges that savaged the senior officer ranks in the same manner: 75 percent of brigadiers and major generals were killed or imprisoned, but only 67 percent of colonels, 50 percent of lieutenant colonels, and only 19 percent of majors. And all of that in a military far smaller than the Red Army of the 1930s, one where major general was effectively the highest rank.[34]

It's worth returning to the example of the Soviet Union, because politicization produced dramatic swings in Soviet military performance at the strategic level throughout the Stalinist era, but had little discernible impact on Soviet tactical forces. Soviet military performance at the strategic and operational levels was awful until well into 1942 as a result of the purges. Soviet victories, such as they were, invariably were the products of exceptional generals or of overwhelming mass, or both. Zhukov's assumption of command was critical to the Soviet victory against the Japanese at Khalkin Gol in 1939, not any superior performance by Soviet tactical forces. Similarly, the Russo-Finnish Winter War was a disaster, in which Moscow only eked out a pyrrhic victory by bludgeoning the Finns with superior numbers. The initial German offensives in 1941 and 1942 were unmitigated catastrophes for the Soviets. Throughout all of these campaigns, Soviet strategic direction was abysmal. The only exceptions to this rule were flukes—competent generals who miraculously survived the purges, such as Timoshenko—and officers who rose to senior command as a result of the "headroom" created by the purges and who just happened to be competent, such as Zhukov. The procession of Soviet military failures finally came to an end in 1942–1943 because Stalin had by then sacked (or shot) most of the political cronies he had appointed during the purges, and promoted capable, lower-ranking officers such as Konev, Malinovsky, Chuikov, Bagramyan, Rybalko, Tolbukhin, Yeremenko, and Rokossovsky to the senior slots. In other words, when commissarism was at its peak, Soviet senior leadership was miserable, but when Stalin loosened the commissarist reins, it improved quickly.

By contrast, from the early 1930s to the end of World War II, Soviet tactical performance also improved, but never to the same extent as the dramatic transformation of its operational and strategic leadership, and for reasons having little to do with politics. Indeed, most of the improvement in Soviet tactical capabilities that transpired during the war can be ascribed to the reorganization of the military between 1941 and 1943 along more effective lines, the development and refinement of Soviet doctrine, the tremendous increase in the quality and quantity of equipment fielded by the Red Army, and the slow accretion of combat experience in the Darwinian process of combat. Soviet tactical commanders began the war with close to zero command competence as a result of their wrongheaded and hopelessly inadequate training before the German invasion. Over time, however, their overall skills improved as poor leaders were killed off (by the Germans or the NKVD), and the ability of the rest grew by dint of painful experience gained in battle after battle.[35] Consequently, the rise and fall of Soviet commissarism produced dramatic changes in Soviet strategic leadership, but had much less impact on tactical performance. Nevertheless, while Soviet senior commanders such as Rokossovsky and Chernyakhovsky were every bit the equal of their German foes, Soviet tactical formations improved but rarely, if ever, matched the skill of their Wehrmacht counterparts until the very end, when shortages in every category gutted the German military.[36]

Indeed, the politicization of the Wehrmacht itself between 1933 and 1945 also illustrates the tendency of commissarism to fall most heavily on senior ranks and to have only very limited impact on lower ranks. Hitler accomplished his initial politicization of the German army in the late 1930s by eliminating and reorganizing the highest ranks of the military, essentially just the Army General Staff, "without alienating the bulk of the officer corps or disturbing the foundations of professional efficiency which had been laid by Seeckt."[37] During the course of the war, Hitler exerted greater and greater control over the German military, issuing orders to lower and lower levels of command, sacking senior commanders who opposed him or conducted even tactical retreats (starting with Field Marshal Gerd von Rundstedt after his withdrawal from Rostov in 1941), and packing the highest slots with sycophants such as Göring, Keitel, and Jodl. However, Hitler's micromanagement of military operations generally remained above corps or division level—although during the Polish campaign he inspected orders down to regiment level and he briefly (and ridiculously) took direct command of Army Group A in late 1942. He rarely interfered with promotions below general officer, and the purely tactical operations of battalions, regiments, and even divisions were still left to their commanders. Not surprisingly, while the strategic performance of the German army became ever more rigid and foolish as a result of the Führer's intrusions, German tactical units performed superbly throughout, only falling off significantly in late 1944 and 1945 when combat losses meant that Germany had to turn to lower quality manpower and short-shrift training to try to make up for skyrocketing losses. Thus, here as well, Hitler's increasingly commissarist politicization had a pronounced impact on Germany's strategic leadership, whereas German tactical performance remained largely constant until other factors unrelated to politicization began to erode it.[38]

The highly politicized militaries of Latin America have demonstrated the same pattern. The Honduran defeat in the 1969 war with El Salvador was largely the responsibility of the inept leadership provided by the Honduran high command. In the aftermath of this conflict, Honduran junior officers pressed for a depoliticization of the military that would allow for an improvement in the senior leadership.[39] Similarly, in El Salvador in the late 1970s, the senior command slots were so horribly politicized that the junior officers attempted a coup intended to install a democratic-technocratic government that would allow the military to disengage from politics and devote itself entirely to combat operations. In the early 1980s, Washington also concluded that the poor performance of El Salvadoran units was a result of inept strategic direction stemming from the severe politicization of the senior officers. The United States pressured the El Salvadoran military command to give up control of these operations to the junior officers who were far more professional and competent. El Salvadoran counterinsurgency operations picked up considerably after this was accomplished.[40] Not surprisingly, when the Salvadoran civil war finally ended, making peace required the removal of virtually the entire top leadership of the armed forces, whereas the lower ranks were left largely untouched.[41] Remarkably, the high command of the Argentine military recognized that they simply were not capable of effectively prosecuting a counterinsurgency campaign, and so in the 1970s, they began to encourage their junior officers to take over fighting the insurgency, precisely because the junior officers were less affected by politicization, and therefore more capable. In the Argentine case as well, the shift in responsibility to the junior officers led to a noticeable improvement in military effectiveness.[42]

Further evidence of this tendency can be found in the experiences of the Iranian military under the last shah. The shah's army was thoroughly politicized in the commissarist vein, and this politicization was greatest at higher levels of command with diminishing impact the lower one went along the chain of command, down to the NCOs and *homafars* (warrant officers) who manifested little if any effects of commissarist politicization.[43] The shah demanded that he personally approve all promotions from the rank of colonel and higher, but not below.[44] Throughout his work on the rebuilding of the Iranian military after the Iraqi invasion, William Hickman explains that under the shah, the higher echelons of the Iranian officer corps suffered heavily as a result of commissarist politicization while the junior levels were affected much less: "[Showing initiative] was the one factor likely to get a senior officer into serious trouble with the Shah. Ever conscious of the possibility of a military coup against him, the Shah constantly manipulated his senior officers, just as he did other politically influential members of Iranian society. If a senior officer attained a position from which he might derive too much power or influence, he was subject to rapid retirement, demotion, or transfer."[45] Edgar O'Ballance found that before the Iran-Iraq War, Iran's senior officers were political hacks who knew little about generalship, but Iranian junior and mid-grade officers were considered by American and British advisers to be "reasonably efficient."[46] Elsewhere, O'Ballance notes that during the first campaigns of the Iran-Iraq War, Iranian junior officers fought very well, especially when compared to their Iraqi opposites, and showed few, if any, of the effects of politicization.[47]

Finally, Stephanie Cronin has argued that the shah's political controls over his senior officers prevented them from acting against the Iranian revolution on their own in 1978–1979—an inaction that led to the defection to the revolution of a great many of the mostly professional junior officers.[48]

After the shah's fall, Khomeini immediately set about building a commissarist military of his own. Like Stalin and other autocrats before him, he purged the standing military and once again concentrated his attention on the higher ranks. Eighty percent of the shah's generals were purged, but only 0.5 percent of his field-grade officers and only 0.2 percent of company-grade officers.[49] Indeed, after Iraq invaded and the Islamic Republic had to scramble to find forces to stop them, Khomeini recalled most pilots and lower-ranking officers to the colors, but none of the shah's generals.[50] Finally, when the mullahs agreed to depoliticize the Iranian high command in 1981–1982, the new Iranian generals proved flexible and capable, and devised highly innovative tactics that allowed them to rout the Iraqis and drive them out of Iran altogether.[51] Again, politicization largely affected the top of the Iranian chain of command, and depoliticization led to improved strategic leadership but had little to no impact on tactical leadership.

Finally, the history of Middle Eastern armies themselves also supports the greater impact of politicization at higher levels of command. In a study of 16 Middle Eastern states in the 1960s, Manfred Halpern found a marked split between criteria for promotion at senior levels of command (primarily colonels and higher) and criteria for promotion at lower levels. Among junior officers, the primary standards for promotion were performance of duty, education level, time-in-grade, and competitive examination. On the other hand, for senior officers the key criterion for promotion was political reliability, and in many armies this was the only criterion.[52] In addition, beginning in the late 1960s, officers of the rank of colonel and below began to lead some Middle East coups. This evidence also supports the contention that politicization is much greater at higher levels of command. The general officer slots, because they are so obviously potential staging grounds for coup-plotters, are thoroughly politicized, but because regimes are less fearful of lower ranking officers and have much greater difficulty determining their political reliability, they often overlook the ambitious major or lieutenant colonel. In David Rapoport's words, lower-ranking coup plotters have the advantage of being "too inconspicuous to draw the government's attention."[53]

In short, in a highly politicized military, especially a commissarist system, the problems with leadership tend to be most pronounced at the top of the hierarchy, rather than at the bottom, and so they manifest themselves primarily in strategic, rather than tactical, decision-making. This is not to say that politicization has no impact on lower levels of command. There are some effects of commissarism that affect lower levels more than higher ones, such as poor morale and unit cohesion, which are overwhelmingly problems of the lower ranks. Politicization pervades the entire military, but its impact is principally felt at the top of the chain of command and trickles down primarily in the form of demoralization and poor unit cohesion.

Assessing the Impact of Politicization

Just as I did with the notion that Arab military ineffectiveness was the fault of the Soviet system, I now want to dig into the history to see if it supports the notion that it was the politicization of the Arab militaries that has caused their crippling deficiencies since World War II. In the next two chapters, I'm going to look at a pair of examples from Arab military history itself where there was some dramatic change in the politicization imposed on an Arab military to see if it led to a corresponding change in its military effectiveness, and if so, how. The two chapters after that look at a pair of heavily politicized non-Arab militaries to see if they had the same problems as the Arabs.

CHAPTER 6 | Arab Militaries and Politicization: Egypt

POLITICIZATION IN ITS various forms has been a pervasive, corrosive feature of the Arab military landscape during the post-1945 era. However, the three different types of politicization shifted over time, as I described in the previous chapter. Most Arab armed forces entered the era with some modest degree of politicization, but many experienced descents deeper and deeper into its different forms over time, with palace guardism giving way to praetorianism, which in turn was superseded by commissarism (and many then returning eventually to palace guards).

However, there were also Arab militaries that depoliticized/professionalized to a very considerable extent at times: some to the point where they were no more politically compromised than Western armed forces (all of which have their own civil-military tensions).

To the extent that politicization was the cause of the persistent Arab military problems during this same period, the effectiveness of Arab militaries should obviously have *improved* with depoliticization. Moreover, since the different types of politicization typically have different effects on militaries, as Arab militaries shift from one form of politicization to another, so too should their problems. If politicization is the source of Arab military problems, then the combat performance of Arab armed forces should wax and wane with corresponding changes in politicization. So in this chapter and the next I am going to look at several key moments when modern Arab militaries experienced significant changes in politicization, to illustrate the impact that the change had on those militaries' effectiveness. I am going to start with the performance of the Egyptian armed forces from the nadir of their politicization in 1967 to the pinnacle of their professionalism during the October War of 1973.

Reform and Rebuilding

The catastrophe of the Six-Day War brought home to the Egyptians that their military capabilities were much less than they had imagined. Moreover, the extent of their defeat was so great that it became impossible for Cairo to rationalize away the disaster as the product of foreign intervention or some other deus ex machina as they had in the past. Faced with the stark realization of their own weakness, Egypt rose to the challenge and made a concerted effort to improve its military capabilities. Of equal importance, Egypt's generals recognized that there were certain inherent handicaps in their armed forces that they would never be able to overcome, so they developed a strategy for war with Israel that would allow Cairo to achieve its political goals given the inevitably limited capabilities that even a retrained and rearmed Egyptian military would be able to achieve.

As part of this, immediately after the Six-Day War, Gamal 'Abd al-Nasser began a lengthy process of depoliticizing the Egyptian military that was continued under his successor, Anwar as-Sadat. Both men grasped that the Egyptian military had been too heavily involved in politics, and that political concerns had been allowed to dictate military affairs to the detriment of military operations.[1] Before 1967, far too many of Egypt's senior commanders had been chosen for their connections to Nasser or 'Amr than for their military acumen. Cronyism in the high command had caused many officers, especially in the senior ranks, to pay more attention to political intrigue than preparing for war. In addition, 'Amr and many of his top commanders had seen the armed forces as their means of asserting power over the rest of the Egyptian government and so had used army units in many nonmilitary assignments such as building housing, excavating the Aswan Dam, and providing internal security. After the war (and a failed coup attempt triggered by the defeat), Nasser removed 'Amr and his colleagues, and sacked nearly 800 Egyptian officers—virtually all of the rank of colonel or higher—who had placed politics above military preparedness. Nasser and Sadat insisted that demonstrated ability and professionalism, not loyalty to the regime or the army commander, would be the primary criteria for promotion.[2]

They also insisted that the military focus solely on preparing for war with Israel and forget its prior involvement in construction, internal security, and other nonmilitary tasks. In pursuit of this, first Nasser and then Sadat appointed the most professional and capable of Egypt's generals to command the armed forces and lead them against Israel, and gave them carte blanche to promote only those officers who demonstrated professional competence. Indeed, to drill home the point that the armed forces had to focus on improving their combat capabilities and ignore politics entirely, they removed any general who demonstrated any interest in politics, no matter how competent he may have been. As a result, by October 1973, Cairo had a first-class team commanding its armed forces led by General Ahmed Isma'il 'Ali, the minister of war; Lt. General Sa'd ad-Din Shazli, the Chief of the General Staff; and Lt. General 'Abd al-Ghani al-Gamasy, the Deputy Chief of Staff for Operations. Moreover, these men put together a superb group of military planners in the Egyptian general staff, who would wage a new way of war for Egypt. In other words, first Nasser and then Sadat removed the commissarist shackles from the Egyptian armed forces and ensured that it had no vestiges of its palace-guard past.

The first priority of General Isma'il 'Ali and his staff was to improve the caliber of Egyptian soldiers and, especially, Egypt's junior officers, who they recognized had performed very poorly in the past. Likewise, Cairo understood that one of its previous problems had been a shortage of personnel who could operate and maintain sophisticated weaponry. To correct these problems, the Egyptian armed forces began recruiting previously exempt college graduates and those with technical training. By 1973, 60 percent of Egyptian officers had at least a university degree, as opposed to less than 2 percent in 1967. Similarly, the percentage of enlisted personnel with at least a high school degree rose from 25 percent in 1967 to 51 percent in 1973. Overall, 110,000 of the 800,000 men in the Egyptian armed forces in 1973 had a university degree or better—a remarkable percentage for any conscript military of the time. Moreover, by the start of the October War, one-half of all of the trained engineers in Egypt had been inducted into the armed forces.[3]

The Limited War Strategy

Sadat's objective for the 1973 October War was to convince the Israelis (and the United States) that Egypt was not impotent and would not sit passively while Israel occupied Sinai, and therefore Israel would have to agree to negotiations if future wars were to be averted. Consequently, all Sadat really needed from his army was to be able to get across Suez and retain a foothold there until a ceasefire could be declared and negotiations begun. To accomplish these modest military objectives, Isma'il 'Ali and his subordinates formulated a limited offensive strategy designed to play to Egyptian strengths, avoid Israeli advantages, and allow the Egyptians to hang on long enough to give Cairo's diplomats their chance.

General Isma'il 'Ali and his chief planner, General Gamasy, envisioned a strategic offensive coupled with a tactical defensive. Two Egyptian field armies (equivalent to Western corps) would surprise the Israelis, cross Suez under cover of a massive artillery barrage, overcome the light Israeli fortifications along the canal, push 5–15 kilometers into Sinai, and then dig-in to repulse the inevitable Israeli counterattacks. Rather than attempting decisive maneuvers of their own, they would stay on the defensive while Israeli armor bashed its head against a wall of entrenched Egyptian infantry. To neutralize Israel's tremendous advantages in armored combat and air power, Egyptian forces would be festooned with new Soviet antitank weapons such as the AT-3 Sagger and RPG-7 rocket-propelled grenade, and surface-to-air missiles (SAMs) like the SA-2 Guideline, the SA-3 Goa, and the SA-6 Gainful.

The most important innovation the Egyptian high command devised for the assault across Suez was to plan the operation in such meticulous detail that Egypt's junior officers were effectively alleviated of the burden of command. The Egyptian General Staff scripted the entire operation down to the very last detail. Every action of every platoon and even every squad in the Army and every squadron of the Air Force was detailed at every stage of the operation by General Staff planners. Nothing was left up to the commanders on the spot to decide. Indeed, Cairo specifically forbade its junior officers from deviating from the script in any way, or taking any action not specifically ordered by the plan.[4]

Egyptian units then practiced their tasks repeatedly on full-scale mock-ups of the Canal and the adjoining terrain in Sinai. Operations were rehearsed incessantly, until every member of every unit knew by heart what he was supposed to do at every step of the operation. Individual units practiced their missions hundreds, if not thousands of times, while the entire two-corps offensive was rehearsed 35 times before the actual attack.[5] Chaim Herzog provides a good description of this process based on what the Israelis learned about it after the war:

> For years the individual soldier was trained in his particular role in war: each unit dealt with its own problem and nothing else. One unit did nothing for three years but train in passing across a water barrier a pipe for transporting fuel; while every single day for three years bridging units would train in backing up trucks to a water barrier, stopping abruptly at the water's edge, causing the elements of the PMP

heavy folding pontoon bridge on the truck to slide by momentum into the water, before they bolted together the two elements of the bridge and drove off. Twice a day during four years these units assembled and dismantled the bridge. Similarly, every day for years all operators of Sagger anti-tank missiles lined up outside vans containing simulators and went through half an hour's exercise in tracking enemy tanks with their missile. . . . This system was repeated right down the line in the army until every action became a reflex action.[6]

Eighty Egyptian engineering units practiced blasting down sand ramparts, such as those Israel had constructed on the east bank, twice a day and twice more every night for two years. By scripting the offensive in such detail and then forcing Egyptian units to learn to execute them by heart, the General Staff was able to write combined arms coordination, tactical maneuver, and synchronized movement into the operations order, thereby obviating the need for tactical commanders to act on their own initiative—at least as long as things went according to plan.

After the Six-Day War, the Egyptian General Staff had conducted a number of extensive studies on the strengths and weaknesses of both the Egyptian and Israeli armed forces, which they had used to guide their preparations for the October War. One important conclusion of these studies was that many of the problems that had proven detrimental to Egyptian forces in past wars were the product of Egyptian cultural patterns and thus could not be solved quickly or easily. (An important Egyptian vote for the cultural explanation.) In particular, the Egyptians concluded that the constant deception and distortion of information they had experienced at all levels in their wars was derived from Arab cultural traits. Their response was to devise a way to skirt the problem altogether by building a massive signals intercept complex on Jebel Ataqah, a large hill west of the Suez Canal, and manning it with large numbers of Hebrew speakers. The Israelis were notorious for broadcasting even the most sensitive information in the clear in battle, and the Egyptians reasoned that they could get accurate reports on the situation at the front by intercepting Israeli situation reports, rather than having to rely on their own troops for the information they needed.[7]

In addition to the unprecedented level of planning that went into the Egyptian assault, Isma'il 'Ali, Shazli, Gamasy, and their men believed that Egypt required both complete surprise and overwhelming advantages in numbers and firepower to ensure that they could dictate the course of the battle to the Israelis and allow their units to methodically implement their rigid, detailed orders. Egypt undertook an all-encompassing, highly sophisticated deception and camouflage campaign to ensure surprise. The operation was kept so tightly secret that even the foreign minister was not informed of its start date. Beginning in 1968, the Egyptians began conducting large-scale exercises simulating a canal-crossing operation. They staged these exercises so frequently that when the actual attack began, the Israelis assumed it was just another drill.

Meanwhile, the Egyptians secretly massed a huge army for the operation while the Israelis kept only a tiny tripwire force along the Canal. By attacking on Yom Kippur, the holiest day of the Jewish year, the Egyptians ensured that the fewest number of Israelis were available on the Canal or in Sinai to meet the initial Egyptian attack. Thus, when the "Badr Offensive" began on October 6, 1973, Egypt had 300,000 troops, over 2,400 tanks, 2,300 artillery pieces, and 540 combat aircraft available for the war. Of these, they massed 200,000 men, 1,600 tanks, and 2,000 artillery pieces for the initial assault. At that moment, this force faced about 18,000 Israeli troops in all of Sinai, with 300 tanks and 80–100 artillery pieces.[8]

Victory—and Defeat

As a result of these Herculean preparations, the Egyptian assault across Suez on October 6 was a stunning success. Thanks to outstanding feats of logistical and combat engineering support, Egypt crossed tens of thousands of men and thousands of vehicles over the Canal with minimal friction on the first day. These units quickly isolated the Israeli fortifications, spread out beyond the Canal, and dug-in in layered antitank defenses. Remarkably, the Cairo correspondent of the *New York Times* reported that "The Egyptian Army has doggedly adhered to a comprehensive, preconceived strategic and tactical plan. Military spokesmen insist that there have been no departures from the plan, no improvisations and no unauthorized initiatives by local commanders."[9] As if that was a good thing.

When Israeli tanks, unsupported by infantry or artillery, charged these lines, they were savaged by barrages of guided missiles, RPGs, and tank and artillery fire. After each Israeli counterattack, Egyptian forces slowly spread outward until all of the brigade and divisional bridgeheads of each army had been linked into a single bridgehead, at which point Cairo's forces began pushing eastward. The Israeli Air Force tried to destroy the bridges across Suez over which supplies and reinforcements were pouring, but they were battered by Egyptian SAMs and anti-aircraft artillery (AAA) pieces, and had little impact. Israeli ground forces repeatedly counterattacked to try to slow or stop the

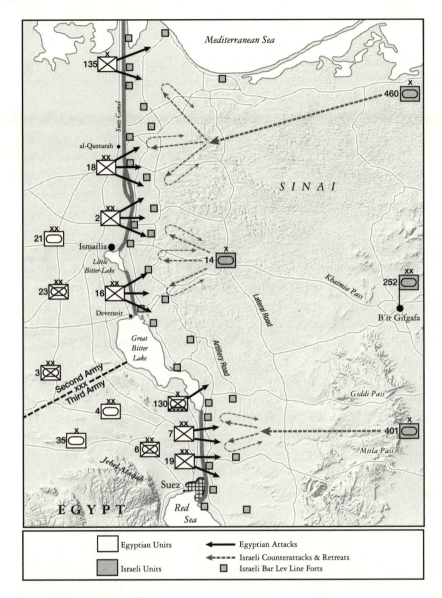

MAP 9 The Crossing of Suez, 1973

Egyptians' methodical advance, but each attack was beaten back with heavy losses, so that by the end of the first two days of the war, the Israelis had lost 200 of the 300 tanks that had begun the war in Sinai.

Between October 9 and October 11, however, the Egyptian attack began to falter. After advancing roughly 8–10 kilometers from the Canal, Egyptian units were able to make less and less forward progress, and Israeli counterattacks began to have a greater and greater impact.

The problem was that the conditions the Egyptian General Staff had created to enable their offensive to succeed were unraveling. First, the Israelis were rapidly reinforcing their army in Sinai; by October 10 the Egyptians still outnumbered the Israelis by sizable margins in terms of men and weapons, but the massive imbalances that had prevailed on October 6 were gone. Second, the effects of the surprise attack had largely worn off and Israeli commanders and their troops had shaken off the confusion and disorientation that had paralyzed them during the initial assault. Third, Israeli commanders across Sinai were quickly improvising solutions to the problems created by the Egyptian antitank teams. Moreover, gaps were appearing between Egyptian units as they advanced—gaps that quick-thinking IDF commanders recognized and launched immediate counterattacks against. Finally, the Egyptians were increasingly forced to operate without a script. To some extent, this was because the Egyptians had only planned and rehearsed the first-phase operation, which they had mostly accomplished by October 10. Of equal or greater importance, however, the vicissitudes of combat were constantly introducing unforeseen events that the meticulously detailed Egyptian orders had not anticipated.

As a result, Egyptian field commanders were being forced to rely on their own initiative and training, with disastrous consequences. The crisp, efficient assaults of the first few days faded into the kind of tentative, plodding, and inflexible movements that had characterized Egyptian operations over the preceding 25 years. Combined arms integration crumbled, with tanks charging ahead and infantry failing to support them. Egyptian artillery units could not find targets, and could not redirect their fire quickly enough to hit those they did identify. Egyptian units found it increasingly difficult to operate in tandem, providing opportunities for Israeli commanders to exploit their confusion and lack of coordination. There was no effort to maneuver on the battlefield, and the antitank screens began to break down. Egyptian advances slowed to a crawl, and Egyptian units reacted sluggishly or not at all to Israeli moves.

On October 14, Egypt renewed its offensive with a major armored assault all along the front. Isma'il 'Ali opposed the new attack because he (correctly) argued that it was beyond the capability of Egyptian forces: they had lost the advantages that had given them success during the first week of the war, and therefore they were likely to be defeated. However, the Syrians cajoled Sadat into ordering the attack to relieve Israeli pressure on Damascus.

The Egyptians launched two armored divisions supported by four separate armored and mechanized infantry brigades at the Israelis. The attack

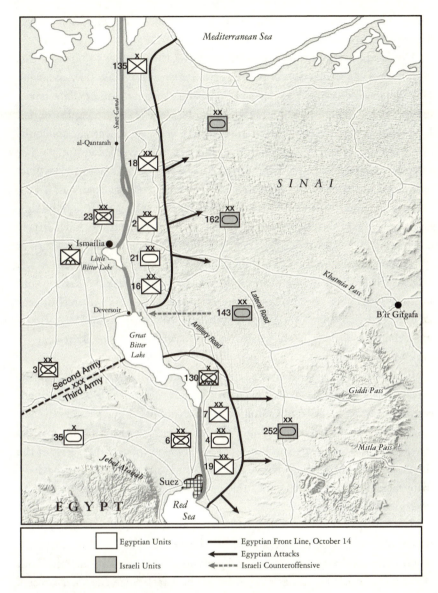

MAP 10 The Egyptian Attack on October 14, 1973

began badly for the Egyptians and got worse quickly. At first light, Israeli air and special forces units destroyed the Egyptian signals intercept facilities on Jebel Ataqah, depriving Cairo of its most reliable source of information on the fighting. Then, as could only be expected, without the advantages in numbers, surprise, and intelligence, or the benefit of carefully scripted and rehearsed orders that had made their initial attacks so successful, the Egyptian ground forces failed miserably.

Unlike the earlier advances on October 6–10, the October 14 offensive displayed all of the weaknesses of past Egyptian offensives. It was slow and rigid. Units attacked piecemeal. Battlefield commanders would neither adapt to unforeseen circumstances nor would they take advantage of sudden opportunities. Egyptian armor, infantry, and artillery could not work together, and units drove straight at the Israelis rather than trying to maneuver for advantage. The Egyptian artillery barrage covering the attack was huge, employing at least 500 guns, but completely ineffective. As the great military historian Trevor Dupuy observed, "Without detailed, prearranged fire plans, such as those they had employed on October 6, the Egyptian artillery concentrations fell largely on empty rock and sand dunes."[10] For their part, the Israelis were astonished at the sudden reversal in Egypt's combat performance. In the words of one Israeli brigade commander, "they just waddled forward like ducks."[11] As a result, in just a few hours, the Egyptian offensive was mauled and sent reeling; the Israelis destroyed over 260 Egyptian tanks and 200 other armored vehicles—more than one-quarter of the attacking force—while losing no more than 25 tanks of their own.

It was a stunning defeat for the Egyptians, which revealed that the successes of October 6–10 had been an anomaly engineered by the brilliant planning and preparation of Cairo's superb General Staff, but one that did not reflect any actual improvement in Egyptian tactical leadership, information management, or weapons handling. These remained the Achilles heels of the Egyptian armed forces, and they resurfaced—and once again became the dominant factor in battle—as soon as the clever workarounds devised by Egypt's strategic leadership ran out.

The day after the disastrous Egyptian defeat, the Israelis launched a major counteroffensive, which seized a bridgehead over the Suez Canal. Rather than report this humiliating development, Egyptian commanders on the west bank of the Canal misled Cairo as to the size of the Israeli force that had crossed. For two days, while the Israelis expanded their bridgehead and built up their strength on the west bank of Suez to several brigades, Egyptian officers reported to the General Staff that the Israelis on the west bank were no more than a raiding force of less than a company. Eventually, Cairo sent the Army Chief of Staff, General Shazli, himself to find out what was going on, and only Shazli's reconnaissance made them aware that this was no raiding party but a multi-division counteroffensive.

For the next two weeks, the Israelis expanded this bridgehead, pushing two armored divisions onto the west bank of the canal. They then developed

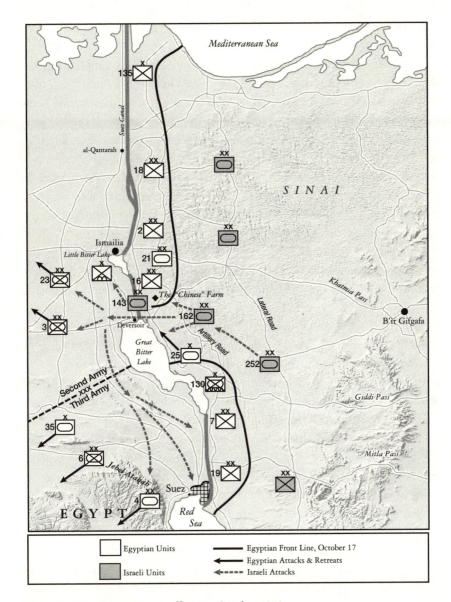

MAP 11 The Israeli Counteroffensive, October 1973

an attack southward that mauled Cairo's operational reserves and cut off the entire Egyptian Third Army. Throughout these battles on the west bank of the Canal, Egyptian forces again proved almost powerless to stop the IDF. They fought bravely whenever attacked, but showed little ability to knit together an effective response to Israeli thrusts. Units would not or could not maneuver or even reorient themselves to meet Israeli envelopments, they rarely counterattacked except when ordered to do so by the military command in Cairo itself, and those counterattacks were inevitably slow, simple, straight-ahead charges that the Israelis quickly dispatched in fluid maneuver battles. As the Egyptian defenses collapsed, the levels of deception and obfuscation from Egyptian tactical formations spiraled, and the Egyptian forces on the west bank quickly descended into confusion and paralysis. Egypt's senior leadership scrambled to try to patch together some kind of defense to stop the Israeli advance, but they were hamstrung by the passivity and dissembling of their subordinates. For instance, on one occasion, an Egyptian brigade commander repeatedly told the Third Army commander that he was counterattacking the Israelis when in fact his forces had never moved from their positions.[12]

As Egyptian forces suffered one defeat after another at the hands of the Israelis, Egyptian field commanders increasingly misled Cairo about the course of the battle. Without the Jebel Ataqah site to learn the truth from the Israelis, the Egyptian high command found it ever more difficult to know what was happening on the ground, further diminishing Cairo's ability to respond to the IDF offensive. Moreover, Israeli ground forces made a concerted effort to overrun Egyptian SAM sites on the west bank of the Canal, freeing up the skies for the IAF to launch air strikes against the Egyptian Army. By the 24th of October, Cairo was desperate for a ceasefire, which Israel accepted under heavy US pressure on October 28.

As with their ground forces, Egypt's ground-based air defenses were highly effective in keeping the Israeli Air Force from seriously disrupting Egyptian ground operations until late in the war, but they were terribly inefficient in doing so. Egyptian SAM and AAA operators had only a limited understanding of their weapons, and their marksmanship was rotten. The Egyptians probably shot down 20–25 Israeli aircraft with SAMs and another 15–20 with AAA.[13] Given that the Israelis flew approximately 6,000 sorties against them, this translates into a loss rate of only .006.–0075 per sortie—a very poor attrition rate from the Egyptian perspective. The Egyptians fired about 1,000 heavy SAMs of all types, plus another 4,000–8,000 SA-7s. Thus, on average, they expended about 40 heavy SAMs and 150 SA-7s for every aircraft shot down.[14] Again, a very poor ratio. By comparison, Soviet metrics expected that downing an enemy aircraft should have required the expenditure of only 5–10 SAMs of all kinds. Egyptian air defenses apparently shot down more of their own planes than Israelis, destroying somewhere between 45 and 60 EAF aircraft during the war.[15]

Egyptian air-to-air performance was no better. Over the course of the war, there were 52 major dogfights between the Egyptians and Israelis. In all, the

Egyptians succeeded in shooting down 5–8 Israeli aircraft while losing 172 of their own to Israeli fighters.[16]

As these figures indicate, the Egyptians were completely outclassed by the Israelis and actually did worse than they had in 1967. While it is true that the Israelis possessed the state of the art F-4E Phantom, which was more advanced than Egypt's MiG-21s, it is also the case that the Israelis generally reserved the Phantoms for strike missions and their older Mirages flew the lion's share of counter-air missions (65–70 percent of all counter-air sorties). So the majority of air-to-air battles involved the same combination of planes as in 1967. However, in the Six-Day War, the Egyptians had suffered about a 1:7 kill ratio to the Israelis, while in 1973 this ratio fell to roughly 1:25.

While IAF pilot skills continued to grow, the Israelis found little improvement among their Egyptian counterparts. As in 1967, Egyptian pilots were inflexible, dogmatic, and slow to react in combat. They stuck closely to doctrinal maneuvers, were heavily reliant on their ground controllers, and panicked when Israeli pilots took unexpected actions or busted up their textbook formations. As a result, when Israeli and Egyptian fighters did tangle, the Egyptians were virtual sitting ducks for the Israelis. For instance, in one battle on the first day of the war, 2 Phantoms took on a strike package of 28 MiG-21s and MiG-17s near Sharm ash-Shaykh, and in a few minutes of dogfighting the 2 Israeli planes shot down 8 MiGs and chased off the other 20 with no losses.

When all was said and done, Anwar as-Sadat got just enough from his military to work his miracles in the diplomatic realm, eventually securing the peace with Israel, the return of Sinai, and the aid from the United States that had always been his goals for the war. This was a masterful performance, and we should take nothing away from him, or from Egyptian generals such as Ahmed Ismail 'Ali and Abd al-Ghani al-Gamasy, who worked similar feats with the Egyptian armed forces.

But what stands out most is just how much Egypt's high command had to do to accomplish so little. It required a *major* improvement in Egyptian strategic leadership—which then translated into strategic surprise, massive advantages in firepower, numbers, and technological surprise—to produce only a *modest* military accomplishment: crossing the Canal and holding two small bridgeheads no more than about 8–12 kilometers deep for about two weeks until one of those bridgeheads was outflanked and encircled. The albatross holding Egypt back from greater success in 1973 was the ineffectiveness of Egyptian tactical formations, resulting from the limitations of Egypt's junior officer corps. This problem was clearly demonstrated in the sudden reversal in Egyptian effectiveness between the first four days of the offensive and the rest of the war. As long as Egyptian tactical formations could follow the superb, meticulously scripted plans of the General Staff, they did well, but as soon as those plans ran out and the direction of operations devolved back to the tactical commanders, Egyptian operations quickly returned to previous patterns of ineffectiveness.

I will address the lessons at greater length after I have gone through the other three cases, but there are at least two critical points worth flagging now about how Egyptian performance in the October War related to the impact of politicization. First, politicization clearly had an impact at strategic levels. Nasser and Sadat's thorough professionalization of the Egyptian military did lead to a dramatic improvement in Egyptian strategic performance over the disaster of 1967. And that improvement in strategic leadership was critical in securing a marginally better military outcome to the war, which Sadat then parlayed into a remarkable diplomatic victory. However, that depoliticization led to effectively zero improvement in Egypt's tactical leadership, tactical information management, and weapons handling. Indeed, probably the greatest achievement of its strategic leadership was to create circumstances where those problems were briefly masked to allow massive advantages in more conventional military measures (such as numbers and surprise) to secure some modest military objectives. Depoliticization produced an improvement in Egyptian military performance, but solely at strategic levels and only a relatively modest improvement overall because the nagging problems at tactical levels proved more important.

| Arab Militaries and Politicization:
Iraq

T HE EGYPTIANS WEREN'T the only Arab state to find that some aspects
of their military performance could be improved by depoliticizing while
others could not. At various times the Iraqi military also saw dramatic changes
in its civil-military relations, and they also shed light on the ways that politicization affected Arab armed forces.

The Lame Blitz, 1980–1982

When Saddam Husayn decided to invade Iran in September 1980, he did
so with one of the most politicized militaries in modern history. Saddam
was a paranoid and would become deeply delusional over the course of his
reign, but he was no fool. He idolized Josef Stalin and studied his methods of
gaining and retaining power. He didn't just replicate Stalin's totalitarianism in
Iraq, he took it to new extremes. Where Stalin had had 3 or 4 security services all watching the Russian people, the Soviet government, the Red Army,
and one another, Saddam would eventually create 16. Where Stalin at times
eliminated his most aggressive and independent-minded generals for fear they
might mount a coup against him, by 1980, Saddam appears to have deliberately chosen some of his generals because they were incompetent and so were
unlikely to succeed if they ever tried. Like Stalin, Saddam kept large security forces to watch the Iraqi army and block any coup attempt. Like Stalin,

Saddam attached political commissars from his Ba'th party throughout the military chain of command. Unlike Stalin, he went so far as to fill the senior ranks of his officer corps with generals who had personal ties (family, tribe) to himself, and to fill key units (such as the Republican Guard) with personnel from his minority Sunni sect. Civil-military relations in Saddam's Iraq were the epitome of commissarist politicization.

Not surprisingly, the Iraqi invasion of Iran in 1980 was one of the most pathetic military offensives of the past century. To begin with, Saddam's incompetent military leaders had no idea how to draw up a proper plan.[1] As several professional Iraqi generals who participated in that operation explained, in the end, Baghdad just moved 9 of its 12 divisions to the Iranian border and ordered them to drive into Iran and not stop until they reached the Zagros Mountain passes that separated oil-rich Khuzestan Province from the rest of Iran. Iraqi tactical formations were not issued any logistical plans, and there were no march order or routes of advance, no maps, and nothing about air support. Not even instructions about how to operate with friendly units on either side of them. As one of those generals put it, "Our troops were just lined up on the border and told to drive into Iran. They had an objective, but no idea how to get there or what they were doing, or how their mission fit the plan, or who would be supporting them."[2]

Having seen the Israelis mount a spectacular preemptive air strike to open the Six-Day War, the Iraqis tried to do the same against Iran, but theirs was a fiasco. Baghdad's planners had no clue how to mount such an operation; they conducted no reconnaissance, and instead relied on outdated (and biased) information from Iranian defectors fleeing Khomeini's revolution.[3] The squadrons were only given their orders two days before the attack and were led to believe that it was nothing but a major training operation.[4] They could only muster about 100 operational planes and pilots, and they assigned them far too many (and too large) targets. Their weaponeers often loaded the wrong munitions on the planes for the missions, and in some cases the pilots were so bad that their bombs fell too far from any nearby military facility for the Iranians to guess at what the Iraqis were trying to hit. Iraqi pilots left untouched Iranian military aircraft sitting out in the open, instead sticking to their assigned missions regardless of these golden opportunities. To top it all off, the air force failed to follow up its initial attacks with post-strike reconnaissance and restrikes against targets insufficiently damaged during the first attacks.

By the end of the first day, Baghdad's surprise air assault had inflicted negligible damage on a handful of Iranian facilities, and overall had no impact on Iranian air capabilities. Iran lost two or three combat aircraft and one transport. Not one of the Iranian air bases was put out of action.

To add injury to insult, the next day, Iraq lost air superiority to the Iranian air force, despite the crippling it had suffered from the revolution. Iranian fighters swept the skies of Iraqi planes. Although Iraq's operational fighter strength was three to four times that of Iran, Iraqi pilots generally aborted their missions the moment they detected Iranian fighters, and in those instances when the Iraqis either accidentally or purposefully engaged in air-to-air combat, the Iranians quickly prevailed. Iran also conducted air strikes against Iraqi military, industrial, and oil facilities. Baghdad reacted by dispersing most of its aircraft (including many fighters) to bases in western Iraq and to foreign countries such as Jordan and Kuwait where they were beyond Iran's reach.

The Iraqi ground offensive was no better. With an overall advantage of roughly 5:1 in available manpower as well as operational tanks, artillery, and other armored vehicles—and a local ratio in Khuzestan even higher than that—the Iraqis should have rolled. Instead, they stumbled forward at a snail's pace against meager Iranian resistance. Iraqi mechanized formations would take up a defensive position and then spend hours or days shelling the area in front of them before moving forward a kilometer or two. (A pattern repeated by Iraqi forces in the war against ISIS in 2014–2017.)

Oftentimes, there was no Iranian resistance in front of them at all, but the Iraqis did not know this because their tactical formations never bothered to patrol or conduct other reconnaissance. Nor could such failings be compensated for by intelligence provided by higher echelons. Baghdad's senior leadership similarly neglected intelligence gathering. The air force had few reconnaissance aircraft, and rarely used those it had. Iraq's ability to exploit photoreconnaissance missions was poor and subject to severe distortion because Iraq's senior military intelligence officers mostly reported whatever Saddam wanted to hear. Moreover, even this information was rarely disseminated to Iraq's field commanders because the senior leadership saw restricting information as a way of keeping control over their subordinates. Consequently, Iraqi tactical commanders rarely knew what was in front of them, and were repeatedly caught off guard by small Iranian deployments and counterattacks.

Even as they fell further and further behind schedule, Iraqi front-line commanders never varied from these patterns. Iraq's tactical leadership simply refused to show any creativity or initiative. Iraqi armored and mechanized formations never used their mobility to bypass Iranian positions, nor did they envelop Iranian defensive positions, nor did they use their shock power to just overrun what were usually small numbers of ill-trained Iranian infantry with little or no antitank weaponry. They had no capacity to perform combined arms operations except when massing all of their firepower against (defended

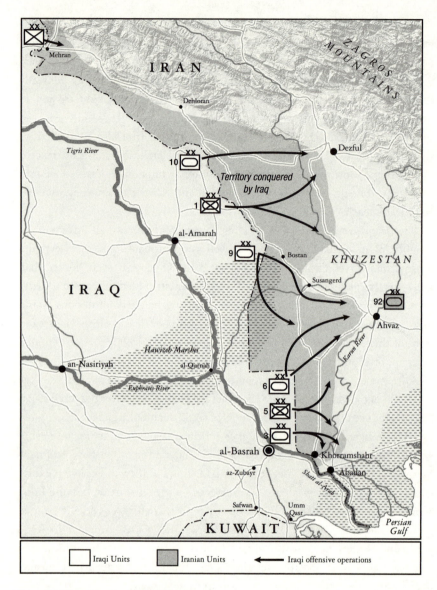

MAP 12 Iraq Invades Iran, 1980

or undefended) terrain. John Wagner, a leading expert on the Iran-Iraq War, marvels that "no attempt was made to use fast-moving armored columns to penetrate and disrupt Iranian rear areas and to capture key objectives before the Iranians could react."[5] Iraqi officers showed little or no aggressiveness, consistently failing to pursue defeated Iranian units, conquer undefended territory, or otherwise exploit opportunities. As a result, Iraq failed to capture a number of Iranian towns early on when they were largely undefended, and even lost several key population centers that they overran but then failed to garrison, only to have small Iranian formations sneak back in to reclaim them.

By November 1980 the Iraqi invasion was over. After two months (not the 14 days originally planned) the only city Iraq had taken was Khorramshahr—and that required a bloodbath because the Iraqis foolishly tried to assault it with tanks unsupported by infantry. Of greatest importance, they had not come close to the passes through the Zagros. Iran was able to bring in reinforcements from all over the country, and by early December Tehran had cut Baghdad's numerical advantage to 2:1. The Iraqi invasion ground to a halt and Saddam offered to make peace with Tehran and return to the status quo ante.

Khomeini would have none of it. He had rallied the Iranian people to his banner and, in January 1981, Iran began a snowballing counteroffensive that would eventually erase all of Iraq's gains and shatter Saddam's brittle army. Iran's armed forces were still hobbled by the effects of the revolution, purges, and civil war—as well as the sudden loss of their American patron. Yet Tehran put together a hybrid military method using the zealous but untrained and barely armed Basij (mobilization forces) and Revolutionary Guards to punch holes in Iraq's defenses with human wave attacks. These were then followed by the remnants of the mechanized and motorized formations of the shah's army to exploit the breakthrough and envelop Iraqi forces. In a series of decisive battles in 1981 and early 1982, the Iranians used this approach time and again to rout the Iraqis and drive them from Iranian soil.

Although some credit must be given to the Iranians who developed a primitive but workable operational doctrine, ultimately it was the Iraqis who lost rather than the Iranians who won. Once again, Iraqi formations refused to patrol or conduct routine reconnaissance, allowing the Iranians to surprise them repeatedly. Iraqi front-line formations were unnerved and overwhelmed by the Iranian human wave attacks. Local commanders refused to reorient, reform, or otherwise shift their defenses to parry what were ultimately slow-moving Iranian breakthroughs. Iraqi tactical and operational reserves would only counterattack when the orders came from the highest levels, and then their moves were sluggish, straight-ahead belly flops onto the spearheads of Iranian penetrations. They showed virtually no capacity to employ maneuver or combined arms, especially at tactical levels. Iraqi tanks were used as moveable pillboxes, their infantry had no idea how to support their armor, and Iraqi artillery could neither shift fire nor provide timely on-call fire support. As a result, in battle after battle, clumsy Iranian penetrations succeeded in enveloping and destroying large Iraqi mechanized formations until by early July the Iraqis had been driven from Iran altogether.

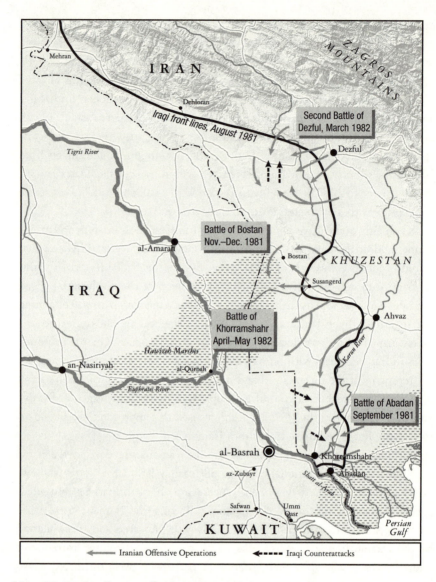

MAP 13 Iranian Counteroffensives, 1981–1982

Depoliticization, 1982–1986

After some debate, Khomeini decided to press his advantage, turning the counteroffensive into an invasion of his own to "liberate" the Shi'a holy cities of Karbala and Najaf and overthrow Saddam as he had overthrown the shah. At that point, the fighting turned Iraq's way again thanks to a confluence of factors. First, Iraqi soldiers (including the vast majority of Iraqi Shi'a) fought much harder to defend Iraq's *Arab* soil from the hated Persians than they did to conquer Iranian territory. Second, Iraq discovered an unexpected ability to engineer formidable defensive fortifications, and its crude logistical apparatus proved able to ensure that threatened sectors had all the replacements, reinforcements, and supplies they needed. Third, the world rallied to Iraq's defense to defeat Khomeini and his frightening revolution. The Arab states provided Saddam with hundreds of billions of dollars, Europe and Russia provided boatloads of weaponry, and the United States provided invaluable intelligence. Nearly all of the major arms producers refused to sell to Iran, with the result that Tehran could not replace its losses and the combat power built up by the Shah and initially exploited by Khomeini's forces slowly withered. Fourth, Iraq started to employ barrages of chemical warfare (CW) agents, which devastated Iran's ill-equipped mobs of infantry.

The last factor that began to turn the tide of battle was that Saddam began to depoliticize his officer corps.[6] The defeats in Iran apparently convinced him that his straitjacketing of the armed forces had hampered their combat power, and with Iran's victorious armies beating down the doors of his realm it was time to put military effectiveness ahead of political reliability. Thus, Saddam began to undo the damage, starting in 1982 with the characteristically dramatic gesture of dismissing or executing 200–300 senior officers who had performed poorly in 1980–1982.[7] In their place, rather than appointing still more of his cronies, Saddam began promoting officers who had fought well in the first two years of the war.

Depoliticization did not come quickly to Saddam's Iraq. The process took several years to show its full results, but as soon as it began, the Iraqis began to experience greater success, and over time the trend accelerated. The emphasis on leadership and demonstrated performance over loyalty and personal ties increased until it became the rule rather than the exception.[8] Saddam went so far as to recall to service hundreds of junior officers formerly dismissed for suspected disloyalty. Baghdad eliminated the political commissars and ceased the practice of frequently rotating the commanders of divisions and corps. Instead, Saddam weeded out incompetent commanders (many of whom were friends, loyal supporters, and even relatives), and when he found competent generals he stuck with them. Over time, this allowed for the emergence of a core of able military leaders such as Hisham Sabah al-Fakhri, Salim Husayn 'Ali, Sultan Hashim Ahmed, Ayad Khalil Zaki, Saadi Tuma Abbas al-Jabburi, Iyad Futah ar-Rawi, and Salah Abud Mahmud, as well as a first-rate General Staff under the Deputy Chief of Staff for Operations, General Husayn Rashid Muhammad at-Tikriti.

Most difficult of all for Saddam, he relinquished control over military operations and began to give greater latitude to the generals. In turn, his generals thoroughly revamped Iraq's training practices. They began to try to teach combined arms tactics to their troops in a more comprehensive and systematic fashion and, recognizing their problems in Iran, they began to try to encourage junior commanders to be aggressive and innovative in combat and to react more quickly and effectively to Iranian moves. Saddam took up this theme himself and in a 1984 meeting with his senior generals, he emphasized that he wanted Iraqi officers to demonstrate initiative, and launch counterattacks and spoiling attacks. He announced, "I have stressed two essential points: Maneuver and the ability to wage attacks to disperse the enemy effort." In the same meeting, he later went on to say, "The solution is [that] field commanders should have the ability to make a decision during the battle without going back to their corps commanders even if there is a 30 percent error rate."[9]

Depoliticization and the concomitant emergence of competent *senior* officers quickly led to a noticeable improvement in Iraqi defensive strategy. Iraq abandoned its previous reliance on forward defenses, which had been so detrimental during the fighting in Iran. Instead, Baghdad deployed infantry well supported by area-fire weapons in defenses-in-depth along the heavily fortified lines that soon spanned the entire length of the border. Increasingly, the Iraqis concentrated their armored and mechanized infantry units in reserves that could be quickly shifted around the country by newly expanded transport battalions to wherever Iran happened to be attacking. These heavy units, well supported by artillery, were used to halt or even counterattack Iranian assaults.

Yet Iraq's problems persisted at tactical levels. The generals might concentrate mechanized reserves and order them to counterattack Iranian offensives, but the counterattacks were invariably slow-to-develop frontal assaults devoid of tactical maneuver. Despite the new training efforts, combined arms coordination remained nonexistent and air support was aspirational at best. Iraqi Mi-24 attack helicopters committed to support Iraqi ground forces had a bad habit of merely flying in the direction of the Iranians, blowing off every piece of ordnance on the helicopter and then returning to base—without making any effort to identify, let alone target, specific Iranian forces. Iraqi armored formations remained clumsy and largely unable to take advantage of the mobility of their tanks, while Iraqi artillery batteries had little ability to perform other than preregistered fire missions against preset coordinates. When they were requested to shift fire to strike unexpected Iranian thrusts they were often as lethal to their own forces as to the enemy.

Still, taken together, these changes were enough to enable the Iraqis to finally start blocking Iranian offensives that had previously been unstoppable.

But Iraq still had no capacity to mount a counteroffensive and force Iran to stop attacking. Saddam tried other approaches such as bombing Iran's cities and attempting to shut down Iran's oil exports to choke off the revenues that paid for Iran's war effort. It all failed, and the war degenerated into a bloody stalemate that dragged on for four years. During this period, Iran launched three to six major ground offensives each year, and the Iraqis brought each one to a bloody halt for little gain.

Defeat into Victory, 1986–1988

What appeared to be an interminable deadlock ended abruptly on the night of February 10/11, 1986. In a rainstorm, Iranian forces crossed the Shatt al-Arab and overran the Al-Faw Peninsula, the southeasternmost tip of Iraq. Baghdad panicked and launched a flurry of counterattacks that went nowhere. Iraqi tanks advanced with minimal infantry support, and these failed to cooperate with the armor, allowing Iranian attack helicopters and infantry to repulse them with ease. In desperation, Baghdad committed its air force, but the Iraqi planes had little impact on the Iranian infantry holding the peninsula, which presented few vulnerable targets. When the initial counterattacks failed, Iraq rushed its best infantry south to al-Faw—special forces and Republican Guards—for another round of counterattacks. These did help stop the Iranian advance, but could not push them back.

On February 22, Iraq launched a major counteroffensive to try to expel the Iranians from al-Faw, mustering three division-strength columns, each commanded by one of Iraq's best corps commanders. The Iraqis threw everything they had at the Iranians. They committed the air force in full, flying as many as 200 CAS/BAI sorties per day, in addition to enormous quantities of artillery, and heavy doses of chemical warfare. However, after three weeks of constant attacks, they had made almost no progress. Despite all of the emphasis in training on combined arms, maneuver, and aggressive tactical leadership, Iraqi formations, even the elite units, continued to perform just as poorly, and demonstrated none of these skills in practice. As before, they just relied on the firepower of their tanks and artillery to grind their way forward. Iraqi armor refused to maneuver. They just tried to force their way south against the dug-in Iranian infantry who were well-armed with antitank weapons. Iraq was unable to suppress or defeat Iranian antitank teams either with artillery fire or infantry, who simply did not understand how to support the tanks. In the end, the Iraqis suffered heavy losses, taking 8,000–10,000 casualties, losing 20–25 aircraft to Iranian F-14s and air defenses, and sustaining 30 percent casualties among the Republican Guards.

The invasion of al-Faw and the dramatic failure of Iraq's counterattacks jarred Baghdad out of its complacency. In particular, it convinced Saddam to remove the remaining fetters on Iraq's generals and allow them to run military operations as they saw fit. Baghdad had been moving inexorably in this direction since 1982, and even before al-Faw, Iraqi senior commanders were mostly free to make all but the most important decisions on their own. After al-Faw, however, the last constraints of Saddam's Stalinist system were removed.

Now free to fight as they liked, and bolstered by the shock of defeat at al-Faw, the General Staff concluded that Iraq could not simply remain on the defensive and hope that at some point Iran would agree to a ceasefire out of exhaustion or frustration. To bring the war to an end, they would have to defeat the Iranian army in the field, but al-Faw laid bare that Iraq lacked the capacity to take the offensive and inflict such a defeat on Iran.

Consequently, Baghdad would have to dramatically reform the Iraqi armed forces to create such a capacity. For this purpose, they secured Saddam's approval to remake the Republican Guard into the instrument they needed. The General Staff first expanded the Guard into the new Republican Guard Forces Command (RGFC), a corps-level formation that would encompass 28 brigades under six divisional commands by 1988. Of greatest importance, the General Staff also won Saddam's consent to stress proficiency over loyalty in recruiting new members for the Guard. While Guard units remained more heavily Sunni than the general population, the General Staff received permission to expand it by taking the best soldiers and officers from regular Army units, rather than the most loyal, even if that meant bringing large numbers of Shi'a into its ranks.[10] The Guard also got the best weapons in the Iraqi arsenal, including Soviet T-72 tanks and BMP-1 infantry fighting vehicles, French GCT self-propelled howitzers, and Austrian and South African GHN-45/G-5 artillery pieces. Finally, Baghdad assigned Lt. General Iyad Futah ar-Rawi to command the RGFC. Rawi was an extremely competent commander with no ties either to Saddam or Tikrit, a first for a Guard commander.[11]

The General Staff then took the Guard out of combat, along with a small number of the best regular Army divisions (basically the 3rd, 6th, and 10th Armored Divisions and the 1st and 5th Mechanized Infantry Divisions), and retrained them. They practiced constantly and began conducting large, corps-level maneuvers. Although it diminished the combat power of the rest of the

Army, this program gave the General Staff a hard core of about 11 divisions with a modest offensive capability.

Along with its new offensive arm, the Iraqi General Staff developed a new approach to operations, extrapolating both from lessons Baghdad had learned earlier in the war and from Egypt's experience in 1973. The most important element of this new approach was detailed scripting of military operations. Iraq's military leadership concluded that attempts had consistently failed to train Iraqi tactical formations to conduct combined arms operations, to employ tactical maneuver, to act creatively and aggressively, and to use the full capabilities of their equipment. Moreover, they recognized that just providing even more rigorous training in these areas was unlikely to fix the problem. Instead, they had to develop a workaround and so, like the Egyptians in 1973, the General Staff would begin extensively scripting major offensive operations.

Deputy Chief of Staff Husayn Rashid gathered a group of Iraq's most talented staff officers and began planning limited, set-piece offensive operations in minute detail. Since they could not count on their field commanders to properly coordinate combined arms operations, the General Staff would do it for them by writing it into the script. Since they could not count on their field commanders to employ tactical maneuver, the General Staff would write maneuver into the script as well. Since they could not count on their field commanders to innovate in battle, they wrote innovative approaches into the script of the operation. In short, they tried to overcome all of the failings of Iraqi junior officers by writing operations orders so smart and detailed that, simply by following this guidance in rote fashion, Iraqi field commanders would do everything they needed to win.[12]

These detailed plans were then given to the Republican Guards and the handful of competent regular Army divisions to learn backward and forward. For months beforehand, these units practiced executing their scripts. The Iraqis built vast, full-size mock-ups of the relevant terrain and practiced conducting their scripted operations on them. The units designated to take part in these offensives would rehearse their specific missions repeatedly. According to the former commander of the Guard's Hammurabi Armored Division, the RGFC regularly trained for 10–14 hours without pause, day after day.[13] Units were trained to perform specific tasks and nothing else, and these specific tasks they repeated again and again. Initially, units would practice their missions on their own. Then later they would be integrated into larger exercises in which they could practice their tasks in conjunction with supporting forces and adjacent units, until eventually the entire operation could be practiced as a whole.

By the time they were committed to battle, the entire operation could be performed from memory.

After one last unsuccessful Iranian offensive against al-Basra in 1987, the Iraqis rolled out their new method of war-making. In the spring and summer of 1988, they conducted a series of five offensives that stunned the Iranians and destroyed their armies. These five Iraqi offensives demonstrated a higher degree of effectiveness than the Iraqi military had ever hinted at previously. Each was preceded by a massive, overpowering barrage of conventional and CW munitions, helpfully directed at weak points in the Iranian lines by American intelligence and Iraq's new strategic SIGINT capabilities.[14] Iraqi mechanized forces followed these barrages by penetrating Iranian defensive positions quickly and usually with a minimum of casualties. Once through the front lines, Iraqi armored columns operating in conjunction with mechanized infantry and combat engineers—and provided with plentiful artillery and air support—conducted relatively deep maneuvers that led to the encirclement of sizable Iranian forces. What's more, all of the Iraqi operations moved crisply and efficiently, proceeding from one phase to the next with little delay and featuring relatively rapid movement throughout.

Nevertheless, like Egypt's initial success in 1973, Iraq's victories in 1988 signified only a modest increase in Iraq's *real* military effectiveness. The five offensives were primarily a testimony to the dramatic improvement in Iraqi strategic-level military leadership. The critical element in each of Baghdad's victories was the detailed scripting by the General Staff. The General Staff was able to rely on its strategic intelligence assets (primarily photoreconnaissance aircraft, signals intercepts, and information provided by the United States) to put together an accurate picture of Iranian deployments.[15] They then used this information to develop a detailed plan to rip apart Iran's front-line defenses, encircle large formations, and defeat its operational reserves. They carefully concentrated overwhelming force against a given sector and convinced Tehran that each attack would come somewhere else so that the Iranians were surprised and misdeployed. The General Staff wrote into these plans combined arms coordination, air strikes, artillery fire-support missions, operational-level maneuver, and the timing and distance of each part of the operation. The Guard and regular Army formations were trained to implement these plans precisely, but no more. Finally, the General Staff was careful to undertake only limited, short-duration attacks (never more than 48 hours long) that could be planned in detail in advance because the limited scope of the operations would keep unforeseen events to a minimum. In short, the planning and preparation for each operation were first class.

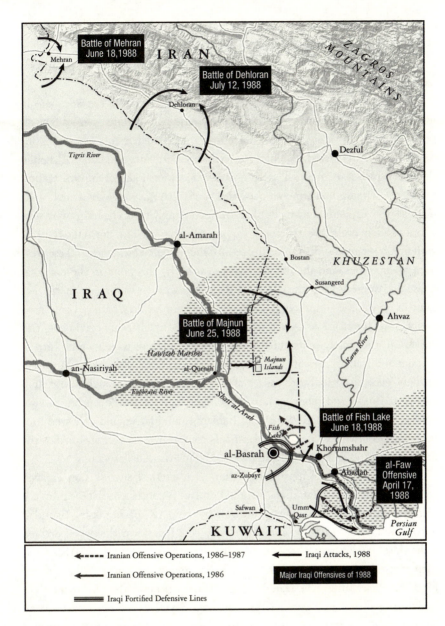

MAP 14 Iraq's 1988 Offensives

The execution of these operations, however, did not always match the high standards of their planning. As long as the advantages they gained from surprise, chemical warfare, numbers, and overwhelming firepower held, Iraq's highly practiced field forces performed admirably executing the plans of the

General Staff, just like the Egyptians during the Canal crossing in October 1973. Yet any time something happened that was not addressed by the plan, Iraq's tactical formations reverted to form and stumbled, just as the Egyptians had on October 14, 1973.

Whereas combined arms integration generally was stilted but adequate in most of the 1988 Iraqi offensives, whenever Iraqi tactical units were caught off guard by an Iranian ambush, counterattack, or unexpected defensive position, this cooperation disintegrated, leading to heavy losses in infantry and tanks. Although the initial phases of an attack often featured operational and even some tactical maneuver by tanks and armored personnel carriers (APCs), once the armor broke free and were exploiting, maneuver became increasingly rare. The Iraqis were slow to react and, in every case, their only response was to try to beat down the Iranians with firepower and numbers. Fortunately for them, their advantages in these areas were so enormous, and the Iranian forces so weak by this point in the war, that it usually worked. Even then Iraqi artillery fire was devastating primarily because of its volume and heavy reliance on CW. Iraqi artillery batteries only fired pre-planned fire missions—even in support of the exploitation operations—and as a result, they rarely contributed if the armored columns took a wrong turn or encountered Iranian resistance where it was not expected. For this reason, Iraqi artillery generally had little impact after the initial breakthrough battle. Iraq committed more and more aircraft to the fight, but these do not seem to have done proportionately more damage to Iranian ground forces, and only won limited air superiority because the Iranian Air Force was by then overwhelmed by the maintenance and logistical problems caused by international sanctions.

These various problems indicate that what tactical success Iraq enjoyed was primarily a function of the detailed and well-conceived planning by the General Staff plus the extensive rehearsals by the participating units. Baghdad got its best forces to the point where they could perform their well-defined tasks close to flawlessly. However, like the Egyptians in 1973, Iraqi troops and their tactical commanders did not internalize any of the concepts that lay behind these carefully orchestrated moves. Thus, whenever the plan went awry and local commanders were left to their own devices, they reverted to form. Whenever it fell to the tactical commanders to take action on their own— particularly when Iraqi forces encountered unexpected Iranian ambushes or counterattacks—they demonstrated that they did not understand combined arms cooperation or maneuver, could not respond or adapt quickly, and were largely incapable of independent initiative or improvisation.

Overall, Iraq's achievements in 1988 were quite modest given the enormous advantages it by then enjoyed over Iran. By early 1988, the Iraqi military outnumbered Iran in every category of military manpower and hardware. Iraq boasted roughly 1,000,000 men under arms while Iran could field only about 600,000; Iraq had over 4,000 functional tanks while Iran had fewer than 1,000; Iraq had over 600 combat aircraft while Iran could surge less than 50. In each of the battles in 1988, Iraqi advantages were even greater with force ratios of 10:1, 20:1, and even 50:1 not uncommon. For instance, in Iraq's penultimate offensive in the Majnun Marshes, Baghdad was able to concentrate 2,000 tanks against just 60 Iranian tanks.[16]

Given these breathtaking disparities, what is surprising is that the Iraqis could not achieve more. In particular, the Iraqis never pushed more than 40 kilometers beyond the front lines, and never let their offensives run for longer than 48 hours, which was about as far and as long as the General Staff felt they could go without reality diverging so far from their script that the entire operation came apart. Nevertheless, the damage Iraq inflicted on Iranian forces in these five battles was so great that, coupled with Tehran's inaccurate but unswerving belief that the United States had become an active belligerent in the war and the fact that the arms embargo meant that Iran could not replenish its weapons stocks any time soon, Ayatollah Khomeini grudgingly agreed to a ceasefire in August 1988.

Victory into Defeat, 1990–1991

A bit more than two years after the end of the struggle with Iran, Iraq was at war again. At just past midnight on August 2, 1990, Iraq invaded Kuwait.

This was the same Iraqi army that had defeated Iran in 1988. Contrary to some claims, Saddam had not repoliticized his military after the end of the Iran-Iraq War. The entire command structure, from top to bottom, was virtually unchanged, with most of Iraq's corps, divisions, brigades, battalions, and companies retaining the same veteran commanders who had risen to their posts during the war. The few changes were overwhelmingly normal rotations and promotions in which one experienced, professional officer replaced another. Saddam had not reinstated political commissars. The army continued to devote extensive time and resources to regular training in the (highly scripted) manner they had learned during the war. Saddam would only reimpose his commissarist controls *after* the Gulf War, when much of the Army revolted against him in the wake of their catastrophic defeat.[17]

There were really only two notable changes to the Iraqi military command after the Iran-Iraq War, and both improved its professionalism. First, Saddam finally sacked General Maher 'Abd al-Rashid, a well-known and self-important but useless corps commander who had only survived Saddam's depoliticization because his daughter was married to Saddam's son, Qusay.[18] Second, in 1989, Iraq's then-defense minister, Adnan Khairallah, was killed in a helicopter crash. It is widely believed that the crash was an execution ordered by Saddam. There's no proof one way or the other, and it is worth noting that Adnan was Saddam's cousin, brother-in-law, and closest friend. It may have been an accident. Some conspiracy theorists claim that Saddam had him killed because Adnan had become too popular with the army. That is certainly possible, but if the crash were deliberate, it is far more likely that it stemmed from a vicious family feud several months earlier in which Saddam's son, Uday, had killed a relative of Saddam's second wife, and Saddam's first wife (Uday's mother) and Adnan (her brother) came to Uday's defense.[19] The man who succeeded Adnan, General 'Abd al-Jabber Khalil Shanshal, was an older but thoroughly professional military officer who had served as Chief of Staff during the latter stages of the Iran-Iraq War.

Moreover, after the invasion of Kuwait, Saddam sacked both his new defense minister and chief of staff. These men were professionals, but long past their prime. He replaced them with two of Iraq's most experienced and competent generals: Saadi Tuma Abbas al-Jabburi and Husayn Rashid at-Tirkiti. Saadi had led the successful defense of Basra in 1987, and Husayn Rashid had been the Deputy Chief of Staff for Operations and the principal architect of Iraq's 1988 offensives.[20] Thus, the changes he made bolstered Iraqi professionalism rather than politicization.

Not surprisingly, the invasion of Kuwait was a highly efficient operation just like the 1988 offensives against Iran. The invasion was conducted by the entire Republican Guard, now expanded to eight divisions. The Iraqis mounted a corps-level attack over multiple axes of advance. They employed maneuver— at least at the operational level—and moved quickly, pushing three heavy divisions 80 kilometers in about 10 hours to take Kuwait City on the first night. Those same formations drove another 75 or so kilometers to reach the Saudi border in the next 24 hours. Although the Guard's four infantry divisions followed the lead armor formations at a slower pace, within 24 hours they too were taking up positions throughout Kuwait. Baghdad staged a large-scale heliborne assault as part of the initial attack that, while clumsy, secured most of its objectives. Of course, the Iraqis were greatly helped by the small size and negligible capabilities of the Kuwaiti forces, and they once again dealt with those units that resisted by applying overwhelming numbers and firepower.

The invasion of Kuwait reflected all the lessons Iraq had learned in 1982–1987 and then employed to such great effect in 1988. It was meticulously planned months in advance. It relied only on the Republican Guard, the most competent force Baghdad had. The Guard rehearsed the entire operation repeatedly during the summer of 1990 until they could perform their tasks like clockwork. Finally, the invasion, like the 1988 offensives, was conducted strictly by the book. It was a set-piece operation well-executed, and the only times it showed any signs of stress were when reality diverged from the plan—for instance when the Kuwaiti Air Force mounted a few air strikes against Iraqi armor, or when Kuwaiti ground units briefly resisted south of Kuwait City. In those situations, the Iraqi response showed far less elegance than the rest of the operation: they ignored the air strikes and simply bludgeoned the Kuwaiti army units into surrender.

But that's when Iraq's luck (and capabilities) ran out. Rather than accept a fait accompli as Saddam had hoped, the United States, its Western allies, and the Western-aligned Arab states formed a coalition to fight back, evict Iraq from Kuwait, and defang the Iraqi military.

After six months of military buildup and diplomatic maneuvering, on January 17, 1991, the US-led coalition unleashed the 43 days of Operation DESERT STORM. The offensive began with a massive air campaign that lasted for five weeks and devastated the Iraqi military. The Coalition air forces quickly tore up Iraq's extensive air defenses. American fighters found that Iraqi pilots were poor dogfighters (many could barely fly, let alone fight) and shot down three dozen Iraqi jets for only one Coalition loss. Coalition strike aircraft shut down much of the country's electricity, water, and oil industry, as well as destroying WMD and arms production factories, bridges, and railroads. Iraq tried to fight back, launching volleys of modified-Scud ballistic missiles at Israel, Saudi Arabia, and Bahrain, but Washington succeeded in keeping the Israelis out of the war and the Saudis in.

Coalition air strikes ultimately destroyed about 1,000 of the 6,500 Iraqi armored vehicles deployed in theater.[21] Of far greater importance, the Coalition air campaign effectively shut down Iraq's logistical system in the Kuwaiti Theater of Operations (KTO) and demolished the morale of many front-line Iraqi units, leading to widespread desertions. Indeed, by the time the Coalition ground offensive kicked off on February 24, Iraqi troops in the KTO had fallen from roughly 550,000 to about 350,000.[22]

The Coalition launched its long-awaited ground assault on February 24. When it came, Iraq's front-line infantry divisions disintegrated in a welter of surrender and flight. The Coalition strategy consisted of a diversionary attack by US Marines into southeastern Kuwait, coupled with a wide outflanking maneuver to the west of the Iraqi lines (the famed "Left Hook") by the US VII Corps, the most powerful armored concentration in history.

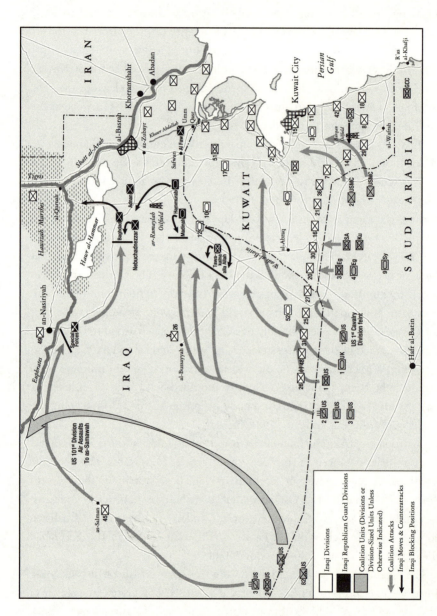

MAP 15 The Gulf War, 1991

On the second day of the ground war, Baghdad made two important realizations. First, that morning they had tried to counterattack the Marines with their 5th Mechanized Division (one of their best regular Army units) only to have it wiped out in a few hours of fighting without doing any real damage to the Marines. This let Baghdad know that even its best formations could not hope to defeat the Coalition army. Second, after several Iraqi units were destroyed by huge American armored formations in the far west of the KTO, Baghdad recognized the Left Hook. In response, Saddam issued a general retreat order to try to get as much of his army out as fast as he could. Meanwhile, the Iraqi General Staff shifted five Republican Guard Divisions and four of the best armored and mechanized divisions of the regular Army to form up defensive screens to the west and south, behind which the rest of the Army was supposed to retreat.

On the third and fourth days of the ground campaign, Coalition forces smashed into these Iraqi defensive screens and fought the hardest battles of the war. In southeastern Kuwait, the Iraqi 1st Mechanized and 3rd Armored Divisions put up a desultory fight around the Matlah Pass and Kuwait International Airport respectively that kept the Marines occupied, but never endangered their advance.

In the west of the KTO, the Republican Guards fought to the death. On February 26, three US heavy divisions and an armored cavalry regiment (a combined force of over 1,000 M1A1 tanks) ploughed into the lines of the Iraqi Tawakalnah 'alla Allah Mechanized Division of the Republican Guard. In roughly 12 hours of vicious combat, the Americans obliterated the Tawakalnah, destroying nearly every one of the division's 300 operable tanks and APCs. But the Americans came away with considerable respect for the Republican Guards, who fought on despite being outnumbered, outgunned, and outmatched in every way. The story was the same on February 27 when other American armored units crushed a brigade of the Madinah Munawrah Armored Division, along with the Adnan and Nebuchadnezzar Infantry Divisions. The Guards did not fight well and inflicted only minimal damage on the Americans, but they fought very hard.

At that point, the Iraqis were saved by the fog of war. The US military leadership (wrongly) believed that the Guard had been completely destroyed. Meanwhile, Washington became concerned about (equally inaccurate) news reports that Coalition aircraft were slaughtering Iraqi soldiers fleeing Kuwait. Consequently, President George H. W. Bush ordered a halt to the ground offensive during the morning of February 28. In reality, over half of the Republican Guard survived the war and would go on to crush the postwar revolts that nearly overthrew Saddam's regime.

Iraqi Military Effectiveness and Ineffectiveness, 1980–1991

Iraq's experience in the Persian Gulf War reinforces and clarifies the changes that occurred at the end of the Iran-Iraq War stemming from Saddam's dramatic depoliticization of the Iraqi armed forces. That thorough depoliticization led to a sea change in Iraq's strategic performance, but virtually no change in the competence of its tactical formations.

Iraq's greatest liability in the Gulf War was the limited capabilities of its tactical formations. Even acknowledging the superior performance of Western equipment over Iraq's largely Soviet arsenal, Iraqi units simply could not fight at the same levels of effectiveness as the British, French, and especially American soldiers and officers who made up the core of the Coalition military forces. Iraqi tactical commanders were inflexible and incapable of adequately responding to the constant maneuvering, deception, and speed of the Coalition forces, and this was as true of their best formations—including the Republican Guard—as it was of their worst. Time and again, the response of Iraqi units to being surprised or outflanked was either to do nothing, to keep doing what they were already doing, or to run. Only rarely did Iraqi junior officers try to devise responses to unforeseen developments. For example, the Iraqi 52nd Armored Brigade was deployed with the rest of the 52nd Armored Division as the operational reserve of the Iraqi VII Corps, and therefore its primary mission was to counterattack a Coalition attack into one of the VII Corps infantry divisions. Late on February 24, the commander of the 52nd Armored Brigade received a frantic message from the headquarters of the 48th Infantry Division *directly in front of his brigade* that they were being overrun by American armored forces. Nevertheless, because he had not received orders from corps or divisional command, the commander of the 52nd Brigade did nothing. He did not execute his primary mission by moving to support the embattled 48th Division. He did not ready his brigade to move or fight; he did not even contact divisional headquarters to report the message and ask if he should counterattack. As a result, the 48th Infantry Division was overwhelmed by the US 1st Infantry Division, and the Iraqi 52nd Brigade was itself overrun by the British 1st Armored Division with barely a fight.[23]

Combined arms at tactical levels was dismal. While the initial deployment schemes of Iraqi units did a good job of weaving together infantry, armor, antitank units, artillery, and other supporting arms into a cohesive pattern, this was the product of the five months that Iraqi division and corps commanders had had to plan and inspect the dispositions of their subordinates. In every other way, Iraqi combined arms cooperation was almost nonexistent. For example, the 5th Mechanized Division counterattack on the morning of February 25 featured large concentrations of armor, infantry, and artillery support, but none of them together. Likewise, when the Republican Guard Madinah and Tawakalnah Divisions redeployed to the west to meet the US VII Corps attack, their new defensive deployments displayed only the most haphazard integration of infantry and armor. The dispositions of the two divisions along their defensive lines show little interspersing of tanks and APCs.[24] While both the tanks/APCs and the infantry of the Tawakalnah were active against the US forces, in any given sector US forces had to worry about T-72s *or* mechanized infantry, but rarely both at the same time. Moreover, their tanks generally refused to leave their defensive positions to maneuver (or even change firing positions), and their artillery could not or would not shift fire from its predesignated fire missions. As a result, it had no significant impact. One story from a meeting between the US VII Corps commander, Lt. General Fred Franks, and the 1st Armored Division commander, Maj. General Ronald Griffith, illustrates the problem nicely:

> Griffith was briefing his commander [Franks] when one of many Iraqi artillery concentrations hit nearby, causing some concern to VII Corps staff officers, one of whom turned quizzically to Griffith's aide and asked, "What's that, some short rounds from our artillery?" Robinson shook his head and offered, "Nah, that's Iraqi artillery." He smiled at the officer's confused expression and said, "Don't worry, that's about the fifth barrage they've fired, but they don't move it. It just goes into the same place every time."[25]

In contrast to this poor tactical performance, Iraq's high command, led once again by General Husayn Rashid (now Chief of Staff of the armed forces), turned in a very creditable performance given what they had to work with. Iraq's greatest mistake was to fight the Coalition at all rather than finding a way to negotiate its way out of Kuwait. This was a political decision, not a military one, ultimately made by Saddam, not the Iraqi GHQ.

If we look past that huge mistake, the Iraqi General Staff's performance was actually pretty good. Specifically, given the limitations of the forces at their disposal, their strategic choices must be considered quite creditable. For instance, a major criticism often leveled at Iraq's plan is that the Iraqis should have realized that a set-piece defense-in-depth would not work against the powerful armored forces of the Coalition. Many critics have argued that Iraq should have employed a mobile defense instead. But the Iraqi Army could not have effectively prosecuted any other kind of defensive scheme, especially not a mobile defense. The dearth of tactical aggressiveness and independence of action among junior officers; the inability of their tactical units to maneuver, to react to unforeseen events, and to conduct ad hoc operations efficiently; the inability of Iraqi tactical commanders to cope with unstructured engagements; and the constant disintegration of combined arms cooperation, all meant that Iraqi forces simply could not have fought with any degree of skill in a mobile defense.

Instead, the Iraqis relied on a strategy based on what their troops were capable of doing. Iraq's engineers could build first-rate fortifications. Iraq's infantry could defend tenaciously when well dug-in and when not expected to maneuver. Iraq's armor could mass firepower when they knew where the enemy was located, and he was located right in front of them. This approach wasn't just Iraq's best strategy: it was their only possible strategy. Asking their tactical forces to do anything more than this would have been a very poor strategic decision. This assertion is borne out by the actual history of the war, in which the Iraqi forces did best when they stuck to these missions, but became helpless when they had to fight in fluid maneuver battles.

Most of Iraq's strategic decisions during the war were also quite sound. In particular, the General Staff's conduct after they realized that the US VII Corps had already flanked their defensive lines in the west was probably the smartest thing they could have done. The General Staff recognized that the US VII Corps was the greatest threat, and moved to place its strongest forces—the Republican Guards—against it. A critical feature of this move was the decision to use the best Iraqi units to conduct the rear guard, while the mass of less-capable units escaped from the KTO. Under different circumstances, Baghdad almost certainly would have preferred to use mediocre units to screen the retreat and allow the better units to escape. In this case, however, the General Staff recognized that this was impossible. The US and Western forces of the Coalition had demonstrated an ability to destroy Iraqi units so effortlessly that only Iraq's best units had a chance to delay the Coalition forces. If Baghdad had used any but its best troops to screen the withdrawal, Coalition forces would have rolled over the rear guard and caught the retreating units from behind.

Despite the enormity of Iraq's military defeat, the manner in which Baghdad's military leadership was able to conduct the retreat from the KTO enabled them to snatch a small victory from the jaws of total defeat. The determined stand by several Iraqi units, mostly Republican Guard divisions, on February 26 and 27 allowed the survival of the forces Baghdad would later rely upon to suppress the Shi'ah and the Kurds when they revolted against Saddam's rule after his defeat in the war. Ultimately, it was the performance of Iraq's junior officers—and the skill of their American and British adversaries—that was the most important cause of Baghdad's defeat, not Iraqi generalship. As the military analyst Murray Hammick observed, "[Iraqi] tactical incompetence would almost certainly have put paid to the best laid strategic plans."[26]

The Collapse of the Iraqi Armed Forces in 2014

After the American invasion of Iraq in 2003 and the decision to disband the Iraqi armed forces and start again from scratch, the United States mishandled the rebuilding of Iraq's military several times before getting it right. Only in 2006–2008 did the United States finally build a large, cohesive Iraqi army and police force with the ability to contribute to Iraq's vast security challenges. This force was primarily trained in counterinsurgency and population security operations, but at that time those were the only threats the Iraqis faced. American military trainers and advisors modestly improved the effectiveness of the Iraqi Security Force (ISF) by introducing rigorous, Western-style training programs and partnering closely with Iraqi forces in ways that allowed US personnel to get to know their Iraqi counterparts. Over the course of many months, the Americans figured out who were the good Iraqi soldiers and officers and who were the bad. Who was connected to the terrorists or militias. Who was connected to organized crime. Who was smart and brave. Who was lazy or cowardly. And the US military then went about systematically promoting the best Iraqi personnel and pushing out the bad ones. Moreover, through constant lobbying, the United States succeeded in creating a more balanced force, with significant numbers of Sunni Arab and Kurdish troops even though the Shi'a were still the majority.[27]

This large, well-integrated, and modestly capable force was a critical, unsung factor in the success of the Surge in 2007–2008. As many American troops as there were in country, they were still inadequate to secure a populace as large as Iraq's without hundreds of thousands of reliable Iraqi troops.[28] The greatest victory of the new ISF came in the spring of 2008, when Prime Minister Nuri al-Maliki backed into a major offensive against the Iranian-supported Shi'a militia, Jaysh al-Mahdi (JAM), which answered to Shi'a firebrand Muqtada as-Sadr. JAM ruled the great southern Iraqi (and overwhelmingly Shi'a) city of al-Basra. Maliki ordered an all-out offensive by the newly reformed ISF to push JAM out of Basra. To do this, he had to bring down largely Sunni brigades from Anbar. Not only did these units defeat JAM and drive them from the city

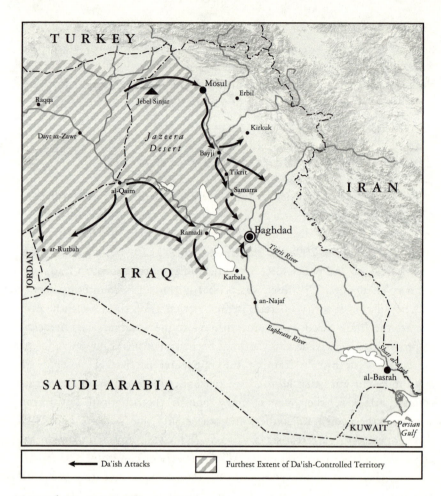

MAP 16 The Da'ish Offensive, 2014

(with a lot of American assistance), but they were welcomed by the Shi'a populace as their saviors in the fight against the Shi'a militia. That operation, called "Charge of the Knights," was a remarkable moment: it demonstrated not only the new strength of the ISF, but their professional transformation and the extent to which Iraq's populace recognized and welcomed it. Maliki seized the moment to run the table on JAM, sending the ISF in to clear them from other strongholds in al-Qurna, al-Amara, and even Sadr City in Baghdad. When the campaign was done, Iraq's civil war was over and the good guys had won.

Of course, it didn't last. Although Maliki styled himself an Iraqi nationalist and a democrat, in practice he proved to be a paranoid and a Shi'a-chauvinist. When the Obama administration began to turn a blind eye toward Iraqi affairs in 2009, and to an even greater extent when American troops departed Iraq in 2011, Maliki began to persecute his political foes and quickly alienated Iraq's Sunni Arab populace.

A critical element of Maliki's political agenda was bringing the ISF fully under his control. For Maliki, the ISF's hard-won professionalism meant that they could not be trusted to do his bidding and, at worst, might side with his political rivals if the Army believed they were in the right. He could not countenance that and starting in 2009–2010 began to systematically politicize the ISF to ensure that it was wholly subservient to his will.

Maliki began to remove the capable, apolitical officers that the United States had painstakingly put in place throughout the Iraqi command structure. He replaced them with men loyal to himself and, in so doing, he invariably removed the most competent officers (because those were the men that the United States promoted) and replaced them with the criminals and mediocrities that the United States had deliberately sidelined. The result was an Iraqi army that was both heavily politicized and far less competent than that which had helped win the Surge.[29] In the words of Michael Knights, after the US withdrawal in 2011, "The leading political parties of the Iraqi government continually re-staffed the senior command positions to ensure that their chosen political appointees were on top. Political, tribal, and family favouritism expanded out of control. The most senior positions in the military—those responsible for the battlefield command, administration, planning, training and logistics functions—were run by unqualified persons. These low quality officers were not interested in continuing the development of the ISF and did not value training or sustaining the morale of their troops. Instead, many were focused on avoiding work and making money through corruption."[30]

Worst of all, the knuckleheads that Maliki promoted saw little need for the rigorous training programs the Americans had put in place. After the last US soldiers left in 2011, they closed most of the training facilities that the United States had built and simply stopped training their troops. When these formations were suddenly thrown into action against Da'ish (the Arabic acronym for ISIS) in 2014, they had not trained for three years. That meant they did not know what they were doing (bad enough) and *knew* that they did not know what they were doing. In addition, the Da'ish attack was a semiconventional assault, something that the ISF had not been trained to fight, which simply added to the ISF's loss of confidence. All of this was poisonous for morale.

Yet these were not the only factors that demoralized the ISF in 2014. Another element was Maliki's use of the ISF to go after his political rivals, many of them leading moderate Sunni leaders. This began literally on the day the last American soldier left Iraq in December 2011 and picked up speed thereafter. It was a critical element of Maliki's alienation of Iraq's Sunni community, and further demoralized the Sunni Arab, Kurdish, and other minority soldiers and police officers. It also disappointed many of the Shi'a soldiers and officers who preferred to be part of an apolitical, national military and had never wanted to become part of "Maliki's militia," as the ISF was increasingly derided during those years.[31]

Not surprisingly, when this force came under stress, it fractured. When Da'ish invaded in June 2014, Maliki's policies had thoroughly hollowed out the Iraqi armed forces. It was nothing like the force that the United States had built in 2006–2008. Several of the Army divisions in northern Iraq had become something like ghettoes for Kurdish and Sunni Arab troops. When the Sunni extremists of Da'ish (and other Sunni militant groups) attacked, the Sunnis in these divisions saw no reason to fight to the death *for* Maliki and *against* Sunni fighters looking to stop him, no matter how abhorrent their beliefs. Iraq's Kurdish soldiers too saw no reason to fight and die for Maliki, who had been threatening to attack the Kurdistan region of Iraq as well. That left only the Shi'a troops. When their Sunni Arab and Kurdish comrades deserted, they saw little point in fighting and dying to hold Sunni cities such as Mosul, Tikrit, Bayji, and Samarra. In many cases, it was Maliki's (Shi'a) senior commanders who fled first and started the entire process.[32] As always in these kinds of cascading events, the first few desertions created a snowball effect. Within days, all of the Army divisions in northern Iraq had disintegrated, with the Kurds fleeing to Kurdistan, the Shi'a fleeing to Baghdad, and the Sunnis either joining Da'ish or going to ground in the hope of avoiding another war altogether.

Politicization and the Lessons of Arab Military History

Before moving on to compare the Arab militaries to two non-Arab militaries, it is worth reflecting just a bit on what these three examples can tell us about the impact of politicization on their performance. The Egyptian armed forces of the Six-Day War were an archetypal example of a praetorian military. Its leadership ruled the country, and in so doing, lost its way, placing politicking and the perquisites that come with it ahead of assiduously preparing for war against a foreign foe. The Iraqi army that invaded Iran in 1980 was a quintessentially commissarist military. Saddam not only replicated Stalin's methods, he took coup-proofing to its illogical extreme, deliberately hobbling his military to ensure that it could not defy his will or unseat him. The ISF that faced the Da'ish assault in June 2014 was a classic palace-guard military. It was wholly focused on internal security and keeping the paramount leader in power, which required little more than selected counterterrorism operations coupled with riot control duties and a willingness to use force against any domestic rival the prime minister wanted silenced. It had never really been trained to face a conventional invasion from across Iraq's borders. To the extent it trained at all, that training had been focused almost entirely on counterinsurgency and other forms of unconventional warfare.

All three then went through a wrenching, extensive process of depoliticization coupled with a new retraining/rebuilding process to develop the skills to fight and win conventional battles against what had previously proven to be a superior foe. The Egyptians experienced this in Nasser and Sadat's determination to purge their armed forces of any politically inclined officers, promote only the most competent, focus the military solely on defeating Israel, and train them relentlessly to do so. Saddam did something similar, stepping back from micromanaging Iraqi combat operations, allowing his best officers to rise in the ranks and command the war effort, and rebuilding the Iraqi armed forces to maximize their ability to defeat Iran even if that meant sacrificing Baghdad's political controls. When Nuri al-Maliki was replaced as Iraq's prime minister by Haidar al-Abadi in 2014, Baghdad brought the Americans back, and the US military once again set about rebuilding Iraq's shattered field formations, training them to fight as a conventional force against a conventional adversary, and helping to promote Iraq's most professional and capable officers while extirpating its political hacks.

In all three cases, when politicization was present, it had a profound impact on the strategic leadership, strategic intelligence gathering, and strategic information management of the Arab armies and a lesser, but still significant, impact on morale and unit cohesion. Egyptian generalship in 1967, and Iraqi generalship in 1980–1982 and again in 2014 were deplorable. Their generals were mostly incompetent and their direction of these various campaigns was disastrous. While there were still many instances when Arab field units hung together and fought to the death in circumstances where other armies might have broken, it was in these wars that the largest number of Arab formations did break and run pell-mell. And in the case of the Egyptians in 1967 and the Iraqis in 2014, it was frequently the hack generals who fled first, causing some—but not all—of the units under their command to unravel.[33] Finally, all three militaries experienced constant problems with information and intelligence, and some aspects were unquestionably the product of the perverse incentives endemic to politicized militaries. In short, and as has been the case in many other historical examples, heavy-handed politicization (of any variety) crippled strategic leadership, hampered strategic information management, and eroded unit cohesion, although the first two were more pronounced than the last.

However, what is equally striking and equally important, is what did and did not change as a product of depoliticization. Strategic leadership improved dramatically. That was especially true of the Egyptians and Iraqis, whose generals and general staffs turned in the finest performances of any Arab military in 1973 and 1988–1991, respectively. These were arguably the greatest achievements of Arab arms during the post–World War II era, and that was largely a product of the capable, professional generals and planners who ran the Egyptian Armed Forces during the October War and the Iraqi Army during the end of the Iran-Iraq War, the invasion of Kuwait, and (Saddam's foolishness aside) even the Persian Gulf War. The performance of Iraq's senior leadership in 2014–2017 was not quite so stellar—and got a big help from the United States—but in the emergence of figures such as General Uthman al-Ghanimi and LTG 'Abd al-Amir al-Lami, they did far better than in the past.

Information management and intelligence collection also improved dramatically at senior and strategic levels. The Egyptian General Staff did a brilliant job collecting information, analyzing friendly and enemy forces, and devising ways to monitor the course of battle in 1973. So too did the Iraqi General Staff in 1988, with more than a little help from the Americans. The same held true after the United States returned to Iraq in late 2014.

Similarly, in all of the post-depoliticization campaigns, the Arab militaries experienced noticeably better morale and unit cohesion. Even after the Israelis had turned the tables and were beginning to carve up the Egyptian forces from October 14 onward Egyptian forces never dissolved the way that some units had in 1967. Obviously, large numbers of Iraqi units eventually did just that in 1991, but two points are worth making. First, those that did, did so only after 39 days of constant bombing during which they were stuck in the desert, cut-off from logistical support, and left to face the army of the world's sole remaining superpower. It is hard to see those Iraqis who deserted or surrendered as anything but men pushed far beyond their physical and psychological breaking point. And second, a number of Iraqi formations, led by the Republican Guard, remained cohesive and fought to the death against the US-led Coalition. They fought so hard that American veterans of Vietnam described these battles as the fiercest firefights they had ever been in.[34] Finally, while the ISF of 2015–2017 still had many problems, it did not fall apart in battle, no matter how fierce the fighting got in places like Ramadi and Mosul, and that was a major change from 2014.

Yet all of these armed forces still suffered from the same crippling problems with tactical leadership, tactical information management, air operations, weapons handling, and maintenance that has bedeviled every modern Arab military. Moreover, they were all plagued by these problems both before and after depoliticization, and despite the fact that their depoliticization efforts were specifically meant to try to address the problems with tactical leadership (and to a lesser extent, information management, air operations, and weapons handling). Miserable generalship, horrendous information problems, and uneven unit cohesion contributed to Egyptian defeat in 1967 and Iraqi defeat in 1981–1982 and 2014, but these were not the only problems they suffered, and it is debatable whether they were more important than the tactical incompetence, endemic lying by front-line forces, hapless air operations, and inability to properly employ or maintain their weapons that plagued these militaries at those times. In truth, I would argue that these other factors ultimately were more important than the failings of generalship, strategic information management, and unit cohesion.

Moreover, all of these problems persisted despite comprehensive depoliticization. This drives home the point that they are not products of politicization. It also makes clear that something else is going on with the Arab militaries beyond politicization. *Politicization has clearly contributed to the poor performance of Arab armed forces over time, but it is not the only factor, and not even the most important factor in their ineffectiveness.* Because what also stands out about the Arab victories in 1973, 1988–1991, and 2015–2017 is how meager they ultimately were, and meager because of the limitations imposed by their poor tactical leadership, poor tactical information management, poor air operations, poor weapons handling, and poor maintenance.

In every one of these examples, the Arab military in question won only a very modest victory despite investing enormous effort and resources to do so. It is striking how hard Egypt and Iraq worked to eke out the minimal successes they achieved in 1973 and 1988. Think about how much Egypt poured into its preparation and conduct of the October War! All of the advantages it created for itself against Israel in terms of strategic surprise, technological surprise, massive numerical imbalances, massive firepower imbalances, and forcing Israel to fight on two fronts. Any one of these advantages has proven decisive by itself in other modern wars, yet all that the Egyptians could achieve with all of them together was an impressive water crossing followed by four days of modest progress that resulted in a narrow bridgehead about 10 kilometers deep. Then they barely held this bridgehead for a couple of weeks and were about to lose everything when the superpowers shut down the fighting. And throughout, the factors that consistently prevented Egypt from achieving more with all of those advantages were the same old problems of tactical leadership, tactical information management, air operations, weapons handling, and maintenance.

The exact same thing was true for the Iraqis against the Iranians in 1988, when they had tactical surprise, obscene numerical advantages, massive firepower advantages, better weaponry, American intelligence assistance, and even chemical warfare. While their five victorious battles (and the 1990 invasion of Kuwait) were very impressive by the standards of that war, they were hardly the German blitzkrieg. They never penetrated more than 40 kilometers into Iran and, like the Egyptian offensive in 1973, only functioned when everything was going exactly according to plan and they did not have to improvise. As long as they were following their well-rehearsed scripts and Iranian forces were on their heels, unable to respond, the Iraqis were fine. The moment the script ended they had to stop. Any time something happened not according to script, Iraqi military performance reverted back to the same incompetence it had evinced in every previous campaign. So too with the Gulf War, where forced to fight on the Coalition's terms, Iraqi formations were defeated effortlessly by Western ground units. Even the Republican Guards fought very hard, but very badly. In each case, combined arms, maneuver, tactical flexibility, and artillery support disappeared.

So too for the Iraqi operations to defeat Da'ish. They did liberate the country but it took them nearly three years to do so despite overwhelming advantages in numbers, firepower, intelligence, air power, weaponry, and logistical support. No matter how hard American advisors and trainers tried to get Iraqi formations to act aggressively, flexibly, creatively, and cooperatively, very few Iraqis would or could do so. At places such as Tikrit, Ramadi, and Mosul, even American-trained and advised Iraqi formations showed little ability to maneuver, conduct combined arms operations, react flexibly to events, or aggressively press forward against a pugnacious but supine enemy. They became heavily dependent on American fire support to make any progress against Da'ish, and often would not advance or fight at all unless the US-led Coalition had plastered the area in front of them with firepower.

What's more, these are hardly the only examples of this phenomenon. I could have presented the experience of the Syrians in 1973, the Saudis in 1991 or 2015–2018 (in Yemen), the Libyans in Uganda in 1979 and throughout their struggle for Chad, or a host of other Arab armies that have tried to improve and professionalize under Western-tutelage since.

The pattern is a strong one. When Arab militaries are politicized, as they often are, this hurts them by affecting strategic leadership, strategic information management, and to a lesser extent, morale and unit cohesion. Not surprisingly, many of the Arab world's most catastrophic defeats correlated with Arab militaries that were heavily politicized.

But politicization is neither the only problem nor the most important one that the Arab militaries faced. Their deficiencies in tactical leadership, tactical information management, air operations, weapons handling, and maintenance persisted regardless of how politicized or professional they were. At some level, that's not surprising because politicization has never produced those problems in other armies at other times. What's more important is that not only did these problems prove immune to depoliticization, they were consistently the decisive factors in Middle Eastern wars, ensuring that Arab defeats turned into fiascoes and constraining their successes to pyrrhic or mere symbolic victories.

| Politicization and the South
Vietnamese Armed Forces

T HE NOTION THAT all of the Arab military problems are caused by politicization has become an article of faith among some Americans, particularly academics. So it is important to delve deeper into this idea. Once
again, it is helpful to look at some non-Arab militaries that have experienced
similar problems with politicization to see if they had the same weaknesses
as the Arab armies. If politicization really is the cause, then the non-Arab
armies should experience the same patterns of poor performance as the Arabs.
It's not just that they should lose most wars and barely win those in which
they somehow prevail, but that their armed forces should manifest the same
patterns of military ineffectiveness that the Arabs did.

With that in mind, in this chapter and the next I am going to discuss
the South Vietnamese experience during the latter half of the Vietnam War
and Argentina's experiences in the Falklands War. Later I will also bring the
experiences of the Cubans and North Koreans discussed in Chapter 4 back in,
since these were also heavily politicized militaries. The key question is the extent to which the Argentines and South Vietnamese (and Cubans and North
Koreans) experienced the same problems in combat as the Arabs.

South Vietnam, 1969–1975

The Republic of Vietnam Armed Forces (RVNAF) were among the most
politicized of the twentieth century. Moreover, because of America's

involvement in that war, their performance—or a caricatured version of it—and their endemic politicization are known to a great many in the West. Nevertheless, while the RVNAF, and particularly the Army of the Republic of Vietnam (ARVN), was a badly flawed military, its flaws were not uniform and the specific nature of its problems help illustrate the ways that politicization affects a military. In that way, it's a good comparison for the Arab militaries.

I am only going to look at RVNAF performance from the start of the American withdrawal in 1969 to the fall of Saigon in 1975. There are several reasons for this. Before 1969, the war was primarily a counterinsurgency fight, but a counterinsurgency waged by US and South Vietnamese militaries that mostly weren't employing counterinsurgency strategies or tactics. That makes it hard to assess the effectiveness of the force. In every case, it begs the question of whether RVNAF failings were a product of poor military practices or of America's insistence on fighting the wrong way—especially since the South Vietnamese understood the right way to fight an insurgency and initially tried to get the Americans to help them do so.[1] Moreover, the United States took over the direction of the war pretty much completely after the assassination of Ngo Dinh Diem in 1963, and American ground and air forces dominated the fighting after 1965, pushing the RVNAF into the background. It was only after the decision to start withdrawing US forces in 1969 that the RVNAF were forced to shoulder the burden of the fight on their own.

Politicization in the RVNAF. Throughout their brief history, the RVNAF were riddled with politics like end-stage lymphoma. South Vietnam's first president, Ngo Dinh Diem, was a civilian who took office in 1955 and consolidated power in the face of several efforts by military cabals to unseat him. Naturally, he adopted traditional commissarist practices to try to coup-proof his regime. He scrupulously promoted only relatives and loyalists, disregarding questions of competence. He ensured that all senior military commands were held by officers of proven reliability. He centralized power and decision-making in himself and a very few trusted friends and relatives. He created overlapping lines of authority so that his senior subordinates (and their organizations) were never quite clear what they were responsible for. He kept ministers and generals isolated from each other and often pitted them against one another. He ultimately created 10 different intelligence services, all of which reported only to him. Diem favored Catholics and former Northerners as the most rabid anticommunists. By 1967, out of 25,000 ARVN officers, 25 percent had been born in the North and 19.4 percent were Catholics even though only 10.4 percent of all South Vietnamese were Catholic.[2]

Diem famously surrounded himself with sycophants and exploded at anyone who presented him with news he did not want to hear.[3] "Diem set two precedents which future Presidents followed. First, he turned the Capital Military District into a fortress with its nerve centre [*sic*] in the Presidential Palace to discourage coups. All governments in South Vietnam spent more time worrying about potential political plots than the war effort. Second, ARVN units such as the Airborne [Division] were extensively used for political purposes which frequently left them unable to complete their normal military responsibilities."[4] Indeed, it was Diem who began to treat the ARVN's elite forces, the Airborne and Marine Divisions, as anti-coup formations that got special attention and privileges but also had political responsibilities that frequently trumped strategic needs. This also meant that Diem paid extra attention to the command of these formations, and to ensuring that their commanders were faultlessly loyal to him regardless of their professional qualifications.[5]

Worst of all, none of it worked. Diem fought off multiple bids to oust him before falling prey to a military putsch (backed by the United States) in 1963.[6] Diem's murder opened the door to a cavalcade of coups—nine of them in just 20 months—that ultimately produced a new government under General Nguyen Van Thieu.[7] Thieu's triumph was also a function of his political skills. As one recent history of the war concluded, "Thieu had risen so high in ARVN not because of a talent for success on the battlefield but because he was essentially a skilled political operator in an army uniform."[8]

Naturally, his regime was a swamp of praetorianism. Under Thieu, "the ARVN had to administer the country as well as defend it. The generals in command of country and army were, with very few exceptions, in power because they had distinguished themselves not in battle but in political intrigue. They possessed neither the technical ability to command large numbers of armed men nor the political talents to ameliorate the problems of a war-torn and underdeveloped country. Indeed, by 1968 ARVN resembled less a national army than a feudal alliance of local armies. Political power rested on command of troops. The movement of a division out of one command area into another therefore became a major political problem, and flexibility in the deployment of ARVN units was consequently almost nil." Political intrigue became a way of life for South Vietnamese generals. Well-connected officers could not be removed from command or disciplined by less well-connected superiors. Worse, many would simply refuse to obey orders they did not like.[9]

Thieu was also deeply corrupt, inflicting this aspect of politicization on the RVNAF as well.[10] In the words of his vice president, Nguyen Cao Ky, "Corruption touched every family."[11] While he retained Diem's practice of personally approving all promotions to general officer, Thieu also forced would-be generals to pay him for their promotions.[12] Senior officers of the ARVN in particular used their commands to insinuate themselves into local political and commercial structures. "Soldiers brought their families to live with them, officers became entrenched in local politics, and regional commanders grew accustomed to predictable campaigning."[13]

Thus, Diem's commissarism gave way to Thieu's praetorianism. But like the Middle East, the praetorian leader (Thieu) picked up all of the commissarist habits of his predecessor and added a few of his own. Indeed, having seen Diem's failure, as well as the demise of those who had overthrown him, Thieu was determined to do better. That meant inflicting even worse commissarist control over the military. As one superb history of the RVNAF explained, in South Vietnam "No government could survive without the support of ARVN's Joint General Staff. Therefore, every President hand-picked his generals. The sole criteria for promotion to General was loyalty, not experience or ability, which resulted in heads of state being surrounded by friends who were incapable of developing effective military policies."[14] Thieu obsessed over the political reliability of his generals, and endlessly fought American efforts to remove his corrupt, incompetent cronies and replace them by promoting more capable junior officers. Unfortunately, many of these American efforts to reform RVNAF leadership came late, as early on the US military was uninterested in South Vietnamese military performance, preferring to just fight the war for them.[15]

Finally, the RVNAF also suffered from important aspects of the palace-guard variant of politicization. The Airborne and Marine Divisions, as well as the armored brigades and armored cavalry regiments, were seen by both Diem and Thieu as special regime protection forces. Yet they were also counted as South Vietnam's strategic reserve. These duties came into conflict at the worst times, particularly in 1975 when North Vietnamese advances created military threats that required commitment of Saigon's strategic reserves, but simultaneously conjured political threats to Thieu's regime that argued for their retention around the capital. Along similar lines, in 1970, as US ground forces withdrew, the American high command recognized that the ARVN needed to build up its forces along the DMZ in what was called Military Region I, or I Corps. But the only divisions that could be spared were either from the strategic reserve or from the politically sensitive Mekong Delta. Not surprisingly, Thieu refused to agree to either, with dire consequences during the 1972 Easter Offensive.[16]

Like other modern politicized militaries, the impact of these perverse practices was felt in various ways throughout the armed forces. First of all, it meant poor leadership, especially at the senior levels, with a diminishing impact lower and lower in the chain of command.[17] A RAND report from 1970 noted that "Political loyalty, rather than battlefield performance, has long dominated the promotion system in the officer corps, with the result that there is often an inverse relationship between rank and military skill."[18] In other words, the higher the rank, the more political and—typically—the less competent the leader. (But the opposite was also true: the lower the rank, the more likely the officer was competent.) South Vietnam's highly regarded Deputy Chief of Staff, General Dong Van Khuyen, said after the war that "Promotion to top positions required connections, not ability, and as a result the Army was denied the wisdom of some very talented men."[19] Thomas Cantwell observes that "Senior Army staff were primarily concerned with ensuring their patrons remained in power. Consequently, they rarely studied the war situation. Some generals were totally ignorant of what was happening in the field."[20]

Fitting the same pattern, South Vietnam did possess many capable tactical commanders. As Cantwell wrote in his exhaustive study of the ARVN, "The average soldier never received inspiration, support or guidance from his senior officers since they were more concerned with Saigon's political equilibrium rather than the welfare of their men. On the other hand, ARVN's best combat officers were its captains and lieutenants who spent their time in the field gaining valuable experience. However, these junior officers lacked the political connections, family ties and financial clout necessary to break into ARVN's elite circles which left the Army with only a small group of senior staff, ranked colonel to general, who had some degree of combat experience."[21] Indeed, it was ARVN junior officers who consistently but unsuccessfully agitated for a greater emphasis on counterinsurgency operations in the face of the American emphasis on conventional firepower.[22]

Politicization also meant poor training and poor morale for the rank and file. In 1969, the Nixon administration announced a policy of "Vietnamization" of the war, which meant building up the ARVN to be able to handle the defense of South Vietnam on their own, thus allowing the withdrawal of American ground forces. That meant that for the first time, the United States had to take seriously the training and equipping of the ARVN. Yet the United States found that at that time, about one-third of all ARVN battalions did no training at all, less than half trained for 2 hours per week, and another fifth trained for 20 minutes per week.[23] Between their incompetent generals and their lack of training, few ARVN troops were optimistic about their ability to win, or willing to risk their lives to achieve it. These reinforcing problems drove crippling desertion rates that plagued the ARVN from the early 1960s right to the end of the war.[24] For instance, in 1972, the year of the North's Easter Offensive, 70 percent of all ARVN personnel losses were from desertion, not enemy action.[25]

Vietnamization: The ARVN Shoulders the Load

In February 1968, during Vietnam's Tet New Year's celebration, Hanoi launched a nationwide offensive to try to shatter its adversaries, the government of South Vietnam and its American protectors. The Viet Cong guerrillas came out of hiding and mounted surprise assaults all across the country. As has been well documented, the Tet Offensive was both a military fiasco and a political triumph for the Communists. The Viet Cong scored some spectacular but ephemeral successes and were slaughtered by ARVN and US combat forces once they had recovered from the surprise. Of roughly 125,000 Communist fighters that participated in the Tet Offensive, anywhere from 30,000 to 90,000 were killed.[26] However, the size, extent, and early successes of the attack seemed to belie US military and governmental claims that the war was effectively won.[27] Both aspects of Tet proved critical, albeit to different parties and in different ways.

For the Americans, what mattered about Tet was its political impact. It forced the Johnson administration to "de-escalate" the war by starting to withdraw American ground troops, a process that once begun proved impossible to reverse. When the Nixon administration took office in 1969, public opinion and congressional action made the process irresistible. No matter how much Nixon wanted to keep the troops there, and he tried mightily, it was impossible for him to do so.

Bereft of American ground forces but determined not to abandon the war or South Vietnam altogether, Nixon was forced to adopt what became known as "Vietnamization." This meant building up the RVNAF, and particularly the ARVN, so that they could fight on. However, at the time, it was widely assumed and formally promised by Nixon and Kissinger that the United States would continue to provide air support, trainers, advisors, and the supplies that the ARVN needed to win.[28]

Washington appointed General Creighton Abrams in place of the disgraced William Westmoreland, and ordered him to build a better ARVN. Abrams adopted a true counterinsurgency strategy, instituted new training programs for the ARVN, and emphasized to his American troops the importance of their training and advisory functions. In general, Abrams and his team made greater progress with ARVN enlisted men and junior officers than they did with the heavily politicized senior leaders.[29] For instance, in III Corps around Saigon, they established a program called Dong Tien ("Progress Together") that paired American and ARVN battalions in combat operations so that the South Vietnamese could learn by doing with the Americans, and found that it "greatly improved the effectiveness of ARVN units throughout III Corps, and they began to show more aggressiveness, better coordination, and more sustained combat effort."[30] By 1970, some ARVN formations were doing so well that they shed their US advisory teams.[31]

Cambodia, 1970

Abrams believed that the United States needed to improve Saigon's military situation not just by enhancing RVNAF tactical capabilities, but also by diminishing some of the strategic threats it faced. Ultimately, the Communists' ability to prosecute the war rested on their ability to move troops and supplies from North Vietnam to South Vietnam along two routes: one overland through Laos via the famous Ho Chi Minh Trail, and the second by sea to southern Cambodia and the port of Sihanoukville, then overland into southern South Vietnam. Although less well known, the latter path was more important, accounting for roughly 85 percent of all supplies to Communist forces in South Vietnam by 1970.[32]

This importance, the shifting politics of Cambodia, and the fact that the Communists' primary headquarters for the war in the south operated out of Cambodia, all led the United States to decide to move first against the southern supply route. A combined force of American ground troops and ARVN units would mount a reinforcing sequence of drives into southeastern Cambodia. The operation involved 32,000 US troops and 48,000 ARVN, and was led by Lt. General Do Cao Tri, commander of the ARVN III Corps. The Americans considered Tri one of the very few aggressive, dynamic, and capable South Vietnamese senior leaders.

In many ways, the Cambodian offensive was a signal achievement by the ARVN. Their troops sliced into the border regions, "scattering VC forces and seizing over a million and a half rounds of small arms ammunition, 300 vehicles, 30 tons of rice, and much else."[33] The operation also killed 11,000 VC and People's Army of Vietnam (PAVN, the North Vietnamese army) fighters, closed down the Cambodian supply route, and even disrupted the Communist offensive in Cambodia. Some ARVN formations had operated without US advisors and fought well. The South Vietnamese themselves were thrilled, and it helped give them the confidence to believe that they could survive without

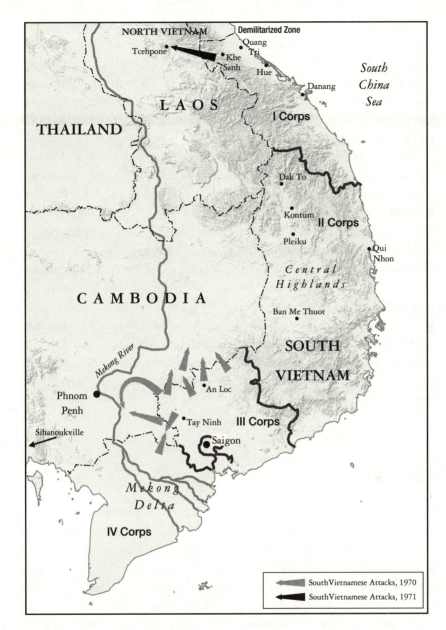

MAP 17 ARVN Offensives, 1970–1971

the Americans.[34] Abrams himself remarked that "The ARVN has done better than I would ever have expected."[35]

Yet this was only half the story. Most of the 40,000–60,000 Viet Cong and PAVN troops in the region quickly pulled back in the face of ARVN and US firepower so there was little real fighting. All of the ARVN formations were elite units, including brigades from the Marine and Airborne Divisions. And even then, there were considerable problems. ARVN formations had difficulty with combined arms coordination and fire support. Their armored units experienced crippling problems with maintenance, logistics, and communications. The ARVN units may have gotten better, but they were still a long way from real proficiency.[36]

Yet the crucial flaws of the Cambodian incursion lay with South Vietnam's generals. As James Willbanks put it, "With the exception of a few aggressive leaders like General Tri, most of the senior ARVN officers, including division commanders and those above them, remained too politicized and were more concerned with Saigon palace intrigue and personal creature comforts than with fighting the Communists."[37] Ultimately, Lt. General Tri succeeded by task-organizing all of the ARVN formations to put colonels and lieutenant colonels in command and so bypass "the politicized division commanders and their staffs, who played almost no role in the operation."[38] After the Cambodian operation, General Westmoreland (then Chief of Staff of the US Army) traveled to Saigon and urged Thieu "to clean house in the senior ranks of the Vietnamese Army." He told Thieu that there were "many young colonels capable of assuming general officer responsibilities and eager to do so."[39] Thieu thanked Westmoreland and ignored him.

Laos, 1971

The next year, Abrams turned his attention to the Ho Chi Minh Trail, which had resumed its critical role in Hanoi's war effort because the Cambodian sea-land route remained closed. Of course, the "trail" was a euphemism for a vast network of roads and paths that led from North Vietnam into the western regions of nearly all of South Vietnam. But there were key chokepoints in northern Laos through which virtually everything had to pass, and the Americans believed it possible for the ARVN to close these bottlenecks to cut the North's supply line to its forces in the south. In addition, Abrams and his staff expected Hanoi to mount a major military campaign in 1972 to try to influence the US presidential election, and they hoped to disrupt or even prevent this attack.[40]

The Laotian incursion, dubbed Lam Son 719 by the South Vietnamese, was different from the Cambodian operation in several important ways. First, American ground forces and even advisors were now prohibited by law from operating outside Vietnam. Second, both the weather and the terrain were much worse than in Cambodia, with the former hampering the air support available to ARVN ground forces. Finally, Hanoi would not back down this time. PAVN had been preparing for the attack for months. They built defensive positions and deployed a force of 30,000 men with another 20,000 in reserve to face an ARVN attack of 19,000. Unlike Cambodia, the North was determined to hold the Ho Chi Minh Trail open.[41]

Even making allowance for all of these challenges, ARVN performance was dreadful. Without the Americans to handle their logistics, South Vietnamese units quickly began to run out of ammunition, fuel, and replacement equipment within days of its start.[42] Laos was the first time that the elite Airborne and Marine brigades had ever operated together as divisions. They had no experience in large-unit maneuver warfare—and it showed.[43] To try to preserve operational security in the face of Hanoi's numerous intelligence penetrations, Thieu and his high command only notified the participating divisions a week before the start of the operation, so they had too little time to prepare.[44]

However, without question, ARVN's biggest failings were command problems stemming from politicization. The offensive was mounted by the ARVN's I Corps, responsible for the northernmost sector of South Vietnam, which at the time was commanded by Lt. General Hoang Xuan Lam. Lam won the command from Thieu entirely for his reflexive loyalty.[45] He was "an officer who epitomized the ineffectiveness of Saigon's command structure. Lam had the political acumen to excel in Saigon's politics, but he was a poor military commander who proved incompetent."[46] To make matters worse, both the Airborne and Marine Division commanders were senior in rank to Lam and, as palace-guard formations, they were protected by Thieu. They resented being subordinated to Lam and according to the senior US advisor to I Corps at the time, "The Marine commander did not accompany his division from Saigon . . . and the Airborne commander refused to attend LTG Lam's command briefings."[47] Lam had never commanded a multi-division operation. Throughout the battle he ignored his subordinate commanders' requests and suggestions, and worked tirelessly to prevent their complaints from reaching Saigon.[48]

Not surprisingly, Lam Son 719 was a disaster, and failed in a much more obvious fashion than the Cambodian offensive. It kicked off on February 8, 1971, but within a week had already come to a halt. Even though the Airborne and Marine brigades fought very well, Thieu got cold feet at the prospect that his palace guards might get butchered so far from Saigon. On February 12, he told Lt. General Lam that he was to proceed with caution and abort the entire offensive if his forces suffered more than 3,000 casualties.

Unwilling to be blamed for incurring casualties, Lam simply stopped issuing orders. With no strategic direction, and an equal unwillingness to become the scapegoat for any losses, Lam's division commanders stopped and dug-in.[49]

By the time the ARVN formations started moving again on February 16, the North Vietnamese had concentrated superior power against their positions and began hammering them. In mid-March, Saigon decided to turn the floundering operation into a heliborne raid to destroy PAVN supply depots farther west, which they more or less accomplished with tremendous American air support. At that point, Thieu pulled his precious Airborne brigades back to Saigon, and ordered the rest of his forces out as quickly as possible. Despite Thieu's imprecations, the ARVN took 7,000 casualties (a 40 percent loss rate), and lost 54 tanks, 87 other armored vehicles, and 96 artillery pieces. The United States estimated that PAVN took 19,000 casualties, 106 tanks, and 13 artillery pieces, mostly to American air power.[50]

There was little to brag about in ARVN's tactical performance. Three of its finest divisions—the Airborne, Marines, and 1st Infantry Division—had shown little ability to maneuver or conduct combined arms operations, although all three had tried to do so. Some of this goes to the fact that they had performed mostly counterinsurgency and palace-guard duties over the past decade, some to the fact that they had learned to fight like American formations and rely on massive firepower and strategic mobility assets—neither of which were available to them in the early days of the offensive because of the weather. South Vietnamese armored formations showed little fire discipline, marksmanship, or attention to maintenance and resupply. On the other hand, ARVN unit cohesion had generally been quite good. Some units had panicked, but the vast majority had fought hard in difficult circumstances and ended up conducting a skillful fighting withdrawal that inflicted heavy casualties on the PAVN forces.[51]

The principal problems once again lay with the ARVN's horribly politicized senior officers, principally from division and corps command up to President Thieu himself. Observers and historians of Lam Son 719 stress the failures of South Vietnam's senior leaders as the key to ARVN failure.[52] In his unmatched history of the operation, Willbanks concludes simply that "There are a number of explanations for the outcome of the operation. Chief among these factors was poor South Vietnamese senior leadership."[53] Likewise, Andrew Wiest concluded in his history of the ARVN that "Perhaps the greatest lesson of the invasion of Laos was that, while the ARVN fighting men and their junior officers fought well and hard, their leadership at the highest levels remained politicized and unsound."[54] General Lam, in particular, bears much of the responsibility for the fiasco, and it is worth noting that his performance was so bad that Thieu actually relieved him of command in late February, only to have to reinstate him when his replacement was killed on the flight in to I Corps headquarters.[55]

The Easter Offensive, 1972

ARVN had shot its bolt in Laos. Now it was North Vietnam's turn, and Hanoi decided to roll the dice. According to North Vietnamese sources, Hanoi decided to shift from an insurgency to a conventional military invasion to conquer the country outright.[56] This reversal derived from four critical conclusions. First, Hanoi assessed that the insurgency had failed. The Viet Cong had been devastated by the Tet Offensive and Abrams's counterinsurgency strategy that followed.[57] Second, the invasion of Laos convinced them that PAVN was now superior to the ARVN in conventional warfare, and they suspected that ARVN morale would crack if it faced a major assault.[58] Third, the North had begun receiving large amounts of new equipment from the Soviets and Chinese, and some of its troops had begun learning Soviet-style combined arms techniques.[59]

Finally, North Vietnam's leaders believed (or hoped) that the strong antiwar sentiment in the United States and the Nixon administration's pursuit of détente with Hanoi's Soviet allies would limit or even prevent Washington's support for the ARVN. Indeed, by March 1972, only about 70,000 Americans remained in Vietnam, and barely 6,000 were combat troops—none of whom were deployed on the front lines anymore. Even the American advisory presence had declined from over 9,400 in 1968 to just 1,000 in 1972.[60]

The North Vietnamese military leadership recognized that the American withdrawal had stretched ARVN thin. Half as many divisions were now defending the same length of front. Hanoi also concluded from the failed Laotian incursion that ARVN could not quickly shift its forces around the country the way that the Americans had, and Saigon had too few strategic reserves. To exploit these vulnerabilities, the North opted to mount simultaneous assaults against three of Saigon's four corps sectors to try to overstress the ARVN. To do so, they launched virtually the entire PAVN field force against the South: 120,000 troops and 1,200 armored fighting vehicles.[61] Although North Vietnam's leaders were unsure that what they dubbed the Nguyen Hue Offensive would conquer the South altogether, they hoped that at the very least it would force the United States to agree to their terms at the desultory Paris peace talks, sink Nixon's chances of re-election, shatter the pacification program, and so weaken the ARVN that it could be finished off in a subsequent offensive.[62]

MAP 18 The Easter Offensive, 1972

The offensive would be opposed by an ARVN that had improved some, but not much. Failure in Laos prompted Abrams and his staff to press Thieu to remove his incompetent generals at the top, and improve and expand ARVN forces at the bottom.[63] They got about half of what they wanted. Thieu would only agree to make cosmetic changes among his senior commanders, but he did agree to establish several new formations, and he approved an expanded training program in combined arms warfare. Even then, the Americans had focused more on the quantitative expansion of the ARVN rather than its qualitative improvement, and in line with the United States' own practices at the time, emphasized increasing firepower as much as improving training.[64]

Initial Assaults. The offensive began on March 30, 1972, in I Corps, in the far north. The North mounted its largest attack here, both from the north across the demilitarized zone (DMZ) and from the west out of Laos. Despite his appalling performance the year before, Lt. General Lam remained in command of I Corps because of his connections to Thieu. He kicked off this campaign by disregarding urgent warnings from South Vietnamese (and American) intelligence of an imminent PAVN attack across the DMZ on Good Friday. He had only the new and inexperienced 3rd Division commanded by Brigadier General Vu Van Giai facing north while the rest of his forces were oriented toward the west. To make matters worse, Giai had decided to rotate two of his regiments despite these same warnings, meaning that two-thirds of his division would not even be in its defensive positions when the North attacked. He then flew down to Saigon for the weekend.[65]

The North Vietnamese started by sending two infantry divisions and two tank regiments directly south across the DMZ, where they smashed into the unprepared ARVN 3rd Division. ARVN problems quickly began to emerge and multiply. Poor weather severely limited American and South Vietnamese air support for the first several days of the campaign. The staffs of the 3rd Division and I Corps proved incapable of coordinating fire support. Between the surprise, improved PAVN capabilities, and the poor disposition of the 3rd Division's formations, some South Vietnamese units broke while others surrendered en masse.

On April 1, Giai ordered the remnants of his 3rd Division to abandon their positions and fall back to the Mieu Giang/Cam Lo/Cua Viet river line. Giai issued these orders from the front, without alerting the Americans or having his staff plan the retreat. He then ordered his own headquarters to pack up and retreat even farther south. These panicked moves prompted his own staff to melt away, the senior officers fleeing first and the junior officers following, leaving no one to organize the retreat. Only the stalwart performance of the 258th Marine Brigade—which stood firm, developed its own battle plan with its American advisors, and then had the initiative to send a battalion to hold the vital Dong Ha Bridge—prevented the complete collapse of I Corps' northern flank. The next day, however, PAVN units assaulted the river line and terrified refugees caused the ARVN 57th Infantry Brigade to collapse. When its sister 56th Brigade surrendered a major defensive position to the North, the Marines were forced to fall back to Quang Tri City.[66]

The South Vietnamese II Corps commander was no better than his counterpart to the north. Lt. General Ngo Dzu was indecisive and changeable, a member of a family of infamous heroin smugglers. The US military considered him the worst corps commander in the ARVN.[67] The main PAVN attack here came at Dak To with 20,000 troops and 400 tanks. It was opposed by the 22nd ARVN Division under Colonel Le Duc Dat, who was also deeply corrupt but had close ties to Thieu. Dat refused to patrol, maneuver, or send reinforcements to units in trouble. Dat's artillery refused to conduct counter-battery missions against PAVN guns, and he placed his armored reserve so far away that it was unable to reach his infantry in time to prevent a PAVN rout. Two of Dat's subordinate formations, the 47th Infantry Regiment and 9th Airborne Battalion, fought hard, but without support and coordination from higher leadership, they were eventually outmaneuvered and overpowered by PAVN forces. By the second week of April, the 22nd Division was hors de combat, and the North Vietnamese forces were pushing on to Kontum, farther east in South Vietnam's central highlands.[68]

On April 5, PAVN commenced its assault against III Corps in Binh Long and Tay Ninh Provinces with over 35,000 troops, tanks and artillery. Despite massive American bombing, the North Vietnamese forces overwhelmed Loc Ninh on April 6, where the ARVN commander, Lt. Colonel Nguyen Cong Vinh, was another political appointee determined to surrender as quickly as he could. Two PAVN Divisions isolated An Loc the next day.[69]

The III Corps was commanded by Major General Nguyen Van Minh, a decent administrator but not a fighting general. Minh was overwhelmed by the situation he faced. An Loc itself was defended by the ARVN 5th Division, commanded by Brigadier General Le Van Hung, a wealthy minion of Minh's with little combat experience. But the reality of being surrounded at a location critical to the defense of Saigon and a forceful team of American advisors stiffened Hung's spine. He would rise to the occasion and conduct a spirited defense of An Loc almost in spite of himself. Hung's efforts were assisted by a poor combined arms performance by the PAVN forces attacking in this sector. He also benefited from astonishing amounts of American air support, including 297 B-52 sorties on a single day in May. But most of all, led by a general willing to command, the soldiers and officers of the 5th ARVN division put up a helluva fight, stopping PAVN T-54s with light antitank weapons and forcing the North Vietnamese to pay in blood for every house and every block they took. For two months, Hung's division held on and bled the PAVN forces dry until they were forced to pull back.[70]

Crises in I and II Corps. While one senior ARVN commander was rising to the challenge, others were failing miserably. Top of that list was General Lam. The initial PAVN attack against I Corps had run out of steam after pushing his 3rd Division back across the Cam Lo-Cua Viet river line, but Lam foolishly assumed that the North was finished. Saigon had sent him most of the Marine and Airborne Divisions to prevent a total collapse in I Corps. Rather than use these forces to shore up his defenses as his subordinates and American advisors wanted, Lam decided to launch a major counterattack to throw the Communists back across the DMZ. Moreover, because he did not trust either the Airborne or Marine Division commanders after his experience with them in Laos, he subordinated all of their brigades to Giai, the 3rd Division commander, along with several ranger and armored battalions. As a result, the battered and inexperienced 3rd Division was forced to try to command 36 maneuver battalions and 18 artillery battalions.[71]

Lam's offensive began on April 14 and ground to a halt almost immediately. Many of the ARVN formations were still exhausted from fighting the initial PAVN attack. Giai simply could not exercise control over so many formations, so none of his units could support one another or act in unison. Then the logistical system of his wounded division broke down trying to support four times as many combat formations as it would normally. Even as the attack fell apart, Lam refused to allow the Marine Division and ranger brigade commanders to take control of their forces so that they could maneuver properly. Meanwhile, the Marine and Ranger commanders continued to check all of their orders with their own chains of command, further delaying and discombobulating their operations. When Lam found out about this, he began issuing orders directly to brigades, battalions, and even lower formations, creating utter chaos in his command.[72]

Sensing an opportunity, the PAVN commanders went over to the attack on April 27. They found that Lam had committed so much to the counteroffensive that he had no depth to his positions and few reserves left to meet the renewed Communist assault. The PAVN forces punched through the exhausted and uncoordinated defenses and cracked the I Corps river line. The Northerners were only slowed by massive, continuous American air strikes. Giai then asked to fall back to establish a new line along the Thach Han River, but Lam forbade it. Within days, the 3rd Division collapsed completely and PAVN was able to take Quang Tri City, the first South Vietnamese provincial capital it had ever taken.[73]

Meanwhile, in the central highlands, the North Vietnamese forces were driving on Kontum to unhinge the northern flank of the II Corps' defenses. Kontum was defended by the ARVN 23rd Division under Colonel Ly Tong Ba, who was not corrupt and considered better than most ARVN division commanders. However, Ba was only a colonel, like most of his brigade commanders, who resented him and were not always willing to obey his orders. Moreover, Colonel Ba had some of the same problems as Brigadier General Giai. Like Giai, Ba had a number of Ranger, Airborne, and Regional Force (the famous "Ruff-Puffs") formations under his command, all of which saw their parent formations as their primary commanders. Inevitably, this made it difficult for Ba to coordinate operations, and on May 1, when PAVN assaulted several positions held by ARVN Rangers, the Ranger Group commander ordered them to withdraw, opening a hole in Ba's lines that enabled the PAVN to overrun most of the defensive positions forward of Kontum.

Yet Colonel Ba did well at Kontum, even more so than his counterpart, Brigadier General Hung, at An Loc. Ba was active and energetic, overseeing the construction of new defensive positions, pressing his subordinates to patrol aggressively, and moving among his troops to bolster their morale and understand their situations. Moreover, although the II Corps commander, Lt. General Dzu, remained paralyzed, his American advisor, John Paul Vann, took over fire support coordination and secured tremendous American air power to help Ba's division hold.[74]

On May 14, Hanoi attacked Kontum itself. A massive tank-infantry force backed by plentiful artillery broke through the ARVN lines but was then pulverized by B-52 ARC LIGHT strikes. The North Vietnamese kept attacking, launching follow-on assaults on May 16 and 19.[75] These had to be stopped by determined counterattacks by Ba's reserves, which acted with "well-disciplined fire and movement."[76] Ultimately, the Northern assault petered out as the constant pummeling from the B-52s hamstrung PAVN's ability to reinforce the attack.[77]

The Tide Turns. By late April, Hanoi seemed to be winning on every front and the ARVN looked close to breaking. This forced Thieu to address the incompetence of his corps commanders. In II Corps, he sacked the ineffective Dzu and replaced him with Major General Nguyen Van Toan. Toan was just as corrupt and politically tied to Thieu, but had an upbeat demeanor helpful to morale, and of greatest importance, he was willing to hand over the conduct of the battle to Vann and Ba.[78] In I Corps, Thieu finally relieved Lt. General Lam and replaced him with South Vietnam's finest battlefield commander, Lt. General Ngo Quang Truong. He also replaced the commander of the Marine Division with a general more willing to work with the corps commanders—and someone more highly regarded by the Americans. Finally, Thieu sacked Brigadier General Giai and had him court-martialed.[79]

These changes in command led to an immediate improvement in Saigon's fortunes. In II Corps, the North launched one last effort to take Kontum on May 25. Once again, a well-designed assault punched through the ARVN lines, but once again massive air power prevented it from wiping out the defenders. Colonel Ba again counterattacked and retook the town. Further attacks in late July regained virtually all of the II Corps territory lost to the Communists. The Northerners left 4,000 dead in Kontum, and ultimately lost 20,000–40,000 troops and about 100 tanks in the fighting in the central highlands.[80]

Farther north in I Corps, Truong turned in a virtuoso performance. He pulled 3rd ARVN Division offline and sent it south to regroup. He replaced it with his own former command, the elite 1st ARVN division, which deployed to defend the old imperial capital of Hue. Truong arrayed the 1st in depth and skillfully employed his reserves, encouraging and enabling his subordinate commanders to react as they saw fit and counterattack aggressively as circumstances required or permitted. Once the 1st Division had blunted the PAVN assault on Hue, Truong launched his own counteroffensive. While the 1st Division mounted supporting attacks on the flanks, the Marine Division moved to retake Quang Tri City itself. The Marines, under their new division commander, Brigadier General Bui The Lan, fought extremely well in bloody house-to-house fighting to clear the Communists from Quang Tri City. Through the summer, Truong mounted a series of small, well-designed attacks that slowly levered the North Vietnamese out of one forward position after another, helped greatly by relentless American air strikes. Although I Corps could not retake all of its lost terrain, Truong pushed PAVN back from the main population centers in the north and reopened all of the key transportation routes.[81]

By September, the Easter Offensive was over. PAVN had taken 100,000 casualties and lost more than half of its tanks and artillery—mostly to American air power. For its part, ARVN took 60,000 casualties and lost 150 tanks of its own.[82] Northern losses were so heavy that the PAVN chief of staff told the Politburo that they would not be able to try another such offensive for three to five years. Nevertheless, the South had come close to disaster, and even in defeat, the North had made significant territorial gains that would enable them to launch their 1975 offensive from better start lines than they had in 1972.

ARVN Performance in the Easter Offensive. It is hard to apportion responsibility for Saigon's victory in the Easter Offensive. The American air effort in
support of the ARVN was simply unparalleled. No army in history has been
pounded as hard from the air as the PAVN during the Easter Offensive: not
the Wehrmacht in Normandy in 1944, not the Iraqis in DESERT STORM
in 1991, not ISIS in 2014–2017. By May 1972, American air forces in the
region had built up to about 600 tactical aircraft, 171 B-52s, and 28 fixed-
wing gunships.[83] During the first 60 days of the campaign, American and
South Vietnamese tactical aircraft still averaged 300 ground attack sorties
per day in poor weather, in addition to 45 B-52 sorties per day. In July 1972
alone, the United States flew a mind-boggling 2,054 ARC LIGHT missions
(each comprising at least 3 B-52s), a daily average of 66.[84] This air campaign
inflicted the vast majority of damage on the PAVN and stopped or hobbled
many of its assaults.[85]

Nevertheless, victory in 1972 was ultimately the result of a hammer-and-
anvil approach: US air power was the hammer, and it was awesome. But it
could not win the campaign on its own. It required an anvil, and that was
the ARVN. South Vietnamese ground units forced PAVN to concentrate in
places where they could be smashed by the B-52s. And in many places, South
Vietnamese soldiers still had to halt the North Vietnamese offensives in hard
fighting on the ground. General Abrams remarked after the invasion, "The
Vietnamese had to stand and fight. [If they hadn't], ten times the [air] power
we've got wouldn't have stopped them."[86]

At the tactical level, ARVN performance was uneven. Some units evinced
excellent unit cohesion, standing and fighting in the worst situations, while
others disintegrated under relatively mild pressure.[87] Ultimately, however,
enough South Vietnamese units held together and held their ground to allow
American air power to slaughter the North Vietnamese. For every collapse by
units such as the 56th and 57th Infantry Regiments, one can point to remarkable performances turned in by units such as the 147th and 258th Marine
Brigades (and the 20th Armored Battalion) at Quang Tri City.[88] Where ARVN
units broke, it was typically because their unit commanders had deserted or
proved incompetent, because they were put in untenable positions by still
higher level leaders, or because civilian refugees had compromised their unit
integrity. There were a number of incidents during the Easter Offensive where
civilian refugees badly undermined the morale of ARVN units.[89] In particular,
the first large-scale instances of what would come to be called ARVN's "family
syndrome"—soldiers deserting their units to try to find, protect, or rescue
their families—emerged in 1972.

On the whole, South Vietnamese junior officers were nothing to brag about, and some were infected by the politicization that plagued their senior ranks. But there were at least as many competent, even skillful junior officers, and on the whole their performance was at least adequate. There are numerous examples of ARVN junior officers employing good combined arms integration, although there were probably an equal number who did poorly.[90] In those cases, the primary culprit was the inappropriate and inadequate American training programs, which still focused overwhelmingly on small-scale search-and-destroy missions to the neglect of large-scale conventional combat.[91] Likewise, the historical accounts of the fighting are rife with instances in which ARVN junior officers demonstrated initiative and aggressiveness, shifting forces in response to PAVN penetrations, counterattacking hard, and maneuvering for advantage. That was particularly true for the Marine, Airborne, and 1st Divisions, but it was also true of line formations such as the 44th and 45th Infantry Regiments at Kontum, the 71st Ranger Battalion at Ben Het, the 47th Infantry Regiment at Dak To, and even the Regional Forces at Kontum, to name just a few examples.[92]

Finally, although ARVN armored formations were very limited in 1972 and its air force was vastly overshadowed by the American air campaign, both performed reasonably well and had some notable victories.[93] The M-48 Patton-equipped 20th Tank Regiment turned in a particularly good performance, repeatedly outflanking PAVN armor and knocking out almost a dozen enemy tanks at roughly 3,000 yards in one engagement on April 2nd. As one of their American advisors pointed out, "That kind of gunnery is on a par with the Israelis in the Sinai [in 1973] and probably better than all but the very finest U.S. tank units could accomplish."[94]

Once again, the key variable throughout the Easter Offensive was ARVN senior officer performance. Whenever ARVN corps and division commanders performed poorly, the forces they commanded collapsed. Generals Lam, Dzu, Minh, and Giai, as well as Colonel Dat were all terrible commanders who presided over disastrous defeats. However, whenever ARVN corps and divisions were well led (or even adequately led in the case of Hung's 22nd Division and Toan's II Corps), their subordinate formations did fine and were able to defeat the North Vietnamese by playing anvil to US air power's hammer.[95] I Corps was the most dramatic example, falling apart under Lam and then roaring back to smash the Northern invaders under Truong.[96] In effect, Toan did the same in II Corps and Hung with the 5th Division, by simply deferring to their American advisors.[97] American military personnel in South Vietnam during the Easter Offensive from top to bottom cited poor ARVN senior leadership as the most important problem—and in April and May, as the problem that could cause the fall of South Vietnam if it were not rectified.[98]

Clearly, ARVN's junior officers were not the primary cause of South Vietnam's problems. Saigon's generals were. When properly led, ARVN units and their tactical commanders performed well enough to defeat their PAVN adversaries with massive American air support. When poorly led, not even massive American air support could save them. Ultimately, Saigon was only able to win out when ARVN's best generals—all of whom were, not coincidentally, apolitical and uncorrupted—took over.

The Fall of South Vietnam, 1975

By the time the North was ready to resume the war in earnest, a lot had changed. For starters, PAVN was considerably stronger than before. The Soviets and Chinese resupplied the North with huge amounts of equipment to make good the losses of 1972. More than that, the Soviets were now providing more training in conventional warfare, and PAVN troops were getting time to practice and internalize the concepts. Although the Easter Offensive was halted with horrific losses, the North had held on to important terrain in western South Vietnam, and Hanoi built a second logistical network, the Truong Son Corridor, in this territory to supplement the Ho Chi Minh Trail and bring PAVN forces closer to South Vietnam's cities. As a result, North Vietnam's military had increased to over 650,000 men, with at least 200,000 troops, 700 tanks, 450 artillery pieces, and 100,000 support troops, already in South Vietnam. At least another 40,000 combat troops and 50,000 support personnel were waiting in Cambodia and Laos.[99]

Of course, the South had not stood still either. Vietnamization had proceeded apace, with an ever-greater emphasis on conventional, combined arms operations. The RVNAF also tried to expand its forces and reached nearly 1 million men, although like their American mentors, far too few were in combat units and far too many were assigned to combat support and combat service support functions. Finally, the United States had managed to convince Thieu to sack a small number of his absolute worst senior officers and replace them with better ones.[100]

There was one big problem, however. The improvement in ARVN's capabilities and its victory in 1972 had convinced Thieu that it could successfully defend the entire country, despite the (greater) increase in PAVN strength. ARVN and US intelligence recognized this mistake, and most of Thieu's best commanders recommended that he cede northern South Vietnam,

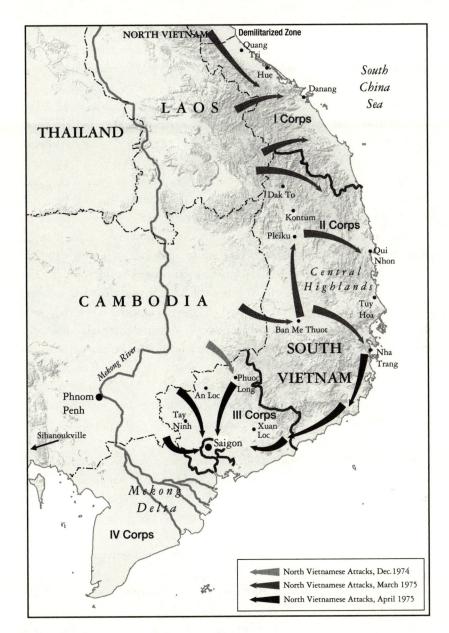

MAP 19 The Fall of South Vietnam, 1975

which was difficult to defend and had less than 15 percent of the population, but Thieu would not hear of it. Yet in 1969, 22 American and ARVN divisions were defending the same territory that 13 ARVN divisions would have to hold in 1975. Moreover, because of the loss of terrain to the North in 1972, ARVN's front was less defensible than in 1969 or 1972. In addition, the ARVN had virtually no strategic reserves to deal with a PAVN breakthrough because both the Marine and Airborne Divisions remained in I Corps, committed to holding the long, thin front lines.[101]

To make matters worse, the United States had truly abandoned South Vietnam after Watergate and Nixon's fall. American advisors and air power were both withdrawn in 1973. Then, at the end of that year, Congress began to drastically cut military assistance to Saigon.[102]

The American withdrawal and aid cuts had a profound impact on South Vietnamese military strength. As George Veith, author of the best history of the 1975 campaign, put it, "A military that depended heavily on firepower and mobility to offset the Communist propensity to mass forces suddenly had its two most important advantages sharply curtailed."[103] In October 1974, Saigon limited all military operations to just one 10-day operation per corps per month. In February 1975, it went further, ordering its corps to only mount battalion-sized or larger operations when they were absolutely necessary. Fuel shortages became so acute that Saigon limited helicopter flights for medevac missions. Ammunition allocations were cut from 100 rounds per day in 1973 to just 4 per day in 1974, and ARVN soldiers were issued only 85 bullets per month.[104] The North's military analysts correctly assessed that ammunition shortages had reduced ARVN firepower by 60 percent, and fuel and spare parts shortages had reduced RVNAF mobility by 50 percent.[105]

Altogether, the material shortfalls and the sense of American abandonment undermined the morale of both the ARVN and the wider populace. Unlike in 1972 where the vast commitment of US air power and the critical activity of US advisors reassured the South Vietnamese that Washington had their back, this time around they felt very much alone. As much as anything, this is why South Vietnamese morale was so fragile, and why small setbacks snowballed into major calamities.[106]

South Vietnamese morale also took major hits from the state of the economy. The withdrawal of American forces and all of the money they spent in South Vietnam, both from soldiers and the US government, crippled the South's economy. Jacked up by the Middle East oil embargo of 1973, inflation hit 92 percent in 1974 while unemployment topped 20 percent. A survey in the summer of 1974 found that 90 percent of ARVN soldiers were not being paid enough to support their families. Meanwhile, pervasive corruption undermined the willingness of people and soldiers to fight for a government increasingly seen as callous and illegitimate. ARVN's annual defection rate increased to 25 percent of total strength in 1973–1974.[107]

Although Thieu may not have believed that America was gone, never to return, the North Vietnamese leadership apparently did. They recognized that the American departure—coupled with the improvement and expansion of their own forces—had shifted the odds in their favor. Nevertheless, Hanoi was still unsure of the military balance and did not want to mistakenly over-commit as it had in 1972. Consequently, the 1975 offensive was merely intended to weaken the ARVN and set it up for what Hanoi hoped would be the knockout blow in 1976.[108]

The North Attacks. Thus, Hanoi's war-winning offensive began small and gathered steam as the North took the measure of its rival and found it wanting. In December 1974, a large PAVN force of armor, artillery, and infantry attacked Phuoc Long in III Corps, north of Saigon. The Communists had a 4:1 numerical advantage and demonstrated greatly improved combined arms integration thanks to their Russian training. They overran the city and nearby positions in less than a month, leading to the fall of the entire province.[109]

The loss of Phuoc Long created a problem for Thieu. Losing a symbolically important provincial capital made South Vietnam look weak and threatened his "defend everywhere" strategy. But he simply did not have the reserves to retake it, and lacked the airlift assets to move large forces from somewhere else quickly even if they were available. He decided that III Corps would just have to handle the problem itself. However, as usual, he saw the political threat posed by the defeat as more dangerous than the military loss. He became anxious about coup plots and focused his energy on uncovering them. He became more secretive than usual and stopped confiding his intentions to his generals, which meant that there was no contingency planning for the events to come.[110]

For its part, the North Vietnamese Politburo saw Phuoc Long as a hopeful sign and decided to press their advantage. They chose to mount a larger attack against Ban Me Thuot, northeast of Phuoc Long in the ARVN II Corps sector. Ban Me Thuot was a critical position in the southern sector of South Vietnam's central highlands and taking it would put PAVN in position to cut the country in two. Hanoi employed a sophisticated deception plan to convince the ARVN II Corps that a major attack was coming, but farther north, at Kontum and Pleiku. Although ARVN intelligence correctly recognized this as a feint, the II Corps commander, Lt. General Pham Van Phu, believed it, and massed his forces in the north, leaving only one regiment to defend Ban Me Thuot.

PAVN attacked on March 1, 1975, with a 5:1 advantage in troops, 1.2:1 advantage in tanks, and a 2:1 advantage in artillery. Moreover, the North Vietnamese force was simply better: its tanks were more capable, its commanders more aggressive, its soldiers more motivated, and its officers understood combined arms warfare better. Lt. General Phu realized his mistake quickly, and begged Saigon for reinforcements to defend the city and the mobility assets to get them there, but the ARVN high command had none of either. Eventually, Phu tried to fly in a brigade of his own but could not get them there in time. By March 11, the city had fallen.[111]

Although it did not seem like it at the time, the fall of Ban Me Thuot was the beginning of the end of South Vietnam. The catalyst, once again, was the mistakes of Saigon's senior leadership, this time in the person of Thieu himself. The easy Northern conquests of Phuoc Long and Ban Me Thuot convinced the general-turned-president that he could not hold everywhere and trying to do so would simply allow the North to pick off key defensive positions at their leisure, eventually compromising the entire defense of South Vietnam. He also recognized that the North could develop its success at Ban Me Thuot into a wider offensive to drive to the sea and cut off I and II Corps from the rest of the country.

In light of this, Thieu made a momentous decision: the ARVN would abandon northern South Vietnam and pull back to defend only Saigon and the Mekong Delta, thereby shortening its defensive lines and freeing up units that could be used as reserves. While this was effectively what his best generals had recommended to him after the Easter Offensive, trying it in the midst of a major PAVN offensive was not at all what they had had in mind. Thieu wanted the withdrawal to happen immediately—in less than 10 days—but neither the ARVN General Staff nor any of the corps had planned for such a massive, sudden retreat. Thieu ordered it anyway, and demanded that Truong's I Corps give up the Airborne Division immediately so that it could be moved back to Saigon to stage for a counteroffensive against Ban Me Thuot.[112]

That's when the ARVN and all of South Vietnam fell apart. In addition to pulling the Airborne from I Corps, Thieu had II Corps try to withdraw to Saigon while the rest of I Corps attempted to pull back into defensive enclaves around Danang and Hue. He added to the confusion by flip-flopping over whether Hue should be defended. All of these moves, beginning with the withdrawal of the Airborne, prompted a torrent of civilian refugees. The unorganized retreat quickly turned into a rout. Redeploying ARVN formations became intermingled and disorganized by the refugee flows. And "family syndrome" resulted in mass desertions by soldiers who went to find their loved ones and escort them to safety.[113]

To their credit, North Vietnamese leaders in the field and in Hanoi recognized what was happening. They were helped enormously by well-placed spies who provided key information on Thieu's decision to evacuate the north, the order of battle of ARVN forces, and the specific retreat orders issued to the field commanders. Northern military leaders pressed their combat formations for greater speed to further disrupt ARVN units and prevent them from reaching new, defensible positions. Here as well, PAVN's new conventional capabilities, coupled with aggressive leadership, allowed them to inflict terrible casualties on both the retreating ARVN units and the civilian refugees, which prompted even more to flee and even more ARVN personnel to look to safeguard their families.

In every instance during the disintegration of the ARVN and the fall of South Vietnam, the stone that started each avalanche was poor strategic leadership. For instance, when Thieu ordered Lt. General Phu to pull II Corps back out of the Central Highlands and down to the Saigon area, Phu did not bother to tell the RF/PF formations, hoping they would remain in place to hold back the PAVN offensive. Instead, when the Ruff-Puffs saw the ARVN formations pulling out with no orders of their own, they bolted. This allowed the PAVN forces to catch many ARVN units from behind and maul them as they retreated. Moreover, because the Ruff-Puffs were so closely tied to the people, it exacerbated the civilian refugee surge southward.[114] Histories of the war also note that in many cases, senior officers simply abandoned their formations after the retreat order was issued, but many junior officers ("battalion commanders and lower officers," according to General Thinh, the commander of II Corps artillery) stayed with their men and tried to fight back against the North Vietnamese or at least keep their units together as they retreated south. Nevertheless, their formations crumbled from panic, refugees, and enemy attack.[115] The retreat led to the loss of 75 percent of II Corps' combat power.[116]

At that point, even Lt. General Truong could not save the I Corps farther north. As usual, Truong led his men well. When informed of the decision to withdraw, he tried to organize a fighting withdrawal to the coastal cities to allow civilians the time to escape and create the military conditions that might make a political deal with Hanoi possible. But when word of the withdrawals from Kontum and Pleiku spread north, South Vietnamese civilians created another surge of refugees out of the I Corps sector, some fleeing south but many others toward the ports of Hue and Danang to find boats to the south. Hanoi attacked the four divisions of I Corps with nine divisions of its own. Nevertheless, Truong's units—the Marine Division, and the 1st, 2nd, and even the 3rd ARVN Divisions—all fought well, and it was neither PAVN numbers nor skill that did them in but the failures of Saigon and the tidal wave of civilian refugees. All four divisions tried to hold back the PAVN forces, and succeeded in delaying them, after which they attempted to conduct staggered withdrawals, leapfrogging their units back toward the coast. Yet one by one, the Marines last of all, they were overwhelmed by the civilian hordes, as well as a hemorrhage of desertions from family syndrome stemming from the avalanche of refugees.[117]

For a few weeks, ARVN resistance stiffened as the PAVN offensive pushed on toward Saigon. In South Vietnam's southern provinces, ARVN formations stood and fought and forced the North Vietnamese units to halt or find alternative routes south. In particular, the ARVN 22nd Division fought "valiantly" in the words of the US defense attaché to defend Qui Nhon, Tay Hoa, and Nha Trang against a larger PAVN force. However, in every case, the North Vietnamese commanders either brought up reinforcements that enabled them to overpower the ARVN units or bypass them.[118]

The best known of these stands was by the ARVN 18th Division at Xuan Loc in mid-April. The 18th was led by a superb commander, Brigadier General Le Minh Dao, whose defensive preparations were smart, creative, and on the mark regarding likely PAVN intentions. For 11 days, the 18th held off three PAVN divisions. By April 20, however, Hanoi's generals had surrounded Xuan Loc, forcing the 18th to retreat. Once again, Dao did a masterful job conducting the retreat, but Xuan Loc was no more than a single stone trying to halt the current of the North Vietnamese invasion. It simply wasn't enough.[119] On April 21, Thieu resigned, throwing the South Vietnamese government into political turmoil.

Five days later, PAVN attacked Saigon itself. By then, the ARVN had only about 125,000 men to defend the capital. Against them, PAVN was able to concentrate 270,000 men with 20 artillery battalions.[120] As expected the Airborne Division and the remnants of the Marine Division fought hard and well in defense of the capital. They inflicted heavy losses and time delays on the Communists as did several other ARVN formations. But the weight of PAVN's numbers, its growing skill, and the preponderance of firepower enabled them to wrest chunks of the city from the defenders with no real expectation that anything short of a miracle would alter the inevitable outcome. Then, on April 29th, the Corps Commander, Lt. General Toan, abruptly fled to a US Navy ship patrolling offshore. With Toan's flight, ARVN command and control collapsed. What had been a vicious battle that seemed likely to grind on for weeks or months was suddenly over, and the Communists had won.[121]

South Vietnamese and Arab Military Effectiveness

It is hard to conclude that the ARVN did anything but underperform. With all of the money lavished on it and massive American support it consistently punched below its weight. But it was not entirely hapless either, and even its final defeat demonstrated both its relative strengths and weaknesses. For our purposes, what matters most is the ways in which the ARVN was both like and unlike the Arab armed forces. Both shed important light on the role of politicization in Arab military effectiveness.

Of greatest importance, the performance of ARVN tactical commanders was not a primary reason for its failures and eventual defeat, nor did it mimic the striking patterns evinced by the modern Arab armies. Overall, ARVN's junior officers were a mixed bag, although they do seem to have improved over time as the US and South Vietnamese governments both came to take their training more seriously. ARVN tactical performance was noticeably better in 1972 than it had been in either the 1970 Cambodian incursion or the 1971 Laotian incursion, and it was arguably better in 1975 than it had been in 1972. It was primarily the Marines, Airborne, and 1st Divisions along with a handful of armored, ranger, and Regional Force brigades that fought well in 1972, and it was primarily US air power that carried the vast weight of effort. In 1975, not only did those same formations perform well again, but so too did the 2nd, 3rd, 7th, 18th, 21st, and 22nd Divisions, along with a number of independent brigades, regiments, and battalions. Certainly, far more ARVN formations stood and fought—and fought better—in 1975 than had been the case in 1972.

Of course, there were still too many South Vietnamese junior officers who performed poorly or simply abandoned their troops and fled in 1975. Politicization did have a "trickle-down" effect to reach some tactical commanders. But like the economic theory of the same name, the impact on those at lower levels was far, far less than imagined by its theoreticians. For instance, Veith observed that "Most Western journalists portrayed RVNAF officers as deserting their men in droves. In reality, very few regular Army or Marine officers commanding troops during the final days left their soldiers."[122] Indeed, to the extent that such flights did occur, senior commanders kicked them off, causing their headquarters staffs to follow suit, and so compromise the combat capability of the field formations.[123]

In the final campaign, ARVN units regularly launched tactical counterattacks, and many succeeded at places like Ban Me Thuot, Ben Cau, Hue, Bong Mountain, the Bo river, Long An, Thua Thua, Can Tho, Du Long, Thanh Son, Phan Rang, and Xuan Loc.[124] For instance, at Xuan Loc, the heretofore belittled 18th ARVN Division repeatedly counterattacked to reverse PAVN gains, including a brilliant counterstroke by a combined arms task force that outflanked and nearly enveloped the most dangerous initial North Vietnamese penetration.[125] ARVN junior officers were often aggressive and creative, and showed considerable initiative, such as Lt. Colonel Le Van But and Major Tran Cong Hanh of 3rd Airborne Brigade, who improvised a remarkable helicopter exfiltration that rescued 800 badly needed Airborne soldiers scattered in the hills around the M'Drak Pass.[126] ARVN tactical commanders also frequently shifted their forces to meet PAVN attacks and maneuvered for advantage against PAVN units.[127] For instance, at Can Tho, Lt. Colonel Mach Van Truong created a combined arms reserve of an infantry regiment and an armored cavalry squadron. When the PAVN 4th Division attacked, his front-line troops stopped the assault with air and helicopter support, and then he swung this reserve into their rear and counterattacked, mauling the PAVN division and forcing Hanoi to bypass Can Tho altogether.[128]

Many ARVN units also demonstrated better combined arms cooperation than they had in the past.[129] Veith has called the performance of the ARVN 3rd Armored Cavalry Regiment (ACR) at Duc Hue "a remarkable combined-arms operation."[130] Within the combined arms teams, ARVN armor appears to have improved somewhat, with the 3rd ACR as the truly standout formation. ARVN fire support had come even farther since their near-total reliance on the Americans in 1972. Throughout the 1975 fighting, ARVN artillery wrought havoc on the PAVN attackers.[131]

Perhaps more surprising still was how much the South Vietnamese air force improved, mounting numerous ground attack missions that were a major problem for Communist forces. North Vietnamese unit histories repeatedly cite South Vietnamese Air Force (VNAF) air strikes as having broken up their advances and beaten up their forces. For instance, a PAVN history of the fighting at Cam Ranh Bay records that "Enemy aircraft savagely bombed and strafed our forces," while another notes that VNAF air attacks turned Route 450 "into a flaming hell."[132] Many VNAF squadrons flew constant sorties, and there is considerable evidence from both sides that VNAF air sorties were highly effective.[133] Indeed, at Xuan Loc, PAVN forces began their final assault by pummeling nearby Bien Hoa airbase with long-range howitzer fire because VNAF strikes from the base had been such a problem for previous assaults.[134] Similarly, before the assault on Saigon, Hanoi waited to concentrate 800 AAA guns plus a regiment of SA-2 missiles and numerous SA-7s to ensure that the VNAF would not be able to hamstring the attack.[135] Ultimately, the VNAF was no substitute for US air power, but it fought well and inflicted considerable damage on PAVN units—far more damage than any Arab air force ever inflicted on any foe, even in similar circumstances in which they had air superiority (Iraq during the latter half of the Iran-Iraq War) or air supremacy (Libya in Chad).

Once again, the best evidence that tactical leadership was not the same Achilles heel for the ARVN as it was for the Arabs is in the exceptions that prove the rule. Namely, whenever ARVN corps and divisions had competent leaders, the units under their command fought well—remarkably well in many cases. It is hard to find examples of South Vietnamese generals let down by the poor performance of their subordinates the way that the Egyptian and Syrian high commands were in 1973, the Jordanians in 1967, or the Iraqis time and again. The consistent pattern was that when South Vietnamese divisions and corps were well led by generals like Truong and Dao (or even adequately led, like Hung at An Loc in 1972), they fought well, but whenever they were led badly by men like Lam, Dzu, Toan, and Thieu himself, they fell apart.[136] The key variable was clearly their senior leadership, which in turn was a product of politicization.

Thieu was the ultimate source of the problems that brought down South Vietnam. Not just in his foolish strategic decisions to defend everywhere and then suddenly withdraw in the face of the PAVN attack—and to insist on doing so immediately so that no plans could be devised to give the withdrawal any chance of success—but also in his handling of more routine matters. Thieu denied his general staff any oversight of the corps commanders and regularly bypassed them altogether, issuing orders of his own directly to the corps commanders. He did this to prevent any general from becoming strong enough to overthrow his regime, but it also kept the ARVN from being strong enough to defend his regime against a conventional invasion.

Three other issues need to be addressed. The first is simply to note that South Vietnam's palace-guard formations, the Marines, Airborne, and armored formations, fought very well. In the vast majority of cases, they fought much *better* than ARVN's line formations, despite their own politicized leadership and the complications this introduced in Laos and the Easter Offensive. This is reminiscent of the better performance of Iraq's Republican Guard, suggesting that palace guardism may not be as damaging as is often claimed.

Then there is the matter of morale, both across the ARVN and among the wider population of South Vietnam. There is no question that both were fragile at the start of the 1975 offensive. But South Vietnamese morale was fragile before the Easter Offensive too, and it did not crack then. Instead, it held to enable the combination of ARVN ground and American air forces to win out. In 1975, the same was largely true. The attack itself did not cause a collapse of morale, thereby engendering a general disintegration. Rather, some small, isolated military failures led to strategic misjudgments that produced a collapse of morale, which caused a general disintegration. Again, ARVN units fought very hard in many places, and more ARVN formations fought well than fought badly.[137] Even the Regional and Popular Forces fought surprisingly hard in many instances.[138] Ultimately, a handful of PAVN successes provoked some terrible strategic decisions that compromised the ability of South Vietnamese units to fight and win, and simultaneously started a tsunami of refugees that engulfed those units. The key was, once again, the strategic leadership.

Finally, as we contemplate what led to South Vietnamese defeat in 1975 that differed from the Arab experience, we have to recognize that what ultimately did in the ARVN was less the PAVN than the refugees. Although Lt. General Truong was incredibly bitter about Thieu's handling of the withdrawal from I Corps, he nonetheless wrote after the war that "The most significant problem facing me were the hundreds of thousands of refugees who moved in an uncontrollable mass to Danang. This force represented a greater danger and contributed more to the defeat of the ARVN than did the enemy. Combat units attempting to deploy . . . were swallowed up in the mass of humanity which choked Route 1 and intermediate land routes. Confusion, frustration and ultimately panic began to grip some combat units."[139] Anthony Joes likewise concluded that "There is no debate that the disintegration of the South Vietnamese armed forces in MRs I and II was due not to the actions of the enemy but to a collapse of morale, and that this in turn was caused above all by the failure of the Thieu government to anticipate or deal adequately with the enormous effusion of refugees let loose by the ARVN redeployment."[140]

CHAPTER 9 | Politicization and
the Argentine Armed Forces

Between World War II and the return of democracy after the
Falklands War, the Argentine military was one of the most heavily
politicized in the world. A military junta composed of the three service chiefs
had ruled since 1976. This was only the most recent in a long series of military
takeovers. Indeed, so bad was the politicization of the Argentine military that
in 1962 the Army and Navy had actually fought pitched battles against each
other that caused several thousand casualties to decide which would run the
government.[1]

By the late 1970s, the military leadership was deeply distracted from military issues by economic and social problems, and was riven by internal factions
spawned by these political dilemmas.[2] Despite the efforts of US military
advisers and an exaggerated threat from Chile, Argentine military forces were
wholly absorbed with internal security problems. The "Dirty War" against
militant factions opposed to military rule had been the central focus of the
military throughout the late 1970s.[3]

Moreover, the immersion of the Argentine military in politics instilled
in the generals and admirals running the government a deep fear of coups
from other elements in the armed forces. To ensure their grip on power, they
imposed heavy loyalty requirements on the officer corps; punished capable,
aggressive senior commanders; warped the command structure to limit the
independence of their subordinates; and shot unsuccessful commanders for
jeopardizing the legitimacy of the regime.[4]

In other words, the Argentines suffered from heavy doses of all three variants of politicization.

Nevertheless, on April 2, 1982, Argentina put teeth into its long-standing claim on the British-ruled Falklands Islands by invading and seizing them outright. The Argentines employed their best units and brought overwhelming force to the islands. The operation was well planned and competently conducted, and even the British were impressed. In particular, intelligence received by Buenos Aires at the last minute indicated that the British garrison in the Falklands was twice as large as the Argentines had originally believed, forcing a rewrite of the invasion plans. The Argentines were able to put together a completely new plan in less than 24 hours, transmit it to the various units, and implement it as designed.[5]

The only part of the invasion that did not go according to plan was London's response. The Argentines were stunned when the Thatcher government refused to abide by Buenos Aires' unilateral annexation of the islands and instead dispatched a very sizable (especially by the standards of the British armed forces of the time) expeditionary force to retake the Falklands. The Argentines had expected the British to reluctantly acquiesce to their invasion and so had made no preparations for defending the islands against a major British military effort. Moreover, Buenos Aires kept most of its best units back to defend against a possible Chilean attack. As a result, the Argentines did not deploy a large force to defend the islands, they did not bother to fortify the islands, and they neither made any effort to improve the Falklands' infrastructure to support military operations nor did they stockpile supplies in case the British fleet blockaded the islands.[6]

After withdrawing the elite formations that had conducted the invasion, the Argentines started sending other units there from all over the country. They brought no armor, and little artillery, helicopters, or motor transport. In addition, they did not bring materials for building barracks, even though the soft ground and harsh weather of the Falklands made it difficult to remain in the field for long. There was little rhyme or reason to their choice of reinforcements, and the final Argentine garrison was a hodgepodge of formations. Elements of different army brigades from all over the country were sent to the islands. Some units had no cold-weather clothing or training. Others were sent without any of their heavy weaponry.[7]

As a result, by the time combat was joined between the two sides in early May, the balance of forces appeared to lean toward Argentina, but actually favored the British. Buenos Aires had roughly 13,000 military personnel on the islands with forty-two 105-mm howitzers, four 155-mm howitzers, and 12 Panhard armored cars. The Argentine air forces boasted over 200 combat aircraft, and the Navy had 25 warships, including one old aircraft carrier. Against them, the British eventually massed 11,000 troops with 30 howitzers and 18 light tanks, 38 aircraft, and 51 warships including five nuclear attack subs and two small but modern aircraft carriers.[8]

Even these numbers were deceptive, however. In actuality, the Argentines had only nine combat battalions on the island—against eight British combat battalions—and the rest of their troops were combat service support, occupation forces, and administrative personnel. Although the Argentines had slightly more artillery than the British, the British howitzers were more modern and were backed by ceaseless fire support from the 4.5-inch guns of their fleet. Helicopters proved to be a critical factor in the combat because the soft terrain of the islands made cross-country movement hard: the Argentines had 26 while the British had over 200. Barely a hundred Argentine aircraft had the range to reach the Falklands given Buenos Aires' very limited aerial refueling assets and of these, only 75–80 were actually committed to the fight, the rest held back against Chile. Moreover, the best Argentine attack aircraft were its 30–40 A-4P Skyhawks—the earliest model of an obsolete plane—because its Mirage IIIs and Daggers (Israeli versions of the Mirage) were not optimal for long-distance ship-attack missions. Argentina had five Super Etendard naval-strike aircraft, but had received them only months before and had only five Exocet anti-ship missiles to use with them. Finally, the British fleet was vastly more powerful and modern than the Argentine Navy, and its nuclear-powered attack subs (SSNs) alone kept the Argentine ships bottled up in mainland ports starting in early May. Thus, the real material balance favored the British by a significant margin.[9]

Initial Skirmishes

The bulk of the British fleet arrived in the South Atlantic in late April, but was not yet ready to mount an invasion of the islands then. Instead, the British feigned an assault in an effort to draw out the Argentine Air Force and Navy and destroy them in advance of any actual amphibious operations. This led to a series of naval and air engagements on May 1–5.

The Argentine Air Force (AAF) conducted strikes against British destroyers and frigates around the islands, impressing the British with their flying skills but doing only minor damage to the ships. On May 2, the British sub HMS *Conqueror* sank Argentina's only cruiser, the aged *General Belgrano*. During the next two days Argentina's carrier task force located the two British aircraft carriers and tried to launch air strikes against them, but poor weather prevented it, and eventually the threat from the British SSNs forced them back to port. On May 4, Argentina's naval air force struck back at the British, sinking the new destroyer HMS *Sheffield* with an Exocet missile launched from a Super Etendard. Although the two sides had sustained about equal damage in these clashes, the British were surprised by the abilities of the Argentines, and pulled back east of the islands to await the rest of their forces.[10]

In two dogfights on May 1, four British Harrier fighters engaged four Mirages and Daggers, resulting in the loss of one Dagger and one Mirage. These engagements convinced the Argentines that trying to take on the highly maneuverable Harriers armed with the advanced AIM-9L Sidewinder heat-seeking missile at very low altitudes and at the extreme edge of the Mirage's range was not a winning proposition. Consequently, after May 1, the AAF flew no more counter-air missions and instead tried simply to avoid the Harriers to concentrate on attacking British ships.[11]

The British Come Ashore

On May 21, the British finally launched their invasion of the islands, landing the reinforced 3rd Commando Brigade on the west side of East Falkland Island. The Argentines responded with a determined air offensive against the Royal Navy. Over the next nine days, the Argentines flew 120 strike sorties against the British fleet. Bad weather, interservice disputes, and maintenance problems prevented a sustained effort from day to day, but on several, the Argentines were able to mount heavy raids. To avoid the SAMs and AAA on the British warships, the Argentine pilots attacked at extremely low altitudes, usually below 250 feet above the water. Although the Argentines lost 21 aircraft to British air defenses in that time—including 12 to Harriers—they sank 3 British warships with iron bombs and the huge British transport *Atlantic Conveyor* with an Exocet.[12] The Argentines might have done far more harm: they damaged another six ships with iron bombs that failed to detonate because they had not been properly fused for the low altitudes at which they were dropped. Given the ease with which small numbers of Argentine bombs sank other British ships, most or all of these other six ships likely would have sunk had the bombs that struck them exploded.[13]

Between May 21 and 27, British ground forces consolidated their beachhead on the west coast of East Falkland Island while the Argentines did nothing. Despite constant prodding from Buenos Aires to counterattack or at least harass the British ground forces while their beachhead was still vulnerable, the Argentine commander on the island, Major General Mario Menendez, remained

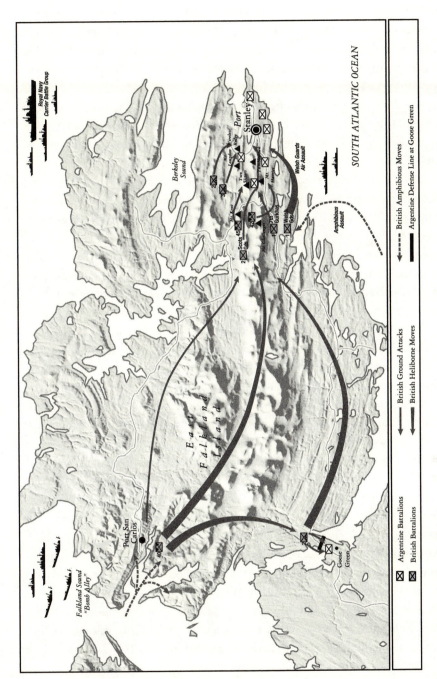

MAP 20 The Falklands War, 1982

inert. Indeed, although Argentine military intelligence had predicted that the British would land at San Carlos and then push overland toward Port Stanley on the east coast, Menendez believed the British landings were a diversion and the main attack would be a direct amphibious assault against Stanley. Consequently, he made little effort even to reinforce the small number of units guarding the line of hills west of Port Stanley.[14]

On May 28, the British began their breakout from the beachhead with an attack by the elite 2nd Parachute Battalion against the Argentine forces at Goose Green. Goose Green was defended by about a battalion's worth of troops, but this force consisted of bits and pieces drawn from three different battalions of at least two different brigades. The Argentine forces there had little in the way of winter clothing or supplies, and less than half their ostensible complement of heavy weapons. Although as many as 1,500 Argentines were at Goose Green, only about 600 were combat soldiers. In addition, the units at Goose Green were commanded by an Army general in Port Stanley who could not get out there to command his troops because the Argentine Air Force and Navy refused to move his headquarters without approval from their service chiefs, which could not be obtained before the battle.

The Argentines had built a formidable defensive system across the isthmus with multiple trench lines dug in depth, reinforcing bunkers and weapons pits, and very sophisticated interlocking fields of fire. However, they were not only defending against a British attack overland from the north, but also had to guard against an amphibious assault from the sea to both east and west. Thus, one battalion was essentially trying to cover 31 kilometers of front. Because the Argentines were trying to cover so much ground with so little force, the British attack at the north end of the isthmus enjoyed a 3:1 advantage in manpower.[15]

The British attacked the Argentine positions during the night of May 28/29 and prevailed in a fierce fight. The "Paras" worked their way through the Argentine security screen despite accurate Argentine artillery fire, but were stopped cold at the main defensive line. They attempted to attack both Argentine flanks simultaneously but the Argentines quickly pulled platoons from the coastal defenses to reinforce the threatened sectors and conducted local counterattacks that held the British. When the Paras regrouped and resumed their attack during the morning of May 29, they were able to force their way through the Argentine defenses by employing tremendous volumes of firepower, including using Milan antitank guided missiles (ATGMs) and Light Antitank Weapons (LAWs) to obliterate Argentine positions. In addition, one British platoon found that with the Argentine troops off the coastal defenses, they were able to wriggle along a low sea wall and turn the Argentine left flank. By noon the Argentines had committed their last reserves and the Paras had cleared many of their lines, but the defenders fought on. Finally, British Harriers hit the Argentine AAA battery at Goose Green airstrip with napalm and cluster bombs. The Argentines had been using these guns to support their final defenses, and only when they were silenced did the Argentine defenses fail.[16]

After Goose Green, the British began their overland march across East Falkland to Port Stanley while the Argentines remained passive. Although Argentine aerial reconnaissance and ground patrols provided a good sense of the movement of British troops across the island and their buildup for a major assault on Port Stanley from the west, General Menendez remained unconvinced. He redeployed a small number of his units to face the British advance from the west, but still kept at least half his forces dug-in along the coast around Port Stanley to repulse the British amphibious landing he was certain would come. The Argentine Air Force continued to conduct strikes against the British fleet when it could, but at a much reduced level as a result of combat losses and maintenance problems.[17]

The Battle for Port Stanley

The balance of forces around Port Stanley was about even, but the British held important advantages in their greater firepower and mobility, plus Argentina's continued neglect of the western approaches to the capital. General Menendez had about 8,400 personnel in and around the city, but only six combat battalions and three of them were still guarding the beaches. Against the three battalions dug-in on the hills guarding the town from the west the British mustered nearly their entire expeditionary force: over seven infantry battalions. Argentine defenses were haphazard. Some positions had been occupied for many weeks and were well fortified, while others had been occupied only days before the British assault and so were protected merely by hasty defenses. When the British attacked the three outermost Argentine positions on Mt. Longdon, Two Sisters, and Mt. Harriet they sent 1,800 crack troops in three battalions against 850 tired, hungry, frostbitten Argentines in five companies. Moreover, the British attack was preceded by three days of constant bombardment from mortars, artillery, naval guns, and Harrier strikes.[18]

The British assault on Port Stanley began on the night of June 11/12. British units conducted small, well-prepared, and heavily supported attacks against Argentine defensive positions and reduced the ring of defenses around Port Stanley bit by bit. The first assault was conducted by the 3rd Parachute Battalion against a company of Argentines on Mt. Longdon. Despite the unfavorable force ratio, the Argentine defenders were clever and active and had fortified their positions well. They forced the British to advance through a narrow killing zone, ambushing and counterattacking the Paras repeatedly, and inflicting heavy casualties on them. Eventually, the British took the position only by employing Milans, LAWs, artillery, and mortars.[19]

The British had a much easier time on Two Sisters. The Argentines had only occupied the position in the last week or two before the British attack, and the units sent there did not have any entrenching tools. Moreover, the Argentines deployed two companies on the hill from two different battalions, and left those companies under the command of their respective battalions. Thus, when the British 45th Commando Battalion assaulted the southern end of the hill and caught the Argentine company there in a double envelopment, the Argentine company on the north end made no effort to come to their aid. Also, the company on the southern end of the hill had no heavy weapons or transport, with the result that they were easily overwhelmed by British firepower.[20]

In the last attack of the night, the British 42nd Commando Battalion found a way through an undefended minefield, allowing them to attack the two Argentine companies on Mt. Harriet from the rear. The British soldiers were in among the Argentine reserves, headquarters, and mortar positions before the fight ever began, and they took the position and quickly scattered the defenders. Several Argentine junior officers tried to pull troops from the front lines to counterattack the British in their rear, but many of their soldiers panicked and fled, while others simply refused to obey any commands to fight or move. One officer managed to pull together a platoon for a counterattack but it was pinned and dispersed almost immediately by British artillery and mortar fire.[21]

The fighting during the first night proved to have been much harder than the British had expected, leading them to postpone the next round of attacks for 24 hours. All day on June 12, British artillery and naval guns continued to pound away at the Argentine second line of defenses, accompanied by constant air strikes from the Harriers. Then, during the night of June 13/14, the British resumed the offensive, attacking the Argentine units on Wireless Ridge and Tumbledown Mountain.[22]

The 2nd Parachute Battalion was responsible for taking Wireless Ridge, and it had learned from the fighting at Goose Green. The Paras arranged for extensive fire support including artillery, naval gunfire, mortars, and light tanks to accompany their attack. British artillery fired 6,000 shells during the 12-hour fight for these ridges. Defending this position, the Argentines had an exhausted company that had fallen back to Wireless Ridge after the British assaults on June 11, so it had not been there long and had not had time to adequately fortify its lines. The Paras conducted a simple frontal assault behind a wall of fire, which blew the Argentines off the northern ridgeline.

The Argentines attempted to fall back and regroup on the southern ridgeline, but the British hammered them with their guns and missiles and then sent a company around the Argentine left flank, allowing them to roll up the Argentine positions along the ridge. The Argentine brigade commander responsible for the defense of the western approaches to Port Stanley, Brigadier General Joffe, desperately scrambled for reinforcements to prevent the British from exploiting beyond Wireless Ridge, but had little luck because Menendez still refused to release any troops from the beaches. Joffe scraped together two small company-sized forces that conducted two uncoordinated counterattacks. These were clumsy efforts that the British quickly repulsed with their firepower.[23] One British parachute officer described these counterattacks as "quite sporting efforts, but without a sporting chance."[24]

The final battle of the war was also the hardest fought. A reinforced company of Argentina's elite 5th Marine Battalion held Tumbledown Mountain. They were attacked by the Scots Guards Battalion, a competent formation, but not the equal of the Paras or Commandos. The Guards hit the southern flank of the Argentine lines but were driven back by accurate Argentine mortar and artillery fire. The British regrouped and this time got onto the left rear of the Argentine positions. However, the Marine platoon at this end of the line quickly redeployed to new positions to cover this unexpected attack and halted the Scots. The Argentines then tried to counterattack to regain their lost positions, but the British enveloped the Argentine assault on both sides and crushed it. Under heavy artillery support, the Guards again assaulted the Argentine lines, this time cracking their defenses and forcing the Marines to withdraw.[25]

At that point the war was essentially over. The defeat of the Marines on Tumbledown caused nearby Argentine units to flee to Port Stanley. Having lost all of the protective hills to the west, and seeing his army retreating in disarray, Menendez surrendered to the British without a further fight. In the end, the Argentine armed forces suffered 655 dead and 1,200 wounded. They lost 25 helicopters and 75 aircraft—45 of which were lost in combat and 24 of these to British Harriers. The British had 256 killed and 777 wounded. They lost 10 Harriers (none in air-to-air combat), 24 helicopters, and had 6 ships sunk and another 18 damaged.[26]

Argentine Military Effectiveness

Overall, Argentine forces performed poorly in the Falklands War, but even at this level of generalization, they appear to have still performed better than most of the Arab armed forces in most of their wars. Of far greater importance, however, much like the South Vietnamese armed forces, the strengths and weaknesses of the Argentine forces were very different from those of the Arab militaries since 1945.

Morale, Unit Cohesion, and Weapons Handling. At the bottom of the military hierarchy, Argentine soldiers performed poorly throughout the course of the Falklands War. In their defense, Argentina's enlisted personnel were ill-prepared for war. Fully 75 percent of the troops in the Falklands were conscripts with less than six months of military service, while many of the remaining 25 percent were reservists called up for duty after the dispatch of the British fleet and sent to the Falklands without any refresher training. Only a few units, notably the 5th Marine Battalion, had troops that had served for more than six months, and even in the case of the Marines, few had served for more than a year. To make matters worse, Argentine Army training was notoriously poor, instilling little discipline or actual military skills in the short time each conscript was in the Army.[27] As a result, Argentine conscripts "didn't know one end of a gun from the other."[28]

Still, not all of the problems among Argentine enlisted ranks can be blamed on the military system. The troops brought other problems with them. Many of the Argentine enlisted men were illiterate. Most were from the tropical regions of the country and so were unused to the Arctic weather of the Falklands. Personal hygiene among the troops was poor, and in the climate of the Falklands, this led to rampant medical problems. Although most Argentines were ecstatic about the seizure of the Falklands, few wanted to fight Great Britain for them. Consequently, many of the troops lacked any commitment to their mission, and the winter weather and supply problems turned apathy into misery.[29] British special forces units reconnoitering the Argentine positions "formed an impression of an indolent, apathetic army careless of military routines, indifferent to their officers, suffering acutely from the weather."[30]

On top of all this, Argentine ground units suffered from severe officer-enlisted frictions. The officer corps was a professional body with tremendous pride in its professionalism. Most officers saw their troops as useless, ignorant "short-timers" possessed of few militarily useful skills. Similarly, the enlisted personnel mostly considered their officers (and NCOs) martinets unconcerned with their well-being and pursuing a profession alien to their own lives. Argentine military culture had developed a severely stratified command structure by which the officers were encouraged to remain aloof from their troops as much to preserve their cherished corporate identity as to maintain a proper air of authority. After deploying to the islands, most Argentine officers made little effort to train their men, house them properly, or even see that they were warm, dry, and fed on a regular basis.[31]

Given this background it should not be surprising that Argentine troops performed poorly in battle; it is actually surprising they did not perform worse than they did. Argentine enlisted personnel generally displayed little personal bravery or commitment in combat, and unit cohesion was mediocre at best. Some units threw away their weapons at the first sign of battle and waited to surrender. On many other occasions, they put up a determined fight at first, but when the British began to push through their lines, they broke and ran. Argentine officers frequently had difficulty putting together counterattacks or shifting forces from quiet sectors to stem British assaults because their troops simply refused to obey their orders to get out of the trenches and go into battle. Nevertheless, there were instances, such as at Goose Green, Mt. Longdon, and Tumbledown where Argentine troops stuck together, fought hard, maneuvered, and counterattacked until they were physically overpowered by the British.[32]

Argentine enlisted personnel had a mixed record with weapons handling. Most Argentine soldiers were not good with their small arms, and neglected regular maintenance and cleaning. However, the British consistently reported receiving accurate fire from enemy machine guns, mortars, and artillery. This seems incongruous given the inadequate training given to Argentine enlisted personnel. One possible explanation is that a high percentage of the small number of career soldiers (or an unusual number of NCOs and officers) were assigned to heavy weapons crews to ensure that they were employed properly.

Tactical Leadership. In contrast to Argentina's enlisted personnel, its junior officers were actually quite good. As noted above, their officer corps cherished a corporate identity that gave them great pride in their skills as military officers, and while they generally disdained their troops, they were committed to their profession and turned out to be reasonably good tactical commanders. In addition, Argentine junior officers (and NCOs) generally remained at their posts and did not desert. Indeed, in most cases, it was the Argentine officers who tried to fight on while their troops fled.[33] In his own account of the conflict, Brigadier Julian Thompson, commander of 3rd Commando Brigade, notes that "On Mt. Harriet, as elsewhere, the Argentine officers and senior

NCOs fought hard and on several occasions towards the end of the battle tried to prevent their men surrendering by firing at them."[34]

Argentine tactical leadership was creative, aggressive, able to act independently in pursuit of the larger goals of an operation, and able to react quickly and efficiently to unforeseen events. Argentine units frequently tried to maneuver on the battlefield to ambush or outflank British units, even though the British were on the offensive. Similarly, many Argentine units reacted rapidly to British maneuvers, repositioning themselves to best meet the assault.[35] Argentine platoon, company, and battalion commanders shifted reserves to bolster threatened sectors and counterattacked entirely at their own discretion.[36] Indeed, in a few cases, Argentine junior officers disobeyed the orders of their superiors to retreat and instead counterattacked to try to retake a fallen position.[37] In many cases, however, their initiative was not rewarded because the troops under their command were unwilling to execute their orders. Argentina's junior commanders also were very diligent about maintaining a constant cycle of reconnaissance patrols. However, Argentine troops hated patrolling: they made only halfhearted efforts and generally came running back at first contact with British forces.[38]

As another mark generally in favor of Argentina's junior officers, Argentine artillery fought quite well during the course of the war. Firsthand accounts of the fighting from the British side make numerous references to the accuracy and lethality of Argentine artillery and its ability to complicate British operations in a wide range of situations and conditions.[39] Argentina's artillery batteries demonstrated a good ability to conduct pre-planned and preregistered fire missions in support of established Argentine defenses. More impressive still, Argentine artillery demonstrated an ability to shift fire quickly and effectively around the battlefield. On numerous occasions, immediately after an Argentine defensive position fell, their artillery would quickly bombard the fallen position to try to prevent the British from consolidating their hold and to allow Argentine troops time to regroup and counterattack or fall back to new lines. When British units attacked from unexpected sectors, and even when they got into the rear of Argentine positions, Argentina's artillery and mortars usually were able to redirect their fire within minutes and take the force under bombardment. Although British artillery usually prevailed in counter-battery duels, this was not always the case, and in some instances the British could not silence Argentine guns.[40] The Argentines also had a small number of Rasit battlefield surveillance radars that they used well and could fire artillery missions accurately based on readings from these systems.[41]

Although the evidence is limited because there were no mechanized units in the Falklands, Argentine forces seem to have done adequately in combined arms warfare. Argentina's combat arms did reasonably well working together both in set-piece and ad hoc operations. As I noted above, Argentina's artillery supported its infantry formations very well. Artillery missions were closely tied to the actions of the infantry and were quite flexible in their ability to support the infantry as the course of battle ebbed and flowed. In addition, the Argentine air force did a good, but not great, job providing support to ground forces in combat. The air force was good about flying reconnaissance missions in support of the ground operations. On a few occasions (most notably at Goose Green), Argentine strike aircraft flew close air support (CAS) missions that were timely and responsive to the needs of ground commanders. The greatest problems for the Argentines was that British command of the air made it very difficult for Argentine strike aircraft to conduct any kind of sustained effort in support of the ground troops. In addition, the Pucaras—Argentina's primary ground attack aircraft—lacked the right munitions and so did little damage when they did fly CAS missions.[42]

Still, Argentine junior officers were hardly perfect. Virtually all of Argentina's tactical commanders appeared to know parts of the right way to conduct modern military operations, but none understood the entire range of command responsibilities and operational methods. For instance, at Goose Green, the Argentines had a good security screen but their counterattacks were weak and ill-timed. By contrast, at Mt. Longdon and Tumbledown, the Argentines failed to deploy an adequate security screen but counterattacked forcefully and immediately. Clearly, these officers were reasonably competent, and mostly had the right idea as to how best to conduct their operations, but they regularly forgot certain elements or executed others improperly.

This pattern of behavior suggests that the greatest problem among Argentine junior officers was inadequate training. They had been taught the proper techniques and seemed to have some intuitive understanding of military operations, but had not had the opportunity to practice frequently enough to get down the mechanics of military tasks to the level necessary to execute them in the chaos of battle. This explanation is supported by numerous references to the limited amount of time Argentine units spent training and exercising.[43]

Strategic Leadership. The performance of Argentina's senior military commanders was mostly awful. The biggest exception to this rule was the planning of the initial invasion, which was quite competent even though it was not a terribly demanding assault. Beyond this, it is difficult to find bright spots. In particular, General Menendez, the supreme commander of Argentine forces in the Falklands, was a political appointee with little understanding of conventional military operations and no desire to command Argentine troops in battle against the British.[44] His leadership was disastrous during the war, and he and his senior subordinates must bear much of the blame for Argentina's poor showing.

The broad patterns of Argentina's senior Army leadership on the island were a constant hindrance to their defense. Argentine tactical commanders enjoyed considerable freedom of action not because Menendez consciously decentralized authority, but because he and his staff mostly failed to exercise command. As a result of this negligence, the Argentines had great difficulty conducting operations involving forces from more than one battalion, nor could they shift forces from different units quickly to aid those in danger. Without the coordinating abilities and command authority of Menendez's headquarters nothing could move, and he and his staff rarely recognized the need for such leadership.

When it did react at all, the Argentine strategic command moved painfully slowly, allowing minor setbacks to turn into major defeats. Part of this problem stemmed from the fact that Menendez never kept a reserve and never expected British attacks at night, even on the eve of the final battle of the war. Throughout the campaign, Menendez and his staff were passive and plodding, demonstrating not the least bit of creative flare or aggressiveness. Whenever he was pressed either by his tactical commanders or by the leadership in Buenos Aires to move against the British, Menendez found excuses to do nothing.[45] Sir Michael Carver remarked with expected British understatement that General Menendez was "particularly unenterprising."[46]

Menendez also made appalling decisions regarding specific aspects of Argentine strategy, preparations, and operations. He opted to defend only Port Stanley, and chose not to contest the landings, when British forces were at their most vulnerable. Menendez then undermined his own strategy by sticking two of his nine infantry battalions on West Falkland Island—where they were cut off by British naval and air power and incapable of supporting the defense of Stanley—and putting another at Goose Green, where it too was out of position to help defend Port Stanley. That left Menendez only six battalions to defend Stanley against eight British infantry battalions possessing far better firepower, training, and motivation as well as air and naval superiority. He simply wasted one-third of his force by deploying them where they could not contribute to his strategy of defending only Port Stanley.

Menendez and his staff created a bizarre and highly damaging command and control scheme. Rather than keep his battalions subordinate to their three organic brigade commands, he sent one brigade commander back to Argentina, placed all six battalions around Stanley under the command of another brigade commander, and then assigned the three battalions at Goose Green and on West Falkland to the third brigade commander. The six battalions around Stanley were more than one brigade headquarters could effectively control, while the other brigade headquarters had tremendous difficulty commanding battalions scattered over several hundred square miles on two different islands. Menendez and his staff exacerbated these problems by constantly dividing up battalions and recombining subunits into new formations. In most cases, those subunits were left under the command of their original formation rather than creating an ad hoc command to control all elements of the new formation. In other instances, such as at Two Sisters, Menendez divided key terrain features between two or more units not under the same commander.[47]

Even in executing his preferred (and misguided) strategy of defending only Port Stanley, Menendez did poorly. First, he failed to defend Mt. Kent and Mt. Challenger, two major heights that dominated the hills around Stanley. The British were astonished that they were able to take these two positions without a fight. They were extremely strong natural defensive positions, and without them the British could never have attacked Stanley. In addition, control of these mountains allowed the British artillery and mortars to hammer the Argentines on the other hills with impunity.

Second, Menendez failed to pull troops off the beaches around the capital to reinforce the line of hills facing west even when it became clear that this was the direction of the main British thrust. Argentine intelligence had predicted time and again that the British would attack Stanley overland from the west. While Menendez was not the first field commander in history to ignore intelligence assessments that later turned out to be accurate, by early June he probably should have realized that they were spot on. Argentine patrols and aerial reconnaissance gave a good picture of the extent of the British buildup around Stanley and made it clear that this would be the direction of the main British assault. This being the case, Menendez should have had more than half his force covering this axis.

Even giving him the benefit of the doubt and assuming that it might have been reasonable for him to have believed that the British could still have had one or more battalions at sea on June 11 for use in an amphibious assault on Stanley, after June 11 there was no possible reason not to reinforce the western defenses. On that day, the British smashed five Argentine companies in the outer ring of hills west of Stanley. Consequently, there was no reason to believe that the remaining four companies defending the inner ring of hills (with less extensive fortifications) could hold back the British. So on June 12 Menendez should have recognized that, regardless of whether the British were going to land on the beaches around Stanley, they were going to cave in his left flank and take the capital from the west if he did not pull troops off the beaches and reinforce this sector. He never did, and three more battalions—another third of his force—were left sitting on the beaches, irrelevant to the battle.

The Argentine high command on the mainland was little better. Reinforcements to defend the islands were plucked from all over the country with little thought given as to whether they were the right forces for the job. In some cases, units were sent for political reasons, such as to ensure the support of particular cities or regions for the war by sending units raised and garrisoned in those areas. None of the units sent had any training in Arctic operations, and very few had any winter clothing or equipment. In general, the Argentine high command failed to think through what forces would be needed to defend the Falklands and then make the necessary arrangements to move them there. The entire 10th Mechanized Brigade deployed without its armor or other heavy weapons, combat engineers were sent without any of their specialized vehicles and equipment, and many anti-aircraft units were sent without their guns or SAMs. Conscript units were sent into battle with little or no training, and reserves were not given any refresher training before being shipped off to the Falklands, while the best units in the army were held back against an unlikely Chilean attack.

Argentine Air Force Performance. The Argentine Air Force (AAF) fought remarkably well during the Falklands War, astonishing the British and much of the rest of the world. The politicization that crippled the rest of the military appears to have been absent from the process of pilot recruitment and promotion as AAF (and Navy) pilots were considered the nation's military elite and were chosen based on very demanding mental and physical standards. Argentine pilots were extremely well-trained, most having been tutored by the French or the Israelis. The Argentines considered themselves to be the equal of Israeli pilots—whom they considered the best in the world—and their flying during the war gave some substance to this boast.[48] AAF pilots were incredibly brave, showing a professionalism and determination that was absent from most of the military.[49] In the words of Max Hastings and Simon Jenkins, "The British were awed by the courage of the Argentine pilots, flying suicidally low to attack, then vanishing amid flashes of pursuing Seacat, Blowpipe, and Rapier racing across the sky behind them. Alone among the enemy's three services, the Air Force seemed highly motivated and utterly committed to the battle."[50]

The Argentines suffered from several disadvantages. First, their bases were roughly 400 miles from the zone of operations, whereas the British carriers could steam in to less than 100 miles to launch and recover their aircraft. At this range, less than half of Argentina's aircraft could even reach their targets, while those that could had only enough fuel for a quick bombing run before heading home. There was simply no loiter time to carefully choose targets, orchestrate complex attacks, or wait for conditions to become more favorable for an attack run.[51] Second, the AAF had only very old planes—many of which, like the Mirages, were not optimized for ship attacks. These planes were outclassed by the British Harriers, and they lacked the physical and electronic capabilities to fend off British air defenses. The newest planes, and those best for ship attacks, were the five Super Etendards of the Argentine Navy. However, they were too new to be counted on, and too few (and with too few Exocet missiles) to really be a formidable threat.[52] Third, with the exception of the five Exocets, Argentina lacked the proper ordnance to go after ships, and so was forced to rely on dumb bombs. Finally, the AAF had never planned or trained to fight a war at sea. Many of their pilots had never even flown over water. Only the handful of Navy pilots had any training in ship-attack missions. Consequently, the AAF pilots had to learn everything on the fly and ended up improvising most of their missions.[53]

Despite these handicaps, the Argentines performed extremely well. Argentine pilots and air staff learned quickly. At bottom, however, the most important reason for the AAF's success was that they proved to be superb flyers. Argentine aircraft on ship-attack missions flew the last 150 miles to the islands as low as 10 feet above the sea. They would cross West Falkland island at tree-top height. Then, at the last possible moment, they would pop up from behind the hills, pick a target among the ships in Falkland Sound, and then dive at the target, releasing their bombs at 150 feet but continuing on down to the deck to try to escape over the waves. The AAF flyers hugged the water and the terrain of West Falkland so well that the British rarely had more than a few seconds between when they detected a plane and when it released its bombs.[54]

Despite their lack of training in ship attacks, Argentine pilots from both the Navy and the AAF proved to be very accurate with their ordnance. By Martin Middlebrook's count, the Argentines launched 150 ship-attack sorties, of which 100 actually made it to the Falklands to mount an attack. Of these 100, 16 were able to put their bombs into British ships. Given the fact that many of those 100 planes were shot down, damaged, or otherwise hindered by British air defenses, 16 percent is a very impressive hit-rate—especially for pilots with no training in ship attacks, in planes not designed for these kinds of missions, with unguided ordnance, and who had never been in combat before. As an aside, those 16 aircraft put 25 bombs into 14 British ships. They sank only 6 British ships, however, because only 11 of the 25 bombs exploded.

This was the great bane of the AAF: bombs improperly fused for the extremely low altitudes at which they were attacking.[55]

In air-to-air engagements the Argentines fared badly, but it is hard to make the case that this was because of poor dogfighting skills. The extreme range drastically diminished the time Argentine fighters could devote to aerial combat, while the low altitudes at which they conducted their attacks were the worst possible for their Mirages and Daggers but best for the British Harriers.[56] However, the single most important British advantage was the AIM-9L Sidewinder, which could be fired from any angle, while the Argentines had only older French and Israeli missiles that had to be fired close-in at the rear of the target. British, Argentine, and American sources all agree that the AIM-9L was the key to British victory in air-to-air combat.[57] On May 1, the Argentines sent several Mirages and Daggers out to escort the strike aircraft only to have them trounced by the Harriers with advanced Sidewinders. Thereafter, the AAF high command decreed that there would be no more dogfighting, and instead, all aircraft would attempt to avoid the Harriers as best they could and concentrate solely on ship attacks. Consequently, it is difficult to hold their air-to-air record (24 Argentine aircraft shot down for no Harriers) against the AAF.[58] Indeed, British pilots remarked that when attacked by Harriers the Argentine pilots proved very good at evasive maneuvering to try to shake their pursuer and proceed with the bombing run.[59]

As noted above, the AAF made some efforts to support Argentine ground forces. However, for a number of reasons, these strikes made little difference to the outcome of the fighting. The great distance from the mainland made it almost impossible for the AAF to use its A-4s and Mirages for ground support missions. Moreover, most of the time, British Harriers made it impossible for the Argentines to fly missions with their Pucara ground attack aircraft. The British all felt that the Pucara pilots were excellent flyers, but they lacked the proper munitions—such as cluster bombs—to harm British infantry.[60]

The direction and planning of Argentine Air Force operations were of a very high caliber. The AAF conducted constant aerial reconnaissance missions, beginning with long-range flights by a specially configured Boeing 707 to monitor the fleet as it made its way across the South Atlantic to the Falklands. Reconnaissance patrols preceded every mission, and their information was quickly and efficiently incorporated into strike planning throughout the process—even updating or redirecting missions as the attacking planes flew into the zone of operations.[61] To overcome British jamming, the Argentines employed spotter aircraft, usually Neptunes, to designate targets for attacking aircraft, illuminate them, and provide any additional guidance needed by the Skyhawks and Mirages. Argentine air strikes were well designed to minimize the effectiveness of British air defenses while still providing the pilots with a reasonable chance of hitting their targets. Their plans were flexible and highly responsive to unforeseen developments. They found creative ways to take the British unawares by disguising strikes, bringing them in from unexpected angles, or suddenly deviating from established patterns.[62]

The AAF leadership cannot go blameless, however. In particular, they made several crucial mistakes in terms of their strategy that undermined the Air Force's contribution to the war effort. The most serious of these was their determination to go after the British warships and ignore the transports. The UK aircraft carriers were clearly crucial to the British operation, and the Argentines were justified in their prodigious efforts to try to get at them. However, the destroyers and frigates were the most expendable element of the British task force: they were the one asset of which the British had more than enough. On the other hand, the British transports were vital, vulnerable, and in very short supply. Throughout the first weeks of the landing, London was terrified that the Argentines would go all out after the transports. The troops, equipment, and supplies for the ground forces were literally crammed onto a handful of ships. Had the Argentines been able to sink three or four more British transports, rather than warships, they might have forced the British to pack it in altogether.[63]

Combat Support and Combat Service Support Functions. Argentina's intelligence services turned in a mostly mixed performance. Strategic intelligence was pretty bad, while tactical military intelligence proved to be quite good. Argentina's national-level intelligence services were heavily politicized and so usually told the junta exactly what they wanted to hear. Their gravest mistake was to predict that the British would not go to war in response to an invasion of the Falklands. This was what the junta wanted to hear, and from this error flowed many other Argentine problems.[64]

At tactical levels, however, Argentine intelligence proved quite good at its job. Army intelligence correctly picked the British landing site, they forecast the British move against Goose Green and then the overland advance against Stanley rather than an amphibious assault, and they gave General Menendez an accurate read on the progress of the British advance across East Falkland and their buildup around Stanley in early June.[65] The Argentine air force and naval intelligence services did an outstanding job tracking British ship movements and relaying them in real time to approaching strike aircraft. In perhaps their finest feat of all, Argentine intelligence tracked radar contacts with British Harriers and then used this information to pinpoint the location of the two British carriers—information that was then used to set up an

Exocet strike on the carriers. The carriers turned out to be right where they were supposed to be, but the missile was decoyed and then shot down by an escorting destroyer.[66]

On the other hand, Argentina's handling of information was very poor but in fundamentally different ways from the Arab militaries. Rather than the endemic lying and obfuscation that crippled Arab operations, Argentine forces suffered from an unwillingness to share information, both among services and within the Argentine Army chain of command. Operational security was lax, greatly aiding British intelligence collection efforts.[67] In addition, because the constant political infighting had taught Argentine officers not to trust one another, none were willing to share information even when the shooting started. This situation was especially pernicious among the senior officers who distrusted each other and their subordinates completely. As a result, it was the general rule that senior commanders (including the high command in Buenos Aires) kept junior officers in the dark about even the most basic information regarding their own or enemy forces.[68]

The record on Argentine logistics was similarly poor. In battle, Argentine troops were frequently hindered by shortages of ammunition, and away from it they lacked food, clean/warm clothing, sleeping gear, tents, medical supplies, weapons' cleaning materials, spare parts, and virtually everything else. Of course, Argentina's greatest logistical problem was the British blockade around the islands, which made any movement of forces and resupply difficult once the British fleet arrived in the South Atlantic.

But Argentine logistics problems cannot all be blamed on the British blockade. Buenos Aires had failed to make any real logistical plans or preparations for supporting a garrison on the island before the invasion, and so were overwhelmed when they were suddenly called on to support a multi-brigade combat force. Consequently, Argentine forces began experiencing shortages of food and medical supplies almost immediately after the invasion and nearly a month *before* British warships ever arrived in the area. Argentine officers were indifferent to the care and well-being of their troops, and even in those cases where their officers were diligent, the Argentines lacked the helicopters or all-terrain transports to be able to get supplies to the front lines in a timely, regular fashion. Whenever Buenos Aires decided to add more troops or equipment to the forces already in the Falklands they invariably failed to make the necessary provisions for the additional supplies these units would need. As a result, reinforcements simply increased the logistical burden on the force defending the islands.[69] As Nora Kinzer Stewart put it, the Argentines "were simply unable because of their inexperience in logistics to distribute these supplies in a rational manner."[70]

Argentine logistical problems were compounded by the crippling interservice rivalry within the Argentine armed forces. Some cross-service cooperation was possible at the highest levels of the junta only because the senior military leaders recognized that their fate would be determined by the outcome of the war. However, at the next rung down the military hierarchy, there was tremendous antipathy and a malicious unwillingness to cooperate. All three services took responsibility only for supplying their own forces on the islands, especially after the British SSNs arrived. Since the Army had no way of getting supplies to the island without the Air Force or Navy's aid, they suffered the worst. Eventually, some high-level discussions forced the Air Force and Navy to carry some Army supplies to the islands, but the Army never received what it needed.[71] Although Menendez was nominally in command of all air, sea, and ground forces in the Falklands, in practice he had great difficulty getting the Air Force or Navy to obey his orders. Both the Navy and the Air Force monitored British ship movements around the islands but refused to share their information with each other.[72]

Argentine technical skills varied greatly. The Argentines demonstrated a fairly impressive capability for employing high-tech equipment, modifying weapons, repairing sophisticated technology, and devising technical solutions to military problems.[73] For instance, when war broke out between Argentina and Great Britain, French technicians had not yet performed the various operations that essentially "married" the Exocet to the Super Etendard and allowed the planes to fire the missiles. In support of their NATO ally, France broke its military ties to Argentina before the Exocets and Super Etendards were properly linked up. Indeed, the French believed this operation so complex that they told the British not to worry about the Exocets because the Argentines would not be able to do it themselves. Yet, the Argentines did it, and did it very quickly.[74] However, the other side of this coin is that routine maintenance among Argentine units was abysmal. Even the Argentine Air Force suffered from maintenance and repair problems that quickly reduced its sortie rate.[75] The inability of Argentine armorers to make the simple adjustment to their bomb fuses to allow them to detonate when dropped from low altitudes also undercuts the image of Argentine technical prowess.[76]

Politicization and Arab Military Effectiveness

The comparison between the Egyptians and Iraqis on the one hand and the South Vietnamese and Argentines on the other highlights the ways that politicization has and hasn't contributed to Arab military deficiencies over the years.

The Argentine and South Vietnamese militaries were among the most heavily politicized of the twentieth century (as were the Egyptians in 1967 and the Iraqis in 1980 and 2014). The Argentines and South Vietnamese performed almost like textbook versions of politicized militaries, evincing all of the problems associated with this influence. The Iraqis and Egyptians did too, but only when they were heavily politicized in 1967, 1980, and 2014, and even then they suffered from other problems as well.

Morale and unit cohesion were problems for all of these armies, but rarely in straightforward fashion. In every case, there were important mitigating factors. The Argentines were probably the simplest: their enlisted personnel had no interest in fighting, let alone dying, for the Falklands or the regime that had seized them. Not surprisingly, they evinced the worst morale and unit cohesion. The disintegration of the ARVN in 1975 was primarily caused by a collapse in morale, but that was a product of the general lack of confidence in Saigon's senior leadership, Thieu's catastrophic strategic decisions, and a range of other factors such as the withdrawal of American support, the economic collapse that followed, the tidal wave of refugees, and family syndrome. For both the Iraqis in 1980 and 2014 and the Egyptians in 1967, unit cohesion and morale were very uneven. In all of these instances, some Iraqi and Egyptian units disintegrated when attacked or encircled by the Iranians, Da'ish, or Israelis respectively, but other units stood and fought in circumstances where many others might have broken and fled. At the very least, the fact that their unit cohesion fluctuated so wildly should tell us that there is something else going on beyond politicization.

There were several other aspects of military performance where the patterns were not perfectly consistent across all of these cases. Egypt in 1967 and Iraq in 1980 suffered from huge problems with strategic intelligence and information management, but these areas were not as problematic for the Argentines and South Vietnamese. In their cases, the problem was more the unwillingness of senior commanders to pay attention to the intelligence. Factionalism and interservice rivalry crippled the Argentine forces and wrought havoc with the ARVN at times (especially in Lam Son 719 and the Easter Offensive). Although these issues were also present to a greater or lesser extent in all of the Arab armed forces, they were never as problematic as they were for the Argentines and South Vietnamese.[77] Likewise, the negligence of Argentine and many South Vietnamese officers who were too distracted by politics to train their forces was a serious problem for them. By contrast, Arab officers did neglect proper training at times, but the fact that their key problems did not abate when they were extremely diligent about training—in 1967–1973 for the Egyptians, and 1986–1991 and 2015–2017 for the Iraqis—demonstrated that simple negligence was not the decisive problem it was for the Argentines and South Vietnamese.

If we turn to the issue of strategic leadership we see, from start to finish, that Argentine and South Vietnamese generalship was abysmal. In the South Vietnamese case, there were a few exceptionally good generals, but they were the exceptions that proved the rule. Egyptian strategic leadership in 1967, and Iraqi strategic leadership in 1980 and 2014 were equally awful. It's also worth noting that when the Egyptians and Iraqis thoroughly depoliticized their systems by 1973, 1988, and (to a lesser extent) 2016–2017, their generalship got much, *much* better. All of this proves the impact that politicization has had on Arab strategic leadership.

Of course, that's where things get complicated again because Arab generalship has not always been poor and has not been the most important problem afflicting the Arab armed forces. Yet the last four chapters demonstrate that politicization has little to no impact on tactical leadership, tactical information management, tactical air operations, weapons handling, or maintenance—the critical, consistent limiting factors on Arab military fortunes. Neither the Egyptians nor the Iraqis experienced any meaningful improvement in these areas, as especially demonstrated by the dramatic downturn in their tactical fortunes in 1973 and 1988–1991 whenever they lost the elements of surprise, numbers, firepower, and the heavily scripted and constantly repeated plans devised by their senior leadership.

In stark contrast, neither the Argentines nor the South Vietnamese experienced the same problems either generally or specifically that the Arabs did in these areas. Neither military was perfect, but most Argentine and many South Vietnamese junior officers were aggressive and creative, counterattacked and reoriented their forces to cope with changing battlefield developments, implemented good combined arms cooperation, employed their artillery flexibly and competently, and proved tactically proficient at air operations. Argentina's junior officers, in both the Army and Air Force, turned out to be the greatest strength of their military and quite capable by any standard despite the incompetence of their senior officers. South Vietnam's turned in a more mixed performance, but the critical variable was the senior leadership. Like the Arab militaries, when ARVN units were led by inept generals, their junior officers disappointed as well, albeit in most cases because they became demoralized and saw no point in trying. Unlike the Arab militaries, when ARVN units were led by competent generals, their junior officers performed much better—at least adequately, in virtually every instance, and quite well in a number of cases. Moreover, in these cases, the South Vietnamese junior officers did not need the extensive scripting and other workarounds that the

Egyptian and Iraqi high commands required to squeeze a few ounces of tactical success from their otherwise hapless subordinate formations.

Moreover, neither the Argentines nor the South Vietnamese lost their wars *because of* poor tactical leadership or poor air operations. In fact, it was pretty clear that whenever an ARVN division or corps had a commander who was even just adequate, its junior officers, NCOs, and enlisted personnel typically fought well. In the case of the Argentines, it was often their junior officers trying to win battles that Menendez and his staff seemed determined to lose. Argentina's air force performed magnificently in 1982, as did the South Vietnamese air force in 1975. This was in marked contrast to the performance of Arab junior officers (including pilots and squadron commanders) who proved utterly incapable time and again, no matter how good their generals were. Their failings were consistently the key weakness leading to Arab defeat or severely limiting their victories.

We can also bring the experiences of Cuba and North Korea back into this discussion. Both of those militaries were also heavily politicized along commissarist lines, and to a lesser extent from praetorianism as well. Castro and Kim Il-Sung both micromanaged military operations, although the former seems to have been a positive and the latter a negative. Both employed political commissars in a parallel chain of command to ensure that military commanders performed as ordered and to identify potential threats to the regime. Both valued loyalty as the highest criteria and fretted over a possible military coup.

Yet, in the Cuban and North Korean cases as well, their tactical leadership, tactical information management, air operations, combined arms cooperation, and even maintenance was far, far superior to that of the Arab armies—even the best Arab armies in their best performances. This too reinforces the point that these are not problems that can be blamed on politicization. Politicization simply does not trickle down enough to affect tactical leadership in meaningful ways. In other words *the greatest problems that the Argentines, Cubans, North Koreans, and South Vietnamese experienced were not those most damaging to Arab operations, whereas the most crippling problems for the Arabs were generally not problems at all for these other, non-Arab militaries.*

What requires a bit of explanation with the Cubans and North Koreans is their superior strategic performance, which does diverge from the norm for politicized militaries. In the case of the North Koreans, the invasion plan itself and much of their combat operations during the early months of the fighting were shaped by their Soviet advisors. And you will remember that Moscow dispatched a new team of grizzled combat veterans to "assist" Pyongyang's war effort once Stalin agreed to the invasion. Thus, early on, much of the competent North Korean senior leadership needs to be attributed to their Russian advisors.

As for the Cubans, they simply produced excellent generals to lead their forces, first among them Fidel Castro himself. This demonstrates an important truth about politicization: that since an army only needs a relatively small number of strategic commanders, the leadership sometimes can find generals who are both competent and loyal. Loyalty to the political leadership does not require stupidity, and it is exceptionally rare to find political leaders who deliberately choose senior commanders for their incompetence. As I noted in Chapter 5, dictators tend to be terrified of losing wars because losing wars can trigger coups and revolutions, as the Argentine junta and dozens of Arab leaders all learned from painful experience. Consequently, most prefer to have generals who are loyal *and* competent, and only when forced to choose between those traits do they default to the former. But there have also been plenty of generals who were both loyal and able—including geniuses from Belisarius to Model. And sometimes, the leader himself proves to be an able general who then doesn't have to trust any but his own wits.

Looking back on all of this history, we can feel confident that politicization played an important role in the problems of the Arab armed forces, but not the most important one. Arab militaries were frequently politicized during the post-1945 era. The more politicized they were, the more they suffered, but primarily in the areas of strategic leadership and strategic information management, with a lesser impact on morale, unit cohesion, and interservice rivalry. At times—such as the Egyptians in 1967, and the Iraqis in 1980–1986 and 2014—the impact of politicization contributed significantly to Arab defeats. Moreover, when determined leaders thoroughly depoliticized their militaries, it did produce a dramatic improvement in strategic leadership. This allowed some of the greatest achievements of modern Arab arms: the Canal crossing in 1973, the defeat of Iran in 1988, and the invasion of Kuwait in 1990.

Yet these victories were impressive largely in a relative sense when compared to the much longer list of Arab military failures. Underperformances were primarily the result of a consistent set of failings of Arab militaries unrelated to the problem of politicization: poor tactical leadership, poor tactical information management, poor air operations, poor maintenance, and poor weapons handling. These proved to be more powerful determinants of Arab military accomplishments, severely limiting or even undoing them.

Thus, politicization has been a cause of Arab military weakness, but it is only one of many, and not the most important. When Arab armed forces are heavily politicized, it heaps another load of damaging problems onto a set of constants that have hobbled Arab combat performances throughout the modern era. When politicization has been eliminated as a constraint, Arab militaries can do better, but not much. In the modern era, they only ever achieved very modest battlefield victories, and then only when depoliticization allowed a superb group of generals to engineer elaborate but limited and temporary workarounds to that more damning set of problems unrelated to politicization.

PART III | Underdevelopment

| Economic Development and
Military Effectiveness

I NOW WANT to turn to the impact of economics on modern Arab armed
forces. The key issue here is the extent to which the chronic underdevelopment of the Arab world during the postwar era has been the source of their
military problems. Many Westerners intuitively believe that Third World
nations simply cannot generate military power to the same extent that advanced societies can. In other words, given the same resource base, a First
World country will generate significantly greater military power than a Third
World country. As part of this, many believe that only advanced societies can
achieve high levels of military effectiveness on the modern battlefield, and the
problems besetting the Arab states are a function of "backwardness."

There is some obvious history to support this idea. As Paul Kennedy famously observed, in the twentieth century, "modern" warfare was effectively industrial warfare, and so those countries that had industrialized had
advantages over those that hadn't.[1] The same would obviously apply to the
information age of the twenty-first century: those countries that have mastered
the information-age economy should be expected to be better at making war
in this century than those that haven't, all other things being equal. Moreover,
there are any number of well-known examples that suggest a broad connection
between economic development and success in war. For instance, the Zulu
were a feared military power among the tribes of South Africa, but were blown
away by much smaller British armies in the nineteenth century. On the other
hand, it is hardly clear that economics is deterministic of military power: the

Roman empire was conquered by Germanic tribes centuries, if not millennia, behind in economic development.

Economic Development in the Arab World

For most of the twentieth century, during the era of most of the wars we have looked at so far, all of the Arab states—even the oil-rich shaykhdoms of the Arabian peninsula—were very underdeveloped in the sense of being pre-industrial. Table 10.1 summarizes some relevant economic statistics for the six Arab states that have participated in the most combat since 1945. It provides snapshots of some of their economies in 1960, 1990, and 2014. I had hoped to provide figures for 1950 rather than 1960 but the Middle East was so underdeveloped in 1950 that there are virtually no reliable statistics in Western, Arab, or international sources. Consequently, 1960 was as early as I could get. I have also included the same statistics for Sweden in 1960 and 1990 to allow for some comparison between the Arab states and a modern industrial society. Table 10.1 illustrates the vast differences separating the advanced industrial nations and the Arab states.

Although per capita GDP is the traditional measure of socioeconomic development, in the case of the Arab states, this statistic can be misleading. As the table demonstrates, the oil wealth of Libya and Saudi Arabia created enormous GDP per capita, but these states were not necessarily any more developed than the rest of the Arab world.

Underdevelopment and Military Effectiveness

This book is trying to answer a question largely about the recent past: Why it is that the Arab militaries have underperformed in combat since 1945? The problem still exists in the present and may persist into the future. That makes this particular question complicated because the economic system of the world is changing very rapidly at the moment. It is no longer what it was during the vast majority of the wars fought by Arab armies treated in this book.

For that reason, while we explore the idea that economics was the source of Arab military ineffectiveness, I am going to need to talk about the economics of the past, even as I am acutely aware that the economics of the present are already quite different. For now, I am going to just ask you to bear with me. The transition from an agriculture-based economy to an industrial economy was a critical development of the twentieth century when most of the wars that we

TABLE 10.1 Socioeconomic Development of Selected Arab and Non-Arab States

Indicators	Egypt 1960	Jordan 1960	Syria 1980	Libya 1987	Iraq 1990	Saudi Arabia 1990	Iraq 2014	Sweden 1960	Sweden 1990
GDP per capita (in 1960 dollars)	145	176	345	1,631	439	1,313	792	1,840	5,358
Literacy (% of pop. over 15 able to read +write)	26	32	58	60	15	62	80	99	99
Infant mortality per 1,000 live births	128	140	73	84	140	59	27	17	5
Life expectancy at birth, in years	48	53	65	57	48	69	69	73	79
Per capita electrical production (in KwH)	102	59	406	3,250	132	3,300	1,684	4,964	16,700
% of workforce in manufacturing	5	26	29	31	5	28	19	45	38
% of workforce in agriculture	58	44	32	18	53	16	22	14	3
Inhabitants per physician	2,500	5,900	2,570	690 (1984)	4,900	770	1,667 (2010)	730	370
Inhabitants per automobile	386	262	109	6	168	21	10	7	2
Inhabitants per telephone	106	67	49	24	122	44	18*	8	1

* This is for fixed telephones. Mobile phones per Iraq were at almost a 1:1 ratio in 2014. The World Bank, World Development Report, 2016. Sources: CIA, The World Factbook, Various years; Angus Maddison, *Chinese Economic Performance in the Long Run* (Paris: OECD Publishing, 1998); Angus Maddison, *The World Economy: A Millennial Perspective* (Paris: OECD Publishing, 2001), The World Bank, World Development Report, Various years; UN Statistical Office, *Compendium of Social Statistics and Indicators*, Various years.

are looking at took place. So it's important to see those wars in that economic context. Later in this book I will turn to the question of how the revolutionary changes in global economics are affecting Arab societies, and what it might mean for their future military power.

With that in mind, it is important to remember that, in the twentieth century, the effects of underdevelopment represented only a *relative* disadvantage of pre-industrial societies compared to the advanced industrial states. The whole concept of "underdevelopment" refers to the absence of something— industrialization, or later the information revolution. During the twentieth century, an underdeveloped society was one whose economy had not undergone the process of industrialization, with all that entailed. Consequently, underdevelopment during this period can only be said to hinder anything in relation to more advanced, industrialized states. Compared to France during the Middle Ages or England during the Renaissance, even as poor a country as present-day Bangladesh would seem an economic superpower. That's important because if this explanation is right, then contemporary Bangladeshi military forces should demonstrate greater effectiveness using their weaponry (not just owning more powerful weapons) than the militaries of medieval France and Elizabethan England used theirs.

The most obvious effect of underdevelopment is its impact on health and nutrition. Underdeveloped societies generally do not have the same kind of access to improved foods (and understanding of nutrition), medicines, and treatment as more advanced societies. Preservation, sterilization, and vitamin fortification of foods (as well as fluoridation of water), more extensive sanitary and waste disposal procedures, and the greater availability of adequate food, water, and shelter led to dramatic differences between industrial and pre-industrial societies, who could obtain these benefits only through trade with (or charity from) the advanced states. While this gap is still readily apparent today, it was even more pronounced 30–40 years ago. Likewise, the success of more advanced societies in determining the causes of illnesses, developing the means to treat those illnesses, and producing far more doctors and nurses per capita, have similarly diminished the toll of disease, injury, and even aging.

For the militaries of underdeveloped states, these health and nutrition standards affect the pool of available manpower upon which the armed forces can draw for its soldiers and officers. By shaping the general health and nutrition of the population, socioeconomic development determines the "fitness" of the eligible (primarily male) population for military service. Countries with poor health and nutritional standards produce larger numbers of people with mental or physical disabilities that preclude them from military service. Although this point may seem minor, it plays a significant role in the developing world. As late as 1992, in most Arab countries only about 55–65 percent of males age 15–49 were mentally and physically fit to serve in their armies.[2]

There is also a well-established relationship between socioeconomic development and education. Richer societies are better able to provide education for their members. They also tend to have a greater division of labor, making it easier for children to be excused from work and given the time to go to school. Education, starting with basic literacy, is an extremely useful quality for officers and soldiers.[3] Widespread illiteracy makes it harder for a military to train its troops because they have to be taught everything by another person. Illiterate personnel cannot be expected to pick things up on their own by reading manuals, nor can they be expected to improve their skills by reading accounts of the methods of other militaries, past or present. It also becomes difficult for a military to standardize knowledge and ensure that this knowledge is disseminated to all who need it. Since the military cannot disseminate the information in written form, instead it must rely on oral transmission with all the inaccuracies inherent in that practice.

Illiteracy can hinder military operations in other ways. Orders cannot always be transmitted or disseminated in writing—including electronic text. Instead, personal or verbal electronic communication is necessary, creating the potential for miscommunication or eavesdropping by the adversary. As with training, the limits involved in providing written orders also increase the likelihood that orders will not be issued uniformly to all taking part in the operation, thereby creating the potential for confusion. Running a logistics system for a sizable, modern army with illiterate personnel is almost unthinkable: How can inventories be tracked and supplies requisitioned?

In addition, illiteracy can hinder the ability of military units to act effectively and efficiently in a variety of smaller, but still important ways. For instance, map-reading is a critical skill in military operations and illiteracy normally makes map-reading difficult if not impossible. Similarly, in the course of military operations, soldiers are likely to come across writing in a wide variety of venues such as street signs, captured enemy documents, weapons and equipment instructions, and clues as to the location of food, fuel, and other supplies. An inability to read makes it difficult for any soldier to take advantage of these things.

At least a limited degree of education is needed to be able to handle high-technology equipment. Beginning in the First World War, military operations have become increasingly dependent on machinery. In recent decades, the complexity of these machines has grown astronomically. While many systems are still relatively simple to employ, and others are so "smart" that almost anyone can use them, many of the most sophisticated weapons available in modern arsenals require some basic understanding of the scientific principles behind them. For example, modern fighter pilots generally benefit from at least a basic understanding of the various physical principles involved in flight. It might be possible to teach a totally uneducated person how to fly a fifth-generation jet fighter, and perhaps even use it to fire its weapons, but his ability to employ the aircraft as a combat system will be limited.

This raises another element of underdevelopment potentially critical to military effectiveness, namely the limited familiarity with machinery of most people in underdeveloped nations. Throughout the twentieth century, and to a lesser extent today, industrialized societies had far more machinery than underdeveloped nations, and it was much more a part of everyday life. Table 10.1 provided some indication of the differences in the ubiquity of machines in day-to-day existence in industrial societies as opposed to that of underdeveloped states. In 1960 there was a car for every seven Swedes, while there was only one car for every 168 Iraqis—and Iraq was the best off of the Arab states at that time. In 1990, the ratio of telephones to people in Sweden was one-to-one while even in oil-rich Saudi Arabia the corresponding figure was 12 times higher. Of course, the information revolution and spread of cheap telecommunications across the planet is leveling that playing field quickly, as the table also shows with the statistics for penetration of mobile phones, which are pretty comparable in the "developed" and "underdeveloped" countries.

Familiarity with machines means greater ease in employing them and working in conjunction with them. Those who have only rarely come in contact with machines are unlikely to be able to operate them, and may well resist employing them. Even personnel taught to use a particular piece of machinery are unlikely to get the maximum utility out of the equipment if they are unfamiliar with machines in general: such personnel probably will lack an appreciation of how machines work, what they need to function properly, and how to avoid breaking them. Conscripts from the central Asian republics of the Soviet Union were generally afraid to fire standard Soviet infantry weapons such as heavy machine guns and grenade launchers. Similarly, officers from these areas frequently refused to employ Soviet automated command and communications systems.[4] Alexander Zuyev, the Soviet MiG-29 pilot who defected in 1990, had this to say about Soviet maintenance personnel:

> *Kolkhoznicki* with the cow manure of the state farms still wet on their boots could not be expected to repair radars and fire-control computers like their American counterparts, who had grown up with their own cars and—we heard on the Voice of America—their own home computers. Instead, we relied on a small cadre of professional maintenance officers

trained in academies supplemented by *praporschiki*, warrant officers who could keep the conscript mechanics from destroying the planes.[5]

Industrialization also demanded a different sense of time. A different pace. Essentially, industrialization demanded a mechanical pace, in the sense of one set by machines and responsive to the needs, limitations, and capabilities of machines. At the most basic level, it required a sense of precision and alacrity that pre-industrial economic systems did not.

This is not to say that time is unimportant to agrarian, maritime, nomadic, or other societies. Clearly time is important for them as well. For example, in an agrarian society, one must plant in spring, harvest in fall, and tend the crops regularly in-between, and this is only the most obvious influence of time.

However, considerations of time in an agrarian society lack the precision and pace of industrial society. Agriculture demands that time be measured in months, weeks, or, at most days. While every farmer may try to time things perfectly, it is almost impossible to narrow the optimal time for an agricultural activity beyond a particular week, or possibly a specific day. Moreover, the marginal benefits of hitting the perfect day as opposed to one day earlier or one day later are slight. While failing to plant or harvest for several weeks can be disastrous, it is exceptional that being off by a day or two would be. Likewise, it is almost impossible to measure the factors relating to timing in agriculture more precisely than on a weekly basis: likely condensation, temperature, the state of the ground, etc., are all important for agriculture, but are very difficult to measure precisely enough to calculate the optimal time for a given activity beyond weeks or (in rare circumstances) days.

By contrast, industrial society has both the means and the need for greater precision and a faster pace. Machines are capable of precise measurements, regular activities, and constant repetition. As a result, it is entirely possible to calculate the optimum timing for an activity down to the minute or even the second. And in the information age, digital and nanotechnology have made timing even faster and more precise. Moreover, because machines can perform tasks much faster than a person, it is possible to do far more in a given amount of time, or to perform any single action much faster than would otherwise be the case. Finally, because most machines are limited to performing only one specific action, accomplishing a given task often requires the use of several machines. The need to ensure that several machines can interact to accomplish a task that none could do individually requires enormous precision and efficiency in timing their activities. Anyone who has seen factory assembly in action will recognize that precise synchronization and mechanical efficiency are not just useful, they are absolutely essential to the functioning of the operation.

In short, machinery creates tremendous time-efficiency, and this time-efficiency becomes its own necessity. A necessity that is greatly exaggerated in combat. Because warfare is by its nature a competitive activity, squeezing the maximum efficiency out of your machinery is vital, which in turn generates even greater pressures for precision and speed. Doing something faster and more accurately than your adversary is invariably an important, even decisive, advantage. Industrialization introduced machines into the process—which made possible greater precision and speed—and it also introduced the mechanical-industrial approach to time that requires soldiers and officers to treat time with greater efficiency and care.

Industrialization changed not only the perception and use of time, it also changed the perception and use of information, in turn paving the way for the information revolution. Just as industrialization required greater precision in the management of time, so too did it demand greater precision in the management of information. It also demanded a far greater *quantity* of information than other economic modes. Information is an "input" into any economic system. If we return to the example of agriculture, we note that the farmer must know about the weather, his crops, his tools, the soil, and a variety of other factors to best be able to determine when and how to plow, plant, irrigate, harvest, etc. But the amount and the precision of information that agricultural economies require are much lower than industrial economies. For a farmer, it is probably enough to know that April is a cooler, rainier month than May. As far as exactly when the rain will fall, and how much will fall, the farmer has only the crudest idea, and because he can—for the most part—adapt to fit the weather, he does not require greater precision. (Obviously, he would like to know ahead of time whether there will be a severe drought or extensive flooding, but even in these cases, all the farmer would really like to know is whether his field will be flooded—not how much water will do the inundating.)

On the other hand, for an engineer or a factory manager, the amount of powder a machine will pour into a bottle must be measured down to the milligram, the number of machines doing the pouring must be known exactly, and their exact rate of production must also be known so that a number of machines can be installed with the exact capabilities required to put the caps on the exact number of bottles being filled with powder by the previous machine. Moreover, this precision in information extends down even to factory workers themselves, who must know how quickly the machines will be producing bottles of powder, how to determine which bottles get which colored caps, how many of each bottle should be sorted and crated, etc.

Because people in societies that have gone through the process of industrialization must interact constantly with machines, and the machines will not adapt themselves to the fairly loose tolerances of human beings, the humans must adapt themselves to the rigid tolerances of the machines. Because machines cannot think (yet), people must think for them, and because machines can do things with great precision, humans must think with great precision when interacting with machines. It is this need for precise decision-making that creates the demand for large quantities of precise information.

Finally, as the above discussion suggests, industrial economies entail far greater complexity and interaction than is the case in other types of economic systems. Put simply, no other economic system requires as much interaction between different people and machines as does industrialization. Industrial societies require an extensive division of labor and a high degree of specialization among its members, far more so than is the case in any other sort of society. Because this specialization requires people to obtain a vast number of goods and services they do not provide for themselves, life in an industrial society is dramatically more complex than is life in any previous kind of society. In particular, life in an industrial society requires all of its members to constantly handle the interactions of various people and machines all doing their jobs and attempting to obtain the goods and services they need. For this reason, it is highly likely that citizens of industrial societies will, on average, be much more accustomed to mediating complex interactions among people and machines than citizens of pre-industrial societies.

An Important Caveat

I want to inject a word of caution here. In the past, some scholars have attempted to argue that underdeveloped or pre-industrial societies all had a common set of behavioral traits including passivity, blind obedience to authority, an unwillingness to act creatively or independently among individuals occupying the lower rungs of a hierarchy, and a constant manipulation of the truth to suit personal interests. These claims, however, are just wrong. None of the scholars who made them were able to offer a reasonable argument why this should be the case. Moreover, the facts overwhelmingly refute these claims.

From a historical perspective, it is difficult to argue that the dynamic civilizations of the past such as ancient Greece and Rome, China, the Islamic civilization of the Middle Ages, or Renaissance Europe were dominated by these traits. Of even greater importance, before industrialization there was not simply one single "culture" that characterized all of the various civilizations of the world. Indeed, efforts to demonstrate that this was the case have ended up concluding the opposite: that these different factors vary immensely from one society to the next, whether developed or undeveloped and having nothing to do with industrialization. Back in 1974, Alex Inkeles and David Smith wrote a book called *Becoming Modern* in which they began their work by assuming that it was industrialization that instilled traits such as independent initiative, improvisation, adherence to the truth, and a capacity for independent action among individuals at the bottom of a hierarchy. However, after studying six different developing societies, they ended up concluding instead that the presence or absence of any of these traits was far more dependent on the preexisting culture of these societies than on industrialization.[6]

In the military realm, this is even more apparent. Countless books have been written about the wide variance in military effectiveness broadly—and the specific ability to innovate, take the initiative, fight aggressively, maneuver, and conduct combined arms operations—among the German, American, British, Russian, and Italian armies of the Second World War. Especially in the case of the Americans, British, and Germans, all were at identical levels of socioeconomic development, and yet the German army was far better on all of these counts than the British army, with the Americans falling in-between and improving considerably during the course of the war.[7] Thus, it is simply not the case that industrialization is responsible for these aspects of modern military effectiveness. The cases I am going to present in the next few chapters will make this point even clearer.

The Effects of Underdevelopment on Military Effectiveness

Even if industrialization doesn't convey a set of traits to the members of advanced societies, it may still be the case that the advantages of living in an advanced society that I described above—better health and education, a greater familiarity with advanced technology, a more precise sense of time, and the ability to operate at a faster pace—affects soldiers and officers in modern militaries. It may also be the case that at least part of the problems that the Arabs have experienced in warfare since 1945 stems from their underdevelopment, and especially from their failure to industrialize fully during the latter half of the twentieth century. So the question for this section is what we should expect to find in the performance of Arab and other "Third World" militaries if they are being hindered by their underdevelopment—and is that what we have found so far?

Weapons Handling. Let's start with the most obvious likely effect of underdevelopment, problems with weapons handling. Because underdeveloped societies, almost by definition, have far fewer machines than do advanced societies, and this is especially true of the most sophisticated machinery, their ability to employ machinery and military equipment is likely to prove limited. In particular, it should be the case that Third World personnel are generally incapable of really employing weapons to the full extent of their capabilities. For example, no matter how well a pilot has been trained to fly her jet fighter, if she had little exposure to machinery before joining the air force, she is unlikely to fully understand the functioning of the plane, its various capabilities and limitations, and the relationship of the aircraft itself to its avionics and weaponry. So, to the extent that Arab military ineffectiveness is a product of the underdevelopment of the Arab world, we should expect to find that their armed forces should suffer from an inability to fully employ the capabilities of their weaponry and a corresponding misuse of machinery.

If you have been paying attention at all to the earlier chapters of this book, you will recognize that weapons handling *has* been one of the big problems of the Arab armed forces since 1945. Time and again, they have proven unable to take full advantage of the equipment at their disposal, which was often superior to that of their foes. So far, in the cases we have looked at and in the general conclusions I presented in Chapter 1, difficulty assimilating and employing weapons and equipment has been a constant problem for the Arabs entirely in keeping with this explanation.

Maintenance and Repair. If you haven't had a lot of exposure to machines, it is difficult to appreciate how much attention and effort is needed to properly maintain them so that they will continue to operate efficiently. More than that, people who don't understand a machine and how it functions rarely understand what maintenance it requires. In other cases, people from underdeveloped societies (or underdeveloped parts of societies) may even be scared of a piece of equipment and so will be unwilling even to take it apart to the extent necessary to perform basic maintenance such as cleaning and lubrication. If your soldiers and officers generally don't understand how machines (including weapons) work and how they are maintained, chances are they won't know how to repair them either. That's why Third World militaries tend to concentrate their mechanics in higher-level depots. Combat formations then must drag their equipment back to these centrally located depots for everything from routine maintenance to extensive repairs.

Here as well, the evidence we have looked at so far seems to line up well with this aspect of the underdevelopment explanation. Arab militaries have had a significant, persistent problem keeping their equipment operational. More to the point, a lack of attention to maintenance and poor repair capabilities have been the critical factors in that problem.

Engineering. Combat engineering is a critical role in modern war, but one hopelessly bound up with technical skills and machinery. To be able to build or clear obstacles for mechanized forces, to be able to breach the defenses of enemy forces equipped with industrial (let alone high-tech) weaponry, and to be able to build, move, or demolish the various facilities required to support modern military forces requires an intimate understanding of machines, as well as a wide array of specialized machinery to get the job done. Here as well, the limited exposure of members of underdeveloped societies to machinery suggests that they would probably have difficulty conceiving and executing the various engineering tasks required for machine-based military forces.

Now we have a problem. In two of the most important Arab cases we have looked at so far, the Egyptians in 1973 and the Iraqis in 1980–1991, their engineers were not bad. In fact, they were very good. Indeed, in my overview of Arab military performance in Chapter 1, I noted that while there was unevenness across the Arab world and across the modern era, the engineering capabilities of their armies were often surprisingly good.

Logistics. In a similar vein, the unfamiliarity of most members of underdeveloped societies with machinery suggests that the militaries of underdeveloped states should find it hard to keep their mechanized forces supplied. First, they may not fully understand the demands of the equipment and so won't provide adequately for their needs. Second, because transport is often motorized or mechanized itself, they may not fully appreciate how to get supplies to the front-line units, resulting in delays and foul-ups. Third, a greater tolerance for imprecision in time may mean that front-line forces do not get the supplies they need when they need them, leading to breakdowns in both vehicles and operations.

This is another one where the logic of the explanation doesn't seem to mesh with the history. As I noted in Chapter 1, there was some degree of unevenness across the Arab militaries since 1945, but most were pretty good at moving forces and keeping them supplied, and some were outstanding. Again, the Egyptians—both in Yemen in the 1960s and in the October War—and the Iraqis—in all of their wars before the fall of Saddam—were terrific. Their logistical procedures may not have been elegant or frugal, but they were effective.

Combined Arms. As its name implies, combined arms operations is the integration of the various capabilities of modern, mechanized armed forces into cohesive units. It is because of their coordination that combined arms units achieve strengths and capabilities greater than the sum of their parts. Thus, effective combined arms operations hinges on the management of complex interactions. Different personnel trained to perform different missions must be integrated with one another and with machines designed to perform different functions. The complexity of this problem is significant, and even the militaries of many advanced industrial societies have difficulty making this coordination work. This being the case, it may be that Third World militaries, composed of men unaccustomed to dealing with the kind of complexity and synchronization common to industrial societies, would have problems effectively integrating their various elements into cohesive, combined arms teams.

Certainly, combined arms were another major, persistent problem for all of the Arab armed forces. Underdevelopment may be playing a role here as well.

Pace of Operations. The slower rhythm of pre-industrial societies also suggests that the armed forces of underdeveloped societies—those that have not gone through industrialization—are likely to operate at a slower pace, and to have difficulty keeping up with an adversary able to operate at a faster pace. It is certainly true that in many underdeveloped countries around the world, people prefer a slower pace in any task, they are more willing to accept delays, and routinely have difficulty adjusting to a faster pace. A common Middle Eastern joke is to explain that the Arabic word for "tomorrow," *bokhra*, carries a similar connotation to the Spanish mañana, but without the same sense of urgency.

And in keeping with that tradition, Arab militaries often had difficulty setting a rapid pace of operations, or keeping up with an enemy who could. Again, underdevelopment may also be at work in this area of military effectiveness.

Training. Finally, widespread illiteracy and the largely rudimentary education of the populations of underdeveloped countries are likely to contribute to problems with training and military education. A high illiteracy rate usually limits the ability of the populace to learn military skills, and therefore limits their utility as soldiers. Likewise, the absence of a technical education also hinders a person's ability to learn how to operate machinery and weaponry.

Consonant with this, Arab militaries did a terrible job training their personnel in some instances. At other times, however, they did a superb job, with the Egyptians in 1973 and the Iraqis in 1987–1991 leading the way. I could easily add the Jordanians in 1948, the Syrians in 1973, and at least part of the

Iraqi security forces in 2015–2017. Moreover, when the Arabs fell down in their training, it was much more about general neglect and lack of interest, not an inability to train personnel. There was some of the latter in the very early parts of this era. The British and French evinced no interest in training Egyptian and Syrian peasants, respectively, and in part excused their inattention to these colonial armies for that reason. However, as time passed, the latter manifestations of inattention seemed to be more associated with politicization, and the distractions from training it created, than with the difficulties created by underdevelopment.

Taking a Deeper Look

So at first blush, there are a number of important aspects of Arab military ineffectiveness that seem consistent with the idea that underdevelopment is the real culprit here. But first glances can be deceiving. We need to look deeper at the question. To do that, I now want to look more closely at two Arab militaries and two more non-Arab militaries to judge to what extent and in what ways underdevelopment has been the source of Arab military problems since 1945.

CHAPTER 11

Economic Development and
Syrian Military Effectiveness

IT IS IMPORTANT to keep in mind some of the overarching ideas embedded
in the claim that Arab military ineffectiveness springs from a set of
problems common to all Third World militaries. In particular, if underdevelopment is really the problem here, then we should expect to find that changes
in economic status are reflected in corresponding changes in military prowess.
Basically, military effectiveness should mirror development.

Another related element of this explanation is that to the extent that Arab
military problems are a product of their underdevelopment, then Arab states
at higher levels of development should be more competent than those at lower
levels of development. It also means that the more an Arab country develops
and modernizes, the better its armed forces should perform.

That's the particular aspect of this explanation I want to look at in this
chapter. During the 34 years between 1948 and 1982, Syria made very significant progress in terms of its socioeconomic development. (See Table 11.1.)
It also fought major conventional wars against the same foe (Israel) at the
beginning and end of that period. To the extent that underdevelopment has
been the main problem (or merely one of the problems, since we know from
previous chapters that politicization also played a role), then Syrian military
performance ought to have improved in a corresponding fashion.

Table 11.1 shows that in all of these basic indicators of economic development—from overall economic activity to basic health to the availability of
technology—Syria experienced a major jump from 1960 to 1980. Most of the

TABLE 11.1 Socioeconomic Development of Syria from 1960 to 1980

Indicators	1960	1980
GDP per capita, in 1960 dollars	198	960
Literacy (% of pop. over 15 able to read + write)	30	58
Infant mortality per 1,000 live births	196	73
Life expectancy at birth, in years	48	65
Per capita steel consumption (in tons)	23	15*
% of work force in agriculture	54	32
Inhabitants per physician	5,200	2,570
Inhabitants per automobile	273	109*
Inhabitants per telephone	90	49

* Figure is for 1990 as no data is available for 1980.
Sources: CIA, *The World Factbook*, 1982, 1992; The World Bank, *World Development Indicators,* 1960, 1980; The World Bank, *World Development Report,* 1960, 1961, 1982, 1990–94; *United Nations Statistical Yearbook,* 1960, 1990, 1991.

indicators either doubled or halved (depending on whether it was positive or negative) during that 20-year period.

Unfortunately, the Middle East was so underdeveloped in 1948 that very few statistics exist for that period. Needless to say, they would be even worse than those I presented above for 1960. There are a few examples I have been able to dig up to illustrate the even more dramatic change in Syrian economic development between Syria in 1948 and Syria in 1982 (or thereabouts). For instance, the amount of railway track in Syria in 1948 more than doubled by 1975, from 867 kilometers to 1,761.[1] Charles Issawi noted that in 1948, Lebanon and Syria combined imported $200 million worth of goods and exported just $40 million. By 1977, however, Syria alone imported $2.7 billion and exported $200 million worth of goods.[2] Even adjusting for inflation (which brings the 1977 figures down to a little over $1 billion in imports and $80 million in exports), it still represents a nearly fivefold increase in foreign trade, a reasonable marker of economic development in the twentieth century.

Syrian Military Performance in the War of Israeli Independence

On May 14, 1948, the Syrian Army invaded Palestine as part of the Arab effort to snuff out the state of Israel at its birth. It was a fight the Syrians were unprepared for, even though they did not know it at the time. The army had been created by the French in 1919 as a constabulary force to help control the Levant after World War I. The *Troupes Speciales du Levant*, as it was then known, was purely an internal security force. France provided the nascent Syrian army with little in the way of either training or weaponry.

Altogether, the Syrian Army had no more than about 12,000 men by 1948. These troops were mostly grouped into three infantry brigades and an armored force of about battalion size. In addition, the Syrians had an air force of about 50 aircraft, of which the 10 newest were World War II–era models. Syrian ammunition stocks were so inadequate that the quartermasters initially could provide only a few hundred rounds for each soldier sent to Palestine.[3]

The Southern Sector. The initial Syrian thrust was directed along the southern shore of the Sea of Galilee (Lake Kinneret). In support of this move, the Syrians set up a logistics depot near the B'nat Ya'acov Bridge north of the Sea of Galilee. As they had hoped, the Israelis detected this and took it as a sign that the Syrians were going to make their major thrust in that area. The few Israeli mobile units in eastern Galilee were deployed near the B'nat Ya'acov bridge and few defenders were left south of the Kinneret to defend against the real Syrian attack.

Despite the success of this ruse, the Syrian thrust south of the Kinneret proved to be something less than a juggernaut. The 1st Infantry Brigade, supported by Syria's entire armor corps—a battalion of armored cars and a company of French Renault 35 and 37 tanks—an artillery battalion, and other units, attacked the Israeli village of Zemach. During the night of May 15/16 the Syrians attacked with infantry supported by armored cars. The infantry moved south of the town to try to flank the Israeli defenses, but the Israelis recognized this move and were able to shift forces to block it, at which point the Syrians fell back to regroup.

In the meantime, the Israelis threw together some hasty defenses at Zemach and began work on more extensive fortifications in the twin Deganyah kibbutzim to the west, which guarded the bridge across the Jordan at Deganyah Alef. On the morning of May 18, the Syrians renewed their assault. They had used the two-day interregnum to carefully plan and rehearse the attack and, as a result, there was a noticeable improvement in their conduct. This time, the infantry hung back and the tanks and armored cars advanced, supported by heavy artillery fire. The Syrian artillery had now plotted and preregistered their fire missions and so their initial volleys were very accurate. This time, the Syrian armor swung south of the town, but the Israelis could not block them because they had only two 20-mm guns that were largely useless even against

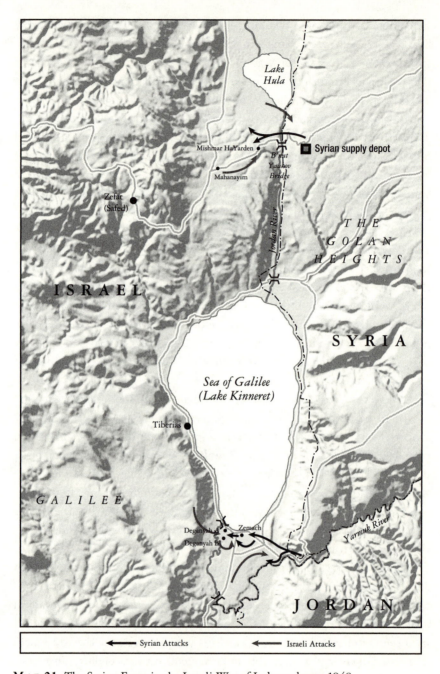

Lake
Hula

Mishmar HaYarden •

B'not
Ya'akov
Bridge

■ Syrian supply depot

Mahanayim •

Zefat
(Safed) •

Jordan River

T H E
G O L A N
H E I G H T S

I S R A E L

S Y R I A

Sea of Galilee
(Lake Kinneret)

Tiberias •

G A L I L E E

Deganyah A
Zemach

Deganyah B

Yarmuk River

J O R D A N

◄─── Syrian Attacks   ◄─── Israeli Attacks

MAP 21 The Syrian Front in the Israeli War of Independence, 1948

the obsolescent Syrian tanks. The Syrians forced the Israelis to abandon the town and retreat back to the Deganyah positions.

With the fall of Zemach, the Israelis realized they faced a serious threat south of the Kinneret. They scraped together reinforcements from all over eastern Galilee and sent them to the Deganyahs under the command of Major Moshe Dayan, who had grown up there. Dayan attempted a counterattack on Zemach but the Syrians fought back hard and repulsed them.

The Syrians began their assault on the Deganyahs before dawn on May 20. It was poorly coordinated at almost every level. First of all, the Syrians failed to synchronize the timing of their attacks on both kibbutzim, with the result that the attack on Deganyah Alef started hours before the attack on Deganyah Bet. At Deganyah Alef, the Syrians committed an infantry company supported by artillery, armored cars, and half the Syrian tank force in a frontal assault against 70 Israeli defenders. Although the Syrian units began moving in tandem, the armor outpaced the infantry and ended up attacking the Israeli lines first. The Israelis had only one Piat shoulder-fired antitank weapon and one 81-mm mortar, and so the Syrian tanks and armored cars were able to break into the settlement itself, but they were then stopped by determined Israeli resistance. The Israelis knocked out four tanks and four armored cars with Molotov cocktails, the Piat, a 20-mm gun, and even the mortar employed as a direct fire weapon. When the Syrian infantry arrived, their tanks had been defeated and were beginning to retreat. The Israelis were then able to redirect their fire on the infantry, and seeing the armor fleeing, the infantry fell back as well.

The attack on Deganyah Bet later that day showed that the Syrians had learned some lessons from their earlier mistakes. This time, they were careful to have their armor keep pace with the infantry. Nevertheless, they again conducted a frontal assault that the Israelis beat back after a short fight. The Syrians tried to regroup for another attack when unexpected Israeli reinforcements appeared: two ancient 65-mm field guns that had reached Tel Aviv by ship only days before. These guns began firing on the Syrian units around Zemach as they formed up for another attack on the Deganyahs. The Israeli crews had never fired their guns before, so their accuracy was poor, but their mere presence had a disproportionate effect on the Syrians.

The sudden appearance of Israeli artillery after having had a total monopoly on heavy weapons unnerved the Syrians. In addition, the Syrian forces around Zemach were low on ammunition, and the resupply they had been promised was diverted to the Syrian 2nd Brigade operating north of the Sea of Galilee. In response, the Syrians pulled back. They abandoned their positions in front of the Deganyahs, as well as Zemach, and retreated back to the foothills of the Golan. Indeed they even left behind a number of lightly damaged tanks that the Israelis were able to repair and employ. Although the Syrians still outnumbered the Israelis by a wide margin in this area—especially in artillery and armor—they never again mounted another attack south of the Sea of Galilee.

The Northern Sector. After their defeat at the Deganyahs, the Syrians redirected their attention to the B'nat Ya'acov bridge north of the Kinneret. Damascus had planned to launch a supporting attack in this area around May 22. However, when the Israelis realized that the main Syrian attack was coming south of the Sea of Galilee, they sent a company of infantry across the Jordan, which overpowered the Syrian forces protecting the supply depot near the bridge and destroyed the Syrian provisions. This loss forced the Syrians to delay their offensive north of the Kinneret until they could rebuild their logistical stocks in the area.

On June 6 the Syrians were finally ready to go, and that morning their 2nd Infantry Brigade, supported by armor and artillery, attacked across the Jordan at Mishmar HaYarden. The Israelis had emplaced some automatic weapons along the river and also were able to call in mortar fire, which prevented the Syrian infantry both from establishing a bridgehead and getting their armor even across the river. The Syrians pulled back to regroup and the Israelis brought in reinforcements.

On June 10 the Syrians renewed their assault on Mishmar HaYarden, and this time they turned in a much better performance. Damascus had reinforced its units here so that it had nearly two brigades. The Syrians began the attack with a determined infantry assault across the river supported by heavy artillery fire from the Golan. In addition, the Syrians brought in aircraft to conduct strikes against the defenders in support of the river crossing. The Syrian guns delivered heavy, accurate fire on the Israeli positions, and their infantry were able to establish three bridgeheads on the west bank of the river. The Syrians then crossed an infantry force north of Mishmar HaYarden and an armored unit south of the settlement. These two forces converged on the settlement while Syrian artillery on the east bank continued to pound the Israeli fortifications. This combined attack succeeded in taking the settlement by about noon, although mopping-up operations continued for the rest of the day.

The Syrians had hoped to continue pushing westward into Galilee from Mishmar HaYarden to link up with Lebanese forces and so sever the Huleh Valley from the rest of Galilee. Indeed, at that point, the road to Zefat lay wide open and the Israelis were trying desperately to rush reinforcements there. After securing the settlement, the Syrians attacked westward toward Mahanayim. However, unlike the last attack, this one was slow and tentative, and their careful combined arms cooperation fell apart. Moreover, they conducted a frontal assault rather than trying to outflank the small Israeli force there, and so were easily defeated.

This rebuff ended the Syrian offensive in Galilee. They retreated to Mishmar HaYarden and dug-in, and did not try to press their advantage to try to drive on to Zefat.

In July, the Israelis concentrated 2,000 troops to try to retake Mishmar HaYarden. For their part, the Syrians had built up their forces to about 2,500 men behind formidable defenses.[4] The Israeli plan was to launch a diversionary attack against the southern flank of the Syrian positions while the main force crossed the Jordan in strength north of the Syrian bridgehead and drove south along the east bank of the river to cut the Syrians off.

The offensive began during the night of July 9. The Israeli diversionary attack was highly successful and the Syrians were unable to prevent them from capturing most of the critical Syrian strongpoints along the southwestern perimeter of the Mishmar HaYarden bridgehead. However, the Israeli main effort failed miserably. The Syrians had observation posts watching the river and realized that the Israelis were trying to ford it to their north. Syrian artillery then fired preregistered barrages at the Israeli fording operations. These bombardments disrupted the Israeli operations so that they were only able to cross a small part of the attack force over to the east bank where they were forced to go to ground.

The next morning, the Syrians launched a series of skillful counterattacks. They sent their armored reserves against each of the Israeli penetrations in turn. Supported by fierce artillery fire, the Syrian armor succeeded in driving the Israelis back from the positions they had taken during the night. Meanwhile, most of the Syrian Air Force was committed to battlefield air interdiction (BAI) missions that prevented the Israelis from shifting forces and so allowed the Syrian armor to defeat each Israeli formation in detail.

The last Syrian counterattack was directed against the Israeli forces straddling the Jordan to the north of the Mishmar HaYarden bridgehead, and was intended to eliminate this threat and then drive north to clear the west bank of the river. The Syrian armor overwhelmed the Israelis at the river and forced them to liquidate their bridgehead on the east bank, but then the Israelis were able to bring up reinforcements and halt the Syrian attack. For the next four days, there was ferocious combat all along the perimeter of the Syrian bridgehead as the Israelis struggled to drive them back across the Jordan, and the Syrians fought to maintain their positions. Ultimately, the Syrian advantages in armor, artillery, and air power allowed them to successfully fend off the Israeli attacks, and by July 15 the lines had essentially returned to the positions at the start of the Israeli offensive.

Syrian Military Effectiveness during the War of Israeli Independence. The Syrians turned in a mixed performance in 1948. In a number of areas, they fared reasonably well. They were extremely brave, repeatedly attacking or counterattacking to take key positions, and fighting hard to hold their defensive lines. Unit cohesion also was quite good, as there were few instances of Syrian units retreating or disintegrating, even under intense pressure. The Syrians fought well on the defensive, particularly at Mishmar HaYarden, where their operations were very skillful by any criteria. In particular, in that battle, Syrian reserves reacted promptly and counterattacked hard with good artillery support. Syrian air support at Mishmar HaYarden also was quite impressive, although the absence of any Israeli aircraft made their missions considerably easier.

Combined arms cooperation was an interesting problem for the Syrians. Syrian officers seemed to appreciate the need for combined arms operations at all levels: in every Syrian attack there was at least some effort to have the different combat arms support one another. Even in their worst performances, the Syrians tried to use armor supported by artillery. However, the success of these operations ranged widely from the excellent coordination displayed on June 10 in the second (successful) attack on Mishmar HaYarden to the awful performances turned in at Deganyah Alef and Mahanayim. To some extent, the critical variable appears to have been whether the Syrians had time to thoroughly prepare their forces for an operation. When they had several days to prepare a set-piece attack, the combined arms coordination generally came off well. Whereas on those occasions when one attack followed close on the heels of the last, forcing them to plan on the fly and attack without extensive rehearsals, their combined arms coordination never came off.

This pattern strongly suggests that only *senior* Syrian field commanders really understood how to make combined arms operations work. When Syrian command staffs could carefully lay out the details of an operation and walk their subordinates through each step of the mission, combined arms coordination worked pretty well. On those occasions when Syrian commanders could only order their troops into battle and improvise the operation as they went, Syrian junior officers seemed to know that they were supposed to try to coordinate with the other combat arms but just couldn't figure out how to do it. Thus, in hastily planned operations, the Syrians tried to employ combined arms but it never worked quite right: the armor would leave the infantry behind or would attack on a totally different axis.

As with combined arms operations, maneuver was another feature that appeared to come and go based on the extent to which senior Syrian officers could plan an operation and conduct it in set-piece fashion. For the most part, when the Syrians had several days to think through an operation they came up with an outflanking maneuver that frequently brought them victory. However, when forced to commit to an attack without adequate preparation time, they generally put in a frontal assault, which only succeeded when their firepower advantage over the Israelis was huge. For example, in the two assaults on Zemach the Syrians relied on flanking maneuvers, and in the second attack—the more carefully planned of the two—they succeeded in taking the town. In contrast, in the attack on the two Deganyahs, for which the Syrians had less than a day to regroup and prepare, they conducted a blundering frontal assault that failed despite significant advantages in numbers and firepower. Moreover, at a tactical level, there was little use of maneuver at all, as Syrian infantry and armor simply charged their objectives and rarely, if ever, tried to jockey for a more advantageous spatial position.

The Syrians generally were more successful in defensive than offensive operations. In all three successful assaults—Zemach, the Deganyahs, and Mishmar HaYarden—victory came only after their initial attacks had failed and they were forced to regroup and conduct a set-piece operation. Syria's limited offensive capability was mostly the product of the sluggishness, inflexibility, passivity, and inability of Syrian tactical forces to coordinate their actions. In particular, their unwillingness or inability to move on Zefat after the fall of Mishmar HaYarden was inexcusable.

Overall, Syrian participation in the War of Israeli Independence was limited and halfhearted. This prevented them from suffering the same humiliations the Israeli *Haganah* inflicted on their Iraqi, Egyptian, and Palestinian allies, but it also ensured that Syrian accomplishments were negligible. The Syrians aborted their offensive south of the Sea of Galilee as soon as they experienced a setback, even though they still had a huge advantage in men and heavy weapons. In the north, they won a small but impressive victory at Mishmar HaYarden, only to give up when their exploitation hit meager Israeli resistance. Thereafter, Syria was content to sit on the defensive and conduct a few minor attacks on small, exposed Israeli settlements, none of which had any impact on the course of the war.

The Israeli Invasion of Lebanon, 1982

Thirty-four years later, on June 6, 1982, the Israel Defense Force invaded southern Lebanon. Ever since the Palestinian expulsion from Jordan in 1970–1971 and their subsequent resettlement in Lebanon, Israel had been harassed, shelled, attacked, and raided by Palestinian guerrillas based in Lebanon. The Palestinian presence had been a major contributing factor to the outbreak of the Lebanese Civil War in 1975, which had caused Lebanon to spiral into chaos and triggered a Syrian intervention and partial occupation. By the early 1980s, key members of the right-wing Israeli cabinet were determined to solve the Lebanese problem by force and began trying to provoke Palestinian actions that could justify a full-scale invasion. In 1982, the Israelis found the pretext they were looking for and sent their military north.

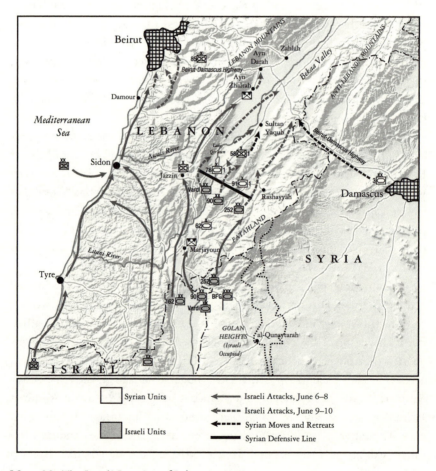

MAP 22 The Israeli Invasion of Lebanon, 1982

It was a desperate move and the plan devised primarily by Minister of Defense Ariel Sharon was a harebrained scheme. Sharon, with the connivance of Prime Minister Menachem Begin and the assistance of Israel's chief of staff, Lt. General Rafael Eitan, claimed that his intent was merely to send Israeli forces 40 kilometers into Lebanon to push the PLO away from Israel's borders. In actuality, his goals were far more expansive. He planned to send Israeli ground forces to Beirut, have them rout the PLO and drive them out of Lebanon altogether, install the pro-Israeli Bashir Gemayel as president of Lebanon, and provoke the Syrian forces occupying the Bekaa Valley into a war that would enable Israel to crush them and drive them out of Lebanon too.[5]

To accomplish this daring set of tasks, Israel put together a massive force including nine divisional *ugdot* plus a variety of smaller formations. These units totaled 76,000 men, 1,250 tanks, and 1,500 other armored vehicles. In addition, the Israelis would have the entire IAF, 650 combat aircraft, at their disposal.[6]

In contrast, the Syrian presence in Lebanon in 1982 was primarily an occupation force, unprepared for large-scale combat with the Israeli military. The Syrians had two substantially reinforced heavy brigades in Lebanon at the time of the Israeli invasion. The 62nd Armored Brigade was bivouacked in the Bekaa Valley, and the 85th Mechanized Brigade was deployed along the Beirut-Damascus highway east of Beirut. In addition, the Syrians had at least 10 battalions of commandos operating throughout Lebanon. Altogether, there were about 30,000 Syrian soldiers with 200–300 tanks deployed in eastern and central Lebanon. The Syrians also had 16 batteries of SA-2/3/6 SAMs deployed in the Bekaa.[7] Later, the Syrians would commit the 1st Armored Division, additional SAM batteries, and then the 3rd Armored Division to the fighting, but when the Israelis first invaded these divisions were still deployed around Damascus and the Golan. In addition, the Syrian forces in Lebanon had been compromised by graft and a general inattention to combat training.

On the other hand, the Syrians had been working hard to improve their forces. In the late 1970s, after they had settled into their occupation of Lebanon, the Syrian military began to make changes in accordance with the lessons it had taken away from its war against Israel in 1973 and its own bumbling invasion of Lebanon in 1976. Syrian dictator Hafiz al-Asad further expanded his army so that by 1982, the Syrian armed forces boasted some 250,000 men, 3,600 tanks, 2,700 APCs, 2,300 artillery pieces, 80 SAM batteries, and 500 combat aircraft.[8] As these numbers implied, the Syrians also made a major effort to mechanize their force, importing huge numbers of tanks and other armored fighting vehicles from their Soviet patron.

After the success Syrian SAM units had had against the Israeli Air Force in 1973, Damascus greatly increased the number and mobility of its tactical air defenses by buying additional SA-6 launchers, as well as newer SA-8s.

Of particular importance, the Syrians concluded that only their commando units had shown any real skill in combat against either the Israelis on the Golan or the Palestinians in Lebanon. In response, the Syrians expanded their commando forces from 7 to 33 battalions. They did this by stripping most of the best personnel from their infantry units and diverting many of the most promising new recruits to the commandos. They began to attach commando units to armored formations, and vice versa. While the expansion of the commandos and their new missions gave Syria a small force of quite competent soldiers, it diminished the skill levels of other Syrian units by stripping them of many of their best personnel.

Israel Attacks. In the west, the Israeli offensive went largely according to plan, but not according to schedule. On June 6, 1982, the Israelis launched their attack only to discover, as the Syrians had six years before, that Lebanon's terrain impeded the movement of large armored forces. Israeli tank columns got jammed up trying to bypass the coastal cities and were further delayed by small groups of Palestinians with rocket-propelled grenades (RPGs) and mines who ambushed Israeli armor as it moved along the narrow roads. Still, with their usual skill and flare for improvisation, Israeli forces found ways to defeat these threats and so made remarkably good time by any standard but their own. The Israelis reached the outskirts of Beirut by June 9 where they encountered much stiffer resistance, but by June 11 they had fought their way into the suburbs and besieged the center of the city.

In the east, things moved in a more herky-jerky fashion, reflecting the bizarre political circumstances of the Israeli invasion, the ongoing mobilization of key units, and command failures on the part of IDF leaders. During the first three days of the invasion, Maj. General Avigdor Ben Gal's corps-sized BFG pushed into southeastern Lebanon to clear out the Palestinians in the area and get into position for the expected showdown with the Syrians. To the BFG's right, the Israeli 252nd Armored Division attacked what was called "Fatahland," the center of PLO operations in Lebanon, and cleared out PLO forces with little difficulty. Only on the third day of the invasion, June 8, would the Israeli General Staff finally order the BFG forward into their jumping off positions for the assault into the Syrian-occupied Bekaa, at which point Ben Gal's divisions hit the forward Syrian screening positions around Marjayoun. The Syrian forces there put up little resistance and were easily driven off.

Damascus was surprised and perplexed by the Israeli invasion. The Syrians were not entirely displeased with the idea of the IDF smashing the PLO, which had become obstinate with them too. But they did not know whether to believe Israel's (disingenuous) claims that it had no desire to fight Syria. Hafiz al-Asad adopted the prudent course: he would stay out of the Israelis' way to avoid war if at all possible, but reinforce his positions in Lebanon in the event they attacked. Because Asad did not want to give the Israelis any pretext to attack his troops, he ordered them not to fire at the Israelis—even if they were fired upon—unless they began taking casualties. Syrian troops were also forbidden from moving any farther forward, even to occupy better defensive terrain, for fear that this would look aggressive to the notoriously trigger-happy Israelis.

Meanwhile, Syria readied its forces in the event the Israelis were looking for a fight. The Syrians ordered their troops in Lebanon to man prepared defensive positions along many of the major routes from the south into their strongholds in the Bekaa and along the critical Beirut-Damascus highway. They dispatched the 1st Armored Division to bolster Syrian forces in the Bekaa. The 1st arrived on June 7 and immediately began to establish a Soviet-style defense-in-depth across the valley. Two days later, Damascus decided to add its 3rd Armored Division as well. Finally, Syria redeployed 3 more medium SAM batteries to the Bekaa, bringing the total number there to 19.

Operations in the Central Sector. While the Syrians were attempting to decipher Israeli intentions, the Israeli 162nd Armored Division was steadily pushing northward into south-central Lebanon toward the Beirut-Damascus highway, the lifeline of Syria's occupation army in Lebanon. Sharon and Eitan hoped this move would force Asad to fight to prevent the 162nd from cutting off the Syrian units around Beirut, thus furnishing Israel with an excuse to attack the Syrian forces in the Bekaa.

At first, the 162nd's route of advance was largely undefended, as the Syrians had only one company of tanks and one commando company watching it. However, the Syrians detected its movement on June 7 and sent several commando companies with armor to set ambushes along the Israeli route. Damascus also dispatched a multi-battalion task force of commandos and armor from the 85th Mechanized Brigade to establish a blocking position farther north at Ayn Zhaltah.

The 162nd began to run into these units on June 8. The Syrian commando-armor teams fought hard and retreated in good order when they were outflanked and driven off by the IDF. While they did little damage to the Israelis, they delayed them. Later, the first Syrian helicopter gunships made their appearance, attacking the 162nd Division along the narrow, winding mountain paths. The Syrian helicopters—French-made Gazelles armed with ATGMs—caused little damage and were easily driven off, but they caused further delays by forcing the Israelis to scramble for cover and then regroup before they could get moving again.

All of these skirmishes, plus additional pauses caused by Israeli command problems, bought the Syrians time to establish impressive defenses at Ayn Zhaltah. When the Israelis reached the town during the evening of June 8, they were hammered by Syrian commandos, well dug-in and generously armed with RPGs and ATGMs and covered by tank and other heavy weapons fire. The Syrians had dug-in on the high ground around the southern entrance to the town, with their tanks at the far end. The Israelis saw the tanks and drove straight at them, destroying three T-62s before they were themselves caught in a crossfire by Syrian commandos with AT-3 Saggers and RPGs hiding among the steep ridgelines on both sides of the road. The Syrians destroyed the two lead tanks and several APCs of the Israeli vanguard before the Israelis could halt the column and pull back from the Syrian fire sack.

Later, the Syrians beat back an Israeli infantry force that tried several times to rescue their wounded. Moreover, when the Israelis pulled back from the village to regroup, Syrian commandos crept forward and again attacked them from several different directions, forcing the Israelis to fight their way back south of the town. Late the next day, the Israelis regrouped and conducted a flanking attack under heavy air support that drove the Syrians from the hills overlooking the town, so that by nightfall on June 9, Ayn Zhaltah was in their hands. The Syrians did only slight damage to the IDF in the clashes at Ayn Zhaltah, mostly because their fire was inaccurate and their armor refused to maneuver against the Israelis, but they delayed the IDF drive toward the Beirut-Damascus highway. Ultimately, this proved to be one of the most important factors in preventing the complete destruction of the Syrian army in Lebanon.

Farther south on June 8, an Israeli armored brigade without infantry or artillery support attacked a reinforced brigade of Syrians in the Lebanese town of Jazzin. The Syrians saw Jazzin as the forwardmost position on the right flank of their defensive lines in the Bekaa and had sent a brigade task force to hold the city. The Israelis had been content initially just to set up a blocking position at the crossroads—which allowed the 162nd Armored Division to pass. On June 8th the Israelis attacked into the town, where they were met by well-placed antitank ambushes manned by Syrian commandos. The Israelis then sent another part of their brigade in a flanking maneuver to roll up the Syrian positions in the outlying hills. The Syrian commando units were deployed to fire into the town and could not quickly reorient themselves to deal with this unexpected move. Thus, it fell to the Syrian armor to try to stop the Israelis. However, the Syrian tanks also had difficulty shifting to face the IDF flanking attack, and the tank battalion was virtually wiped out in a quick firefight, prompting the other Syrian units to pull back.

The events of June 7–8 had important effects in both Jerusalem and Damascus. For the Syrians, the powerful Israeli attacks on Ayn Zhaltah and Jazzin convinced Asad that the Israelis were lying when they claimed only to want to punish the PLO. He recognized that they were looking to drive Syria out of Lebanon. In response, he sped up the deployment of the 3rd Armored Division to the Bekaa and sent additional commando battalions to Lebanon.

Nevertheless, the fighting at Ayn Zhaltah and Jazzin, the movement of Syrian reinforcements into the Bekaa, and the participation of a few Syrian MiGs in dogfights with IAF jets over Lebanon, were enough for Sharon to persuade the Israeli cabinet to approve the offensive against the Syrians. On the afternoon of June 9th, Ben Gal was ordered to drive the Syrian army out of the Bekaa. Simultaneously, the IAF was ordered to implement its long-planned contingency operation to knock out the Syrian SAM network in the Bekaa Valley.

The Israeli SAM Suppression Campaign. The IAF had meticulously studied the lessons of the 1973 war and developed a comprehensive operation involving over a dozen different ground and air-based systems to suppress and destroy Syria's medium-range SAM units. Although the Syrians had bought even more advanced models than they had possessed in 1973, they had not kept pace with Israel's countermeasures. Syrian SAM operations were very predictable. Their command and control was primitive, slow, and lacked redundancy, making it susceptible to Israeli attack and incapable of adequately responding to the fast-paced, multifaceted Israeli assault. Syrian radars, transporter-erector-launchers (TELs), and support equipment rarely moved from their positions, and Syrian radars were left on for long periods of time, making it easy for the Israelis to locate and target them. The Syrians also had inadequate early-warning radars— they had less than a quarter of the radars called for by Soviet doctrine—and did not recognize that terrain masking from Lebanon's mountains degraded the coverage of the radars they had deployed. All of these problems left them vulnerable to the Israeli attack.

The Israelis began the assault with flights of unmanned drones and electronic spoofing of the Syrian radars to convince the Syrians that large numbers of attack aircraft were overhead. These deceptions prompted Syrian SAM crews to turn on their targeting radars and fire off a huge salvo of missiles at the drones, at which point the Israelis unleashed a swarm of air- and surface-launched anti-radiation missiles that homed in on the Syrian fire control radars and destroyed them. With the Syrian SAM units blinded and "unloaded," Israeli strike aircraft and artillery attacked the early warning radars and TELs themselves, pounding them for several hours with highly accurate strikes.

The Syrians mostly panicked during the attack, showing little ability to respond to this unexpected set of Israeli tactics. Some Syrian SAM crews tried to fight back as best they could, but few turned off their radars or tried to pack up and move, which were the only solutions to their problems. Syrian SAM batteries also had difficulty communicating with each other and with the small number of AAA units supposed to defend them, so that they could not coordinate their responses to the Israeli attack. By night on June 9 the Israelis had destroyed 17 of the 19 SAM batteries in the Bekaa without losing a plane, and by the end of August, subsequent Israeli air strikes had destroyed another 12 SAM batteries.[9]

When Damascus realized that the IAF was destroying its SAM batteries, it ordered the Syrian Air Force into the fray to protect its air defense forces. The Syrians dispatched as many as 100 aircraft, which were met by a similar number of Israeli fighters. The Syrians labored under several disadvantages. Syrian command and control was incapable of coordinating the operations of air forces and ground-based air defense units, so that each could only fight either at different times or in different areas, but could not integrate their efforts. Damascus also had no particular battle plan or operational concept for employing its fighters. They were simply sent to the Bekaa and told to drive off the IAF without much thought. The Syrians were flying MiG-23s and MiG-21s and their pilots were heavily dependent on guidance from ground-controlled intercept (GCI) sites, while the Israelis flew more advanced F-15s and F-16s armed with far more capable air-to-air missiles. The Israeli fighters also were supported by E-2C Hawkeye airborne warning and control aircraft, which vectored Israeli aircraft to intercept Syrian planes before they could sneak up on Israeli aircraft or flee the battlefield.

Nevertheless, Syria's technological disadvantage became almost beside the point because Syrian pilot performance was so poor. When the Syrian Air Force rose to defend the SAMs, the Israelis jammed their GCI links. Deprived of GCI guidance, the Syrians pilots "went stupid." Syrian formations dissolved as their pilots could not handle flying in formations larger than pairs. The Syrians were unimaginative and showed no creativity or flare for improvisation; they flew into combat mindlessly, making little or no effort to maneuver in dogfights with the Israelis. Some pilots simply flew figure eights because without the orders of their GCI operators they literally had no idea what to do and made no effort to try to think for themselves. Those few pilots who did try at least some air combat maneuvers employed only simple, predictable tactics and were slow to react to Israeli moves.

The result was a slaughter. In three days of air battles, the Israelis shot down 82 Syrian fighters without losing any of their own. By the end of September the Syrians still had not shot down a single Israeli plane, and their losses had reached 86 MiGs.[10]

The performance of Syria's Air Force was stunningly inept. A senior Israeli Air Force officer asked to comment on the capabilities of the MiG-23 replied:

> I can't compare it when a MiG-23 is flown in a tactic that I can't understand or in a situation that I would never get into. The problem is that their pilots didn't do things at the right time or in the right place . . . the pilots behaved as if they knew they were going to be shot down and then waited for it to happen and not how to prevent it or how to shoot us down. . . . It wasn't the equipment at fault, but their tactics. They could have flown the best fighter in the world, but if they flew it the way they were flying we would have shot them down in exactly the same way. I don't mean they were sitting ducks, but in our view, they acted without tactical sense.[11]

The outstanding RAND analyst, Ben Lambeth, concluded:

> The Syrians were simply outflown and outfought by vastly superior Israeli opponents. Without question, its sophisticated American hardware figured prominently in helping Israel emerge from the Bekaa Valley fighting with a perfect score. Nevertheless, the outcome would most likely have been heavily weighted in Israel's favor even had the equipment available to each side been reversed. At bottom, the Syrians were not done in by the AIM-9L's expanded launch envelope, the F-15's radar, or any combination of Israeli technical assets, but by the IDF's constant retention of the operational initiative and its clear advantages in leadership, organization, tactical adroitness, and adaptability.[12]

However, by the same token, one Israeli pilot who fought in the June air battles stated that the Syrians "knew they stood no chance against us, yet they kept coming in and coming in as if asking to be shot down. They showed such remarkable dedication and courage, and I have nothing but respect and admiration for them."[13]

The Battle of the Bekaa Valley. On the ground, when the Israelis finally launched their main assault, the Syrians were ready for it. The 1st Armored Division, reinforced with additional artillery and commando units, was fully deployed in the valley and had been improving its defensive positions for two days. The Syrians deployed with their 76th and 91st Armored Brigades forward, dug-in across the valley floor, anchoring their lines in the mountains on either side. In addition, the Syrians had worked the natural obstacle of Lake Qir'awn into their defensive scheme in the western Bekaa. The 1st Armored Division's mechanized brigade, the 58th, was deployed in-depth, dug-in behind the two armored brigades, where it could serve either as a secondary line of defense or a reserve that could be brought forward to aid the armored brigades. The Syrians also deployed teams of commandos backed by armor in antitank ambushes farther south to delay, disrupt, and attrite the Israeli forces before they hit the main defense line. Meanwhile, the T-72-equipped 3rd Armored Division was en route to the Bekaa and was expected to arrive some time on June 11.

During the afternoon of June 9, while the IAF was butchering Syria's air and air defense forces, the Israeli Bekaa Forces Group slogged their way along the narrow roads of the southern entrance to the valley. On a number of occasions, Syrian helicopter gunships—and occasionally fixed-wing aircraft—attacked the Israeli columns, causing little damage but forcing them to take cover and slowing their advance. In addition, the Israelis constantly encountered Syrian commando ambushes, which further slowed and frustrated them. The Syrian commandos were usually well-deployed and tough to root out. Several Israeli units lost armored vehicles and men to these ambushes, while all were slowed by the need to move cautiously and clear out the stubborn Syrian defenders whenever they did trip an ambush.

The Israelis had learned to use infantry, air strikes, and armor when possible, to clear the surrounding hills when they encountered dug-in Syrian antitank teams, but this was a time-consuming process, and the Syrians fought hard and mostly retreated in good order when their positions became untenable. Nevertheless, Syrian aim was poor and the commandos and their armor rarely tried to get out and maneuver against the Israelis. These problems, and the superb gunnery and quick improvisational skills of the Israelis, tended to minimize the actual damage the Syrian commandos were able to inflict, but the lost time was important. Especially since Israel knew that the destruction of the Syrian SAMs would bring immense superpower pressure on them to agree to a ceasefire.

The Israelis finally attacked the main Syrian defense line in the Bekaa in the early morning of June 10. The Syrians were outnumbered in the assault: the reinforced Syrian 1st Armored Division had 350–400 tanks, 150 artillery pieces, and approximately 150 ATGM-equipped BRDM-2s, while the Israeli *ugdot* had over 650 tanks and about 200 artillery pieces. However, the Syrians had the advantages of their dug-in defenses and the superb defensive terrain of the Bekaa.

Two of the Israeli *ugdot* struck the Syrian lines in the west, on either side of Lake Qir'awn, while the 252nd Armored Division hit the eastern flank of the Syrian lines anchored on the Anti-Lebanon mountain range. Although all three Israeli attacks were frontal assaults against dug-in Syrian units in excellent defensive terrain, which prevented the Israelis from deploying more than a fraction of their forces for the assault, the Israelis punched through rapidly on all three axes. In the far west, the Syrians deployed only light covering forces, believing the terrain too rough for an Israeli armored drive, with the result that the Israelis quickly broke through the Syrian lines and began driving deep into the Bekaa along the eastern slope of the Lebanon range.

The main battle, however, took place to the east of Lake Qir'awn where the Israeli 90th Armored Division attacked up the main north-south road in the Bekaa. The Syrian high command recognized this as a critical threat and fed in ever more reserves to try to stop the Israelis. Although the terrain prevented the Israelis from deploying their full force and the Syrians were well entrenched on the surrounding hills, the Israelis constantly worked against the Syrian flanks, maneuvering for advantage and using their superb gunnery skills to pick off Syrian armored vehicles and grind down the Syrian forces. By 1500 hours, the Syrian lines had buckled and the 90th Division had broken through. In the east, the Israeli 252nd Armored Division drove through the Syrian lines fairly easily, and by late afternoon they were threatening to link up with the 90th Division and encircle the remnants of the forward brigades of the Syrian 1st Armored Division.

Yet the trap never snapped shut, and much of the 1st Armored Division was able to escape as a result of Israeli mistakes. Of greatest importance, most of the Israeli units did not aggressively pursue the retreating Syrians and moved at an almost leisurely pace. Despite the urgency in Tel Aviv for the BFG to reach the Beirut-Damascus highway before nightfall, Ben Gal's units moved slowly and deliberately. Without Israeli pressure, the Syrians retreated reasonably well, conducting fighting withdrawals all across the front and maintaining good unit cohesion, except among those formations that had suffered most in the combat with the Israelis earlier in the day. On one occasion, a Syrian commando unit conducted a spoiling attack against an Israeli armored unit near Rashayyah, which only destroyed one APC and killed a few soldiers, but still disrupted the Israeli formation and delayed its advance. In addition, the Syrians threw their helicopter gunships into the melee to slow down the Israelis and cover the retreat of their ground forces. The Syrian Gazelles and Mi-24 Hinds generally caused only minor damage to the Israelis, but they further slowed the already cautious advance.

For the most part, the sluggish pace of the Israeli pursuit appears to have been the product of their experience over the previous four days, during which they had been constantly ambushed by Syrian commandos. This seems to have made the IDF reticent to engage in any sort of headlong advance through the hills of the Bekaa, even after cracking the main Syrian lines and putting the 1st Armored Division to flight.

This caution was further reinforced when an Israeli battalion accidentally ran into several battalions of the Syrian 58th Mechanized Brigade, plus other elements of the 1st Armored Division regrouping around the town of Sultan Yaqub during the afternoon of June 10. Most of the Syrian units were part of the second line of defense, and they were not aware that the Israelis had gotten so far north. The vanguard of an Israeli armored brigade pushed into the town against no resistance and then out the other side only to suddenly find itself in the midst of the Syrian forces.

Although the firefight became quite fierce and the Syrians had the advantage of being deployed in hills surrounding their prey on three sides, they did remarkably little damage to the trapped Israelis. The Syrian armor and APCs sat in the hills and were content to fire down on the Israelis, rather than coming down to destroy the Israeli armor in a close assault. Twice, the Syrians did send small antitank units down to attack the Israelis, but they were driven off easily by automatic weapons fire. Finally, at around 2100, the Israelis concentrated virtually every artillery piece in the Bekaa on the Syrians around Sultan Yaqub, creating a "box" of fire through which the trapped battalion was able to withdraw. The Israelis lost only eight armored vehicles at Sultan Yaqub, but the ambush had preoccupied Ben Gal's command staff and deprived the rest of his corps of artillery support, further slowing the Israeli pursuit. Thus, by night on June 10, the Israelis had routed the 1st Armored Division, but they had not finished it off, nor had they reached the Beirut-Damascus highway.

Despite the IDF's problems on June 10th, the defeat of the 1st Armored Division, coming on top of the destruction of Syria's air and air defense forces, threw the Syrian high command into a state of panic. The Syrians recognized that the Israelis had powerful forces threatening to cut the Beirut-Damascus highway, which would split the Syrian forces in Lebanon. The General Staff also could not be certain that the Israelis did not intend to drive up to the Beirut-Damascus highway, turn right, and push into the Damascus plain in conjunction with an assault from the Golan. This fear prompted the Syrians to alert their forces around the capital, dispatch two independent armored brigades to block the Beirut-Damascus highway as it debouched into Syria, and order the 3rd Armored Division to establish a defensive line south of the highway with the remnants of the 1st Armored Division.

Although one of its brigades suffered heavy losses to IAF air strikes on June 10 and 11, by 1000 hours on June 11, the 3rd Armored Division was in the Bekaa and heading south to take up defensive position forward of the Beirut-Damascus highway before the Israelis could get there. The Israelis meanwhile had finally gotten going after a late start and were similarly racing north to get to the Beirut-Damascus highway before noon, when a US-brokered cease-fire was due to take effect. Shortly before then, lead elements of the 82nd Armored Brigade of the 3rd Armored Division collided with the vanguard of the Israeli corps. In the ensuing firefight, the Israelis quickly gained the upper hand through superior marksmanship and maneuver and destroyed as many as 30 T-72s before the Syrians pulled back.[14] The Syrians were unable to knock out any of the Israeli tanks in this exchange. Nevertheless, the fight was still a sort of victory for Syria because the 3rd Armored Division had prevented the Israelis from reaching the Beirut-Damascus highway before the noon deadline.

The Syrians took at least 4,500 casualties and lost 300–350 tanks, 150 APCs, nearly 100 artillery pieces, 12 helicopters, 86 aircraft, and 29 SA-2/3/6/ 8 batteries. Against the Syrians, the Israelis suffered 1,067 casualties, 30 tanks lost (with another 100 damaged), and 175 APCs destroyed and damaged.[15] Thus, the Syrians were on the wrong side of a 4:1 exchange ratio in casualties, a 10:1 ratio in tank losses, and an 86:0 ratio in aircraft losses.

Syrian Military Effectiveness during the Israeli Invasion of Lebanon

Syrian combat performance in Lebanon showed improvement over past wars in some respects, while in other ways it showed no improvement whatsoever.[16]

Strategic Performance. Given the conditions under which they were forced to operate—and despite Asad's continued commissarist politicization of his armed forces—Syrian generalship was fine, even good, although not brilliant. Syrian moves in the first few days were wise given their desire to avoid provoking Israel while preventing the IDF from securing a decisive advantage and then attacking the Syrian forces in Lebanon. Syrian units were placed on alert right away and ordered to begin preparing and repairing defensive positions along key axes of advance. Damascus bolstered its air defenses in the Bekaa and redeployed two of its best armored divisions plus several more commando battalions to reinforce its units in Lebanon, many of which had been on occupation duties for so long that they were not combat ready.

When the Israelis began pushing up the spine of the Lebanon range toward the Beirut-Damascus highway, the Syrians recognized the danger of this move and decided to block it, regardless of the potential for provoking a war with Israel. This too was probably the right move: as badly as the fighting in the Bekaa actually went for Syria, it almost certainly would have been worse had the Israelis been able to cut the Beirut-Damascus highway and then attack into the Bekaa from behind the main Syrian defense lines.

Syria's strategy for fighting the Israelis once it became clear that war was unavoidable was also reasonable. Damascus deployed its commandos forward with armor support in ambushes along the narrow paths into the Bekaa. They were ideally placed to contest the Israeli advance. The alternative, deploying all of the commandos with the reinforced 1st Armored Division along the main Syrian defense lines in the Bekaa, would not have taken full advantage of the commandos' capabilities, and their impact would have been diminished.

The Syrian defensive strategy in the Bekaa was straightforward: a standard, Soviet-style defense-in-depth with two brigades up and one back, but entirely appropriate for the situation. It may be the case that a truly brilliant general might have found a better approach, but the Syrian strategy was not bad, and it is unclear that Syrian tactical forces could have implemented a more sophisticated defensive scheme. For instance, any kind of elastic defense strategy would have given up the enormous advantage of the terrain. It also would have required Syrian units to prevail over the IDF in fluid maneuver warfare. Given the drubbing the Syrians took when they were defending in place and had all of the advantages of the terrain, and how badly their forces fared when they tried to maneuver against the Israelis, it seems likely that any such mobile defense would have failed far worse.

Finally, although the decision to commit the Syrian Air Force to defend the SAMs and the ground forces in the Bekaa Valley resulted in the destruction of about a quarter of the Syrian Air Force, it too was probably the best move. Not sending out the Air Force to confront the Israelis would have been a severe blow to morale throughout the Syrian armed forces. Moreover, the Syrian Air Force did succeed in keeping much of the Israeli Air Force occupied on June 9–10, the key days of the battle. In fact, the IAF was so intent on killing Syrian MiGs that they concentrated most of their effort on the air battles. As a result, the IAF did not provide much support to Israeli armor in the Bekaa until late on June 10 when the Syrian lines had already been broken. Of course, what can be faulted in the decision to commit the Syrian Air Force was the absence of any real strategy that took into account the well-known shortcomings of Syrian planes and pilots and so might have allowed the Syrian fighters to accomplish something more than merely serving as a punching bag for the IAF to distract it from the ground battles.

Tactical Performance. The real variations in Syrian military effectiveness were at the tactical level. Specifically, there was a sizable gap between the performance of Syrian commandos and that of the rest of the armed forces. Syria's commando forces consistently fought markedly better than any other units of the Syrian military. They chose good ambush sites and generally established clever traps to lure the Israelis into prepared kill zones. The commandos showed a decent ability to operate in conjunction with tanks and other armored vehicles, integrating them into their own fire schemes and doing a good job protecting the tanks from Israeli infantry. The Syrian commandos also were noticeably more aggressive, creative, and willing to take initiative and to seize fleeting opportunities than other Syrian units. Their surprise counterattacks on Israeli armored columns at Ayn Zhaltah and Rashayyah in the Bekaa stand out in particular. Finally, the Syrian commandos did an excellent job disengaging whenever the Israelis began to gain the upper hand in a fight, at which point they usually pulled back to another ambush site farther up the road.

In contrast, the rest of Syria's armed forces performed very poorly, manifesting all of the same problems that had plagued them in their previous wars. In the words of Major General Amir Drori, the overall commander of the Israeli invasion, "The Syrians did everything slower and worse than we expected."[17] Without a doubt, the Syrian Air Force performed worst of all the services, but having discussed their problems in some detail above, I will concentrate on the Syrian Army.

As opposed to the competent performance turned in by their commandos, Syria's line formations had little to brag about other than their stubborn resistance and orderly retreat. Syrian armor consistently refused to maneuver against the Israelis, with the result that in every tank duel, no matter how much the terrain or circumstances favored the Syrians, it was only a matter of time before the Israelis' superior marksmanship and constant efforts to maneuver for advantage led to a Syrian defeat. Chaim Herzog has echoed this assessment, observing that the Syrian military's greatest problem was its chronic "inflexibility in maneuver."[18] Syrian artillery support was very poor and had little effect on the fighting. Syrian artillery batteries showed almost no ability to shift fire in response to changing tactical situations or to coordinate fire from geographically dispersed units. Syrian armored and mechanized formations recognized the need to conduct combined arms operations, but showed little understanding of how to actually do so. Infantry, armor, and artillery all failed to provide each other with adequate support, allowing the Israelis to defeat each in detail. In general, the Syrians relied on mass to compensate for their tactical shortcomings, but Israeli tactical skill proved so overwhelming that even where Syrian armored and mechanized formations were able to create favorable odds ratios, they were still easily defeated by the Israelis.

Damascus's ground forces had other problems as well. Syrian units were extremely negligent in gathering information and conducting reconnaissance. Many Syrian commanders simply failed to order patrols to keep abreast of Israeli movements in their sector, instead relying on information passed down from higher echelons. Those patrols that were dispatched seemed to have little feel for the purpose of reconnaissance and rarely gathered much useful information. As a result, many Syrian units blundered around Lebanon with little understanding of where the Israelis were, sometimes with fatal consequences. Syrian units showed poor fire discipline, squandering rounds so quickly that they were forced to retreat because they were out of ammunition. Despite extensive training in night-combat from their Soviet advisors, Syrian units were almost helpless after dark. Syrian personnel at all levels could not night navigate, their units lost all cohesion in the darkness, and morale dropped accordingly. Only some of the commando units showed any ability to actually apply the training they had received and operate after dark but, fortunately for the Syrians, the Israelis generally halted each night.

The Syrian Gazelle helicopter gunships made a huge psychological impact on the Israelis, but did little actual damage. The Gazelles were not able to manage more than a few armor kills during the war, and although they employed proper "pop-up" tactics, they could only delay the Israelis. Although this was useful in slowing the Israeli advance to the Bekaa and then hindering the Israeli pursuit after they had broken through the Syrian lines, the Gazelles were unable to prevent Syrian defeats, even when they were committed in large numbers as in the fighting around Lake Qir'awn. One Israeli officer observed that the Syrian Gazelles were "not a problem" because they did not employ them creatively, had bad aim, and operated only individually or in pairs, making it easy for the IDF to handle them.[19] Anthony Cordesman has commented that Syrian helicopter operations in Lebanon suffered from "The same tactical and operational rigidities, training, and command problems that affected its tank, other armor, and artillery performance."[20] Consequently, their contributions were negligible.

Syrian combat support was another impediment to their tactical performance. In particular, Syrian logistics were appalling. Damascus had established huge stockpiles of spares and combat consumables in the Bekaa, yet during the combat operations many Syrian units could not get resupplied (although part of the problem was their wasteful expenditure of ammunition). Graft had riddled the Syrian quartermaster corps with the result that a lot of things that were supposed to have been available were not. In addition, the Syrians did not understand their Soviet-style "push" logistics system, with quartermasters demanding formal requests for provisions, rather than simply sending supplies to the front at regular intervals as intended.

Maintenance was another problem area for the Syrians. Most Syrian soldiers were incapable and unwilling to perform even basic preventive maintenance on their weapons and vehicles. Instead, these functions had to be performed by specialized technicians attached at brigade and division level, and for most repairs, equipment had to be sent back to a small number of central depots around Damascus. These facilities were manned in part by Cuban technicians who handled the more advanced Soviet weaponry. The Israelis reported capturing a fair number of Syrian armored vehicles abandoned because of minor mechanical problems.

The fact that Syria's commandos performed so much better than Syrian units ever had in the past should not obscure the fact that, in an absolute sense, when compared to the forces of other armies, Syria's commando battalions were still mediocre. In general, the Syrian commandos were content to sit in their prepared positions, fire down on Israeli forces that wandered into their ambushes, and then retreat as soon as the Israelis recovered and began to bust up the Syrian defensive scheme. Incidents such as the commando counterattacks at Ayn Zhaltah, Rashayyah, and a few other minor engagements were still exceptions to the rule. They are noteworthy because they were among the only times that even the commandos tried to get out and upset Israeli operations. The rule, however, was for the commandos to establish ambushes and then wait passively for the IDF to come to them.

The commandos also weren't terrific with their weapons: on any number of occasions, Israeli units were completely trapped by Syrian commando ambushes, and subjected to a hail of gunfire, grenades, and missiles, only to emerge having suffered just a handful of casualties. In addition, like other Syrian formations, the commandos frequently neglected to cover their flanks or were too quick to conclude that terrain was impassable. As a result, many Syrian ambushes were cleared by Israeli flank guards or bypassed altogether when Israeli combat engineers found a way through terrain the Syrians had deemed impassable.

Unit cohesion among Syrian formations in Lebanon was actually quite good. For the most part, Syrian units stuck together and fought back under all circumstances. Few Syrian units simply disintegrated in combat. The rule was that Syrian units fought hard and then stuck together and retreated well. Although it is true that Israeli pressure was uncharacteristically light on the Syrian armored forces withdrawing up the Bekaa after their defeat on June 10, there were still many instances of Syrian units showing good discipline and retreating in good order under heavy pressure. The commandos in particular showed outstanding unit cohesion. In many fights they clung to their defensive positions until they were overpowered by Israeli infantry units, and in several clashes, Syrian commando units fought to the last man to hold particularly important positions or when acting as rear guards to allow other forces to escape.

Syrian Combat Performance and Underdevelopment

It's easy to get distracted by the better performance of Syria's commandos in 1982 and see it as evidence that the Syrians had improved dramatically over their performance in 1948 (and 1967, 1970, 1973, and 1976). It's just as important not to. The commandos represented no more than about 5 percent of the Syrian forces that fought against the Israelis in Lebanon. They were better than the other 95 percent, but not dramatically so. They never proved the equal of their Israeli opponents. They were always beaten, sometimes badly, sometimes very badly.

Meanwhile, the rest of the force was pretty disastrous and showed no marked improvement over the conduct of their predecessors back in 1948. It's not that there weren't any differences between the Syrian Army of 1948 and that of 1982. There were. And in some important areas and in some very noticeable ways. But overall, it's hard to make the case that Syrian combat effectiveness had improved much.

Syrian *strategic* performance was notably better in 1982 than it had been in 1948, but that had nothing to do with underdevelopment. If anything, it is another bit of evidence regarding the impact of politicization. Asad had found a handful of generals who were both competent and loyal to command his forces before the October War, and these men largely remained in charge in 1982.

Syrian tactical leadership, however, demonstrated the same set of problems that plagued their forces in 1948 and all of the wars in-between.[21] Their junior officers would not act aggressively or creatively, could not execute ad hoc operations, did not bother to patrol or otherwise try to collect information, could not maneuver for advantage or even shift their forces to react to enemy maneuvers. They rarely counterattacked, and when they did so it was generally a clumsy frontal assault. Time and again, Syrian tactical forces just sat in their defensive positions and blasted away (inaccurately) until the Israelis killed them or maneuvered them out of position. And while the commandos did noticeably better with combined arms, an ability to improvise defensive positions quickly, and a somewhat greater reactivity to Israeli moves, so too did some of the Syrian forces in 1948, notably in their second assault on Zemach and the fighting at Mishmar HaYarden. Moreover, the performance of the Syrian Air Force in 1982 was absolutely dreadful, more than compensating for any plaudits the commandos might have won. In terms of tactical leadership, there was little, if any, improvement among Syrian forces despite Syria's significant economic development from 1948 to 1982.

A variety of other problems persisted or actually got worse as Syria developed economically between 1948 and 1982. Syrian logistics were not great in 1948, but neither did they have to be. Very little was asked of them. Syrian logistics were awful in 1982, although corruption was a big part of the problem. Syrian maintenance and operational readiness rates did not improve much, nor did Syrian weapons handling. To some extent, all of these issues need to be seen in relative terms: in 1982, the Syrians were operating far more sophisticated equipment requiring far greater logistical needs than they had in 1948. They were still bad, but they seemed to be keeping pace, staying at the same mediocre level, even as the sophistication of their equipment increased. That suggests an improvement that paralleled their rising level of development.

The one area where that didn't seem to apply was Syria's air force pilots. In 1982, they were utterly incapable of flying (let alone fighting) their planes when they lost their GCI guidance. There is no parallel in 1948, and this suggests that the MiG-23 and even the MiG-21 may have been beyond the ability of even a better-developed Syria to employ properly.

In an absolute sense, the Syrian military of 1982 was vastly more powerful than that of 1948. It was better armed, better trained, more professional, larger, and had more combat experience. If they somehow could have fought each other, the Syrian military of 1982 undoubtedly would have beaten the Syrian military of 1948. Two things are noteworthy for our purposes, however. First, many of the most crippling problems that the Syrians (and other Arab militaries) have consistently experienced since 1948 in tactical leadership and information handling remained unabated. If anything, *they got worse*. Second, despite the significant improvement in

Syria's socioeconomic circumstances, its problems with logistics, mainte-nance, weapons handling, and even combined arms operations did not im-prove much, if at all. At best, they kept the same mediocre pace with the increasing sophistication of Syria's Soviet-supplied kit.

All of this suggests that underdevelopment probably did have an impact on the effectiveness of Arab militaries since World War II, but like politici-zation, it came in certain areas, and not necessarily those that were the most deleterious.

CHAPTER 12 | Economic Development
and the Libya-Chad Wars

T HE STORY OF the Libyan wars with Chad is a twofer. Libya is, obviously,
an Arab state while Chad is not only *not* Arab, but at the time of these
wars, was one of the poorest, least developed countries on earth. At the time of
their conflict, Libya was vastly better developed than Chad. (See Table 12.1 for
some comparative statistics.)

That's great, because to the extent that underdevelopment is to blame for
the problems of Arab militaries, we should expect to find that the armies of
more developed Arab countries fight better than the armies of less-developed
non-Arab countries (and vice versa). In particular, if underdevelopment is the
culprit, then underdeveloped non-Arab states should demonstrate the same
patterns of military problems as the Arabs. In fact, all underdeveloped states
should have all the same problems, Arab or not.

So the questions before us are: Did the Libyans perform better than the
Chadians, since the Libyans were much more developed than the Chadians?
Did the Chadians and Libyans experience similar problems, since both were
relatively underdeveloped? And were those problems worse for the Chadians
than for the Libyans, since the Chadians were still much less developed than
the Libyans?

The First Libyan Intervention, 1978

The story of Libya's repeated invasions of Chad is a convoluted one, like most
things related to the reign of Muammar Qadhafi. Libya had an irredentist

TABLE 12.1 Socioeconomic Development of Chad and Libya in 1987

Indicators	Chad	Libya
GDP per capita	$90	$6,260
Literacy (% of pop. over 15 able to read + write)	17	60
Infant mortality per 1,000 live births	138	84
Life expectancy at birth, in years	44	57
Per capita electrical power production (in kWh)	12	3,250
% of work force in agriculture	85	18
Inhabitants per physician	38, 360*	690*
Inhabitants per automobile	215	6
Inhabitants per television	1,082	19
Inhabitants per telephone	929	24

* Figure is for 1984 as no data is available for 1987.

Sources: CIA, *The World Factbook*, 1987; MVMA Motor Vehicle Facts & Figures
'89; The World Bank, *World Development Report*, 1987, 1990; UN Statistical Office,
Compendium of Social Statistics and Indicators 1988.

claim to the Aouzou Strip, the northernmost border region of Chad, roughly
100 kilometers wide, that was said to contain uranium deposits. However,
Aouzou was also a convenient excuse for Qadhafi to involve himself in Chad
as part of his grandiose vision to make Libya the dominant power in North
Africa and claim Nasser's mantle as leader of the Arab world.[1] Soon after he
took power in 1969, Qadhafi began to support Chadian dissidents seeking to
overthrow its government.[2]

Chadian politics in the 1970s (and 1980s) were unstable to say the least.
Numerous groups vied for power, creating opportunities for Libyan meddling.
By the late 1970s, the primary split was between two rival opposition leaders
from the Toubou—an African ethnic group that follows Islam. Personal and
policy differences (including Chad's relationship with Libya) drove apart the
two primary Toubou leaders: Goukouni Oueddei and Hissène Habré.

In 1978, Goukouni's forces attempted to take over the country by force,
with help from Qadhafi and still another rebel army of Chadian Arabs. In
their first offensive in January of that year, Goukouni's forces overran the
mountainous Tibesti in extreme northwest Chad. Then they turned south,
and Qadhafi dispatched Libyan combat units to fight alongside them. In a
pattern that would become the norm over the next nine years, the Toubous
provided the infantry, which did the bulk of the scouting and fighting, while
the Libyans provided armor, artillery, and air support.

In February, an army of 2,500 Toubou fighters, with possibly as many as 4,000 Libyans providing fire support, attacked the crossroads town of Faya-Largeau in north-central Chad. The 5,000-man garrison there lacked the weaponry to contend with Libyan firepower, particularly Libyan tanks and air strikes, and they collapsed after a brief battle. The Toubous and Libyans resumed their drive south in April, smashing small government units with Libyan armor and airpower and heading directly for N'djamena. This threat to the capital prompted the Chadian government to ask France, Chad's former co-lonial master, to rescue the country. Paris agreed, dispatching a force of 1,000 men and 20 Jaguar fighter-bombers. The Jaguars in particular turned the tide because the Libyan MiGs and Mirages would not engage them. As a re-sult, the government suddenly possessed the complete air superiority that the rebels previously had enjoyed, and the results were equally decisive. In a pair of battles along the northern approaches to N'djamena at Ati in May and Djedaa in June, the government and French forces routed the rebels and Libyans and drove them back to the Aouzou Strip.

The Second Libyan Intervention, 1979

Goukouni and his Toubous had always been uncomfortable with the Libyan presence, chafed at the Libyan occupation of the Aouzou Strip, and regarded their partnership as nothing but a temporary alliance to get rid of the gov-ernment. Thus, after the poor performance of Libyan forces at Ati and Djedaa, Goukouni began to re-evaluate the relationship. This created a rupture with the Chadian Arabs (now known as the Volcan Army) who saw Libya as their natural ally. Yet at Ati, the Volcans had proven to be the weakest military link in the alliance because they had neither the firepower of the Libyans nor the tactical skill of the Toubous.

Then, in February 1979, Habré managed to topple the Chadian govern-ment. Goukouni hurried south with his own forces to contest power with Habré. However, rather than fight a knockdown, drag-out battle in the cap-ital, the two Toubou armies struck a deal. The result was a new government of national unity, the Government d'Union Nationale de Transition (GUNT).

The Libyans were incensed that the new GUNT did not include the Arabs of the Volcan Army, nor did it recognize Libyan claims on the Aouzou Strip. Qadhafi ordered another invasion to compel the new government to recognize his claims. He sent a force of several thousand Libyan troops with armor and air support along with elements of the Volcan Army to retake Faya-Largeau. This time, however, the Libyans were opposed by Goukouni's forces. Without

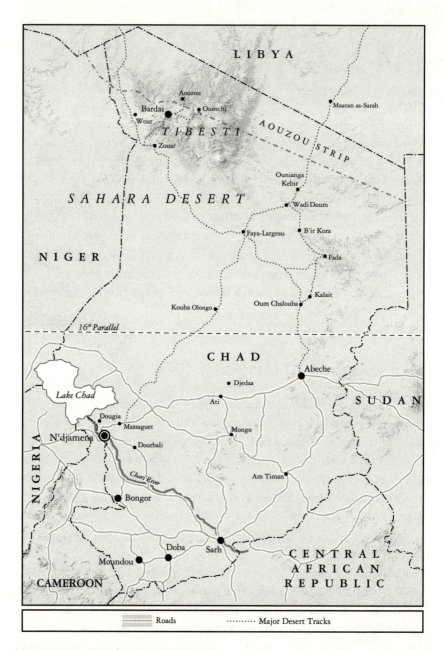

MAP 23 The War for Chad, 1978–1987

the Toubous to provide infantry and reconnaissance, Libya's firepower proved impotent. The Libyans and Volcans again proved their incompetence in combat and were smashed by Goukouni's forces—backed by French airpower—in a series of clashes around Faya-Largeau from April to August 1979.

The Third Libyan Intervention, 1980–1981

Of course, victory simply bred division. After the Libyans were ousted, Habré turned on Goukouni, and in March 1980, he expelled the GUNT from N'djamena. Habré and his forces, now called the Forces Armée du Nord (FAN), then set out to gain control of the rest of the country. After a few small setbacks, Habré's FAN drove the GUNT out of north-central Chad, seizing the major towns of Faya-Largeau and Ounianga-Kebir as well as much of the northern Toubou lands. Once again, Goukouni was forced to turn to Tripoli for aid.

For his part, Qadhafi was eager to get back into the Chadian game, although he was also determined to put it on a firmer footing than before, having recognized that Goukouni would never be more than an ally of convenience. He now had the leverage to get what he wanted as GUNT forces regrouped in southern Libya where they rested and were re-equipped by the Libyans. At that point Goukouni even accepted a Libyan officer, Mansur 'Abd al-Aziz, as commander of the GUNT forces. Starting in August 1980, Tripoli mustered an army of Libyan regulars and Islamic Legionnaires—poorly trained paramilitary forces—at Sabha in southern Libya to prepare for the next round.

In October 1980, before Habré could consolidate his rule, the Libyans, Volcans, and GUNT invaded. They had every advantage. Qadhafi sent 7,000 Libyan regulars with 300 T-55s and several batteries of BM-21s, backed by much of the Libyan Air Force (LAF), along with 7,000 members of the Islamic Legion. The GUNT and Volcan Armies added another 6,000–7,000 soldiers to the invading force while Habré had only 4,000 men with no armor, aircraft, or even heavy infantry weapons to resist the onslaught.[3] Moreover, the FAN soldiers were terrified of the firepower the Libyans were able to bring to bear, especially because the FAN had no anti-aircraft or heavy antitank weapons with which to fight back.

Tripoli began the invasion by airlifting large numbers of troops into the Aouzou Strip and then striking directly at Faya-Largeau while Habré's forces were still scattered and consolidating their control over the country. Beginning at Faya-Largeau in October, the Libyan/GUNT advances developed into a predictable routine. Seasoned GUNT warriors would probe ahead of the main columns looking for FAN concentrations. When they were located, the Libyans would bring up their armor and artillery, dig-in in front of the defenders, and then unleash a barrage from their tanks, artillery, and rocket launchers, accompanied by heavy air strikes for good measure. The Libyan bombardments were usually very inaccurate, but because Habré's men had never encountered such volumes of firepower before and had no answer for the Libyan armor and fighter-bombers, they completely unnerved the FAN defenders. On many occasions, FAN soldiers simply fled during the initial Libyan barrage. Libyan airpower, free to roam the skies without fear of the French Air Force or SAMs, proved particularly devastating, winning numerous engagements single-handed by scattering the defenders before the ground units even came to grips.

On those rare occasions when Habré's defenders were not driven off by the initial bombardment, Libyan armor and Islamic Legionnaires occasionally put in a straight-ahead charge at the main FAN positions. Although these attacks were clumsy affairs and Libyan armor and Legionnaires had no understanding of how to coordinate their actions, because Habré's men lacked any antitank weapons, the attacks usually succeeded in breaking FAN resistance. Otherwise, the GUNT infantry would conduct a determined assault, which usually resulted in their overwhelming the disoriented FAN units in bloody hand-to-hand fighting.

Using these inelegant but effective tactics, the Libyans and the GUNT swept all resistance before them. By early November, Tripoli's army had driven the FAN from Faya-Largeau. The Libyans quickly turned the town into a staging base, airlifting in vast quantities of supplies, replacement troops, and equipment to make good their losses. In late November, the Libyans and GUNT resumed their advance south toward N'djamena. Habré's men did not stand a chance. Outgunned and outnumbered, they fled back to the capital to try to make a stand. At the end of the month, the Libyans and the GUNT conquered Dougia, just 60 kilometers north of N'djamena. Here they paused to set up another forward logistics depot and airbase, and again built up supplies for the impending offensive against the capital.

With all troops and logistical support in place, the assault on the defenses of the city began on December 8 and was conducted largely by the GUNT. However, the Libyans committed about 5,000 troops and nearly all of their heavy weapons (including 200 T-55s and all of their artillery and MRLs in support of the attack. The fighting was ferocious between Goukouni and Habré's men, and the Libyans kept up a steady barrage, lobbing 10,000 artillery rounds into the city in the last three days of fighting alone.[4] As before, because the FAN units were outnumbered, had no air defense weapons, and had only a handful of rocket-propelled grenades (RPGs) for antitank weapons, they were slowly beaten down under the weight of GUNT numbers and Libyan firepower. N'djamena fell to the Libyans and the GUNT on December 15.

Qadhafi had finally achieved his goals: N'djamena and the government were in the hands of Goukouni, who was not only beholden to him for conquering the country, but was effectively hostage to the nearly 15,000 Libyan soldiers deployed across Chad. What's more, the Libyan offensive had been a stunning accomplishment, if only as a logistical feat. A Libyan army operating over 2,000 kilometers from its principal bases along the Mediterranean had conducted a sustained armored advance over 1,000 kilometers through hostile territory in a victorious seven-week campaign. However, this victory was hardly cost-free for the Libyans. As many as 1,500 Libyan soldiers were killed in the fighting, and probably another 4,000–6,000 were wounded.

The Fourth Libyan Intervention, 1983–1986

Once again, the victory did not last long. In January 1981, Qadhafi tried to coerce Goukouni into a merger of the two countries, prompting Goukouni to break with Qadhafi and setting off a firestorm of criticism against Libya in the Organization of African Unity (OAU), whose support Qadhafi needed for his African aspirations. Realizing that he had overplayed his hand, Qadhafi forgot the merger and withdrew all Libyan troops from southern Chad in October 1981. The withdrawal was another remarkable logistical accomplishment, equal to its efforts during the invasion in the fall. The entire Libyan force pulled back to the Aouzou Strip and southern Libya in just three weeks with a minimum of problems.

Of course, Goukouni's rule over Chad did not last long either. While the Libyans licked their wounds in the Aouzou Strip, Habré and the FAN retreated to Sudan where they regrouped, retrained, and recruited new soldiers. With covert aid from Sudan, Egypt, France, and the United States, Habré was able to rebuild the FAN into an efficient fighting force by early 1982. In May of that year, he invaded Chad from Sudan and routed Goukouni's forces. The GUNT army disintegrated and headed for their homeland in the Tibesti. Two days later, on June 7, 1982, Habré re-entered N'djamena and proclaimed himself president of Chad.

The Libyans sat on the sidelines during this fight. Qadhafi had been badly burned by his experience the year before. He needed to maintain the support of the OAU, and was loath to sustain heavy casualties for ephemeral political gains as he had in 1981. Nevertheless, he also began to prepare to re-intervene in Chad in the near future, renegotiating an alliance with Goukouni and building up Libyan forces in the Aouzou Strip.

In early April 1983, they were ready and the GUNT, the Volcans, and the Libyans invaded yet again. Although the Libyans had roughly 11,000 men in the Aouzou Strip—the vast majority of whom were Libyan regulars, the Islamic Legionnaires having fought poorly and taken heavy casualties in 1981—Tripoli committed only a few thousand to the invasion. Most of these were artillery and logistics units. Qadhafi meant to minimize his losses this time by further relegating Libyan troops to pure support roles, forcing the GUNT to shoulder an even greater share of the actual combat.

At Dourbali, in April 1983, the GUNT/Libyan force beat a small government garrison. In June, the GUNT took Faya-Largeau, overran Abeche, and then marched on N'djamena. However, Habré responded quickly, rallying the rest of his army (now called the Force Armée Nationale Tchadien, or FANT) and marching north to meet the GUNT/Libyans outside Abeche in early July. Once again, Habré proved to be the better general with the better army, smashing Goukouni's forces at Abeche and then launching a counteroffensive of his own. On July 30, Habré hit the GUNT/Libyan army at Faya-Largeau and routed them, retaking the town and threatening to drive north on the Tibesti and the Aouzou Strip.

Goukouni's defeat prompted Qadhafi to re-enter the Chadian fray in force. The string of losses in the late spring and early summer had demonstrated that without Libyan armor and airpower, the GUNT could not prevail alone against Habré's FANT. Yet Qadhafi could not allow Goukouni to be defeated; not only would this be an intolerable blow to Libyan prestige, it would leave Chad in the hands of the rabidly anti-Libyan Habré who could be expected to support all manner of opposition to Qadhafi from Chadian territory. So in August 1983, Qadhafi ordered another general Libyan invasion of Chad, with the regrouped GUNT leading the way.

This time the Libyans committed 11,000 troops, most of them regulars, to the operation, and airlifted virtually the entire force, complete with tanks and artillery, directly into the Aouzou Strip. Although Tripoli again dispatched large numbers of tanks and APCs as well as roughly 80 combat aircraft (a considerable portion of the operational Libyan Air Force) for the offensive, Libyan forces still played their traditional roles providing fire support and the occasional headlong tank charge for GUNT assaults. The GUNT probably contributed 3,000–4,000 men to the invasion force. Meanwhile, Habré had dug-in a sizable FANT army—perhaps as many as 5,000 men—at Faya-Largeau to await the inevitable Libyan/GUNT assault along the traditional invasion route between Libya and Chad.

In August, the GUNT and Libyans attacked, battering the FANT with MRL, artillery, and tank fire as well as almost continuous air strikes by Libyan Su-22s and Mirages operating from Aouzou, as well as Tu-16 bombers flying from Sabha. Although the FANT troops mostly held their positions, by the time the GUNT launched its main infantry assault supported by slow-moving Libyan armor, the heavily outnumbered FANT troops were in no shape to put up a fight. Without antitank or anti-aircraft weapons, their main line of defense crumbled and Habré retreated south. Despite their crushing victory, the Libyans failed to pursue the FANT, allowing Habré's forces to escape to N'djamena.

This proved to be a crucial mistake. While the Libyans milled around and took their time regrouping at Faya-Largeau, Habré pulled his troops back to N'djamena to regroup and rearm. Of greater importance still, Habré realized that the FANT alone could not hold N'djamena against a GUNT-Libyan force of this size. So he appealed to Paris for help. Thanks to pressure from the United States and the African outcry against the renewed Libyan intervention, the French dispatched 3,500 troops and Jaguar fighter-bombers to Chad. By the time the Libyans and Chadians resumed their march south, the French had established a defensive line along the 16th Parallel, effectively bisecting the country.

The French defensive line provided Habré with a secure base from which to mount a counteroffensive against the GUNT and the Libyans. In early September, he attacked Oum Chalouba in central Chad, southeast of Faya-Largeau. Although no French ground troops participated, French aircraft flew defensive counter-air missions to keep the Libyan Air Force at bay. Moreover, Habré had had the time to rally his forces once again, and with the assurance that Libyan Mirages and Sukhois were out of the picture, the FANT troops rose to the challenge. On September 6 they drove the GUNT and Libyans out of Oum Chalouba, and a few weeks later retook Faya-Largeau. Habré then attacked northward toward the Aouzou Strip. However, the French refused to fly combat air patrols for this offensive. In addition, the FANT was tired and its ranks depleted from the constant campaigning. On the other hand, the Libyans had had a chance to regroup, resupply, and dig-in in familiar territory. As a result of these complimentary factors, Habré's offensive quickly ground to a halt in a few small, desultory battles.

With the fighting petering out, French president François Mitterrand proposed a mutual withdrawal to Tripoli. Qadhafi accepted, but while the French eagerly departed, the Libyans covertly remained. In fact, far from evacuate, they built new roads from Libya into northern Chad and a major new airbase at Wadi Doum, north of Faya-Largeau. France's departure stirred Qadhafi and Goukouni to make yet another go at Habré and the conquest of Chad.

So as not to spark a French redeployment, the Libyans and the GUNT moved more cautiously this time, pushing into northern Chad in measured advances and keeping north of the 16th Parallel. By mid-1985, the Libyans had built up their forces in Chad to approximately 7,000 troops with 300 tanks, and 60 combat aircraft. Like the FANT, the GUNT had taken heavy losses in the battles from 1980 to 1983 and was reduced to no more than 2,000–3,000 full-time soldiers. As a result, the Libyans shouldered more of the burden than in the past, and tended to rely even more heavily on sheer firepower to dislodge FANT units from their positions. However, the Libyans found that Habré had decided not to contest northern Chad. Without French airpower, and still lacking the weapons to defeat Libyan tanks and jets, Habré chose to conserve his forces and concentrate on defending N'djamena and southern Chad. Consequently, the Libyans had little difficulty reasserting their control over the northern half of the country in 1985 and 1986.

The Change in the Balance of Forces

The political and diplomatic context of the Libya-Chad wars continued to churn. Qadhafi experienced repeated military coups in the early 1980s, including one that led to fighting in the streets of Tripoli in 1984. In response, he imposed ever greater commissarist controls over his military, including some that affected his troops in Chad. In particular, Qadhafi would not permit the creation of divisions, so all formations larger than brigades had to be formed on an ad hoc basis in the field. He attached militia and reserve units to regular formations to try to shore up the loyalty of the line units. He even limited the size and scope of field training exercises and virtually prohibited live-fire exercises for fear that the troops would use the ammunition to overthrow the regime.

Nevertheless, like other dictators before him, Qadhafi also feared that losing a war would trigger a wider move against him, and this meant that he required a certain degree of efficiency from the forces in combat in Chad. Consequently, despite his fears of the military, Qadhafi was forced to place well-regarded and experienced officers in command of his forces in the field. This may have been easier for him because Chad was so far away, making it difficult for these men to threaten his reign. Yet, even this consideration had its limits, and there were still numerous command and control eccentricities stemming from his fear of a coup. For example, Libyan garrisons in Chad were sometimes manned by battalions from different brigades, all of which were left under the command of their parent headquarters, making it nearly impossible for the garrison to act in a concerted manner.[5]

In 1985 and 1986 there was a crucial, but initially undetectable, shift in the military balance in Chad. Although the increasing political shackles on the Libyan armed forces were part of this change, in truth, they were only a minor aspect of it. Libyan tactics—relying on massive doses of firepower coupled with the occasional, slow-moving, frontal assault—were not terribly demanding, and therefore a great deal of inefficiency could be tolerated without "diminishing" Libya's ability to conduct such simplistic operations. Moreover, the Libyans generally executed these tactics so poorly throughout their involvement in Chad that it is difficult to detect any significant further decrease in their abilities as a result of the increased politicization of the early 1980s. Instead, the key changes were in the capabilities of the FANT.

Throughout the early 1980s, the Reagan administration had grown ever more bellicose toward Libya and ever more willing to support Habré's FANT as Libya's enemy. In 1985, the United States and France (in part because of US pressure and in part because of Mitterrand's embarrassment at having been duped into withdrawing by Qadhafi) began providing the FANT with training, weaponry, and extensive logistical support.

To their credit, Habré and his subordinates recognized which equipment would be useful to them and which would simply be a hindrance. They declined offers of tanks, APCs, and heavy artillery. They felt that their troops lacked the technical skills to operate them. Instead, they requested light armored cars, trucks, automatic weapons, grenade launchers, recoilless rifles, mortars, antitank weapons, and anti-aircraft weapons. In particular, the FANT asked for US-made Redeye shoulder-launched SAMs and French Milan antitank guided missiles (ATGMs).

These new weapons made possible new tactics for Habré's forces. With the Milan and Redeye, the FANT finally had weapons that could take on Libya's tanks and fighter-bombers. This knowledge gave Habré's soldiers the courage to stand and fight. At that moment, the conflict ceased to be a one-sided contest in which the Libyans could simply stand back and frighten off FANT soldiers with their firepower. Suddenly, the FANT could fight back.

However, the key tactical change that the new weapons made possible was to reintroduce the rapid movement and concentration that were the hallmark of traditional Toubou warfare. The large numbers of Toyota four-wheel-drive trucks equipped with crew-served weapons restored to the Chadians the strategic mobility and tactical maneuverability they had lost when they had adopted modern infantry weapons, organization, and tactics. With their new mobility, the FANT's tribal warriors were then able to employ their traditional desert warfare tactics in a way that they had not been able to before.

In battle, Chadian forces employed "swarming" tactics. They used the speed of their armored cars and Toyotas to dart around the battlefield, hitting Libyan armored vehicles in the flanks, and often from several angles simultaneously.

The Chadians maintained a very high pace of operations, relying on the speed and flexibility of their units to confuse the slow-moving and slow-to-react Libyans, isolate them in smaller units, and then crush them suddenly with attacks from all sides. The Chadians maneuvered constantly on the battlefield to prevent the Libyans from bringing their heavier firepower to bear and to get flank shots at Libyan armor and fortifications. Indeed, the Chadians moved so quickly that Libyan tank crews often had difficulty moving the turrets on their T-55 tanks fast enough to accurately target Libyan Toyotas.

In addition to the new weapons, the change in US attitudes toward the war in Chad also brought other important benefits. In particular, although the Chadians did not employ Western soldiers or even advisers in their campaigns in 1986–1987, they benefited from Western personnel (mostly French) manning their logistical system. Inadequate logistics had hamstrung previous FANT offensives, and the added burden of large numbers of motor vehicles further increased the FANT's supply difficulties. By taking over the FANT's logistical system and seeing to its effective functioning, Western personnel greatly enhanced the speed and range of Habré's forces.[6]

The last element in the improvement in FANT military capabilities was the development of a cadre of outstanding battlefield commanders, whom Habré had found to lead the FANT against Libya and the GUNT. Over the course of the campaigns in 1983–1986, Habré identified a number of leaders from among his forces and increasingly used them to command key units. By 1986, Habré had a corps of aggressive, flexible, seasoned field commanders such as Idris Deby, Ahmed Gorou, Muhammad Nouri, and Hassan Djamous. Djamous, in particular, proved to be an outstanding commander, practicing maneuver warfare with a skill that led several Western observers to compare him to Erwin Rommel.[7] In 1986, Habré made Djamous the commander of the FANT's main field army.

The 1986 Campaigns

At the beginning of February 1986, the Libyans and the GUNT attacked south from their positions in north-central Chad. This offensive was larger and more ambitious than Libyan/GUNT operations over the past two years. The Libyans committed 5,000 troops with large formations of armor and artillery, backed by considerable airpower and 5,000 GUNT and Volcan Army soldiers. On February 10, the Libyan/GUNT forces attacked Kouba Olonga, Kalait, and Oum Chalouba. They took Oum Chalouba and Kalait the next day, despite fierce resistance by the FANT.

However, FANT patrols had long-before detected the Libyan buildup and so Habré had forces already in place to meet the attack. On February 13, the FANT counterattacked, retaking Oum Chalouba and Kalait and crushing the Libyans and the GUNT with their new weapons and tactics. The Libyans were beaten so badly that they were forced to pull back to the Aouzou Strip to regroup, and were not able to resume the offensive until March. By then, Habré had concentrated considerable forces in the Oum Chalouba area and the Libyans were repulsed with heavy losses. Moreover, Habré used the size and power of the initial Libyan thrusts (as well as Mitterand's humiliation from Qadhafi's false withdrawal in 1984) to convince the French to redeploy 2,000 troops and several squadrons of Jaguars to Chad. Although the French still refused to join the FANT in a counteroffensive, they began conducting air strikes against Libyan airbases in Chad, ostensibly to suppress the Libyan Air Force while French troops and supplies were airlifted into the country. The unexpected reversals on the ground at the hands of the FANT, plus the French air strikes, prompted the Libyans to call off the invasion and retreat back to their positions in the north.

Of course, these setbacks only convinced Qadhafi to redouble his efforts. Immediately after the March offensive, Libya began a massive reinforcement of its army in Chad. Moreover, by late 1986, the Libyan forces in Chad were equipped with more powerful weapons than ever before, including T-62 tanks and BMP-1 infantry fighting vehicles. Tripoli did not recognize that the FANT's new Western arms and the new tactics that they made possible were the cause of their defeat, and instead blamed inadequate numbers. Libya concluded that the 1986 invasion force had been too small: with only 5,000 Libyan troops it had been unable to accomplish the same objectives as the much larger forces that had overrun Chad in 1980 and 1983. Consequently, Qadhafi doubled the size of his army in Chad, principally augmenting its armor, artillery, and air components, in expectation of resuming the offensive in the fall.

But events conspired to preclude an autumn Libyan offensive. In August 1986, before the Libyans had completed preparations for a new campaign, Goukouni's GUNT and Qadhafi's Libya had a final falling-out. The GUNT retreated to their traditional strongholds in the Tibesti, ousting Libyan garrisons from Bardai, Wour, and Zouar. In early December 1986, the Libyans sent a brigade task force of 2,000 men with T-62 tanks and heavy air support to smash the GUNT and retake the Tibesti. Because of this firepower, to which the GUNT had no answer, the Libyans were able to force the GUNT out of Bardai, Wour, and Zouar once again.

Hissene Habré recognized this moment as his opportunity to unite all of Chad behind him and drive the Libyans from the country. He sent 2,000 FANT troops to the Tibesti to link up with Goukouni's forces. The infusion of these newly equipped and trained troops allowed the Chadians to stop the Libyan advance, but they found it hard to pry the Libyans out of the Tibesti. Libyan units proved tenacious when conducting simple, static defensive operations in the difficult terrain. Moreover, the channeling effect of the mountains minimized the extent to which the Chadians could employ flanking maneuvers against Libyan defensive positions, while maximizing the Libyan advantage in firepower. Consequently, the fighting in the Tibesti turned into a slogging match. Although the Chadians retook Zouar and Wour by January 1987, the Libyans were really only forced to pull out of the region altogether in March because of Chadian victories elsewhere.

Nevertheless, the split between Goukouni and Qadhafi was another watershed in the local military equation. Without the GUNT soldiers, Libyan formations lacked adequate infantry and reconnaissance elements. Libyan units were brought in as replacements, but they were very poor compared to the GUNT's Toubous. Libyan formations were forced to scout for themselves—which they rarely did—and, in combat, they could no longer sit back and blast away while the GUNT soldiers did all the dirty work. Now the Libyans had to engage the tough FANT warriors themselves and the Chadians, relying on their traditional swarming tactics, proved to be much better in combat than the slow, inflexible Libyans.

The Chadian Offensive of 1987

By the beginning of 1987, Tripoli had massed nearly 8,000 regulars with 300 tanks, large numbers of artillery and MRLs, Mi-24 helicopters, and 60 combat aircraft in northern Chad. Roughly 2,500 of these troops were engaged in the Tibesti, as part of a task force known as Operational Group South because Qadhafi continued to refuse to allow his commanders to establish divisions. The rest of the Libyan expeditionary force was concentrated in Operational Group East (under then-colonel Khalifa Haftar, who has led the Libyan National Army since the fall of Qadhafi in 2011) with its headquarters at Faya-Largeau. The theater headquarters for all Libyan forces in Chad was located at Wadi Doum.

Against them, Habré had now built an army of 10,000 regulars backed by another 20,000 tribal irregulars who could be called up for short periods of time to conduct operations in their native regions. In their final offensive, the Chadians would rely primarily on a force of 4,000–5,000 regulars led by Hassan Djamous and Ahmed Gorou. These troops fielded 70 French Panhard and American V-150 armored cars plus about 400 Toyota trucks equipped with machine guns, recoilless rifles, mortars, grenade launchers, and Milan ATGMs. With Tripoli distracted by its battle with the GUNT, Habré sent this army north to evict the Libyans from Chad.

The Chadian offensive began with an attack on the Libyan garrison at Fada, which the FANT captured on January 2, 1987. Although there were 1,200 Libyan troops with armor and artillery in fortified positions around Fada, the Chadians conducted a series of swift pincer movements, enveloping the Libyan positions and crushing them with sudden attacks from all sides. Fada fell in just eight hours, costing the Libyans 784 dead, 81 captured, and 100 destroyed tanks. The FANT had only 50 killed and 100 wounded in the battle. The French, still deployed in southern Chad and flying combat air patrols along the 16th Parallel, took no part in the operation, but under pressure from Habré, they conducted an air strike against the main Libyan airbase at Wadi Doum, which prevented the Libyan Air Force from playing much of a role in the battle.

The defeat at Fada stunned the Libyans. They had assumed that their heavy weapons and fortifications made their garrisons virtually invulnerable to the lightly armed Chadians. In response, Qadhafi ordered still more forces south. Tripoli dispatched several battalions immediately—including units from his elite Jamahiriyah Guard—to shore up its positions around Faya-Largeau and Wadi Doum, while the Libyan high command put together more substantial reinforcements. By March, the Libyans had roughly 11,000 troops in northern Chad.

On the other hand, after the fall of Fada the Chadians were forced to pause. Because of the difficulty of supplying large mechanized forces in the desert, they had to "hop" from one inhabited place to the next. To the northwest of Fada, the next major population center was Faya-Largeau, heavily fortified and garrisoned by several thousand Libyans. On the other hand, north of Fada, and a bit closer than Faya-Largeau, was the even more heavily garrisoned and fortified Libyan base at Wadi Doum. Habré and his commanders reasoned that if they could take Wadi Doum, Faya-Largeau would be in an untenable position and would fall without a fight, whereas if they took Faya-Largeau, Wadi Doum would still need to be reduced before they continued moving north. Consequently, despite its more formidable defenses, they opted to strike directly at Wadi Doum.

In March 1987 Wadi Doum was garrisoned by 6,000–7,000 Libyan troops with 200–300 tanks and APCs. Moreover, it had all-around defenses as much as six kilometers wide at points and an airbase with several squadrons of fighter-bombers and attack helicopters inside the perimeter. The Libyans believed it impregnable, and the Chadians felt it necessary to weaken the garrison both numerically and psychologically before attacking. Thus after they had consolidated their position at Fada, the FANT began harassing the Libyans in and around Wadi Doum to try to goad them into launching a counterattack against Fada.

In mid-March, the Libyans took the bait. They dispatched an armored task force of about 1,500 men to retake Fada. Chadian scouts trailed them all the way down from Wadi Doum. On the evening of March 18, the Libyans stopped their day's march and went into laager near B'ir Kora. Djamous immediately brought up a unit of FANT regulars and surrounded the Libyans during the night. At dawn the next day, the Chadians attacked. They began by launching a diversionary attack on one side of the Libyan position, which panicked the task-force commander, prompting him to shift all of his reserves to bolster the threatened sector. At that point, the Chadians unleashed their main assault against the opposite side of the Libyan lines. This attack caved in a large area of the Libyan perimeter, and the Libyans proved too slow and inflexible to shift forces to cover the gap or counterattack to blunt the Chadian penetration. As a result, the Chadian main force fanned out and struck the rest of the Libyan positions from the rear, in conjunction with frontal assaults by the Chadian diversionary force.

The Libyans were butchered in the fighting, but their pleas for help caused Haftar, the Operational Group East commander, to dispatch a second battalion task force from Wadi Doum late that day to aid the trapped unit. It took so long for the Libyans to get organized and move south, however, that the battle at B'ir Kora was already decided before the relief force even set out. During the night of March 19, the Chadians caught the Libyan relief force 12 miles north of B'ir Kora, surrounded it, and demolished it in identical fashion on March 20. Altogether, the Libyans suffered 800 dead, and lost 86 destroyed and 13 captured tanks in the battles at B'ir Kora.[8]

Wadi Doum was now ripe for Chadian attack. Although the garrison still boasted 4,000–5,000 men with ample armor and air support, the Libyans were demoralized by the annihilation of their forces at B'ir Kora. The Chadians decided to capitalize on this advantage by striking quickly. Toward the end of March, Habré sent a force of about 2,000–3,000 men under Djamous to attack the stronghold. Although the Libyans were on alert and became aware that a Chadian army had surrounded the base, they did not scout the Chadian deployment and so had no idea from which direction the FANT planned to attack. In contrast, the Chadians carefully reconnoitered the stronghold and uncovered all of the Libyan weak points, including pathways through the extensive minefields.

On March 22, the Chadians attacked. The hardest part of the fight was breaching the outer ring of Libyan defenses, but the Chadians attacked simultaneously at two opposing points and blasted their way through the Libyan lines. The Libyans were slow to commit their reserves, allowing the Chadians to penetrate their forward defenses and fan out before the breakthroughs could be sealed. Indeed, despite their extensive armored reserve, the Libyans failed to counterattack at all—allowing Chadian forces to roam at will once they were inside the Libyan perimeter. According to Lt. General Bernard Trainor, USMC (ret), who served as a military correspondent with the Chadians, between the unexpected routes taken by the Chadians and the speed of their advance, the Libyans were incapable of reacting, and not one Libyan artillery round was fired during the battle.[9] Four hours later, the Libyans had lost the entire base.

The Libyan forces regrouped that night and launched a sloppy, slow-moving, and uncoordinated—yet very determined—counterattack the next day. It was smashed by the FANT, leaving Wadi Doum firmly in their hands. Libyan airpower had little impact on the fighting because the Chadian Redeyes forced them to remain above 10,000 feet where they could do little against the dispersed formations of fast-moving Chadian trucks. In all, the Libyans suffered 1,269 dead and 438 taken prisoner, while losing over 300 tanks and APCs, 20 Czech-made L-29 light aircraft, four Mi-24s, and several batteries of SA-13 and SA-6 SAMs. Against these losses, the Chadians had 29 dead and 58 wounded.[10]

The Battle for the Aouzou Strip

The loss of Wadi Doum and its garrison were a major blow to Tripoli. Its fall forced the Libyans to abandon central Chad and pull back to their strongholds in the Aouzou Strip. The Libyan high command hurried south both the units they had already earmarked for deployment to Chad, along with large numbers of additional forces to try to find some level of mass and firepower that would halt the Chadians. By the spring of 1987, Tripoli had rebuilt its forces there to nearly 13,000 troops—over one-third of the entire Libyan Army. And to make up for the loss of Wadi Doum, the Libyans began a major effort to turn Maatan as-Sarrah airfield in southern Libya into a base capable of supporting large-scale air operations to defend the Aouzou Strip.

The battle for the Aouzou Strip began in late July 1987. The FANT retook several Libyan-held positions in the Tibesti to secure its western flank for the offensive. In early August, however, the Libyans put together a counteroffensive of reinforced-brigade strength (3,000 men) to try to regain the Tibesti. On August 8, the Libyans drove toward Bardai, but were intercepted by a FANT cohort of roughly equal size at Oumchi, 80 kilometers southeast of Aouzou. As they had at B'ir Kora and Wadi Doum, the Chadians located the Libyan force, surrounded it, and then attacked on multiple axes. And as *they* had at B'ir Kora and Wadi Doum, the Libyans could not act as quickly as the Chadians, nor did they maneuver, counterattack, or commit reserves in time to prevent Chadian units from penetrating their lines and then hitting the remaining forces simultaneously from front and rear. The result was predictable: the Chadians demolished the Libyan force.

Sensing a larger victory, Hassan Djamous urged on his forces, aggressively pursuing the defeated Libyans. As the beaten and demoralized Libyan units fell back in disarray, they caused other Libyan units to flee positions they passed through, turning the retreat into a rout. The pursuing Chadians were able to occupy the town of Aouzou late on August 8 without much of a fight. Between Oumchi and Aouzou the Libyans suffered 650 killed, 147 taken prisoner, and 111 military vehicles captured, in addition to at least 30 tanks and APCs destroyed.

Qadhafi would not abide the loss of Aouzou and ordered its recapture. He continued to feed reinforcements into Chad until there were nearly 15,000 Libyan troops pitted against the FANT. In addition, he sent 'Ali ash-Sharif, widely considered Libya's most capable general, to organize a counteroffensive to retake Aouzou. Libya began a preliminary bombardment of artillery and air strikes to soften up the Chadian positions at Aouzou days before the counterattack. Nevertheless, despite all this firepower, when the Libyans attacked on August 14 they were soundly beaten, suffering over 200 dead and captured. The Libyans regrouped and attacked again, only to be defeated once more. In both cases, the Libyans conducted simple, slow-moving frontal assaults that were easily broken by fast, enveloping Chadian counterattacks.

After these reversals, ash-Sharif concentrated even greater firepower against the town and brought in a number of Libyan commando units and formations from the Jamahiriyah Guard. He used these forces as shock troops in a set-piece assault featuring tremendous firepower, which finally succeeded in forcing the Chadians out of Aouzou on August 28. In this final attack, the Libyans greatly benefited from the fact that Djamous, Gorou, and other key Chadian commanders—along with most of their troops—had pulled out of Aouzou in preparation for another offensive. This left the town with a garrison of only about 400 FANT soldiers led by a novice commander who deployed his force poorly and was overwhelmed by Libyan numbers and firepower. Still, the fighting for the Aouzou Strip in August cost Libya 1,225 dead and 262 wounded.[11]

Habré too was determined to regain the Aouzou Strip but had a more sophisticated strategy to do so. He had withdrawn Djamous and most of his veteran troops from Aouzou to rest and refit them for the next offensive, which Habré hoped would allow him to secure the Aouzou Strip against further Libyan attacks. This he hoped to accomplish by smashing the major bases in southern Libya from which Tripoli was supporting its operations in Chad. Habré and his generals concluded that without those bases to provide air and logistical support, Libyan forces would be unable to further contest the Tibesti or Aouzou. The Chadians decided to begin by eliminating the main Libyan base at Maatan as-Sarrah.

For their part, the Libyans hoped to follow up on the limited success of their victory at Aouzou. In early September, they sent a brigade-sized force to attack Ounianga Kebir. Simultaneously, Habré dispatched Djamous with several thousand FANT soldiers to drive 200 kilometers into Libya and wreck Maatan as-Sarrah. The Libyans moved noisily through the desert, launched a frontal assault on Ounianga-Kebir on September 5, and were quickly defeated by rapid Chadian counterattacks. Djamous's force by contrast carefully followed the wadis to stay under cover, while Tripoli's forces in southern Libya made little effort at security or patrolling, allowing the FANT to sneak up on the base undetected. On September 5, the same day the Libyans were being smashed at Ounianga Kebir, the Chadians attacked Maatan as-Sarrah, taking its defenders completely by surprise. Although Maatan as-Sarrah had a 2,500-man garrison including a brigade of tanks, artillery, and extensive fortifications, the Chadians quickly crushed the slow-reacting Libyan defenders. They took control of the airbase, demolished it and all of the equipment they could not carry back with them, and then melted back into the desert. It was a stunning defeat for the Libyans. The Chadians killed over 1,700 Libyans, captured another 300, and destroyed 26 Libyan aircraft, 70 tanks, 30 APCs, and numerous SAMs, radars, and electronic equipment. The FANT suffered 65 dead and 112 wounded.[12]

The Chadian raid on Maatan as-Sarrah proved to be *too* successful, however. The French became concerned that it was the first stage of a general Chadian offensive into Libya proper, something Paris did not want to see. Thus, after the attack on Maatan as-Sarrah, Paris forced Habré to agree to a ceasefire. Over the entire course of the 1987 campaign, the Libyans suffered at least 7,500 dead and nearly 1,000 captured soldiers, in addition to losing nearly $1.5 billion worth of equipment including 28 aircraft and over 800 tanks and APCs. On the other hand, in all of these battles combined, the Libyans killed less than 1,000 FANT soldiers.[13]

Chadian Military Effectiveness, 1986–1987

Chadian forces fought brilliantly against the Libyans in the later stages of the war. They were not without flaws, but their commanders recognized both the strengths and weaknesses of the forces at their disposal and built an army well suited to those characteristics.

Chadian Strategic Leadership. Chad's senior military commanders performed well throughout the fighting. Much credit must go to Habré himself, who conceived and planned most of the Chadian operations. Nevertheless, his senior field commanders, particularly Hassan Djamous, also performed superbly. The Chadian high command stressed reconnaissance and patrolling, and Chadian moves were made with an excellent understanding of the situation. Despite moving sizable forces over hundreds of kilometers of open desert, the Chadians rarely had logistical problems, and their victories were smooth and quick despite high degrees of complexity and improvisation in their actual conduct.

During the victorious 1986–1987 campaign, Chad's overall operational concept, as well as each of its strategic moves, were excellent. Habré and his lieutenants seized on the opportunity presented by the GUNT split with Libya to launch their offensive. They reinforced Goukouni to hold the Libyans in the west while striking their main blow against the Libyan garrisons in central Chad. They recognized that Wadi Doum was too strong to be assaulted so they lured part of the garrison away and destroyed it, making the stronghold an easier target. They took Fada and Wadi Doum and, as a result, Faya-Largeau fell into their hands without a fight. They astutely recognized when the Libyans were broken and pursued aggressively, often capturing additional prizes as a result. At other times, when the Libyans were able to retreat in some semblance of order or could fall back on good defensive positions, the Chadians were careful to regroup and prepare their forces before striking the next objective. Finally, the deep raid against Maatan as-Sarrah to eliminate Libyan air support before launching a new assault on Aouzou was brilliant.

Particularly praiseworthy was the fact that Habré and his subordinates recognized both the strengths and the weaknesses of their forces and carefully tailored their war effort to these capabilities. Chad's war leaders knew that their forces would do best if they could employ their traditional desert warfare techniques, and so they bought weapons and other equipment that would allow them to implement such tactics. They purposely turned down offers of heavier weapons such as tanks and artillery because they recognized that their troops would not be able to operate and maintain these systems.

In this respect, the Chadian generals were very much like the Egyptian high command of 1968–1973 and the Iraqis of 1986–1991. However, the difference between them was that the Chadian generals had far more capable forces under their command than did the Arab generals, and the Chadians fought far less competent foes.

Chadian Tactical Leadership. The performance of Chad's tactical commanders was also outstanding. The Chadians relied on a highly decentralized command structure in battle. Before a fight, Chadian officers would gather with their commander to share information about the enemy, hear his plans for the battle, and learn how their units could be best employed in that plan. However, once combat was joined, actual operations were left entirely to the discretion of battalion, company, platoon, squad, and vehicle commanders. How best to achieve tactical surprise, how to maneuver, and how to coordinate the operations of different units were all left up to the individual commanders. Consequently, the Chadian approach placed a tremendous burden on Chad's junior officers. Had they failed, the Chadian armies would have failed too. Chad's successes were very much their successes.

The Chadian swarming tactics demanded that commanders at the lowest levels be quick-thinking, highly aggressive, creative, and able to act with little or no guidance from higher authority—and the Chadians more than fulfilled these requirements. They used the speed of their armored cars and Toyotas to dart around the battlefield, hitting Libyan armored vehicles in the flanks, and often from several angles simultaneously. The Chadians maintained a very high pace of operations, relying on the speed and flexibility of their units to confuse the Libyans, isolate them in smaller units, and then crush them suddenly with tremendous firepower from all sides. Whenever the Chadians ran into a problem it was up to the individual commander on the spot to find a solution to it with whatever was at his disposal.

The Chadians maneuvered constantly on the battlefield to prevent the Libyans from bringing their heavier firepower to bear, and to get flank shots on Libyan armor and fortified positions. Indeed, no matter how much the Libyans tried to orient their forces in an all-around defense, the Chadians were forever on their flanks and in their rear. When the Chadians faced Libyan strongholds with all-around fortifications—such as at Wadi Doum—they probed for weak spots, then quickly committed overwhelming force there, penetrated the Libyan lines, and spread out to hit nearby units in the flank and attack artillery positions and command posts.

Chadian tactical commanders also showed a knack for the intelligence aspects of war. They conducted constant patrols. They scoured the immediate vicinity of their forces. They placed a huge emphasis on camouflage, concealment, and deception (CC&D). Unit commanders and vehicle crews were responsible for getting their men and machines out of sight so that there would be nothing for Libyan aerial reconnaissance to see. When moving, the Chadians used surreptitious or unlikely routes of march to prevent the Libyans from learning of their approach. As a result of these efforts, the Chadians almost always surprised the Libyans, but were rarely surprised by them.

Since the Chadians had no tanks, no true artillery, no combat engineers, or other combat support elements, it is harder to assess their combined arms integration. They certainly did integrate the Toyotas with their crew-served weapons, armored cars, leg infantry, and mortars well. In particular, they recognized that each system had its strengths and weaknesses, and they were good at using each to cover the weaknesses of the other. Thus, on those occasions when Chadian armored cars and trucks ran into Libyan or GUNT infantry with rocket-propelled grenades (RPGs) and other light antitank weapons, they would try to suppress their fire with mortars and bring up their infantry to clear away the enemy antitank teams before the light armor resumed its advance.

Unit Cohesion. It is even more difficult to gauge the cohesion of Chadian units in combat. The problem is that Chadian tactics were to attack hard and quickly and then break off if the enemy was not crushed. On a few occasions, mostly in the Tibesti, Libyan units put up fierce resistance from fortified positions and hung on despite Chadian swarming tactics. The Libyans were able to hold their ground longer than the Chadians expected, and the Chadian formations fell back. Moreover, in the words of one US government official knowledgeable about the course of the war in Chad, the Chadians "just didn't do defense." Chadian units almost never tried to hold static positions against enemy attacks, instead preferring to counterattack and turn any battle into a meeting engagement. The Chadians were at their best when combat was fluid and they could maneuver freely, and they avoided defending fixed lines whenever possible. Thus when the Chadians were on the offensive and were winning, their unit cohesion was great, but when they were losing or forced to defend fixed positions, their unit cohesion was poor.

Chadian Technical Skills. Chadian military personnel had almost no technical skills or exposure to machinery and so their ability to handle modern military equipment was very low. This translated into poor weapons handling. The Chadians probably shot down no more than four Libyan aircraft with

Redeyes and fired off scores of Milans for each Libyan armored vehicle they destroyed. It also meant that Chadian troops often simply did not understand key aspects of modern combat. For instance, Chadian truck drivers attempted to drive straight through Libyan minefields, not because they expected to self-lessly clear a lane for their comrades behind them at the risk of their own lives, but because they believed that if they drove fast enough, the mines would detonate behind them.

Chadian maintenance was terrible. At some level, Chadian personnel understood that their vehicles and weapons had to be carefully cleaned and repaired. However, it rarely occurred to them to perform maintenance and when it did, few understood how to do so properly. So for instance, the Chadians tried hard to maintain their armored cars and Toyota trucks because these were so important to their mobility. But they had only very modest success and frequently had large numbers of inoperable vehicles. Similarly, the Chadians realized early on that they just did not have the trained man-power to handle the logistics required for moving sizable motorized forces over long distances in the open desert. Few Chadians could read or write, let alone calculate the supply requirements of hundreds of vehicles with several thousand troops and their weaponry. Thus, logistics and repairs had to be left to the French.

In these areas, Chad's underdevelopment was a considerable hindrance. However, what is of far greater importance is that the Chadians never let it be an obstacle preventing them from achieving their objectives. Instead, they procured the weapons they could handle and that fit their preferred tactics. They turned over those functions such as logistics and maintenance that they knew they could not perform to their Western advisers and developed their operations with this constraint in mind. The Chadians also were helped in this area by the fact that their opponents were equally bad off.

Along these lines, it is important to recognize that their prowess on the battlefield was achieved almost entirely through the tactical skills of Chadian soldiers and junior officers: their weaponry contributed very little to their victory. This is not to suggest that the new weapons Chad received from France and the United States in 1986 were unimportant. Clearly they were not. Without the Milan, the Redeye, and the other heavy infantry weapons, Chad could not have defeated Libya because without them the FANT had no answer to Libyan tanks and aircraft. But it was not the weapons per se that allowed the Chadians to beat the Libyans. All the new weapons did was to "level the playing field" between the two sides. Once the Chadians had a counter to Libyan armor and airpower they were able to employ their superior tactical abilities to beat the Libyans. It was Chadian generalship and tactical leadership, not Chadian weaponry or the ability of their soldiers to handle those weapons, that brought them victory in combat with the Libyans.

Ultimately, Chad's stunning defeat of Libya was the product of the combination of Chadian strengths and Libyan weaknesses. The Chadians forced the Libyans to fight a war of rapid maneuver, which came naturally to them and did not come at all to the Libyans. In this way, the Chadians were able to do to the Libyans what the Israelis were able to do to their Arab opponents in virtually all of the Arab-Israeli wars, and what the United States was able to do to the Iraqis during the Persian Gulf War and the invasion of Iraq.

That it was Chadian strategy and tactical abilities rather than any superiority in weaponry that was most important in their victory over Libya is further demonstrated by comparing the Chadian experience against Libya with the Cuban experience against South Africa in 1987–1988. The Libyans and the Cubans were armed almost identically: they both used large numbers of older Soviet-style tanks, APCs, artillery, aircraft, etc. Both sides also relied on Soviet military practices to a greater or lesser extent. Moreover, they both fought foes with similar styles of warfare and accouterment. The Chadians and the South Africans both favored light, quick formations centered on armored cars and swarming tactics in battle to defeat the enemy's heavy units with speed and maneuver. In fact, the South Africans were actually far better armed than the Chadians because they had improved Centurion tanks, more and better armored cars, modern jet fighters, and the incomparable G-5 and G-6 artillery pieces. Thus, the Cubans faced a tougher foe than the Libyans. The fact that the Cubans and South Africans essentially fought to a draw while the Libyans were crushed by the Chadians demonstrates that the caliber of the weaponry on either side, and even the ability of one side or another to take full advantage of the capabilities of that weaponry, was not nearly as important in determining the outcome of combat as were the strategic and tactical skills of the two sides.

Libyan Military Effectiveness in Chad

Although Libya's military fortunes in Chad rose and fell in dramatic fashion over the nine years of its involvement there, the performance of Libyan military forces remained remarkably consistent. Libyan tactical forces performed extremely poorly from start to finish. Libya's generals proved to be a varied but mostly adequate lot: their qualities as strategists ranged from fairly impressive to middling, and their qualities as leaders of men ranged from uninspiring to reasonably effective. On the other hand, Libya's logistical operations were consistently excellent—at times outstanding—throughout the course of its wars in Chad.

The principal causes of Tripoli's varying fortunes in Chad were not the performance of Libyan arms at all, but the changing political alignments on either side and the eventual development of Chadian military forces that were able to exploit the limitations of Libyan tactical forces. Ultimately, the performance of Libyan forces closely resembled that of the other Arab armies, although it fell on the worse end of that spectrum. They won at first because their adversary was even weaker than they were, but ultimately lost because their opponent improved dramatically and they could not.

Strategic Performance. Libya's generals were rarely spectacular and must bear part of the blame for certain Libyan defeats, but they were hardly terrible and deserve credit for many of Libya's victories. Overall, they can hardly be considered a principal element of Libya's eventual failure.

In general, the various Libyan invasions of Chad were well directed, if simple. Libyan strategy in each offensive was to move from one population center to the next on the best routes from southern Libya to N'djamena: ounianga kebir and then either Faya Largeau to Kouba Olongo, or Fada to Abeche. These routes were determined largely by logistical considerations: the need to secure each population center (and its crucial water supplies, energy supplies, road crossings and airfields) before moving on to the next. Moreover, the directness and predictability of these routes proved to be an advantage for the Libyans insofar as Libya's main operational goal was to bring the Chadian army to battle in open terrain outside of N'djamena where it could be smashed by Libyan firepower. Thus, the fact that the Chadians could anticipate the Libyan route of advance and would often send their main army out to try to halt the Libyan invasion frequently meant that the FANT was right where the Libyans wanted them.

For the better part of their involvement, this strategic approach worked fine. By carefully securing each population center before moving on to the next, the Libyans ensured their logistical and communications lines and frequently were able to draw out sizable Chadian formations to fight them in the open where Libyan armor and airpower typically proved decisive. In 1980–1981, Libyan forces successfully conquered Chad, and only Qadhafi's mishandling of the post-ceasefire political arrangements forced the Libyans out again. Likewise, in 1978 and 1983 there is every reason to believe the Libyans would also have overrun the country had it not been for the French interventions. In 1984–1986 the Libyans solved that problem by deceiving the French into withdrawing and then moving slowly with minimal force so as not to give the French sufficient provocation to return.

Ultimately, the key limitation on Libyan operations was not poor generalship but the incompetence of Tripoli's tactical formations. Libyan units had such limited effectiveness in combat that only under perfect circumstances could this strategic approach succeed. Specifically, only when Libyan forces were called on to provide almost nothing other than stand-off fire support, air strikes, and the occasional tank charge could they prevail over their Chadian adversaries. Thus, only when the Libyans had sufficient numbers of Goukouni's Toubous to serve as reconnaissance and assault infantry, only when the French Air Force did not ground the Libyan Air Force, and only when the Chadian forces had limited tactical mobility and no antitank or anti-aircraft weapons could the Libyans prevail in tactical engagements. Any time that any of these conditions were not met, the Libyans lost. Badly.

Consequently, it is hard to fault Libya's generals, at least for Libya's inability to secure its objectives up till 1986. During that period of time, it was reasonable for Tripoli's strategic commanders to believe that they could create the right conditions under which their forces could defeat the Chadians in battle, and indeed they were frequently proven correct.

After 1986 it is more difficult to make a case for Libyan strategic leadership. Specifically, the Libyan high command must bear at least part of the blame for the inability of the Libyan armed forces to recognize or adapt to the change in the balance of power on the battlefield. To some extent, the inability of Libya's generals to properly react to the dramatic improvement in FANT capabilities can be attributed to surprise. Beyond that, the Libyan high command at least appears guilty of arrogance and/or inertia: they almost certainly had become either so contemptuous of FANT capabilities or so accustomed to the limitations of the FANT that they could not accept that the Chadians were beating them.

By the same token, it is difficult to imagine what Libya's generals might have done differently had they been less pigheaded and more willing to adapt. Like the Iraqis in the Gulf War, the "right" military answer to the problem created by the FANT's new capabilities was probably to have evacuated northern Chad, but this was a political decision that Qadhafi almost certainly would have forbidden even if his generals had recommended it. Once their new weapons and motor transport allowed the FANT to return to their traditional swarming tactics, Libyan forces were simply incapable of defeating them. Again, like the Iraqis in 1991, the Libyans could not have adopted a mobile defense and tried to match Chadian maneuver warfare techniques because Tripoli's tactical formations simply could not execute them. Consequently, the only strategy practicable for the Libyans was to dig in deep at key population centers to force the Chadians to attack heavily fortified positions defended with tremendous firepower and hope to bleed the FANT white. Ultimately, Libyan tactical forces proved unable to accomplish even this, and the Libyans were routed.

Still, Libya's generals must be faulted for the numerous counteroffensives they conducted during 1987, which clearly ran counter to the logic that made the static defensive posture a reasonable option. Static defense was the appropriate strategy for the Libyans after 1986 because they lacked the ability to defeat the Chadians in meeting engagements and maneuver battles, and therefore it made some sense to try to wear down the FANT by forcing it to repeatedly assault heavily fortified positions defended with massive firepower. This logic should have ruled out large-scale counteroffensive operations such as those the Libyans conducted in 1987 at B'ir Kora, the Tibesti, and Oumchi. Sending large forces out of their fortified bases to try to assault Chadian positions exposed them to the risk of ambush and massacre by FANT units en route, which of course is exactly what happened.

Tactical Performance. Libyan tactical forces performed extremely poorly in Chad throughout the entirety of Tripoli's involvement there. Libyan tactical incompetence was the Achilles heel of the Libyan war effort, the key vulnerability that the FANT was ultimately able to exploit to defeat them. Libyan tactical forces were so limited in their capabilities that they squandered the opportunities offered by Tripoli's superb logistical efforts, and severely constrained the strategic choices available to Libyan generals.

Without doubt, the greatest failure of Libyan tactical forces was their rigidity. Libyan units parroted Soviet tactics in the most stereotyped manner, and without taking advantage of even the limited flexibility inherent in Soviet doctrine. For example, Libyan mechanized infantry always fought mounted—regardless of the terrain, mission, or other conditions. As a result, Libyan mechanized infantry usually did not dig-in on defense nor would they dismount to clear out entrenched Chadian infantry or antitank teams. Any number of Libyan APCs were incinerated by the Chadians with full infantry squads inside them (54 such APCs were found at Wadi Doum). Libyan tanks rarely maneuvered or attempted to flank an enemy: when defending, they sat immobile in prepared positions, and when attacking they simply rolled straight ahead, in both cases firing almost indiscriminately until the enemy ran away or they were themselves destroyed. Libyan artillery proved adept at conducting preregistered, pre-planned barrages, but that was it. So if the initial Libyan bombardment did not shatter the Chadian defense, Libyan artillery could contribute little more, and the battle had to be turned over either to the armor to launch a charge, or else to the GUNT infantry (when available) to push forward and dislodge the FANT defenders. On defense, especially in 1986–1987 when the FANT's new mobility allowed them to attack suddenly from any quarter, Libyan artillery proved largely useless since it could not accurately shift fire around the battlefield.

In addition to the individual failings of each of Libya's combat arms, its junior officers could not integrate these forces into concerted, combined arms operations. In every case, the infantry, artillery, armor, engineers, etc., were left to fight separate battles. About the best they did was to coordinate tank, artillery, and rocket launcher fire with air strikes in indiscriminate bombardments of fixed targets. They could not provide fire support to actively maneuvering forces. Indeed, Libyan fire support units really could not even conduct rolling barrages in support of armor or GUNT infantry advances; either they bombarded or they assaulted, but not both simultaneously.

As this suggests, the majority of Libyan problems can be traced to ineffective tactical leadership. Libyan junior officers proved inflexible and unaggressive, and therefore had little ability to cope with either the rapid maneuvers of FANT units at the end of the Libyan involvement, or even the slower, more ponderous infantry tactics of Habré's forces before 1986. In contrast to the fairly aggressive leadership displayed by the senior levels of the Libyan command structure—who insisted on counterattacking all through 1987 despite considerable evidence that such operations could not succeed—Libyan tactical forces almost never counterattacked except when ordered to do so by higher authority.

In similar fashion, Libyan defenders rarely shifted their forces to plug breakthroughs, shore up sectors under pressure, or meet a flanking attack. In those few instances when Libyan local commanders did make such an effort, their forces did so too slowly and rigidly to make the action worthwhile. Nor did Libyan units attempt to maneuver for an advantageous position in battle. The Libyans really tried not to move at all, instead preferring to knock Chadian units out of their positions with firepower. On those occasions when Libyan forces did finally resort to an assault (and when they lacked GUNT infantry to conduct it for them), they launched sluggish, rigidly prescribed frontal attacks directly at the main Chadian positions. Finally, when the Libyans were successful, they rarely pursued defeated FANT units, with the result that they never scored as great a tactical success as was possible and never exterminated Habré's forces, allowing them to regroup and fight again another day.

The Libyans also experienced debilitating problems managing information throughout their command structure, but again, these lapses were greatest at tactical levels. Libyan senior commanders rarely provided adequate information either about Libyan operations or enemy deployment and capabilities to their subordinates. However, they generally recognized the need for accurate assessments of Chadian forces and so employed either GUNT scouts or LAF reconnaissance planes to gather such information. The Libyans were not very thorough even when they did make the effort to find out where Chadian forces were and what they were up to. Libyan strategic intelligence often left significant gaps in their coverage and seldom kept abreast of developments in Chadian politics and military affairs. Tripoli's junior officers did not even perform up to this level.

Libyan tactical units simply did not conduct reconnaissance. The most obvious example of this was at B'ir Kora, where neither Libyan column commander bothered to scout his route of advance or deploy forces to screen his flanks. Yet this was a constant of Libyan operations in Chad. Libyan forces were notorious for failing to even keep an alert watch around their fortified bases and field encampments. To make matters worse, Libyan tactical commanders regularly misled their superiors for fear of bringing shame on themselves, their men, their colleagues, or their superiors; they overstated the scale of victories, failed to report defeats, and exaggerated the size of enemy forces. As a result, Libyan strategic commanders frequently had little idea what really was happening on the battlefield.

Unit Cohesion. The cohesion of Libyan formations in Chad and the degree of commitment and bravery evinced by Libyan soldiers fluctuated considerably over the course of the Libyan intervention, correlating to a certain extent with the highs and lows of Libyan morale. When Libyan morale was high, unit cohesion was stronger, and more Libyan soldiers were willing to risk their lives for their comrades and their missions. On the other hand, when they were dispirited, units broke under less pressure and fewer troops were willing to sacrifice for their mission or one another.

Nevertheless, there were other patterns of unit cohesion and individual commitment that did not fit the oscillations in Libyan morale. For example, Libyan forces invariably displayed better unit cohesion when defending fixed positions than in any offensive operations or meeting engagements. When the Libyans had a chance to dig-in and allow their men to fight from fortified lines, Libyan units from squad to battalion level hung together, fought hard, and clung to their trench lines. This was equally true of Libyan forces battling in N'djamena when riding the crest of their victorious advance in 1980 as it was when they were desperately trying to hold on to the Tibesti even after the crushing defeats of 1986 and early 1987. Moreover, it was generally a rarity when Libyan regular units simply collapsed in battle; although the militia and

Islamic Pan-African Legionnaires might run at the first sign of battle, Libyan line formations usually had to be beaten before they cracked.

Of course, it should be kept in mind that Libyan unit cohesion—even at its best—had little impact on the success of Libyan forces in combat. Although poor unit cohesion often contributed to Libyan setbacks, it was never a singular cause of defeat. Nor was it ever the case that good unit cohesion alone led to a Libyan victory. The limitations of Libyan junior officers left their tactical formations so inutile that this dwarfed other considerations such as unit cohesion. When attacking, all that mattered was how much firepower the Libyans could bring to bear and whether the Chadians would sit and take it. Because if the Chadians were able to either limit Libyan firepower or maneuver against them, the Libyans were doomed to defeat. Similarly, when defending, all that mattered was whether the Chadians were forced to conduct a slow-moving frontal assault, or could conduct quick flanking maneuvers. Because if the Chadians could maneuver, the Libyans were going to lose. Only when the Libyans were conducting static defensive operations against a Chadian frontal assault did it become at all relevant whether the Libyan units would stand and fight or break and run.

Combat Service Support. The Libyans had a strangely mixed record in terms of supporting their forces in Chad. On the one hand, Libyan maintenance was awful. Libyan soldiers and junior officers seemed to have no understanding of the need for regular preventive maintenance on major weapons systems, nor did they have the desire or the skills to perform repairs to broken equipment. Tripoli tried to compensate by importing large numbers of Cuban and East European technicians who were assigned to large, centralized workshops that deployed forward with the Libyan combat forces to Chad. At Wadi Doum, a number of Cubans, North Koreans, and East Germans were captured by the Chadians. These personnel had been assigned to the maintenance crews of the airbase and the major refit facility the Libyans had established there for armored vehicles. Nevertheless, because the Libyans never had enough Warsaw Pact technicians to attach them to every field formation down to battalion or company level, and because the Libyan vehicle crews were unwilling and unable to perform basic maintenance, Libyan operational readiness (O/R) rates remained poor. For example, even though over half of Libya's combat aircraft were kept in storage because they had inadequate numbers of trained pilots to fly them, Libyan line squadrons were still rarely able to achieve readiness rates better than 50 percent.[14]

On the other hand, Libyan logistics were first-rate throughout the history of their intervention in Chad. In every Libyan campaign, Tripoli's forces were kept well-supplied. They never were defeated—or even hindered—by shortages of ammunition, food, fuel, water, or other combat consumables. Instead, Libyan forces typically had ample supplies of everything they needed to prosecute combat operations, no matter how difficult the conditions. Indeed, Libyan maintenance problems cannot be blamed on logistical shortcomings; in 1987, when Chadian forces overran major Libyan forward bases at Faya-Largeau, Wadi Doum, and Aouzou oasis, they discovered vast warehouses full of spare parts, repair tools, repair manuals, and replacement equipment. Similarly, the low morale of Libyan forces cannot be blamed on neglect or inadequate provisioning, because Qadhafi's quartermasters took superb care of the combat forces, lavishing them with all variety of creature comforts. For instance, in 1980, the Libyan garrison at Abeche was provided with piped-in music, sports facilities, air conditioning, an irrigated wheat field, and even a Guernsey cow for the commander's milk.[15]

Libyan forces deploying south to Chad moved quickly and efficiently, arriving where they were supposed to when they were supposed to. On several occasions, the Libyan Air Force demonstrated the extraordinary ability to airlift vast Libyan mechanized forces into Chad at the start of an offensive. The best examples of this were in 1980 and 1983, when Qadhafi began his invasions by airlifting thousands of troops complete with tanks, APCs, artillery pieces, and MRLs into the Aouzou Strip. On both occasions, these operations were conducted quickly and skillfully and allowed the Libyans to steal a march on Habré.

Libyan logistical accomplishments appear even more impressive when the circumstances are taken into account. It is over 1,100 kilometers from N'djamena to the Aouzou oasis on the Libyan border. Moreover, it is a further 1,000-plus kilometers from Aouzou oasis to the main Libyan military bases along the Mediterranean coast. Thus, Libya's most successful campaigns were waged over 2,000 kilometers from the main Libyan depots. Moreover, although Chadian terrain is ideal for tactical armor and air operations, it constitutes an extremely forbidding strategic logistical environment. Much of the northern two-thirds of the country is desert, scrubland, or dry savannah with little water, cultivated lands, or population. Chadian infrastructure was primitive. There were few roads or airfields, and essentially no rail lines for the movement of large military forces.

The Libyans overcame all of these obstacles both in meeting immediate requirements in the short term, and making their presence in Chad sustainable over the long term. Libyan engineers and logisticians built roads, airfields, and all manner of logistical bases, slowly developing a considerable transportation network from the Mediterranean coast south into north-central Chad.

When the Libyans were finally evicted from Chad, it was not because they lacked the capacity to supply their forces there. Although it is true that Libyan combat formations did not advance at a particularly torrid pace, it is nonetheless remarkable that their combat service support elements were able to conduct these operations as smoothly and quickly as they did, displaying a skill in sustainment capabilities that most Third World armies (indeed, that many First World armies) lack.

Libyan Air Force Performance. For roughly seven years, the Libyan Air Force was probably the most important arrow in Tripoli's quiver in Chad. When free to participate in combat operations, Libyan aircraft often proved the decisive element in any battle. Nevertheless, the actual combat performance of the LAF was just as dismal as that of the Libyan Army.

Libyan air strikes, no matter how heavy or protracted, rarely caused any physical damage to the target. Troops of the FAN or FANT suffered few casualties from Libyan air strikes, nor did they lose many pieces of equipment. In particular, in 1986–1987, the LAF could not destroy or impede the fleet of Toyotas that were instrumental to the Chadian victory. The one exception to this rule were Libyan air strikes on Chadian villages, which did cause large numbers of civilian casualties but were counterproductive because they incited large elements of the Chadian population against Tripoli. Libyan air strikes rarely ever caused any physical damage because few Libyan pilots actually understood their planes and munitions well enough to put ordnance accurately on target.

Indeed, the incompetence of Libyan pilots was the single greatest problem of the Libyan Air Force in Chad. Because the Chadians had no air force— and the French never sent more than a couple of squadrons of Jaguars to oppose them while the Libyans regularly committed 5–10 squadrons of Mirages, Su-22s, MiG-23s, and MiG-21s—the LAF invariably had the edge in terms of numbers, firepower, and equipment. But its pilots squandered these advantages, even when unopposed in the air. In Anthony Cordesman's words, the Libyans had "a serious shortage of even mediocre pilots."[16] One US government expert on the Libyan military estimated that no more than about 10 percent of Libyan pilots would have been considered even adequate flyers by Western standards.[17]

As was the case for Libyan ground forces, the one bright spot in Libyan Air Force performance was in the logistical field. Tripoli's quartermasters and East-bloc technicians were usually able to sustain a reasonable sortie rate for Libyan fighter bombers. In key battles, this meant that Libyan aircraft were over the battlefield for long periods of time and Chadian troops were under some form of air attack almost continuously.

Finally, the command and control of Libyan Air Force operations were characterized by a tremendous degree of amateurism. The Libyans had a lot of planes, which they used frequently, but had little appreciation of how to employ them in a systematic fashion to achieve the maximum impact. In most cases, the LAF did not bother to fly reconnaissance missions over a target before striking it. The LAF neglected proper air planning, often sending out strike missions with minimal information about the target to be struck, its location, or air defenses. The Libyans regularly dispatched inadequate numbers of planes to targets, and often provided them with inappropriate ordnance for the mission. When allocating strike assets, the Libyans made no allowance for the poor skills of their pilots, nor were Libyan strikes accompanied by appropriate measures to suppress enemy air defenses (with more serious consequences after 1986). Finally, the Libyans rarely conducted post-strike reconnaissance to assess whether additional strikes were required to destroy a target. By and large, Libyan pilots reported that the target was destroyed, and the chain of command accepted their word.

Chadian Military Effectiveness and Arab Military Effectiveness

In 1986–1987, the Chadians were poorer and more backward than the Arabs were at any time during the postwar period, yet Chadian forces fought better than Arab armies. There were some important similarities in the performance of the Chadians and Libyans: neither army could handle or maintain its weaponry very well. But that's where it ended. Instead, the Chadians were effectively the reverse of the Libyans, and of the Arabs more generally. The one bright spot in Libya's war effort was logistics, which the Chadians did not share. There, time and again, the Libyans proved remarkably good, running completely contrary to the expectations of the underdevelopment explanation. In contrast, whereas Libyan forces demonstrated their greatest strengths in unit cohesion, set-piece offensives, and static defenses, these were the aspects of military operations in which the Chadians were weakest. The Chadians' greatest strengths were the flexibility, initiative, creativity, and independence of their tactical commanders and the quickness and maneuverability this brought to their units in battle. The Chadians proved superb at maneuver warfare and information management, their junior officers far exceeding the abilities of their Libyan counterparts. The absence of these same traits was the greatest weakness of the Arab armies during the postwar era. Ultimately, the Libyans were defeated principally because Chadian strengths were perfectly suited to exploiting the common Arab weaknesses that the Libyans manifested to an extreme.

CHAPTER 13 | Economic Development and
Chinese Military Effectiveness

T HE LAST NON-ARAB military I want to look at is the Chinese military's
performance during the Korean War, 1950–1953. China was an extremely
underdeveloped state in 1950, arguably worse off than Chad in the 1980s. It
was considerably more backward than the Arab states in 1960. (See Table 13.1
for a comparison of Chinese socioeconomic indicators for 1950 with those of
Iraq and Jordan, two representative Arab countries, in 1960.) Korean War vet-
eran-turned-historian Patrick Coe has called the Chinese army he fought, "a
huge but primitive force."[1]

China's size suggests that it might have been able to recruit only a small
percentage of the healthiest and best-educated men in its population to field
a large but unrepresentative army, but it never did so. Since the beginnings
of the Chinese Civil War, the Chinese Communists always opted for a mass
conscription army. As a result, Chinese military personnel closely reflected
Chinese society in general. In 1950, the Chinese army was largely illiterate,
uneducated, and unfamiliar with machinery and modern industrial life.[2]
In Coe's words, "The appearance of the Chinese soldier was not impressive.
A U.S. recruiter would have turned away most of them."[3] Russell Spurr
has noted that during the Korean War, the small number of radios in the
Chinese army had to be operated by former Nationalist soldiers who had
been trained as signalers by the United States during World War II, "because
their own revolutionary farm lads could hardly flush a toilet, let alone replace
a radio tube."[4] In less colorful language, the US Defense Intelligence Agency

TABLE 13.1 Socioeconomic Development of China in 1950 and Iraq and Jordan in 1960

Indicators	China 1950	Iraq 1960	Jordan 1960
GDP per capita (in 1960 dollars)	144	233	176
Literacy (% of pop. over 15 able to read + write)	10	15	32
Infant mortality per 1,000 live births	130	140	140
Life expectancy at birth, in years	38 (1952)	48	53
Per capita electrical power production (in KwH)	8.4	132	59
% of workforce in manufacturing	5	5	26
% of workforce in agriculture	77	53	44
Inhabitants per physician	34,469 (1946)	4,900	5,900
Inhabitants per automobile	10,940	168	262
Inhabitants per telephone	2,430	122	67

Sources: CIA, *The World Factbook*, 1987; Angus Maddison, Chinese Economic Performance in the Long Run (OECD Publishing, Paris, 1998); The World Bank, *World Development Report*, 1987, 1990; UN Statistical Office, Compendium of Social Statistics and Indicators 1988.

commented that "The Chinese Communist Army of 1949 was basically a peasant-infantry force organized and trained mainly for guerrilla-type operations in which conventional military science and technology played a lesser role. Its firepower, mobility, communications, and logistics were limited and for the most part archaic."[5]

Chinese Operations in the Korean War, 1950–1953

When China's peasant army intervened in the Korean War in October 1950, all of the material factors favored the UN armies. Led by Marshal Peng Dehuai, the Chinese attacked into Korea with roughly 380,000 men commanded by two army groups, the 13th and the 9th.[6] The 13th Army Group with about 180,000 men faced the main UN force, the US Eighth Army marching up the western side of the Korean peninsula, while the 9th Army Group faced the US X Corps on the eastern side with only about 120,000 men. In addition, the units assigned to the 13th Army Group were all veteran formations from the

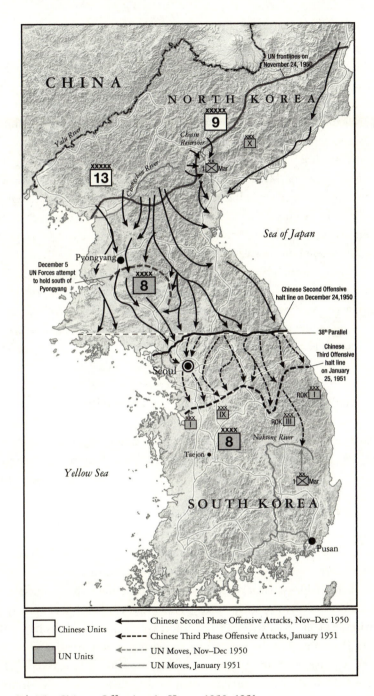

CHINA

NORTH KOREA

UN frontlines on
November 24, 1950

XXXXX
9

XXX
X

Yalu River

XXXXX
13

Chosin Reservoir

Chongchon River

X Mar

Sea of Japan

December 5
UN Forces attempt
to hold south of
Pyongyang

Pyongyang

XXXX
8

Chinese Second Offensive
halt line on December 24, 1950

38th Parallel

Chinese
Third Offensive
halt line
on January
25, 1951

ROK I
XXX

Seoul

XXX
IX

ROK III
XXX

XXX
I

XXXX
8

Naktong River

Taejon

Yellow Sea

1 X Mar

SOUTH KOREA

Pusan

☐ Chinese Units

◼ UN Units

⟵ Chinese Second Phase Offensive Attacks, Nov–Dec 1950

⟵--- Chinese Third Phase Offensive Attacks, January 1951

⟵---- UN Moves, Nov–Dec 1950

⟵ UN Moves, January 1951

MAP 24 The Chinese Offensives in Korea, 1950–1951

Chinese civil war.[7] Against them, the UN forces consisted of 450,000 men, of which about 225,000 were Republic of Korea (ROK) troops.[8]

In addition to their slight numerical edge, the UN armies, and particularly their American backbone, possessed an incalculable advantage in equipment, mobility, and firepower. Chinese units were laughably underequipped compared to their American counterparts. Only one-quarter to one-third of the Chinese infantrymen even had rifles. The vast majority went into battle with only grenades. The Chinese armies attacked without any artillery. They had a few Katyusha MRL batteries but held these in reserve at first. They had no antitank weapons. Instead, every Chinese platoon carried enough TNT for 8–10 five-pound satchel charges that had to be placed in the wheels of a tank or thrown through an open hatch to have any effect. The heaviest weapons Chinese units possessed were a handful of 120-mm mortars per regiment and only light mortars and light machine guns at lower echelons. Those weapons the Chinese did have were a heterogeneous assortment captured from the Japanese and the Guomindang and so consisted of older US, European, Japanese, and some Russian small arms. The Chinese had no radios below regimental headquarters, and had so few of these that divisions generally relied on runners for communications. Finally, the Chinese entered Korea with a logistics system that had to rely entirely on porters except for about 800 old trucks, of which only 300–400 were operational on any given day.[9]

The Chinese Intervene. The initial Chinese assault began on October 21, 1950. They struck with total surprise. Chinese CC&D efforts were phenomenal, and US intelligence never detected the movement of their vast armies into Korea. The Chinese also were greatly aided by the self-deception of UN-commander General Douglas MacArthur's headquarters. MacArthur adamantly believed that the Chinese would not intervene (and if they did that they would be easily defeated by US air power), and so he and his subordinates repeatedly disregarded evidence of an impending Chinese offensive.[10]

When the Chinese attacked, UN forces were caught spread out all over northern Korea and completely unsuspecting. The Chinese hit so quickly and so hard that many units were overrun before they knew what was happening. Initially, the Chinese deliberately targeted South Korean formations, believing them to be weaker than American or other non-ROK formations.[11] They enveloped the ROK 1st Infantry Division, attacking simultaneously from the rear and both flanks before the division ever knew they were there. The South Koreans fought their way out only because they were able to call on enormous US firepower to cover their retreat. The Chinese then smashed the ROK 6th and 8th Infantry Divisions, caving in the right flank of the ROK II Corps and causing the entire corps to collapse. The Chinese armies kept pushing west, trying to roll up the lines of the US Eighth Army. They enveloped and mauled the US 8th Cavalry Regiment at Unsan, before the Eighth Army commander, Lt. General Walton Walker, ordered the entire army to fall back to the Chongchon River. At the Chongchon, the United States was able to regroup and bring to bear its overwhelming firepower to halt the Chinese advance.[12]

Marshal Peng concluded that it would be too costly to try to break through the UN lines along the Chongchon and instead opted to pull back in hopes of luring the UN armies back north. Peng's intention was to coax the UN forces out of their fortified lines and get them on the move where they would be easier prey for another Chinese offensive.[13] In addition, the Chinese started to suffer from logistical problems almost immediately. Within days of the initial attacks, Chinese combat units had outstripped their man-powered supply columns. Chinese units carried only three days of food, and after a week of combat were tired and starving. This too argued in favor of a withdrawal and preparation for a new offensive.[14]

The Chinese Second Phase Offensive, their main assault against the UN, began in late November 1950. By that time, Marshal Peng had regrouped and resupplied his forces and believed he had his support services in better shape for a new offensive. He would commit 388,000 Chinese troops against a UN force in northern Korea that now numbered only 342,000.[15] To make matters worse, the Americans had interpreted the withdrawal in early November as an indication that the Chinese had been beaten—despite the fact that they had won nearly every battle they fought—and had run back to Manchuria. Consequently, on November 24, MacArthur ordered a renewed offensive to the Yalu River, despite the misgivings of some of his more clear-headed field commanders. Once again, UN forces pushed back up the peninsula, spread out, and paid little heed to forward reconnaissance. The Chinese struck on November 25th like a hurricane. They attacked with complete surprise and their operations were devastating.[16]

Contrary to popular belief, Chinese forces rarely employed "human wave" attacks. Human wave assaults entail hurling masses of lightly armed infantry against an enemy position in an effort to take that position through shock and attrition. The idea is that the horde of soldiers will simply swamp the position despite their paucity of skills or weaponry. The Chinese regularly employed massed infantry tactics, but rarely human wave attacks. The differences are subtle but important.

In Korea, Chinese forces were so lightly armed that they could not generate adequate firepower for virtually any military operation. Consequently, the Chinese had to employ masses of infantry for those roles in which better-equipped armies would normally use firepower. Specifically, Chinese armies could not use firepower to cover the movements of a unit or to pin an adversary while another force maneuvered against it. Instead, the Chinese had to use infantry assaults for all of these tasks. In addition, the Chinese at times employed what they called the "short attack"—a variant of the Soviet echelon attack, albeit without tanks. In a short attack, Chinese infantry formations would repeatedly attack a narrow enemy defensive sector in hope of wearing down the defenders and creating a breakthrough they could exploit.[17] While manpower-intensive, both of these approaches represented more sophisticated uses of light infantry than what is traditionally meant by a "human wave attack."

The most common Chinese tactic was to employ masses of infantry to keep constant pressure on a position—just as a Western force would use firepower to do the same—while other elements outflanked and enveloped the enemy position. Obviously, this resulted in terrible casualties because keeping pressure on a UN position required the Chinese to send large numbers of lightly armed infantry into the heavy firepower of US and allied units. The Chinese only employed true human wave attacks on occasion late in the Korean War, when so many of their veteran soldiers had been killed that they had to rely largely on raw recruits who lacked the training and experience to employ more sophisticated tactics.[18]

Bloody or not, Chinese tactics were highly effective, securing victory after victory despite the lopsided imbalance in weapons and equipment. Chinese units employed a constant screen of reconnaissance patrols to locate enemy positions. Chinese patrols would then further probe the enemy lines looking for unit boundaries, flanks, gaps, and other weak points. Under cover of darkness, infantry units would infiltrate through these gaps or around the enemy's flanks. These forces would be employed in the attack to surround front-line combat units; overrun enemy command posts, artillery, and other support units; and set up ambushes deep in the rear to cut the enemy's escape route. Other Chinese units, employing painstaking CC&D, would sneak up as close to the enemy defensive positions as possible without giving themselves away. The purpose of this was to be able to rush the defender from a short distance to get into close combat immediately. This was advantageous because the Chinese were superb in hand-to-hand combat and because this hindered UN units from bringing their artillery and air support to bear.

Whenever possible, the Chinese would begin their attack suddenly and under cover of night. Ideally, Chinese infantry infiltrated earlier would combine with formations in front of the enemy to launch assaults from all sides simultaneously. When this was impossible, some units would launch a frontal assault to pin the enemy as other forces conducted a double envelopment of the position. Then, while some reduced the encircled enemy positions, others would bypass them and push on into the rear to attack the enemy's depth. As soon as one sector was secured, Chinese forces would press on quickly deeper into the enemy's rear or into the flanks of nearby enemy units. When enemy forces were put to flight, Chinese units pursued aggressively for as long as they could.[19] These tactics were employed at every level of the Chinese military, from army group and army right down to company and platoon, and proved highly successful throughout the war.[20]

The Chinese used these tactics in November 1950 to tear huge holes in the UN lines. The main Chinese attacks were directed against the center of the UN front, where the Eighth Army in the west and the X Corps in the east were separated by the impassable mountains of central Korea. The Chinese 13th Army Group attacked the ROK II Corps and the US IX Corps on the right flank and center (respectively) of the Eighth Army advance while the 9th Army Group attacked the US 7th Infantry Division and the 1st US Marine Division holding the left flank of the US X Corps.

Chinese successes were spectacular. In the west, the Chinese split and then destroyed the two forward divisions of the ROK II Corps, allowing two entire Chinese armies to push around the right flank of the Eighth Army and envelop the US 2nd Infantry Division as well as the right flank of the US 24th Infantry Division. The 2nd Infantry Division took 4,000 casualties and lost over 50 percent of its equipment fighting its way out of the Chinese encirclement. A Turkish Brigade rushed north to hold the collapsing right flank was butchered, and the US 1st Cavalry Division also took heavy losses when it was brought forward for the same purpose. Chinese forces penetrated and enveloped parts of the US 25th Infantry Division and the ROK 1st Infantry Division, forcing both back with heavy losses. In the east, Chinese forces outflanked and mauled the US 7th Infantry Division. The only significant reverse the Chinese suffered during the entire campaign was against the US 1st Marine Division, which conducted a brilliant fighting withdrawal. Although the Chinese threw two entire field armies against them, the Marines fought phenomenally and, with plentiful fire support, they crippled the Chinese 9th Army Group and cut their way south.[21]

The Marines aside, UN forces fell back in panic and confusion and the Chinese pressed them as hard as they could. However, the Chinese advance simply ran out of steam south of Pyongyang. Several factors were at work. First, Chinese forces could not advance as quickly as the UN could retreat. Without any motor transport, the Chinese could not keep pace with the fully mechanized UN units. The Chinese lost contact with the UN on December

3 and did not catch up to them again until December 20 when the UN had regrouped and formed a new defensive line north of Seoul. Second, China's ramshackle logistical system could not support an advance even as quick as the Chinese infantry could march. As in October, Chinese units quickly began to run out of food and ammunition. As winter crept in and they had no warm clothing, they also began to suffer heavy losses from frostbite and exposure. Many units showed superhuman endurance and kept moving south without resupply, but eventually they too had to halt. Finally, US air power prevented the Chinese from advancing during the day and complicated Chinese logistical problems by working over roads, bridges, and rail lines, and destroying many of the precious few trucks and rail cars the Chinese had.[22]

Continuing the Offensive. The Chinese resumed their assault on New Year's Eve. This "Third Phase Offensive" was a virtual replay of its predecessor. The Chinese again took the UN forces largely by surprise, launching 280,000 men against a 100-mile assault sector. In the center of the peninsula, Chinese units again concentrated on the ROK II Corps, again smashing through it and then turning onto the flanks of the American units on either side. In the west, the Chinese mostly broke through the ROK divisions deployed between the American divisions, and then conducted double envelopments of the US units. Once again, in the first weeks of the offensive, the Chinese inflicted heavy losses on the UN forces and sent them reeling backward. However, almost immediately, logistical problems and China's dearth of motor transport—compounded by the relentless pressure of US air power—prevented the Chinese from turning local successes into strategic victories. Time and again, Chinese units could not move fast enough to close their encirclements before the UN units slipped from their grasp. By mid-January 1951, the Chinese had taken Seoul and pushed the UN south of the Han River, but they ran out of steam before they could obliterate the UN armies altogether.[23]

The Third Phase Offensive was China's last shot at victory in Korea, and when it failed, stalemate became inevitable. By late January 1951, several important changes had deprived the Chinese of the capability to achieve a decisive victory. First off, Chinese losses were staggering. According to Marshal Peng, by the end of the Third Phase Offensive, China had lost roughly half of the force originally deployed to Korea in October and November 1950. Most of these casualties were the result of combat, logistical problems, and winter weather, with combat losses being the *smallest* of the three categories. What mattered was that so many of those killed were the hardened veterans of World War II and the Chinese Civil War. Consequently, Chinese armies increasingly were filled out with raw recruits sent to Korea with virtually no training.

Meanwhile, Chinese logistical problems continued to worsen. American air power prevented the Chinese from effectively using the railroads inside Korea, so supplies had to be carried by porter from the Manchurian border 300 kilometers away. Chinese divisions required remarkably few provisions compared to their American counterparts, but as soon as they went on the offensive, the extra distance from the Manchurian railheads began to weigh down their advance. At the end of the Third Phase Offensive, Chinese troops were attacking UN units primarily to seize their rations rather than to take their positions or drive them out of Korea.

In addition, Lt. General Matthew Ridgway took command of the US Eighth Army in late 1950 and then succeeded General MacArthur as theater commander in 1951. Ridgway was a brilliant general who rebuilt the UN armies and devised new tactics for fighting the Chinese. With Ridgway in command, UN forces were far more dangerous than they had been in the past.[24]

In early February, Ridgway launched a limited counterattack that made little progress and took heavy casualties. Less than a week later, the Chinese responded with their Fourth Phase Offensive. Through outstanding CC&D efforts the Chinese again surprised the UN units, but the declining strength of the Chinese armies and the growing strength of UN forces with Ridgway in command made this offensive even less successful than the last. Surprise and Chinese tactical prowess again combined to bring some short-term successes: Chinese armies again routed several ROK divisions, allowing the Chinese to penetrate and envelop nearby American units. The US 2nd Infantry Division, finally back on line after its drubbing in November, was once again encircled and mauled. This time, however, Ridgway had devised tactics that allowed the UN to employ its firepower more effectively to kill Chinese and break up their assaults. Chinese units suffered appalling losses as a result of these tactics, and again their logistics failed them, forcing pauses that let UN units slip away before they could be cut off and destroyed. After only a week, the Chinese were forced to pull back to regroup.[25]

It took the Chinese over two months to recover from their Fourth Phase Offensive. During this time, Ridgway launched a series of limited counterattacks that succeeded in retaking Seoul. Then on April 22, the Chinese commenced their Fifth Phase Offensive. This was Peng's last bid at victory, and for it he had assembled 500,000 Chinese and North Korean troops. Yet it too followed the trend of accomplishing less than its predecessor.

The Chinese again achieved tactical surprise, and again aimed their initial assaults at ROK units. However, Ridgway had begun a program to retrain and re-equip ROK troops and, this time, the ROK divisions were pushed back, but not routed. UN troops also had learned to defend their positions in-depth and from all sides so that Chinese infiltration was much harder and less effective. In addition, the UN now had roughly 650,000 troops (227,000 US, 400,000 ROK) defending a much shorter front, making it far more difficult for the Chinese to find gaps between their units. Finally, Ridgway had concentrated unprecedented levels of firepower and simply obliterated everything in front of the UN lines. American artillery batteries were employed to bombard suspected Chinese assembly points whenever an attack seemed possible, while the US air forces conducted over 7,000 ground attack sorties in support of UN troops.

Chinese manpower reserves and tactical skills were such that they were again able to penetrate the UN lines, but they could not translate these breakthroughs into strategic victories. Mobility and logistics problems hobbled the Chinese advance from the start, giving Ridgway time to bring up American divisions held in reserve that proceeded to check and then reduce the Chinese penetrations with overwhelming firepower. As their supplies dwindled and their casualties soared, Chinese morale disintegrated and whole units began to crack under American pummeling. The Chinese pushed to the outskirts of Seoul, but were unable to retake the city.[26]

The War Drags On. After the failure of the Chinese Fifth Phase Offensive, the fighting in Korea bogged down into a bloody stalemate. Both Peng and Ridgway recognized that they could not score a decisive victory over the other. Chinese maneuver skills and manpower resources essentially balanced out American firepower, mobility, and logistics. Both sides conducted frequent limited offensives meant to secure more advantageous defensive terrain, but neither attempted another grand "end-the-war" offensive.

Instead, the Chinese dug-in deep. They built elaborate trench and tunnel complexes with interlocking fields of fire, strongpoints, minefields, and hidden exits from which the defenders could launch sudden counterattacks from unexpected locations. According to Marshal Peng, the Chinese dug 1,250 kilometers of tunnels and 6,240 kilometers of trenches by war's end.[27] In the late summer of 1951, after the failure of China's great offensives, the USSR began to provide Beijing with modern weaponry. The Soviets sent tanks, artillery, trucks, infantry weapons, and advanced fighter aircraft such as the MiG-15 to China. This new arsenal gave the Chinese considerably more firepower than in the past and a better ability to hang on to their defensive positions.[28]

As a result of the sudden influx of Soviet equipment into China, the war in the air over Korea became interesting just as the war in the ground deadlocked. The Chinese Communists had never had an air force before, and their pilots had no more than a year of training before they took to the skies, so Beijing set only modest objectives for the new service.[29] Essentially, Marshal Peng asked only that the Chinese Air Force provide air defense for his ground armies. At first, the Chinese fighters tried to intercept US bombers—mostly B-29s—attacking the Chinese logistics network in northern Korea. The B-29 was no match for the MiG-15 and thus Chinese pilots began doing considerable damage to US bomber formations in late 1951. However, these operations prompted the United States to deploy advanced F-86 Sabre and F-84 Thunderjet squadrons to Korea to escort the bombers and clear out the MiGs. In dogfights with the US fighters, especially the Sabres, the Chinese were initially mauled. The Sabre was a slightly more capable aircraft than the MiG, but the big difference was that virtually all of the US pilots were veterans of World War II while the Chinese were brand new to flying. Nevertheless, over time the Chinese pilots gained experience, and some became quite good.[30]

As the size of China's air force grew and the experience of its pilots improved, Beijing tried more ambitious air operations. First, in April 1951, the Chinese attempted to make a major air effort in support of their Fifth Phase Offensive by employing large numbers of IL-10 Sturmovik ground-attack aircraft they had received from the USSR. However, in ferocious battles with the US Sabres and Thunderjets, the MiGs could not clear the sky for such a ground-support campaign.[31]

Next, the Chinese attempted to halt the US air campaign against Chinese lines of communication that was hampering the flow of supplies south to the front lines. In the summer and fall of 1951, the Chinese deployed 690 combat aircraft in Manchuria, of which 525 were MiG-15s, to try to gain air superiority over the battlefield. At that time, the United States had only one wing of Sabres and another of F-84s in Korea. United States' pilots reported that the Chinese were better led, better trained, better organized, and employed better tactics than in the past. In some cases, this was because the Soviets had dispatched some of their own veteran pilots to fly the MiGs for the Chinese (and North Koreans).[32]

Although the Chinese continued to be on the losing end against the Sabres, they were able to put up such huge numbers of aircraft that they began to seriously interrupt the US tactical air campaign against their logistics system. In response, the US air forces threw all their assets into a massive offensive counter-air campaign consisting of fighter sweeps and constant attacks on Chinese forward air bases. The MiGs rose in defense and fought huge, swirling dogfights with the American fighters. Although the US Air Force was unable to knock out the Chinese airbases altogether, they shot down hordes of MiGs in this way. Nevertheless, in 1952, the Chinese Air Force became even more aggressive, deploying ever greater numbers of aircraft (1,800 aircraft, including 1,000 jet fighters) and flying them farther and farther south. Still, although Chinese dogfighting skills continued to improve, they could never beat the Sabre pilots, and so over the course of 1952 and 1953, attrition began to wear down the Chinese Air Force, forcing it back on the defensive, and reducing its ability to interfere with other US air operations.[33] Ultimately, the American Sabres would shoot down 566 MiGs for the loss of about 100 of their own.[34]

With the fighting deadlocked on the ground and the United States having defeated the Chinese air threat, both sides agreed to peace talks in 1951. Nevertheless, it took two years of on-again, off-again negotiations to produce a ceasefire agreement on July 27, 1953, largely because of disagreements over the handling of prisoners of war. Actual costs for the Chinese remain unknown, but the most recent assessments suggest that probably around 450,000 Chinese were killed in the fighting. On the other hand, the South Koreans suffered 137,899 killed and the Americans 36,516 dead, most of whom were killed fighting the Chinese.[35]

Patterns of Chinese Military Effectiveness

Overall, Chinese military forces fought very well during the Korean War. Chinese forces labored under a variety of important disadvantages, many of them derived directly from the poverty and underdevelopment of Chinese society at the time. Yet they scored major victories, knocking the UN armies out of North Korea and then fighting them to a draw around the 38th Parallel. Of greater importance, the specific performance of Chinese military forces in battle showed little similarity to that of the Arab armies. Although there were areas of overlap, primarily related to limited technical skills, even in these cases the similarities were not identical.

Chinese Strategic Leadership. China's generals mostly showed a high degree of competence. Peng Dehuai obviously stands out as a first-rate commander, but Beijing's strategic direction in general was very good.[36] Allan Millett has argued that if Peng had deployed more of his force east of the Chongchon River in the November 1950 Second Phase attack, it would have produced an even more crushing victory than Peng achieved. That may be a correct appraisal, but it still does not detract from Peng's performance under difficult conditions, nor the scope of what he did accomplish on this and many other occasions.[37] In particular, Peng and China's other generals seemed to have had an excellent understanding of the strengths and weaknesses of their own forces and carefully crafted their operations to suit those capabilities.

Peng's various offensives in Korea were well conceived, and had UN forces been less mobile and his own logistical system been more robust, the UN might easily have been thrown off the peninsula altogether. Even working under these constraints his operations achieved remarkable results. His offensives always featured a single-minded concentration of force against the decisive points coupled with deft maneuvers to confuse and cut off enemy formations. Nor would it be fair to criticize Peng for failing to incorporate his own logistical weaknesses and the enemy's mobility into his planning: Peng's mission, throw the UN off the Korean peninsula, probably was unattainable given the capabilities of his forces, yet he came remarkably close.

The direction of Chinese operations also was first class in every category. China's military moves were thoroughly planned and meticulously prepared. Chinese generals used feints, deception, disinformation, and maneuver in superb combinations to achieve surprise and defeat otherwise superior opponents. They were extremely diligent about reconnaissance and intelligence operations. Although willing to pay heavily in casualties, it is difficult to say they squandered lives: Chinese operations were well-thought-through and there was a clear, well-reasoned purpose to their sacrifices. Chinese strategic leaders kept the control and organization of their forces simple and straightforward and commanded enormous armies with remarkably primitive communications systems. Chinese offensives were noteworthy for consistently securing surprise, uncovering the weak sectors in an enemy's defense, concentrating overwhelming force at the decisive point on a battlefield, and forcing the enemy to fight at a disadvantage through rapid maneuver. On the defensive, Chinese operations were marked by a thorough appreciation for the terrain, extensive and well laid-out fortifications, and an ability to sense the flow of battle and shift forces appropriately in response to changes.[38]

Before we move off the topic of China's strategic leadership, it is worth noting that the People's Liberation Army (PLA) was heavily politicized at this time in commissarist fashion.[39] Political officers were present down to company level, and numerous officers and soldiers were Communist Party members who enforced party dogma. Chinese officers generally assumed that the political commissars were more powerful than they were since all military orders had to be countersigned by the ranking political officer.[40] Patrick Coe has noted that in the Chinese military of the Korean War, "Decisions in combat (and elsewhere) not only had to be militarily or tactically correct; they also had to be politically correct."[41] Mao Zedong was a notoriously paranoid, capricious, and bloody-minded dictator who terrified his generals. Peng's own rise was primarily a result of his steadfast loyalty to Mao, yet Mao endlessly micromanaged Chinese operations, often pushing strategically foolish ideas that drove Peng and his staff to distraction.[42]

All of this reinforces the point from previous chapters that while politicization can be an impediment to military effectiveness, it is not inevitable, and various armies have found ways to compensate. Likewise, emphasizing the promotion of loyalty over competence does not mean that every general in a politicized military will be incompetent. There are brilliant loyalists too, especially in armies with considerable recent combat experience where the audit of battle can help sort the wheat from the chaff.

Chinese Tactical Leadership. Chinese junior officers performed equally well, perhaps even better, than their generals. The Chinese employed a highly decentralized command system that placed a heavy burden on tactical leaders. Because Chinese operations were often conducted at night, involved large-scale infiltrations, had few radios, and placed a premium on stealth, it was often impossible for senior commanders to direct their forces in the midst of battle. The Chinese also placed a premium on decisions made on the spot in response to immediate circumstances. In particular, they emphasized the immediate exploitation of gaps and weak points such as unit boundaries, which meant that junior officers were expected to recognize such opportunities and act on them without direct orders. As one historian observed, "The nature of the Chinese Red Army, with its paucity of modern military equipment, placed a great deal of responsibility on unit commanders, they were to follow the general plan if they could, but not be afraid to deviate if it seemed appropriate."[43] To facilitate this, the Chinese army conducted extensive pre-attack briefings, with senior officers providing remarkable amounts of information to their subordinates to ensure that more junior commanders would be able to make smart decisions during the battle based on a full understanding of the plan and the intelligence regarding enemy forces and intentions. Indeed, virtually all Chinese operations were planned only at general levels, and the specifics were typically left to the commanders in the field to decide as the circumstances dictated.[44]

Chinese junior officers performed extremely well in this system. They kept up a constant stream of patrols to find the enemy, and then to probe for routes of attack, flanks, gaps in the line, unit boundaries, etc. Once they had a reasonable picture of enemy dispositions they formulated a plan of attack and put it into action. They showed tremendous individual initiative and aggressiveness. They rarely seemed to let an opportunity pass, and reacted quickly and flexibly to the ebb and flow of combat. At times, they did miss opportunities to exploit, but typically because their logistics failed them or they had suffered such heavy casualties taking the position that they had too little left to follow through. When one approach failed, Chinese junior officers devised a new plan of action and then put it into effect. They also showed a real flare for improvisation in their approach to combat situations. As just one example of this, in 1950 one Chinese company commander had his men light the dried grass near an American position on fire when they could not find a way to flank the American lines. The grass burned straight up the hill the Americans were holding, forcing them to abandon the position.[45]

Chinese tactical units operated at a quick operational tempo, especially given their lack of motor transport. Chinese junior officers fully recognized the need to hit hard and fast and to keep hitting the enemy with rapid blows so that he could not recover. Consequently, they bypassed resistance when possible and drove as far and as fast into the rear as they could to overrun command posts and keep the enemy reeling. In one incident, Chinese troops smashed the ROK 15th Infantry Regiment and then pursued so quickly that they passed the retreating South Korean troops, overran the regiment's command post, and then turned to ambush the combat units (again) as they fled south.[46] Even when one Chinese unit might stop to regroup on an objective, other elements of the force—or other units of the same formation—would take it upon themselves to keep moving forward to maintain the pace of advance and not give the enemy any breathing space.[47]

One of the greatest strengths of the Chinese military at every level was their predilection for maneuver. Shu Guang Zhang notes that the PLA itself believed that its forces could overcome American advantages in firepower because they were "good at maneuvering, flexibility and mobility and, in particular, good at surrounding and attacking [the] enemy's flanks by taking tortuous courses, as well as dispersing and concealing forces."[48] The PLA's favored form of attack—and counterattack—was what Lin Biao referred to as the "one point, two sides" maneuver, which consisted of a frontal assault to pin the enemy coupled with a double envelopment. Chinese forces at every level from army group to squad employed this approach, and when it proved impossible, they found other ways to maneuver against their foe, performing a single envelopment or simply attacking from an oblique angle to the defender's lines. American, South Korean, Turkish, British (and in 1962, Indian troops) reported being constantly outflanked and hit from the rear by Chinese units.[49]

These traits were equally apparent in defensive operations. Chinese tactical commanders were just as diligent about reconnaissance when on the defensive. They were careful to disguise their positions and built ingenious defensive networks. Chinese forces were also extremely active on defense and rarely sat passively in their trenches while being attacked. In battle, Chinese units would abandon their positions if they thought that they could move into a better one, preferably one from which they could fire or counterattack into the attacker's flank or rear. Chinese units counterattacked vigorously and quickly at every level. Indeed, many Chinese defensive positions were designed to lure the enemy in and crush him with a devastating counterattack (often from several sides simultaneously).[50] Whenever possible, the Chinese attempted to conduct flanking counterattacks to cut off the attacking force and crush it. Moreover, if they repulsed an attacker, Chinese units frequently seized the opportunity to pursue or even launch an immediate attack of their own.[51]

The Chinese appear to have done adequately in combined arms operations when their very limited experiences are taken into account. In Korea, the Chinese initially employed pure infantry formations, but by the end of the war they also fielded considerable numbers of artillery batteries. By and large, the Chinese did well in employing their artillery to support their infantry formations both when attacking and in defense.

Chinese Rank and File Performance. China's soldiery did all that could be expected of them. Personal bravery among Chinese units was very high. The Chinese Army attacked with great confidence and enthusiasm. In Korea, this remained the case until the cold, the lack of food and other supplies, as well as the terrifying losses in combat began to set in during 1951.[52] Chinese unit cohesion was likewise excellent. Although numerous Chinese units did begin to crack in 1951 at the end of the Fifth Phase Offensive, what was impressive was just how much hardship and adversity these formations endured before that happened. By that time, many of the Chinese soldiers were literally starving to death, clinically exhausted, and numbed by five months of attacks into the teeth of UN firepower. Most armies would have fallen apart long before.[53]

Chinese weapons handling was mostly poor, albeit with several bright spots. Chinese marksmanship was lousy across the board. Chinese infantrymen could do little with their small arms. One exception to this rule was that Chinese units were often inexplicably good with light machine guns.[54] Chinese forces also suffered heavily from the limited technical skills of their personnel. Consequently, few could handle electronics equipment, heavy weaponry, or other technology-intensive machines. To at least some extent, the Chinese had to forgo certain weapons that were simply beyond the technical skills of their men. Moreover, Chinese troops rarely got the maximum performance out of even the relatively simple weaponry they employed.

By contrast, Chinese artillery and mortar operations were very competent. Although Chinese forces entered the war with only light mortars and almost no artillery, by 1952 they had learned to employ their new Soviet-supplied indirect-fire weapons in a fairly sophisticated manner. As the war progressed, the ability of Chinese mortar and artillery units to mass their fire became an important element in their defensive operations. Chinese artillery batteries could rapidly combine their fire even when geographically dispersed, their fire missions were often very accurate, and they could quickly and flexibly shift their fire from one target to the next as required by front-line commanders. Chinese mortar units even got so good that they could silence US mortars in counter-battery duels.[55]

Chinese Combat Support and Combat Service Support Performance. Above all else, logistics was the bane of Chinese military operations. In Korea, China might have scored one of the most impressive victories in modern history had its supply services been able to keep pace with its combat units and had its combat units been able to move faster than they did. As one historian has said of Marshal Peng, "It was not the Americans who were defeating him; it was winter, and the Chinese inability to fight this sort of war on a straight offensive basis. The logistics of an attacking army are perhaps six times more difficult than those of a defending army, and Marshal Peng's logistics, by his own statements, were so ridiculous as to be laughable."[56]

The causes of these logistics problems may not be as clear as they may seem. The most obvious problem the Chinese faced was that they had too few trucks and trains to supply their army, and too few air defenses to protect the logistical network from air attack. In addition, they had other material complications. For example, in Korea, Chinese forces used a multitude of small arms, none of which were manufactured in China and most of which were no longer manufactured at all. Consequently, providing ammunition and spare parts to the combat units was a nightmare. However, it is unclear whether Chinese logistics problems also were related to China's low levels of education or other socioeconomic factors. Logistics for an army that is even crudely modern requires quartermasters able to read and do arithmetic and often more complicated mathematics. In addition, supplying such a vast army, over such great distances with such a multitude of different weapons, is a complex project to say the least.

Very little information exists regarding China's maintenance capabilities. During October and November 1951, the Chinese generally were able to keep 300–400 of their 800 trucks running on any given day.[57] A 50 percent operational readiness rate is usually considered very poor, and this would fit well with the pattern of difficulties the Chinese experienced in other aspects of military operations related to technical skills. Still, it would be rash to conclude based on this single scrap of evidence that Chinese armies experienced considerable problems with maintenance and repairs. The Chinese were using mostly very old trucks captured from the Guomindang and the Japanese. It is unclear what kind of shape they were in when the Chinese Communists got them, or what kind of an inventory of spare parts and lubricants they had by 1950. Moreover, 800 trucks is an absurdly low number to try to support an army of over 300,000 men, so those trucks may have been driven to death. For all of these reasons, this meager evidence on its own cannot support the conclusion that Chinese maintenance practices were poor, even though this would fit the pattern suggested by Chinese problems with logistics and weapons handling.

Limited evidence suggests that Chinese combat engineers were reasonably good. Although the Chinese were known to use infantry battalions to clear paths through minefields by having them walk across in line-abreast, they generally could rely on a competent corps of engineers. In Korea, Chinese engineers built impressive fortifications very quickly. Chinese engineers showed a tremendous ability to cross water obstacles. The US Air Force was constantly frustrated by the speed and ingenuity of Chinese engineers building, repairing, and circumventing bridges knocked down by US air strikes.[58]

Chinese Air Force Performance. China's air force made a reasonable effort given its newness. The Chinese did not necessarily do "well" in any category of air operations, but deserve high marks for learning quickly.

The planning and direction of Chinese air operations was reasonably good. Chinese Air Force leaders initially recognized that their squadrons were only capable of defensive counter-air missions, and so they concentrated on trying to disrupt the US campaign against Chinese logistics. Later, as the forces available to them improved, they took on more ambitious missions. The Chinese quickly deduced the weaknesses of the F-86 Sabre, specifically its limited range, and designed tactics to try to take advantage of that problem. Although the United States quickly countered, the Chinese in turn devised a counter to the Americans' counter-tactic. The United States ultimately prevailed in this contest, but this rapid interplay indicates that Chinese Air Force leaders were intelligent, creative, and resourceful and actively tried to shape aerial encounters, rather than passively accepting situations as they occurred.

Chinese air forces concentrated almost exclusively on counter-air missions; consequently, this is the only category of air operations in which the Chinese performance can reasonably be assessed. The Chinese began very poorly but had made major improvements by war's end. The chief factor was the experience of Chinese pilots. At the start of the war, the Chinese Air Force was brand new and had only a handful of qualified pilots, none of whom had participated in air-to-air combat before. When these men went up against the World War II veterans of the US Air Force they were slaughtered. The Chinese began sending large numbers of pilots to the USSR for training, and over time, they began to give the American pilots a harder time. There was never a month during the Korean War when Chinese MiG squadrons did more damage to the Americans than they sustained themselves, but by 1952 they had reduced the number of losses they were taking and had increased the number of US planes they were shooting down.

Nevertheless it is still the bottom line that, throughout the war, the Chinese never performed as well as the Americans in air combat maneuvering. They fought aggressively, and they maneuvered, and some of their pilots were able to really exploit the capabilities of their aircraft, but they were never able to do it at the same level as the Americans. As a result, US Sabre pilots racked up at least a 5:1 kill ratio against the Chinese for the war.[59]

Decisive Factors in the Korean War. Chinese forces did as well as they did in combat for several reasons. Chinese leadership at both strategic and tactical levels was unquestionably the most important factor in Chinese successes. China's generals did a superb job employing the resources at their disposal to achieve Beijing's political objectives. In many of their campaigns, the Chinese achieved spectacular results that almost certainly would have been beyond the reach of less competent generals commanding the same forces. Similarly, it is difficult to fault Beijing's generals for Chinese failures. Ultimately, the tasks set for them by their political masters may well have been unachievable.

Chinese tactical competence was just as important as the skill of their strategic leadership. In battle, the Chinese were an extremely dangerous foe, and what is so incredible is that they achieved this level of tactical prowess despite pitiful weaponry and illiterate soldiers mostly incapable of taking full advantage of the meager equipment they possessed. It is remarkable that Chinese infantry companies of roughly 100 men equipped with no more than a few dozen rifles, perhaps three or four light machine guns, and maybe a light mortar or two, could attack and defeat entrenched American units of roughly equal size but lavishly armed with the most modern weapons and backed by fearsome air and artillery support. Chinese tactical formations maintained a torrid pace of operations, although this inevitably outstripped what their logistical train could support. Their units displayed this tactical excellence from squad to division levels, and the credit for this has to go to China's tactical commanders. With only a few exceptions, the Americans were never able to match Chinese tactical skills in Korea, and only were able to achieve a stalemate through the application of overwhelming firepower to bleed the Chinese army white—and they could do so only because Chinese logistical failings prevented them from overrunning the peninsula altogether.

Another important aspect of China's victories was its superb intelligence capabilities. In Korea, China won the intelligence war, and in doing so, went a great distance toward winning the entire war. China's constant attention to reconnaissance and its persistent efforts to gather information on its adversary in any way possible usually gave Chinese military leaders at all levels an excellent understanding of the adversary they faced. On the other hand, China's meticulous attention to operational security and CC&D prevented their enemies from knowing much if anything about their own operations. At the grandest strategic level, the Chinese moved over 300,000 men into Korea without the United States realizing it. At tactical levels, Chinese platoons and battalions often passed right under the noses of US, ROK, and other Western units before and during a battle.

Chinese military setbacks were largely the product of two weaknesses: logistics and weaponry. Chinese deficiencies in supplying and moving their forces were literally crippling because they led to widespread starvation and frostbite. In 1950–1951, this failing was unquestionably the most important factor that prevented China from turning a remarkable victory into a decisive one.

China's arsenal was its other great problem. The Chinese simply lacked the equipment that their adversaries possessed, both in terms of quantity and quality. The gap between the arms of a US, or even a ROK, unit and those of comparable Chinese units was immeasurable. Nevertheless, China's deficiencies in terms of arms should not be exaggerated: the Chinese armed forces achieved stunning successes despite this problem, and their defeats do not seem to have been the result of deficiencies in weaponry. Had the Chinese been better armed, their operations almost certainly would have been even more successful, but there is no reason to believe that this would have compensated for the logistical problems that brought their Korean offensives to a halt.

An important aspect of this issue is whether Chinese deficiencies in weaponry and logistics were purely the product of their poverty, or the result of an inability among Chinese personnel to read and write, to understand machinery, and to handle the complex requirements of a modern army. Was the problem simply that the Chinese could not afford to build or buy adequate numbers of modern arms, trucks, and combat consumables? Or, was the problem that even had Beijing been able to acquire adequate supplies of this materiel it would have made little difference because Chinese soldiers and officers would have been unable to employ them properly?

This is a crucial question to understand the impact of underdevelopment on military effectiveness. If the problem is simply one of availability, then this says little about the impact of underdevelopment on the performance of the personnel themselves. Of greatest importance, it would argue that underdevelopment probably was not a very good explanation for Arab military ineffectiveness, because in most of their wars the Arab armies had a surfeit of weapons, mobility assets, and supplies. Unfortunately, very little evidence is available, and what is available is contradictory. For example, the poor dogfighting skills of Chinese pilots suggests that the problem was an inability to fully exploit modern technology. On the other hand, the excellent machine gunning and artillery skills of Chinese ground forces indicate just the opposite, that the problem was simply the inadequacy of the available hardware.

As a final note, although China's enemies have often blamed their losses on Chinese numerical superiority in manpower, I find this excuse unconvincing. In Korea, Chinese quantitative advantages were not great. The Chinese often had fewer men in the field than the UN forces. Of course, the UN armies had a much lower "tooth-to-tail" ratio so the Chinese frequently had more combat soldiers available than did the United States. But these imbalances should not have been decisive. For instance, in November 1950, China fielded 388,000 men against 342,000 UN soldiers. Even if one assumes that as much as 80 percent of Chinese manpower were combat troops while only 50 percent of UN manpower were, the net figure is 310,000 Chinese soldiers against 205,000 UN soldiers. Given the immense material disparity between the two sides, such a difference in manpower should not have been decisive. In 2003, an Anglo-American army of about 75,000 troops with similar material advantages crushed an Iraqi army of 300,000 and conquered their country in under a month.[60] If the issue were merely mass versus materiel in Korea, the Chinese advantage in mass should not have outweighed the UN advantage in materiel.

Regardless of the raw balance of manpower, the crucial point is that the Chinese did not win by overwhelming numbers. The Chinese were forced to employ mass as a substitute for firepower in their tactical maneuver schemes. This should not take away from the fact that their victories over the US-led armies in Korea were achieved by superior tactical competence. The Chinese won battles by deceiving, confusing, and outmaneuvering their opponents, not by drowning them in a sea of manpower. Especially prior to Ridgway's reforms, American military units in Korea were very mediocre, and weren't even as competent as their World War II antecedents. For the Americans, having more such units would not have made nearly as much difference as having more capable ones.

Chinese and Arab Military Effectiveness. Comparing Arab military performance since 1948 with the Chinese military experience in the Korean War shows pretty much the same thing as the Libya-Chad case: vast differences in military effectiveness existed between many Arab and non-Arab forces despite comparable levels of socioeconomic development. China's extreme backwardness does not appear to have produced the same patterns of ineffectiveness in Chinese forces that characterized Arab operations during the postwar era.

Aside from those categories related to limited technical skills, the only areas in which Chinese and Arab armed forces appeared comparable was in the high degrees of unit cohesion and personal bravery displayed by both. Other than this, it is difficult to find areas in which the Arabs fought as well as, or even just similar to, the Chinese. In particular, the Chinese manifested none of the problems the Arabs had with information management and tactical leadership in terms of initiative, creativity, flexibility, responsiveness, etc. Instead, these were areas in which the Chinese excelled. For the Chinese, maneuver warfare and information management were arguably their greatest strengths, whereas for the Arabs these were their greatest weakness.

CHAPTER 14

Economic Development and
Arab Military Effectiveness

W E NOW HAVE a lot of information to assess the extent to which Arab
military problems were the result of the underdevelopment of the
Arab world. In addition to the Syrians from 1948 to 1982 and the Chadians
and Chinese, it is important to recognize that Argentina, Cuba, North Korea,
and South Vietnam were all pre-industrial or "proto-industrial" societies
during the wars we looked at. Table 14.1 provides a comparison of the socioeconomic indicators for these six non-Arab countries at the various times they
were at war during the postwar period. In addition, it gives those same statistics for five of the Arab states as well as Sweden in 1960 and 1990.

A comparison of these statistics demonstrates that all of the Arab states
and all six of the non-Arab states we looked at were underdeveloped. While
the Arab states experienced considerable growth, as late as 1990 none had
even come close to the level of Sweden 30 years earlier, and therefore none can
be considered advanced, or industrialized societies by any stretch of the imagination. The same is true for Argentina, Chad, China, Cuba, North Korea,
and South Vietnam. Although Argentina in 1980 and Cuba in 1975 were a bit
more advanced than the Arab states during this time frame, the difference is
not dramatic. Argentina and Cuba were much closer to the level of the Arab
states than they were even to 1960 Sweden.

So the question then becomes: Did we see similar patterns of military effectiveness among these six non-Arab states and the Arab militaries? In some
areas yes, and in other areas no. There were some things that all of them

TABLE 14.1. Socioeconomic Development of Selected Arab and Non-Arab States

Indicators	Argentina 1982	Chad 1987	China 1950	Cuba 1975	DPRK 1950	South Vietnam 1970	Egypt 1960	Jordan 1960	Libya 1987	Syria 1980	Saudi Arabia 1990	Iraq 1990	Iraq 2014	Sweden 1960	Sweden 1990
GDP per capita (in 1960 dollars)	363	23	144	173	174	189	145	176	1,631	345	1,313	439	792	1,840	5,358
Literacy (% of pop. over 15 able to read +write)	94	17	10	78	35–40	50	26	32	60	58	62	15	80	99	99
Infant mortality per 1,000 live births	33	138	130	25	116 (1944)	37	128	140	84	73	59	140	27	17	5
Life expectancy at birth, in years	70	44	38 (1952)	72	49	70	48	53	57	65	69	48	69	73	79
Per capita electrical production (in kWh)	1,454	12	8.4	876 (1978)	NA	41	102	59	3,250	406	3,300	132	1,684	4,964	16,700
% of workforce in manufacturing	34	5	4	18	NA	NA	5	26	31	29	28	5	19	45	38
% of workforce in agriculture	13	85	77	29	71	77	58	44	18	32	16	53	22	14	3
Inhabitants per physician	370	38,360 (1984)	34,469 (1946)	115 (1968)	4,545	12,236	2,500	5,900	690 (1984)	2,570	770	4,900	1,667 (2010)	730	370
Inhabitants per automobile	6	215	10,940	125 (1973)	613	425 (1969)	386	262	6	109	21	168	10	7	2
Inhabitants per telephone	12	929	2,430	20		500	106	67	24	49	44	122	18*	8	1

* This is for fixed telephones. Mobile phones per Iraq were at almost a 1:1 ratio in 2014. The World Bank, *World Development Report*, 2016.

Sources: CIA, *The World Factbook*, Various years; Angus Maddison, *Chinese Economic Performance in the Long Run* (Paris: OECD Publishing, 1998); Angus Maddison, *The World Economy: A Millennial Perspective* (Paris: OECD Publishing, 2001), The World Bank, *World Development Report*, Various years; UN Statistical Office, *Compendium of Social Statistics and Indicators*, Various years.

experienced as problems, but ultimately they were more dissimilar than they were alike. The evidence doesn't line up perfectly—and I will discuss some of the outliers below—but the patterns seem pretty strong.

Weapons Handling and Maintenance

First and of greatest importance, there were areas of similarity among all of these armies. These lay in their handling and upkeep of equipment, which was poor across the board. From the Syrians in 1948 to the Chinese in 1950 to the Cubans in the 1970s and 1980s, to the Argentines and Syrians again in 1982, and even the Chadians in the late 1980s, none of these militaries was able to employ advanced weaponry to the full extent of its potential. Syrian fighter pilots in 1982 seemed to define the nadir of this problem; they could barely fly their MiG-23s let alone fight them as well as they could be fought. In contrast, in that same year, Argentina's fighter pilots demonstrated that a small, elite group could make full use of a similar generation of warplanes in their commendable performance against the British in the Falklands. But the Argentines defined the apogee of the same curve, and it was noteworthy that their counterparts in the Argentine Army could not even approach their level of performance. They were the exceptions to the rule.

The other Arab states performed uniformly badly. Throughout the Iran-Iraq War, Iraqi pilots and tankers were outfought by their Iranian counterparts (not that the Iranians were particularly good). During the Persian Gulf War of 1990–1991, Iraqi pilots were so bad that many were killed because they flew into the ground and, like the Israelis in 1982, American fighter pilots achieved a badly lopsided kill ratio in air-to-air combat. The same was true for Libyan pilots facing American pilots over the Mediterranean in the 1980s, let alone when they tried to conduct air strikes against Chadian troops in the 1980s or Tanzanian troops during Qadhafi's bizarre intervention in Uganda to save Idi Amin.[1] As I noted in Chapter 3, very few modern Egyptian pilots even know how to employ the avionics on their F-16s.

The same pattern was also present when it came to maintaining those weapons. Whether it was the Chadians or the Libyans, the Iraqis or the Chinese, the Vietnamese or the Egyptians, they all had great difficulty maintaining their equipment, and the more sophisticated the system, the worse the problems. As a result, operational readiness rates were low across the board. Throughout the Iran-Iraq War, Iraqi mechanized formations rarely had operational readiness rates above about 60–65 percent for their armored vehicles. Likewise, at critical moments throughout the later campaigns of the Vietnam War, the South Vietnamese were hamstrung by poor maintenance—crippling their armor during the 1971 invasion of Laos and grounding their CH-47 helicopter fleet during the fighting in the Central Highlands in 1975.[2] In the former instance, the ARVN lost 37 of 62 tanks and 98 of 164 other armored vehicles during Lam Son 719, overwhelmingly from vehicle breakdowns and running out of gas. Dale Andrade noted that South Vietnamese armor training was hampered by maintenance problems, which in turn were a function of "a lack of technical understanding by South Vietnamese tankers."[3] In short, none of these underdeveloped societies could produce enough personnel with the technical skills needed to maintain sophisticated equipment.

There was at least one exception to this rule: the Cubans. Although the Cubans were not outstanding at maintenance or weapons handling, they did notably better than the rest of their Arab and non-Arab peers. In particular, Soviet bloc countries regularly employed Cuban mechanics and technicians to handle the very maintenance and repair tasks that they couldn't. (The North Koreans also seem to have done better, and *in later years* also provided technicians to other Soviet clients, particularly Arab states.) Moreover, the South Africans regarded the Cubans as decent pilots and decent tankers, albeit not as good as they were. Anecdotally, we have all heard stories about the remarkable Cuban mechanics—professional and amateur—who keep American cars made in the 1950s running 60 or 70 years later. So there is something about the Cubans that has made them better in their handling of technology than seems to be the norm with the militaries of underdeveloped societies. Nevertheless, this one exception should not blind us to the otherwise strong pattern of underdeveloped societies, including the Arab states, suffering in combat because of poor weapons handling and maintenance.

Indeed, the two Syrian cases offered further proof of the connection between weapons handling and underdevelopment. Although the Syrians in 1982 were terrible compared to the Israelis (and to the Argentines, at least in some areas) they were still better than their own predecessors in 1948. The Syrian Army of 1948 could not possibly have handled the jet fighters and tanks that the Syrian military employed in 1982, no matter how badly. Likewise, while the Syrians did not do a very good job of maintaining their equipment in 1982 (and when a Syrian pilot defected with his MiG-23 in the late 1980s, the MiG was found to have rats' nests in its air intakes) they did not necessarily do worse than when they were maintaining the much simpler weapons of 1948. In other words, although the Syrians never did well with maintenance compared to First World armies, they "kept pace" with evolving technology, reflecting the increased development of Syrian society from 1948 to 1982.

Bigger Exceptions: Engineering and Logistics

Cuban exceptionalism in maintenance and weapons handling doesn't seem like a meaningful one. The world is full of exceptions because humans and their societies are complicated and quirky. There's something about the Cubans that gives them an advantage in this area. That's fine and we can live with that.

But there were two other patterns that were more troublesome as we try to understand the role that underdevelopment played in poor Arab military performance since 1948. The problem is that most or all of the non-Arab states were bad in these two areas, as we would expect of underdeveloped societies where relatively fewer people have exposure to more advanced technology. But the Arabs proved good in them.

The first of these was combat engineering. The Arabs were consistently quite competent in this area. In 1948, Egyptian combat engineers improvised a makeshift road across the beaches of the Gaza Strip to help extract their main army before an Israeli flanking maneuver could cut it off completely. Natanel Lorch has remarked about their efforts that "Egyptian engineers demonstrated a degree of initiative and improvising ability completely at variance with that shown by their [combat] commanders."[4] Iraqi engineers proved remarkably good during the Iran-Iraq War, building extensive and elaborate fortifications that thwarted countless attacks, and doing so in record time. They even began constructing new defensive lines behind the original ones as the Iranians attacked the front lines. They built massive water barriers, such as Fish Lake to protect Basra, and came up with ingenious methods such as pumping high-voltage electricity into the Majnun marshes (and Fish Lake) to prevent Iranian infantry from crossing. Most noteworthy of all, the Egyptian engineering effort that made the crossing of the Suez possible in 1973 was nothing short of brilliant: after the first wave of troops crossed the Suez in assault boats and rafts, 40 combat engineer battalions began building two heavy vehicle bridges, one light vehicle bridge, and two pontoon bridges in each of five division sectors. The Israeli Air Force pummeled these bridges but the engineers replaced each damaged section quickly and efficiently so that there was only minimal disruption in moving Egyptian follow-on forces across the Canal. Then, to overcome a 60–80-foot sand wall Israel had built all along the Canal, the Egyptians employed the novel approach of using high-pressure water pumps to blast their way through. On the day of the assault, Cairo's engineers cut through this massive barrier in less than an hour.[5]

Several of the non-Arab militaries proved pretty good at combat engineering as well. The Cubans improvised defenses in Angola quickly and efficiently in 1975 that were critical in halting the various offensives against

Luanda. They did even better at Cuito Cuanavale in 1988, where Cuban engineers laid down new minefields and fortified positions in real time, during South African offensives. The Chinese did well in Korea too. They too built effective fortifications and did so in short order. While they never had to accomplish anything like the crossing of the Suez, their water-crossing operations were always excellent and never impeded their ground operations—just as they repaired damage from American air strikes with similar speed. It's hard to fault Argentine engineers since they were sent to the Falklands without their specialized equipment, yet they seem to have done a decent job building fortifications in the uncooperative terrain of the islands. Likewise, South Vietnamese engineers were not necessarily the strength of the ARVN, but they too did a creditable job improvising water crossings and fortified positions as needed.

All of which suggests that perhaps good combat engineering does not require a highly developed society. Perhaps, like Argentina's fighter pilots, you can always find a small group of people with the requisite technical skills for a discrete task such as combat engineering.

Then there is the matter of logistics. Here, the differences are more striking. With the possible exception of the Cubans, all of the non-Arab armies were pretty bad at logistics, whereas with the exception of the Syrians, all of the Arab armies were quite good at it. On the non-Arab side, the South Vietnamese were consistently hobbled by supply problems that proved the undoing of nearly all of their major offensives and counteroffensives. It was even worse for the Chinese and North Koreans, whose combat forces scored a series of remarkable battlefield victories, but could never finish off their adversary because their attacks so consistently ran out of gas (metaphorically and even literally in some cases). The Chadians were fortunate enough to have the French handle their logistical requirements for them because there is little evidence to suggest that they could have done it themselves, and this might have hamstrung their entire 1987 campaign if they had been left to their own devices. Argentine logistics were a similar mess, although a significant part of this must be blamed on their paralyzing interservice rivalries and foolishness in defending islands for which they lacked the fleet and/or air force to maintain lines of communication to and from. Once again, only the Cubans stand out as an exception. Their logistical efforts moving large forces to Africa were remarkable, as was their ability to sustain large, mechanized forces across hundreds of kilometers of the African bush and Ogaden desert.

In contrast, most of the Arab militaries did remarkably well when it came to logistics. Only the Syrians in 1948 and 1982 (and 1976 when they invaded Lebanon) really experienced logistical problems that fouled up their combat operations. Since 2003, the Iraqi army has experienced all kinds of problems with logistics but that may be a product of the American efforts to computerize and shift them from their traditional hybrid push-pull system to a typical American pull system. In addition, between 2003 and 2011 and again since 2014, the Iraqis have been able to rely on the Americans to handle logistics for them, so they haven't needed to figure out how to do it themselves—a problem that seems to have contributed to South Vietnamese logistical problems as well. Other than these few exceptions, other Arab armed forces in combat since 1948 just haven't experienced supply problems.

Moreover, in many cases, the Arabs demonstrated some remarkable logistical abilities. Perhaps most impressive of all was the Libyan performance in its wars with Chad. Although the Libyans may have been the most incompetent of the Arab armies in terms of combat performance, they arguably turned in the best performance in the logistical field. Time and again, the Libyans would airlift what amounted to a reinforced mechanized division 1,000 kilometers away from its bases, and then support it on an overland drive of another 1,000 kilometers across the Sahara Desert—one of the most inhospitable places on earth. Their quartermasters were smart and efficient, staging supplies at various points, quickly building forward logistical bases, even pre-positioning supplies en route. Right behind them would have to be the Iraqis, who in October 1973 deployed and sustained a mechanized corps (two armored divisions, two infantry brigades, and a special forces brigade) roughly 1,000 kilometers from their own bases across the Syrian desert. Not only did the Iraqis sustain this force in combat with the Israelis, they also delivered tens of thousands of tons of additional fuel to replenish empty Syrian planes and tanks.[6] Only slightly less impressive was Iraqi logistical performance in the Iran-Iraq War, when they kept a million-man army with horrible fire discipline well-supplied and developed the transport capacity to move an entire corps the length of the country in a matter of days. And once again, Egyptian logistical support for the Canal crossing was similarly remarkable.

In short, the non-Arab militaries appear to have performed as expected in the field of logistics, while the Arabs did not. It isn't entirely clear why the Arabs proved so good at logistics, and it is worth noting that none of their logistical efforts were anything less than ugly and wasteful. But all military operations tend to be ugly and wasteful, even the most brilliant. If the Iraqis and Libyans moved and sustained their forces in an even uglier and more wasteful manner than the American army would have in similar circumstances, that's not much of a criticism. We can't argue that other First World militaries would also have been tidier and more efficient than the Iraqis and the Libyans because, as I have noted already, most First World militaries could not do what they did, efficiently or not.

The Dissimilarities

Ultimately, the Arab armed forces had *less* in common with the performance of other Third World militaries than they had in common with them. And, of greatest importance, none of the non-Arab militaries experienced the same difficulties that were the greatest problems of the Arab armed forces. This argues that while underdevelopment was a problem for the Arab militaries and did limit their military effectiveness, it was not the principal source of their shortcomings.

Ultimately, the combat performance of Argentine, Chadian, Chinese, Cuban, North Korean, and South Vietnamese armies during the postwar era bore little resemblance to that of the Arab armies. Of greatest importance, these six non-Arab states did not show the same patterns of difficulty in the areas of tactical leadership, air warfare, and information management that proved so debilitating to the Arab armed forces. The Argentines, South Vietnamese, and North Koreans did reasonably well in terms of the aggressiveness, creativity, flexibility, and initiative shown by their junior officers, while Chinese, Chadian, and Cuban tactical commanders excelled in these areas. While their employment of combined arms operations varied, some handled them reasonably well, and none demonstrated the same consistent failings as the Arabs. Similarly, none of these militaries suffered from the same problems of dissembling, obfuscation, and compartmentalization of information as the Arabs. The Argentines and South Vietnamese had problems with information flows, but these were not the same as those of the Arabs, suggesting other factors were at work in the Arab cases. Contrary to what we would expect from underdeveloped militaries, none of them had the same problems as the Arabs in maintaining a rapid pace of operations. In fact, North Korean, Chinese, Cuban, and Chadian tactical forces all demonstrated an ability to maintain a very rapid operational pace. Finally, while none of the non-Arab militaries handled their aircraft as well as the Americans or Israelis, the Argentines, Cubans, South Vietnamese, and eventually even the Chinese all handled theirs far better than the Arab air forces. Moreover, none of them manifested the same shockingly inept tactical performance as Arab air forces did time after time.

In fairness to many of those making the argument that underdevelopment was to blame for poor Arab military performances, they never specifically claimed to be able to explain such problems (although a few did). However, the fact that these aspects of tactical leadership and information management proved to be the most problematic for the Arabs but were not problems at all for the other six non-Arab states indicates that underdevelopment is not the best explanation for Arab military ineffectiveness from 1945 to 1991. Like politicization, it too played a role, but was only part of what was going on—and not the most important part.

Again, I don't want to throw the baby out with the bath water. Underdevelopment clearly played a role in hobbling Arab militaries from employing their weapons to the full extent of their theoretical capabilities and removed large numbers of others from poor maintenance. These were significant problems and certainly contributed to the painful defeats and limited achievements of Arab arms from Ashkelon in 1948 to the Golan in 1973 to Kuwait in 1991 and Mosul in 2017. In these ways, underdevelopment was an element of modern Arab military ineffectiveness, and arguably an important one—just not the *most* important one.

The combat histories of the Argentine, Chadian, Chinese, Cuban, North Korean, and South Vietnamese militaries make clear that they bore little resemblance to the Arabs, and that the deeper one digs in attempting to understand the patterns of their military effectiveness, the less they look like modern Arab combat experiences. It strongly suggests that there is no "Third World Way of War," as claimed by many who have argued that underdevelopment was the root cause of Arab military problems. Only in those areas of military effectiveness related to technical skills was there a significant similarity among these many armies, Arab and non-Arab alike. Even then, the similarities were less than we might have expected.

So if it is not Soviet military practices that have been the bane of Arab military operations, and politics and economics are only partly to blame—and not for their greatest problems—what is it that has been going on with Arab armed forces for all of these years?

PART IV | Culture

CHAPTER 15 | War and Culture

B Y NOW YOU have probably guessed that I believe that the most important problems that Arab militaries have experienced in battle since
1945 derive from behavioral patterns associated with Arab culture. It starts
from the fact that the other explanations just don't cover the full extent of the
problem. The Russians probably helped the Arab armed forces more than they
hurt, and while politicization and underdevelopment played important roles,
they cannot explain the most damaging and consistent shortcomings of Arab
militaries in the modern era. But it's not enough just to demonstrate that the
other explanations don't fully explain the problem.

There is a compelling case to be made that the primary weaknesses experienced by the Arab armed forces since 1945 derive from culturally motivated
patterns of behavior inculcated by Arab educational processes. In this last Part
of the book, I am going to try to make that case.

That said, dealing with culture is like working with nitroglycerin: it may
be necessary to do so, even useful, but you have to handle it with great care.
This is one of those instances. Culturally driven patterns of behavior are a
critical element of the story of Arab military ineffectiveness, but culture lends
itself too easily to all kinds of abuse. So I need to start out with a number of
cautions and caveats. Like nitroglycerin, you have to treat culture with a lot of
respect if you want to use it without doing a lot of damage.

To do that, I want to start by explaining the broad relationship between
warfare and culture.

The Development of War-Making

Human beings have been waging war for longer than we can remember. Warfare literally predates civilization and written history.[1] Yet the methods of war-making have changed radically over time as technology and human organization have evolved. Unorganized bands of spear-throwing men gave way to organized formations of spear- and shield- (and sword-) bearing men, which gave way to bands of armored men mounted on horses, and so on up to the age of drones, cyberwar, and stand-off precision munitions.

Over the millennia, it has been this interaction between technology and human organization that has defined war-making in each era. Of course, the technology has been more unpredictable and harder to control than the organization. The technology typically comes into being for reasons having little to do with war-making, and rarely at the opportune moment for war leaders. Yes, Oppenheimer and company harnessed the atom in time to help the United States win World War II, but they were able to do so only because Rutherford, Bohr, Einstein, and others had discovered the basic scientific principles by then, and those discoveries had nothing to do with warfare. Generals have probably always wanted to be able to wage war from the air, but that was effectively impossible before the Wright brothers figured out how to fly.

Humans have often adapted scientific principles to develop new weapons for a war when those principles were known, but that's about as far as it goes. German scientists devised the Snorkel to make their U-boats more survivable in response to Admiral Dönitz's pleas during the Second World War, but Nelson, Andrea Doria, and even Themistocles would have loved to have had submarines too; their wants had little impact on the progress of technological development. When the scientific principles are unknown, they are unknown, and a general cannot demand that they advance the way that he can his armies. As a result, technology has really only ever been marginally responsive to the desires of the warrior, even though it is one of the most important factors driving the evolution of warfare.

Instead, the part of warfare that humans have been best able to control has been our own organization, and there the demands of war have weighed heavily. Throughout history, war leaders have sought and experimented with new and better methods of organizing (and employing those organizations) to defeat their foes. Although there are often difficult political and bureaucratic fights to be won to institute a new organization, it has typically proven far easier to increase military power by changing organizations (and the tasks that those organizations perform) than to try to do so by demanding new weapons.

Indeed, as many starting with Charles Tilly have noted, organizing for war has been an important element in the development of states themselves.[2]

Thus, technology can be said to be an "objective" condition of war-making, proceeding largely at its own pace and only modestly susceptible to human manipulation at any given time. In contrast, organization and the employment of military organizations—what we call tactics and strategy—can be seen as a "subjective" condition that humans can change far more easily to try to gain advantages with the technology at hand. Another way of putting it is that at any given moment in time, the technology available to mankind makes it possible to fight in many different ways, and different societies and militaries will try to organize themselves and use those organizations to act in different ways to gain advantages in battle.

The Dominant Mode of Warfare

Warfare is a competitive activity. For that reason, if only in theory, there will always be a "best" way to organize and act in battle given the available technology. I refer to that best way as the "dominant mode of warfare" of the time. Few societies ever perfect the dominant mode of warfare, but those that do typically enjoy great success on the battlefield. Even those that come closer to the dominant mode than their foes secure an advantage, possibly a decisive one. Indeed, it is ultimately what we mean when we talk about one country having greater military effectiveness than another. The Chadian armies of the 1980s were hardly the epitome of twentieth-century warfare, yet they were much better at practicing the dominant mode of warfare of that era than their Libyan foes, and that enabled them to defeat Libya despite all of the Libyan advantages in firepower, air power, fortifications, and logistics. The Chadians demonstrated greater military effectiveness, and that is why they won.

The concept of military effectiveness itself ultimately derives from an unstated conception that there is just such a "best" way of doing things at any point in time given the technology available. It is what US military personnel implicitly mean when they refer to "best military practices." That is why it is useful to have a concept such as the dominant mode of warfare, because it establishes a constantly evolving but absolute ideal that the relative concept of military effectiveness can be measured against. The great military historian John Lynn has made a similar point, suggesting the idea of "paradigm" armies that define the height of military effectiveness at any given time, the best practices to which other militaries aspire.[3] These armies define the paradigm because they have proven best at practicing the dominant mode of warfare of their era.

Of course, those nations with the highest military effectiveness—those best able to perform the dominant mode of warfare—are not inevitably bound to win at war because other factors such as numerical balances, generalship, etc., can trump military effectiveness. But like the Chadians, they have an important advantage that can prove decisive. For that reason, most militaries endlessly (and rightly) pursue the dominant mode of warfare of their time, and the best try to refine or even reinvent it, trying new technologies or new organizations and methods to take advantage of existing technology.

The Role of Culture

The notion that there is always a dominant mode of warfare to which most militaries will aspire is a way of placing military effectiveness in the context of time and circumstance. This is important because it points out that what constitutes military effectiveness at any given time and what it takes to be a dominant military change over time as the dominant mode changes. Because technology changes and because humans are constantly innovating new ways to organize and employ that technology, the best practices that constitute the epitome of military effectiveness are constantly changing too, mostly evolving slowly but sometimes very quickly in what have been called revolutions in military affairs.

The reason that this is important is that what is required from groups of humans to achieve the dominant mode of warfare at any given time is also constantly changing. Human beings are not all alike, nor are groups of human beings. Just as individuals have different abilities and ways of doing things, so too do groups and societies, inculcated by the culture of the society. Those traits are enormously important to war-making, and always have been throughout human history.

Spears, swords, and shields were some of the earliest weapons known to mankind but there are lots of different ways to use them in battle. The Greek phalanx was a far more effective way to use those weapons than the way most ancient civilizations had previously. But not every society could field a competent phalanx. Really only a very few could, and some—notably Sparta—were much better than others. That is because what it took to field an effective phalanx was men steeped in certain patterns of behavior that caused them to act in a certain way and that in turn allowed them to perform the way that the organization and tactics of the phalanx required. Really only Greek city states (and their colonies) could produce enough such men to field a phalanx.

Sparta famously engineered its entire culture to produce the maximum number of men who would act in exactly the best manner possible to make the phalanx effective. So for a period of time, the Greeks figured out the best way to employ the war-making technology of the time (spears, shields, and swords). But only the culture of the Greek city state produced large numbers of men able to function effectively in a phalanx. No other ancient society of the time could do so.[4] And Spartan culture took that to its absolute extreme, making the Spartan phalanx the most effective of all.

In other words, what made Sparta the greatest military of its era was its culture. Spartan culture was consciously engineered to produce large numbers of men who would axiomatically perform in the manner that was most conducive to success in the phalanx, and as long as Spartan culture continued to produce large numbers of such men, and as long as the phalanx was the dominant mode of war-making, Sparta was the greatest military power.

The same phenomenon was at work in later eras with English longbowmen, Parthian cataphracts, Mongol horse archers, Swiss pikemen, British men-of-war, German panzer divisions, and any number of other dominant military forces that won not because of better technology, but because their societies produced relatively large numbers of men with a skill set that enabled them to use the existing technology in the best way possible. And because they produced considerably more such men than their rivals, in some cases having men uniquely able to employ the military technology of the era, they had an enormous advantage over their foes.

What this demonstrates is that culturally derived traits and behavior can be absolutely critical in determining military effectiveness, but what matters is the extent to which those traits mesh with the technology and organization (including the tactics) being employed by the armies of that era. When the culturally driven traits of a society mesh well with the demands of the dominant mode of warfare of the era, the armies of that society will tend to be more effective, and in some cases may prove all-conquering. When they do not mesh, the armies of that society will tend to do worse and—unless saved by other factors such as numbers, wealth, favorable geography, powerful allies, etc.—the society may be wiped out altogether.

Inevitably, the traits and behavior that allow a military to succeed will change over time as the dominant mode of warfare changes. Some societies may deliberately adapt, and adopt cultural practices that serve the dominant mode of warfare, as the Spartans (and arguably the Prussians and Israelis) did. Most won't do so consciously, but they will nevertheless be helped or hindered anyway based on the extent to which the dominant mode of war suits the behavioral patterns fostered by their society—their culture—which typically will have evolved for reasons unrelated to war-making.

The Mongols did not become great horse archers *purposely* so that they could conquer Eurasia. The Mongols became great horse archers because those were the skills they needed to survive on the twelfth-century Eurasian steppe. However, once their society developed this skill and Mongol culture began to produce large numbers of skilled horse archers, it gave Mongol warlords such as Genghis Khan a military tool that enabled him to conquer Eurasia. The Mongol army defined the dominant mode of warfare of the time. Although the technology they employed—the horse and composite bow—were readily available to other societies, no one was able to use it to make war as well as the Mongols. This gave them an overwhelming tactical advantage over so many other societies whose cultures did not produce large numbers of skilled horse archers, not by any mistake on their part, but simply because their physical and historical circumstances did not create a need for large numbers of skilled horse archers.

The Mongols are an extreme example, useful to illustrate the point. Let me turn to another example that shows the more normal course of how culture and warfare interact over time. In the eighteenth and early nineteenth centuries, European wars were fought largely with muzzle-loading, smooth-bore muskets; flat trajectory cannon; and horsemen armed with swords, lances, and pistols. This technology defined the dominant mode of warfare for that era, and over time, the best armies learned how to organize themselves, train, and devise tactics to get the greatest performance when using that technology. Specifically, they learned to organize large groups of infantry in tight formations to maximize firepower. Because muskets were horribly inaccurate, it was possible to have such formations walk slowly, in formation, to a point on the battlefield, then shift from a marching formation (column) to a firing formation (line) and begin firing at the enemy, reloading, and firing again. The cavalry of the time was typically held back, waiting for an opportunity to charge forward and terrorize, disorder, and break enemy infantry formations, as well as overrun enemy artillery. The artillery sought to slaughter and disorganize enemy infantry (and cavalry) to render them more vulnerable to friendly infantry and cavalry.

All of this called for a very particular set of skills and behavior to produce military effectiveness, let alone victory. If we just stick with the infantry of that time, we see that they had to be able to move in formation and not become disorganized. They had to be able to fire and (of even greater importance) reload their muskets while being fired at by their enemy counterparts often no more than 50 yards away. And they had to be willing and able to eventually fix bayonets, charge the enemy, and kill him in hand-to-hand combat. For the soldiers, that meant that they needed to be brave (or inebriated); highly disciplined; well-practiced at marching in formation, firing, and reloading; and competent in hand-to-hand combat. For junior officers, it meant that they needed to be able to organize the formations of their men, shift from one formation to another at a moment's notice, and move them quickly and efficiently around the battlefield. In particular, they had to maintain iron discipline among their troops in the maelstrom of an eighteenth-century battle, which required that their men fear them more than the enemy. And they had to be brave enough to stand or charge, as directed *when directed*, setting an example for their men to follow. It is important to note that field officers in eighteenth- and early nineteenth-century European armies were not expected to show lots of creativity and initiative. Indeed, they were generally trained and encouraged to be unquestioning martinets because that was what was needed from lower-ranking officers for an army to be successful in this mode of warfare.

The deprecation of independent action by junior officers was in large part a result of the fact that the general commanding an eighteenth-century European army could (theoretically) see the entire battlefield, and it was his responsibility to formulate strategy, look for opportunities, and maneuver his forces in response to the actions of his adversary. The last thing that an eighteenth-century general wanted was a subordinate acting on his own— or refusing an order from the general orchestrating the battle. (General Seydlitz's famous act of insubordination to Frederick the Great at the battle of Zorndorf was a salient exception proving the rule.) An eighteenth-century army would have been pulverized if all of its captains and majors made decisions for themselves and acted independently, even if in pursuit of their commander's overall objective. The strength of such an army was in the co-ordination of its forces and the ability of a general to see (or create) an opportunity—a mistake by his adversary—and then quickly concentrate superior force against it. Napoleon's victory at Austerlitz, achieved by separating the Austrians and Russians and then crushing each in turn, is a perfect example. On the other hand, if some English major at Waterloo had seen a hole in Napoleon's line and charged in with his battalion, it would have created a battalion-sized hole in the English lines, through which Napoleon would have quickly pushed a division or a corps. As Wellington would have been the first to warn, nothing could have been more disastrous, and why the Iron Duke would never have countenanced it.

Indeed, one of the most famous instances of such independent and creative officering from that time—Sir John Colborne's defense against the French

Guard at the end of the Battle of Waterloo—is a perfect exception proving the rule. Colonel Colborne commanded the 52nd Regiment of Foot at Waterloo and during the final attack by Napoleon's Middle Guard, he led his men out of the line of British infantry regiments and turned them at a right angle to fire into the flank of the French, helping to rout one of the French battalions. It is worth noting that this only came at the very end of the battle, when the French had completely shot their bolt and were making one last, desperate attempt to break the British lines. Had Napoleon anything left to counter Colborne's move, it could have been disastrous. But he didn't and so it worked. Moreover, Colborne's feat is legendary because he was the only battalion commander who did so. There were several dozen others manning the ridgeline all afternoon, facing repeated attacks, and none of them (including Colborne earlier) had tried this stunt. Moreover, even when Colborne did it, he was the only one. None of his peers thought to do the same. Colborne was a celebrated exception, but he was very much an exception to the rule of the time, and he was only celebrated because he tried it in exceptional circumstances that allowed it to succeed.

Fast forward to the twentieth century and everything has changed. New technology has emerged: automatic weapons, indirect fire artillery, trucks, tanks, airplanes. They have transformed the battlefield and defined a new dominant mode of warfare. Firepower has become so lethal that armies must disperse and rely on camouflage at all times. Demographic and political changes have also placed far larger armies at the disposal of the generals. Ground forces must deploy in open order, concealed as best they can, and moving very quickly whenever forced to do so. Given the C³I (command, control, communications and intelligence) available at the time, no supreme commander could possibly control such forces in real time let alone orchestrate a battle the way that an eighteenth-century general would. As a result, the skills required of soldiers and (especially) field officers to succeed have changed dramatically. Now, junior officers (including even NCOs) are expected to understand the strategic plan of their commander but act independently to try to accomplish the commander's objectives, the famous German principle of *auftragstaktik*. In this mode of war, tactical commanders have to show initiative and creativity to win tactical victories. The job of the general is now to recognize the pattern of tactical victories, reinforce success by committing reserves, and so turn the tactical victories won by his subordinates into strategic victories (largely by breaking through the enemy's front lines, routing his reserves and rear area services, and either surrounding or causing the logistical and psychological collapse of the enemy army). For those familiar with it, Stephen Biddle's concept of the "modern system" of warfare captures this approach, representing the dominant mode of warfare of the twentieth century.[5]

The point of this comparison is to illustrate that what it means for a military to be effective changes over time as the dominant mode of warfare changes. The skills that allowed the British Army to thrive on both eighteenth-century European and nineteenth-century colonial battlefields were the same skills that caused it to consistently underperform in the wars of the twentieth century. It was largely the same British Army—with new kit—fighting largely the same way. But the skills, methods, and approaches to warfighting that produced success at Blenheim, Waterloo, and Omdurman produced disaster at the Somme, Gazala, and Goodwood. The dominant mode of warfare had changed, but the British Army had not, and its military effectiveness suffered as a result.[6]

It should not be surprising that some societies (and some military organizations) will be better able to produce the skills required by the dominant mode of warfare than others. Those that do demonstrate greater military effectiveness than those that don't. Those that produce these skills in the greatest abundance tend to be Lynn's paradigm armies. As the great French philosopher Raymond Aron once observed, "An army always resembles the country from which it is raised and of which it is the expression."[7]

To some extent, this explains the rise and fall of some countries and their militaries. Of course, economics explains a lot of that, but there are always countries that punch far above their weight militarily in any given historical period: the Swiss during the sixteenth century, the Swedes during the seventeenth century, the Prussians during the eighteenth century, the English and American Confederacy during the nineteenth century, and the Germans and Israelis during the twentieth century. I would argue that in every case it was because their society just happened to produce large numbers of men with the traits required for success by the dominant mode of warfare of the era. Of course, over time, technology shifted, the dominant mode of warfare changed, and what was required to succeed in war changed, disadvantaging those who had once been dominant and bringing to power new countries whose societies produced large numbers of men with the requisite skill sets (or behavioral patterns) needed to succeed in the new dominant mode of war. Thus the Swedes were the terrors of the seventeenth-century battlefield and that made them a major player in European international relations at that time. But by the eighteenth century they were no more potent than any other European country, and so they declined to a second-rank power as befitting their economic, demographic, and other endowments.

People's behavioral traits can be shaped by many different factors. Every kind of human grouping has a culture, but different kinds of groupings have greater abilities to inculcate that culture than others. The community or society we are born into (the country, nation, state, empire, etc.) typically has the greatest ability because it dictates childrearing practices and the educational methods employed with children and adolescents. Nothing is a more potent means of socializing people into a set of cultural norms.

But institutions and organizations within a society develop their own cultures too. Often these cultures are themselves influenced by the wider society's culture. In other circumstances, they may employ a variation on that wider culture, or develop something quite different—even directly contrary to the wider culture. Militaries can be very powerful agents of socialization because they take relatively young men (overwhelmingly men in the past, still mostly at present) and put them through ferocious forms of education—what we call training—to try to get them to think and act differently than they did as civilians. Indeed, military training is a deliberate form of cultural socialization. It is how armies get people to think and act in the ways considered most conducive to warfighting by that society at that time.

So it is important to recognize that while the traits and behaviors that provide an advantage or disadvantage to militaries at any time given the dominant mode of warfare of that era are inevitably derived from culture, that culture may be national/societal, it may be the organizational culture of the military (which may replicate that of the wider society or diverge from it in important ways), or it may be the culture of some important subgroup—a particular tribe or ethnicity, an elite military formation, etc.[8] Indeed, it is a fascinating question how much the culture of the British Army—which produced such incredible success from 1689 to 1898 and then so many stunning failures from 1914 to 1945—was a product of the wider British culture and how much the product of the unique features of the British Army (like the regimental system) as it evolved over time.

No Judgments

Because it is culture—dominant or national, local or subcultural, institutional or organizational—that determines which societies, or which groups within societies, generate the largest numbers of men (and increasingly, women) with the skills needed for success in the dominant mode of warfare of the time, culture can obviously play a critical role in determining military fortunes. However, none of this should be seen as applauding one culture or denigrating another. Cultures, especially the cultures of nations and other societies that lie beyond mere military organizations, emphasize some traits and behavioral patterns over others based on the circumstances of the society, both physical and historical. The traits and patterns of behavior the culture favors make sense for its society in that place at that time.

In other words, culture can grant some advantages to a society in certain activities where two societies are competing, but that does not mean that one is superior to the other except in that narrow area of competition. Remembering both the Mongols and the Romans is helpful here. The Roman empire that stretched from the second century B.C. to the fifth century A.D. and the Mongol empire of the thirteenth century A.D. were both phenomenal conquerors. Both invaded numerous neighboring states and crushed their armies, fought vast wars, and were consistently victorious. In both cases, there were cultural aspects of their societies that were critical to their military successes. Both societies contained cultural tendencies that allowed them to generate much greater military power than their neighbors—whether it was the tactical excellence of the Roman legion or the Mongol archer, or the strategic ability of each society to keep generating large numbers of both. Both were often superior to the societies they conquered in this narrow aspect of human activity: warfare. That narrow superiority turned out to be extremely important, especially to peoples conquered by these empires, such as the Carthaginians and Chinese.

However, it does not follow that Roman or Mongol society was superior in general, or in every way, or in any other way other than war-making to other societies, even to those societies they conquered. Culture encompasses a vast range of traits related to an equally vast number of human activities. Just because the Mongols were better than the thirteenth-century Chinese at war-making does not mean that they were superior in any other way. The Chinese generally believed they were far more sophisticated, creative, and knowledgeable than the Mongols. They may well have been, suggesting their own culture was superior to that of the Mongols in producing many other desirable skills. That sophistication did not save them from conquest because the Mongols were superior in the one area that mattered when they clashed: war-making. (Had the Mongols and Chinese competed in poetry or pottery rather than killing, the outcome probably would have been very different.) But their competition was military, and the Mongols proved far superior in that one area. Similar arguments could be made about the relative advantages of Roman and Greek cultures—arguments in which many Romans would have agreed on the superiority of Greek philosophy, sculpture, rhetoric, etc., just not war-making.

There is also an important difference between the Romans and Mongols. Whereas Roman culture seems to have given the Romans an excellent ability to hold, retain, and integrate its conquests such that their empire lasted for centuries, Mongol culture, so equally superb at conquest, did not grant the same advantages to their empire. Mongol society did not do as well at holding and building on what they had conquered, and so the Mongol empire did not endure the way that the Roman empire did. Just because two great nations were equally adept at conquest did not mean that they were equally adept at other aspects of human endeavor. The advantages that culture may grant to warfare does not mean that that culture or its society are somehow superior in any way except in war-making at a particular moment in time.

Nevertheless, what should be clear from this discussion is that culture—national, subnational, and organizational—is an important element in military effectiveness. Moreover, just as we recognize that some cultures have proven instrumental to battlefield success by enhancing military effectiveness at certain periods of time, we should also recognize that other cultures can be just as critical to martial weakness by undermining military effectiveness. For every Sparta, Rome, Mongol horde, Wehrmacht, and Israel Defense Force there is likely to be another society badly hamstrung because its culture is not producing sufficient numbers of people with the traits best suited to the dominant mode of warfare of the time. In the late twentieth and early twenty-first centuries, that was exactly what happened to the Arabs.

CHAPTER 16

Arab Culture as an Explanation
for Military Ineffectiveness

E NGLISH IS A marvelous language, but its ambiguities can be maddening. The word "culture" has lots of meanings, and people are often sloppy when they use it. As I already have begun in the last chapter, throughout this book, I use "culture" in the anthropological sense of learned, shared values and patterns of behavior developed by a community over the course of its history.[1] Culture is both the practice of how things are done in a society *and* the values that suggest how things should be done by the members of that society.[2] Among the most important and discernible elements of a culture are its religion, language, family life, hierarchies, and other groupings. These are simultaneously sources of culture, products of the culture, and methods for the transmission of culture.

In that sense, culture is what humans have where animals have instinct. Animals react to situations instinctively and most have only a very limited ability to modify those instincts by learning, if they have any ability to do so at all. Humans have instincts that guide our reactions to a small range of the most basic circumstances, such as Sigmund Freud's famous "fight or flight" situations. However, far more human behavior is guided by culture, by notions of how to do things based on the collective experiences of our societies. That, in turn, develops through a Darwinian process of determining how best to deal with the many challenges that nature and other humans have posed to our societies over time. What works is kept, what doesn't is discarded. Those who learn best thrive and pass on their solutions to future generations.

Those who fail to learn tend to end with a whimper or a bang, their remnants assimilated into other, more successful cultures.

This constant cultural development and revision has been critically important to the success of the human species because it makes culture infinitely more adaptable than instinct. Recent scientific studies have demonstrated that major genetic changes (which drive instinct) can take place in as little as 30 generations, but culture can change dramatically in just a few generations. It is this adaptability of culture that has allowed human beings to live and prosper in virtually every climate and so take over the planet. It is also why every society's culture is different, because it developed in response to the community's specific geographic, topographic, and climactic settings as well as its historical experiences over time.[3]

A crucial point that should not be missed is that *culture is not congenital*. You are not born with it. It is not written in a person's DNA. It is acquired behavior, learned by members of a community over the course of their lives. The anthropologist Clyde Kluckhohn summed this up in writing that "Culture is a *way* of thinking, feeling, believing. It is the group's knowledge stored up for future use."[4] Culture is transmitted from generation to generation in a community through the formal and informal education of its members, primarily during the process of maturation from child to adult. Recent work suggests that the period of late childhood (roughly ages 7–13) is when humans do the most assimilation of cultural values and patterns of behavior.[5]

The history of a community is key to the endless development and revision of its culture. Culture is an accumulated set of behaviors derived from the common experiences of the society over time. What that means is that *culture is not static*. In fact, it is constantly changing, evolving as the community reacts to new experiences.[6] That said, this change is slow and can be imperceptible. It happens much faster than biological evolution, but it still happens at the pace of generations, not years or months. Embedded in a people's culture is their history, and in a sense, the behavioral patterns embodied in a culture are simply the responses of the community to significant historical events and influences. In the words of Issa Boullata:

> The culture of any human group is its collective experience in time. As the group moves in time from generation to generation, it continuously meets with new needs that challenge it. The response of the group shapes its experience of reality, which in turn, adds to its culture. The group learns to acquire new cultural elements and discard others, so that its culture continues to develop in the service of group survival and enhancement. Culture is thus continually changing and accommodating

the group's institutions, beliefs, and values, to its ever-rising needs, both material and otherwise. Certain cultures may be more open to change than others. But there is no culture that does not change.[7]

Moreover, it is the middle-term historical experiences of a community that are most important in shaping its culture at any particular time. Cultural traits developed in response to historical experiences of the distant past tend to be superseded by those defined by more recent events. Very recent experiences, on the other hand, are not immediately absorbed by the fabric of a society's culture, but take time to seep in.

The Influence of Culture

Culture influences an individual's preferences and priorities, which in turn drive his or her behavior. By shaping what the individual is likely to consider important, culture affects an individual's preferred outcome in a given situation. For example, although the common trait of self-preservation generally will prompt an individual to prefer outcomes that do not result in death, earlier Japanese cultures relegated this preference to a secondary status behind honor. Consequently, during the Second World War, an unusual number of Japanese soldiers chose death rather than the dishonor of surrender.[8] Similarly, culture will shape the courses of action and methods an individual is predisposed to employ to secure a goal. Culture has a tendency to suggest that certain ways of doing things are better than others; thus culture shapes both ends and means. Finally, culture may actually shape the way in which an individual thinks and how he or she approaches different situations.

Each society believes that its way of doing things—its cultural values and patterns of behavior—are "right" and "natural" because that is what the members of that society were taught by their parents, teachers, clergy, etc. It is "how they have always done things," as far as they know, and they assume and insist that it is right. Of course, there is rarely any objective evidence that one culturally prescribed way of doing things is better than another, but it does not stop members of every society from believing that their way is the best. As the cultural anthropologist Andrea Rugh has observed, "Each view is so deeply engrained in the cultural consciousness of a people that it is difficult for people to stand outside their own cultural perspective and project themselves into the consciousness of those holding the opposing view. People conceive of their own world view as representing logic, common sense, and other valued characteristics, and, indeed, given the whole social system within which the world view functions, it *is* the view with the best 'fit' to provide coherence for the society as a whole."[9]

Culture can seem ethereal, but it can be remarkably powerful for all its intangibility. Marwan Dwairy, a Palestinian psychologist, explains what happened when he tried to employ Western psychotherapeutic practices to help his Arab clients:

> The main experience I remember from my first year of work in Nazareth is that my clients seemed to be different from those described in the context of [Western] psychological theories. They reacted differently to my diagnostic and therapeutic interventions. They tended to focus on their external circumstances and were unable to address internal and personal issues. Terms such as self, self-actualization, ego, and personal feelings were alien to them. They emphasized duty, the expectations of others, the approval of others, and family issues. In conversation with my clients, the task of distinguishing between the client's personal needs, opinions, or attitudes and those of the family was almost impossible.[10]

Not surprisingly, repeated encounters along the same lines led him to write a book designed to help psychologists understand the psyches of their Arab clients, which were shaped by the preferences of Arab culture, not the Western culture that gave rise to the psychoanalytic methods that Dwairy had been trying to employ. The cultural psychologist Gary Gregg noted the same thing in explaining why he had written a 600-page book describing Arab culture and its impact on individual psychology: "Just as psychological development is rooted in family and social relations, so it is rooted in a culture's primary value systems."[11]

In many areas, culture's primary function is merely to prioritize values that are common to every society; but that prioritization can have huge impacts.[12] For instance, both American culture and Arab culture value honesty and loyalty. However, American culture tends to promote the idea that when the two are in conflict—such as when a person knows that his friend has done something wrong and he must decide whether to tell this to some authority figure—then "honesty is the best policy," and he should tell on his friend because in the end that will be the best for everyone, including his friend. In the Arab world, loyalty is the higher virtue, at least if the two people have a close relationship, and so the person in question should demonstrate his loyalty by staying quiet.

Of course, there is no empirical evidence anywhere that suggests that a society that values honesty over loyalty when the two are in conflict is somehow "better" than one that values loyalty over honesty.[13] Nevertheless, this prioritization does have important ramifications for how people behave toward each other in all kinds of circumstances, which can be incredibly important in the most dangerous and stressful human endeavor of all: warfare. As just one example of this, during the period of the American occupation of Iraq after the fall of Saddam, the Iraqi Interior Ministry conducted a survey of its police officers. Not surprisingly, "The survey indicated that Iraqi police valued loyalty, service, honor, and duty over justice, religious commitment, and trust." This provided an explanation to the Americans as to why so many honorable Iraqi police officers would stand idly by and do nothing while their colleagues committed horrendous human rights violations or indulged in obvious corruption.[14]

As contemporary anthropologists have noted, cultural systems are also contradictory and contested.[15] Every cultural predilection also has its opposite because a complex and unforgiving world always poses dilemmas, and few rules are uniformly correct. Every axiom has its antithesis: in the United States, we say both that "A friend in need is a friend indeed" (you should help your friends) and "God helps those who help themselves" (you should look out for yourself). Or "strike while the iron is hot" (act quickly before an opportunity passes) but "measure twice, cut once" (think before acting). Such countercultural tendencies exist within every society as a source of balance and growth. Societies rarely survive by doing everything just one way. And over time, cultures must change, and countercultural values are the kernels of change—shifting over time from what is disparaged to what is promoted as the society's circumstances require new values and patterns of behavior.

In similar fashion, recent work in social and cultural psychology has demonstrated that individuals themselves often act in culturally contradictory manners, sometimes conforming to the dominant cultural predilections and at other times or in other circumstances deviating from them—even acting in antithetical fashion.[16] Thus, as I noted above, Arab culture values both loyalty and truth even though they are often in tension with one another. Arab culture tends to favor loyalty over truth when an individual or a group faces the dilemma of choosing one over the other, while American culture favors the opposite. But Arab culture does value truth, there are pressures against lying, and plenty of individual Arabs will opt for truth over loyalty in many cases.

Of course, some members of a society may consistently favor the antithetical or countercultural behavior over the cultural norm. They tend to be outliers in their society—literally nonconformists, and perhaps "bohemians," rebels, or others singled out as different. Their consistent deviation from what is considered the norm typically makes them seem to be extremists by the majority, who tend to adhere to the cultural norms, and when they deviate from them, do not do so as frequently. Culture merely specifies how most people will act in most situations.

The existence of these inevitable contradictions should not detract from recognizing an overall coherence to any cultural system. As William Sewell Jr. has noted in an important essay, even the countercultures and dissenters within a culture are responding to the predilections of the dominant culture; they are not random, but draw meaning from the themes of the dominant culture.[17] In America, individualism is not much of an act of rebellion because it is a critical element of the dominant culture, which sees it as a virtue and promotes it. American parents often worry when their child *isn't* expressing his or her individuality. In Japan, where conformity is a major theme of the dominant culture, American-style individualism is an act of rebellion.

Within a larger society, such as the Arab world, culture also will vary from community to community and from nation to nation. These differences are often subtle and sometimes imperceptible to an outsider; nevertheless, they exist and can be important. Halim Barakat observes that "Arab society has its own dominant culture, constructed from what is most common and diffused among Arabs. In addition it has its sub-cultures, those peculiar to some communities, and its counter-cultures, those of alienated and radical groups."[18] While I am going to focus on what Barakat and others call the "dominant" Arab culture, it is important to remember the existence of both the subcultures and countercultures. Thus, even culturally regular Arab behavior should be understood as a regional mean around which national and subnational cultural means will vary.

For all of these reasons, culture *influences* the behavior of the individual, but does not autocratically *determine* individual behavior. Culture is only one of many influences on the individual. Consequently, discussions of the impact of culture on collective undertakings reflect tendencies rather than iron-clad laws. As the Lebanese sociologist Sania Hamady writes, "(Culture) stands for a common denominator of national characteristics, with individuals varying from it in different directions and degrees. This concept does not correspond to the total personality of an individual, but describes the pattern of the culturally regular character."[19] Thus culture should be seen as a mean around which individual behavior varies.[20] As Gregg put it, culture should be understood "not as a way of life *shared* by all those who live in it but as a constellation of values, meanings, and practices unevenly *distributed* to its members."[21]

Consequently, it is critical to bear in mind that *culture is least useful in understanding the behavior of an individual, and appears most readily in the behavior of large groups over time.* The larger the number of people, the more likely that their collective actions will reflect culturally regular patterns of behavior.

Conversely, the collective actions of smaller groups, let alone individuals, are more likely to be shaped by idiosyncratic factors. This is because individual personalities can more easily shape group actions when the group is small. As groups get larger, their collective personality tends to increasingly reflect the culturally regular persona, rather than the quirks of individual members of the group.

This point also should make clear why stereotypes are both so dangerous and so foolish. As Yehoshofat Harkabi has warned:

> We must be cautious when generalizing about national character; the ground beneath our feet is often shaky and we run the risk of generalization based on prejudices. However, in discussing social groups, there is no escape from assigning a collective personality to the group under discussion. . . . It should be borne in mind, (however), that not every individual in the group need possess these characteristics.[22]

Harkabi's use of the terms "national character" and "collective personality" makes me cringe. They reflect an outmoded way of understanding culture. However, he is spot on in warning against reliance on stereotypes while still recognizing that there are important behavioral tendencies in every society that affect a large number of individuals to a greater or lesser extent, and it is dangerous to make *either* mistake.

Finally, in addition to its impact on the individual, culture also influences the collective action of groups by shaping interpersonal behavior. As one of its most important tasks, culture teaches members of a society how to treat other people and how a person should behave when part of a group. It establishes what is permissible and what is desirable behavior in public or within smaller groups.

Of greatest importance, culture defines how people should behave toward one another in hierarchies.[23] Every human society has hierarchies. They are a foundational element of civilization. But every society organizes its hierarchies differently, encouraging members to behave in different ways when they occupy different roles within an organization. In the words of one massive, decade-long study on the subject, "Societal culture influences and regulates human behavior in the society. Cultural values and practices help identify socially acceptable and unacceptable behavior. Two specific arenas for the impact of these values are organizational culture and effective leadership attributes. Organizations are a micro version of the society in which they operate. They are populated by individuals who have grown up in the host culture, and their success in external adaptation and internal integration depends on their ability to assimilate their broader environment."[24]

In other words, every culture values leadership, but what leaders are expected to do and how they are expected to do it can vary dramatically from one society to the next. The same is true of both mid-level managers (like junior officers and NCOs in a military) and low-level workers (or enlisted personnel). For them as well, different cultures prescribe different roles and responsibilities and different ways of behaving toward one another.

As a result, some societies have hierarchies that tend to function in a more top-down manner, others are more bottom-up, and still others have hybrid approaches. All of these hierarchies function, but they all function in different ways driven by these cultural patterns, and some are more efficient at doing some things than others. That is critically important in a competitive activity like warfare. In combat, the ability of one culture to make its organizations function more efficiently in keeping with the dominant mode of warfare of the time than the organizations of another culture can be the difference between victory and defeat.

Arab Culture and the Arab World

As I noted at the beginning of this book, the Arab world as cultural unit consists of 18 nations: Algeria, Bahrain, Egypt, Iraq, Jordan, Kuwait, Lebanon, Libya, Morocco, Oman, the Palestinians, Qatar, Saudi Arabia, (North) Sudan, Syria, Tunisia, the United Arab Emirates, and Yemen. Across them, there is a common, overarching "Arab" culture—what Barakat refers to as the dominant culture. Each nation constitutes a subculture that is subtly different from the larger, dominant Arab culture, but the similarities exceed the differences.

Although this view was once disputed by some academics it is now overwhelmingly accepted and supported by Arab and other experts in every meaningful field.[25] Perhaps the best evidence of this is the six Arab Human Development Reports produced under the auspices of the United Nations between 2002 and 2016 and jointly authored by scores of the brightest minds of the Arab world in a wide range of fields from anthropology to economics to political science, all of which treated these countries as a single "culture area" in Gregg's terminology.[26] Indeed, psychologists, sociologists, and cultural anthropologists routinely and uncontroversially treat all of the Arab countries as part of a single cultural system, one in which individuals and groups share basic behavioral and psychological traits.[27] In his comprehensive study of the subject, Gregg simply notes that "The societies in this region share many characteristics with each other that they do not share with neighboring regions." He further cites Abdelhamid Jabar's study of psychological needs across Arab countries: "Jabar concludes that the data show a common Arab culture with relatively small variations resulting from ecological factors."[28] Likewise, the highly regarded cultural anthropologist Philip Carl Salzman notes that "All knowledge is based on abstraction, and abstraction draws on commonalities and averages that exist beyond the acknowledged variation of the particulars. For example, there are different species and varieties of camel, but we would not therefore conclude that we cannot validly distinguish camels from horses. . . . As regards cultures, there are variations both between and within Arab and Middle Eastern cultures, but anyone who argues on that basis that it is impossible to distinguish Arab culture from Hindu culture would not be frank."[29] Meanwhile, as you will see in this chapter and the next, cultural anthropologists and psychologists have conducted work all across the region—from Morocco to Iraq, Sudan, and Yemen, to Jordan and Syria—and the cultural patterns they describe are remarkably similar. Indeed, with allowances for important subcultural distinctions, they are far more like than unalike.[30]

Within the Arab world, there are regional subcultures (the Maghreb, Levant, and Gulf), topographical (desert, mountain, urban, agricultural), national, and other varieties. However, for my purposes, it is the dominant Arab culture that is of greatest importance.[31] Only the dominant culture has an influence across the entire Arab world—although local subcultures almost certainly have their own distinctive impact and may be responsible for some variations in military effectiveness among Arab militaries. Moreover, as most Arab writers have observed, the dominant culture is quite pronounced across the region while the subcultures are often modest in their diversity, and the countercultures are mostly confined to small, often marginalized groups and consequently have little impact on the behavior of large Arab military forces.[32] Thus, while I recognize the cultural variations within the region, it is the set of broad cultural similarities that extend across it on which I have focused.

What the Dominant Arab Culture Is and Is Not

I'm certainly not the first person, or the first Westerner, to write about Arab culture. Unfortunately some who went before me treated it in a cavalier fashion that veered off into stereotyping, racism, and other problems. Moreover, in the West, there are many common notions associated with the Arab world that are exaggerated, outdated, or just inaccurate. One of the rules for handling a topic as ineffable and potentially dangerous as culture is to be precise. So let me be precise.

I consider the dominant culture of the Arab world to be that of its settled communities—the cities and towns—and the agricultural and artisan-based economies that characterize them. The most important distinction I draw here is that between the settled communities and the Bedouin of the Arab world. While many Westerners still tend to associate Arab society with a nomadic existence, the vast majority of Arabs live in towns and, increasingly, cities. The proportion of the population that can still be considered Bedouin is extremely small: As long ago as 1970 nomads comprised less than 1 percent of the population of the Middle East, and even before World War II Bedouin comprised less than 15 percent of the population.[33] Although the values and lifestyle of the Bedouin subculture still exert a powerful sway over the imagination of many Arabs, the reality of the dominant culture has been moving steadily away from that of the Bedouin for at least the last eight centuries.[34]

Just as I do not consider the dominant Arab culture to be the traditional Bedouin culture, I also do not consider Arab culture to be identical to the religion of Islam. Although the overwhelming number of Arabs are Muslims, a textual evaluation of the Islamic religion does not provide the key to patterns of culturally regular Arab behavior. This is a critical point in the post-9/11 world in which so many have tried to identify Islam as the source of the West's troubles with the Middle East, and some have tried to claim that it is the enemy itself.

Contrary to the common wisdom, religions are essentially products of a culture, or even vessels of it. They tend more to espouse the ideals and values of a community than to shape those values. While it is true that, once created, religions tend to exert an independent influence on the culture, they are not immune from constant, additional molding by the culture. After the birth of a religion (or its importation into a society), there is an almost constant struggle between the theoretically static religious dogma and the constantly changing culture, and the culture wins far more than it loses. It is generally the case that a religion is constantly reinterpreted to meet the changing needs of its community—needs that are expressed in its culture. One need only look to the ever-evolving doctrine of the Catholic Church to see this in action. More to the point, Clifford Geertz has demonstrated that Islam as it is practiced in Morocco (the western end of the Islamic world) is a remarkably different religion from the Islam practiced in Indonesia (the eastern end of the Islamic world). In both societies, Islam has been interpreted so that it meshes with the underlying, dominant culture. Again, there is no question that Islam has had an impact on Indonesian and Moroccan cultures, but the impact of the cultures on the religion has been much greater.[35]

Thus, Islam is a product of Arab culture.[36] However, its sacred texts can serve as only a vague and nebulous guide to current Arab culture because those texts were shaped largely by the culture of seventh-century Arabia—where the Quran was written—and the seventh- and eighth-century fertile crescent—where the Hadiths were compiled. In the 13 intervening centuries, Arab culture itself has changed dramatically, and as a result, classical Islam and contemporary Arab culture have grown apart. While many Middle East societies claim to live strictly according to the laws of Islam as set down in the Quran and the Hadiths, the divergences from these traditions are at least as noteworthy as the areas of true conformity. Despite the best efforts of orthodox Jews, Christians, and Muslims, it is ultimately impossible for a twenty-first-century society to live exactly as demanded by medieval religious doctrine. Even in Saudi Arabia and Iran, perhaps the two most fundamentalist of current Middle East societies, it is difficult to make the case that Saudis and Iranians are living their lives as prescribed by the Quran.

The Quran is interpreted slightly differently in virtually every Arab state, and even wider gaps exist between Arab states and non-Arab Muslim states. In every case, these differences can be explained largely by the differences in the underlying cultures.[37] For instance, Andrea Rugh has noted how Islam has "provided the moral authority that helps give patterns of behavior such persistence," but not that it is the source of those patterns.[38] Many practices closely associated with orthodox Muslim society are not specified in the Quran, and are instead a product of Arab cultural practices and later interpretations. Patrick Porter notes that the Quran forbids suicide, yet suicide bombing has become a common practice in the region—and too many Islamic clerics have accommodated their dogma to tolerate or even accept it because it is culturally popular.[39] Consequently, attempting to describe Arab culture by a textual exegesis of classical Islamic religious documents would not present an accurate portrait of modern Arab society.

This last point brings up another issue regarding Arab culture. I have focused on the culture of the Arab world only as it existed since the end of the Second World War. As noted above, cultures are not static or timeless; in fact all cultures are constantly changing. Arab culture during this period was subtly different from Arab culture as it existed before World War II, which in turn was different from the Arab culture of the nineteenth century, and so on back into the depths of time. For any culture, there are strong carryovers from one period to the next. However, it would not be at all correct to assert that Arab culture after World War II was identical to Arab culture during the Middle Ages. Indeed, after the Second World War, the Arab countries experienced a series of profound changes brought about by decolonization, efforts toward industrialization, and greater contact with the West that produced a fairly dramatic break with the culture of the past.

Moreover, there have been important changes in Arab culture even (or especially) during the period since the Second World War. Just as it is true that Arab culture during the modern era is not identical to the Arab culture of millennia ago, neither has it remained unchanged since World War II. Arab culture in the 1940s and 1950s was (inevitably) closer to the culture of older Arab society than that of today. The infusion of modern telecommunications and social media has ushered in profound changes in Arab culture, and has triggered an all-out culture war across the generations in the Middle East. For that reason, some of the cultural traits I consider in this book were more applicable in the first half of this time period than in the latter. That said, it is still true that all of the traits I consider did have a powerful influence on Arab behavior throughout this period, and the distinction between the earlier and latter periods is a relative one. This is particularly the case because culture is transmitted to members of the community primarily during the process of maturation from child to adult. Thus even the Iraqi, Egyptian, and Saudi soldiers who fought in the Gulf War of 1990–1991 began the process of cultural inculcation in the late 1960s and early 1970s, just as most of the Iraqi, Libyan, Yemeni, and Syrians fighting in the civil wars of today largely imbibed the culture of the 1980s and 1990s.

It would also be a mistake to assume that the various traits identified as elements of the dominant Arab culture are necessarily unique to the Arabs. It is entirely possible, indeed highly likely, that many traits considered culturally regular for the Arabs are also important elements of other cultures, or of subcultures within other societies.[40] Numerous cross-cultural studies in anthropology, sociology, and psychology have demonstrated as much.[41] Cultures are the responses of communities to a wide variety of influences, including geography, topography, demography, economics, and history, to name only a few. To the extent that other societies share similar geography with the Middle East, or perhaps suffered analogous historical events, it would seem plausible that they would share cultural patterns with the Arabs developed in response to these common experiences.

However, it is equally crucial to recognize that the cultural patterns developed by another society will invariably be different from those of the Arabs, no matter how close they may seem at first glance.[42] Culture is a hopelessly complex phenomenon, subject to an enormous range of influences, and it is effectively impossible that two different societies living in two different areas of the world and experiencing two different histories (no matter how similar) would produce identical cultural traits. At most, they may be crudely similar. Gregg warns that "On a daily basis, a Westerner may experience moments of 'self-esteem,' 'propriety,' and 'embarrassment' in a manner that roughly parallels a Middle Easterner's experiences of honor, modesty, and shame, but the resemblance does not run very deep."[43]

Likewise, for the same reasons, no other society is likely to have the same complete "set" of culturally regular behavioral predilections. There may be overlap in the cultural traits of different societies—reflecting similar historical experiences, environments, economic systems, etc.—but the entire sets will not be identical. For instance, the cultural anthropologist Michael Herzfeld has demonstrated that every Mediterranean society had important values attached to the concepts of honor and shame, but these had very different meanings and connotations from one society to the next, and so produced very different behavioral patterns.[44]

Finally, it is crucial to remember that culture can be a nebulous subject. It is often like a will-o'-the-wisp: always just out of reach, slipping from our grasp whenever we try to pin it down. Unfortunately, the necessities of analysis require a certain amount of concreteness. Consequently, in the pages that follow, I am going to treat it in a more precise and clearly delineated fashion than it realistically deserves. To some extent, this "reductionism" may have distorted my treatment of culture. I see this as an unfortunate necessity. However, I tried not to do grievous damage to the concept despite having to overlook many of the subtleties, connections, and distinctions of Arab culture. To adjust for some of the distortions arising from the need to treat culture more concretely and simplistically than is the case in reality, I have tried to temper my conclusions to reflect this artificial process. In the end, I am a military analyst and an expert on the Middle East trying to explain how the culture of the Arab world has affected its military performance. Doing so has required a certain amount of simplification, if only so that this book did not run to thousands of pages to encompass hundreds of nuances, warnings, and exceptions.

CHAPTER 17 | Arab Culture:
Patterns and Predilections

A NY CULTURE IS difficult to measure and difficult to categorize. In
addition, depictions of Arab culture have been controversial over the
last 60 to 70 years. For these reasons, how I arrived at my portrait of Arab
culture is an important question. Because my expertise is in Middle Eastern
military and political affairs rather than Arab culture per se, I chose to rely
on what is often called the "Delphi" method. Rather than attempting to delve
into the subject on my own, I instead relied on the analysis of Arab behavioral
patterns by true experts on the cultural anthropology, sociology, and cultural
psychology of the Middle East.

In a similar fashion, instead of trying to judge the validity of sociological,
psychological, or anthropological theories that purport to explain the origins
of Arab cultural traits, I have limited my analysis to the observed behavior
itself. The latter is much less controversial than the former. Moreover, it was
just unnecessary for this book. I am trying to explain the causal connections
between the patterns of behavior of Arab society and the historical patterns of
Arab military performance. The origins of these behavioral patterns in the environment of the Middle East or events in Arab history, while interesting, are
not really relevant to this book, and therefore I have left them out.

So for example, Arabists such as Edward Said have argued that the impact of Ottoman and European imperialism had a profound impact on Arab
culture. Based on both my research and my own experiences in the region,
I tend to agree, and suspect that many of the predilections and patterns of

behavior I will describe below were a product, at least in part, of that colonial experience. In fact, a number of Arab sociologists, anthropologists, and cultural psychologists such as Mahmoud 'Awda, Jamal Hamdan, Abdellah Hammoudi, Tarik Sabry, and Mustafa Hijazi have made a similar case to Said's—without his vitriol—arguing that centuries of subjugation under the Ottomans, Europeans, and then the post-independence autocrats have fostered passivity, dependency, resignation, deception, dissimulation, and quietude as powerful tendencies within Arab culture.[1] However, others disagree about the causes, ascribing these same traits to other sources. Ultimately, it just isn't relevant to this book. What is relevant is the patterns and predilections themselves, not the debate about how they became infused into the culture.

In relying on the Delphi method there were a number of important criteria that guided my work. The first was to only include behavioral patterns cited by experts and to discard traits suggested only by amateurs or generalists. There are a huge number of travelogues, journalistic accounts, and armchair pseudo-psychology of the Arab world that claim to give insight into the "Arab mind" based on the experiences of the author in the Middle East. I tended to disregard the suppositions of such accounts except in those rare cases where the traits cited were also supported by true scholarly work by respected experts, and in those cases, it was the expert studies upon which I relied.

That included my own experiences, by the way. While I have spent a lot of time in the Middle East, I am absolutely not an expert on Arab sociology, and I recognize that my own firsthand experiences provide merely one set of (inexpert) observations. I let the expert literature, not my idiosyncratic experiences, drive my portrait of the dominant Arab society.

This standard led me to exclude from consideration many "folk theories" regarding Arab culture for which I could find no support in the scholarly literature on the Middle East. For instance, I have not included a "disregard for human life" as a common trait of the dominant Arab culture, despite frequent claims by journalists and some military analysts that this is a central feature of an "Islamic Way of Warfare."[2] I found very little in the scholarly literature on Arab culture to suggest that this most Islamic of societies places little value on human life and that Arabs are more willing than others to sacrifice lives in pursuit of minor goals.

Another consideration in putting together a list of patterns of behavior considered culturally regular for Arab society was to include only those on which there was a consensus among Middle East experts regarding the behavior derived from the trait. In a number of cases, I found a substantial amount of support that a particular trait was an element of Arab culture, but disagreement as to exactly what kind of behavior the trait produced. For example, a great many authors see a pervasive fatalism among Arabs (something I and other frequent visitors to the Middle East have certainly encountered). However, I could find no agreement on how this caused Arabs to act. Some authors argued that this fatalism tended to make Arabs inattentive to long-term considerations, unwilling to make sacrifices in pursuit of a greater gain in the future, apathetic, and even lazy.[3] Other authors argued equally persuasively that although Arabs tended to be fatalistic, this had no impact on their behavior because a great many worked hard, sacrificed for the future, and believed that their labors would eventually bear fruit—or at least, that not working hard would certainly doom them.[4] (Personally, I have seen both.) So while I am willing to accept that fatalism may be a component of the dominant Arab culture, because there was no clear consensus among the experts as to the behavior prompted by this belief, I chose not to include it in my treatment of Arab culture as an explanation for Arab military problems.

I also chose to exclude culturally regular patterns of behavior that appeared unlikely to have a meaningful impact on military operations. Ultimately, my task is not to sketch an encyclopedic list of the elements of the dominant Arab culture but to explain the performance of Arab militaries in combat. I came across any number of behavioral patterns derived from Arab culture that seemed to have only the most distant potential connection to the behavior of Arab soldiers and officers in battle. Consequently, I chose to exclude from consideration such Arab traits as generosity, hospitality, particular sexual codes, and the gender roles of Arab society, for instance. In each of these cases, while I found a considerable amount of scholarly support for these traits, and agreement on the behavior that typically flowed from them, I could see only the most tenuous links between them and behavior on the battlefield. There is little or no reason to believe that how Arab couples are expected to deal with sexual matters will influence how Arab men act in battle. Therefore, although including a discussion of this subject might have made this book infinitely more interesting to the reader, because it had no clear bearing on Arab military effectiveness, I chose not to include it. Sorry.

Given all of these criteria for inclusion, the reader should beware that my treatment of Arab culture can only be considered a partial list and is far from a comprehensive picture of even the dominant Arab culture, let alone the entirety of Arab society. Setting aside the subcultures and countercultures, the dominant culture alone possesses scores, if not hundreds or even thousands of behavioral predilections. I have culled from that universe a small subset that I feel comfortable including in a list of features of Arab culture that should produce persistent patterns of behavior among Arab soldiers and officers in combat. But it does not depict the totality of Arab culture.

As a final point, please bear in mind that I am looking at Arab military effectiveness since 1945, and so have tried to identify cultural patterns that existed more or less throughout that same period of time, even recognizing that the culture shifted throughout. While, inevitably, there is more continuity than discontinuity, some of the patterns were more prevalent in earlier days than at present. Moreover, I deliberately used scholarly sources from that entire period. I did so to demonstrate that these patterns were present at the start of the post–World War II era and persisted throughout, even though they may have evolved over time (and may diminish or change in the future).

Conformity

When reading the anthropological, sociological, and psychological literature on culture in the Arab world, the behavioral emphasis that comes up most frequently is the promotion of conformity to group norms as a guide for individual behavior. Within the dominant Arab culture, the group typically takes precedence over the individual. Individual desires and interests are often underplayed in favor of the good of the group. Indeed, many Middle East experts write of the general "submergence of the individual within the group."[5] Afif Tannous asserts that "The individual learns to identify himself with [his] family group from the moment of birth and his behavior is patterned accordingly."[6] According to Halim Barakat, "Arabs tend to interact as committed members of a group, rather than as independent individuals who constantly assert their apartness."[7] A comparative study of Jewish and Arab high school students in Israel in 1976 showed that the "Arab subjects displayed a significantly higher need for social approval than their Jewish counterparts," and were far more concerned with remaining committed members of the group by obtaining its collective approval.[8]

The principal act by which the individual achieves the support and approbation of the group is by conforming to the values of the group. Consequently conformity is an important value of the dominant Arab culture. Hamed Ammar stated in his study of Egyptian village life that there is a "Compelling moral law that the individual, to be in line with the group, should express group-sympathy; if the group is angry, he should be angry, if it is insulted, he must feel insulted."[9] Levon Melikian has remarked that "Arabic movies in general center around a moral issue and the consequences of breaking the accepted codes and patterns of behavior. In general they stress conformity."[10] Indeed, the Iraqi sociologist Sana Al-Khayyat titled the first chapter of her book on the role of women in Iraqi society, "The Pressure to Conform."[11]

The importance of conformity is related to and reinforced by a reverence for tradition. There is wide agreement among Middle East experts that elements of the dominant culture encourage the individual to live his or her life in conformity with the extensive body of traditions Arab society has for virtually all activity.[12] Tarek Heggy writes that "Arabic-speaking societies belong to a culture that venerates the past, and sets great store by traditions and customs established through long usage. This makes for a mindset that is averse to change in general, and for any change to be perceived as a threat to their traditions in particular."[13] In the words of the great French Arabist Jacques Berque, Arab society is "intentionally tradition-alist."[14] Urban Egyptians characterized a respect for tradition as one of their salient cultural traits, according to Laila Shukry El-Hamamsy.[15] Abdullah Lutfiyya considers "A deep-seated respect for tradition and the past" as a central facet of Arab society.[16] Elsewhere, Lutfiyya has argued that " 'Good' and 'Bad' acts are so defined in the light of the traditional norm. Thus, if an act is in accord with custom, it is good; if not, it is bad. In the absence of a specific traditional norm, one's behavior is expected to be guided by the spirit of tradition in general."[17]

One result of this constant pressure to conform is a corresponding stifling of originality. If all behavior must conform to established, traditional patterns, then there is little room for innovation and creativity. Indeed, there is a con-sensus among Middle East scholars that although there are many individuals and even important countercultures of great creativity within the Arab world, the dominant culture works to suppress originality and innovation.[18] Heggy bemoans "the strong resistance to change in the Arab culture."[19] The result is that many Arabs show little flare for—or interest in—creative or novel approaches to a situation. "Conventional values . . . emphasize conformity over creativity," in the words of Halim Barakat.[20] Likewise, El-Sayyed Yassin sees Egyptians "as characterized by conventional rather than creative thinking."[21] Hisham Sharabi decries that "In putting conformity above originality and obe-dience before autonomy, [Arab society] crushes creative talent and encourages only those powers that help to maintain it."[22] Berque writes that "Arabic cul-ture purposely resists innovation," and Ernest Gellner has noted the "proscrip-tion of innovation," in Arab society.[23]

The dominant culture consistently suppresses creativity, innovation, im-agination, and all similar divergences from established patterns of action and thought. "Innovators are always the objects of shame and ridicule. Invariably there is an outright rejection of anything new that appears to conflict with tradition," according to Lutfiyya.[24] These claims are echoed by the famous Syrian poet Ahmed 'Ali Sa'id (known as Adonis), "The group has always been more highly valued than the individual, and stability has been sought at the expense of risky change and creativity. Innovators have been silenced, while static values and attitudes have been preserved."[25] Similarly, Hamed Ammar recounts that, in Egyptian village life:

> One should not think in terms of "if" or "as if," as according to the prophetic tradition, "'if' opens the path for the devil's advance." It is also interesting to mention that the classical Arabic word for imagination (*Khayal*) is used in the village to denote "shadow," and does not refer to a mental process, except of course, to some literate persons. This does not mean that some children are not imaginative, and they are recognized by other children who may sometimes sneer at them by asking them to relate some of their fantasies (literally "pinches"). Children would tell you that such flights of fancy run through certain families, adults, however, do not expect children to use, much less exercise or enrich, their imagination as this would hamper their social and economic maturity.[26]

The tendency of the dominant culture to discourage innovation and creativity is among the more striking features noted by many Western observers of the Middle East. For example, American educators who have taught Arab students both in the United States and the Middle East generally have found that Arab students are "Shrewd, politically astute to the nuances of human behavior but non-creative and non-analytical in thought-processes."[27] Similarly, Melikian's study of Saudi college students found that, despite various other differences between them, both Saudis who had not gone to college as well as Saudi college students ranked the statement "accept new ideas" as the last or second to last priority of Saudi culture out of a group of 10 statements reflecting different potential cultural values.[28] Likewise, the American educator Joshua Mitchell noted of his twenty-first-century Arab students, "This attentiveness to family obligations often has deleterious consequences for their studies, though in vain does the teacher implore them to place their own self-interest at the forefront. Many do not understand themselves first and foremost as individuals but rather as bearers of a family name. More accurately, while they are increasingly coming to think of themselves as individuals, they nevertheless continue to understand themselves as occupying a specific and largely unalterable role in their families and, by extension, in their societies."[29]

Edward Said also noted this predilection. He argued that the West values individual freedom, in part to promote individual creativity, whereas Arab society promotes "participating with the people in cultural creation." That is, Arab culture emphasizes that it is the society that should be *collectively* creative, progressing and achieving by collective activity, rather than the Western concept of fostering individual creativity, progress, and achievement, which Westerners believe leads to societal creativity, progress, and achievement.[30] Commenting on the same concept, Andrea Rugh observes that in the Arab world, "individuals realize themselves through immersion in the group." A concept she notes that seems counterintuitive, even contradictory, to the Western mind.[31]

The preference for conformity over creativity has been institutionalized in unwritten but well-known codes in Arab society and in formal prohibitions in the Shari'a. Fatima Mernissi notes that "The words that mean 'to create,' like *Khalaqa* and *Bid'a*, are dangerous and stamped with bans. All innovation is a contravention of the order of things." She further points out that the word for Satan (*Shaytan*) comes from *shatana,* which means "Straying from usual human behavior and becoming conspicuous by stepping out of the ranks in some way or another."[32] Bassam Tibi goes even further in noting that "The [Arabic] term for innovation is *Bid'a*, which is tantamount to heresy."[33] According to Lutfiyya, "Islam sanctions traditional behavior and gives it precedence over innovations. This view finds a legal support in the *Sharia* doctrine that declares, '*al-qadim yabqa zala qidamih,*' i.e. anything of the past has precedence (over innovation)."[34]

In short, free thought tends to be discouraged by the dominant culture. Hisham Sharabi "sees Arab children as discouraged by their upbringing from exercising independent judgment. They are taught to accept unquestioningly the view of others."[35] Barakat writes that Arab children "Avoid taking risks and trying new ways of doing things, for independence of mind, critical dissent, and adventure beyond the recognized limits are constantly and systematically discouraged by parents and other members of the family."[36] Likewise Saad Eddin Ibrahim and Nicholas Hopkins have commented that "To behave properly meant to learn to suppress individual impulses. Since individuals had to take the clues of proper behavior from traditional authority and heritage, and since they were not to choose or judge outside that framework, independent thinking and analytical abilities remained undeveloped, if not deliberately stunted."[37] Marwan Dwairy links this tendency precisely to the pattern of behavior we have seen time and again among Arab armies since 1945, noting that "self-control among Arabs is not an independent personality construct. The ego functions as a controller, but it is specific to control rather than problem solving and functions only in understanding and following authority in Arab society. *Serious difficulties are encountered by the ego when facing new situations in which one needs to make personal evaluations and decisions.*"[38]

Centralization of Authority

For the most part, the dominant Arab culture favors the centralization of authority and information in hierarchically organized social groupings. Indeed, Arab subordinates are regularly characterized as submissive and obedient to their superiors. When placed within a hierarchic structure the dominant Arab culture inclines individuals to keep to their assigned place, to not usurp authority from those higher in the chain, and to wait until provided with direction from above. As a result, many Arabs demonstrate constant obedience and respect for their superiors, often regardless of circumstances. Most Middle East scholars concur that this pattern is characteristic of Arab organizations and social groups, from families to business enterprises to government bureaucracies, a topic I address at greater length in the next chapter.

This tendency starts in most Arab families, which in turn set the example for behavior in other hierarchies later in life. Despite the many changes in Arab society since the Second World War, the family remains the basic social unit of the Arab world, although globalization is slowly stressing the model. Life in the cities makes it harder for extended families to live together, but relatives still try to live close by and frequently remain the primary support network for individuals.[39] According to Daniel Bates and Amal Rassam, "When one hears of reference to the decline of the family in the Middle East, it is usually in reference to the break-up of large residential entities and not necessarily to the diminution of the viability of the kinship grouping itself."[40] Writing in the 1990s, Donna Bowen and Evelyn Early found that:

> The family into which one is born, the natal family, is the most important social group in one's life. It provides protection, food, shelter, income, reputation, and honor. The family is the reference for assistance as one grows up, finds a spouse, job, and home, raises one's own family, and adjusts to changing social circumstances. The family mediates between the individual and the outside world, and Middle Easterners naturally assume that relatives will be favored. One's family name is a ready-made identification which reveals to all both one's reputation and one's access to assistance.[41]

In an insightful essay on Arab youth from 2013, Suad Joseph noted that "I have found that children and youth rarely spend time together alone. Overwhelmingly they spend time with a wide generational mix, based on family and neighborhood. Spending time with grandparents, who, in this village, are often in the same building or very close by, spending time with uncles and aunts, spending time with older siblings and cousins (as well as parents) is usually the preferred activity. In individual interviews in July of 2011, I asked two women in their early twenties and their two teenage brothers whom they wanted to spend their leisurely (sic) time with. All of them replied that they preferred their own siblings and family as leisure-mates and best friends. . . . Children grow up with their grandparents, uncles and aunts, and cousins as their immediate, and at times, often exclusive social world."[42]

Moreover, the Arab family largely has clung to its traditional features throughout the postwar era although it too is changing as modernity comes to the Middle East. Nevertheless, it is typically an extended family, characterized by patrilineal descent, and a patriarchal system.[43] In Halim Barakat's words, "The family is the basic unit of social organization and production in traditional and contemporary Arab society, and it remains a relatively cohesive institution at the center of social and economic activities. It is patriarchal; pyramidally hierarchical, particularly with respect to sex and age; and extended."[44]

The father is the head of the family, and he expects "respect and unquestioning compliance with his instructions."[45] In her study of a middle-class Egyptian family, Ilse Lichtenstadter found that the father "is treated with respect and deference, and even the grown-up and married sons submit to his authority."[46] Lutfiyya agrees that "The youngster learns early in life to obey the father's orders without questioning them, and looks at his father as the mighty giant who rules unchallenged in the family's world."[47] Indeed, the Arab family is frequently a rather severe hierarchy in that the father makes most decisions regarding the external activities of the family, and he expects his wife and children to obey without dissent.[48] As the Dutch sociologist C. A. O. Van Nieuwenhuijze put it, "The family father is the centre [sic] of the family in all respects. . . . Operationally speaking, the family father is the fountain head of authority and decision-making. . . . He is the one who knows how to decide; in doing his bidding the family, as an extension of him, will survive."[49] Likewise, according to Hamed Ammar, the father is not only "expected to make all of the important decisions," but he "usually plans the work of his sons" in village communities.[50] Pergrouhi Najarian has noted that this pattern of paternal dominance of decision-making for the family holds true in even many of the most liberal, Western-minded middle-class families of urban Arab society.[51] So heavy is the father's control over decision-making that sons are taught to be submissive to their father and generally are discouraged from taking any decisions of consequence without paternal approval.[52]

Because of the dominance of the family as the primary social structure in the Arab world, the patterns of intra-family behavior have been expanded to virtually every aspect of Arab society.[53] Sania Hamady sums this up by saying, "Arab society starts with the family and is patterned on it."[54] In a study of Jordanian bureaucracies, Jamil Jreisat noted that "heads of departments rule their units as chiefs of tribes; they hold all powers, real or symbolic . . . "[55] Barakat writes that:

> The continued dominance of the family as the basic unit of social organization and production has contributed to the diffusion of patriarchal relations and to their application to similar situations within other social institutions. Specifically, the same patriarchal relations and values that prevail in the Arab family seem also to prevail at work, at school, and in religious, political, and social associations. In all of these, a father figure rules over others, monopolizing authority, expecting strict obedience, and showing little tolerance for dissent. Projecting a paternal image, those in positions of responsibility (as rulers, leaders, teachers, employers, and supervisors) securely occupy the top of the pyramid of authority.[56]

Rugh makes a virtually identical point from her observations on Egyptian (and Saudi and Qatari) society: "One sees this phenomenon in offices, religious groups, universities, and other institutions and organizations as well. Chiefs, bosses, sponsors all are expected to play fatherly roles that go far beyond what is required by the dry routine of office work. They provide mediation services, loan money, provide advice, listen to problems. . . . The employee assumes the role of son, dutifully performing menial tasks, and when necessary seeking the intervention of the powerful father-figure who usually has the means to resolve his small problems."[57]

Gregg and Abdoullah Hamoudi, among others, argue that the persistence of authoritarian politics in the Arab world into the twenty-first century ultimately derives from its prevalence in Arab family life.[58] Because the typical Arab family concentrates decision-making authority in the father, and the Arab family is the model for the rest of society, there is a pronounced tendency for other organizations and institutions in the Arab world to similarly centralize authority in the hands of the chief executive, who effectively assumes the role of the father. Gregg has pointed out that "Moroccan investigators have emphasized the fact that relationships so pervasively take the form of *subordination and domination*. Indeed, classlike layers objectively exist and lead to the pervasive formation of hierarchical patron-client networks."[59]

Deference to Authority, and Passivity

A cultural trait closely related both to the promotion of conformity and the tendency toward hierarchic centralization in Arab society is the tendency among individuals occupying the lower rungs of hierarchies to defer decision-making to higher authority and to remain passive, even refusing to make trivial decisions on their own. Because organizations in Arab societies are so often modeled on the family, and because in a traditional Arab family the father is expected to make most if not all important decisions with his wife and children expected to execute these orders without question, delegation of authority is rare and often superficial.[60] Instead, decisions are constantly referred back to the highest executive levels, just as they would be referred to the father in a family.

This is the flip side to the centralization of authority and the unwillingness of leaders to delegate authority: virtually all authority is concentrated at the top of the hierarchy, and not even mid-level officials are expected to act independently, nor do they believe it incumbent upon them to do so. While this can ensure that Arab social groupings do not suffer from "schizophrenic" behavior—one part of the group acting in a manner opposite to that of the rest of the group, or opposite to that desired by the leadership—it also fosters a widespread lack of initiative among subordinates.

Once again, a wide consensus of opinion exists among Middle East experts that initiative and decision-making in Arab groups is expected to come from the top of the hierarchy, and those at the bottom of a hierarchy are expected to remain passive, acting only as and when specifically directed to do so.[61] For instance, Raymond Cohen found that "Psychological tests have shown that Egyptians score significantly higher in tests of obedience and unquestioning respect for authority than do Americans," and that such scores were found to be "culturally normal in an Egyptian context."[62] Cohen's own work led him to conclude that "Denied freedom of choice, children learn to do only what they are told. Self-reliance and personal initiative are not encouraged because they do not contribute to group needs."[63] Similarly, in the 1950s, Edwin Prothro and Louis Melikian tested university students in Lebanon and Egypt and found that in both cases, the Arab students gave more "authoritarian" responses on issues related to authority and obedience than Americans. Likewise, Gregg has noted that various, more recent, studies have shown that Arabs "*value* authority more highly than do Westerners."[64] In Marwan Dwairy's words, "Arab children, as well as adults, are guided by strict norms. External authority such as parents and teachers are the agents that ensure fulfillment of norms. These authorities allow very little space for personal choices. Almost everything is determined a priori. The only mission left to an individual is to learn what he or she is expected to do and to adhere to these norms. People in these societies do not have many personal choices and are not involved much in decision-making processes."[65]

Another powerful cultural factor fostering deference to authority and passivity among subordinates in Arab hierarchies are the forces of honor and shame. Honor and shame, essentially two sides of a coin, are powerful influences on behavior in the Arab world. Honor is a driving motive in many (some would say all) aspects of Arab life, and a failure to act honorably is punished with shame, which is to be avoided at all costs.[66] In Gregg's words, "honor and shame indeed are crucially important features of [Arab society], in that they shape the personality development of perhaps most individuals."[67] Maxime Rodinson states simply that "Loss of honor, shame, or debasement was a terrible punishment."[68] Or as Philip Carl Salzman has put it, for a great many Arabs, "the search for honor and the avoidance of shame becomes a goal in its own right."[69] Because shaming is the primary instrument by which Arab society enforces conformity, and because shame is considered an unbearable punishment, "worry about external dignity is (the Arab's) continual concern."[70] Ammar remarks on the "almost morbid fear of shame" in Egyptian village life.[71] Pierre Bourdieu, in his treatment of Algerian society, similarly found that "the sentiment of honor, like its reverse, the fear of shame and group censure, can affect . . . deeply the most trivial action of daily life and can dominate all relations with other people."[72]

Honor and shame have a strong impact on proclivities toward action and initiative. In Arab society, to do something wrong generally is much worse than to do nothing at all. Because the dominant Arab culture focuses identity on groups rather than individuals, responsibility is generally considered to fall on the group in its entirety, rather than on any particular individual. As a member of a group, some event may be the responsibility of the group, but it is not necessarily the responsibility of any particular member of the group. In Rugh's words, "Individual initiative is rewarded primarily as it enhances the prospects of the status of the group. Without great effort outside the group, one can be an appreciated group member by dutifully fulfilling obligations of roles and relationships within the group. This is clear in television serials where good and bad events befall the heroes and heroines and they are judged not so much by their effort to overcome events as by their intentions toward others and their unfailing fulfillment of their expected roles."[73]

In this way, the dominant Arab culture creates a disincentive for taking initiative or action, especially for those who occupy lower rungs in a traditional hierarchy. Because responsibility is collective, no individual necessarily has any more responsibility to take action to avert disaster than anyone else. By taking action, the individual takes responsibility and risks failure, and the individual is blamed for failure because failure reflects badly on the group. However, simply discharging one's obligations to the group is always honorable and praiseworthy and can never be a source of shame. Dwairy hauntingly concludes that in this way, "A mere shadow of an individual who has no autonomy is thus created."[74]

Hence, by acting, an individual invites the risk of shame, but by doing nothing he or she runs no such risk.[75] On this point, Hisham Sharabi comments that children are taught to believe themselves weak—weak before the commands of their father and the judgment of the group. Having such limited capabilities, the child can only have very limited responsibilities and is encouraged to believe that virtually everything is always someone else's responsibility. Consequently, because the child is taught to believe that he or she is neither responsible for, nor capable of, doing most things, he or she finds little reason to act in most circumstances.[76] Similarly, Hamady argues that "Instead of striving toward doing the good, [the culturally regular Arab] seeks only to avoid doing the disapproved."[77]

Indeed, in the patriarchal hierarchy of typical Arab society, it is normally the father—or father figure—who is solely responsible for acting or ordering actions, a pattern repeated in other organizations. Lichtenstadter sums this up succinctly in noting that "The father carries the full responsibility for the well-being of his family."[78] Thus only the father has the responsibility to take action. The only responsibility of the led is to obey the leader. Moreover, taking any action without the expressed consent of the leader would be disrespectful, and worse, might put the family or group on a different track from that which the father or leader would have chosen. Consequently, these two cultural criteria are strong forces prompting Arab subordinates to remain passive, and to act only when specifically ordered to do so.[79]

The net result of these various forces is that most members of Arab hierarchies tend to expect action and initiative to come from higher authority—the father, teacher, supervisor, boss, general. The powerful fear of shame combined with the expectation of complete obedience to authority encourage the led to not take any actions that are not specifically requested by higher authority. When a decision must be made, Arab culture stresses *Naql* (traditional authoritative transmission) from higher authority over *Aql* (reasoning) by subordinates.[80] American educators who have taught large numbers of Arab students report that a strong sense of shame makes many Arab students "timid and unadventurous."[81] A RAND study on the subject found that, among most Arabs, "Outcomes that are unfortunate are regarded as personal failures, whereas in other cultures they would be regarded as risks worth taking in the deliberate search for novel solutions."[82]

Group Loyalty

Another highly valued trait of Arab society is group solidarity and loyalty, particularly loyalty to family. As noted above, the family remains the basic unit of Arab society, generally superseding the individual in importance.[83] In the words of Ahmed Al Suofi, writing after 9/11, "One of the central goals of an Arabic person is to build, strengthen, and protect his family."[84] In fact, Dwairy began his 2006 book on the practice of psychotherapy in the Arab world by warning, "Western counselors and therapists who work with Arab and/or Muslim clients usually realize immediately that they are not dealing with an independent individual, and discover the tremendous impact of the family, culture, and heritage on the client's thoughts, attitudes, feelings, and behavior."[85] In study after study, Arab countries score very high in surveys of collective thought and behavior.[86]

For these reasons, Rugh—a cultural anthropologist who has worked in a half-dozen Arab states—noted in her book on Egyptian families that "Individualism has little positive value in Egyptian society, and often is equated with a number of negative outcomes." She also relates a revealing story about an Egyptian class at an Egyptian university taught by an American professor, which had just read Thoreau's *Walden*: "The consensus of the class was that Thoreau was not accomplishing anything useful by his anti-social behavior; he had abrogated his role as a social being. He should in fact be considered 'crazy' and would be so considered if he should try to live in this way in the Egyptian context. The concept of self-realization and self-reliance were totally lost on the students."[87]

Rugh goes on to explain that Westerners tend to see groups as "collectives," assemblages of individuals who unite for a common purpose for as long as that purpose exists. In contrast, Arabs tend to see groups as "corporate," having a role and existence beyond the individuals and persisting for their own sake, with individuals joining and leaving only when necessary, including by birth and death. Individual rights supersede group interests in a collective, but the opposite is true in the corporate groups common to Arab society. In the corporation, "the group comes first and the individuals are expected to sacrifice their own needs for the greater good of the group. The personal status of individual members is defined by the group and not more than incidentally by individual achievement. Individual behaviors are evaluated primarily by how they reflect on the group, the group taking the blame or the rewards for these behaviors. Personal lapses in behavior, if kept secret, are of little consequence; it is only their public acknowledgement and association with the lowering of group status that causes an individual a sense of shame and personal guilt," for dishonoring the group.[88]

An interesting facet of the urbanization of Arab society, and the attendant changes in economics and demographics is that, in many cases, the neighborhood has begun to replace the clan or tribe in the lives of most Arabs.[89] While it is true that many members of the extended family live in the same neighborhood when possible, it is also the case that even where no kinship tie existed previously, residence in a common urban neighborhood has led to bonds of fellowship and community that traditionally only were extended to members of the same clan or tribe. In Barakat's words, "What the tribe is to the Bedouin and the extended family is to the village, neighborhoods and institutions are to the city."[90]

This last point illustrates an important element of the bonds of group solidarity and loyalty in Arab society. Although the family and other kinship groups—clan and tribe—are the primary poles of loyalty, there is flexibility. Distant cousins, friends, classmates, workers, and neighbors can develop bonds of loyalty as strong as those between close family members. The old Arab saying, "My cousin and I against a stranger; my brother and I against my cousin," is often used to illustrate the progressive "circles" of kinship and loyalty. The proverb enjoins Arabs to remain loyal to their kin against non-kin, but also to remain loyal to nearer kin rather than more distant relations when intra-family disputes arise. However, another Arab proverb reminds, "Your near neighbor before your distant brother." This second saying indicates that the ties of loyalty, while most often extended to kin, are not meant exclusively for them. Rather, what is important is to extend loyalty to those most important to the individual's well-being—the people who make up the individual's primary support group. In many cases, friends, neighbors, and co-workers will fall into this category in addition to, or in some cases even as substitutes for, family members. For example, in his study of Saudi college students, Levon Melikian found that in Saudi society, "Expectations of support from other members of the family and dependence upon them are generalized to one's closest friends."[91]

Because folk wisdom has it that only bonds of kinship can truly be counted on for loyalty in times of duress, kinship ties are sometimes fabricated, denied, and manipulated as needed to accommodate social realities. In Nieuwenhuijze's words, "Under certain conditions, the self-perpetuating process of family life may broaden out somewhat and embrace people who are not kin."[92] Two people living together in the same city who become close may fabricate a kinship tie as an explanation for their closeness, and to some extent, to cement the relationship. Bedouin regularly alter genealogies and histories to show common ancestry between newly allied tribes, or to show that no kinship exists between new adversaries. For them, history is malleable and is made the servant of social and political needs.[93] Dale Eickelman relates that an ideological representation of tribal social organization is not necessarily based upon actual historical persons and is used primarily to explain contemporary social relationships. Ancestors not needed to provide links between actual groups are "forgotten," just as other linking forebears are "remembered" when realignments in present-day groups require the existence of a common ancestor to give form and legitimacy to their cooperation.[94]

There is a slightly different dynamic among individuals than among groups. In the Arab world, loyalty to other members of a group, particularly members of a primary group such as the family or clan, tends to be extremely strong. Because of the focus on the group as the primary actor, obligations of group members to one another are wide, varied, and extremely powerful. Hamady observes that Arabs are often slow to make friends, particularly by Western standards, but are more often willing to make extreme sacrifices for their friends for this reason.[95] According to Lutfiyya, in rural Jordan, "Loyalty to relatives is expected at all times and under all circumstances."[96] El-Hamamsy reports that the same belief was evident among urban Egyptians, who universally asserted that a salient characteristic of the typical urban Egyptian is that "He is deeply loyal to his kin and neighbors and is always there to help when needed."[97] Melikian found that these bonds extended to "cousins and uncles several steps removed," as well as "one's closest friends."[98]

The final point to note here is that when a corporate group is formed—either because it already existed because of blood ties, or it developed among a group of otherwise unrelated people—it takes on the general characteristics of the Arab family: a hierarchy with a leader who is to be obeyed, obligations among the members (and between the leader and the led), and strong ties of loyalty among the members. Such groups can form in a variety of places, and when they do, they tend to be very tight-knit. However, where no such "in-group" exists, many Arab populations tend to see less of a connection to one another than Westerners might, with few or no obligations or ties of loyalty. In short, group solidarity tends to be more stark in the Arab world than in the West. Where most Arabs feel themselves to be part of such an in-group, they tend to be more cohesive than a similar group of Westerners. Where such a "familial" in-group does not exist, then a group of Arabs often evinces less cohesion than a similar group of Westerners.[99]

Manipulation of Information

The dominant Arab culture places a premium on group loyalty and socially "correct" behavior. A failure to demonstrate loyalty, to respect obligations, and to act appropriately to others in all situations invites shame. In addition, the prioritization of loyalty described above typically enjoins the individual to place the needs of kin and friends ahead of responsibility to the abstract concept of "truth." Many experts have linked these tendencies with the powerful injunctions favoring conformism and obedience to authority.[100] They also invite conscious distortions, because to do otherwise would be shameful. While these traits have brought Arabs an unrivaled reputation for courtesy, loyalty, and hospitality, they are fostered at the expense of others. In particular, they contribute to a tendency to manipulate and compartmentalize information.[101]

One of the most commonly cited manifestations of such behavior comes in the form of saying "yes" when one really means "no." As Hamady bluntly states, "The Arab avoids a blunt refusal to any demand. He tries to get around the word 'no.'"[102] Because it would be shameful and impolite to tell a superior that something he or she has requested cannot be done, subordinates may agree to do things they recognize are impossible. "When the individual is unable to accomplish the task he will have no recourse available but to prevaricate, invent excuses, or fail to appear."[103] In a study found of US educators who had taught Arab students, the professors indicated that Arab students often evinced a much higher rate of cheating than their American counterparts because to refuse to help a classmate was considered shameful among the Arab students.[104] In situations where something bad has befallen an individual, the tremendous aversion to shame may produce tendencies to exaggerate the obstacles the individual encountered when attempting to perform the deed.[105]

Another, related manifestation is reflected in the Arabic term *taqiyyah*, which means dissembling, and refers to when it is permissible to lie according to the Shari'a. In particular, it refers to the denial of certain feelings and beliefs to avoid persecution.[106] In this, it has come to be associated with Shi'ism and the widespread notion that Shi'a readily practice *taqiyyah* to avoid persecution by the majority Sunnis.

Fear of dishonor also contributes to tendencies toward secrecy and compartmentalization of knowledge. Shame attaches only when the sin becomes public. "The public aspect is essential for shame; the loss of '*ird* (personal honor, including for female chastity) is a judgment of the public. . . . 'Shame is not when someone's daughter has illicit sexual relations; the shame is when it is public knowledge that she has had illicit sexual relations.' Families, of course, do their best to keep misbehavior secret, but in face-to-face communities this is very difficult."[107] Several highly regarded studies on the subject have concluded that many, perhaps most, cases of female sexual infidelity are not punished with murder and often with mild or no punishment at all. Women are typically only punished if the indiscretion becomes public, or is expected to become public.[108]

In order to conceal mistakes that would result in shame, features of Arab culture encourage the individual to exaggerate, lie, and/or remain secretive. They also encourage the family or other in-group to help conceal the transgression. In her study of Egyptian families, Rugh found that "The villain for the individual Egyptian is almost always perceived as an outside aggressor rather than the Egyptian himself, his failings, or the failings of someone of his committed inner circle. This allows projection of problems on outside others rather than on introspective self-doubts or vital group members. The greater good requires that these kinds of deceptions be sustained by everyone concerned lest the solidarity of the group be threatened."[109] Hamady cites several Arab proverbs in this vein: "He who has done a shameful deed must conceal it for revealing one disgrace is another disgrace" and "A concealed sin is two-thirds forgiven."[110] Raymond Cohen encapsulates this cultural pattern in the following passage:

> Loss of face, to be shamed before one's peers, is an excruciating penalty which one seeks to avoid at all costs. Once again, child-rearing practices condition the individual from an early age to acute awareness of the norm. Punishment is administered in public and intensified by deliberate belittlement or ridicule. The humiliation is worse than the pain or the admonition itself. The effect of the punishment, one may conclude, is not simply to discourage misbehavior as such but to inculcate an abiding aversion to being disgraced in front of the group. In effect, the child is taught that the penalty for wrong-doing is public disgrace rather than a sense of personal remorse. He is conditioned, therefore, to escape humiliation as much as sin. Since shame results from being found out and ridiculed, it can be avoided as well by concealment as by rectitude.[111]

Sharabi notes the same behavior, observing that "In practice, shame ('Ayb) is what 'people say' (shu bi'ulu n-nas). The implication is clear: what people do not see or hear is all right. This is not merely to distinguish what one does and what one ought to do; it involves an attitude of concealment."[112] Likewise, in her study of the slums of Cairo, Unni Wikan notes that poor Egyptians believed that "The best protection for a man is to practice information control—by keeping other people at arm's length—and by 'stopping friends/acquaintances coming to your home.' Each visit offers the guest the possibility of going out and revealing the family's secrets, saying that 'the furniture was ugly, the wife was ugly, etc.' "[113] One Saudi college student in Melikian's study explained that "Every person has two characters, one he displays in public, the other in his private life. Thus when given a chance to do things that are forbidden by religion (without being exposed) one does not force himself not to do it."[114]

The fear of shame generates great pressure to shift blame for even the most routine errors. Because being at fault is considered so dishonorable, there is a powerful incentive to shift responsibility for problems away from oneself—and often from close friends or relatives—and to distort or even falsify to serve this purpose. Barakat comments that within the ubiquitous Arab social hierarchies, "upward communication may be accompanied by crying, self-censorship, obfuscation, and deception."[115] The Lebanese psychiatrist Haig Katchadourian concluded that the fear of dishonor often leads to such evasion and subterfuge that an individual's adopted "mask" becomes indistinguishable from his true self because the individual tends to lose track of the distinction.[116]

Finally, this same set of cultural pressures also make self-criticism exceptionally difficult in the Arab world.[117] Time and again, American military advisors and trainers in Iraq, Egypt, Jordan, Saudi Arabia, and elsewhere in the Arab world have been frustrated by the unwillingness of their charges to engage in honest appraisals of their own conduct—either individually or in groups. This is problematic because it is critical to proper learning. If a soldier or unit cannot recognize his/its mistakes and then learn how to correct them, there is little hope that he/they ever will improve. I can certainly remember sessions I attended at Iraqi training ranges in 2005–2011 where getting the Iraqis to admit to even one thing they could have done better was like trying to get blood from the proverbial stone.

Atomization of Knowledge

Some Middle East scholars have used the term "atomization of knowledge" to describe a tendency among Arab populations to see knowledge as a grouping of discrete details without acknowledging the connections between those details. It is an over-attention to parts, "without integrating them into a composite and well-organized whole."[118] Bernard Lewis refers to the "Tendency to view life and the universe as a series of static, concrete, and disjunct entities, loosely linked in a sort of mechanical or even casual association by circumstances or by the mind of an individual, but having no organic interrelation of their own."[119] Lewis believes this perspective leads many Arabs to view knowledge as composed of distinct, unrelated elements. Many do not see disciplines of knowledge as related and overlapping, but as "Separate and self-contained compartments holding a finite number of pieces of knowledge, the progressive accumulation of which constitutes learning."[120] Lewis specifically applies this problem to traditional Arabic literature, which "achieves its effects by a series of separate observations or characterizations, minute and vivid, but fragmentary, linked by the subjective associations of author and reader, rarely by an overriding plan."[121] The result of this tendency is a greater difficulty moving from the specific to the general and grasping the whole as more than the sum of its parts.

This tendency has been noted by a number of other Middle East experts as well, starting with Lewis's nemesis, Edward Said:

> It isn't knowledge as a product or commodity that we need; nor is it a matter of remedying the situation by having bigger libraries, a greater number of terminals, computers and so forth, but a qualitatively different knowledge based on understanding rather than on authority, uncritical repetition, mechanical reproduction. It is not facts, but how facts are connected to other facts, how they are constructed, whether they relate to hypothesis or theory, how one is to judge the relationship between truth and interest, how to understand reality as history. These are only some of the critical issues we face, which can be summed up in the phrase/question, how to think?[122]

Morroe Berger has likewise observed that Arab philosophy is characterized by an "inability to take a complete, organic view of human experience," and that "Arab Moslem civilization has emphasized structure, repetition, and perfection in detail at the expense of meaning, originality, and the joining of parts into a related unity."[123] Similarly, Manfred Halpern approvingly cites H. A. R. Gibbs's remark regarding the "Atomism and discreteness of the Arab imagination."[124] To make the same point, Hamady notes that it is common in Arab poetry for the author to describe details with "inimitable poignancy," but to fail to portray the entirety of the person or object, while Arab folk tales "show no consistency of sentiment or content, lacking organic continuity, they are a mere 'string of episodes.' "[125] In a 1960 study of Jordanian civil servants, Jamil Jreisat found that they were preoccupied with "small and routine matters, but were unable to even suggest answers to the larger bureaucratic issues facing their departments."[126]

More recently, Alexander Abdennur has written extensively on what he calls the Arab tendency toward "isolating" information and knowledge, divorcing one aspect of a thing from its whole, or isolating like things and considering them separate and unrelated.[127] As part of this, he describes a tendency among Arabs toward the "breakdown of a configuration into its constituent parts, with each part treated as a discrete entity in isolation from other parts of the whole."[128] He goes on to describe what he sees as a tendency among Arabs to "split" knowledge: "The process involves separating aspects of a unit from one another and perceiving or reacting to them as distinct entities. The individual also fails to reunite the split parts when needed."[129] Likewise, Tarek Heggy has argued that this tendency to see differences rather than connections contributes to difficulties that Arabs have in acting as part of a team and subordinating their egos to it.[130]

Closely related to the atomization of knowledge, and in part an outgrowth of it, is the difficulty that many Arabs experience with interdisciplinary subjects. A rigid teaching style that relies on rote memorization and the tendency to atomize knowledge hinders many Arabs in seeing relationships between seemingly disparate subjects. As one manifestation of this proclivity, the 1979 RAND report cited multiple studies of Arab and American students in which the Arabs scored significantly higher in vocabulary tests than they did in tests based on analogies. The vocabulary tests basically measured the ability to memorize information, whereas the analogy tests measured the ability to generalize.[131] The 2002 and 2003 Arab Human Development Reports focused on the same set of problems, warning that "Arabic thought has refrained from engaging with multidisciplinary issues, which are of great importance within the knowledge society. For example, Arab philosophical thought, especially in theology and philosophy, has been isolated from other disciplines, despite the marked attention paid by traditional scholastic theology, philosophy, and traditional jurisprudence to language, concepts, and terminology."[132]

Personal Courage

Within the dominant Arab culture, an important element of a man's honor is his courage. "Manliness" is a highly regarded commodity in the Arab world. Manliness includes injunctions to come to the aid of family and friends no matter what the circumstances, an element of the obligations of members of a group to one another. Of equal importance are notions of personal bravery and a willingness to bear extreme hardships. Maxime Rodinson refers to a "cult of honor" that includes strength, material or moral power, courage, and the "capacity and the will to defend the independence of the group and the chastity and freedom of its women."[133] In a similar fashion, El-Hamamsy points to the values of *shahamah*—gallantry, boldness, nobility—as well as *muruwwah*—courage, fierce loyalty to one's kin, generosity and hospitality—both of which are synonymous with manliness.[134]

Numerous sociologists—as well as casual observers—have noted that the ideals of courage exert a considerable influence on the actual behavior of Arab men. In his comprehensive assessment of the cultural psychology of the Arab world, Gary Gregg writes that the "vigilance and courage of its teenaged boys is a source of (a family's) strength." It is an important aspect of a family's honor, and he argues that it inspires physical bravery in boys in the same way that it inspires modesty in girls.[135] Along with group cohesion and honor, Mansur Khalid includes endurance, in the form of self-control and physical and moral discipline, as one of the three values most important to Arab society.[136] El-Sayyid Yassin has similarly cited "patience and perseverance in the face of hardship" as a defining trait of the culturally regular Egyptian persona.[137]

Themes of the need for toughness and personal courage pervade the various studies of Arab village life in Egypt by Hamed Ammar, in Iraq by Phebe Marr, and in Jordan by Richard Antoun and Abdulla Lutfiyya.[138] The same themes are echoed—albeit in subtly different forms—in the work of Nawal Nadim and Unni Wikan on urban populations in Egypt.[139] Finally, John Bagot Glubb (who built and commanded Jordan's Arab Legion) wrote with characteristic enthusiasm that "With the Arabs in particular, it is vital to remember the existence of a capacity for passionate and heroic courage concealed beneath their everyday venality. . . . All of a sudden appears a cause or a leader possessing the flaming quality which can inspire the exalted courage that lies hidden deep in the Arab character. Suddenly they throw away money in disgust or exaltation, and develop a courage which staggers, if it does not sweep away, their astonished opponents."[140]

Ambivalence toward Manual Labor and Technical Work

The last pattern of culturally regular behavior I want to raise is also the trickiest. This is how Arab society values technical work and manual labor. There is a consensus within the scholarly literature that Arab culture evinces a disdain for both. Moreover, the educational practices of the Arab world (discussed in greater length in Chapter 20) demonstrate unequivocal flaws in scientific and technical teaching that reflect a disregard for the scientific method and critical scientific concepts. However, a number of other commentators, and a variety of other facts suggest that, at the very least, many Arabs have no choice but to engage in menial labor, and many do see technical degrees such as medicine and engineering as quite prestigious. It's not impossible to reconcile these disparate tendencies, but it requires some effort.

In the anthropological, sociological, and cultural psychological literature on the Arab world there is an undeniable consensus that Arab society, as it developed over the centuries, came to see manual labor as dishonorable.[141] "There is a common and very deep-seated feeling that manual or rural forms of work mean drudgery and nothing more; that furthermore, there is an element of degradation in them, so that they must be avoided by all and any means," according to John Gulick.[142] Gellner observes that the crafts of most artisans, such as blacksmiths and dyers, are "morally suspect," and Arabs have tended to leave such occupations to foreigners.[143] In Abdennur's words, "Manual work or crafts came to be called *mihnat*, which is derived from *mahanet* or humiliation."[144] Berger noted that "The prejudice against technology and engineering is still intense and the attraction of clerical work, administration, and law very strong."[145] Fahim Qubain said of technical and vocational training in the Arab world, "For untold generations a strong prejudice has existed throughout the Middle East against hard work. It was regarded as undignified, degrading, and menial. . . . With the gradual rise of industry, the disdainful attitude toward vocational training and manual labor has begun to wane, but it is still very much in evidence."[146]

Obviously, many cultures consider manual labor to be a less desirable occupation than white-collar work, but there were two facets of Arab culture's treatment that bear on our inquiry. The first is that traditional Arab culture's disdain for manual labor appears stronger than most. The second is that technical and scientific work more broadly were lumped in as forms of manual labor because they were seen as "working with one's hands." Perhaps not surprisingly, a number of studies found that Arab populations were often willing to sacrifice material benefits (including better pay) to avoid taking a job considered as "manual labor."[147] For instance, an Egyptian government study from the 1990s found that Egyptian children were very reluctant to go into technical occupations. They sought out white-collar jobs over blue-collar jobs, "even though the latter type of occupation provided more opportunities, better pay and promotion."[148] Likewise, a former personnel adviser to the Iraqi Petroleum Company remembered that "While Iraqi oilfield laborers were eager to educate their children, they were reluctant to have them learn technical skills which were in *tremendous* demand and therefore offered very significant material rewards."[149] Bowen and Early found that in the Arab countries, "While white-collar jobs may bring prestige, skilled and unskilled labor are in higher demand and in many cases bring higher salaries than do positions as clerks, professionals, and bureaucrats."[150] Meanwhile, the World Bank has repeatedly warned that too much of the workforce of the Arab states is concentrated in the public sector, too much of the small private-sector work force is foreign, and too much of the population is either unemployed or out of the workforce altogether.[151]

A number of authors argue that Islam, as it has come to be taught—although not necessarily as it was originally conceived—has worked against the spread of rationalism and technical knowledge. This has translated into the teaching of science by rote memorization with little attention to scientific methods of inquiry in many Arab primary and secondary schools. Pervez Hoodbhoy despairs that "Although Muslims form one-fifth of the world's population, they are barely noticeable in the world of scientific research, and Muslim countries are the most abjectly dependent among developing countries upon Western technology and know-how."[152] Indeed, no less a scholar than Albert Hourani has written that in the dramatic expansion of education following independence in the 1950s, "there was a tendency to concentrate on academic education which would lead to government service or the liberal professions," because "the use of the hands as well as the mind, was alien to the concept of education" in Islamic culture.[153] Tarek Heggy echoes the notion that this trend is a product of the twentieth century: before independence, few Arabs could afford the education and idleness of a government job, but post-independence, the establishment of public education and government guarantees of public-sector jobs for all college graduates suddenly made this a viable option for huge numbers of people.[154]

Of course, a great many Arabs have been forced by economic necessity to swallow their pride and engage in manual labor. However, because the middle and upper classes of Arab society could afford the luxury of pride, their children—who were more likely to become officers in Arab militaries than those of the lower classes—tended to opt for careers in more prestigious, nontechnical fields during the twentieth century. The cultural anthropologist Unni Wikan writes that "from the time they are small, children will say they are going to school to become a *muwazzaf(a)* (a government employee)."[155] Indeed, until very recently, Arab students generally showed little interest in pursuing further studies in engineering or the sciences. Arab law schools, however, overflowed with applicants.[156] Constantine Zurayk bemoaned an "absence of a scientific spirit and a predominance of literary concerns in intellectual life," in Arab society.[157] Joseph Jabbra also observed this phenomenon, remarking that "For a long period of time and for cultural and cost reasons, the Arab world has neglected technical fields of study. This situation has resulted in a shortage of qualified technical people and a surplus of people in the social sciences and the humanities."[158] To place this trait in a quantitative context, in 1979, Mohamed Rabie found that 50 percent of all university graduates in the Arab world were in the humanities or law, "leaving Arab societies in dire need of expertise in almost all technical fields."[159] Similarly, the 1979 RAND study noted that few of the Arab students who studied abroad pursued scientific or technical education.[160]

Nevertheless, there was an important counter trend, by which many other families, particularly from the lower and lower-middle classes, viewed technical subjects such as engineering and medicine as pathways to social and economic advancement. This was especially true when secular, autocratic regimes such as Nasser's in Egypt and Saddam's in Iraq took power and saw technical education as a way to catch up to the modern world. The problem then was that the desire for more doctors and engineers did not necessarily translate into better scientific and mathematical education, with the result that there was a significant increase in people with technical degrees, many of whom lacked the full range of skills their degrees supposedly conferred.[161]

The result has been a widely observed dearth of high-quality scientific work from the Arab world. In a 1980 study, *Science and Science Policy in the Arab World*, A. B. Zahlan presented a compelling argument that the Arab world produced fewer trained scientists and engineers than other regions of commensurate wealth and development and, of greatest importance, these scientists and engineers produced far less *quality* work than their colleagues elsewhere in the world. For example, Zahlan noted that on a per capita basis, Arab scientific contributions (measured in terms of numbers of scientists publishing in scientific journals per year) were 1 percent of the Israeli contribution in 1980. Likewise, Zahlan argued that based on the global average, the 7,000 scientists and engineers in the Arab world in 1973 should have produced between 8,000 and 14,000 papers that year, but they actually produced only 847. He concluded, "No matter what method is utilized to assess the productivity of scientific workers, the gap between what is actually produced and what is to be expected from the research and development manpower and the academic staff of existing institutions is exceedingly large."[162] Zahlan also condemned the quality of what little scientific work is published in the Arab world: "The work reported in the basic sciences is actually poor and limited in scope. . . . Most of the work is relatively dull and routine, and seems to be out of touch with activity and progress elsewhere. The pages of most of the professional journals attest to the notable absence of scientific contributions from Arab institutions."[163]

This same issue has been a principal alarm sounded by the UN's Arab Human Development project, which published the six Arab Human Development Reports (AHDRs) between 2002 and 2016. These have warned that in recent decades, the Middle East has been on a par with sub-Saharan Africa in its production of scientific and technical articles in journals and patent applications by residents.[164] Between 1980 and 2000 Israel, with a population less than one-tenth that of Egypt's, registered nearly 100 times as many patents. During that period, Israel registered 44 times as many patents as Saudi Arabia.[165] For 270 million Arabic speakers, "the usual published number of any given novel or short story collection ranges between 1,000 and 3,000 copies. A book that sells 5,000 copies is considered a bestseller."[166] The 2003 AHDR concluded, "Innovative capabilities can, however, be gauged by demonstrating the widespread presence of innovations in national and foreign markets that can be counted and evaluated. On that criterion, there are virtually no Arab innovations on the market, a fact that confirms that Arab scientific research has not yet reached the innovation stage."[167]

Since the turn of the millennium, a new generation of Arab students has shown a greater interest in technical subjects, suggesting that the disdain of traditional Arab culture is losing its hold. Globalization and modernity are proving to be powerful transformative agents, as they have everywhere. But the great question facing the Arab world is whether its educational systems can be transformed, as King Abdallah of Saudi Arabia tried with his efforts to reform Saudi curricula and his founding of King Abdallah University of Science and Technology. It is a process that the United Arab Emirates, Qatar, and now with greater determination, Saudi Arabia, have all embraced in years, but that have so far borne mixed results.[168] Yet it is a shift that will be critical to the future of the region, and would represent a major change to the behavioral patterns emphasized by the dominant culture.

CHAPTER 18

Arab Culture and Arab Military
Effectiveness

I HOPE THAT by now the relationship between the patterns of behavior
emphasized by the dominant Arab culture and the patterns of behavior
evinced by Arab armed forces in combat since 1945 is starting to become
clear. It is striking how much the Arab armies and air forces have performed
in keeping with those patterns of culturally regular behavior identified by
anthropologists, sociologists, cultural psychologists, and other experts on Arab
society. It is easy to match these cultural predilections with the problems (and
some of the strengths) manifested by Arab militaries time and again during
the modern era.

Matching Patterns

It is hard to imagine that the general cultural injunctions in favor of conformity at the expense of creativity and innovation aren't producing the same
general phenomena experienced by Arab military units. It appears self-evident
that the promotion of conformity at the expense of innovation, adherence to
traditional patterns of behavior, and the fear of deviating from those patterns
of behavior that are important facets of the dominant Arab culture are what is
dampening innovation and encouraging dogmatic adherence to tactical doctrine. It is entirely consistent with these cultural patterns that Arab tactical
units would have difficulty reacting, counterattacking, reorienting themselves,

or otherwise adapting to unforeseen developments on the battlefield, such as when their defensive lines have been penetrated by an adversary.

The fear of shame evinced by Arabs in daily life and the concomitant belief that to do nothing is better than to risk doing something wrong, appear perfectly correlated with the remarkable passivity, especially among subordinates, demonstrated by modern Arab armed forces. This tendency toward passivity within the patriarchal hierarchies of Arab society unquestionably contributed to—and may have wholly produced—the widespread dearth of initiative evinced by Arab military personnel, which worsened as one moved lower in the chain of command. Enlisted personnel and junior officers acted as the subordinates in a traditional Arab patriarchal hierarchy, and so it is not surprising that they were so consistently passive while general officers, as the "patriarchs," were more willing to try to take advantage of opportunities. Similarly, in accordance with the cultural patterns, decisions in Arab armies typically had to be referred up to the highest levels of command, which badly slowed the pace of operations and meant that Arab tactical formations were often reluctant to act on their own in response to the vicissitudes of combat by counterattacking, reorienting, shifting forces, or exploiting opportunities.

Of course, the heavy injunctions against taking initiative by low- and mid-level personnel were interwoven with the cultural preference for heavily centralized hierarchies, both of which combine to furnish an obvious explanation for the rigidity and inflexibility of Arab militaries. Although the perverse civil-military relations of most Arab states may have played a role in this tendency toward over-centralization, the cultural tendencies of Arab society were at least as important if not more—the fact that the heavily politicized Argentine, Chinese, Cuban, North Korean, and South Vietnamese armies did not experience the same problems strongly suggests that it was far more Arab culture than politicization. Moreover, Arab militaries experienced the same over-centralization regardless of the political system they employed, or the degree of internal threat their leadership faced.

The same tendencies to avoid giving offense and to shift blame through secrecy, exaggeration, deception, or dissembling mimic the poor transmission of information along the chain of command displayed by one Arab military after another. As the cultural predilections would predict, Arab subordinates demonstrated a tendency to conceal, mislead, and even lie to their superiors about failures and reversals. At the same time, and again entirely consistent with the patterns of the dominant culture, superiors in Arab military chains of command were routinely reluctant to provide information to subordinates, preferring to retain the control that more extensive information bestowed.

These patterns together also appear to explain the unwillingness and inability of Arab armed forces to employ maneuver, especially at tactical levels. Maneuver is an inherently creative act requiring action on the part of an officer. The use of maneuver on the battlefield to gain an advantage over the adversary requires that the commander be able to imagine circumstances different from his present situation, one in which he has an advantage over his enemy derived from a different spatial arrangement. It demands that the commander quickly develop an operational plan that will allow him to place his forces into the newly imagined, spatially advantageous position, and that anticipates the likely reactions of his adversary. And it requires that he take action to make that imagined situation a reality. Given the cultural injunctions against creative behavior, initiative, and even flexibility in Arab hierarchies, it is not hard to recognize that maneuver, especially tactical maneuver conducted by junior officers, would be a major challenge for Arab militaries. Again, it is not at all surprising to find that Arab armies and air forces made so little use of maneuver, especially at tactical levels, in war after war. Men taught not to act creatively, not to imagine things differently from how they are, and not to take action but to wait for orders probably would not easily take to the idea of attempting to purposely create a new situation—even one that might be helpful to themselves. Indeed, the idea of altering the situation through maneuver probably wouldn't occur to them at all.

This same combination of proclivities, as well as the difficulties with efficient information management driven by Arab cultural preferences, would also appear to explain why Arab armies had such difficulty with ad hoc operations—but also why they did much better when conducting set-piece operations. Ad hoc operations are the very definition of flexibility for any military. What's more, on the battlefield, they require commanders from top-to-bottom able to think quickly, fill in gaps, communicate clearly, seize opportunities, intuit the right move in circumstances where they may not have clear orders, and then take action to accomplish it. All of this appears to run directly contrary to Arab cultural norms.

On the other hand, set-piece operations that can be planned and rehearsed ahead of time would appear to lend themselves much better to people conditioned to this manner of behavior. Moreover, while poor information flows are always a problem for any military operation, they are far less damaging for set-piece operations, when the high command should have the opportunity to rely on its own intelligence collection and analysis assets to gather the needed information prior to the start of the operation rather than having to rely on combat reports from front-line commanders in the midst of the battle.

The manner in which Arab culture compartmentalizes knowledge (its "atomization") and the difficulties with interdisciplinary subjects that flow from it seems like an obvious explanation for the consistent problems that Arab militaries have shown with combined arms (and joint) operations. Combined arms operations require the integration of knowledge from widely disparate fields (from infantry operations, armor operations, air operations, etc.) and the ability to intellectually integrate the interactions of these different forces. In effect, combined arms operations are the military's equivalent of an interdisciplinary subject. Understanding combined arms requires not only understanding the capabilities and missions of each combat arm, but more importantly, understanding their interaction. It isn't surprising that some Arab officers were aware of the need for combined arms coordination, or that so many of them were still unable to implement the concept properly. Although laborious efforts by command staffs were able to produce better combined arms integration in a small number of Arab set-piece operations, it is noteworthy and predictable that in every case, once the plan broke down because of unforeseen circumstances, the combined arms cooperation came apart with it.

To a great extent, these problems taken together explain why Arab militaries have experienced such tremendous difficulties conducting fluid, mobile operations, with disastrous results in war after war. To fight effectively on a modern, fluid battlefield, an army must show good use of tactical maneuver, an ability to quickly and easily shift forces and artillery fire, as well as an ability to improvise and immediately exploit fleeting opportunities. In addition, the rapid pace of modern operations and the transient nature of engagements demand a smooth, rapid flow of information and the delegation of authority to the lowest levels of command to ensure those who are "at the point of the spear" are responsible for decision-making and have all the information they need to make the best decisions. Finally, junior officers, the mid-level managers of modern war, are crucial to maneuver warfare, because in fluid combat, decisions must be made by the local commanders on the spot. Thus, passive, unimaginative junior officers tend to make maneuver warfare impossible. Because Arab armies have shown enormous difficulty in all of these various categories of military performance, and because these are critical components of effective mobile operations, it is only to be expected that Arab armies would experience tremendous difficulty conducting mobile, maneuver warfare exactly as they have, time and again.

The same problems with maneuver, initiative, creativity, flexibility, and communication—plus an ambivalence toward technical subjects—also furnish a powerful explanation for the consistent problems that Arab air forces have experienced, particularly in air-to-air combat and air-to-ground operations.

Success in dogfighting requires that pilots have tremendous independence and confidence in their decision-making. A pilot must be willing and able to constantly and instantaneously re-examine her situation and decide on the best course of action. Similar to the problems to be expected of maneuver on the ground, air-to-air combat requires the imagination to constantly conceive of possible alternative spatial arrangements, and the willingness to act quickly and decisively to create favorable situations. In addition, in air-to-air combat, it is crucial for the pilot to fully understand the capabilities of his aircraft and weaponry so that he can take full advantage of their capabilities and avoid their weaknesses. Clearly, personnel who have had little exposure to machinery and do not have a grasp of the basic mechanics involved in air warfare are unlikely to get full advantage of their planes and weapons, so underdevelopment probably played a role here as well. Yet, the constant deference to a rigid hierarchy suggests that the overreliance on GCI is neither accidental nor the fault of the Soviets/Russians, but a culturally comfortable routine. The fact that pilots in such systems (such as the Syrians, Libyans, and Iraqis) were unable and unwilling to fight for themselves when GCI was cut further reinforces the point.

The same considerations largely hold true for air-to-ground operations as well. Especially in the era before remote sensors and precision-guided munitions, it was a rarity when a pilot could count on having ample intelligence on a target, a detailed mission plan, and precision-guided munitions that made it unnecessary for him to do anything but launch the weapon—not to mention a flight so uneventful that he needed to do nothing but execute the plan. Almost invariably, intelligence on a target was incomplete or inaccurate, the mission order was more a general course of action than a precise flight plan, and the weapons being employed demanded that the pilot maneuver the aircraft into an advantageous launch position and then select a target or aimpoint upon arrival at the target area. In short, before the current era—and even today for air forces that lack the latest technology—the success of an air-to-ground mission depends on the ability of the pilot to understand the nature of the mission, the capabilities of her aircraft and weapons, what targets would be most valuable to the strategic plan, what targets would be most vulnerable to her weaponry, and the best way to bring those weapons to bear against the target. In addition, an air strike, like a dogfight, requires the pilot to maneuver his aircraft to accommodate these competing considerations and a high degree of creativity and aggressiveness on the part of the pilot to adjust for problems and still accomplish the mission. Once again, personnel with little familiarity with machinery, a tendency to refrain from innovating or taking initiative, and a tendency to concentrate on details to the neglect of the larger picture could only be expected to have difficulty conducting successful air strikes.

Just as a number of traits combine to explain Arab difficulties in maneuver war, so do a number of the traits of the dominant Arab culture help explain why Arab armies enjoyed somewhat better performance in static, defensive operations. For starters, static defensive operations place the least demand on those areas of military effectiveness in which Arab militaries have experienced the greatest difficulty (consistent with the predilections of the dominant Arab culture). A static defense requires less initiative and innovation from junior commanders because the stationary nature of the fighting, the slower pace of operations, and the clearer delineation between attacking and defending forces should allow senior commanders to keep greater control over the course of the battle without hindering the operations of their forces. While rapid, accurate transmission of information is always important, it is less so for static defense because there is less movement, defense lines are better defined, there is less intermingling between attacking and defending forces, less information is needed by the defender, and the defender's commander is more likely to be able to dispatch trusted aides to gather the information he requires. Static defenses also alleviate a number of other problems consistent with Arab cultural patterns: artillery can be preregistered and fire-missions pre-planned, there is less need for units to maneuver, and tanks can even be dug-in and employed more like armored antitank weapons. Again, although it would be better to employ maneuver and use armor and artillery flexibly even in support of static defensive operations, success in these missions relies on those skills less than other types of combat operations.

Strengths Derived from Arab Cultural Patterns

Even though the main purpose of this book is to understand why Arab militaries have tended to underperform in combat since 1945, it is still important to note how aspects of Arab culture appear to have contributed to some of the strengths evinced by those same armed forces. That's important both because it is worthwhile to understand that the Arabs were not unmitigated disasters and because the cultural patterns appear to explain at least some of these areas of strength, something that the other explanations mostly don't. That should give us further confidence that the cultural patterns are exerting a major influence on Arab military performance, bad *and* good.

Unit cohesion seems like the best place to start. As I discussed in Chapter 1, and noted in many of the subsequent historical examples, Arab armies evinced fairly uneven unit cohesion during the modern era. At times it was disastrously bad, but in other instances it was remarkably good. Moreover, the differences tended to be within Arab armies waging specific battles, not across them or differing from war to war. Whether it was the Egyptians, Jordanians, and Syrians during the War of Israeli Independence or the Six-Day War, the Iraqis during the Iran-Iraq and Persian Gulf Wars, or the Libyans in Chad, cohesion varied dramatically from unit to unit within these armies during these wars. Some units melted away on first contact with the enemy while their neighbors fought like lions even after they were surrounded.

The predilections emphasized by the dominant Arab culture offers a cogent explanation for this phenomenon. The consensus among Middle East experts appears to be that Arab interpersonal bonds tend more toward the extremes (at least when implicitly compared with Westerners): Arabs tend to feel greater loyalty and obligation to friends, relatives, and others with whom they have clear in-group ties, but feel considerably less attachment or obligation to those with whom they are unable to make such a link. That is most often true when there is kinship or other preexisting bonds among them. However, many of the experts have noted that the kind of loyalty normally associated with kinship can be extended to friends, coworkers, and neighbors, and so we should expect that it can also apply to the other members of a soldier's unit. It seems relatively straightforward to imagine that in many cases platoon-buddies, wingmen, squadron-mates, and fellow crew-members could become extremely close. There is no reason to believe that an entire unit could *not* take on the characteristics of an Arab primary group (effectively an extended family) in the manner that many Middle East experts have noted that offices, institutions, clubs, and other groups do. In these instances, we should expect Arab units to continue to fight as a cohesive unit under extreme pressures, likely even in situations where military formations from other cultures would disintegrate.

The other side of the coin would also appear to be true. Although military units obviously could take on the dynamics of such a primary group, there is no reason they have to. Extrapolating from the experiences of businesses, universities, factories, and other civilian organizations, it would appear that the role of the leader is very important—whether he (or conceivably she) acts the way that a "good" Arab leader is expected to act, honoring the obligations that work in both directions of Arab primary groups. If such an in-group does not emerge in a military unit, again the modal behavioral patterns of the dominant culture would suggest that soldiers in such groups might feel even less loyalty to their comrades and officers than is the case in other armies. Whenever that happens, we would expect that the unit would likely disintegrate under even light enemy pressure. An anecdotal study by the US Army War College of Iraqi soldiers after the 2003

US invasion of Iraq demonstrated that strong unit cohesion was typically a product of tribal or regional ties among Iraqi soldiers in a formation. Where those were present, Iraqi units evinced some degree of cohesion; when they weren't there was little to none.[1] Thus, Arab culture offers a powerful argument for the highly uneven unit cohesion demonstrated by Arab armies since 1945.

One last point on the positive side: contrary to the slander that Arabs were cowards in battle, quite a few demonstrated extraordinary bravery, from the Jordanian defenders of Latrun in 1948 to the Iraqi Republican Guards in the battle of the Wadi al-Batin in 1991. Moreover, there was no pattern of Arab soldiers systematically abandoning the fight. If anything, especially given their poor performance in most battles, Arab soldiers evinced higher than normal levels of personal bravery. Remembering the emphasis that aspects of the dominant Arab culture places on male courage, this is not terribly surprising.

Mixed Evidence: Technical Subjects

Then there is a set of military topics where Arab military history only conformed partially to what we would expect given the predilections of the dominant culture. These are the elements of military operations related to technical matters: maintenance, logistics, engineering, and the ability of personnel to properly employ the machinery of war. In some ways, Arab experiences in combat did mirror cultural patterns, but in other ways they did not. That said, in these same areas, they did not perform exactly the way that we would expect if underdevelopment were the problem either. In fact, both underdevelopment and Arab cultural patterns were probably both working to produce bad performance in these areas, making it even more striking that Arab militaries often did quite well, at least with some of them.

Maintenance has been a consistent problem among the Arab armed forces in the modern era, as I discussed in Chapters 1 and 11. Arab militaries just never understood the need to perform regular maintenance on their equipment, and too few of their personnel actually knew what to do, with the result that the operational readiness rates of Arab formations have been consistently poor. In similar fashion, every Arab military had considerable difficulty assimilating new weaponry and getting their personnel to take full advantage of the capabilities of their equipment. They got more out of simpler pieces of equipment than with more complex weapons; Egyptians and Syrians flying MiG-19s and -21s were more dangerous opponents in their day than Syrians and Iraqis flying MiG-29s in later years. All of this squares perfectly with both the cultural ambivalence toward technical work and the lack of familiarity with machines that is common to underdeveloped societies. Again, some combination of both was probably at work in these areas.

However, where Arab military performance defied all expectations was in the areas of logistics and combat engineering. In the words of Lt. General Gus Pagonis, the chief American quartermaster for Operation DESERT STORM, "Logistics involves getting your hands dirty."[2] Logistics means moving forces, moving supplies to the forces, and making sure that there are sufficient supplies available for operations. Much of what is required to make logistics work falls into the realm of technical work and even manual labor, or close to it. Consequently, you would expect that the disdain for such work inherent in traditional Arab culture would mean that many Arab personnel would find logistics an unpleasant and undesirable task and would leave it to those least worthy of combat positions. Particularly among officers, you would expect that only those unfit for the highly coveted combat commands or other prestigious posts would end up in the logistical services. The end result should have been pretty dreadful logistical capabilities.

In the same fashion, you would expect that an aversion to manual labor and technical work would also mean that few Arabs would want to serve in their armies' corps of engineers, and that the skills of those who did find themselves in engineer units would be low. Since Arab culture creates disincentives for students to pursue scientific interests and hampers the teaching of basic technical skills (discussed in Chapter 20), you would expect that Arab armies would find it difficult to field sizable numbers of competent engineers.

But Arab military history has consistently demonstrated the exact opposite. Only the Syrians and the Iraqis *after* the fall of Saddam have had real problems with logistics. Most Arab militaries did fine with logistics and engineering. Some performed superbly in these areas, particularly the Iraqis and Libyans, as I discussed in Chapter 11.

In both of these areas, actual Arab experiences were far better than what you would have expected based on either the predilections of Arab culture or how underdevelopment has affected other militaries. The fact that Arab armies still demonstrated the expected problems with maintenance and weapons handling should reassure us that both the culturally driven and economically driven problems were present. Yet the unexpectedly good performance of Arab logisticians and engineers should make us suspect that, at least in these limited areas, something else was going on that helped out Arab armies—something that could not help them in other areas of military effectiveness.[3]

The Big Picture

Clearly, the patterns of behavior emphasized by the dominant Arab culture mesh perfectly with the most important patterns of military problems evinced by Arab armed forces since 1945. In particular, their problems with tactical leadership, maneuver warfare, combined arms operations, air operations, and information management are easily explained by well-understood patterns of culturally regular behavior. Reading the cultural anthropological, sociological, and cultural psychological work on Arab society, it feels like it was purposely written to explain the problems that Arab militaries have experienced on the modern battlefield.

There is something else that we can usefully conclude at this point about the effects of Arab cultural patterns, politicization, and underdevelopment. That is that they have their greatest impact on different parts of the chain of command. As I explained in Chapter 17, the impact of culture becomes more and more pronounced in the actions of large numbers of people over time. It is least pronounced in the behavior of any individual in any given situation. For the latter, the idiosyncrasies of that person in that set of circumstances are going to vastly outweigh the impact of culturally inculcated patterns of behavior. But the more that we observe lots of people taking lots of actions, the more that those actions should conform to the cultural mean.

What that means for any military is that actions in conformity with cultural patterns of behavior are going to be most pronounced at the lower end of the chain of command because that is where the largest numbers of people are. The more people, the more actions taken, the more likely those actions will conform to culturally regular behavior. So enlisted personnel, NCOs, and junior officers should demonstrate far more culturally regular behavior than generals should because there are so many fewer generals than lower ranks. By way of comparison, in 2016, the US Army had 68,113 lieutenants, captains, and majors, but only 347 generals of all kinds.[4] We should expect the cumulative and collective behavior of those 68,113 lieutenants, captains, and majors to conform far more closely to American cultural predilections than that of the 347 generals. It is also worth remembering that, as Chapter 17 also described, the dominant Arab culture prescribes very different behavior patterns for those at the bottom or middle of any hierarchy than for those at the very top—to the extent those at the top conform to cultural behavior patterns at all because there are so many fewer of them than there are enlisted, NCOs, and junior officers.

This is very different from how politicization works, and somewhat different from how underdevelopment works. As I discussed in Chapter 5, politicization has its greatest effects at the top of a chain of command and then diminishes as you move lower in the rank structure. Indeed, the vast historical evidence shows that this "trickle-down" phenomenon attenuates very rapidly after the rank of brigadier or perhaps colonel, depending on the military. That is both because it is far easier to keep track of the political views of the small number of generals, and far easier to find known loyalists for that smaller number of positions, and because regimes care far more about the loyalty of their generals than they do about their junior officers (let alone their NCOs) because it is so much harder for junior officers to overthrow a government. It's not to say that junior officers, such as Captain Muammar Qadhafi, don't overthrow regimes, it is just that it happens far less frequently, and requires very peculiar circumstances, so nervous regimes just worry about it far less. Indeed, the historical evidence discussed in Chapter 5 shows a very significant disjuncture between the impact of loyalty requirements on promotions at about the rank of colonel/brigadier for exactly this reason.

Finally, underdevelopment's impacts on a chain of command largely correlate with two factors: the educational level of the personnel and the importance of handling equipment, particularly complex equipment, to their jobs. The better educated a person, the less likely he or she will suffer from the military-related problems associated with underdevelopment. Likewise, the more that a person has to handle complex machinery, the greater the impact of those problems. In the Arab militaries since World War II, both of those patterns indicate that the impact of underdevelopment should be worst at the lower levels

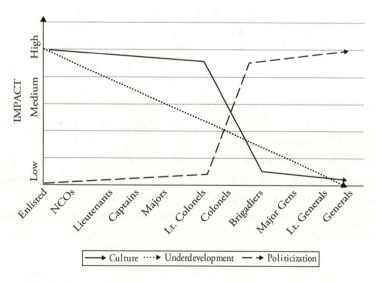

FIGURE 18.1 Graph of Explanations and Impact on Chain of Command

of the chain of command, and least at the top levels. Why? Because Arab generals tend to be far better educated than Arab enlisted personnel and NCOs, and because Arab generals don't fire artillery pieces or drive tanks (although they sometimes fly airplanes, expressly because they are the best educated). Thus, the problems of underdevelopment should be felt strongest at the lowest levels of Arab chains of command, diminishing almost evenly at higher levels of the hierarchy.

Figure 18.1 illustrates these differences. It further bolsters the conclusions of Part II that politicization was responsible for the poor performance of Arab generals, when there was such a poor performance. Simply put, the ability of underdevelopment and now Arab culture to explain poor Arab generalship is very limited. It is true that politicization can cause problems at lower levels of the chain of command by creating poor morale and poor unit cohesion, but as both this chapter and Chapter 1 (and the many examples throughout the book) have all pointed out, there simply was no pattern of poor morale or poor unit cohesion among the Arab armies, and both were more frequently good than bad. By the same token, only culture or (to a much lesser extent) underdevelopment can explain the poor performance of Arab tactical forces although the cultural patterns described in Chapter 17 are more consistent with the most important patterns of poor Arab military performance than the impact of underdevelopment on weapons handling, maintenance, or even pace of operations.

| Arab Culture and
Civilian Organizations

I T SEEMS UNLIKELY that it is mere coincidence that the most damaging
problems that Arab armed forces have suffered in battle just happen to conform perfectly to patterns of behavior emphasized by the dominant Arab culture. But we can look deeper. If the worst problems besetting Arab militaries
are born of cultural tendencies related to how hierarchical organizations
function, it is worth asking whether other Arab organizations function in the
same way. If they do, that's more evidence that Arab military issues are the
product of generalized societal patterns of behavior rather than something specific to the militaries. Moreover, few other Arab organizations adopted Soviet
managerial practices, nor did they suffer from coup-proofing or other forms
of politicization as Arab armed forces because civilian organizations lack the
ability to overthrow or defy the political leadership that militaries innately
possess.

So it is further evidence of the impact of cultural patterns of behavior that
the experience of businesses, utilities, schools, government agencies, and other
organizations in the Arab world reveals the same patterns of behavior as their
militaries: rigid top-down decision-making, little initiative or innovation at
lower levels, a propensity for underlings to avoid taking responsibility and to
await decisions from above, and problems with information flows both verti-
cally and horizontally across the organization, to name a few.

Of course all organizations—whether militaries, hospitals, or businesses—
have incentive structures that cause broadly similar patterns of behavior among

their employees across cultural divides. The behavior of people who work in, for example, banks in the Arab world has much in common with the behavior of people who work in banks in America because banks serve the same purposes in both societies and those purposes come with common notions about how people should behave when discharging those functions. However, those who work in any institution are also subject to incentive structures created by their unique cultures regarding behavior in all hierarchic organizations regardless of their function. And there are important differences derived from the different cultural strictures regarding how individuals are supposed to act within hierarchies, which is why experiences in an American bank often feel *very* different from those in an Arab bank. In other words, the same cultural predilections that have shaped modern Arab military operations affect a vast range of other activities too.

Arab Organizational Experience at a Macro Level

Numerous assessments have found that Arab governmental bureaucracies evince all of the same patterns of behavior as their militaries, albeit without the same disastrous impact since government bureaucracies are not engaged in lethal competition with one another. For instance, in a study of the bureaucracies of Egypt, Saudi Arabia, and Sudan a team of mostly Arab social scientists found that "Supervisors in the Middle East tend to concentrate as much authority as possible in their own hands. Little authority is delegated. . . . Innovation and risk taking are not reinforced. Many supervisory personnel in the Middle East prefer subordinates who keep a low profile and who 'don't rock the boat.' Subservience often brings greater rewards than hard work." The study authors found that "bureaucratic regulations in the Middle East focus on sins of commission rather than sins of omission. It is far more dangerous to stick one's neck out than it is to do nothing." They also reported that 90 percent of the senior bureaucrats interviewed in all three countries believed that "their subordinates were simply unqualified to innovate."[1]

In short, there is a constant tendency in Arab agencies toward highly centralized hierarchies in which authority is concentrated at the top, and rarely, if ever, delegated.[2] A 2010 OECD study of human resources management practices in the Middle East found that "All of the countries are wrestling with a set of intractable HRM issues that are perceived as barriers to improved governance both inside and outside the human resource area." In particular, the study singled out across-the-board problems of "Rigid personnel systems that do not motivate or reward good performance and that rely too heavily on seniority for advancement. . . . A rigidly hierarchical, regulation-based approach that places the Human Resources rulebook ahead of either the employees' best interest or the objectives at hand. . . . Low managerial delegation and decision-making that is strongly-centralized."[3]

One area where these same patterns of behavior have loomed large because they have entailed recurrent failure in a competitive struggle is in the economic practices of the Arab world. The reason that the first Arab Human Development Report in 2002 was so earth shattering was that a group of the best and brightest minds in the Arab world, meeting under the auspices of the politically correct United Nations, stated unflinchingly that the fundamental reason the Arab states were lagging ever farther behind the rest of the world (including even sub-Saharan Africa) was because of a set of culturally derived patterns of behavior that inhibited the development of the kind of "knowledge-based" economy necessary to compete in the twenty-first century.[4]

The second AHDR, published in 2003, was entirely devoted to this "knowledge gap" between the Arab world and the developed (and successfully developing) world. In their words, "The first AHDR highlighted how weak knowledge bases and stagnant knowledge development condemn many Arab countries to fragile productive power and reduced development opportunities. It is now a commonplace that the knowledge gap, rather than the income gap, determines the prospects of countries in today's world economy."[5]

Of course, the AHDR is not the only study to find that economic and business practices in the Arab world are heavily infused by the same culturally driven patterns of behavior as their armed forces, and that they tend to create similar hindrances. This is striking because, until relatively recently, Western economics and management theory took as a bedrock assumption that universal factors such as the availability of technology and the profit motive would produce similar organizations and methods of operation in any business regardless of cultural factors. This has been challenged broadly by new studies of the impact of cultural preferences on organizations, management, and leadership, such as the massive Global Leadership and Organizational Behavior Effectiveness (GLOBE) study of such practices in 62 different countries. The GLOBE study found that societal culture had a far greater impact on leadership, management, and organizational behavior than market forces and industry effects (i.e., industry-wide practices across societies).[6] This and other such studies have increasingly demonstrated that, despite the Darwinian competition of the marketplace (akin to the competition of combat), organizations function very differently in different societies. They have found that this holds true even for businesses nominally owned by foreign entities, which have to take on the patterns of behavior of the host country to survive and thrive.[7]

Moreover, the same outdated ideas about the homogeneity of organizational behaviors have been challenged specifically in the Arab world by a new generation of experts who have demonstrated how differently Arab businesses are organized and operate compared to the same kinds of enterprises in the Western world.[8] Moreover, they note the inefficiencies and economic failings of the Arab approaches, but also how they persist even though to an outsider their failings are obvious. As Samer Shehata warned in his brilliant book on the impact of culture and politics in Egyptian factories:

> The social organization of production—the way the factory and work are organized—profoundly shapes how individuals come to think of themselves and others. The significance of this should not be lost. How work is organized is not exclusively or even primarily the result of particular technologies or production processes. It is a contingent social arrangement, something that could always be otherwise. Thus, different ways of organizing production (and different rules and procedures governing social interaction in the factory) can have profound effects on what it means to be a worker and how this identity is understood.[9]

It is for this set of reasons that the Arab economies have performed so poorly compared to those of so many other regions and countries. The 2003 Arab Human Development Report warned that "rates of productivity (the average production of one worker) in Arab countries were negative to a large and increasing extent in oil-producing countries during the 1980s and '90s. The gross national product per worker in all Arab countries is less than half of that in two advanced developing countries: South Korea in Asia and Argentina in Latin America."[10] In fact, GDP per worker was negative during the 1990s for both oil-producing and non-oil-producing Arab states.[11] The bottom line is that worker productivity in the Middle East is the lowest in the world.[12]

In a similar vein, the International Labour Office found in 2007 that worker productivity in the Middle East and North Africa had grown, but only by 9 percent between 1996 and 2006—very low compared to the global average of 26 percent. Only Latin America showed lower growth.[13] A year earlier, the ILO warned of "stagnant productivity" in the region because while GDP grew by 5.5 percent annually between 1993 and 2003, productivity had increased by only 0.1 percent annually. While this rate was better than sub-Saharan Africa, it was only 1/10 of the global average of 1.0 percent annual growth in productivity during that same time frame.[14] To the extent that any of the countries in the region showed real increases in worker productivity, this tended to come in the Gulf countries, largely because of their reliance on large numbers of foreign workers.[15]

Arab Organizational Experience at the Micro Level

If you do any reading about organizations in the Arab world, whether government bureaucracies, factories, universities, corporations, or small businesses, the word that keeps coming up over and over again is "authoritarian." Arab organizations are characterized by a severe over-centralization of power and decision-making. Ideas and directives are expected to flow from the top down. They are not solicited from the bottom. Authority is not delegated downward, and mid-level managers overwhelmingly act as nothing but glorified couriers and overseers, conveying orders from the top and ensuring that those orders are obeyed. In the rare circumstances when authority is delegated, typically because a problem has temporarily disconnected the top-level leadership from the rest of the organization, those lower in the hierarchy often have no idea what to do, and either do nothing or keep doing whatever they were last told to do.[16]

A few examples will have to suffice for what is a vast literature on the topic. Samer Shehata worked in two different Egyptian factories as an ordinary worker on the shop floor to understand their functioning and corporate culture. A principal theme of his remarkable work is that, in both, "Rigid hierarchy and authoritarian social relations were the norm, and they came across not only in obvious ways such as the CEO's power or the shift supervisor's physical abuse of workers, but also in smaller, more subtle practices, mannerisms, and codes of behavior. Relations of superiority and subordination had become so internalized that they appeared natural and were taken for granted."[17] He was amazed at how the CEO "infantilized the company's top executives."[18] Abbas Ali's survey of Arab managerial practices found the same: "Managerial behavior, which remains strictly within the framework of the authoritarian and hierarchical structure of the organization, seeks to prepare subordinates to accept decisions already made by managers and to improve the individual managers' images."[19] As another example from a very different kind of organization, Tony Pfaff observed from his time as an advisor in Iraq during the US occupation that the Iraqi police force had a particularly hard time after Saddam because of the need to operate as a more decentralized force—with hiring, firing, and organization devolved to the provincial level, not kept in Baghdad as under Saddam.[20] Likewise, the massive 10-year GLOBE study of organization and leadership found that the Arab countries showed the highest preference for a high "Power Distance" (i.e., a rigid, top-down, and highly stratified chain of command) of all of the regions. The Arab states stood out in their preference for a high power distance, whereas every other society wanted less.[21]

Not surprisingly, the authoritarian style of management of Arab organizations has meant that there is very little initiative, innovation, creativity, or autonomy anywhere along the hierarchy except at the very top. Contrary to what is considered routine in the West, most lower level managers and employees simply do not see it as their place to try to improve the performance of the organization or to act without direct orders to do so.[22] The GLOBE study noted that its Middle East cluster "largely rejected the notion of autonomous leadership," which it described as "individualistic, independent, unique and autonomous."[23] They also found that the Middle East cluster had the lowest interest in "Performance Oriented" leadership, which tends "to value education and learning, emphasize results, set high performance targets, value taking initiative, and prefer explicit and direct communications. In contrast, societies whose respondents report low Performance Orientation are reported to value social and family relations, loyalty, tradition, and seniority, and use subtle and indirect language."[24] The organizational culture Shehata encountered in the Egyptian factories in which he worked produced "tremendous risk-aversion on the part of subordinates, especially at the level of middle management. Many CEOs and senior managers at other companies where I conducted research complained that subordinates were unwilling to make decisions and take responsibility. Instead, people constantly deferred to their superiors. Organizational cultures characterized by tremendous hierarchy and the concentration of power do not reward risk-taking or independent decision-making."[25]

Information flows are also problematic for Arab civilian organizations, as they have been for their militaries, albeit without the unparalleled stress of battle. One study of managers from all six of the Gulf Cooperation Council states found that they generally scored low on the importance that they attached to providing information to subordinates as well as on the autonomy that they enjoyed as middle managers.[26] In a study of Arab business communications practices, Rhonda Zaharna argued that Arabic communication often failed to provide critical information, believing that it was either already known to the recipient or unnecessary to that person. "The result is that he will talk around and around the point, in effect putting all the pieces in place except the crucial one."[27] Shehata also noted that the "Overly hierarchical systems of organization prevent the exchange of information that could potentially lead to trouble-shooting and higher levels of productivity and innovation."[28] The GLOBE study found that the Middle East cluster all favored "self-protective leaders," whereas Western countries saw them as an impediment to effective operations.[29] According to the study's terminology, "self-protective leadership focuses on ensuring the safety and security of the individual and group through status enhancement and face saving."[30] Such leaders are "characterized by self-centeredness, elitism, status consciousness, narcissism, and a tendency to induce conflict with others."[31] And the determination of managers to save face and embellish their own status inevitably produced "distortions" in the transmission of information up, down, and across the organizations.

Moreover, Arab civilian organizations have shown a similar, dichotomous pattern with regard to "cohesion" or group chemistry, just like the uneven unit cohesion of their militaries. Where an organization or a department cohered into an "in-group," loyalty was fierce.[32] Shehata found this in his Egyptian factories, as did Pfaff dealing with the Iraqi police, where officers were "less likely to be willing or even able to break apart the close relationships which drive many other decisions, such as hiring, firing, disciplining, and promotions, even though those decisions may not always be compatible with the creation of a just and effective police force."[33] Of course, an important element in this was whether the leader of the organization or department measured up to the cultural ideals, where the GLOBE study found the Middle East to be the "most unusual of all" of the global regions. The leadership dimensions that Middle Easterners favored to an extent that no one else did were "familial, humble and faithful," as well as self-protective and considerate.[34]

Cross-national comparisons such as the GLOBE study are important because they demonstrate that these tendencies in Arab business and organizational practices are not shared by other societies—even societies at similar levels of economic development or with similarly autocratic forms of government. All of the Arab states demonstrate these same tendencies, but they are not shared by all underdeveloped countries or all autocratically governed countries. Some countries have similarities with the Arab states, others do not, but there is no political or economic correlation with these behavioral patterns outside the Arab world, and none of the non-Arab states are as similar to the Arab states as they are to one another, even those with similar economic or political profiles.

It is not surprising then that those pressing for economic reform in the Arab world, like the authors of the various Arab Human Development Reports, have so consistently warned that doing so will require significant cultural shifts. Indeed, even Saudi Arabia's "Vision 2030" reform agenda calls for cultural change, both implicitly and explicitly, as part of the core shifts necessary to transform Saudi society and make it economically competitive and socially contented.[35]

A Clear Pattern

The case that the most debilitating problems Arab conventional forces suffered in combat during the modern era stemmed from organizational factors inherent in Arab society becomes even more compelling when we add in the experience of nonmilitary Arab organizations, particularly businesses, factories, and government bureaucracies, which function in an identical fashion to their militaries—despite having their own set of incentives not to do so. As I wrote at the start of this chapter, it seems unlikely that it is mere coincidence that the most damaging problems that Arab armed forces have suffered in battle just happen to conform perfectly to patterns of behavior emphasized by the dominant Arab culture. It gets even harder to buy given that Arab organizations in other walks of life experience precisely the same patterns of behavior as their armies, despite the fact that those other organizations were not trained by the Soviets, nor were they subject to coup-proofing or other forms of politicization, nor did they behave like similar organizations in other developing countries.

For instance, the notion that commissarist politicization is behind Arab military ineffectiveness stems from the notion that the political leadership fears that the military will mount a coup against it, and takes steps to emasculate the officer corps. Well, no Arab leader fears being overthrown by the employees—or even the leaders—of the Ministry of Tourism, let alone the workers (even the CEO) of a textile factory like the ones that Shehata worked in. Yet all across the Arab world, in all of these different organizations, the patterns of management and behavior by personnel at different levels of the hierarchy are identical. And identical to those evinced by Arab militaries in combat. *And* they are also identical to the pattern of relations in the average Arab family. *And* they just happen to be the same patterns of behavior that all of the cultural anthropologists, sociologists, and cultural psychologists say are indicative of the emphases of the dominant Arab culture. So if someone wants to argue that the cause is something other than those culturally driven incentives, they have a lot of explaining to do.

Moreover, just as these culturally driven patterns of behavior have proven extremely difficult to overcome in Arab armed forces, so too have they bedeviled Arab economies. In both cases, the necessities created by competition and failure have so far not been enough to produce meaningful change. Indeed, the sense that the Arab world is falling badly behind in the competitive arena of international economics, conveyed by the various Arab Human Development Reports from 2002 to 2016, perfectly reflects what has happened to the Arab militaries in the competitive arena of international warfare in the modern era. Especially since the economies and militaries are losing those battles in the exact same ways. And just as the AHDRs identified education as the critical arena where the fight is being lost—and needs to be turned around if it is ever going to be won—so too is it now time to look at Arab educational practices and how they inculcate these cultural predilections, causing both the economic problems that the AHDR has identified and the military problems that every Arab foe has revealed since 1945.

CHAPTER 20 | Culture and Education:
          | The Causal Link

T HE NEXT PIECE of the puzzle I want to address is how the patterns of
     culturally regular Arab behavior *cause* the patterns of Arab military per-
formance. This link can be found in the informal and formal education of Arab
military personnel during their maturation from child to adult as well as their
formal military training once they have been inducted into the armed forces.

Culture is learned behavior. It is a set of conditioned preferences and
comportments that all members of a community learn over time. Some adopt
it wholesale; others reject part or all of it; most adopt much but ignore parts
or reject aspects at certain times and situations. Nevertheless, people are not
born with embedded cultural patterns. They learn them from their parents,
relatives, friends, teachers, etc. This learning takes place both informally—
within the family, among friends, at the workplace, even from sources of
entertainment—as well as formally, in school, where a culture's values are
imparted along with knowledge.

All societies have particular methods of imparting knowledge, values, and
patterns of behavior to successive generations.[1] But cultures can have very
different methods of education, methods that made sense for the community's
needs in certain circumstances at some point in the not-too-distant past.
A crucial problem for Arab society in both the globalized marketplace and
modern warfare has been that the cultural method of education that their
community devised is not preparing its young men and women for these competitive endeavors.

In this chapter I am going to demonstrate that Arab education, in all its various forms, teaches the values of the dominant Arab culture. Education in the Arab world, both formal and informal, constantly seeks to mold the actions and thinking of the individual along the lines of the culturally regular patterns of behavior described in Chapter 17. Arab families and schools teach conformity, deference to authority, loyalty to the group, etc. It isn't found in the formal curriculum. You won't find a class in any Arab school called "Conformism 101." *Instead, you will find it in the teaching method itself: in how students are taught to think, to learn, and to behave.* This is why Arab civilian organizations function in the same fashion as their militaries. The people who make up both have been taught to behave in the same way in any hierarchical organization, regardless of the role or purpose of that organization.

I'm also going to show that these same methods were employed in Arab military training, thereby reinforcing in Arab soldiers and officers the values and behavior first learned in the family and then at school. Military training is another formal educational process. Not only do recruits learn how to fire a gun or drive a tank, they also learn how to think like a soldier or an officer. Thus, the fact that Arab military training also reinforces the same cultural values and behavioral patterns as other educating institutions further demonstrates that the performance of Arab militaries in combat is largely the product of a set of internal incentives that Arab personnel bring with them to warfare, rather than a set of external values imposed upon them by their politics, a foreign military doctrine, or other circumstances. It is the same set of incentives that most Arabs bring with them to factories, universities, bureaucracies, etc., and that cause those organizations to function in similar fashion.

Given that Arab educational methods, formal and informal, civilian and military, teach individuals to act in conformity with Arab cultural patterns throughout the course of their development, it becomes clearer still that Arab cultural patterns are not just correlated with key Arab military patterns, but are causing them. After all, if Arab personnel are taught to behave in a certain manner all their lives, how could one expect them to do otherwise in the midst of combat when there is little opportunity to think rationally, and officers and troops alike tend to fall back on what they know best?

As a caveat before delving in, the reader should be aware that, by necessity, I must again deal in generalized behavior, the kind that is often abused by stereotyping. In doing so, I am going to have to gloss over many of the regional, class, national, and other differences in Arab educational practices both across the Middle East and over time. To a certain extent then, these descriptions constitute a gross oversimplification of education in the Arab world, focusing on the lowest common denominators among Arab families, schools, and military training. Please understand that these descriptions may or may not apply to any specific Arab family, school, or military training program, and instead describe the regional mean, around which individual experiences vary.

Quantity versus Quality

The reason that Arab educational practices have left the Arab states at a competitive disadvantage with other countries in various fields of human activity has little to do with the *quantity* of education provided, especially since the 1980s or 1990s. Since then, virtually all of the Arab governments have made major investments in education, and as a result, there has been a remarkable improvement in the amount of education provided to their people.[2] Literacy is way up on average, as is average years of schooling—from 1.3 in 1970 to 4.5 in 2000.[3] Enrollment rates have increased markedly, especially for high school students.[4] Per capita spending on education across the region is the highest of any region in the world other than Western Europe and North America.[5] The teacher-pupil ratio has declined very respectably.[6] As the 2003 AHDR stated, "ultimately, the quality of education does not depend on the availability of resources or on quantitative factors but rather on other organizations of the educational process and the means of delivery and evaluation."[7]

Despite the quantitative increase in education across the Arab world, Arab educational levels have not improved commensurately. In various "International Mathematics and Science" studies conducted since 1995, a number of Arab states have participated, and the results were noteworthy in two ways: (1) all of the Arab states did poorly, with only one country in one of the tests (Jordan in science in 2003) exceeding the global average, and most falling at the very bottom of the list; and (2) the wealthy Gulf states did just as poorly as other Muslim Middle Eastern countries. For example, in 2003 out of a field of 46 countries, in the math test, Lebanon came in 31st, Jordan 32nd, Tunisia 35th, Bahrain 37th, Morocco 40th, and Saudi Arabia 43rd. In science, Jordan ranked 25th—just above the global average, the only Arab country to do so—but Bahrain came in 33rd, the Palestinians 34th, Egypt 35th, Tunisia 38th, Saudi Arabia 39th, Morocco 40th, and Lebanon 41st.[8] In 2008, the World Bank looked at an even wider range of math and science tests for a wider range of Muslim Middle Eastern states (eight Arab states plus Iran) and found that the average Middle Eastern score of 399 was well below the international average of 489, as well as that of East Asia (466) and Latin America (408).[9]

There are plenty of other indicators of the poor quality of Arab education. The Arab Human Development Report famously pointed out that although Arabs constitute 5 percent of global population, on average the Arab states produce only 1.1 percent of the books published in the world each year.[10] A 2008 RAND study that looked at the educational reforms of Lebanon, Oman, Qatar, and the UAE found "low performance levels on internationally benchmarked student assessments; (a) low share of students whose studies at the secondary and post-secondary levels concentrate in the critical fields of science, mathematics, engineering, and technology; and low rates of obtaining post-secondary degrees, especially for male nationals in the Gulf states."[11] A World Bank report also from 2008 authored by Ahmed Galal and a team of economists and education experts noted the major increase in the quantity of education being provided, but nevertheless lamented that "Notwithstanding these successes—and the considerable resources invested in education—reforms have not fully delivered on their promises. In particular, the relationship between education and economic growth has remained weak, the divide between education and employment has not been bridged, and the quality of education continues to be disappointing."[12] Or as Delwin A. Roy put it when discussing Saudi educational problems, "Although the government can point to dramatic increases in the numbers who have passed through the various educational levels, there is considerable doubt as to the degree to which it might be said that students have actually been 'educated.' "[13]

Education within the Family

Education, like charity, begins at home. Long before they ever set foot in a school, children begin to learn from their parents and families not just knowledge, but values, behavior, and ways of thinking and understanding the world. In Gary Gregg's words, "In every society, psychological development is embedded in the organization of families and styles of familial interaction."[14] Not surprisingly, the methods of Arab informal education, the education that takes place in the home and social settings, is effectively identical to the formal methods employed in Arab schools from kindergarten through graduate schools. Moreover, because education often has the greatest impact at the earliest ages, many sociologists, psychologists, anthropologists, and educators believe that the informal education received in the home is the most important of all in creating patterns for behavior and learning later in life.[15]

The child-raising practices of most Arab families forcefully ingrained culturally regular patterns of behavior into Arab children throughout the modern era. The culturally regular Arab family emphasized deference and obedience to authority, loyalty to family and friends, and the manipulation of information to avoid shame, while denigrating creativity and imagination, manual labor and technical learning, and the assumption of responsibility by any but the head of the family. Arab educational methods within the family mostly discouraged generalization and inquisitive learning, instead fostering a passive absorption of knowledge.

Most experts on Arab culture and society note that the cornerstone of educating a child in Arab families is teaching him or her complete obedience to authority. "Studies also indicate that the most common style of child rearing within the Arab family is the authoritarian accompanied by the overprotective," according to the 2003 Arab Human Development Report. "This adversely affects children's independence, self-confidence and social efficiency, and leads to an increase in passive attitudes and the deterioration of decision-making skills, not only with respect to behavior, but also to how the child thinks. For starting in early childhood, the child becomes accustomed to suppressing her or his inquisitive and exploratory tendencies and sense of initiative."[16] Studies conducted in Sudan and Egypt both found that "parents in general do not encourage curiosity, exploratory and manipulative behavior of their young children. . . . Parents insist on prompt obedience; children are taught to be polite and submissive."[17] Other studies in Egypt, Bahrain, Kuwait, Jordan, and Morocco concluded "that an authoritarian or abusive socialization style is adopted toward Arab children."[18] The Lebanese psychologist 'Ali Zayour, in his monumental study of the *Psychoanalysis of the Arab Ego*, says that the Arab family is "relentless in its repression. . . . The young are brought up to be obedient, well-mannered and subservient to those above them."[19] Halim Barakat remarks that "Children are constantly, and on so many kinds of occasions, reminded that they should obey their parents and never answer back or argue with them even in cases where the parents may be wrong. Moreover, obedience to parents and other members of the family is generalized to all kinds of figures of authority be it a teacher, an employer, a president, a leader, etc."[20] Not surprisingly, Gregg has noted that various psychological studies have found a higher emphasis on parental control and respect for authority in the Arab world than in the United States.[21]

This relentless effort to force children to defer decision-making and judgment to authority figures worked to depress creativity, critical thinking, and initiative among Arab youth. In essence, within the family structure, children were taught to obey rather than to think for themselves. Ammar concludes his work by summing up that Egyptian childrearing worked "to produce submissive, obedient children who lack the spirit of enterprise and initiative. Adults continuously wean their offspring from flights of imagination and spontaneity of action till they almost completely achieve their end by the time their offspring reach adolescence."[22] Raymond Cohen concurs with Ammar's findings that "the personal initiative and autonomy characteristic of child-rearing and education in the Western world, is neglected by Egyptian culture, as it is indeed throughout the Arab world."[23] Cohen goes on to say that "denied freedom of choice, [Arab] children learn to do only what they are told. Self-reliance and personal initiative are not encouraged because they do not contribute to group needs."[24] Hisham Sharabi argues that "Arab children [are] discouraged by their upbringing from exercising independent judgment. They are taught to accept unquestioningly the view of others."[25] Finally, Marwan Dwairy's work has led him to conclude that Arab childrearing practices produce children whose "egos are specifically constructed to understand and follow the rules and social codes of Arab society and are unable to cope independently in new or novel situations without social directives."[26] Likewise, Arab children "learn the accurate solutions for certain problems but not how to think about and solve problems. Arab children do not have problems answering *how* questions while they display significant difficulty in answering *why* questions."[27]

For the most part, Arab families and other primary groups taught their children that their identity came from belonging to a particular primary group: their family, their group of friends, and perhaps their place of work. Arab families tended to teach that group affiliation was the most important thing in the world, and acceptance by the group was achieved by conforming to the accepted behavioral norms of the society. Thus teaching children to suppress their own judgment and needs to that of the larger group also contributed to a suppression of creativity and initiative among Arab children. According to Saad Eddin Ibrahim and Nicholas Hopkins, "[Arab] children learned not only to expect emotional and material support from an expanded kinship group, but also that any of them was nothing by himself outside that group. The child's personality was not only shaped by, but also submerged in the kinship group. His loyalty to it was therefore very intense. He hardly questioned or entertained independent judgment, He developed a reflexive deference to authority."[28] Likewise, the educational specialist Karen Walker has written that "Another feature of Arab students that would puzzle an educator working from a Western world-view is their conformist and dependent behaviour. In Western society where independence is highly regarded, dependence is likewise interpreted as immaturity. In a society that does not encourage individual independence and where conditions support conformism, conformity and dependency are natural results."[29]

Arab children were taught to feel shame as an excruciating punishment, and to avoid it in any way possible. Indeed, there was no prohibition against distortion or fabrication to avoid shame, and Arab children generally were socialized to believe this was acceptable, even desirable, to escape shame.[30] In Barakat's words, "In effect, the child is taught that the penalty for wrong-doing is public disgrace rather than a sense of personal remorse. He is conditioned, therefore, to escape humiliation as much as sin. Since shame results from being found out and ridiculed, it can be avoided as well by concealment as by rectitude."[31] According to Sharabi, parents taught their children that it was okay to do wrong, as long as no one saw it, thus "A double-standard of conduct is not only implicitly sanctioned, but encouraged in the pattern of [child-]rearing."[32]

Like all families, Arab families taught their children that certain occupations and skills were to be valued more highly than others. For much of the post–World War II era, white-collar jobs as government officials, clerks, financiers, and other business managers were considered among the most prestigious careers by many Arab families, and children were encouraged to pursue them. Those who successfully attained such positions were treated with pride and respect by their relatives and friends. On the other hand, jobs involving menial labor, working with your hands, and—by extension, until very recently—technical skills, were often considered not terribly prestigious. Indeed, for most of this period, much technical work was often lumped together with menial labor.[33]

The primary method of teaching children in most Arab families was rote memorization enforced by arbitrary punishment. Halim Barakat and Hisham Sharabi both observe that, "The typical urban, Muslim, middle- and lower-middle class family . . . uses the principal techniques of shaming, physical punishment and rote-learning (*Talqin*) in socializing its children."[34] Elsewhere, Sharabi and Muktar Ani have written that "the learning process in the Arab family (and beyond it) may be characterized by two aspects: it de-emphasizes persuasion (and reward), and it emphasizes physical punishment and rote-learning (*Talqin*)."[35] Both of these methods dampened analytical skills, degraded the ability of children to see beyond specifics, and discouraged independent thought and action. Children were forced to memorize information without necessarily being taught to use it as a starting point for extrapolations to other situations. Information was considered useful only for the specific purpose and context for which it was taught. Similarly, since punishment was arbitrary and frequently no explanation was given for the action that prompted it—or what other action would have entailed a reward—children became wary of all independent action and instead were conditioned to take action only when specifically sanctioned by an authority figure.

This effect has been noted by numerous Middle East experts. For example, Ibrahim and Hopkins conclude that "To behave properly meant to learn to suppress individual impulses. Since individuals had to take the clues of proper behavior from the traditional authority and heritage, and since they were not to choose or judge outside that framework, independent thinking and analytical abilities remained undeveloped, if not deliberately stunted. Instead, the socialization process over-emphasized rote-learning and memorizing."[36] Sharabi likewise argues that, for Arab children, "Rote-learning and punishment had this in common: both excuse understanding and emphasize authority; they both cultivate passivity and inhibit change. The child was conditioned to accept without question the hegemony of the powerful and the learned."[37] Sharabi also writes that "The aim of *talqin* (rote-memorization) is to transmit the institutionalized values of the society and to preserve its established habits of dealing with the world. The subject is confronted with finished models which he appropriates without criticism or understanding; and in the process he acquires a pattern of seeing and valuing which strengthens conformity and discourages creativity and innovation."[38] Sana al-Khayyat's study of village life in Iraq led her to conclude that the constant disciplining of Iraqi children without explanation, and their punishment for asking questions left them incapable of acting independently. In her words, "parents commonly give children commands rather than explaining. Thus children do not grow up to make their own decisions and develop as independent people."[39] Finally, Dwairy relates that for many years he has given the Wechlser intelligence test (the WISC-R) to both Arab and Jewish students in Israel and he has consistently found that:

> Arab teenagers exceeded Jews on the information subtest that measures the amount of knowledge they have stored in their memories. They know more about their physical and social environment. This knowledge is absorbed from home and school environments that emphasize memorizing over thinking. On the other hand, Jewish teenagers exceeded Arabs on the similarities and comprehension subtests. These two subtests require analytical and flexible thinking, with which Arab students are not as familiar. For the similarities subtest, they are asked to compare two concepts to find a similar property. This kind of thinking is uncommon in Arabic classes, which adopt rote learning techniques rather than reasoning and discussion. On the comprehension subtest, students are offered problematic situations such as, What would you do if you saw smoke coming out of your neighbor's house? To answer this question, the student must evaluate the situation and the

options to make a personal decision. Arab students, who are not used to this and are discouraged from evaluating situations and making personal decisions, will find these questions difficult to answer unless they have, by chance, been in similar situations before and were told what they should do.[40]

Education in Arab Schools

These patterns of education continue seamlessly in the formal educational processes of the Arab world: primary and secondary school, college, and even graduate programs. The process of formal education in the vast majority of schools in the Arab world during the postwar era relied on a method that instilled these same cultural values in Arab pupils, reinforcing the lessons taught by the family. Arab schools relied almost entirely on passive learning techniques, specifically rote memorization. More than that, it was most often the case that little or no effort was made to engage the student, nurture his or her intellectual curiosity, or encourage active participation in the educational process. Questions were discouraged in the classroom, and information was to be accepted without explanation. Independent, creative thought and personal initiative were largely discouraged, and subjects were taught as discrete bodies that did not allow for comparison or "cross-pollination." Science, mathematics, and other technical subjects were taught in the same fashion with especially deleterious effects.

The educational system of all the Arab states still derives ultimately from the Quranic schools—the *kuttab* and the madrasa—that were essentially the only formal education in the Arab states for many centuries until the twentieth.[41] Alan Richards and John Waterbury observe that when it comes to the problems of education in the Arab world, "Far too often, education in the region mimics traditional madrasas (Islamic schools, where boys memorize parts of the Koran), with their emphasis on rote learning, rather than stressing problem solving, writing skills, or creativity."[42] As the educational psychologist Gerald Miller described in his study of Moroccan schooling in the 1970s, the primary purpose of the Quranic school was to pass on to the child the culture in the form of values, priorities, and proper ways of behavior. Actually learning any of the Quran was a secondary consideration. Miller notes that many Arab parents told the teacher, "Teach my son politeness and manners. As for the rest [i.e., the Quran] God will provide it."[43]

Throughout the postwar period, the educational method of Arab schools remained remarkably constant. Beginning in the 1950s and 1960s most of the Arab states instituted mass public education as part of a general economic development program. In many countries, primary schooling became mandatory for all children, and elsewhere, strong incentives were established to encourage attendance. Nevertheless, when the public schools took over the task of education from the Quranic schools they changed the curricula being studied but not the manner in which subjects were taught. The teaching method remained identical to that of the Quranic schools. Gregg writes that Arab public schools merely embedded the traditional learning practices, particularly rote memorization, in "modern-looking institutions."[44] In recent decades, there has been some movement toward reforming the educational method in some parts of the Arab world, with the larger reform agendas of Saudi Arabia, Qatar, and the UAE singling out education as key targets for fundamental transformation. However, such efforts have still been modest so far, and it remains to be seen how far the changes will go and whether they will last.

Passive Learning. Most Arabs who grew up after the Second World War (and before it) have been taught throughout their schooling to absorb knowledge, rather than discover it. Indeed, the central notion behind the teaching method was that knowledge is revealed, not created.[45] Like child-rearing, teaching was conducted in Arab schools in mostly authoritarian fashion, and students were generally discouraged from asking questions or actively participating in the process of education.[46] Little effort was made to engage the student in understanding concepts and principles underlying the material: all that was considered important was the ability to memorize details verbatim.[47] Leonard Binder despaired that in Arab schools, "Educational practices emphasize the authority of the teacher, rote learning, formal curricula, uniformity, discipline and routine. . . . In these respects, the school resembles all non-family organizations and simply carries the general culture of social relations into the imported and adapted modern educational structure."[48]

The traditional method of education in the Arab world was for the students to remain entirely passive and simply absorb what the teacher presented. The course of study was expected to come entirely from the lesson plan of the teacher, and students were discouraged from showing initiative or creativity in pursuing their education.[49] All information came from the textbook, and teachers did not dare to improvise or add to the prescribed lessons. For example, Gerald Miller relates that one Moroccan primary school teacher taught his students that 3 x 4 = 11 because there was an obvious misprint in his official lesson plan. The teacher admitted to Miller that previously he had taught

3 x 4 = 12, but now that the lesson plan was different, he assumed that "Now this has been changed."[50]

Gregg has noted in his comprehensive study nearly 40 years later that the same problems that Miller found remain the bedrock of Arab educational practices.[51] Tarek Heggy captured the problem incisively: "A system in which the teacher is relegated to the role of a transmitter and the student to that of a receiver can only instill a spirit of apathy in its recipients, inhibiting any creative impulses they may have, reining in their imagination and stifling their intellectual curiosity and initiative."[52] In 1991, Pervez Hoodbhoy wrote that Arab Islamic schools showed no interest in trying to excite their students or to develop an attitude of questioning. In particular, they worked hard to discourage the notion that authority might be wrong. Knowledge of all kinds was viewed as unchangeable, and all books tended to be memorized.[53] According to Fahim Qubain, the curricula of Arab schools were "non-functional and divorced from the life and environment of the student. Moreover, teaching techniques tend to be authoritarian, dependent on learning by rote, and lacking in the development of curiosity and the thinking faculties of the child."[54]

Indeed, Arab educational institutions at all levels relied heavily on traditional methods of rote memorization as the primary means of learning. In the classrooms of Arab schools, the teacher presented the information to be learned without explanation, and the students were taught to simply memorize this information and be able to parrot it back on demand. The incentive structure of Arab schools encouraged the student to memorize lessons without internalizing them and left them little room to explore their imaginations or sharpen their analytic faculties.[55] "Arab/Muslim schools adopt authoritarian educational means, too," according to Dwairy, "Teachers expect students to memorize information. They allow limited space for dialogue and critical thinking. They do not encourage initiative or creativity. . . . The major functions that students learn at schools are to memorize and to follow directives and orders, on the one hand, and to be detached from their own feelings and avoid self-expression on the other."[56] Likewise, Derek Hopwood commented on teaching in Syrian schools in the 1980s that "The teacher's authority is unquestioned and emphasis is laid on the reproduction of memorized facts. This method stunts initiative and the attitudes instilled at school are carried over into working life, the desire not to disturb the system and a reluctance to assume authority."[57] In his work on Egypt, Hopwood tells the story of a primary school in Cairo in the 1980s where the teachers and students boasted that the students could "read" their primers without even looking at the pages![58] The authors of the 2003 Arab Human Development Report bluntly stated, "In Arab countries, lectures seem to dominate. Students can do little but memorize, recite, and perfect rote learning. . . . Communication in education is didactic, supported by set books containing indisputable texts in which knowledge is objectified so as to hold incontestable facts, and by an examination process that only tests memorization and factual recall."[59]

Indeed, advancement from one grade level to the next depends upon annual standardized tests that measure only the ability of the students to memorize their standardized textbooks.[60] Mohamed Rabie describes the typical method of teaching in Arab schools in the following manner:

> Students are given thousands of facts to memorize instead of the research skills that will enable them to find the facts when needed. Teachers and professors tend to cling to specific innovations instead of applying the principles of innovation, thus rendering the system rigid and conserva- tive. Memorization, together with the authoritarian method of instruc- tion, serves to inhibit rather than encourage students' ability to think and take the initiative. Material memorized will be regurgitated on paper during examinations. A hypothesis may go long untested and be accepted as fact. The students' ability to develop realistic and imagina- tive solutions to whatever problems they may have to deal with is very much limited.[61]

Arab students in the vast majority of schools, including universities, generally were discouraged from asking questions, delving deeper into areas of interest, or otherwise actively participating in the educational process.[62] Gerald Miller's study of a Moroccan primary school revealed that the children were required to do everything in a rigidly prescribed manner. If the child failed to adhere to every last detail of that manner her work was considered wrong—with no ex- planation given—even if the work itself was substantively correct. In general, he found that the children were strongly encouraged to conform to models of prescribed behavior and were harshly punished for failing to do so.[63] Rabie observed that "Instead of leading students to alternative answers, only one an- swer is expected and accepted as being correct."[64] The research conducted by a 1979 RAND report found that Arab students and teachers frequently avoided asking questions altogether: the students to try to avoid showing ignorance, and the teachers to avoid humiliating the students by exposing their ignorance. They noted that American instructors in the Middle East had to go to great lengths to design special programs to allow real give-and-take between the students and teachers.[65] More recently, the Arab Human Development Report bemoaned that "Most present-day educators have graduated from institutions that follow an approach to teaching based on rote learning, which is not especially conducive to critical thinking."[66]

Compartmentalized Learning. The education system of the Arab world also largely promoted the treatment of subjects as discrete and unrelated entities, and discouraged generalization or interdisciplinary comparison. Because facts were simply memorized and were not synthesized into larger frameworks, Arab education generally did not teach students how to see trends or connections between facts. Developing an understanding of the underlying and essential characteristics shared by events or ideas, as well as broad theoretical generalizations, were not considered part of an Arab child's education.[67] In his vast study of education in the Arab world, Joseph Szyliowicz noted that Arab curricula made no attempt to integrate the variety of courses offered.[68] Constantine Zurayk bemoaned the "limited and fragmented education" of Arab schools and universities, which he concluded prevented the individual from developing a comprehensive perspective on a subject.[69] The 1979 RAND study noted that Arab students generally did very well in vocabulary tests, but in tests based on analogies they scored low, and consequently, Americans who had taught in the Arab world felt that it left Arab students with underdeveloped "powers of analysis and generalization."[70]

Not surprisingly, American Peace Corps volunteers in Morocco found that Moroccan students often had great difficulty adjusting to foreign educational systems that tried to promote independent, creative thought, intellectual curiosity and initiative, interdisciplinary comparisons, and learning by understanding rather than simple absorption: "The Moroccan *Lycée* student finds himself in a situation in which he must 'think for himself.' The young French and Americans who make up the majority of the faculty of secondary education [in the Lycée] often encourage innovation. The result is that the [Moroccan] students are either incapable of making the necessary responses or they just go overboard, causing bedlam in the classroom. . . . The students are thrown into a situation where the traditional behaviors will no longer help them to cope."[71]

In his 1994 survey of the contemporary Middle East, Milton Viorst relates the following anecdote regarding the state of education in the Arab world:

> An Arab professor at a West Bank university, a Muslim who taught for many years in the US, told me that his Palestinian students, though more highly motivated and more conscientious than American students, were far more timid about exploring the bounds of knowledge. "They cannot free themselves from the habit of learning by rote," he said. "They are more sensitive to community opinion. They are more dependent on the

teacher. Most striking to me, their training in the Koran teaches them that all knowledge is in the book. One can memorize the book; one can even interpret it. But a book is not a point of departure; one cannot add to it. The Islamic tradition holds that learning is fixed. My students resist going beyond the book, any book."[72]

It is not hard to understand why an educational system that teaches in this fashion is failing its students. It is this obsolete method, more than any other problem, that accounts for the vast disparities in the quality and impact of education between the Arab world and other regions. A system that favors rote memorization of facts, that discourages innovation and initiative, that insists that subjects remain discrete (rather than promoting interdisciplinary thinking), that emphasizes conformity over independence, and that promotes hierarchic rather than critical thinking, is not an educational method well-suited to the demands of the modern, globalized world—or to modern, mechanized warfare. Indeed, Dwairy concludes with the damning assessment that:

> The major ways of socialization used by teachers and parents are lecturing, rote memorization, and punishments. Arguing or debating are not encouraged, and may even be punished. In such an educational system, children memorize what they are to learn and may pass exams, but the content does not become an active part of their own individual system of thoughts. They still are unable to enrich their thoughts and use this knowledge to be creative. A well-educated child is an obedient, conformist one. Many parents and teachers consider a child impertinent if he or she argues, is curious, or creative. Children are not encouraged to develop their own values, thoughts, or opinions; they are expected to adopt the family's.[73]

Technical Education

Science, mathematics, and other technical subjects consistently suffered in Arab educational systems throughout the postwar period, right on to the present. Arab schools applied the same teaching methods to these subjects as they employed for all teaching, hindering their students from developing an accurate understanding of scientific knowledge or the scientific method. Science too was taught by rote memorization, with little emphasis on internalizing the material so that it could serve as the basis for independent inquiry. For the most part, the teachers performed all "experiments" as demonstrations without giving their students the opportunity to conduct them and learn for themselves. Little effort was made to convey to students the more general principles behind experiments or the general applicability of scientific principles and methods.[74]

In Arab schools, "A student . . . learns natural science or technology exactly as if it were sacral knowledge from the Koran and Hadith," according to Bassam Tibi.[75] He has elsewhere written, "In Muslim societies, where higher institutions of learning have a deeply-rooted procedure of rote learning, the content of positive sciences adopted from Europe is treated in a similar fashion. Verses of the Quran are learned by heart because they are infallible and not to be inquired into. Immanuel Kant's *Critiques* or David Hume's *Inquiry*, now available in Arabic translation, are learned by heart in a similar manner and not conceived of in terms of their nature as problem-oriented inquiry."[76] Derek Hopwood has observed that even at modern Syrian universities there is an "Overemphasis on the reproduction of knowledge and examination-passing. Students complain that on graduation they are not good engineers or computer programmers, but that they have learned how to pass examinations."[77]

Fahim Qubain illustrated problems in Arab teaching of science by summarizing the practices employed in Iraq: "As in most Arab countries, the methods of instruction leave something to be desired. The instructor usually delivers a lecture to a large number of students. Class discussion and quiz sections are the exception rather than the rule. The student relies heavily on passive memorization of textbooks and lecture notes. A considerable part of the laboratory work consists of demonstration rather than actual student experience."[78] Indeed, Qubain notes that these same problems were evidenced throughout the teaching of science in the Iraqi school system despite the fact that Baghdad's oil wealth meant that there was no shortage of modern laboratory equipment in most urban high schools and universities.[79] Overall, Qubain's study of science education in the Arab world led him to conclude that "The methods of instruction tend heavily toward classroom lectures, booklearning by rote, and memorization of facts, equations, and formulas. Recitation usually consists of repeating without questioning what the book or instructor has stated. There is very little or no outside reading, and many students go through high school without having read a single book on science aside from the assigned textbooks."[80]

The prejudices of Arab society against science and technical work contributed to a denigration of scientific education generally and to tremendous problems in recruiting students for engineering, basic science, mathematics, and other technical disciplines.[81] The 1969 UNESCO conference on education in the Arab world concluded that Arab schools tended to allot less time to math, science, and practical activities than any other region, and the gap was growing worse.[82] In the 1990s, Peter Wilson and Douglas Graham found that in Saudi Arabian schools, "Long hours are devoted to Koranic memorization, while relatively little time is spent on science or mathematics."[83] Similarly, Hopwood notes that despite the Syrian government's emphasis on producing larger numbers of scientists, engineers, and technicians, this had little impact on the teaching of science and mathematics in Syrian schools:

> In intermediate schools, math and science subjects took only 23 percent of the curriculum and technical subjects a mere six percent. Technical education was separate from general education and was regarded as second best. Only those who could not continue general education entered technical schools. The number of technical students was some 8–12 percent of the total secondary body. . . . Higher education showed a similar bias and was not geared to the needs of the country. The majority of students read [Brit: studied] arts and humanities, and Islamic law, although employment opportunities in these fields were scarce. Posts in technical fields remain unfilled. . . . Only 3–4 percent studied medicine and slightly more science and engineering.[84]

In the 1990s, Roy noted that in Saudi Arabia, "There is little sentiment for having one's children enter the technical or vocational stream where one 'works with one's hands.' There is no prestige or status to be derived and, generally speaking, the wages and working conditions are far less attractive."[85] The 2003 AHDR still found that "Statistics indicate a sustained increase in the number of students in higher education institutions in Arab countries over successive years, with a noticeable increase in the number of female students. These statistics indicate, however, that only a small number of students and graduates have opted to specialize in basic sciences, engineering, medicine and other scientific subjects. . . . In general, the ratio of students enrolled in scientific disciplines in higher education in Arab countries is small, compared to advanced countries in the field of knowledge, such as Korea."[86] And a 2008 World Bank survey found that only 29.3 percent of university students from Muslim Middle Eastern countries were studying medicine, science, engineering, or other technical subjects, compared to 34.3 percent of Latin American and 37 percent of East Asian students.[87]

In fact those who did graduate with any sort of technical degree often did not want to practice their skill. Andrea Rugh has written that Arab undergraduates tend to "major" in subjects based on their scores on standardized tests. Medicine and engineering require the highest scores—as determined by the government—and so are prestigious, but most people do not go on to practice the subjects they majored in. "Interest has little to do with the degrees people take, and indeed the majority who find their way into the private sector choose jobs in fields other than those they were trained in. The engineer becomes a public relations person, the agricultural student a secretary."[88] Delwin Roy warned that because of the poor technical education at Saudi universities, there are "hundreds of Saudis with engineering degrees who, in fact, know little about engineering."[89]

Far too many Arab students forced into technical fields by government fiat still hoped to join the federal bureaucracy, and many who couldn't would try to return to the university for a more respectable humanities degree.[90] As a last resort, they might turn to teaching, but even then they preferred non-technical subjects, and science or math only if there were no other alternative. Actually practicing a technical skill was rarely a student's first priority even when salaries were higher in those fields.[91] An official Egyptian government report in the late 1960s stated:

> The United Arab Republic [Egypt] is rapidly becoming an industrial country. . . . this led [*sic*] to a great demand of specialized personnel. . . . The government finds great difficulty in preparing these numbers, on the other hand a big surplus of unemployed graduates of theoretical faculties are with no work at all. Another notable phenomenon is that the occupations that we called the "white collar" are always preferred to the "blue-collar type." . . . *All the second type are better paid and enjoy much better chance of promotion, yet it has always been noticed that secondary school graduates who fail to join higher education prefer the white-collar job.*[92] [Emphasis added.]

A survey of Qatari secondary school seniors in 2008 still revealed that 77 percent of them wanted to work in a ministry or government-owned company. Only 3.4 percent wanted to work in a private company.[93] Indeed, the World Bank found that overhiring in the public sector actually worsened between 1965 and 2003.[94]

Consequently, in Sharabi's words, "The institutions of higher learning which mushroomed throughout the Arab world in the post-independence period produced scientists but not science, medical doctors but not medical science, social scientists but not social science, and so forth."[95] The same has proven true for mathematics. In the 2007 Trends in International Mathematics and Science Study, only 47 percent of Egyptian eighth-grade students achieved even the lowest international benchmark in mathematics. In the 2015 version of the study, only 36 percent of Moroccan eighth graders could achieve the lowest benchmark, and of 42 countries surveyed, none of the 11 Arab states in the study were even in the top half of the results, with 7 of the last 11 spots occupied by Arab countries.[96]

This pervasive anti-scientific atmosphere in the Arab states prompted many technically skilled Arabs to leave their home countries and move to the West. In her study of the Egyptian "brain drain," Saneya Abdel Wahab Saleh concluded that the major reason for this phenomenon was the lack of moral and social recognition for scientists in Egypt.[97] They were stifled by the intellectual atmosphere in both the academic and private arenas of Egyptian society and were looked down upon as performing necessary but unattractive services. As she put it, "They did not feel wanted here."[98] Focusing on medical doctors and engineers who emigrated to the West, Saleh found that many left for "opportunities to be creative, a chance to use professional training effectively, to work in their specialization by carrying out research in a scientific atmosphere. What really frustrated and pushed them to emigrate can be stated thus: feelings of uselessness in their home or native community, of time and energy lost, of lack of recognition and esteem, of loss of self-respect and sense of identity."[99]

The Persistence of the Traditional Educational Method

These methods remained the dominant, and often only, educational practices employed in all of the Arab states during the post-1945 era. At least three comprehensive surveys of Arab educational practices have been conducted during this period, and it is remarkable how consistent their findings were despite over 50 years between the first and the last.

In 1949, Roderic Matthews and Matta Akrawi (the Director General of Higher Education in Iraq) surveyed education throughout the Arab Middle East. They found that in Iraqi schools, for example:

> The children rarely take the initiative in the classroom, and they are not encouraged to inquire about things which interest them. Questions of a type to provoke original thought are rare. Thus, teaching in these schools is principally a matter of presenting facts and demanding that they be memorized, this in spite of the fact that the primary course of study eschews such practice.[100]

> Methods of teaching in secondary schools do not differ in their essentials from those of the primary schools. . . . Great stress is laid on the teacher's explanation in class by inductive, deductive, lecture, and demonstration methods according to the subject. Not enough emphasis

is laid on student activity which should develop understanding and knowledge of what the students are studying. They, therefore, come to rely on the teacher for clarifying the subject. Theirs is to learn what has been explained and be ready to recite it back when required. In this way the "spoon-feeding" of the primary school is carried over to the secondary school, and the students do not as a rule acquire a habit of self-reliance and self-instruction.[101]

It is largely a textbook method of teaching. . . . The textbook is followed closely lesson by lesson and chapter by chapter, the students relying on it and on the teacher's explanation in preparing their lessons. Little, if any, reading is done outside the textbook, since most of the teachers do not assign reference work. It is the rare teacher who tries to stimulate students' interest in reading outside magazines and books, fiction or otherwise.[102]

Matthews and Akrawi found the same methods of education in every other Arab state they examined, including Egypt, Jordan, Syria, and Lebanon. In Syria, for example, they noted that "Through the use of readers and textbooks and discussions in class, subject matter is methodically imparted to the children. The teacher is the prime mover, and few, if any, classroom activities are initiated by the children."[103] While in Lebanon, "Teaching consisted of imparting knowledge and skills to the pupils, the initiative being largely that of the teacher, pupils taking the passive, receptive role."[104]

In the early 1970s, Joseph Szyliowicz conducted a comprehensive study of the educational systems of the Arab Middle East at all levels as a means of probing Arab problems with economic development. Szyliowicz found that the same methods of education persisted that had been employed by Arab society for centuries and that these methods were producing men and women ill-suited for economic and cultural transformation. For instance, Szyliowicz noted that:

The educational system . . . produced thousands of graduates who have been described by an Egyptian scholar who has analyzed the school system as lacking in initiative and adventure, social intelligence and vision, the ability to think independently, and an appreciation of knowledge and culture [i.e., the arts, literature]. He pointed out that all students sought to obtain an administrative position, regardless of its routine nature or low salary, that they were incapable of understanding or participating in the national life, let alone directing it, that they lacked the ability for creative, innovative thought, and that since they had forgotten the information with which they had been stuffed they were practically illiterate.[105]

Thus whether the child was an Egyptian, an Iraqi, or a Jordanian, he usually had to memorize a mass of data with limited applicability to his environment or to the national situation in order to pass the appropriate examinations. Seldom was the curriculum geared to local needs. Syllabi were decreed by the central ministry and did not permit any gradation or variation in the choice of courses.[106]

For most teachers, the only pedagogical technique is memorization, and at all levels, little attention is paid to stimulating students to think for themselves. The normal pattern is for the teacher to condense textual materials into notes that they either dictate or hand out for the student to further abridge and memorize them as thoroughly as possible in order to pass the final examination. Various efforts to mitigate the traditional emphasis upon memorization of facts so as to provide independent, flexible thinkers have been largely unsuccessful.[107]

On university-level education, Szyliowicz found that:

In Egypt, the emphasis remains upon formal lecture, and students are accorded little opportunity for discussion, questioning, or meeting with the professor. Moreover, the student is graded only upon his success in the annual examination, so that once again the aim of the student is not to learn creatively or to exercise his mental faculties in a disciplined manner but to prepare for examinations by cramming and memorizing the factual information contained in the lecture notes or the textbook.[108]

Most recently, the Arab Human Development Reports of 2002–2016 have once again catalogued educational methods across the Arab world, and what is perhaps most stunning about their conclusions is the consistency and persistence of these same educational methods into the twenty-first century. It was the 2003 edition that focused entirely on the "knowledge gap" that had led to the dearth of "human capital" that the authors of the AHDR concluded was the principal drag on development across the Arab world—the reason that the Arab states were falling farther and farther behind the rest of the world. While the later reports of the AHDR project continued to echo the same findings, it is the 2003 version that deserves to be quoted from because of its specific focus on this problem:

Most present-day educators have graduated from institutions that follow an approach to teaching based on rote learning, which is not especially conducive to critical thinking. . . . The curricula taught in Arab countries seem to encourage submission, obedience, subordination and compliance, rather than free critical thinking. In many cases, the contents of these curricula do not stimulate students to criticize political or social axioms. Instead, they smother their independent tendencies and creativity.[109]

There are various means for conveying information: lectures, seminars, workshops, collaborative work, laboratory work and many others. In Arab countries, however, lectures seem to dominate. Students can do little but memorize, recite and perfect rote learning. The most widely used instruments are schoolbooks, notes, sheets or summaries. Communication in education is didactic, supported by set books containing indisputable texts in which knowledge is objectified so as to hold incontestable facts, and by an examination process that only tests memorization and factual recall.[110]

The quality of education, a long neglected priority in Arab societies, is as important as the availability of education in building the foundations of knowledge. Improving quality will involve inculcating basic capacities for self-teaching and developing people's cognitive, analytic and critical faculties, all of which spur creativity and innovation. It implies a profound reform of Arab educational systems, particularly education methods, which need to become more student-centered, through teams and projects, and more self-evaluating in all dimensions of learning.[111]

Politics Is Not the Problem

It is important to understand, especially in light of current fads to blame everything on politics, that this approach to learning has absolutely nothing to do with the politics of the Arab world. There are some who have tried to blame this educational method on the autocratic governments of the Arab world, claiming that they employed this method to deliberately instill obedience and docility into their populace so that they would not rebel. However, all of this is just flat out false.

To start, the educational method predated all of the Arab dictatorships and the vast majority of the monarchies. As the Matthews and Akrawi study published in 1949 detailed, Arab schools have employed these methods for centuries, since long before the current regimes of the region ever took power. It was the method employed in Quranic schools, mass public schools, and elite private schools without distinction. The regimes universally inherited these educational methods.

Likewise, it is a teaching method identical to that employed by most Arab families. If it were notably different from the common childrearing practices, we might wonder where it came from, and even speculate that it may have been the product of political machinations. But it wasn't. Given that education in families and schools was identical, it makes it difficult (to say the least) to claim that the latter was a product of politics but the former was somehow the product of something else, and it was mere coincidence that the two were identical.

Next, as all of the comprehensive studies of Arab educational practices demonstrated, it is the teaching method employed across the entire Arab world, and has been regardless of the type of government or its degree of fear from its populace. It was the teaching method employed in Lebanese schools during the height of Lebanese democracy in the 1940s–1970s. It was the teaching method employed in Syrian schools before the coups ever began in 1949 and in Egyptian schools before the overthrow of the (utterly incompetent) monarchy in 1952. It has been the teaching method in Oman despite a government that barely rules at all. It remains the teaching method in Saudi Arabia because the Al-Sa'ud agreed to allow the clergy to determine educational practices in return for their support. (In other words, the Saudi ulema determined the teaching method, not the government.) And it remains the teaching method in Iraq even long after Saddam's demise.

In actuality, dictators such as Saddam and Nasser before him wanted vibrant, productive, and creative populations who would increase the wealth and power of their states. If they had wanted to keep their populations docile, they might have tried limiting education altogether, but instead they did everything they could to improve and expand the education of their people and to encourage them to build a rich and vibrant society.

Moreover, a number of these same autocratic governments recognized that the teaching method was deleterious and complained about it, although they were typically too preoccupied, incompetent, or inert to correct them. Hammed Ammar found this in his work, reporting that "the resort to rote learning has been the bane of education in modern schools. Criticisms of students' parrotlike work are abundant in many of the official government reports."[112] And many leaders—from Nasser to the late King Abdallah of Saudi Arabia—have tried to modernize the teaching method to no avail. Indeed, in contemporary Qatar, the government does not fear or seek to control its people at all—it has tried hard to modernize and Westernize its educational system—and yet Mitchell's experience teaching there over the past decade still left him appalled that "the acquisition of knowledge is often measured by how well students memorize the material their teachers have presented and repeat it back to them verbatim."[113] Moreover, Mitchell's experience is backed up by a massive RAND study of education reform in Qatar from 2008, which found the persistence of these methods despite a major effort by the Qatari regime to end them.[114]

In short, the educational method of Arab schools had nothing to do with politics. It existed long before the autocracies, it existed in every state autocratic or not, it was identical to the method of education employed by most families, and to the extent that politics affected it at all, this came in the form of peripatetic efforts to reform, improve, and modernize the educational practices, not to retain or reinforce them.

The Inculcation of Culture

It is hard to escape the conclusion that typical Arab educational practices relentlessly inculcated the values, preferences, and preferred behavior—the culture—of the wider society. It's also not surprising because this is what every educational system, what every teaching method, does. When we begin to learn from our family and then when we go to school, we are not merely taught knowledge, we are taught how to act, how to think, and what is important according to the wider society we have been born into. American children are taught to honor George Washington for his honesty and integrity, Arab children to honor Salah ad-Din (Saladin) for his bravery and loyalty. Western schools mostly teach their students to create knowledge; Arab schools generally teach their students to imbibe it. Again, there are plenty of American students who pass through their educations doing little more than imbibing, and plenty of Arabs determined to create regardless of what their parents and teachers might think (and even many Arab parents encouraging their children to create). There are always rebels, and always multiple lessons to be learned in any educational process, but the overarching patterns are there, and they weigh heavily on their graduates, precisely as they are meant to. It is how societies socialize their members to the patterns of behavior considered most advantageous to their circumstances so as to produce large numbers of people who think and act in a more or less similar manner.

That is the role of culture in human society and the role of education in passing on culture to each new generation. The evidence is compelling that Arab educational methods during the postwar era played their assigned role in shaping how Arabs think and act, how they are taught to behave in most circumstances. It should not be surprising that what they were taught closely reflected how they behaved in battle. In the terror and confusion of combat soldiers and officers are most likely to fall back on what is most deeply ingrained in their psyches. That is, unless they have been relentlessly trained by the military itself to act in some other way. That is why the next topic we need to turn to is Arab military training, to see if that too promoted these same, culturally regular patterns of behavior, or if it tried to teach Arab soldiers and officers to think and act in some different way.

| Arab Military Training Methods

T HE PATTERNS OF teaching described in the last chapter reflect the Arabic cultural idea of how to impart knowledge in the most general sense, not just how to teach in the specific circumstances of the family or school. While it is possible that powerful socializing institutions such as the armed forces can teach their members to think and act differently from the wider society, it is not the norm. Throughout history, most militaries have trained their troops in ways that tended to mirror that of their wider society. When that happens, military training reinforces the behavioral patterns inculcated by civilian education, formal and informal. In the case of the Arab states since the Second World War, their military training overwhelmingly mimicked the family childrearing and school-teaching practices of their wider society. In this way, military training in the Arab armed forces reinforced the behavioral patterns emphasized by the dominant societal culture.

As a side note before diving in, every one of the aspects of Arab military training I describe below, often backed up by various historical examples, is something that I have had repeatedly confirmed to me by American or Western trainers (and often experienced myself) in Iraq, Jordan, Egypt, Kuwait, and Saudi Arabia during my 30 years of experience with Arab militaries.

How Training Mirrored Teaching

Just as most Arab schools taught academic disciplines by rote memorization in the decades since the Second World War, so too did Arab armed forces teach military skills. Most training in the Arab states was taught by the enforced memorization of basic skills. Arab soldiers and officers were generally made to repeat the same set of actions over and over again without any variation. Little or no effort was made to have the personnel understand the purpose of the skill or how it might be adapted to suit different circumstances. Indeed, it was the norm among Arab armies that memorizing the steps needed to perform the task was emphasized to the exclusion of actually attaining the goal the task was meant to accomplish.[1] The relatively good Egyptian and Iraqi combined arms operations in 1973 and 1988 followed by their complete inability to perform these very same operations whenever the course of battle diverged from their set-piece plans was the epitome of this pattern of learning specific operational plans by rote rather than internalizing the general principles so that they could be applied and adapted to any situation.

For the most part, operations in Arab militaries are conducted "by the book." Arab armed forces teach their soldiers and officers there is only one right answer to any military problem, and only one right way of handling a situation. This right answer is then practiced constantly until it can be performed unthinking from memory. This approach is employed in battle regardless of other factors such as terrain, mission, the forces available, or the enemy's strength and disposition.[2] For instance, one UN observer on the Golan Heights in 1973 was amazed at the rigidity of the Syrian attack, remarking that "It wasn't like an attack, it was like a parade-ground demonstration."[3] The Gulf War Air Power Survey pointed out that "The Iraqis conducted basic [air force] instruction on a rigid and inflexible pattern. Pilots and instructors executed their maneuvers, 'solely by reference to instruments with little attention paid to outside, visual references.'"[4] Likewise, Chaim Herzog has opined that "The training of the relatively few good [technically competent, that is] people in the Arab forces has been rigid and not conducive to exercise of the ingenuity required during times of stress."[5]

Arab military personnel are typically taught that the "school solution" is not one they are expected to figure out on their own on the spot. Instead, the correct approach will be told them by higher authority. Arab soldiers and junior officers are generally taught not to act on their own, but to wait for orders from their superiors.[6] Like sons in a traditional Arab family and students in a traditional Arab classroom (or middle managers in an Arab factory), Arab junior officers are trained to remain passive and simply follow the guidance of higher authority. In the words of Egypt's general Saad al-din Shazli, "Our practice had always been to keep junior officers under stultifying strict supervision."[7] For this reason, the Arab air forces took readily to the Soviet practice of ground controllers directing all fighter operations. Indeed, the Arabs took this practice farther than the Soviets ever had, making their pilots so totally reliant on their ground controllers that when deprived of this guidance they simply had no idea what to do, as displayed by the Iraqis in 1991 and the Syrians in 1982.[8] On the effects of this tendency, Edward Luttwak and Daniel Horowitz commented that "In Arab armies, junior officers are used to operating on the basis of written orders rather than on their own responsibility; in combat they seemed to lack the personal initiative and mental flexibility required by a fast-moving mechanized war. When plans were disrupted, most Egyptian units broke down into a leaderless mass of individuals; their officers could pass on orders but failed to provide leadership in the absence of specific guidelines."[9]

Arab soldiers and officers almost universally have been taught only a small range of specific skills narrowly related to their mission. Just as Arab schoolchildren are taught to consider different subjects discrete and unrelated, so too Arab military personnel have been taught to consider the different elements of modern armed forces to be discrete and unrelated. While observing Iraqi operations at the end of the Iran-Iraq War, General Bernard Trainor found that Baghdad's soldiers and officers were "trained to do their specialty and nothing else."[10] Infantrymen were taught to fire their weapons, to dig-in, to camouflage their positions, to attack, and a handful of other very basic skills. However, they were rarely taught how to operate in conjunction with other combat arms, or to perform other skills not specifically related to their basic mission. Often they were not taught anything about how to operate even simple weapons or equipment not directly related to their specialty. The Egyptians took this tendency to its logical conclusion prior to the October War when they specifically decreed that every soldier should have one task and one task alone, and should only be trained in that one task.[11] The training of each combat branch was strictly limited to the specific operations of that branch, and little or no effort was made to explain the operations and missions of the other branches or the interaction among the different branches—this even in small units with organic infantry, armor, and artillery complements of their own. Consequently, Arab personnel were narrowly specialized and had tremendous difficulty integrating their various skills and forces into effective combined arms teams.[12]

Arab armed forces generally suffer from having too little practical field exercises to hone their skills. Like Arab schoolchildren, Arab military units are taught skills but haven't always been allowed to practice them. Instead, skills and operations are typically demonstrated to them by instructors, and the trainees are made to practice only the simple sub-elements that would have to be combined into more involved procedures in battle. Field exercises tend to be insufficient or nonexistent among most Arab armies, while Arab pilots regularly log far fewer flying hours than their Israeli or NATO counterparts. Live-fire exercises are extremely rare for both armies and air forces, and were so throughout the postwar era. Moreover, exercises, when they were conducted, were held at small unit level and only very infrequently involved large formations as would normally be employed in battle. Thus, on the ground, most Arab army exercises were conducted at battalion-size at best, and usually smaller, while Arab air forces rarely practiced larger than two versus two engagements, and almost never practiced even squadron-level operations.[13] In this area, the massive exercises conducted by the Egyptians between 1967 and 1973 and by the Iraqis after 1986 were noteworthy exceptions and important aspects of their more substantial accomplishments.

Arab training and exercises were hopelessly unrealistic. For instance, into the twenty-first century, the Egyptian Air Force's standard pattern of attack called for two planes to approach nearly simultaneously from either side of a target, *on a collision course*. Consequently, even in training exercises, one plane out of every pair had to sheer off at the last minute to avoid a midair collision—causing that pilot's bombs to go far from the target. Because the Egyptians did not record their missions or debrief, let alone actually critique their own performances, and no one at operational levels wanted to rock the boat by pointing out that their tactics were suicidal and their training practices rigged, all of these practices became institutionalized elements of EAF training and US pilots reported constant frustration trying to convince the EAF that their school solutions were not only wrong, but potentially fatal.[14] One US officer observed that it is "probably good" that the Egyptians didn't use live ordnance in practice, because if they did, they would lose a lot of their aircraft and pilots to these ridiculous tactics and distorted training practices.[15]

At every level, Arab drills and maneuvers are heavily scripted. The exercises conducted by Egyptian F-16 pilots of the 1980s and 1990s—in which every pilot knew what he was facing, what he would do and when, what his opponent would do and when, and who would "win" in simulated dogfights—were the rule, rather than the exception, and largely persist to this day. In all Arab units in all Arab armies and air forces, the same scripts tend to be repeated over and over again from month to month and year to year. Consequently, Arab personnel simply had to figure out the specifics of the exercise, memorize them, and then perform them from memory to successfully complete their task. Even worse, Arab soldiers and officers are frequently graded on how they perform their specific task and not whether they accomplished the overall goals of the exercise. So for example, ground units are typically judged on how closely they conformed to the plan of attack, rather than whether they took the objective, and pilots are judged on how well they executed the preset flight profile rather than whether they hit the target.

As one example of this, at least up until the October War, the Syrian and Egyptian armies had "obstacle courses" for their tanks and armored vehicles that were never changed, nor were there ever any other surprises involved: the course was always the same and what was expected of the vehicle crews was always the same. Vehicle crews were graded based on how well they conformed to the strict guidelines of the course and not how well they actually handled their vehicles. Thus a typical course for armor might have called for a tank to drive forward for 200 meters, cross a hill, then drive around an enemy minefield, turn right, drive 30 meters, traverse the turret to the left, fire at a fixed target, traverse the turret back, drive forward another 100 meters, etc. However, tank crews were evaluated based on how they performed these maneuvers and not on whether they actually avoided all of the mines, or found the best way to get from one side of the hill to the other, or even if they hit the targets. All the crew had to do was to memorize the distance to drive in each direction, where to turn, where and when to fire each weapon, etc. In no way did these drills actually teach Arab soldiers and officers how best to fight and defeat their enemies.[16]

In general, Arab training has rarely, if ever, attempted to simulate the real problems of battle by unexpectedly changing familiar activities, introducing novel forces or situations, or otherwise surprising the participants. Instead, training drills remain absolutely unchanged from one iteration to the next, and training maneuvers followed the same scripts time and again with little variation.[17] Indeed, American trainers in Iraq in 2003–2011 and 2014–2017 complained endlessly about these problems and their frustration in trying to get the Iraqis to change their ways.[18]

Just as the Arab educational system has resisted reform, so too the military training systems of most of the Arab countries have proven difficult to change. On a number of occasions, senior-level commanders recognized the need for change, particularly to encourage greater initiative and creativity among junior officers, and tried to encourage their subordinates to integrate this new emphasis into the training. However, real changes along these lines were virtually nonexistent, and fleeting on the rare occasions when they occurred. The Arab militaries simply did not know how to change their training methods to produce different results. Consequently, reform programs often led to changes in rhetoric and curricula, but because the methods did not change, neither did the products.[19]

As an example, the Egyptians tried mightily between 1967 and 1973 to get their tactical commanders to show greater independence of judgment, improvisational ability, and aggressiveness in combat. Senior commanders were directed to encourage their subordinates to act in this fashion and to reward them for doing so. However, because the Egyptian method of training continued to focus on rote memorization of basic skills, rigid adherence to tactical doctrine, and the compartmentalization of information and command authority, there was no discernible change whatsoever in the initiative or creativity of their junior officers.[20] As one US military officer commented after many months working with the Egyptian armed forces, "You get over there and you think the problem is the training. But then, after a while, you realize that the training is just the symptom, and the problem is how they think about things."[21]

Evidence from Iraqi Military Manuals

In virtually all of the Arab militaries, training manuals are typically Arabic translations of British, Russian, and (increasingly) American manuals that are rarely read or taught, let alone put into practice. For most, doctrine is simplistic, rigid, and unwritten, to the extent that there is doctrine at all. There were times when Arab militaries got serious about doctrine—the Egyptians and Syrians in the run-up to the October War, for example—but as I have already noted, in those cases they tended to import someone else's doctrine and misapply it in a cartoonish fashion never intended by the originating military. In those instances where Arab armies did not employ painstakingly detailed manuals it was generally the case that their armies and air forces had tremendous difficulty following the doctrine. In these cases, Arab armed forces generally acted in such a way in battle that they appeared to have no doctrine at all. For example, Iraqi armored formations during the October War could not comprehend or put into practice British bounding-overwatch techniques with the result that Iraqi armored and mechanized formations simply charged at the Israelis in disorganized masses. This almost certainly was the product of Iraq's reliance on translated British armor manuals, which provided only general guidelines and principles, rather than a step-by-step explanation of how to act.[22]

For this reason, Iraq's experience offers a fascinating window into Arab military training. As I discussed in Chapter 7, during the course of the Iran-Iraq War, the Iraqis realized that their performance was miserable and made major exertions to remedy it. As part of that effort, the Iraqis recognized that their "doctrine" such as it was, was useless. Their manuals were a hodgepodge of translated British (mostly), French, American, and Soviet texts that they had never really paid attention to. During the Kurdish wars of the 1960s and 1970s, they had developed a set of tactics that they brought with them to the war against Iran, but found them hopelessly wanting against the Ayatollah's determined and resourceful legions. At that point, their capable General Staff began to write new manuals of their own, which then became the basis of the retraining of the Iraqi armed forces—particularly the Republican Guard—for their victorious campaigns in 1987–1988, as well as the successful invasion of Kuwait in 1990.

During Operation DESERT STORM, the US military captured a significant number of these indigenous Iraqi manuals (along with a number of older, verbatim translations of Western, mostly British, manuals).[23] They make for fascinating reading (well, for someone like me) because they demonstrate the rote, unimaginative, and unchallenging training methods of Arab forces.[24] They are simplistic, step-by-step, how-to procedures for conducting even the most basic military tasks—at far greater levels of detail than corresponding British manuals. In most cases, in the indigenous Iraqi manuals, tactical situations are depicted as having only one possible "solution." Many of the Iraqi manuals tell a commander exactly how to handle a given situation with little allowance for, or encouragement of, flexibility and improvisation.

For instance, in a May 1986 manual on how Iraqi armored formations were to conduct counterattacks against hasty Iranian defenses (especially earthen berms) erected after breaking through an Iraqi defensive position, the manual takes the reader through every last step in the operation, including actions that should be standard procedure in all military operations and all counterattacks. Indeed, the parts of the manual related to specific features of this particular kind of operation—how the Iranians attack and set up their hasty defenses after a penetration, their weaknesses while conducting such an operation, and how to go about attacking them—actually make up a very small percentage of the manual. Instead, the vast majority of the manual is a detailed account of how to conduct any armored offensive operation: information that should be covered in the basic manuals on armored operations and not in a supplementary manual on a specific type of operation. Although the manual is intended for brigade-level operations, it still contains instructions for the brigade artillery commander to make his registration fire appear to be part of normal operations so as not to tip-off the enemy, it warns tank and mechanized infantry formation commanders to redirect their fire to the flanks so as not to kill friendly infantry when they dismount and advance in the center, and it explains precisely when tanks are to start and stop firing.[25] As an example of the level of detail contained in this manual, the section on preparation for the attack admonishes the commander:

Fourth, in order to gather information for developing objectives, the following sources of information are tapped, from which information is gathered and analyzed to come to conclusions, or they may be converted to intelligence reports by the intelligence cell at the corps or division levels or below.

1) Our front troop observation points, including reserve points for observing our artillery.
2) Overlays featuring fire plan targets for our defensive troops.
3) The overlay showing the location of the enemy mortars and artillery, kept by the artillery commanders.
4) The overlay for immobilizing enemy concentrations. The areas of his effectiveness as defined by land observation radars.
5) Aerial photography, after scrutinizing them and highlighting the information they contain about enemy troop concentration on the maps.
6) Air reconnaissance for commanders and consultants or information obtained by air observation points if available.
7) Analyzing the movement area and available information in the headquarters to use them in gathering information about the terrain, critical terrain, features, obstacles, and so on and so forth.
8) Prisoners of war who have been interrogated or those who surrendered as refugees to our troops.
9) Areas of enemy activities and his daily routine as detected by our front troops, such as distribution of rations, approaches, departure and return time for patrols and time of their return, ambushes areas, screen line, etc.
10) Headquarters location and areas of his effectiveness as determined by the technical equipment system.
11) Documents such as maps that can be obtained by our troops during a raid, combat patrol or an ambush.[26]

Likewise, in the 10 pages of instructions on how to conduct the artillery bombardment prior to the counterattack one finds a seemingly endless series of instructions such as this:

The concealing fire is taken off the second cover by the observation officers accompanying the attacking infantry when our troops start the attack to occupy the first cover [the first Iranian defense line] for a distance not less than 400 meters for the dismounted infantry and 200 meters for the mounted infantry. At this point the infantry soldiers prepare the assault hand grenades to hurl at the cover or behind it before climbing the cover to keep the enemy in hiding. A switch is then made to dog fight [hand-to-hand combat] and close engagement to kill the remaining enemy elements in their positions, on or behind the dirt cover [earthen berm] with a view to purging the cover. Meanwhile, firing continues at the second dirt cover during the dog fight at the first cover and the time it takes to open passes, which is about 10–15 minutes. . . .[27]

In short, the manual is a "cookbook" that a tactical commander can use as a step-by-step guide to conducting these operations without having to rely on any basic understanding of armored counterattack operations.

This level of detail might seem excessive in Western armed forces if found in a company-level manual, and would be simply unheard of in a brigade-level manual. Overall, the impression one gets from reading Iraqi manuals from the later years of the Iran-Iraq War is that the Iraqi high command had by then figured out how to beat the Iranians but they just could not get their tactical formations to do the things needed to win. Consequently, their training and doctrine became ever more detailed in hope that they could lead their tactical commanders by the nose through the specific actions necessary to defeat the Iranians in battle.

To give a sense of how different the indigenously produced Iraqi manuals are from the mostly British manuals they ostensibly relied on beforehand, let me give a quick comparison. The paragraph below is from an Iraqi artillery manual based on the artillery course at the Iraqi General Staff college, and is a verbatim translation of British material—indeed, the Iraqis did not even bother to change the names of equipment used in the material from British army weaponry to the mostly Soviet guns used by the Iraqis.

No attempt should be made to launch assaults with mechanized infantry without support from artillery and tanks. The tanks provide reliable support to infantry even though they might be moving on a different axis. Tanks may precede infantry in advancing toward the target or they may provide fire support from a nearby side position. All this depends on the terrain and on the ability to resist hostile tanks. Anyhow, if the tanks cannot advance because of the anti-tank fire, the armored personnel carriers cannot advance either. In this case, if the terrain is suitable, the infantrymen should dismount and advance on hidden approaches to clash with the enemy. After the sections are dismounted, the armored personnel carriers usually remain on or near the target to provide fire support. But they may have to move backward to hide in what is called the "main assembly of carriers." The line at which dismounting occurs may be predetermined or determined by the commander during the assault.[28]

The next pair of paragraphs come from the (indigenously developed) 1986 manual on counterattacking hasty Iranian defenses (fortified earthen berms) at brigade-level.

> After the tanks begin the attack, they will [each] be followed at a distance of 300–600 meters by an armored personnel carrier carrying mechanized infantry. This carrier will proceed at the same speed. When the tanks arrive at a point 700–800 meters from the cover [berm], their gun firing will not be effective. They will therefore have to use their pivotal machine guns, at which point the armored personnel carrier will accelerate its speed to catch up with the tanks, and then go through them and pass them by. In the last 300 meters all weapons mounted on the carrier will start firing, including the infantry weapons. When the carrier is 10 meters from the target, the two soldiers at the front hurl grenades at the target while the infantry carriers dismount and the tanks reach the target at the same time. Any surviving enemy infantry will be killed then and a foothold at the target will be (illegible, [probably "secured"]).[29]
>
> . . . The attack is so designed with the infiltration of carriers through the tanks in order to define the role and responsibilities without leaving such crucial matters loose and up to the two specialties to decide who should reach the target first. For it has been established from analysis of previous battles that when there is a joint attack on the same target, infantry personnel wait for the tanks to reach the target first. Therefore, the carriers reduce their speed in the final phase of the assault to go behind the tanks, while the tank crew wait for the carriers to reach the target before them. Therefore, the tanks would reduce their speed to let the carriers go ahead of them. As a result they advance very slowly and the attack loses its momentum in the last phase. This gave the enemy a chance to fire at our tanks and carriers with its weapons. Once one or two of them is hit, the whole force comes to a halt and is compelled to turn around and return and the assault would then be defeated. For this reason and to prevent this from happening again, the tactic already mentioned has been developed whereby each specialty has a defined responsibility as to what is expected of it.[30]

The difference between the generalities and adaptability of the first paragraph and the rigidity and specificity of the second pair of paragraphs is striking. Indeed, the paragraphs from the indigenously developed manual indicate that Iraqi senior commanders were having such difficulty getting their subordinates to conduct combined arms properly that their solution was to go into even greater detail and to specify exactly when and how each element of a mechanized force (in this case a brigade) was to arrive at the target.

As these samples demonstrate, the Iraqis wrote their own manuals to cover very specific situations repeatedly encountered by their forces during the Iran-Iraq War. Thus, the Iraqi manual on Desert Operations is a verbatim copy of the British version, just as the Iraqi General Staff College lectures on artillery are drawn from British staff officer courses. By contrast, the Iraqis developed their own manuals for operations like defending against human wave attacks, how to counterattack to retake their own earthworks after they had been overrun in an Iranian attack, and how to use tanks to defeat light infantry using small boats to cross marshlands.

This strongly suggests that when push came to shove, the Iraqis found the British approach inadequate for their needs. For those critical battle situations in which Iraqi forces repeatedly found themselves while fighting the Iranians, Baghdad went back and drafted its own "cookbooks" to explain in great detail to its tactical commanders exactly how to deal with the situation, leaving little or nothing up to the judgment of the commander on the spot. It suggests the Iraqis were dissatisfied with the British manuals, not because they found the doctrine misguided, but because they left too much up to the judgment of the commander on the spot, which their junior officers just could not handle. Baghdad tried to remedy this problem by detailing actions far more precisely and by expunging the flexibility encouraged by the British approach. This almost certainly reflects the trend throughout the war with Iran toward greater micromanagement and scripting of operations by Iraqi senior commanders to relieve tactical commanders of the need to make decisions—which the disasters of the early part of the war demonstrated they were simply incapable of doing.

Culture, Education, and Arab Military Training

In retrospect, the pattern by which Arab culture was transmitted to Arab soldiers and officers seems obvious. Over the centuries, Arab culture developed a method of teaching that inculcated the values of the dominant culture. Over time, this method became the model for all teaching. This is true of all cultures: every society has its own ways of passing on knowledge from one person to another. That way of teaching is so "natural" to the members of the society that they use it in all ways to convey all knowledge to anyone in any situation. It is simply how one teaches something to someone else. It is only after exposure to the educational method of another culture that a person is likely to even recognize that there is more than one way to teach something to someone.

For all of these reasons, it wasn't just natural that Arab militaries would employ the teaching method of the larger Arab society to train men to be soldiers and officers, it was probably inevitable. Indeed, it would have been remarkable if Arab militaries trained their men in a manner that differed from the method of teaching in the broader society.

These findings make for a powerful argument. They demonstrate that Arab culture has a specific educational method that produces the patterns of behavior identified as elements of the dominant culture. They demonstrate that Arab personnel are taught to act and think in certain ways as a result of the long process of education both within the family and then in their schools. Although it is conceivable that a process of military training could condition them to act differently from the manner encouraged by the society at large, Arab military training does not do so. Instead, Arab military programs, modeled as they are on the educational methods of the larger society, *reinforce* these patterns of behavior. The result are soldiers and officers conditioned to act and think in certain ways—ways that reflect the values and priorities of the dominant culture.

Given the fact that these men have been trained to act and think in such a way for 18 years or more before they come to the armed forces and then have those behavioral patterns reinforced by their military training, how could they possibly be expected to act otherwise? Indeed, given that they have been taught to behave in this fashion for so many years, it requires a great deal of explanation to claim that something else could be producing corresponding patterns of behavior on the battlefield. At most, other factors—incentive structures imposed on the military from the outside such as those derived from politicization—can only be said to have a complementary effect. Likewise, it is clear that Arab battlefield behavior does not necessarily result from the absence of certain experiences—such as exposure to machinery or work in an industrial economy—but from the constant inculcation of cultural values found in the educational methods of the Arab world.

It also indicates that Arab culture is a better explanation than the others for the most debilitating Arab problems, at least when it comes to tactical leadership, maneuver warfare, air operations, and information management, but possibly including maintenance and weapons handling as well. Both the notion that the problem is the Soviet method and the three different variants of politicization claim that Arabs behave in certain ways on the battlefield because of incentive systems imposed on Arab military personnel that encourage certain kinds of actions and not others. However, the overwhelming evidence regarding Arab educational practices, informal and formal, demonstrate that most soldiers and officers in Arab militaries bring an "internal" incentive structure to battle—an incentive structure embedded in them by the lengthy process of education, civilian and military, and derived from the values of the dominant culture—which will interact with or even supersede any incentive structures imposed on the military system. Similarly, those who argue for underdevelopment contend that patterns of Arab performance in combat simply reflect the absence of certain skills and ways of looking at the world that can only be developed by exposure to an industrial society. However, the evidence regarding Arab educational practices makes clear that it is not so much the *absence* of specific skills and ways of thinking about the world, but the *presence* of other ways of thinking about the world that prompt Arab soldiers and officers to act as they do.

CHAPTER 22

Exceptional Arab Militaries:
State Armed Forces

E XCEPTIONS ALWAYS MAKE for the most interesting discussions. Exceptions can demonstrate that an idea is false. They can also demonstrate that an idea is spot on, if they are exceptions that prove the rule. Or, they can sometimes prove to be inexplicable outliers because human behavior sometimes defies explanation. In this chapter and the next, I am going to look at a number of exceptional military performances, first by the armies of various Arab states, and then by several non-state Arab militaries, to see if these confirm or contradict the evidence that the predilections of the dominant Arab culture were the most important source of Arab military problems during the post–World War II era.

There have been at least four occasions during this period when elements of the militaries of various Arab states have performed notably better than the norm. The Jordanian army in 1948, the Egyptian army in 1973, Syria's commandos in 1982, and the Iraqi armed forces in 1987–1990 all stood out from the pack. It is important to understand that none of them fought "well." Even the best of them achieved no more than a mediocre level of military effectiveness. All of them won modest victories, impressive only compared to the catastrophes that were the outcome of most modern Arab military endeavors. Nevertheless, they did fight better, and their better performances need explaining.

Jordan, 1948

In May 1948, when the Jordanian army—then known as the Arab Legion—marched into Palestine, it was the most professional indigenous military in the Middle East. Jordan's army was trained and led entirely by British officers or Jordanian officers trained in the British manner. In fact, all but five of the officers of the rank of major or higher were British, including its commander, John Bagot Glubb.[1] The British saw to it that the Legion was prepared for conventional military operations. Jordanian soldiers and officers practiced regularly, and during the Second World War the Legion had fought to crush a pro-Axis coup in Iraq and to liberate Syria from Vichy.

On the outbreak of war in May 1948, the Legion had 9,000 men, 45–50 British armored cars, and about 24 artillery pieces. It rushed into the West Bank with 4,500 men and all of its armor and artillery. The most significant material problem the Legion faced was a shortage of ammunition. Before the outbreak of fighting, Glubb estimated that he had only enough for one short battle if it involved the entire army.[2]

As paltry as this force may seem, it still overawed its foe. In May 1948, the Israeli Haganah could field less than 30,000 poorly armed and mostly untrained troops—men *and* women—to fend off six Arab armies, including the Legion.[3] The core of the Haganah, constituting less than half its strength were nine *Palmach* and Haganah field brigades, able to be deployed anywhere in Palestine. The rest were regional militia that could only be used to defend their own town or settlement. At the start of the war, the Israelis had no real armor, artillery, aircraft, or even heavy crew-served weapons to speak of. For example, in the initial battles around Jerusalem, to which the Legion committed nearly half its strength, the heaviest weapons the Israelis possessed were two medium machine guns and two Piat shoulder-fired antitank weapons.[4]

There is considerable uncertainty regarding King Abdallah I of Jordan's intentions when he ordered the invasion of Palestine. At first, in 1947, Abdallah hoped only to occupy the parts of Palestine reserved by the UN commission to the native Palestinians and annex them to his own state. At that time, Abdallah opened secret negotiations with the Israelis to divide the territory without bloodshed. As time went by, however, his ambitions seem to have grown. He apparently began to desire that the new Jewish state be reduced to an autonomous region of Jordan. Barring that, Abdallah hoped to increase the amount of territory under Jordanian control and, in particular, seems to have wanted to own Jerusalem rather than leaving it an international city as specified by the UN partition plan. It might be most accurate to say that

Abdallah intended to conquer the West Bank territories, and then take whatever else he could if opportunities arose.[5]

Abdallah's intentions were complicated by the limited military forces at his disposal and by the divided loyalties of his British officers. The Arab Legion simply was not large enough to occupy all of Palestine. It was not even large enough to conquer the various parts assigned to the Palestinians by the UN. The Israelis could be expected to fight tooth and nail, and Jordan could not be sure how its ostensible Arab allies would react to such blatantly self-serving moves. Beyond this, Abdallah was completely dependent on Glubb and the other British officers whose loyalties were divided between Amman and London. The British government made it clear that, although they had little love for their erstwhile Jewish subjects in Palestine, they would not tolerate actions that contravened the UN settlement. London ordered all of the British officers seconded to the Arab Legion "to abandon their units if these invaded Jewish territory."[6]

So Jordanian strategy tried to straddle these competing positions. Glubb meant to push into the West Bank immediately and occupy it up to the borders declared by the UN. He would then shift to the defensive. One final consideration in Glubb's approach was the need to minimize his own casualties. He knew he could not easily replace losses to his small, long-term service professional army. Consequently, Glubb wanted to avoid bloody battles, particularly in the streets of Jerusalem, where the training of his troops would be discounted and many might be killed in house-to-house fighting.[7]

The Battle of Kfar Etzion. The first Jordanian combat operations actually occurred before the outbreak of war on May 14, 1948. Israelis from the four Etzioni settlements outside Jerusalem began harassing Arab military movements during April 1948. The British considered these actions intolerable and sent British regulars with tanks, backed by a reinforced company of the Arab Legion plus Arab irregulars to attack these settlements in early May. Remarkably, the Jews held their positions against the British assault, but the British still decided that they had taught the Jews enough of a lesson and so withdrew. The Arab Legion company and the Palestinian irregulars remained, however, hoping to get orders from Amman to resume the attack.

A week passed and on May 11, the company commander, 'Abdallah at-Tal, took matters into his own hands and ordered an attack on the settlements.[8] The Jews had about 500 able-bodied settlers (men and women) in the four settlements, but had only small arms. While the Arab force was somewhat smaller, it was centered on the Legion company and was backed by a squadron of armored cars as well as considerable artillery and mortar support. In three

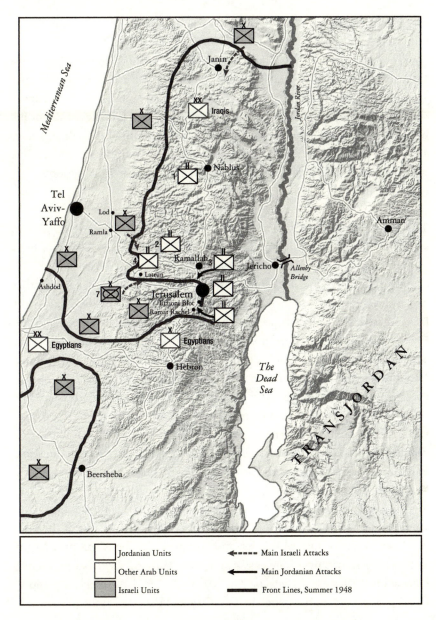

MAP 25 The Jordanian Front in the Israeli War of Independence, 1948

days of fighting, the Arabs succeeded in isolating the four settlements, and then the Legion company assaulted the main settlement of Kfar Etzion with heavy fire support. The Legion used part of their force to pin the Israeli defenders along their main line of defenses, and then sent another force with the armored cars to outflank the primary defensive positions. On May 13, at-Tal was able to take Kfar Etzion, prompting the other three settlements to surrender.[9]

The main body of the Arab Legion crossed over the Jordan River into Palestine on the morning of May 14, 1948. There they linked up with the Jordanian troops already operating south of Jerusalem and quickly occupied the superb defensive terrain of the Samarian Hills. Glubb deployed one of his brigades to cover the entire area from Jenin to just north of Ramallah, which allowed him to concentrate his other brigade, plus a number of independent infantry companies, in and around Jerusalem with the brigade headquarters at Ramallah.

The Battle of Jerusalem. On May 17, King Abdallah ordered Glubb to attack Jewish Jerusalem in strength. This was a clear contravention of both the UN plan and the orders of the British government. Nonetheless, Glubb complied, rationalizing it as intervention to end the confused fighting that had been raging between the Arab and Jewish residents of the city for the past three days. Glubb detached one of the battalions sent initially to Samaria, the 3rd Infantry, and ordered it south to Jerusalem to take part in the attack. This enabled him to mount a double envelopment of the city, with the 3rd Battalion—reinforced with armored cars, artillery, and heavy mortars—thrusting south into the Shaykh Jarrah area of northeastern Jerusalem, and the Jordanian units that had taken the Etzioni bloc (now reinforced to battalion strength) attacking the southwestern settlement of Ramat Rachel on the road to Bethlehem. Meanwhile, Glubb sent several Legion companies and Palestinian irregulars to assault the isolated Jewish quarter of the Old City and so hold the Israeli center.

The Legion's northern thrust met initial success, but then was brought to a halt by fierce Jewish resistance. The Israelis had only 70 members of the *Irgun Zvi Leumi*, the freelance militia/terrorist group headed by Menachem Begin, in Shaykh Jarrah. These were easily overpowered by the Legionaries, thereby cutting off the Jewish garrison on Mt. Scopus. The Jordanians then attempted to drive westward to surround the Old City and cut it off from Jewish territory. However, though the Legion had a huge advantage in firepower—the defenders had only a pair of light machine guns and two antitank weapons—they could not break through the Israeli positions.

In response, the Jordanians shifted their effort closer to the Old City. In this new assault, the Legionaries employed good combined arms tactics, moving in teams of infantry and armor supported by mortar fire and, occasionally, artillery. Nevertheless they found the going tough against the under-armed but resourceful Israelis. Eventually, the course of the fighting coalesced around the Israeli-held monastery of Notre Dame de France at the northwest corner of the Old City. Although it was defended by only a handful of Israelis with one Piat antitank weapon, the Jordanians could not take the monastery. The Jordanians lost several armored cars to the Piat and Molotov cocktails, and their battalion suffered nearly 50 percent casualties.[10] Late on May 24, Glubb called off the attack fearing additional losses. The Legion effort north of the Old City then slacked off considerably, until the first UN-brokered ceasefire halted the fighting altogether on June 10.

The southern thrust, against Ramat Rachel, was conducted in conjunction with Egyptian units coming up from the Negev to the south and was even less successful than the northern assault. On May 21, the two Arab armies launched a combined assault against the small Israeli force defending Ramat Rachel on the hills south of Jerusalem. They succeeded in driving out the defenders by sheer weight of numbers. However, later that day, a company of the Haganah's Etzioni brigade reinforced the Israelis, who counterattacked and retook the village.

Over the next three days the Arabs attacked the settlement over and over again, recapturing it several times, only to lose it to Israeli counterattacks each night. On May 24, reinforcements dispatched by Glubb arrived at Ramat Rachel to revive the flagging offensive. In the ensuing attack, the Legionaries and Egyptians once again managed to storm the Kibbutz, but the Israelis also brought up reinforcements and retook it early the next day. In that counterattack the Israelis also succeeded in taking a nearby monastery that dominated the surrounding terrain and that had served as a jumping-off point for the Arab attacks. With the loss of this key base of operations, the Egyptians and Jordanians called off their attack and dug-in, ending their joint effort to envelop Jerusalem from the south.

Only in the center, against the Old City, was the Arab Legion able to win a clear victory. The Jewish Quarter of the Old City had the disadvantage of being surrounded by Arab-controlled territory, cut off from the Jewish section of the new city. However, it had the advantage of being an ancient Middle Eastern *madina*, overbuilt with adjoining houses and cut by narrow winding streets that were easy to block or defend. While the British remained in Palestine, the Israelis had smuggled some supplies as well as Haganah and Irgun soldiers into the Old City so that it could withstand the inevitable assaults and likely siege the Israelis expected would follow their declaration of independence.

The Arab Legion attacked the Old City on all sides on May 16, slowly overpowering the small number of defenders and forcing them to give ground. The Israelis attempted a relief operation during the night of May 17/18. This effort was badly bungled and turned into a frontal assault on Legion positions. The Jordanians proved to be excellent marksmen and inflicted heavy casualties on the Israelis. Nevertheless, the main Israeli attack so diverted the Legionaries that another Jewish force was able to surprise and overpower the Arab irregulars guarding Mt. Zion, and then breach the Zion Gate into the Jewish Quarter. Although the Legion was surprised by the Israeli operation, they quickly regrouped and counterattacked the Israeli forces holding open the Zion Gate. In a brief, fierce fight during the day, the Jordanians defeated the Israelis and again shut off the Old City from the Jewish-held sector.

For the next 10 days the Israelis tried to open a corridor to the besieged Jewish Quarter but all of their attacks failed. The Legion devised an effective tactic of allowing Israeli soldiers and sappers to penetrate through the Zion Gate and then trap them in a kill sack in the small courtyard on the Arab side of the gate. Meanwhile inside the Old City, the Legion inexorably cleared out the Jewish defenses. They used armored cars in conjunction with small infantry teams and support from mortars and direct-fire weapons on the city walls. The Legion pushed deeper and deeper into the Jewish Quarter, defeated several more Israeli relief efforts, and finally compelled the defenders to surrender on May 28.

The First Battle of Latrun. As part of his effort to conquer Jerusalem, Glubb also deployed Arab Legion forces to try to cut the narrow corridor that ran from the Jewish cities along the coast to Jerusalem. In late May, Glubb ordered his 2nd Infantry Battalion, then deployed northwest of Jerusalem, to move south and take up positions around Radar Hill from which it could interdict Israeli traffic on the Tel Aviv-Jerusalem road.[11] Farther west, the commander of the Legion's 4th Infantry Battalion, Lt. Colonel Habas al-Majali, seized an opportunity to block the Tel Aviv-Jerusalem road at the critical Latrun police fort. The Israelis had initially driven out a small force of Arab irregulars from this position, but then had to draw down the garrison to send reinforcements to deal with the combined Egyptian-Jordanian assault on Ramat Rachel. On his own authority, Majali moved forward and retook the police fort on May 20, blocking the road to Jerusalem where it could not easily be bypassed.

The Latrun police fort is a formidable position, built on a rock promontory that juts out to the southwest from the Samarian Hills. Lt. Colonel Majali deployed his battalion in the fort itself and dug-in along the promontory. He was well prepared for the main Israeli attack. The assault itself was awful. It began at midnight of May 24/25 with a short bombardment from a handful of old 65-mm field guns, but immediately ran into problems. Some of the Israeli units were four to six hours late moving into position. Consequently, the initial bombardment merely alerted the Jordanians, and the sun rose in the midst of the Israeli advance. Two of the four attacking Israeli brigades were composed of European refugees fresh off the boats who spoke eight different languages and were given less than a week of training before being thrown into battle. Not surprisingly, these two battalions blundered around in the darkness and then managed to get themselves pinned by Jordanian fire after dawn. Their feeble efforts allowed Majali to concentrate his efforts on the veteran Haganah battalion attacking his right. The Legionaries were protected by the walls of the police fort and were well dug-in on the flanks of the hill. Their fire was heavy and accurate against the exposed and clumsy Israelis. The attack turned into a slaughter. The Jordanians broke it by noon, inflicting heavy casualties on the Israeli attackers.[12]

Five days later, the Israelis attempted another equally ill-conceived operation against Latrun. This time, they attacked with two veteran battalions from the south. One of the Israeli battalions was able to take the village of Dayr Ayub at the foot of the Latrun position, before they too were repulsed by Jordanian fire. Once again, the rapid defeat of one Israeli unit allowed Majali to concentrate his forces against the other, in this case the armored infantry of the 79th Battalion. The Israelis bravely attacked into the teeth of the Jordanian defenses, but the Legionaries held their ground and put up a murderous fire. In particular, Majali found that by reinforcing his troops along the parapets of the police fortress, his well-trained marksmen could pour fire down into the Israeli half-tracks, which had no protection from above. Again the Jordanians beat back the Israelis with heavy losses.

The two defeats at Latrun were so decisive that the Israelis decided to build a bypass around Latrun to allow vehicular movement between Tel Aviv and Jerusalem without having to use the main road in that area. Nevertheless, the Israeli leadership had become fixated on Latrun, and so decided to try once more to take the position. During the night of June 8–9, veteran battalions of the Harel and Yiftach brigades assaulted the Latrun position on both sides of the promontory but farther to the northeast, along its "neck" rather than its tip. However, the Israelis were unaware that Glubb had reinforced the Latrun position with the 2nd Infantry Battalion and additional artillery. While the 4th Battalion continued to hold the fort and its flanks, the 2nd dug-in along both sides of the neck of the position.

Thus what the Israelis thought would be a double envelopment to get behind the 4th Battalion's positions, turn both its flanks, and cut it off from Samaria, turned into a pair of frontal assaults against the 2nd Battalion's positions. As in the past, the Jordanian soldiers concentrated a heavy volume of fire on both Israeli attacks. The Israelis fought with great determination in the face of Jordanian fire, and they were able to break into the Legion's lines on both sides. However, by that point they had suffered heavy casualties and were thrown back by aggressive, well-timed Jordanian counterattacks. The Israelis tried again the next night but one of the battalions got lost in the dark while the other took heavy casualties from Jordanian fire during the advance and was forced to retreat before they could come to grips with the Legionaries.

The Israeli Ten Days Offensives and the Second Battle of Latrun. On June 11 the first UN ceasefire put an end to combat around Latrun. During this truce, both sides reorganized for battle. The Arab Legion, however, suffered a devastating loss when London demanded the return of all British officers seconded to the Legion because of Abdallah's violation of the UN partition plan by attacking Jewish Jerusalem. Although those British officers under contract to the Arab Legion remained, including Glubb, London's edict suddenly deprived him of both his brigade commanders, three of his four battalion commanders, and many other officers. Replacements were quickly promoted and assigned the vacant commands—most of these were also British—but it took some time to work out new command and control arrangements.

Nevertheless, the truce gave the Legion a breathing space to regroup, reorganize, and improve its defenses. Its various independent infantry companies were integrated into two new battalions, the 5th and 6th. The Jordanians continued to fortify their positions around Latrun. They also used the ceasefire to repair and perform overdue maintenance on their vehicles, especially their armored cars. Of particular importance, King Abdallah was able to secure large stocks of arms and ammunition to replenish Glubb's magazines.

As far as strategy was concerned, Glubb concluded that his troops were spread too thin and so decided to confine future operations to small-scale offensives intended mainly to improve his defensive position. His situation also improved because a large Iraqi expeditionary force had arrived in northern Samaria, enabling Glubb to withdraw the remaining Legion battalion from the Nablus area, and bring it south to reinforce Latrun. Consequently, by the end of the first truce, the Jordanians had three battalions plus a considerable number of artillery pieces, armored cars, and mortars well-fortified at Latrun.[13]

When the first truce expired on July 9, the Israelis launched a major offensive against the Jordanian forces defending both Jerusalem and the corridor. In the city itself, the Israelis mounted drives southward to secure their right flank, into the Old City, and northeastward to try to retake the Shaykh Jarrah area and re-establish contact with the garrison on Mount Scopus. The southern Israeli effort was the most successful, driving a small force of Arab irregulars and Legionaries off of Mt. Herzl. In the center, a clumsy Israeli attack against the Old City was stopped quickly with heavy losses by Legionaries along the city walls. Against Shaykh Jarrah, not only did the Legion halt the Israeli assault, they pushed it back and launched a counterattack of their own that succeeded in taking a few small strips of territory.

The heaviest fighting, however, once again came at Latrun. The Israelis remained determined to recapture it to reopen the main Tel Aviv-Jerusalem road. They launched their new assault on the night of July 14/15. They sent a battalion from the Harel Brigade to make a diversionary attack against the Legion force at Radar Hill. Meanwhile, the main body of the brigade would assault the Latrun salient from the southeast while the Yiftach Brigade would hit it from the northwest. The Israelis were unaware of the extent of Jordanian reinforcements, or that Glubb had again extended his lines both north and east to guard the shoulders of the salient. Thus the Israelis again believed they were bringing overwhelming force to bear against the undefended flanks of the Jordanian positions but were actually attacking dug-in Jordanian units head-on. Once again, the odds were fairly even (three dug-in Jordanian battalions supported by considerable artillery and armored cars against five Israeli battalions with only a handful of guns and armored cars), the Legion was entrenched in good defensive terrain, and the Israelis were conducting what amounted to frontal assaults against the Jordanian lines.

For three days there was ferocious fighting around Latrun. The Israelis were surprised to find the Jordanians waiting for them on the supposedly unoccupied ridges north and east of Latrun, and their first attacks were repulsed with heavy losses. In particular, the Jordanians counterattacked with armored cars and badly mauled several Israeli units that had not expected to face armor and had few antitank weapons. In a few areas, the Jordanians were surprised by Israeli units that stealthily approached their positions at night and then attacked suddenly out of the darkness. However, the Legionaries recovered quickly and counterattacked with "unparalleled fury," in the words of Israeli Lt. Colonel Netanel Lorch.[14] The battles were fierce and seesawed back and forth between the two sides. At one point, the Israelis forced the Jordanians to relinquish a key village by outflanking their positions and rolling up their line, but the Jordanians mounted a sudden counterattack with armored cars and infantry supported by mortars that drove the Israelis out of another important village. By July 17, the Legion's dogged resistance and counterattacks finally brought the two Israeli pincer thrusts to a halt—although they had come within three kilometers of linking up.

The next day, the Israelis tried one last attack, this time launching a frontal assault against the main Latrun position itself, in the hope that the previous fighting had so weakened the garrison that it would fall if given one last push. The Israelis pulled together a company from the exhausted Yiftach Brigade, with mechanized infantry and a small number of tanks. The Jordanians were equally exhausted, and much of their strength had been drawn away from the police fort to block the thrusts against the shoulders. Nevertheless, Jordanian artillery laid down a heavy barrage against the Israeli armor as they approached the Legion positions. The Israeli tanks still made good progress at first, until a communications problem caused the entire unit to mistakenly retreat. The abrupt departure of his tanks caused the Israeli commander to pull back his infantry for fear that without armored support they would be slaughtered by the Jordanians. At that point, the second truce intervened to prevent further combat.

When the second truce ended in late August, neither Tel Aviv nor Amman had any desire to keep fighting each other. Glubb recognized that the military situation had degenerated into a stalemate with neither side able to make much of an impression on the other's lines. Any additional territory he might capture could only come at an exorbitant cost in casualties. For their part, the Israelis chose to concentrate on the Egyptians instead. As a result, fighting gradually halted along the Israeli-Arab Legion lines. Local commanders on both sides continued to encourage sniping and raids against their opponents, but neither military command undertook any large operations. By November, King Abdallah had unilaterally opened up truce negotiations with the Israelis leading to a full ceasefire on December 1, 1948.

Understanding Jordanian Military Effectiveness in 1948

The conduct of the Arab Legion against the nascent Israeli army in 1948 may well have been the best performance of any Arab military against any foe of the post–World War II era.[15] Alone among the Arab armies, the Legion acted and fought like a modern, professional military. Legion units demonstrated remarkable cohesiveness, sticking together and clinging to their positions even under the most severe pressure, such as in the Second Battle of Latrun.[16] The Jordanians demonstrated a good grasp of combined arms operations, regularly integrating infantry, armored cars, and artillery better than the Israelis. The Legion's marksmanship was excellent. Jordanian units covered their flanks well and were not paralyzed when the Israelis did succeed in turning them. The Legion patrolled constantly, often precluding Israeli surprises, and even surprising the Israelis on several occasions. Jordanian junior officers showed real initiative, seizing fleeting opportunities—such as occupying Latrun—that proved to be critical to their war effort. Jordan's tactical leaders led well-timed and effective counterattacks that frequently were the decisive factor in combat.

Finally, Legion officers regularly employed operational maneuver to gain an advantage in combat, although at the tactical level, many Jordanian attacks were simple frontal assaults.

Why? Why did the Jordanians fight so much better than any of their Arab counterparts, or even than they themselves would fight 19 years later on the same terrain against the same foe, when they were crushed in barely four days? Ultimately, four factors combined to produce this exceptional outcome: the British influence, the unique (countercultural) nature of the Arab Legion in 1948, its small size and manning practices, and the weakness of the Israelis.

The British Role. It really all starts with the British. You cannot understand Jordan's exceptional performance without understanding the impact of the British. The Legion relied wholly on British tactics, organization, training, and doctrine. And the British believed in training, working assiduously to inculcate their methods into their Jordanian charges. As noted above, most officers in the Arab Legion were British (until 1956), either seconded from the British Army or "retired" and on contract to Amman. Those who weren't were Jordanians educated in Legion schools, trained by the Legion, and then sent to Sandhurst, Camberley, and other British military schools to learn the art of command British-style. It is worth noting that the British did not treat any of their other Arab charges in the same manner: the Egyptian, Iraqi, Libyan, and other Arab armies were utterly neglected by the British, who saw no point in building them up and feared that if they did, these forces would eventually challenge British rule in their countries. Jordan's Arab Legion was the one exception to that rule.

The pervasive British influence was, on its own, a major factor contributing to Jordanian military effectiveness. There is a consensus among experts on the Jordanian military and the 1948 war that it was the British influence/presence that was the single most important element of Jordanian military effectiveness. For instance, Brigadier S. A. El Edroos, an unabashed admirer of the Jordanian military, remarked that "The credit for the excellence of the Arab Legion's performance during the war of 1948 and later, during the border wars of 1951–1956, must in all fairness be given to Glubb Pasha and the contingent of British officers who served with the Arab Legion from its formation in 1921 to the exodus of 1956."[17] The great military historian Trevor Dupuy similarly noted that the principal source of Jordanian military effectiveness has been "decades of British leadership and military tradition," and that Jordan's proficiency has declined over the years since the expulsion of the British officers in 1956.[18]

There is a great deal of validity to this assessment. Most of the successes the Jordanians enjoyed, and most of the competent military practices they demonstrated were attributable to an officer corps comprised entirely of Brits and a smaller number of Jordanians with long years of schooling and military training by the British. Many of both were veterans of combat during the Second World War. The aggressive counterattacks, battlefield maneuvers, flexible operations, and acts of opportunistic initiative were all exercised by this British-dominated officer corps. Likewise, the high level of individual soldiering skills found in the Legion, such as its excellent marksmanship, is directly attributable to the British emphasis. The very competent strategic direction of the war, itself another element of Jordan's praiseworthy showing in this conflict, was entirely the product of British officering.

As a result of this British influence, the Jordanian military was initially very different from that of other Arab militaries, and therefore suffered significantly less from some of the problems of military effectiveness associated with culturally regular Arab behavior. Jordanian units emphasized the combat skills, discipline, and readiness of individual soldiers that is a hallmark of the British military system. Jordanian training emphasized the development of its personnel as professional soldiers, and this training was frequent and strenuous. Finally, Jordanian training stressed the objective communication of information, inculcating the notion that the honor of a Jordanian soldier demanded accuracy in reporting to his superiors.

A Distinct Military Culture. As this last point begins to make clear, the success of the Arab Legion in 1948, was not just the *direct* British role in introducing members of a foreign culture and giving them command over the military. It also played a crucial *indirect* role in building a Jordanian military culture that was very different from that of the wider Arab culture and much more like the organizational culture of the British Army.

Of greatest importance, the British established their own schools for the Arab Legion. Most of the young men who came to the Legion right after World War I had had no formal education whatsoever. In response, the British established their own school system, which had a unique (British) curriculum, relied on a British educational method, and was largely staffed by British or British-trained teachers. Boys started in these schools at the age of about 10, and when they graduated they were then inducted into the Legion.[19] This, of course, is precisely the age that cultural anthropologists and psychologists have identified as the critical period when children assimilate cultural patterns of behavior.[20] This system persisted until the 1950s when the British officers were dismissed and Jordan's public education system grew large enough that

Amman felt it no longer needed the Legion schools. Yet, while it lasted, Jordan's Legionary school system took Arabs and socialized them to the culture—the "way of doing things"—of the British Army.

In addition, Jordanian recruits came to the Legion different from most of the recruits of the other Arab armies. During the early years of the Legion, essentially between Glubb's arrival in 1930 and his departure in 1956, the Jordanian armed forces were dominated by Bedouin tribesmen, and not the settled *hadari*. The Bedouin were a subculture of the Arab world, and their culture was different from the dominant Arab culture. The Bedouin were considered to be extremely individualistic and egalitarian, showing much less of the emphasis on hierarchy and deference to authority of the dominant society. Indeed, Bedouin tribes (and armies, when they were formed) were far less centralized and hierarchical than the institutions of the settled population. Moreover, the Bedouin particularly cherished a "warrior" ethos that encouraged personal bravery, loyalty to kin, and tolerance for hardship. While these last three values were also found in the dominant culture (as a result of the Bedouin legacy on the settled populations), they were always strongest among the Bedouin.[21]

The more individualistic and egalitarian traditions of the Bedouin, as well as their dislike of strict, centralized authority appear to have made Bedouin personnel more willing to take the initiative and react to battlefield developments using their own judgment. The fact that they were less likely to defer decision-making to higher authority probably meant that junior officers of Bedouin origin were more willing to take advantage of opportunities presented by the vicissitudes of combat—such as at Kfar Etzioni and Latrun in 1948, where junior officers of Bedouin origin seized upon sudden opportunities to secure two of Jordan's most important achievements of the war. Their traditions of egalitarianism and decentralized authority almost certainly made Bedouin commanders more willing to give their subordinates free rein. Also, the "warrior" ethos of the Bedouin undoubtedly contributed to the levels of personal bravery and unit cohesion among Jordanian forces, which were high even by Arab standards.

In these ways, the Arab Legion effectively broke the transmission mechanism outlined in Chapter 20. They recruited young men from a subculture rather than from the society at large, and therefore started with recruits who did not necessarily espouse the values of the dominant Arab culture, particularly as it pertained to notions of behavior in hierarchical organizations. During the early days of the Legion, recruits began as young boys and were taught in Legion schools that used a different teaching method than that employed in the schools of the larger Jordanian (and Arab) society. The Legion itself used a very different military training method than that of other Arab armies, further differentiating the values and behavioral patterns of Jordanian military personnel from those of other Arab soldiers and officers.

Size and Manning Practices. The Arab Legion in 1948 was a highly motivated elite body of long-term service professionals. Glubb purposely insisted that the Legion remain all-volunteer so that it could retain its carefully nurtured esprit de corps. At the time, Jordan was one of the most backward regions of the Arab world, and the pay of an enlisted man was a princely sum. In addition, the military was considered a prestigious career among the Bedouin. The combination of the Legion's prestige, economic benefits, and esprit contributed to a very high retention rate, with many personnel serving for decades and many sons of Legionaries following their fathers into the king's service. Moreover, by keeping the force small, the Legion had its pick of new recruits and was able to man its ranks largely from the minority Bedouin population. Last, the small size of the army allowed Jordan to continue to provide high-quality training for its troops.

Possibly the most important advantage of Amman's approach was that the small size and professional character of the Jordanian military essentially allowed Jordan to train many Arab cultural traits "out" of its soldiers. The Jordanian military's emphasis on extensive training over long periods of time (coupled with the experience of the Legion schools) allowed the military to socialize its recruits to its own culture—the culture of the Jordanian military—which was very different from the culture of the larger Jordanian society because of its heavy British (and Bedouin) influences. It takes a long time to train a person to think and act in a way different from his or her accustomed manner. If Jordan had opted for a large conscript military, it probably would have proven extremely difficult to inculcate the British traditions into so many soldiers and officers serving for brief periods of time. In such a mass army, Arab culture would have quickly reasserted its dominance as British-trained personnel were cycled out of the force and new recruits were brought in. This is precisely what happened in Jordan after King Hussein evicted the British in 1956 and then more than doubled the size of the Jordanian Army.

The Relative Military Balance. Finally, it is important to keep in mind the various military advantages that Jordan held over Israel in 1948 that also contributed to its more impressive performance. The Jordanians were able to defend the superb terrain of Judea and Samaria, while the Israelis were mostly forced to attack from the coastal plain up into the central hills. The Legion was well-trained and had some combat experience from the Second World War.[22]

Myths of Israeli invincibility aside, the Haganah of early 1948 was a mediocre force. Its unit capabilities were uneven, with some brigades performing well and others giving a rather poor account of themselves. The Israelis were inadequately armed and trained. They suffered from political infighting. They had all kinds of problems with personnel and languages, and with the incompatibility of their hodgepodge of weaponry. Some amateurish Haganah units paid too little attention to reconnaissance and so were surprised by Jordanian actions that might easily have been discovered and averted. Finally, the Israelis also had to fight five other Arab armies, which prevented them from concentrating decisive force against Jordan.

Despite all of these advantages, the Jordanians only succeeded in fighting the Israelis to a draw. The Legion consistently defeated Israeli attacks against their prepared defensive positions. Most of the successful Israeli offensives in the Jerusalem area (such as at Lod, Ramla, and Mt. Zion) were conducted against small Arab Legion forces, while larger Jordanian units in the Old City and Latrun held their ground against numerous determined Israeli assaults.

Although the Legion defeated most Israeli attacks, they fared little better in their own offensives. The only significant gains the Jordanians were able to make against Israeli resistance were the conquests of the Etzioni bloc, the Jewish Quarter of the Old City, and the Shaykh Jarrah area. All of these successes came in the first weeks of the war, and all were modest achievements. In none of these battles did the Jordanians face a large, well-armed, and adequately trained force. For example, in Shaykh Jarrah, a Legion infantry battalion backed by artillery and armored cars defeated 70 infantrymen from the Irgun militia. Even with the advantage of urban terrain on the Israeli side, this was a mismatch, and the Legion's victory wasn't much of an achievement. Conversely, the moment that the Jordanians ran into better-trained or larger Israeli units—such as in the Mandelbaum Gate area and at Notre Dame— their attacks went nowhere. In short, while the Jordanians almost certainly fought better than any of the other Arab armies, and they often fought as well as or better than the Israelis, their performance does not exactly rank as one of the great campaigns of military history.

The Impact of a Military Subculture. The combination of all of these factors allowed Jordan to mitigate certain aspects of the influence of Arab culture on its personnel. Essentially, the unique educational background, small size, and long terms of service of Jordan's armed forces allowed the Jordanians to fully inculcate highly motivated volunteer soldiers into a culture that was different from that of mainstream Arab society because of its strong Bedouin and, especially, British influences. Thus, in many areas of military operations, Jordanian forces did not exhibit the patterns of military ineffectiveness associated with Arab cultural patterns of behavior. In addition, the Jordanian military system endowed Jordanian forces with certain strengths that generally were not found in other Arab militaries. These strengths sometimes allowed the Legion to compensate for weaknesses derived from Arab culture that their system was unable to mitigate.

Perhaps the strongest proof of the relationship of these patterns of better military effectiveness to British and Bedouin cultural patterns can be found in the slow erosion of these same skills in the 1950s and 1960s after the Jordanians expelled the British. King Hussein did so to appease nationalist and Nasserist agitators who demanded that the Arab Legion become a bigger, more Arab force. As a result, the British officers were removed from command and from day-to-day training. The Legion schools were closed. And the renamed Jordan Arab Army was expanded from 20,000 men in 1955 to 55,000 men in 1967, which could only be done by accepting far greater numbers of *hadari* and even Palestinians.[23]

Not surprisingly, the impact on Jordanian military effectiveness was considerable. Almost immediately after the loss of their British officers, Jordanian forces at Qalqilyah in the fall of 1956 displayed greater rigidity and passivity than ever before. At as-Samu in 1966, during the Six-Day War of 1967, Black September in 1970, and the October War of 1973, Jordanian tactical commanders showed even less initiative, creativity, and independence of action. Similarly, in 1967 and 1970, Jordan encountered tremendous difficulties with distorted reporting from the lower echelons of the chain of command, over-centralization of command, and a dearth of tactical maneuver. Moreover, unit cohesion was worse than it had been, although individual soldiering skills remained good. In later battles, many of these same problems grew increasingly more pronounced. Nevertheless, Jordanian performance in all of these areas remained somewhat better than those of most of the Arab armies, in part because of the continuing ties between Jordan and Britain—and later with the United States—and in part because the small size and devotion to professionalism in the Jordanian armed forces helped preserve some British traditions long after the British were gone.[24]

Ultimately, by 1948, the British had built the Jordanian Army in their own image, or at least in the cherished image of Britain's vanished colonial armies. Just as Britain traditionally relied on a small, long-term service professional army, so too did Jordan. Just as Britain traditionally relied on a purely volunteer force, so too did Jordan. Just as the British emphasized the quality of their manpower rather than its quantity, so too did Jordan. Just as the British stressed the skills of the individual soldier honed in constant practice over many years, so too did Jordan. In Nadav Safran's words, "excellently drilled and ably commanded by British officers it was then [1948] a model of the level of effectiveness that could be achieved with Arab soldiers through careful training and organization."[25] It is not surprising then that the Jordanian military of 1948 would fight much less like other Arab armies—even like the Jordanian Army it would become by 1967—and much more like a small British colonial army, which was a more accurate description of what it was in 1948.

Syria's Commandos, 1982

As I described in Chapter 11, after the 1973 October War, Damascus decided that its leg infantry formations were close to useless and decided to demobilize some and convert the rest to mechanized infantry. On the other hand, Syria's commandos had fought well in 1973, noticeably better than either its leg infantry or armored formations. Consequently, the Syrian regime decided to expand its commando force and place greater reliance on it in battle.

Eventually, the Syrians created as many as 33 battalions of commandos. They did this by stripping most of the best personnel from their infantry units before they were converted to mechanized formations. They also diverted many of the most promising new recruits to the commandos. Over time, Damascus learned to use them as both special forces teams employed in non-conventional missions as well as "shock" troops to spearhead offensives and man key defensive positions.[26]

Although 33 battalions sounds like a lot, this isn't really the case. Syrian commando battalions comprised only 200–300 men. There were 9–10 brigade headquarters to command these battalions, but there were no divisional commands, and the brigade commands were very light, having few of the support assets attached to maneuver brigades.[27] Consequently, the expansion of Syria's commandos entailed an increase from about 1,500–2,000 commandos in 1973 to about 10,000–15,000 by 1982.[28]

The commando battalions soon became the main combat force of the Syrian army. In 1976, commando units spearheaded nearly all of the major operations during the Syrian invasion of Lebanon. In 1982, the Syrians attached commando battalions to all of their large armored and mechanized formations in Lebanon. Moreover, small units of Syrian commandos—with attached armor, artillery, and engineers—were used to harass and block the Israeli advances through the Lebanese mountains. In all of these battles, the Syrian commandos performed very well. They were hardly invincible and still manifested many of the same problems as the rest of the Syrian army, but they fought far more effectively than the rest of the military. In particular, Syrian commandos showed considerably better combined arms integration and unit cohesion, as well as somewhat greater aggressiveness, creativity, weapons-handling skills, and flexibility than Syrian line formations in Lebanon. In fact, the Syrian commandos performed so well that some commentators have claimed that they—not the Jordanian Army of 1948—were the toughest foe Israel ever faced.[29]

Explaining Syrian Commando Performance. Syria's commandos were a relatively small, elite force. As such they derived a number of advantages from this "eliteness." Members of elite units are typically selected for their combat skills. They also invariably have higher morale and higher unit cohesion because of the esprit de corps of all elite formations. They often receive better, longer, more intense, and more specialized training. In the Arab world they typically get more plentiful and more advanced weaponry. For these reasons alone, it should have been no surprise that elite Arab units (and air forces small enough and selective enough to be considered elite forces) would perform more effectively in battle than line units. All of this was true for Syria's commandos.

In addition, there are also certain aspects of "eliteness" that probably served to mitigate the specific effects of Arab culture on military effectiveness. First, elite units are "picked" bodies, meaning that their members are specially selected for their outstanding martial skills. Although there is little unclassified information regarding the selection criteria used for elite Arab units, it is reasonable to assume that they were similar to those employed for elite forces elsewhere. For instance, we do know that when Iraq decided to build its Republican Guard into a true, elite force, it did so by transferring the best soldiers and officers from line formations into the Guard. Assuming that the Syrians did the same, which seems very likely, then the criteria for assignment to their commandos would have included aggressiveness and creativity in combat, as well as other traits such as personal bravery, leadership and superior weapons-handling skills. Moreover, elite ground units intended for special forces–type missions, such as the Syrian commandos, require the ability to operate independently in very small formations. They tend to place an even greater emphasis on selecting personnel who have demonstrated individual initiative and improvisation.

This strongly suggests that there were a disproportionate number of soldiers and officers in elite Arab units such as the Syrian commandos who were *not* culturally regular. These men, who may still have represented only a minority even among the commandos, were nevertheless probably selected specifically because they possessed traits that were not encouraged (some would argue, actively denigrated) by the dominant Arab culture, and thus were not strongly manifested in most Arab soldiers and officers. Thus these men entered the military different from their peers, and there was a greater percentage of them among the Syrian commandos than in line formations.

They then received different training from line formations, which would have sharpened the differences between their behavioral patterns and those of the rest of the military. Elite units frequently receive different, more rigorous and more demanding training than line units. Any special-forces-type training these personnel received almost certainly would have further encouraged these traits because independent missions by small, self-contained units are the hallmark of special operations. In short, it is reasonable to believe that the training of Arab elite forces such as the Syrian commandos also would have been quite different from the training received by other personnel slated to join combat formations with no special need for a capability for independent action.

As a final note, the size of an elite Arab force relative to the size of the general population almost certainly was an important determinant of just how much better the elite forces were than the regular, line formations. Because a relative minority of people in Arab populations are likely to manifest *strong* traits of independent initiative, creativity, etc., the smaller the elite force relative to the population, the more likely it can have larger proportions of individuals who strongly manifest these traits and therefore the greater the likelihood that these men will end up as commanders and otherwise able to influence the performance of these units in combat. In other words, the smaller the elite force the more likely that Arab commanders will be able to fill it with the culturally non-regular personnel needed to make it an effective force. On the other hand, the larger the force, the fewer culturally non-regular personnel it is likely to have, and therefore the more likely it will reflect the culturally normal behavior patterns. The larger an elite force, the less likely it will perform better than other formations, and the smaller an elite force the more likely it will perform better than other formations.

These patterns are clearly illustrated by a comparison of the Syrian commandos and Iraqi Republican Guards. Syria's commandos accounted for about 5 percent of total military manpower and 0.13 percent of Syria's population in 1982, whereas the RGFC accounted for about 12 percent of total Iraqi military manpower and about 0.72 percent of Iraq's population in 1988. In short, the Syrian commandos represented less than one-fifth of the percentage of their relative populations as the Iraqi Republican Guards. The smaller size of the Syrian commandos relative to the size of the Syrian armed forces and to the general Syrian population compared to the greater size of the Iraqi RGFC relative to the size of its military and population suggest that the

Syrian commandos should have been more effective on a unit-by-unit basis. The special-forces mission of the Syrian commandos—implying even less culturally regular selection criteria and training—also suggests that the Syrian commandos should have been more effective in battle than the RGFC on a unit-for-unit basis. And, as a matter of fact, they were: on a unit-for-unit basis, the Syrian commandos demonstrated considerably greater skills in battle than the Iraqi Republican Guards, although they were still not great units and *far* less skillful than typical Israeli or American infantry units.

The Syrian commandos were small enough relative to the overall manpower pool to be able to select a disproportionate number of culturally "nonregular" personnel along with a similarly disproportionate number of soldiers and officers who were uncommonly brave, charismatic, skilled with their weapons, or had other superior combat capabilities. All of this produced their abnormally good performance. On the other hand, the Iraqi RGFC was so large relative to its potential manpower pool that it could not be as selective in choosing personnel as the Syrian commandos. As a result, the RGFC units were more capable than the units of the Iraqi Regular Army, but not as good as the Syrian commandos on a unit-for-unit basis, nor was the difference between the Iraqi RGFC and Iraqi line formations as great as that between the Syrian commandos and Syrian line units.

Egypt in 1973 and Iraq in 1988–1990

At least two Arab militaries, the Egyptians in 1973 and the Iraqis beginning in 1988, adopted a unique method of military operations that allowed them to avoid traditional areas of Arab weakness in combat. This approach was deliberately developed to try to compensate for the limitations derived from culturally regular patterns of behavior.

As I explained in Chapters 6 and 7, the Egyptians in 1973 and the Iraqis after 1987 ultimately came to rely on six basic elements in their military operations that allowed them to avoid the problems of poor tactical leadership, poor air operations, and information mismanagement. First, they attempted to remain on the defensive whenever possible to capitalize on their greater skill in static defense operations. Second, when it was necessary to attack, their attacks were conducted as set-piece operations. Third, these set-piece operations were scripted in great detail by the highest military planners. Fourth, they attempted to maximize their advantages in firepower, manpower, surprise, novel technology, and (in the Iraqi case) chemical warfare, to put the adversary on his heels and force him to fight at a disadvantage. Fifth, they relied on information from external sources—intercepts of Israeli communications for the Egyptians, and US intelligence for the Iraqis. Last, operations were kept very limited, both in terms of time and space, so that they did not run out of "script" or lose their other military advantages.

By remaining on the defensive whenever possible, the Egyptian and Iraqi militaries were able to capitalize on the various cultural traits that aided their conduct of static defensive operations as well as the inherent advantages that accrue to any defender. Similarly, by employing only set-piece offensives when forced to attack, the Egyptian and Iraqi militaries were able to avoid getting involved in the fluid, unstructured battles in which their culturally derived weaknesses in ad hoc operations, flexibility, creativity, information handling, and tactical maneuver were most damaging. In addition, relying on set-piece battles greatly improved the ability of the Egyptian and Iraqi generals to script their operations and keep them limited.

The detailed scripting of Egyptian and Iraqi set-piece offensive operations, and their constant rehearsal by the field formations, was the single most important reason for the relative successes enjoyed by the Egyptians and Iraqis. Essentially, the combination of meticulously detailed orders from the senior planning staffs plus endless practice of these plans by the tactical formations relieved junior officers of many of the responsibilities of command. Egyptian and Iraqi tactical commanders did not need to be able to think independently or creatively, they did not need to be able to take the initiative and seize fleeting opportunities, they did not need to understand how to integrate their various forces into cohesive combined arms teams, and they did not even need to actually understand the purpose of their actions. By scripting their offensives and having their forces learn to execute them by rote, the Egyptian and Iraqi high commands effectively assumed the burden of all decision-making—and made all necessary decisions ahead of time. The Egyptians employed hordes of surface-to-air missiles to avoid having to contest air superiority with the Israelis, while the Iraqis were relieved of the same need by the arms embargo against Iran that crippled its air force just as effectively. And by relying on external sources of information, they did not have to trust their subordinates to provide them with timely, accurate reporting. In this way, they avoided the crucial failings of their tactical commanders in leadership and decision-making.

Keeping their offensive operations limited in scope and duration was an important addendum to scripting operations. The one great flaw in this method of warfighting was that it was a deliberate attempt to subvert what Clausewitz called "friction." In these operations, the Egyptians and Iraqis drew up elaborate plans and then attempted to execute them dogmatically. Every military academy and staff college worth its salt warns against this because, in war, nothing ever goes as planned. Unsurprisingly, the bane of these Arab operations were unexpected developments, such as the actions of the enemy or even simple human error, that would cause the course of battle to diverge from the plan. Because friction increases exponentially with each additional increment of time, the Egyptians and Iraqis had to keep their operations limited to minimize friction and thereby minimize the extent to which their meticulously scripted and rehearsed plans were likely to diverge from reality.

Egypt's experiences in the 1973 October War paralleled Iraq's experiences at the end of the Iran-Iraq War and the 1990–1991 Persian Gulf War, and both demonstrated that their successes derived from the extent to which this operational method allowed them to avoid culturally derived military problems. For both armies, their operations went extremely well as long as they had overwhelming advantages in manpower, firepower, technology, and surprise over their adversaries *and* their forces were able to simply execute the extensively scripted and exhaustively practiced set-piece operations crafted by their superb general staffs. When this held true, both armies seized and held the initiative, demonstrated reasonably effective combined arms coordination and maneuver, moved quickly and crisply, and achieved (limited but still) impressive results. Yet in both cases, whenever the scripted, set-piece operations ran out, the enemy forced them to deviate from those scripts, or they lost their overwhelming material advantages, the Egyptians and Iraqis reverted back to form. They became just as clumsy, sluggish, and incompetent as they had always been. Combined arms cooperation and maneuver evaporated, they lost the initiative and any ability to react quickly and creatively to enemy moves, and they lost disastrously. This is why the Egyptian army that crossed the canal on October 6, 1973, seemed like a juggernaut for the first four days of the October War, but was then carved up effortlessly by the Israelis in the weeks that followed. Similarly, the Iraqi military that repeatedly routed Iranian ground forces in 1987–1988 and then overran Kuwait in barely 24 hours in 1990, turned into the hapless mob that was crushed in six weeks in January–February 1991.

The performance of both the Egyptian and Iraqi armed forces is still more evidence of the contribution of Arab cultural patterns to the poor performance of modern Arab militaries. As long as the Egyptians and Iraqis avoided ad hoc operations and fluid maneuver battles, scripted their operations to avoid the necessity of having their tactical commanders make decisions, removed air power from the combat equation, and kept their operations limited to minimize the ability of friction to subvert their scripting, they enjoyed considerably greater military effectiveness. On the other hand, whenever their operations were disrupted by friction or else simply ran out of script, the patterns of poor military performance common to Arab armies and air forces suddenly reasserted themselves.

Thus, only when the influence of culture upon their armed forces was diminished by reliance on external sources of information coupled with limited, set-piece missions and heavily scripted operations to alleviate the need for aggressive, creative tactical leadership did the Egyptians and Iraqis perform well. Whenever they were prevented from employing these methods, they reverted immediately to form. What this demonstrates is that this operational method did not eliminate the problems of military ineffectiveness associated with culturally regular Arab patterns of behavior, but merely cloaked or avoided them. The moment they were forced to deviate from these rigid strictures or the enemy otherwise pulled off their cloak, the same old problems suddenly reappeared like Cinderella's rags at the stroke of midnight.

What all of these examples demonstrate is that the armed forces of various Arab states were only able to achieve better-than-usual military effectiveness by finding ways to mitigate the impact of culturally derived patterns of behavior. Jordan's Arab Legion developed its own, quite different, organizational subculture. Syria's commandos (and to a lesser extent Iraq's Republican Guard) benefited from the advantages of eliteness. The Egyptian and Iraqi militaries of 1973 and 1987–1991 respectively found a way to (briefly) take decision-making and information management out of the hands of their tactical commanders. While clever and effective, none of these workarounds permanently eliminated the problems or produced more than marginally better results. Moreover, all of them are exceptions proving the rule that the principal shortcomings of modern Arab military effectiveness have been behavioral patterns driven by the dominant Arab culture.

CHAPTER 23 | Exceptional Arab Militaries:
Nonstate Armies

WARFARE HAS BEEN a constant in the modern Middle East. But the
nature of these wars has shifted over time. In the first four or five
decades after the Second World War, the Middle East was dominated by inter-
state conflict. But the Arab governments slowly realized that they lacked the
military capacity to advance their foreign policies by war-making. In effect,
they learned that no matter how hard they tried, they generally lost when they
went to war against other states, and those defeats typically threatened their
hold on power, so the smart thing to do was to stop attacking other countries.
Jordan and Egypt learned this lesson after the 1967 and 1973 Arab-Israeli
wars, respectively, when they went to war seemingly with every advantage and
still lost, badly. Hafez al-Asad of Syria probably recognized the same, but felt
compelled to intervene in the Lebanese Civil War to try to forestall a revolt in
his country, only to learn an even harder lesson about the limits of Syrian military power in 1976 and 1982.

Of course, it took Qadhafi and Saddam a bit longer. The former had to
be humiliated by the Chadians in 1987 before he understood that his armed
forces were not going to win him anything. Saddam was similarly humiliated
by the United States in 1991, but even then, he clung to the belief that force
could work for him—threatening to attack Kuwait (again) in 1994 and Israel
in 2000.[1] Ultimately, the 2003 US invasion of Iraq removed him from power,
perhaps the last leader of an Arab state to believe that his armies could win
him power and glory.

Yet warfare has hardly abated in the Middle East in recent decades. It has merely changed its form. Today, the region is wracked by internal conflict. Civil wars and insurgencies have taken the place of inter-state war. That's not accidental. First, some Arab leaders recognized that conventional combat against foreign foes such as Israel and the United States was bound to fail for all of the reasons detailed in this book. In response, Arabs who still wanted to fight back adopted guerrilla warfare instead. For them, the goals remained the same, but they shifted from conventional to unconventional means to try to achieve them.

Second, the failure of Arab armed forces presaged the failure of many Arab states, demonstrating as the Arab Human Development Reports warned, that the inability of Arab society to compete in a globalizing world would undermine the political stability of Arab states along with their economic welfare—and their military capabilities. In Syria, Yemen, Libya, Egypt, Bahrain, and Iraq, the governments either collapsed (toppled by the Americans in the case of Iraq) or were severely weakened, creating complete or partial security vacuums that led to the spontaneous generation of militias, insurgencies against what was left of the government, and terrorist groups. In these cases, state weakness or outright state failure produced both conventional and unconventional warfare.

What is important about this history is that some of the Arab insurgencies and militias have proven unexpectedly capable, handing notable defeats to seemingly more powerful adversaries. For over two decades, Hizballah has given Israel fits in Lebanon—in addition to effectively "winning" the Lebanese Civil War and proving to be a formidable participant in the Syrian Civil War. Al-Qa'ida fighters were highly regarded in both Afghanistan in the 1980s and 1990s, and Iraq after the American invasion. Their Iraqi-Syrian offspring, the Islamic State of Iraq and ash-Sham (*Da'ish*, in its Arabic acronym), stunned the world by gaining control of much of eastern Syria in 2012–2013 and then overrunning most of northwest Iraq in 2014. That same year, Houthi militias conquered the Yemeni capital of Sanaa and drove on its second city, Aden, before being stopped by a small but well-equipped Emirati mechanized force. Al-Qa'ida's Syrian offshoot, Jabhat Fatah ash-Sham (formerly the Nusra Front), has also acquitted itself well throughout the civil war. All of these nonstate militaries achieved greater battlefield success—and in some cases demonstrated greater combat effectiveness—than virtually any of the armed forces of the Arab states themselves.

Before we go any further, it is critical to understand that the vast majority of nonstate Arab militaries have not been this good or this successful.[2] In fact, the overwhelming majority have been weak and failed to achieve much at all.

For every al-Qa'ida there have been at least a dozen terrorist wannabes who never accomplished anything before they were snuffed out or disbanded. For every Da'ish there have been a dozen militia groups who were crushed and absorbed into others. For every Hizballah, there have been a dozen insurgencies that just went nowhere.

Moreover, many of those who persisted did not enjoy the same degrees of success, let alone the same military effectiveness, as these few. Even well-known militias such as Fadhila and Jaysh al-Mahdi in Iraq, AMAL and the Phalange in Lebanon, Ahrar ash-Sham in Syria, and well-known insurgencies such as the Polisario in the Western Sahara, the Gamaat Islami in Egypt, Hamas in the Palestinian territories, and the GIA in Algeria, never demonstrated the same kind of effectiveness as their more famous brethren. Likewise, older militias and insurgencies—the PLO against Israel in the 1960s and 1970s, against Jordan in 1970–1971 and in Lebanon in 1975–1982; the Royalists in Yemen in the 1960s; the Dhofaris in Oman in the 1970s; and the Muslim Brotherhood in Syria in 1976–1982—evinced similarly unimpressive performances. Iraq's Hashd ash-Shaabi militias were able to hold Baghdad in the spring of 2014, but against a Da'ish army that had shot its bolt and had never expected to conquer as much as it did. Moreover, after that, they proved incapable of retaking towns from Da'ish on their own, failing miserably at Bayji, Tikrit, and Fallujah, before US-backed Iraqi government formations moved in to get those jobs done.

Still, the impressive performance of some Arab militias and insurgencies needs explaining. They are exceptions that should and can be shown to prove the rule of culturally driven Arab military ineffectiveness. So below I am going to look at the two most successful Arab militias/insurgencies, Hizballah and Da'ish.

Hizballah

Hizballah was born of strange parents, an unexpected product of Israeli patronizing and Iranian mothering. Although Lebanon's long-neglected Shi'a community initially welcomed the Israeli invasion in 1982 as a way of ridding themselves of the hated Palestinians, over time the occupation grated on them. Small incidents turned the community against the IDF, convincing more and more Shi'a to take up arms against Israel. In the famous words of former Israeli prime minister Ehud Barak, "When we entered Lebanon . . . there was no Hezbollah. We were accepted with perfumed rice and flowers by the Shia in the south. It was our presence there that created Hezbollah."[3]

Meanwhile, Iran remained in the throes of its revolutionary fervor in the early 1980s, looking to spread the ideas of its revolution abroad and to combat what it saw as the enemies of Islam wherever it could. Lebanon was a twofer for Tehran: many important young Lebanese Shi'a clerics had studied with Khomeini during his exile in Iraq and pledged their allegiance to him, while the Israeli military intervention furnished a perfect target for Iran's revolutionary ire and the frustration of its new Lebanese allies. Consequently, between 1982 and 1985, Iran assiduously cultivated its ties to militant Lebanese Shi'a, pulling them away from the dominant but non-committal AMAL militia, encouraging them to form their own armed groups and take more aggressive action against Israel, and then convincing them to unite under a single banner, the party of God, *Hizballah* in Arabic. Iran then provided extensive training to Hizballah, including the deployment of as many as 1,500 Revolutionary Guards. Iran also provided weapons and cash, which Hizballah rewarded with loyalty—and support to Iranian terrorist operations outside of Lebanon.[4] Ultimately, Hizballah would grow to play an outsized role in the wars of the Levant.

Most Americans tend to think of Hizballah as a terrorist group, which it is. But far more of its resources and effort have been invested in its insurgency against the Israeli occupation of Lebanon from 1985 to 2000 and its role as a militia fighting in the Lebanese Civil War, controlling Lebanon after the Syrian withdrawal in 2005, intervening in the Syrian Civil War since 2012, and fighting Israel throughout. It is this military role—conventional and unconventional—that is both most important to Hizballah, and most important to this book.

Hizballah Performance in the Lebanese Civil War. The vast majority of Hizballah's fighters, resources, and effort have been consumed by its conventional wars. While these have often been overlooked in the West, they have led to some of Hizballah's most important victories. Some of the most vicious fighting during the Lebanese Civil War was Shi'a on Shi'a (and Sunni on Sunni, and Christian on Christian). In 1987 and 1988 Hizballah and AMAL engaged in a series of brutal battles as part of what was called "the War of the Camps." Eventually, Hizballah emerged as the dominant power in Lebanon through its victories over AMAL in the spring of 1988.[5]

In truth, Hizballah performed only moderately better than its rivals in Lebanon. Its fighters tended to win as a result of their Iranian support, their strong commitment and unit cohesion, and the problems of their adversaries. For instance, Syria might have wiped them out in 1987 but for Iranian entreaties to Damascus to show restraint. Ultimately, it was these political ties that proved decisive for Hizballah.

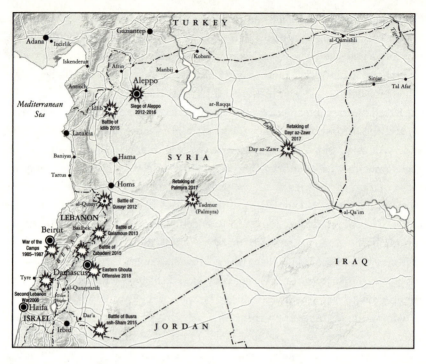

MAP 26 Hizballah's Wars, 1985–2017

When the civil war finally ended in 1991, Hizballah was allowed to retain its arms so that it could dominate Lebanese politics as the local ally of Iran and Syria. Hizballah's status as the only remaining armed militia became even more important after the Syrian withdrawal in 2005. However, during this time, Hizballah did not have to engage in much fighting. The other Lebanese militias were disarmed and cowed by Hizballah's size, arsenal, reputation, and alliances with Iran and Syria. Consequently, it largely refocused on fighting Israel, and most of the personnel and military assets that were not required for that mission were demobilized—although held in reserve and able to be remobilized when needed.

Hizballah Performance against Israel, 1985–2000. Hizballah's reputation derives primarily from its battles with Israel, which have been both unconventional and conventional. It mostly employed guerrilla warfare tactics against IDF forces in Lebanon from 1985 to the Israeli withdrawal in 2000. These included many operations that Israel refers to as "terrorism," although they targeted Israeli military personnel participating in military operations and so do not technically rate that description.

After the Lebanese Civil War ended, Hizballah reorganized to better fight Israel, splitting its forces between a terrorist branch and a military branch. The latter was focused on the fight against the Jewish state in southern Lebanon and northern Israel. To that end, it was divided into sections that dealt with guerrilla warfare, hiding and firing its extensive rocket arsenal, surveillance, logistics, and sabotage—the last of which developed a respected reputation for manufacturing and emplacing booby traps and improvised explosive devices of all kinds.[6]

A critical element of this reorganization was a radical reconceptualization of Hizballah's size. As Daniel Byman has written in his superb history of Israeli counterterrorism, *A High Price*, Hizballah "improved its forces in part by getting smaller."[7] Hizballah's leadership recognized that the thousands of militiamen it had needed to fight the Lebanese Civil War were not only unnecessary to fight Israel, but could prove a liability. Consequently, they demobilized and shifted most of these to the reserves. They kept only those soldiers and commanders who had proven to be the best and bravest during the civil war, leaving them with about 500 full-time and 1,000 part-time fighters for the war against Israel. These men, Hizballah's best of the best, were then provided with extensive new training, much of it conducted in Iran. The Iranians taught them basic soldiering; weapons handling; small unit tactics; leadership; guerrilla warfare tactics; logistics; reconnaissance; intelligence collection and counterintelligence; explosives manufacture, emplacement, and clearing; and air defense operations.[8] In the words of former Israeli Mossad chief Shabtai Shavit, Hizballah became "an Iranian division deployed inside Lebanon."[9]

As a result of all these changes, Hizballah's performance in Lebanon against Israeli troops improved dramatically from the 1980s to the 1990s. Initially, Hizballah military operations against Israel had been sloppy and incompetent. "They failed every time," former intelligence official Barak Ben Zur told Byman about Hizballah's military operations against Israeli targets in the mid-1980s.[10] But in the 1990s, after their reorganization, downsizing, and retraining, Hizballahis became tenacious and resourceful fighters, and the organization became exceptionally creative, adaptive, flexible, and responsive. Every time the Israel Defense Force came up with a new tactic, Hizballah would devise a counter, and would generally do so quickly and effectively. As one piece of evidence of this turnaround, between 1985 and 1995, Hizballah took five times as many casualties as it inflicted on the IDF. After 1995, that casualty ratio fell to just two-to-one.[11]

As always, we need to keep these achievements in perspective. I don't want to belittle Hizballah's triumph, but neither should we exaggerate it. Between

1985 and 2000, 300 Israelis were killed in Lebanon. That's really not a lot of people, even by Israeli standards. But it was still a price too high for the Israeli public, and in 2000, Ehud Barak pulled the IDF out of Lebanon, handing Hizballah its signal victory. There is no question that Hizballah's skill played an important role, but it was also Israel's extreme casualty sensitivity that made Lebanon "Israel's Vietnam."[12]

Hizballah Performance against Israel, 2006. Six years after Israel withdrew from Lebanon the IDF mounted a punitive operation, ostensibly in response to Hizballah's kidnapping of two Israeli soldiers (and killing three others) on July 12, 2006, but also to try to eliminate many of the thousands of rockets and missiles Hizballah had stockpiled in southern Lebanon for use against Israel. Thus, Israel's initial response on July 13 was limited to a massive air campaign that would ultimately amount to 5,000 strike sorties against Hizballah and Lebanese targets to try to destroy Hizballah's military infrastructure, particularly its rockets and missiles, and put pressure on the Lebanese government to crack down on Hizballah.[13] Hizballah responded by firing hundreds of rockets back at Israel, something that the IAF could not stop. In response, Israel began mounting ground incursions into Lebanon on July 19 to try to prevent the rocket firings. These ran into much heavier resistance than expected and led to some fierce firefights. On July 31, the Israeli cabinet approved a larger ground operation involving 10,000 men to take and hold a security zone several kilometers deep in Lebanon. When that too failed to halt the rocket firings, on August 11, Jerusalem escalated further, committing to expand the security zone up to the Litani River. But Israeli ground operations suffered a series of embarrassing setbacks to Hizballah fighters, and so on August 14, both sides agreed to a UN-brokered ceasefire.

The war was humiliating for the IDF and exhilarating for Hizballah, greater even than their triumph in evicting Israel from Lebanon in 2000. Hizballah fighters once again performed well in combat. Nevertheless, this too needs to be kept in perspective. The war lasted 34 days and, on the ground, was largely waged by several thousand Israeli soldiers against roughly 3,000 Hizballah fighters including 1,000 Hizballah "Special Forces," their elite guerrilla fighters whose job it is to defend southern Lebanon and the Hizballah rocket forces against Israeli ground attack.[14] During the course of the fighting, Israel suffered 119 killed, while Hizballah lost 650–750 dead (from their rocket forces and support personnel as well as their Special Forces).[15] In other words, the loss ratio was 6:1 or 7:1 in Israel's favor.

Any discussion of what happened in 2006 needs to start with the Israeli side. Quite simply, the Israelis were completely unprepared for the war—strategically, operationally, and tactically. Jerusalem had gone to war in the mistaken belief that its air force would *on its own* be able to do tremendous damage to Hizballah's arsenal and either suppress retaliatory rocket fire or coerce Hizballah into desisting by destroying other targets. Israel moved on the ground only when it became clear that that strategic concept was completely wrong. Jerusalem had not planned for a ground invasion and had not readied the troops to do so. As a result, the Israelis attacked with a half-baked plan taken off the shelf and hastily revised—and then revamped again when the first revision failed—that never identified a clear Hizballah center of gravity and so had Israeli troops blundering around southern Lebanon to little purpose.

On top of all that, the IDF had badly neglected its training for conventional military operations, focusing excessively on the kind of counterterrorism and population security operations that IDF forces regularly performed in the West Bank. Israeli armor and artillery crews had been turned into light infantry to serve in the West Bank, so they had little experience with their equipment. IDF infantry units had never trained to fire their mortars because they never used them in the West Bank. Even the Israeli Air Force had stopped training to do CAS and had actually eliminated forward air controllers from combat brigades. Their combined arms operations were appalling because most Israeli units had had no combined arms training.[16] Israel had even neglected its intelligence collection on Hizballah with the result that they knew very little about Hizballah forces and deployments in south Lebanon, and IDF forces were repeatedly surprised by Hizballah's deployments, fortifications, tactics, doctrine, and other aspects of their method of fighting.[17] Thus, tactically, Israeli troops performed worse than at any time since 1948.

In contrast, Hizballah had done nothing but prepare for a rematch with Israel. Since 2000, they had built a remarkable network of trenches, bunkers, fighting positions, tunnels, and hide sites across the superb defensive terrain of southern Lebanon, and cached supplies throughout to enable their fighters to carry on autonomously even if they were cut off.[18] They had assiduously studied both Israel's way of war from their experiences in 1985–2000, and their own actions against the IDF to try to learn from their mistakes. They had done a good job of identifying both Israeli weaknesses and their own, and developed workarounds to the latter to try to exploit the former.[19] In particular, and like the Egyptians and Syrians before them, Hizballah had bought thousands of antitank guided missiles (ATGMs) from old Soviet AT-3 Saggers to modern Russian AT-14 Kornets, which they learned to deploy in roughly 100 teams of 5–6 men trained in tank killing.[20] They had trained extensively in Lebanon, Syria, and Iran on individual and small-unit combat.[21]

Moreover, the Hizballah fighters were highly motivated, seeing themselves as defending their homes and families against the hated Israelis who had repeatedly invaded their country. As a result, they fought exceptionally hard at places such as Maroun al-Ras and Bint Jubayl, and only 20–30 of them were taken prisoner.[22]

By all accounts, Hizballah forces fought well. They knew how to maintain their weapons and generally did so.[23] They handled some quite well— their mortars were said to be very accurate, as were some of their ATGM teams, which scored hits on IDF armor 4–5 kilometers away.[24] Their unit cohesion was outstanding.[25] They employed signals intercepts to hack into Israeli command nets and set ambushes, and used UAVs to target IDF formations.[26] Their command and control system proved durable and flexible, and higher-level Hizballah commanders were able to shift forces around the battlefield to hold or give ground in some areas while counterattacking in others.[27] Yet they also employed a decentralized, cellular command structure. Most striking of all, they encouraged initiative and creativity among their small-unit commanders (at least to some extent) and their subunit commanders demonstrated some of both. Far more than any other Arab army, state or non-state, Hizballah units in Lebanon in 2006 shifted positions when flanked by the Israelis, counterattacked on a number of occasions, and even tried to flank the IDF in some instances.[28] Indeed, some of Hizballah's Special Forces units demonstrated a limited ability to employ tactical maneuver in places such as Marun ar-Ras, Bint Jubayl, Ayta ash-Shab, and Dayr Siryan.[29] As a result, Hizballah probably inflicted more Israeli combat casualties per Arab fighter than any of Israel's opponents in 1956, 1967, 1973, or 1982.[30]

Nevertheless, Hizballah was hardly the Wehrmacht. Its marksmanship with small arms was generally atrocious, and even its vaunted ATGM teams had a terrible hit rate overall—possibly as low as 8 percent—and most had to use volley fire to compensate. To the extent that Hizballah employed maneuver and counterattacks, these were not consistent and typically at no more than squad or platoon level. Moreover, only one of the Hizballah counterattacks succeeded. Most Hizballah forces kept to static defensive operations, and reserve movements were small-scale when they happened at all. Its combined arms cooperation was similarly limited. They did use ATGMs, machine guns, and small arms simultaneously, but almost never combined these direct fire weaponry with indirect fire from mortars or rockets.[31] I will give the last word to Stephen Biddle and Jeffrey Friedman, who have written the most insightful analysis of Hizballah's conduct during the 2006 war. See if the following passages sound familiar:

Few Hezbollah units showed much apparent ability to react to changing conditions. Counterattackers taken under surprise fire from previously concealed IDF positions away from the assault objective, for example, often halted and fell back in disorder rather than reorienting to the new threat, redirecting suppressive fire, and continuing the advance. Where Hezbollah organized linear defenses these were often flanked by Israeli attackers; the defenders, however, typically either fought in the same positions or simply withdrew, rather than forming a new front to meet the assault.[32]

Hezbollah . . . fell far short of contemporary Western standards in controlling large-scale maneuver, integrating movement and indirect fire support, combining multiple combat arms, reacting flexibly to changing conditions, and small arms marksmanship. Hezbollah appears to have attempted a remarkably conventional system of tactics and theater operational art, but there is a difference between trying and achieving, and in 2006 at least, Hezbollah's reach in some ways exceeded its grasp.[33]

Hizballah Performance in the Syrian Civil War. It was the outbreak of the Syrian Civil War that forced Hizballah to rebuild the (fairly) large conventional military structure it had employed during the Lebanese Civil War. At first, Hizballah merely sent trainers and advisers to Syria to assist in the creation of pro-regime militias to supplement the remnants of the Syrian Army. However, this proved inadequate. Lacking in both skill and manpower, the regime's forces quickly lost control of much of the country.

In response, Bashar al-Asad called on his Iranian friends, and in turn Tehran called on its key ally across the border. Hizballah combat units first began fighting in Syria in 2012, initially to secure crucial border crossings into Lebanon such as al-Qusayr and then to assist Syrian government operations in Damascus and the nearby Qalamoun mountains in 2013.[34] Yet as the tide slowly turned against the Asad regime, and the Alawis began to run out of manpower to hold their extended front lines, Hizballah was forced to commit more and more ground troops as part of the Iranian-organized Shi'a coalition. By June 2013, the Hizballah contingent had grown to at least 2,000.[35] This trend only continued as the regime lost manpower and evinced little ability to compensate with maneuver or firepower. Consequently, by late 2015, Hizballah's expeditionary force in Lebanon had grown to 4,000 and then to about 8,000 in early 2017.[36]

In Syria, Hizballah personnel have functioned as everything from trainers and advisors, to partnered units with Syrian regime forces and Shi'a militias, to main force units engaged in high-intensity combat.[37] Increasingly, Hizballah and Iranian Revolutionary Guard formations have been called in to buttress vital regime defenses and spearhead major offensives. Accordingly, they played a critical role in the regime's defense of Damascus in 2013 and its conquest of Aleppo in December 2016, and had taken at least 2,000 casualties by early 2017.[38]

Hizballah's value to the Shi'a coalition and its superior military effectiveness are both nicely illustrated by its role in the Battle of Qusayr in April–June 2013. This was an operation that Hizballah planned and fought from start to finish with its own commanders and combat formations. The regime provided some fire support and a small number of troops and armor, but these were entirely under Hizballah control. The offensive was reasonably well reconnoitered, although the rebels proved to be stronger and more committed than Hizballah realized. Hizballah committed roughly 1,500 troops to the battle, many of them members of their "Special Forces," the elite units tasked with fighting an Israeli incursion into Lebanon.[39] Reportedly, many of these soldiers were veterans of the 2006 fighting; Syrian opposition fighters interviewed by Nick Blanford described their Hizballah opponents as "professional," "tough," and said that "none of them were under 35-years-old."[40]

Hizballah and regime forces converged on Qusayr from at least three sides and initially tried to move rapidly, assuming the opposition would fold under pressure. When they didn't—and inflicted some heavy casualties on the attackers—Hizballah stopped, regrouped, and changed their approach to a more methodical clearing operation. Their fighters employed good urban warfare tactics, for instance avoiding doors and windows and instead blowing holes in walls to advance into a building or room. The Hizballah infantrymen worked reasonably well in conjunction with Syrian artillery and air, but did best when fire support was provided by their own short-range rocket systems.[41] They fought very hard, and "The rebels noted how the Hizb Allah [*sic*] fighters were constantly trying to advance, even under heavy fire, and outflank their positions."[42]

Overall, Hizballah's performance in the Syrian Civil War has been good, but not flawless. In the words of longtime Middle East military analyst Jeff White, "Hizb Allah's combat performance in Syria has been at least fair. Its forces have the training and experience to conduct attacks and defensive actions with skill, and they have demonstrated a willingness to accept the casualties necessary to achieve their objectives. Nevertheless, Hizb Allah's forces have not always proved successful in offensive actions, suffering some tactical setbacks in the fighting for Qusayr, and may have failed in some defensive actions in the eastern Damascus suburbs during heavy fighting there in late November 2013."[43] Yet there is no question that Hizballah forces have proven considerably better than Arab state militaries (including the Syrian regime's own forces) at employing tactical maneuver and combined arms operations.[44] They have shown considerably better tactical initiative, discipline, and commitment to the fight, and there are numerous reports of the disdain Hizballah evinces for the incompetence of the Syrian army.[45]

Yet neither has Hizballah proven invincible. Initially, in Qusayr and Damascus, Hizballah forces fought well, in large part because they were mostly Special Forces and veterans of the 2006 war against Israel. They still took heavy casualties, and when these high-quality troops were rotated out, Hizballah formations did not enjoy the same kind of success, for instance in the fighting for Aleppo in late 2013 and 2014.[46] Since then, Hizballah's battlefield fortunes have improved as it has committed more and more troops to Lebanon and these have passed through the Darwinian process of combat in which it is learn or die. As a result, they have improved and are now considered one of the keys to the slow success of the regime (along with Iranian advisors, Russian firepower, and foreign Shi'a manpower), but that remains a relative standard in Syria's clumsy militia brawls.

Explaining Hizballah's Better Performance

So why did Hizballah perform relatively but still notably better than the armed forces of most of the Arab states? A number of factors were at work.

The first of these is the weakness of many of its adversaries. AMAL and the other Lebanese groups that Hizballah fought from 1985 to 1991 were largely ill-trained militias—and Hizballah did not do as well fighting more disciplined forces, such as the Druse, or those with heavier firepower, such as the Syrian army. The Israel Defense Forces were not in any shape to take on Hizballah in 2006 and had no business invading southern Lebanon then. While some of the Syrian opposition groups have demonstrated modest capabilities during the Syrian civil war, none have proven to be highly competent. Ultimately, the best adversary Hizballah ever fought was the IDF from 1985 to 2000, where it ultimately prevailed, but it did so simply by inflicting casualties on the Israelis in protracted guerrilla warfare, and even this it did at an overall 4:1 disadvantage. Hizballah learned to fight well against the Israelis, much better than most other Arab armies have, but they appear to have risen to the level of the Jordanians in 1948 and probably better than the Syrian commandos in 1982. That is still high praise, but only in a relative sense.

The second factor has been zeal. In every war that it has fought, Hizballah fighters have been uniformly described as extremely committed to the fight. During the Lebanese Civil War, this was one of the only advantages that Hizballah possessed over other militias. Of course, in civil wars where most of the combatants are untrained militiamen, having a greater commitment is often all that is needed to win out. That has also been part of Hizballah's success in Syria since 2012. In the 1990s and again in 2006, Israeli soldiers and officers marveled at the determination, bravery, and self-sacrifice of Hizballah fighters, as well as the strong unit cohesion of Hizballah formations.

The zeal of Hizballah fighters is itself a product of two reinforcing elements. The first of these is Hizballah's religious ideology, which is a core component of its training and daily routines. As Nick Blanford has related from his extensive interviews with Hizballah personnel over the years, the organization indoctrinates potential recruits with their ideology from childhood to build their dedication to its mission.[47] Beyond this, Michael Eisenstadt and Kendall Bianchi have demonstrated in a remarkable study of Hizballah personnel that another critical element in the commitment of Hizballah fighters, and the cohesion of their units, is that Hizballah deliberately recruits fighters from common families, clans, and groups of friends. By closely examining the biographies of over 2,000 Hizballah fighters killed in combat from 1982 to 2017, Eisenstadt and Bianchi demonstrated "Hizballah's reliance on family, clan, and local solidarities (or *asabiyya*, the concept of in-group solidarity made famous by the medieval Arab thinker Ibn Khaldun) to recruit members, motivate fighters, create cohesive and effective units, and enhance operational security."[48] The result has been to transfer those fierce bonds of loyalty so common to Arab families, clans, and groups of friends to Hizballah tactical formations, cementing their unit cohesion.[49]

Iran's generous backing is another reason for Hizballah's superior performance. The Iranians have been devoted bankers, trainers, and advisors for Hizballah, in everything from guerrilla warfare to conventional operations, and from actual combat skills to logistics, communications, and other forms of combat service support.[50] However, we should not pin too much on Iranian training. Iran was probably more devoted to Hizballah and worked harder with it than most foreign services working with most Arab armed forces, but it still begs the question of why Hizballah actually learned from the Iranians when (1) the Iranians aren't terrific themselves, and (2) so many other Arab militaries—including other nonstate militaries—have been unable to improve under the tutelage of other foreign militaries. Is Iran truly a better trainer—or its doctrine truly superior—to the Americans, British, Russians, and French? Did Iran really do a better job training Hizballah than the United States has done training the Iraqi armed forces since 2007? Was Iran the reason that Hizballah has performed more effectively than Iraqi forces since the United States got serious about training Iraqi forces at the start of the Surge?

We might give Iran some credit for the difference, but it seems likely that it was more about the nature of Hizballah than about the magic of Iranian training and doctrine. A superb study of this issue by Marc DeVore and Armin Stähli demonstrates that Iran's training actually did very little for Hizballah, although its weapons, financial aid, and sanctuary did. In their words, "The IRGC's members possessed neither the training nor the experience needed to guide an irregular military campaign when they deployed to Lebanon in 1982."[51] At first, Hizballah copied IRGC tactics from the Iran-Iraq War— human wave attacks—that failed horrifically. This caused Hizballah to send most of the Iranian trainers home and then reform its tactics on its own, which helped produce its successes in the late 1980s.[52] Hizballah's superior effectiveness were mostly "a product of tactics devised and implemented by its Lebanese cadres, who drew more heavily on their prior experience in Lebanon's civil war than on the inexpert advice offered by Iran's revolutionary Guards Corps."[53]

One unquestionable source of Hizballah's exceptional prowess has been its reliance on eliteness. During the Lebanese Civil War, Hizballah fighters were somewhat better than the other militias because of their zeal, better tactics, and Iranian weaponry, but not by much. At that time, they had a force roughly 10,000 strong (from a Lebanese Shi'a population of just 1.3 million). To drive Israel from Lebanon, they slimmed down to just 500 full-time fighters (with another 1,000 part-timers who were rarely called on to do any fighting). Those 500 were the men who had demonstrated the greatest ability in battle and represented less than .04 percent of the larger population. By 2006, their Special Forces had only grown to 1,000 men, with perhaps another 2,000 in various support functions. Their experiences in Syria after 2012 make the case further: at Qusayr and Damascus in 2013 and Yabrud in early 2014, Hizballah did very well because it committed many of its veteran Special Forces. However, when losses among these troops caused it to pull many of them back to Lebanon and instead deploy reservists and new recruits—even lowering the recruiting age to find adequate manpower—Hizballah's combat fortunes declined accordingly.[54] Yiftah Shapir notes that the only way that Hizballah could expand from its 2006 field force of 1,000 fighters to its 2017 strength of nearly 20,000 was to lower its recruiting and training standards.[55] Thus, eliteness, a way of avoiding culturally driven problems in part by selecting for those who have least manifested those predilections, has clearly been one important aspect of Hizballah's better performance when it has in fact performed better.

Another has been Hizballah's command and control architecture. Hizballah started out as an amalgam of Iranian-backed terrorist organizations, and although it has grown over time and built a more conventional chain of command, it is still not just another Arab hierarchy. Terrorist organizations employ a cellular structure in which the organization is broken up into lots of small, highly autonomous groups. The cells do not know each other well so that the exposure and capture of one does not compromise others, and they are meant to identify, plan, develop, and conduct operations largely on their own with only minimal guidance from the senior leadership and little or no cooperation from other groups. Members of a cellular organization cannot expect orders from the top; they have to do everything themselves.

Hizballah still has a somewhat flat and cellular command and control architecture derived from its terrorist roots. DeVore and Stähli note that Hizballah was begun by a cadre of highly experienced Shi'a commanders who had fought with the PLO and AMAL in the Lebanese Civil War, and "who had proven their competence in the crucible of Lebanon's civil war." They built Hizballah as a flat, decentralized, and flexible organization from the start, and then sought out Shi'a fighters who could operate in such a command structure.[56] Thus, in 2006, Hizballah divided south Lebanon into several sectors, which were in turn divided up into sub-sectors of just 2–3 villages each, and the forces and leaders in each sub-sector had the capacity and authority to act wholly independently. Indeed, they were expected and encouraged to do so. It was this semi-cellular structure that promoted the greater initiative, aggressiveness, and creativity among Hizballah tactical commanders in Lebanon in 2006.[57] In this area as well, the additional manpower needs of the Syrian civil war have forced Hizballah to move from its flat, three-rung command structure (the 3,000-man *wahidah*, the 200-man *qism*, and the 6–12-man *fara'*) to a more rigid five-rung hierarchy with new units introduced between each of these formations.[58]

Moreover, the semi-cellular command and control structure points back to another important aspect of eliteness. Hizballah fighters had to be able to operate as part of a flat, cellular structure. They could not expect to function like typical members of a typical Arab hierarchy. A cellular organization is not a typical Arab hierarchy. In fact, it is the polar opposite of a culturally regular Arab hierarchy. Those best able to function in such an organization are unlikely to be culturally regular themselves. Thus, by relying on only very small numbers of personnel, Hizballah was able to select those who were least culturally regular and therefore best able to function in its non-culturally regular organization. This was further hardened by the Darwinian process of combat, where only the fittest survive, and those who can't are killed or sent to the reserves. Here "fit" would be defined as those best able to function in Hizballah's non-culturally regular semi-cellular hierarchy. Again, the fact that the combat performance of Hizballah formations has declined as its force structure in Syria expanded and became more traditional to accommodate larger numbers of fighters speaks to the importance of this semi-cellular organization to Hizballah's better performance against Israel in 1985–2000 and 2006, and in Syria in 2012–2013.

Finally, I am going to raise one more possibility, but can do no more than raise it because the evidence is inadequate at this time. Hizballah is, of course, Shi'a Muslim. Pretty devoutly Shi'a Muslim for that matter, which has caused problems with the mostly secular Syrian armed forces.[59] An important difference between Shi'a and Sunni Islam is the concept of *ijtihad*, meaning independent reasoning or interpretation. Most schools of Sunni Islam argue against ijtihad, insisting that the Quran should be taken literally—and that all of the necessary interpretations or supplementary materials are contained in the Hadiths, which should also be followed to the letter, without additional interpretation. In contrast, Shi'a Islam is more amenable to the idea of ijtihad, although when it comes to matters of religion, this is meant to be conducted only by someone with the proper religious training, known as a mujtahid (literally, someone able to practice ijtihad). Many Iranians and Shi'a Arabs (and Israelis, for that matter) claim that this instills a greater willingness among Shi'a to think for themselves, rather than simply waiting for an authority figure to tell them how to act. It is certainly true that Iranian forces showed greater initiative and battlefield innovation than the Iraqis ever did, and Iranians are overwhelmingly Shi'a. However, Iranians are also overwhelmingly non-Arab (they are mostly Persians, Azeris, and Kurds and only about 2 percent are Arabs), and there is no evidence to show that, for instance, Iraqi Shi'a performed better in combat than their Sunni brethren. Moreover, the scholarly literature supporting this conjecture is weak.[60]

In short, Hizballah's relatively better performance—and it has been better—can be explained by a number of different factors. Some of them were very conventional military advantages such as facing a weak opponent and having highly motivated troops. Others, however, specifically enabled Hizballah to mitigate the impact of culturally regular patterns of behavior that had hobbled the armed forces of the Arab states during the modern era and similarly crippled the vast majority of Arab nonstate militaries, forces that never achieved the same success as Hizballah. Finally, Hizballah found clever ways to take advantage of strengths derived from the dominant Arab culture, particularly its ability to generate much stronger unit cohesion and personal bravery by creating a force structure built on the powerful in-group loyalties, the asabiyya, of Arab culture.

Da'ish

If Hizballah is the great Shi'a nonstate Arab bogeyman, Da'ish* is its Sunni counterpart. Da'ish is the latest iteration of the group we once knew as al-Qa'ida in Iraq. At its peak, AQI led the coalition of Sunni groups simultaneously waging an insurgency against the US occupation and a civil war against Iraq's Shi'a community. So great was their success that they felt comfortable declaring themselves the new "Islamic State of Iraq" (ISI). When the group was devastated by the success of the Surge in 2007–2008, they reverted back to terrorism and retreated to Iraq's hinterlands to survive. However, by 2010 they had become little more than a lethal nuisance, and the group was in danger of dissolving altogether as recruits dried up and Iraq's communities unified against them.[61]

In 2011, two things dramatically reversed their fortunes. First, the Arab Spring swept the Middle East. In Syria, it produced a popular revolt against Bashar al-Asad, who managed to turn a secular uprising into a sectarian civil war by convincing his (quasi-Shi'a) Alawi power base and other Syrian minorities that the rebellion was actually a plot by violent Sunni extremists to overthrow his regime and slaughter all of the non-Sunnis. The Syrian Civil War proved to be a godsend for AQI, most of whose remaining cadre fled to Syria to use their hard-won combat skills to build a new Sunni militia in Syria. Since few Syrian Sunnis had the experience of these Iraqis, they were welcomed and quickly became the leaders of a powerful force in eastern Syria. In recognition of their new role in Syria, the group changed its name, adding "ash-Sham" and turning ISI into ISIS, or Da'ish.[62]

Then, at the end of the year, the United States military withdrew its combat formations as part of a larger disengagement from Iraq by the Obama administration. The departure of the Americans let Iraq's Shi'a prime minister, Nuri al-Maliki, run wild. He consolidated power the way that he had always wanted,

---

* This is the widely used Arabic acronym for their name—ad-Dawlah al-Islāmiyah fī'l-ʿIrāq wa ash-Shām, which means the Islamic State in Iraq and ash-Sham. "Ash-Sham" is an older name for a part of the ancient Islamic empire that mostly corresponds with Syria, but can also include much of the Levant. Hence, some call it the Islamic States of Iraq and Syria (ISIS) or the Islamic State of Iraq and the Levant (ISIL). To simplify matters, I will simply use the Arabic acronym, which many non-Arabs have also adopted for simplicity's sake.

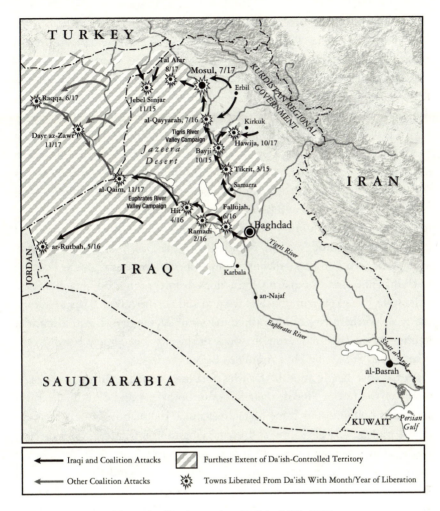

MAP 27 The Iraqi Counteroffensive against Da'ish, 2015–2017

purging the senior ranks of the Iraqi military and government of anyone that he did not consider loyal to himself; arresting, exiling, and intimidating his political rivals; subverting the Iraqi judiciary; and alienating Iraq's Sunni population, which Maliki viewed with enormous suspicion. To make matters worse, Maliki ignored all of the carefully brokered deals between Sunni and Shi'a that the United States had put in place as part of the Surge. Iraq's Sunni community increasingly saw Maliki as their greatest enemy, and the (increasingly Shi'a) Iraqi army as nothing but his militia. By late 2013, Iraq's Sunni community was in a state of near revolt, with large-scale protests in Fallujah and Ramadi, which Da'ish infiltrated and enflamed.[63]

In June 2014, the group unleashed a long-gestating plan to grab territory in Iraq and Syria. That plan succeeded beyond their wildest dreams. In Syria, Da'ish was able to wrest control of much of the northeast from various other civil war combatants, including nearly all of the middle Tigris River Valley and the cities of ar-Raqqa and Dayr az-Zawr, as well as chunks of terrain near Damascus.[64] But their greatest successes came in Iraq. There, Da'ish pushed into Salah ad-Din and Ninewah provinces, expecting to gain control of smaller cities such as Samarra and Tal Afar where they had been developing extensive relationships with the unhappy Sunni populations. As they advanced, however, the Iraqi army collapsed before them (discussed in Chapter 7). Da'ish forces numbering only around 1,000–2,000 men made contact with other Iraqi Sunni militant groups and disgruntled Iraqi tribes, and quickly hammered out a rough coalition with the Da'ish fighters at the core. With their own numbers growing, Sunni tribes and fighting groups flocking to their banners, and Iraqi army formations disintegrating, Da'ish and its new allies were able to overrun much of western and northern Iraq. They even took the great northern city of Mosul in a matter of days and with a minimum of fighting as the two Iraqi army divisions in the city (one largely Kurdish, the other mixed Sunni and Shi'a Arab) fled before them.

After that heady month, Da'ish's fortunes waned. Within just a few weeks of the fall of Mosul, their forces in both Iraq and Syria had largely shot their bolt and now came up against much tougher foes that were dug-in and waiting for them. Iraq shifted its remaining military forces to defend Baghdad and supplemented them with large numbers of Shi'a militiamen determined to prevent the murderous Da'ish troops (and the other Sunni militias) from reaching the great Shi'a population and religious centers of central and southern Iraq. In addition, first Iran and then the United States began to provide much-needed military support to the Iraqis. Da'ish did gain some additional successes—surprising Iraq's Kurds and briefly threatening their capital of Erbil at the end of the summer of 2014, taking Palmyra and Ramadi in the spring of 2015—but these proved to be blips in an otherwise steady decline. In particular, after the Da'ish attack on Erbil, the United States committed itself to a campaign to destroy Da'ish altogether by rebuilding Iraq's military, creating a Syrian opposition force able to defeat Da'ish, and committing considerable air power and fire support to the fight. Because the Americans were largely "punching with someone else's fists," as Lt. General Sean MacFarland, the commander of US forces in Iraq and Syria, liked to say, it took over two years to roll back Da'ish's gains, but ultimately, the end proved inevitable and Iraq declared Da'ish defeated in December 2017.

How Good Was Da'ish?

Like Hizballah, Da'ish was considerably better than most Arab armies of the modern era, state or nonstate. But also like Hizballah, their successes were magnified by both the weakness of their opponents and the low expectations that the world has for any Arab military after the long history of subpar Arab military performances.

2014: The Da'ish Blitzkrieg. A great deal of Da'ish's outsized reputation still derives from its stunning offensive across northern Iraq (and eastern Syria) in the spring of 2014. So that's where we need to begin to assess Da'ish's combat performance.

For starters, Da'ish had some very conventional advantages over its opponents, especially in Iraq. The first of these was surprise. The Iraqi government had badly underestimated Da'ish's conventional military power, having ignored its operations in Syria, deriding it as just the latest iteration of AQI, which it decidedly was not. Baghdad was not expecting a significant conventional assault in June 2014, and it was entirely unaware of the extent to which Da'ish had infiltrated personnel into many towns and army garrisons in northern Iraq, or that it had subverted numerous Sunni tribes and military personnel, and had even made contact with other armed Sunni groups. As a result, Iraqi forces were not deployed, prepared, or even ready to face a conventional assault.

Moreover, as I described in Chapter 7, the Iraqi Security Forces (ISF) were in no shape to fight anyone at that point. They had been horribly politicized by Maliki, who had removed many of the most competent commanders, replaced them with incompetent hacks previously sidelined by the Americans, diminished the numbers of Sunni Arabs and Kurds in the military (except in the divisions in the north, perversely), and allowed corruption to run rampant. As a result, the army had literally ceased training, relations between senior officers and their subordinates were close to nonexistent, Sunni and Kurdish troops had no interest in fighting (let alone dying) for Maliki and his Shi'a chauvinist regime, and few Shi'a had any interest in dying to prevent Sunni attackers from taking over Sunni towns that seemed eager to embrace them. Consequently, taken completely by surprise by Da'ish's fanatical warriors, Iraq's senior officers in the north deserted their troops, the Sunni and Kurdish troops refused to fight (with many Sunnis joining the attackers), and the Shi'a troops fled.

In other words, the ISF, especially in northern Iraq, had become a hollow shell, and it only required one sharp blow to cause it to crumble. The Da'ish attack was that sharp blow, and that was its primary role—causing the final collapse of the ISF after it had been systematically hollowed out for three-plus years. It is critical to note that the two Iraqi Army divisions in Mosul, with roughly 20,000 troops, collapsed in a single day when they were attacked by no more than a few hundred Da'ish fighters.[65] This makes clear that their collapse had almost nothing to do with Da'ish or its operations; a fall that rapid with such an absurd imbalance of forces could only be the result of a collapse in morale, one long in coming.

The self-disintegration of the ISF in the north is a very important element of what happened, and attributing too much credit to Da'ish has been part of why its prowess has been significantly exaggerated since then. Da'ish still did some interesting and impressive things, but all of them were made infinitely easier because of the collapse of morale among the ISF across northern Iraq. In many, many cases, Da'ish fighters simply had to show up somewhere— or announce that they were coming via social media—and far-larger ISF garrisons would flee. That means that there was little to no pressure on Da'ish, virtually no challenge, and nearly anything they did resulted in victory.

Nevertheless, there were some aspects of the invasion that should be recognized. First, Da'ish did a good job of planning its initial moves, and even if the Iraqis had fought back, Da'ish probably would have had some important albeit smaller successes, including being able to secure control of several towns. In particular, they did an excellent job of identifying weak units and potential defectors, infiltrating their own people, and reconnoitering local battlefields. What was arguably more impressive was the ability of Da'ish's high command to improvise when it became clear that the original plan was irrelevant because the ISF was collapsing. They demonstrated an ability to reroute units, shift forces, and push forward new attacks. Likewise, at least some tactical Da'ish commanders also demonstrated real initiative and aggressiveness in recognizing that ISF units were collapsing in front of them, relaying this to higher headquarters and/or continuing their attacks beyond what had originally been planned to win greater victories.[66] Again, all of this was much, much easier than in typical combat situations because the ISF was not fighting back effectively (or at all), but it still requires a certain amount of capable leadership to take advantage of it. In 1980, a different Iraqi army faced almost no opposition in invading Iran, but those formations showed zero capacity to take advantage of those similar circumstances.

Likewise, some Da'ish units employed mortars and artillery to bombard ISF positions to soften them up before attacking them. Others used some degree of maneuver, surrounding ISF garrisons or assaulting them from multiple axes. Still others had infiltrated their people into ISF positions (or turned ISF personnel), but had them wait until Da'ish forces were attacking to have the traitors turn, causing the maximum surprise and confusion.[67]

Indeed, it was in their use of psychological warfare techniques that Da'ish truly excelled, regardless of the collapse of their foe. Da'ish personnel cultivated an image of invincibility and terror. They deliberately committed atrocities to terrify their opponents into fleeing for fear of being captured (as well as because their perverse ideology sanctioned it). They made superb use of social media, broadcasting their triumphs and massacres and warning ISF soldiers ahead of them that they were next. Again, most of the morale collapse of the ISF in the north was a product of Maliki's blunders, but Da'ish still deserves credit for having accelerated that process with its masterful exploitation of fear.[68]

Other Da'ish Offensives. Although it is the best known and most successful, the June 2014 attack was hardly the only time that Da'ish went on the offensive. Indeed, the uniqueness of that campaign is easily illustrated by comparing it to other Da'ish offensives at Kobani, Dayr az-Zawr, Ramadi, Palmyra, Fallujah, Bayji, Erbil, and elsewhere against the Kurdish front lines in 2014 and 2015, none of which unfolded like their astonishing victories in June 2014.

At the strategic level, Da'ish gets mixed marks for these attacks. In some cases—Dayr az-Zawr, Ramadi, Palmyra, Fallujah, and Erbil—Da'ish picked out important targets that were vulnerable to their attack. They planned the operations well, massed their forces quickly and covertly, and concentrated sufficient force to get the job done. In the words of Jessica Lewis of the Institute for the Study of War, Da'ish was "able to plan, adjust, consolidate, and initiate phased campaigns."[69] Kobani and Bayji were mistakes, however. They proved to be meat grinders where the initial Da'ish assaults failed, and rather than live to fight again, Da'ish doubled down and lost large numbers of fighters in fruitless battles of attrition against an adversary possessing superior firepower and logistical capabilities.

At the tactical level, Da'ish was also a mixed bag in these assaults. In all of these major operations and consistently throughout its campaigns, Da'ish has been excellent at aggressive patrolling to identify weak spots in enemy defenses as well as strongpoints to be bypassed. As Michael Knights and Alex Mello have noted, Da'ish's approach to ISR had other purposes as well as it relied on "fighting patrols to dominate no-man's-land, fix the enemy, and prevent enemy intelligence-gathering, and reconnoiter attack routes."[70] At least some Da'ish tactical commanders proved able to concentrate force against weak spots they had identified, although others relentlessly attacked in sectors where they could get no traction.

A consistent strength of Da'ish in the attack has been their manipulation of surprise and ability to set the psychological conditions of battle before an attack. Da'ish routinely exploited its role as Sunni "liberators" come to aid the locals against oppressive Shi'a regimes in Damascus and Baghdad. That allowed them to infiltrate their own personnel forward and persuade local tribes to come over to their side before their assaults began.[71] Likewise, Da'ish's major attacks have typically been accompanied by feints and other efforts to distract the defender and create confusion regarding the real target.[72] Beyond this, Da'ish has continued to employ social media effectively, complemented by their campaign of atrocities and cruelty, which they use to demoralize their enemies in the hope that they will crumble when they find out that a Da'ish attack is headed their way.[73]

One of the more interesting Da'ish innovations has been their integration of suicide bombers into conventional military operations. Da'ish uses suicide bombers (both car/truck bombs and people wearing suicide vests) as a simple version of a precision-guided munition. The local Da'ish commander designates a target and the suicide bomber goes and tries to blow it up. While not terribly sophisticated, they were the first to think of doing this, and it has been an important part of their tactical operations, both attacking and defending.

Most Da'ish tactical attacks conformed to a pattern.[74] They would begin with a preliminary bombardment. At first, they used mortars or artillery until the US-led Coalition stripped away these assets through constant air attack. This forced Da'ish to instead rely on waves of suicide bombers (car bombs or individuals wearing suicide vests). The preliminary bombardment was typically coupled with the advance deployment of snipers and machine guns to soften up the target. After the bombardment and sniper fire, Da'ish typically launched a determined infantry assault supported by whatever armor they possessed— often just armored trucks, bulldozers, or tractors acting as armored personnel carriers to carry infantry through the initial defensive lines. American, Iraqi, and Kurdish military personnel who have fought against Da'ish noted that it was the rare Da'ish unit that actively maneuvered in battle, and while their typical assault tactics sometimes allowed them to break-in to the defender's lines, they rarely were ready or able to exploit these break-ins and turn them into true breakthroughs. Moreover, faced with unexpected resistance or a counterattack from an unexpected direction, Da'ish tactical units typically had just two responses: keep trying to grind forward, or retreat. They rarely tried to adjust their attack to deal with the problem. It is for this reason, for instance, that it took Da'ish eight months to finally conquer Ramadi in 2014–2015.[75]

Moreover, combined arms coordination was both uneven and limited. In some sectors in some battles, Da'ish did a reasonable job integrating its version of armor (armored trucks and tractors), infantry, and fire support (usually suicide bombers or mortars). In other sectors—often in the same battle—the three seemed to be fighting separate battles altogether. For instance, American military officers found that, in some sectors, any time the ISF began to gain some momentum, the local Da'ish commander would quickly start sending suicide bombers against it to try to disrupt, slow, or halt it and give his infantry a chance to regroup and reset, in effect acting as suppressive fire. In other sectors, the car and truck bombs just attacked randomly—not necessarily in coordination with the infantry or even with one another.

For all of these reasons, Da'ish attacks have proven most successful when their psychological warfare techniques have demoralized the enemy so that they can be broken quickly by a few determined blows, possibly involving a few deft maneuvers, and always employing some form of surprise or shock. When they cannot do so, as Gabi Siboni noted in discussing their failure in the attack on the Kurds, "On that occasion, the Islamic State troops were exposed as being average to below average in terms of operational capability."[76]

Da'ish on the Defensive. Early on, Da'ish tried to be aggressive, active defenders. They utilized their interior lines of communication effectively and shifted forces to threatened sectors rapidly and smoothly.[77] They also tried hard to retain the strategic initiative and so did not want to be forced into a wholly reactive, defensive posture.

In particular, Da'ish's strategic leadership demonstrated both a willingness and ability to counterpunch, hitting its adversaries somewhere else whenever they made a gain. The most famous instance of this came in 2015, when the ISF finally liberated Tikrit with American assistance and Da'ish immediately attacked Ramadi in response. However, especially in 2016 and 2017, the US-led Coalition air campaign largely deprived Da'ish of its strategic/operational mobility. At that point, it became far harder for Da'ish to shift forces around its territory, to concentrate them secretly for an operational counterpunch, or to deploy strategic reserves to meet a new offensive. Consequently, the Da'ish leadership was forced to just try to push as many resources as possible to their most important territorial assets and then have those forces dig-in deep and try to hold on.

Da'ish's strategic leadership also deserves credit for recognizing in numerous circumstances that it was not going to be able to successfully defend terrain and so opted to withdraw its forces rather than lose them in a fruitless battle. At Jurf as-Saqr in October 2014 and again at Jalula in November 2014, Da'ish commanders pulled their fighters before many could be killed.[78]

One thing that Da'ish has continued to emphasize and do well at is intelligence, surveillance, and reconnaisance (ISR). In 2016–2017 Da'ish may have lost its strategic and operational mobility, but it gained additional tactical ISR capabilities by deploying its own simple, but effective drones, which proved to be a menace in defense of both Raqqa and Mosul. In addition, they continued to try to patrol aggressively when possible, both to try to ascertain what their enemies were up to, and to try to keep them on their heels to disrupt enemy attacks.

Tactically, Da'ish has proven that it can be a tenacious defender when it wants to be, but it is ultimately a doomed one, like the Japanese in late 1944 and early 1945 because they have no ability or plan to wholly defeat an enemy attack except to bleed them and hope that they give up. It is for this reason that Knights and Mello remarked in April 2015 that "The Islamic State has been on the defensive in Iraq for more than eight months and it has lost practically every battle it has fought."[79]

Da'ish has typically defended in depth, with layer upon layer of IEDs, obstacles, snipers, and infantry fighting positions, often backed by the "firepower" of suicide bombers. They built trenches, tunnels, and berms to enable their own forces to move and impede that of an attacker. Their fighters tended to fight very hard, and they were difficult to root out, especially when they had embedded their defenses in urban environments—and even more so if there were large numbers of civilians around to provide them with human shields.[80] Especially early on, in 2014 and 2015, Da'ish tactical commanders did react aggressively and counterattacked frequently, probably in the hope that they could regain the initiative or that their aggressiveness would paralyze their (typically less committed) adversaries. However, especially against Iraqi and Kurdish (and later Syrian opposition) forces seeded with Western combat advisors and supported by suffocating Coalition air power, this approach proved costly. In some early cases, Da'ish even attempted to employ maneuver in its counterattacks—operations that could have proven disastrous to their foes, but instead turned into defeats because they created "target rich environments" for Western air strikes.[81]

Later in the war, in 2016 and 2017, Da'ish counterattacks tapered off significantly, especially at the operational level. Instead, their tactical commanders dug-in deep and released waves of suicide bombers against an enemy attack, which should be viewed as a response by firepower, not maneuver, as suicide bombers were effectively their version of a defensive artillery barrage. At times, they did try to suck an attacker into a kill zone, but they had effectively lost the ability to maneuver against the adversary, or launch large-scale counterattacks that might have defeated the assault. Again, like the Japanese, their only objective became bleeding the attacker in hope that that would be enough to get him to stop. And also like the Japanese, this approach inflicted some heavy casualties on their adversaries in places such as Bayji, Mosul, and Raqqa, but since they would not or could not maneuver or mount counterattacks at anything more than squad or platoon level, there was no real danger that Da'ish would do more than temporarily halt an assault. If the attacker was willing to pay the blood price, the result became a foregone conclusion.

Explaining Da'ish Successes

Ultimately, six factors have been responsible for Da'ish's battlefield triumphs.

Poor Adversaries. Warfare is a competitive activity, and to win you don't have to be good, just better than your opponent. Neither the Iraqi security forces, the Syrian regime's forces, nor most of the Iraqi and Syrian militias have been much competition for Da'ish. In fact, most have been dreadful. The best evidence of this has been how quickly Da'ish's fortunes turned around as a result of the rather modest improvement in the capabilities of the ISF and some Syrian opposition forces thanks to the advisory assistance and training provided by the US-led Coalition.[82] In the words of Israel's former chief of Military Intelligence, Lt. General Amos Yadlin, "From a military perspective, the Islamic State's mode of operation is not groundbreaking. . . . Its attempts to use heavier and more sophisticated weapons captured in battle have not led to significant battlefield achievements. . . . It has thereby acquired the ability to concentrate forces quickly and surprise remote enemies. Still, these tactics and tools are not suitable for fighting a modern Western Army."[83]

Zeal. One of the most important advantages that Da'ish fighters bring to the battlefield is their commitment. This directly feeds into the disparity between Da'ish and its adversaries. Da'ish fighters—especially its foreign fighters, discussed further below—fervently believe that they are fighting a holy war on behalf of the Almighty. They are completely committed to the fight, and many are not just willing but enthusiastic to die for their cause. Moreover, Da'ish as an organization understands the military value of such fervor and consciously works to instill and enhance it. As Siboni explained in an important essay on Da'ish's military power, Da'ish "deems military training of secondary importance as compared to the effort that it puts into cultivating the combatants' desire to fight."[84]

Especially in the kind of amateurish militia combat that has characterized much of the fighting in the Middle East, merely being willing to keep fighting, killing, and dying is often a decisive advantage. "Its operational capabilities are not stellar, but the high level of its fighting spirit and the readiness with which its followers embrace self-sacrifice have allowed it to expand its control over the region," in Siboni's words.[85] More than that, Da'ish fighters are often, but not always, willing not just to keep shooting at the other guy and absorbing losses, but to *advance against fire*. That is a very unusual trait in these kinds of wars, something that also gave Hizballah an advantage over other militias during the Lebanese Civil War. It is less that such an assault can result in taking an enemy position (which it certainly can) and more that doing so can be terrifying to troops who know that they would never be willing to do the same, which often causes the morale of less committed formations to crack. That is often the surest path to victory in these kinds of militia firefights.[86]

Darwinian Selection. Again, like Hizballah, Da'ish has been able to rely on a reasonably competent cadre of commanders. And again, both at strategic/operational and tactical levels, this has been uneven. Yet Da'ish's victories, where they have come, have often been the product of some very smart strategy and/or able battlefield leadership. Moreover, Da'ish has proven itself to be a learning organization, a trait that has to come from its leadership, especially its senior-most leaders.[87]

In the media, this is often attributed to a group of about 100–150 former Iraqi military officers who have acted as key commanders, planners, and generals for Da'ish.[88] It is frequently claimed that this group brought expert planning and leadership, military discipline, and a genius for war-making to Da'ish's military operations.[89] That's mostly nonsense. First, Da'ish was a pretty big military organization—with about 10,000 fighters at the time of their greatest successes in 2014, and perhaps as many as 50,000 fighters at their height in 2015—and such a small number of highly competent officers is unlikely to have had that kind of impact on so large a force. Second, we have a great deal of information indicating that many of Da'ish's best commanders were not former officers in Saddam's army, and were not even Iraqis. Finally, let's remember that Saddam's army was pretty rotten. Just having been an officer in Saddam's army was no guarantee that you knew what you were doing.

The vast majority of them didn't. Not even at their height in 1987–1991 did the Iraqi military evince much military genius. (Understand that for many Iraqis, this is another way of blaming the United States and Nuri al-Maliki for Da'ish: the United States for disbanding Saddam's army in 2003, and Maliki for refusing to retain Sunni officers in the ISF, both of which pushed many Sunni former Iraqi military personnel out of the Iraqi armed forces into the arms of AQI and Da'ish.)

Please understand that I am not denying that these men exist or that they did not make important contributions to Da'ish's military fortunes, only that their role has been exaggerated and the reason that they have contributed has little to do with their service in Saddam's army. There are tens of thousands of former Iraqi soldiers who fought with Da'ish, and before that with AQI. What is important about those who have become key leaders of Da'ish is that they were the ones who survived and thrived through the American occupation, the 2005–2008 Iraqi Civil War, the Surge, and then the Syrian Civil War. The vast majority didn't. They got killed. They got injured. They got tired. They got sidelined. Unlike all of the rest, these 100–150 men figured out how to fight, how to stay alive, and how to succeed in this kind of warfare. *That* is why they advanced through Da'ish's ranks and why they became important members of Da'ish's command staff.

They seem to have some degree of camaraderie as a result of this shared apprenticeship in Saddam's army, and some no doubt learned some useful things there, but it was not their service in Saddam's army that made them able military commanders. It is the fact that they had innate qualities that enabled them to get something out of service in the Iraqi army—which millions of other Iraqis who also served in the Iraqi army lacked and so got nothing from—that made them successful. In an army as large as Saddam's was, with hundreds of thousands of troops and tens of thousands of officers, it is not surprising to find several hundred very good officers. And placed in the right circumstances, those very good officers can emerge, demonstrate their abilities, learn from experience, and become quite formidable strategists, planners, and field commanders.[90] That is what happened with these men and what made them good commanders, *not* anything they got from Saddam's army—which millions of others had passed through without benefit, either to Saddam or Da'ish.

Finally, to the extent that they deserve credit for Da'ish's greater effectiveness, their impact was probably greatest in the early days of Da'ish's success. At that time the organization was smaller, allowing a relatively small group of competent leaders to have greater impact. They also had far greater freedom of action then. At first, none of their primary foes—the Iraqi government, the

Syrian regime, the Kurds, the Iranians, the United States—took them seriously, and so they could do more with the limited resources at their disposal. Once they had shocked the world with their run of victories, they quickly lost those early advantages and their limitations became far more pronounced.

An Unorthodox Hierarchy. You may have noticed that I used the phrase "placed in the right circumstances" in the last paragraph. That was not an offhand reference. It isn't just that these competent officers succeeded in the Darwinian struggles of the Iraqi and Syrian civil wars, it is that Da'ish's structure enabled them to emerge and then took advantage of their qualities in ways that other militaries (including Saddam's) did not.

Like Hizballah, Da'ish as a conventional army grew out of a terrorist group (AQI and al-Qa'ida before that). That is a very different pedigree from most militaries, and certainly from most Arab state armies. Because of it, Da'ish's organization was very different from that of most conventional militaries. In particular, it retained a highly cellular structure like the terrorist group it once was. Even as a conventional army, it was broken up into platoon-sized formations that had a high degree of autonomy.[91] As Knights and Mello have described it, "A typical attack force comprises 20–40 foot soldiers—historically the size of the average insurgent cell, including indirect-fire, IED-laying/triggering teams, RPG/ambush teams, etc.—plus three to five armored and unarmored utility vehicles, with a couple of heavy support weapons. When larger attacks are undertaken, it is usually coordinated, simultaneous but only loosely connected activity by these small war bands, not a larger unit action per se."[92]

This structure had both advantages and disadvantages.[93] As Knights and Mello point out, it made it hard for Da'ish to coordinate large operations, especially attacks, and is part of the reason most of their attacks were clumsy, except in the perfect conditions of June 2014. However, they also required and relied on tactical commanders willing and able to think and act for themselves with little direction from higher authority.

Hopefully, the link with Arab cultural patterns is becoming clear again. The point is that Da'ish is not a typical Arab hierarchy. It does not function like a typical hierarchic organization in the Arab world. As with Hizballah, many "culturally regular" Arabs would have a very hard time relating to such a structure. Others, those who are not culturally regular, who deviate significantly from the cultural mean, might thrive in such circumstances (people who probably felt smothered in traditional Arab organizations). Moreover, Da'ish as an organization is clearly led by such people, which is part of the reason their group has survived and become a major player in the Darwinian struggle across Iraq and Syria. They then seek out others like themselves, men who can think and act independently, and they put those men in positions of command because that is what they need for this organization to function properly. Da'ish's leaders are clearly not culturally regular themselves. That has been a key element of their survival and success, and they deliberately seek out other, non-culturally regular individuals for their organization, which requires such people for its continued success.

Joining Da'ish is not a "normal" thing for any Arab to do. There are 300 million Arabs and, at most, only about 100,000 have been part of Da'ish in any way, and many of them were forced into it.[94] The small minority of Arabs who join Da'ish are very unusual. They clearly represent a highly rebellious minority. It should not be surprising to find that (1) they have created a hierarchy that does not function like a traditional Arab hierarchy, (2) that the system selects for people who do *not* behave in culturally regular ways, and (3) that the organization does not perform in culturally regular ways on the battlefield. Indeed, there is an extensive body of sociological and psychological work demonstrating that Arabs who join terrorist and insurgent groups have "emerged mainly in milieus where the culture has been distorted or destroyed," in Gary Gregg's words.[95] In other words, *Da'ish takes Arabs who are not "normal" by the standards of Arab society and then places them in a hierarchy that is also not "normal" by those same standards.* It should not be surprising then that the organization does not perform the way that "normal" Arab organizations perform, and since warfare is an area where the normal Arab organization performs badly, it should not be surprising that this abnormal organization performs better.

Foreign Fighters. A related piece of the puzzle is the high number of foreign fighters and how they have contributed to Da'ish's success. Foreign fighters have clearly played a huge role in Da'ish, far more so than for any previous such group. Although the numbers are very soft, it may be that half or more of Da'ish fighters are from somewhere other than Iraq and Syria. For instance, in September 2014, the CIA estimated that Da'ish had 31,000 fighters altogether. Five months later, the chief of the US National Counterterrorism Center testified that 20,000 foreign fighters had gone to Iraq and Syria, most to fight with Da'ish.[96]

The foreign fighters are important for two reasons.[97] First, many of the foreign fighters are fellow Arabs from outside Iraq and Syria. Again, they are not "normal." One could make the case that for a young, unemployed, Sunni Iraqi or Syrian male, joining Da'ish in 2012–2015 made some sense: their communities were enmeshed in civil war, they had no reason not to fight, they could justify doing so to protect their family or community, and Da'ish was the coolest gang in town. It is a lot harder to make that case for a Saudi, Tunisian, Algerian, or Egyptian. Again, tens of thousands did, but hundreds of millions did not. And not surprisingly, those who did were not culturally regular. As a result, some made for competent military commanders, such as Abu Jandal al-Masri (Egyptian) and Abu Huzayfa al-Yamani (Yemeni). Others may not have demonstrated the same military competence, but brought tremendous zeal with them instead. Thus, the foreign fighters have been a critical element of the high morale that has been an important aspect of Da'ish's success. Moreover, for many, zeal made them prime candidates to become suicide bombers, a very important role for Da'ish, but again something utterly abnormal for Arab society. Thus, by attracting large numbers of non-culturally regular people from across the Arab world, Da'ish has benefited by having a larger pool of people with useful military skills, whether it be leadership abilities or a reckless devotion to the cause.

One of the more interesting things about Da'ish is how many non-Arab Muslims it has attracted to its cause. This started with al-Qa'ida, but its offspring, Da'ish, really took it to unprecedented levels.[98] These non-Arabs are important because they too show extraordinary commitment to the cause and because they do not evince any Arab cultural predilections. Talk about *not* being culturally regular Arabs, these people aren't Arabs at all. Perhaps not surprisingly, many of the most dangerous Da'ish fighters are from this group. The Chechens in particular stand out as superb fighters, feared across Syria and Iraq. Indeed, Da'ish's greatest battlefield commander was a man named Tarkhan Batirashvili who went by the nom de guerre Abu Umar al-Shishani, or "Father of Omar, the Chechen."[99] If Da'ish had a truly gifted tactical commander, one able to wage maneuver warfare with the skill of Chad's Hassan Djamous, it was al-Shishani. No other Da'ish commander even came close. None proved themselves able to fight and maneuver the way that he did. Moreover, not only he himself, but all of his key lieutenants were Chechens.[100] When he was finally killed in 2016, his elite command was transferred over to a unit of Uzbeks, and he was succeeded as Da'ish "War Minister" by a Tajik.[101]

Emphasizing Culturally Derived Strengths. Just as Hizballah benefited from the strong bonds of cohesion aspects of the dominant Arab culture can produce within groups, so too did Da'ish benefit from other aspects of Arab culture. The personal bravery of so many Da'ish fighters speaks for itself, for instance. However, two other features are worth noting, both of them first pointed out by Norvell DeAtkine, who spent many years as a specialist in the

Middle East for the US Army. DeAtkine has noted that Da'ish's superb psychological warfare techniques hearken back to the earliest days of the Islamic conquests. He notes that the Quran promoted the use of psychological warfare to undermine enemy morale and win bloodless victories. Of 28 battles fought by the prophet, the enemy fled in 20 of them, very much along the lines of how ISIS used social media in 2014.[102]

Likewise, DeAtkine argues that irregular warfare is more consonant with traditional Bedouin methods of waging war. Indeed, Arab irregulars do tend to function more like Bedouin tribes, with their greater emphasis on egalitarianism, consensus, and reciprocal responsibility than the dominant Arab culture, which is overwhelmingly the product of settled, *hadari* society. Among the Bedouin, "Leaders are responsible to their tribe or families for the successes of their missions and lives of their unit's members. Very often they are considered only the first among equals and are subject to removal for incompetence or wasting lives." And DeAtkine goes on to point out that "the Arab in a guerrilla unit is able to exhibit his imagination and initiative in a way never allowed in the conventional unit."[103] It is certainly true that Da'ish did have fewer problems in these areas, and that many of its Arab fighters were Syrian and Iraqi Sunnis either from Bedouin tribes, or from small towns that retained strong Bedouin traditions, allowing them to harness the strengths of this subculture in their nontraditional organizations.

Why Some Arab Insurgencies and Militias Have Fought Better than Arab State Armies

Hizballah and Da'ish were the two most potent Arab nonstate militaries and the reasons for their success were consistent with the experiences of other nonstate militaries that enjoyed (lesser) degrees of success, such as the Houthis in Yemen, al-Qa'ida itself, Jabhat Fatah ash-Sham in Syria, and the Hashd ash-Shaabi in Iraq. Their successes were borne of a combination of factors. First of all was a set of traditional military advantages: surprise, the tremendous commitment and morale of their troops, and the blessing of fighting against weaker foes.

However, even taking into account these commonplace military advantages, it is still the case that both Hizballah and Da'ish fought better than the vast majority of Arab state and nonstate armies. They may have fought as well or even better than either the Jordanians in 1948 or the Syrian commandos in 1982, and they unquestionably fought better than the Iraqi Republican Guards in 1987–1991. In particular, they performed notably better at information management, and command and control. With regard to the latter, at the strategic/operational level, Hizballah and Da'ish were more consistently proficient and insightful than their counterparts in the state armies. More interesting still, Da'ish and Hizballah tactical commanders showed greater initiative and aggressiveness, willingness to innovate, ability to react to unforeseen events, ability to maneuver and counterattack, and determination to collect intelligence on their adversary. They were not at the same level as the best Western militaries, and Da'ish was more uneven than Hizballah, but they both performed much better than the norm for modern Arab armies.

This better performance was the product of several elements, all of which worked either to avoid or eliminate the culturally driven problems that plagued the Arab state armies or to take advantage of culturally derived strengths. Part of it was the advantages of eliteness: a Darwinian selection process that determined who survived and rose to command positions based on who performed well in combat, and thus in many cases selected for those individuals least inclined to behave in culturally regular fashion. Hizballah honed this further by reducing its combat forces to just 500–1,000 men (at least against Israel), which further allowed them to select only those who had demonstrated the greatest abilities.

Both benefited greatly from a nontraditional organization, a cellular structure derived from their terrorist roots. This was in part a product of the first advantage because both organizations were founded by veteran commanders who had thrived in combat by learning to act in unorthodox (by Arab cultural standards) fashion, and who thus recognized the need for an unorthodox command structure based on their past experiences. Such a flat, atomized organization was the polar opposite of a traditional Arab hierarchy. It meant that both Hizballah and Da'ish selected individuals for leadership positions who demonstrated that they could function in such an atypical hierarchy, and so had the capacity to think well beyond their cultural frameworks or routinely behaved in a culturally non-regular manner. Both took people who were not culturally "normal" Arabs and placed them in organizations that did not function in a "culturally normal" Arab way. Not surprisingly, they did not behave or perform like culturally normal Arab militaries.

Both were also able to capitalize on culturally derived military strengths. For Hizballah, recruiting from families, clans, and preexisting groups of friends enabled it to capitalize on the strong bonds of loyalty and cohesion typically found in Arab in-groups. For Da'ish, this came from their reliance on psychological warfare and irregular warfare, both of which appear more consonant with the traditions of the Bedouin subculture of the Arab world. I will also add that Eisenstadt and Bianchi note that Da'ish also tries to recruit family members and groups of friends for the same reasons, albeit without the same emphasis or success as Hizballah.[104]

Finally, Da'ish could also count on large numbers of foreign fighters, many of them from Europe, Central Asia, South Asia, and the West. Even if they were Muslims, they had been raised in non-Arab societies and so did not bring with them Arab cultural predilections. Not surprisingly, the foreign fighters made a critical contribution to the Da'ish war effort, and many of their best fighters and commanders were non-Arabs.

Like the exceptional Arab state militaries, the best nonstate militaries achieved greater military effectiveness by finding ways to mitigate or eliminate the problematic influences of Arab cultural predilections from their personnel and emphasize those aspects of culturally driven behavior that lent advantages in battle. None of these approaches were completely successful, and while the tactical leadership of both Hizballah and Da'ish were much better than the norm in modern Arab armies, they were still too uneven and too limited to rank with the best Western armies. Yet these were arguably the two most able and successful Arab armed forces of the modern era, and other insurgencies, militias, and terrorist groups were more or less successful to the extent to which they replicated Hizballah's and Da'ish's methods of diminishing the cultural predilections that have so consistently hindered Arab military operations since 1945.

The Past, Present, and Future
of Arab Military Effectiveness

S INCE THE SECOND WORLD WAR, the armed forces of the Arab states
have struggled in battle. Moreover, the manner in which they have
struggled has proven remarkably consistent over time and across the region.
Only a handful of notable but modest exceptions stand out from this tableau
of misfortune. These are interesting mostly for how they reinforce the rule, a
pattern that has been the product of several deep, intermingled sources.

The most readily apparent of these is the malignant politics that have
prevailed across the Arab states since gaining their independence from the colonial powers after World War II. The politicization of Arab militaries, in all of
its variants, praetorian, commissarist, and palace guard, has certainly played its
part. When politicization has been at its worst, it has unquestionably hobbled
Arab war-making, principally by saddling Arab armed forces with incompetent
senior leaders and by undermining the morale and cohesion of their forces. At
times, these problems have badly hamstrung Arab militaries.

Nevertheless, the role of poor civil-military relations needs to be kept in
perspective: the impact of politicization varied considerably over time and, in
several important instances, Arab governments thoroughly depoliticized their
armed forces. On those occasions, their militaries fared better, but only relative to their usual disasters. Even the best Arab military performances accomplished little and fell far short of the standards of the best non-Arab armies.
That pattern speaks to the fact that politicization *was* a factor hindering Arab
military operations, but it was neither the only one nor the most important.

The underdeveloped state of Arab economies also played a role. Industrialization was late coming to the Muslim Middle East and it never reached anything like what it would achieve in the West or, later, in East Asia. That meant that relatively few Arab personnel had the kind of basic understanding of machinery necessary to enable them to take full advantage of the equipment used to wage war in this era. Arab armies, navies, and air forces could not get their weaponry to perform to its full potential. Moreover, they often brought only a fraction of it to the battlefield because they had failed to give it the care it required. Difficulties understanding the requirements of various weapons systems may also have hampered their combined arms operations, although the evidence is not as clear or strong in this area. These gaps hampered Arab operations in every war, even against adversaries less developed than themselves. Against more modern foes that suffered none of these problems, these failings could have been decisive on their own.

Ultimately, however, the greatest problems that Arab armed forces suffered during the modern era (and continue to suffer to the present day) have been driven by patterns of behavior derived from the dominant Arab culture. Just as Spartan, Macedonian, Roman, and Mongol culture produced large numbers of men with the requisite skills best suited to war-making in their times, so Arab culture did the opposite in the modern era, producing too few men with the skills needed to succeed in industrial-age warfare. That is not a condemnation of Arab society or its culture, which emerged from the specific geographic and historical situation of the Arab world at the time and worked for those circumstances. But the behavioral patterns it emphasized were simply not those best suited to success on the modern battlefield.

As a result, Arab armed forces consistently underperformed, and underperformed in the same ways time and again, regardless of who they fought or where, the state of their politics, or the relative state of economic development between them and their foe. Arab militaries were consistently crippled by passive and unimaginative tactical leadership, an inability to conduct effective air operations, and badly distorted flows of information across their chains of command but especially at tactical levels. Arab cultural preferences also hindered their combined arms operations, weapons handling, and maintenance.

All of this reflects the emphases of their dominant culture. No matter how hard Arab militaries tried to overcome these culturally derived problems, the most they could do was to mask them for some time in certain situations. Consequently, even when the Arabs did everything within their power to create the perfect circumstances for military victory—like the Egyptians in 1973 and Iraqis in 1988, who had overwhelming numerical, firepower, surprise, and technological advantages that could easily have proven decisive by themselves, as well as a set of workarounds to limit the culturally driven limitations—they still ensured that Arab successes were modest and short-lived.

If the patterns of behavior derived from the dominant Arab culture were the most important shortcomings of Arab armies, they were only first among equals. Many of the relatively better performances of Arab armed forces were accompanied by reduced politicization. And in the case of the Egyptians in 1973 and Iraqi in 1988, politicization was a prerequisite for them to develop the workarounds to the culturally driven limitations of their tactical forces that made their limited successes possible. Likewise, terrible though they may have been, the Libyans were still able to handle their weapons well enough to defeat Chadian forces (with a lot of GUNT assistance) until the transformation of the Chadian military in 1986.

Thus, the impact of politicization and underdevelopment should not be dismissed or underrated either. That is not the point of this book. Ultimately, the Arab armies suffered some of their worst defeats—in the Six-Day War of 1967 and in Iran in 1980–1982, for instance—when all three sets of problems afflicted their armed forces. In these instances, the culturally derived problems were still the most important, but severe politicization and the problems associated with underdevelopment also played critical roles. Each might have resulted in defeat by itself. Together they produced catastrophic failure.

I have seen this firsthand on many occasions. For instance, in the fall of 2015, I was part of a small group of experts who went to Iraq to provide some advice to the US and Iraqi militaries in the war against Da'ish. At the time, the battle for Ramadi was burning hot, but not particularly fast. There were problems all across the Iraqi Security Forces—the same kinds of problems that have come up throughout this book. The US military had succeeded in removing many of the worst of Maliki's political hacks from the chain of command, but enough still remained to gum up the works. One of those, an Iraqi general in charge of an important city, was notorious for seizing control of any military units moving through his city and then refusing to release them to continue to their intended destination, instead integrating them into his own defenses. Since his city was a key transit point for units moving from southern and eastern Iraq to Ramadi, the number of Iraqi troops at Ramadi was significantly less than what it should have been. That was an important impact of politicization.

Nevertheless, the Iraqis still outnumbered Da'ish by at least 10 to 1 at Ramadi, and possibly as much as 20 to 1. They also had overwhelming firepower and Coalition air support. All of that should have been more than enough to take the city, and it infuriated US military personnel at all levels.

Moreover, the Iraqis had several dozen M1 tanks at Ramadi, which Da'ish essentially had nothing to stop. When we started talking to American and other Coalition personnel about why the Iraqis were not making better use of the M1s, we heard a litany of horror stories about Iraqis mishandling their tanks—driving them into pits and wadis, not understanding what the tank could do, failing to maintain them properly despite large numbers of foreign contractors handling most of the repair and higher-level maintenance work. That was an important impact of underdevelopment.

Yet in the end, what the American and other Coalition military officers found most frustrating was the complete lack of initiative or creativity on the part of Iraqi junior officers, who had absolutely no understanding of maneuver, would not react to Da'ish moves, could not employ the M1s in conjunction with infantry and artillery support, and just would not attack despite their enormous advantages in numbers and firepower. This despite the fact that their own officers and the Coalition advisers were all urging them to be more aggressive and opportunistic. The only way that the Coalition could get the Iraqis to mount attacks at brigade, battalion, company, or platoon level was to have them ordered to do so by the very highest levels in Baghdad *and* have US air power obliterate every living thing in front of them. Only then would they launch a slow, creeping, frontal assault on a Da'ish position. They would then halt and go to ground the moment they had taken the objective. It drove the Americans working with them to distraction. It was no surprise to our team that the battle of Ramadi dragged on for over a year in spite of the ridiculous imbalances in manpower and weaponry in favor of the Iraqi military.

Intertwined Sources

It is also important to bear in mind that the divisions between politics, economics, and culture are not nearly so well defined as I have treated them throughout this book. Instead, the three interact constantly, each shaping the other, especially over the long term. As I noted earlier, there is a widespread conviction among cultural anthropologists, sociologists, and cultural psychologists specializing in the Arab world that the behavioral patterns of the dominant Arab culture incline Arab societies toward authoritarian government, over-centralization, compartmentalization, and the hoarding of information. As far as they are concerned, the political problems of the Arab world—and the politicization of their militaries it produces—are largely the product of these cultural proclivities.[1]

Of course, the interaction of culture and politics (and economics) is always circular and self-reinforcing. Thus, many scholars of the Middle East argue that Ottoman and European imperialism pushed Arab culture toward passive, submissive behavior, which in turn made autocracy an easier fit, and may well have predisposed Arabs to authoritarianism, which then enabled and encouraged the establishment of the post-independence autocracies, which then reinforced those cultural proclivities.[2] Thus, over time, politics helps shape culture, just as culture shapes politics.

As another example of the intertwining, one of the mistakes that those who focus on civil-military relations often make when trying to understand the military effectiveness of Arab armies is that they note the practice of Arab leaders in placing members of their family, clan, tribe, and sect in key positions throughout the military and assume that their doing so is always about loyalty and control, and therefore that those chosen are likely to be less competent. That isn't untrue, but it is exaggerated, badly so in many cases.

It misses the point that such behavior is the typical, traditional Arab method of patronage. When a man (or less often, woman) comes to power of any kind in the Arab world, it is expected that he will bring his relatives, clansmen, tribesmen, and coreligionists/co-ethnicists in with him and give them plum positions within the hierarchy he controls.[3] It happens across the Arab world in every organization imaginable, from businesses to civil society groups. While it is certainly true that this has a dimension of loyalty and therefore is desirable for an insecure autocrat, there is a tremendously strong element of cultural obligation on the part of the leader to his family and other affiliations. Indeed, in many cases it would be dangerous for a leader of any kind *not* to give such posts to members of those groups, because those groups see them as rightfully theirs, and they would object *strenuously* if they did not get them.[4]

Which of these is more important to those holding high governmental office: the utilitarian political incentive or the cultural obligation? It is impossible to know. Both are likely at work. Moreover, throughout history, including modern Arab military history, there have been plenty of military commanders appointed because they had preexisting ties to the leader and then proved to be highly competent. Rakan al-Jazi, Hassan at-Turkmani, Tawfiq al-Jahani, 'Ali Aslan, and Husayn ar-Rashid at-Tikriti all spring immediately to mind as senior Arab officers chosen in part because of an affiliation with the leader, but who proved to be excellent commanders in battle.

Culture and economic development are not distinct topics either. Cultural values and behavioral patterns play a considerable role in shaping a country's economic development. Likewise, a society's economic system is a critical influence on its culture over time. In many ways, this has been the central revelation and battle cry of the Arab Human Development Reports published from 2002 to 2016, in which the authors have called on their people to break out of the cultural shackles that have kept them from real economic development and prosperity.

Like politics and culture (and politics and economics), economics and culture have a powerful impact on each other, and it is sometimes hard to disentangle the two. Indeed, even where it is possible to ascribe a particular pattern of activity to one over the other, it may be that the other is still exerting an indirect influence. Therefore, it is important to keep in mind that during the period since 1945, at the broadest levels, Arab culture shaped the course of Arab economic development, just as changes in the Arab economy exerted an influence on Arab cultural patterns.[5] In researching this book, I came across one study of economics and culture that argued that aircraft cockpit layout should be culturally adapted because people from different cultures intrinsically approached different pieces of equipment and gauges differently, and a pilot from one society in a plane built by another "leads to degradation in the performance of the aircraft as well as that of the pilot."[6] I only raise this example as a way of pointing out that people are finding relationships between culture and economics in all kinds of places they never expected.

For analytic purposes, I have been forced to separate politics, culture, and economic development more discreetly than they deserve. While this separation is unfortunate, I do not believe it has been excessively harmful, and I have made every effort to address problems created by this artificial distinction. Culture, politics, and economic development interact heavily, but they are not the same thing. They operate in separate realms and their effects on human behavior can be distinguished. It is possible to say that a particular set of incentives on a people's behavior derive more from the specifics of an economic system than their culture, or vice versa. Since politics, culture, and economic development are ultimately different phenomena, it is reasonable to argue that one had a greater impact on Arab military effectiveness than the other, at least in the immediate sense and in the short term, as I have done throughout. However, it is also important to remember that they are not so discreet as I have painted them to illustrate my points. That is particularly so over time, as all three interact with one another, changing one another in important but ineffable ways.[7]

Additional Observations

Before moving on to consider what the findings of this book have to say about the future of the Middle East, I want to stop to note a few more points that emerge from this long inquiry into the sources of Arab military ineffectiveness.

The first is a point about generalship. That is that one element of great generalship consists of knowing the abilities of your own forces (and those of the enemy) and conducting operations in ways that play to the strengths and capabilities of your own forces and do not demand that they accomplish things that are beyond them. This insight is at least as old as Sun Tzu, but it is too often forgotten in discussions of military leadership. These often revolve around questions of strategy, logistics, and weaponry, all of which are undoubtedly important. But as important as whether a particular strategy was the best one—or was logistically possible—is the question of whether the forces under a general's command were capable of executing it. Or if it played to their strengths and away from those of their enemy. Most of the operations devised by the most successful Arab generals weren't necessarily brilliant feats of strategy. Some were logistically impressive, but that too was only tangentially related to their success. These operations succeeded largely because the generals in question understood the forces under their command, their (limited) strengths and (significant) weaknesses, and they carefully crafted plans that their forces could handle, and eschewed strategies that might in theory have brought great rewards, but in practice were far beyond the abilities of their troops. It is all well and good to argue that Iraq *should have* employed a mobile defense against the US-led coalition in 1991, but it's also absurd because Iraqi forces could not have executed one. Saddam's generals understood this and did the best they could, and in so doing, they salvaged a small but important victory from the wreckage of DESERT STORM.

The second is a general point about alliances. Any number of wartime leaders from Churchill on down have remarked on the difficulty of fighting as part of an alliance. This book illustrates one often overlooked aspect of that difficulty: understanding your allies' abilities. It is hard enough for a military or political leader to understand the strengths and weaknesses of his or her own military, and history is replete with examples who failed even in that. It is harder still to understand the capabilities of an allied power, and that misunderstanding can create friction when one alliance partner expects its ally to act and perform in one way and it turns out that the ally won't or can't.[8] America's own experiences in the Middle East run up against this problem time and again, from our frustration with the Egyptians during the Persian Gulf War to our frustrations with the Iraqi security forces during the war against Da'ish. The United States has repeatedly expected its Arab allies to fight in one way and at a certain degree of effectiveness, only to have them fall short. It is incredibly difficult to "punch with someone else's fists," and that is an inherent tension in alliances.

This brings me to the last point I want to raise, the question of American security assistance to the Arab world and what this book has to say about that vast topic. As I noted at the outset, for many Americans the question of Arab military effectiveness is of more than academic curiosity because the United States has been trying to build more competent Arab armed forces for over 40 years. Our failure to do so has meant that we have had to fight wars for them or invest excessive resources to try to help them do the job themselves.

I hope that many of this book's lessons on that topic are already apparent. In particular, it has been possible to improve the combat performance of Arab militaries, but it has also been very difficult. It requires considerable effort to better structure the forces themselves and the operations they will undertake, and has proven exceptionally hard to help them acquire more than modest capabilities, even with enormous exertions.

It has certainly been possible to build Arab military forces with relatively better military effectiveness, but doing so requires keeping the forces small compared to the overall population to gain the benefits of eliteness and ensure an unusually high proportion of soldiers and officers with the right, non-culturally regular skills. This is effectively the approach that the United States took in Iraq after 2014, investing heavily in the small, elite Counterterrorism Service, which then spearheaded every major Iraqi fight against Da'ish.

An alternative approach that the United States might employ in other circumstances would be to encourage Arab militaries to focus on doing what they do well—heavily scripted and rehearsed set-piece offensives or static defensive operations—and leave the rest to more capable Western forces. Certainly the United States did some of that in the war against Da'ish too, relying on Coalition air power and special forces to do as much of the scouting and killing as possible to minimize the demands on the ISF. A better example, however, would be the way that the United States tried to structure Arab operations as part of Operation DESERT STORM, although in that instance even the unchallenging missions assigned to Egyptian forces proved too much for them.

Where and when it is possible, there are other ways to skin this cat. To the extent that the United States can influence officer promotions and command assignments, as we did in Iraq in 2006–2010 and 2014–2017, that can help to diminish the impact of politicization and empower commanders with much-needed but culturally non-regular skills. At an even deeper and harder level, the more that the United States can do to affect the education of future Arab soldiers and officers from the earliest ages, the more likely that there will be larger numbers of those with the right skills available.

Unfortunately, as four decades of trying has demonstrated, just bringing Arab officers to Western military training programs does not seem to have enough impact. To a great extent it is already too late by then. Arab officers sent to Western training courses often view the methods they are taught in those programs to be relevant for Western militaries, but not for their own. Even if they perform them well, rather than try to change their military cultures to reflect Western practices when they go home, they more often just revert back to the accustomed practices of their home military.[9]

Overall, foreign military assistance unquestionably helped Arab militaries since the Second World War, but never as much or in the ways expected. The Soviets/Russians have been just as frustrated as their Western counterparts trying to improve the effectiveness of their Arab allies. Yet, on balance, they were pretty helpful. Probably more so than the Western powers. In part that derived from their willingness to provide more advanced weapons at key moments in time, as well as the maintenance personnel to maintain that equipment. However, another part does seem to derive from their providing the Arabs a simple but functional military doctrine that some of the Arab armed forces could adapt to their own proclivities. While the Russians may have gnashed their teeth at the rigidity the Egyptians, Syrians, and Libyans injected into their methods, it worked better than the Western approaches they had previously employed and that their personnel clearly could not relate to whatsoever. In contrast, I have been struck over the years by the endless frustration of American advisors and trainers who repeatedly try to force Iraqi, Egyptian, Jordanian, and Saudi tactical units to debrief objectively after a training exercise like an American unit would, only to find it impossible because no one will criticize anyone else (especially not the commander, even indirectly) for fear of shaming them.

A lesson that Americans might take from this is that rather than try to force Arab military personnel to do it our way, we should look for ways to simply help them do what they do somewhat better. That seems to be what they got from the Soviet system. They won't get to our levels of effectiveness that way, but then again, trying to force them to think and act like Americans has not succeeded so far either, and probably never will.

The Evolution of the Arab World

All this said, you should not take from this book that the Arabs are doomed to military weakness for all eternity. If anything, I would hope that you take the exact opposite lesson from it. I hope that this book demonstrated that the problems Arab armed forces have experienced in combat with industrial-age and early information-age warfare were a product of a combination of political, economic, and especially cultural factors present in their society during a particular period of time. Those same influences could well usher in a very different future.

The Arab world is changing. Dramatically so. The unrest and revolts of 2011, often referred to as the "Arab Spring," were the most obvious punctuation mark in a process that has been ongoing since the late 1990s. These changes will undoubtedly transform Arab politics, economics, and culture. They are already beginning to do so.[10]

After gaining independence following World War II, all of the Arab states installed similar systems. Economies driven by oil revenues, either directly pumped by the countries themselves, or indirectly accrued via trade, aid, and worker remittances from the oil-producing states. Autocratic political systems (dictatorships or monarchies) that treated the citizenry as unwanted dependents. Traditional sociocultural systems that were allowed to persist largely untouched by the changing world around them. This tripartite arrangement never worked particularly well, but it clunked along for several decades until the triple blows of a demographic explosion, the information revolution, and the collapse of oil prices undermined it altogether.

The result has been unprecedented change across the Middle East. The economic impact came first. Most of the Arab states are financially unstable. More than that, their citizenry is infuriated by the lack of decent jobs—jobs that they believe their educational achievement merits, but because the quality of their education is so lacking, jobs they cannot obtain. Meanwhile, the influx of personal telecommunications and social media has not only made Arab populations realize how far they have fallen behind the rest of the globalizing world, it has enabled them to talk to one another without government controls and exposed them to new cultural, political, and economic systems that some desperately desire and others just as desperately fear. For many Arabs, globalization has left them feeling that their culture is hopelessly backward, and for others that it is under assault by alien values.

Inevitably, these changes and pressures have hammered away at the outmoded Arab autocracies and their sclerotic bureaucracies. The first major revolts came in Bahrain in 2006–2008, spurred by the democratic experiment in Iraq, and in Iran in 2009 with the Green Revolt against Mahmud Ahmedinejad's suspect re-election. Neither succeeded, but they were followed in 2011 by revolutions in Tunisia, Egypt, Yemen, Syria, and Libya, and unprecedented unrest in Oman, Jordan, Morocco, Iraq, and Bahrain again. All of this produced failed states and civil war in Syria, Yemen, and Libya (and Iraq too, albeit from other causes). It eventually convinced the governments of Morocco, Egypt, Saudi Arabia, Qatar, and the UAE to propose far-reaching political and economic reform programs, although little has been done in Morocco and Egypt yet, and it is unclear how far the others will go.

Nevertheless, all of this marks out the Middle East as a region confronting profound political change, and that change is already affecting its culture. The great Daniel Patrick Moynihan once remarked that "The central conservative truth is that it is culture, not politics, that determines the success of a society. The central liberal truth is that politics can change a culture and save it from itself." As Moynihan understood, politics can reshape culture over time. The Arab Spring is testimony to the political change building in the Arab world, a product of globalization, and *that* is affecting its culture.

Indeed, globalization has had a profound impact on the Arab world already. It made the Arab Spring possible, and it is now reshaping Arab culture. Thus economic change bred political change that is now evolving into cultural change. There is a growing willingness of people to speak their minds. The younger generation is less willing to blindly follow authority figures. More are willing to take action to change their circumstances (a trait that Hizballah, Da'ish, and other new model Arab armies have doubtlessly benefited from). Experts on the Arab world note that childrearing practices are changing in response.[11] "The available data consistently show . . . fewer parents viewing obedience as their primary goal, and more saying they encourage independence and use praise and reasoning to shape their children's behavior," according to Gregg.[12] Other anthropologists have found that better-educated parents are becoming more concerned with the success of their children in school rather than just instilling loyalty to the extended family.[13]

In other words, the politics, economics, and even the culture of the Arab world is changing, and changing in some remarkable ways. Thus, the fact that these three features of the Arab states conspired to cripple Arab armed forces in the past should not be taken as a sign that they will continue to do so in the future. At some point, they may no longer produce the same patterns of behavior that were so deleterious to Arab military effectiveness in the prior era. It will likely take several decades, but if the trend lines for change in the Arab world bear out, someday they may even benefit Arab armies in combat.

The Evolution of Warfare

Nevertheless, predicting the future of Arab military power is complicated by another unknown variable: changes in the dominant mode of warfare. Just as the onset of the information age is having a heavy impact on the economies, politics, and culture of Arab society, so too is it having an equally profound impact on warfare. These changes have been long in the making, some with antecedents reaching back deep into the twentieth century. But they are finally maturing in ways that augur for equally profound changes in war-making in the future.

For instance, the advent of new technologies resulting in "smart" and "brilliant" sensors, communications, battle management systems, and munitions is driving an equally dramatic transformation of the military sphere. We are fast approaching the point where the capabilities of the munitions may be far more important than (because they far exceed) the capabilities of the platforms that launch them. As recently as the turn of the millennium, having a highly capable fighter aircraft such as an F-15 or Su-27 was critical in air-to-air combat. More and more, what matters is the capabilities of the missiles the fighter carries—their range, maneuverability, sensors, and ability to defeat enemy countermeasures.

Toward the end of the Cold War, Soviet military thinkers theorized about a future "reconnaissance-strike complex." By this they meant a small, highly mobile force with the most advanced sensors and communications gear, which could move quickly around the battlefield, identify enemy forces, and then call in massive firepower from long-range, stand-off, precision-guided systems. The United States already has something close to this capability. American drones employ an array of sophisticated sensors that can transmit information long distances to stand-off attack platforms that can launch high-precision strikes on whatever the drones identify.

At present, there are still lots of humans in the loop, but there don't have to be. The US Navy's AEGIS air defense system is an example of another networked system that takes it to that next level. AEGIS links together all of the sensors in a Navy battle group. The information they collect is then fed into a computerized battle management program that identifies threats, prioritizes them, and assigns them to various weapons in the battle group—on planes, ships, subs, or drones—for interception. Because of the speed at which modern attacks can come in, AEGIS can go on full auto, removing humans completely from the decision-making and leaving it entirely to the computers to make nanosecond decisions to launch any (and potentially every) weapon in the battle group.

There are many other emerging trends in warfare, but I have chosen to high-light these because they could work to the advantage of the Arab militaries, at least in their post–World War II configurations. In a world where technology and munitions do most of the reconnaissance and threat analysis, make most of the tactical decisions, and even do most of the maneuvering against the foe, the Arab armies might suddenly do very well. Such a battlefield would obviate the need for effective information gathering and sharing among personnel, skillful tactical commanders, maneuverable combined arms formations, and personnel willing and able to seize fleeting opportunities. In such a world, computers would do all of that instead. It might only require a handful of ex-ceptional personnel at the top to devise an overarching strategy, and the Arabs have demonstrated that they can handle that.

Even the need for personnel to man, maintain, and repair the weapons is diminishing. With modern ergonomics, the weapons increasingly adapt them-selves to the people manning them, rather than the people having to adapt their behavior to what works best for the weapon, as was the case during the industrial era. Similarly, most repair of high-tech systems now consists of removing a modular component and replacing it with another. Even mainte-nance is getting easier in a world of smart phones and disposable high tech-nology. Moreover, whether the changes in the Arab economies will get them to the point where they can manufacture such systems may prove irrelevant if they can buy them off the shelf from China, India, or other countries, and maintain them simply by buying new ones or periodically replacing subcomponents.

Since the Second World War, Arab armed forces have fared exceptionally poorly in combat. That has primarily been because the dominant mode of war-fare as it has been practiced during this era required skills that Arab society did not produce in abundance. In fact, the economies, politics, and (especially) culture of the Arab world conspired to produce far too few personnel with the requisite abilities for success on the modern battlefield. Industrial-age warfare was well beyond the capacity of contemporaneous Arab society to master. But this history may not prove to be destiny. Arab politics, economics, and culture are all changing dramatically. So too is warfare. And all are changing in ways that it is impossible to foresee.

The future of Arab military power will be determined by how well its new political, economic, and cultural systems mesh with the new, domi-nant mode of warfare. As the information age transforms Arab society and warfare alike, it may reshape Arab military power—and everyone else's too. Whether the relationship between information-age Arab society and information-age warfare is a good fit or a bad one is impossible to know. The Arabs could find themselves just as hapless as they were during the industrial age, they could emerge as the Prussia of the twenty-first century, or they might just find themselves somewhere in-between. All that we can say for sure is that while the match between their society and warfare was a disastrous misfit during the industrial age, the information age might be something else entirely. If it is, one thing we can say for certain is that it will transform the security and international relations of the entire Middle East.

NOTES

Introduction

1. On popular Israeli fears that a war with the Arabs would be disastrous or even apocalyptic, see Ahron Bregman, *Israel's Wars: A History since 1947*, 2010 Edition (London: Routledge, 2010), p. 78; Guy Laron, *The Six-Day War: The Breaking of the Middle East* (New Haven, CT: Yale University Press, 2017), pp. 156–159, 208, 263, 266–267; Michael B. Oren, *Six Days of War: June 1967 and the Making of the Modern Middle East* (Oxford: Oxford University Press, 2002), esp. pp. 18, 80, 88–91, 97, 123–124, 133–136. On Arab expectations that Israel would be destroyed, see Dani Asher, *The Egyptian Strategy for the Yom Kippur War*, trans. Moshe Tlamim (Jefferson, NC: McFarland, 2009), p. 14; Oren, *Six Days of War*, pp. 69, 83, 92, 95, 97, 99, 163. On the perception of others that Israel was likely to lose and might be destroyed, see Laron, *The Six-Day War*, p. 209; Oren, *Six Days of War*, pp. 118–119, 136.
2. Ronen Bergman, *Rise and Kill First: The Secret History of Israel's Targeted Assassinations* (New York: Random House, 2018), p. 113; Laron, *The Six-Day War*, pp. 159, 266; Oren, *Six Days of War*, pp. 136, 168–169.
3. Laron, *The Six-Day War*, p. 263.
4. Kenneth M. Pollack, *Arabs at War: Military Effectiveness, 1948–1991* (Lincoln: University of Nebraska Press, 2002), pp. 58–59, 293–294, 460–461. The IDF had a total mobilizable strength of 264,000 while the Egyptians, Syrians, Jordanians, and Iraqis had a total strength of nearly 550,000. I have chosen to focus on the numbers deployed as being most relevant since that reflects the numbers of troops that actually engaged in combat.
5. Oren, *Six Days of War*, pp. 79–80, 134. On the concurring US view, see ibid., p. 110.

6. The following section is based on Pollack, *Arabs at War*, esp. pp. 62–64; and Kenneth M. Pollack, "Air Power in the Six-Day War," *The Journal of Strategic Studies*, Vol. 28, No. 3 (June 2005), pp. 471–503.

7. Bregman, *Israel's Wars*, pp. 84–85; Oren, *Six Days of War*, p. 176; Pollack, *Arabs at War*, p. 63.

8. Oren, *Six Days of War*, pp. 176–178; Pollack, *Arabs at War*, pp. 63–65.

9. Colonel Eliezer Cohen, *Israel's Best Defense*, trans. Jonathan Cordis (New York: Orion Books, 1993), p. 220.

10. A myth persists that "most" or the "best parts" of the Egyptian Army were in Yemen at the time of the Six-Day War. By May 1967, no more than five to eight Egyptian combat brigades were left in Yemen—and some of these were withdrawn and redeployed to Sinai during the crisis that preceded the war. Thus, at least 29 of the 45 maneuver brigades of the Egyptian Army and all of its divisional commands were deployed to Sinai by June 5, 1967. Moreover, these included many of the finest formations in the Army: the elite 4th Armored Division, and the 3rd Infantry and 6th Mechanized Divisions, considered Cairo's next best. There were a number of commando brigades and battalions in Yemen—as appropriate for a counterinsurgency war—and these were considered good units by the Egyptians. However, lacking heavy weapons, these units were not likely to make much of a difference to the outcome in Sinai and, in fact, the Egyptian commando formations deployed there did not distinguish themselves during the war. For the Egyptian order of battle, see Defense Intelligence Agency, "Order of Battle Summary, Foreign Ground Forces, United Arab Republic (Egypt)," AP-220-1-4-67-INT, 1 January 1967, Declassified.

11. See for instance, Yousef H. Aboul-Enein, ed., *Reconstructing a Shattered Egyptian Army: War Minister Gen. Mohamed Fawzi's Memoirs, 1967–1971* (Annapolis, MD: US Naval Institute Press, 2014), pp. 49–50.

12. Author's interview with Lt. General Mordechai Hod, IAF (Ret.), Tel Aviv, September 1996; History Branch, Israeli Air Force, correspondence with the author, September 10, 1997. Hod was the commander of the IAF in 1967.

13. Author's interview with General Avraham "Bren" Adan, Tel Aviv, September 1996; R. Churchill and W. Churchill, *The Six-Day War*, p. 112; Col. Trevor N. Dupuy, *Elusive Victory*, Third ed., Paperback Ed. (Dubuque, IA: Kendall Hunt, 1992), pp. 263–264; Eric Hammel, *Six Days in June* (New York: Scribner's, 1992), pp. 223–226; Ministry of Defense, *The Six-Day War* (Tel Aviv: Israel Press, 1967), pp. 67–68; Edgar O'Ballance, *The Third Arab-Israeli War* (Hamden, CT: Archon Books, 1972), pp. 135–136; Nadav Safran, *From War to War* (New York: Pegasus, 1969), pp. 342, 346; Emanuel Wald, *The Wald Report: The Decline of Israeli National Security since 1967* (Boulder, CO: Westview, 1992), p. 84.

14. History Branch, Israeli Air Force, correspondence with the author, September 10, 1997.

15. Ibid.

16. Exactly why Damascus issued this false report remains a mystery. Most speculation focuses on the possibility that the Syrians were trying to secure a ceasefire, perhaps by misleading either the superpowers or the Israelis into believing the IDF had conquered the Golan.

17. Israeli casualties and Arab prisoners from "The Six-Day War," Israel Ministry of Foreign Affairs, available at http://mfa.gov.il/MFA/AboutIsrael/History/Pages/The%20Six-Day%20War%20-%20June%201967.aspx, accessed on May 10, 2018. Arab casualties from Pollack, *Arabs at War,* pp. 74, 315, 468.

18. On the impact of Soviet-style military systems see Brigadier Syed A. El Edroos, *The Hashemite Arab Army, 1908–1979* (Amman: The Publishing Committee, 1980); Jon D. Glassman, *Arms for the Arabs* (Baltimore, MD: Johns Hopkins University Press, 1975); Aharon Levran and Zeev Eytan, *The Middle East Military Balance, 1987–1988*, The Jaffee Center for Strategic Studies (Boulder: Westview, 1988); R. D. McLaurin, "Military Operations in the Gulf War: The Battle of Khorramshahr" (Aberdeen Proving Grounds, MD: US Army Human Engineering Laboratory, July 1982); Roger Owen, "The Role of the Army in Middle Eastern Politics: A Critique of Existing Analyses," *Review of Middle East Studies*, No. 3 (1978), pp. 64–71; and Abraham Wagner and Anthony Cordesman, *The Lessons of Modern War, Volume II: The Iran-Iraq War* (New York: Westview, 1990).

19. On excessive politicization of Arab militaries see Eliezer Be'eri, *Army Officers in Arab Politics and Society* (New York: Praeger, 1970); Anthony Cordesman, *The Arab-Israeli Military Balance and the Art of Operations* (Lanham, MD: University Free Press, 1987); the essay on Syria in Richard Gabriel ed., *Fighting Armies: Antagonists in the Middle East* (Westport, CT: Greenwood Press, 1983); Mark Heller, *State- and Regime-Maintenance and Military Incompetence in Iraq*, Paper prepared for the conference "Iraq under the Ba'th," University of Haifa, May 26–29, 1991; David C. Rapoport, "The Praetorian Army: Insecurity, Venality, and Impotence," in *Soldiers, Peasants and Bureaucrats: Civil-Military Relations in Communist and Modernizing Societies,* ed. Roman Kolkowicz and Andrej Korbonski (London: George Allen and Unwin, 1982); James T. Quinlivan, "Coup-Proofing: Its Practice and Consequences in the Middle East," *International Security*, Vol. 24, No. 2 (Fall 1999), pp. 131–165; Caitlin Talmadge, *The Dictator's Army: Battlefield Effectiveness in Authoritarian Regimes* (Ithaca, NY: Cornell University Press, 2015).

20. On arguments that Arab military problems are the result of low levels of economic development, see Anthony Cordesman, *Jordanian Arms and the Middle East Military Balance* (Washington, DC: Middle East Institute, 1983); Efraim Karsh, *The Iran-Iraq War: A Military Analysis*, Adelphi Paper 220 (London: IISS, 1987); and Owen, "The Role of the Army in Middle Eastern Politics," pp. 64–71.

21. On Arab recognition of cultural problems hindering their combat operations, see Fouad Ajami, *The Arab Predicament* (Cambridge: Cambridge University Press, 1981), pp. 25–30; Asher, *The Egyptian Strategy for the Yom Kippur War*, pp. 13, 18; Raymond W. Baker, *Sadat and After: Struggles for Egypt's Political Soul* (Cambridge, MA: Harvard University Press, 1990), p. 188; Cordesman, *Jordanian Arms*, p. 128; Col. Dupuy, *Elusive Victory*, pp. 346–348; Fuad I. Khuri, "The Study of Civil-Military Relations in Modernizing Societies in the Middle East: A Critical Assessment," in *Soldiers, Peasants and Bureaucrats*, ed. Kolkowicz and Korbonski, p. 13; Constantine Zurayk, "Cultural Change and Transformation of Arab Society," in *The Arab Future: Critical Issues*, ed. Michael C. Hudson (Washington, DC: Center for Contemporary Arab Studies, Georgetown University, 1979), p. 11. For Israeli comments to the same effect, see the comments by Generals Dayan and Adan quoted in G.P. Armstrong, "Egypt," in *Fighting Armies: Antagonists in the Middle East*, ed. Richard Gabriel (Westport, CT: Greenwood Press, 1983).

22. This book is primarily concerned with Arab military effectiveness. Military effectiveness refers to how well an army, navy, or air force performs military operations. How well they employ the weapons and other technology available to them. How well they fight. That is not the same thing as winning and losing wars. Military effectiveness is always a factor in who wins and who loses, but it is only one factor, and not always the most important. Material differences such as numbers or the quality of weapons, intangibles such as surprise and luck, intelligence breakthroughs, the contribution of allies, and a hundred other factors also interact with military effectiveness in complex ways to determine victory and defeat.

23. Actually, that's not entirely true. I did just that in my doctoral thesis. This book is a revised and updated version of that work. See Kenneth M. Pollack, "The Influence of Arab Culture on Arab Military Effectiveness, 1948–1991," PhD thesis, The Massachusetts Institute of Technology, Cambridge, MA, 1996.

Chapter 1

1. This chapter draws heavily on the conclusions of my 2002 book, *Arabs at War: Military Effectiveness, 1948–1991* (Pollack, *Arabs at War*) in which I provided a detailed combat history of the Egyptian, Iraqi, Jordanian, Libyan, Saudi, and Syrian armed forces from the Israeli War of Independence through the Persian Gulf War. For those looking for the historical evidence for the conclusions provided in this chapter, that is a good place to start. The numerous cases of post-1991 Arab militaries in conflict presented in this book are also part of the evidence for these findings.

2. David A. Korn, *Stalemate: The War of Attrition and Great Power Diplomacy in the Middle East, 1967–1970* (Boulder, CO: Westview, 1992), p. 92; Keith

Kyle, *Suez* (New York: St. Martin's, 1991), p. 369; Pollack, *Arabs at War,* pp. 361, 414.

3. For the evidence behind all of the judgments in this section, see Pollack, *Arabs at War.*

4. Most post–Gulf War assessments of Iraqi manpower strength in the Kuwaiti Theater of Operations (KTO) are incorrect because they employ an incorrect order of battle for Iraqi forces. The Iraqis deployed 500,000–600,000 troops in the KTO, only to have this force melt to about 325,000–350,000 men as a result of deaths and desertions during the Coalition air campaign. The most accurate statistics on Iraqi forces can be found in Barry D. Watts, "Friction in the Gulf War," *Naval War College Review,* Vol. 48, No. 4, Sequence 352 (Autumn 1995), pp. 94 and 106, fn. 5.

5. For a terrific, firsthand discussion of this problem, see Michael Zacchea and Ted Kemp, *The Ragged Edge: A U.S. Marine's Account of Leading the Iraqi Army Fifth Battalion* (Chicago: Chicago Review Press, 2017).

6. Oren, *Six Days of War,* p. 163.

Chapter 2

1. In addition to the work I did on this subject in my doctoral thesis, I also pursued the topic of the Soviet role in Arab military effectiveness in a later piece coauthored with Michael Eisenstadt. See Michael Eisenstadt and Kenneth M. Pollack, "Armies of Snow and Armies of Sand: The Impact of Soviet Military Doctrine on Arab Militaries," *Middle East Journal,* Vol. 55, No. 4 (Autumn 2001), pp. 549–578.

2. Quoted in Owen, "The Role of the Army in Middle East Politics," p. 70.

3. Glassman, *Arms for the Arabs,* p. 50.

4. Moshe Dayan, *Diary of the Sinai Campaign,* First Paperback edition (New York: Shocken Books, 1967), pp. 4–5; and Safran, *From War to War,* p. 209.

5. This summary of Soviet doctrine and operational art is drawn from William P. Baxter, *Soviet Airland Battle Tactics* (Novato, CA: Presidio, 1986); Christopher Donnelly, *Red Banner: The Soviet Military System in Peace and War* (Alexandria, VA: Jane's Publishing, 1988); John Erickson and E. J. Feuchtwanger eds., *Soviet Military Power and Performance* (Hamden CT: Archon Books, 1979); Richard W. Harrison, *The Russian Way of War: Operational Art, 1904–1940* (Lawrence: University of Kansas Press, 2001); Raymond L. Garthoff, *How Russia Makes War: Soviet Military Doctrine* (London: George Allen and Unwin Ltd., 1954); David M. Glantz, *Colossus Reborn: The Red Army at War, 1941–1943* (Lawrence: University of Kansas Press, 2005), esp. pp. 63–124; Herbert Goldhamer, *The Soviet Soldier: Soviet Military Management at the Troop Level* (New York: Crane Russak, 1975); Benjamin Miller, "The Development of Soviet Armor, 1926–1982," unpublished Ph.D. dissertation

manuscript, Cornell University, 1984; Roger R. Reese, *The Soviet Military Experience* (London: Routledge, 2000); Col. Ghulam Dastagir Wardak (compilation and transcription), *The Voroshilov Lectures: Materials from the Soviet General Staff Academy,* Vol. 1 (Washington, DC: NDU Press, 1989).

6. John Erickson, Lynn Hansen, and William Schneider, *Soviet Ground Forces: An Operational Assessment* (Boulder, CO: Westview, 1986), p. 20.

7. Donnelly, *Red Banner,* p. 85, also see p. 221.

8. Anthony H. Cordesman and Abraham R. Wagner, *The Lessons of Modern War, Vol. III: The Afghan and Falklands Conflicts* (Boulder, CO: Westview, 1990), p. 122. On the general rigidity of Soviet tactical doctrine, also see Steven L. Canby, "The Alliance and Europe, Part IV: Military Doctrine and Technology," Adelphi Paper 109 (London: International Institute for Strategic Studies, 1975), pp. 10–11; Cordesman and Wagner, *The Lessons of Modern War, Vol. III,* pp. 116–117, 206; Donnelly, *Red Banner,* pp. 179–185, 216–217, 223–225; Goldhamer, *The Soviet Soldier,* pp. 97–98, 100–101, 311–315; and John Hemsley, "The Soviet Ground Forces," in *Soviet Military Power and Performance,* ed. John Erickson and E. J. Feuchtwanger (Hamden CT: Archon Books, 1979), pp. 32–33; Erickson et. al., *Soviet Ground Forces,* p. 10. For descriptions of the real initiative, flexibility, and creativity Soviet commanders were capable of at all levels during the Second World War, see Historical Evaluation and Research Organization, *Studies in Soviet Combat Performance,* hereafter referred to as HERO (McLean, VA: NOVA Publications, 1977), esp. pp. 2, 17, 41, 63–64, 73–74, 109, 202.

9. See Robert Forczyk, *Tank Warfare on the Eastern Front, 1941–1942: Schwerpunkt* (Barnsley, UK: Pen and Sword, 2013); and Robert Forczyk, *Tank Warfare on the Eastern Front, 1943–1945: Red Steamroller* (Barnsley, UK: Pen and Sword, 2016).

10. Erickson et al., *Soviet Ground Forces,* p. 205; Goldhamer, *The Soviet Soldier,* p. 102.

11. Alexander Zuyev with Malcom McConnell, *Fulcrum* (New York: Warner Books, 1992).

12. On the development of Soviet ground tactics in Afghanistan, see Lester W. Grau, translator and ed., *The Bear Went over the Mountain: Soviet Combat Tactics in Afghanistan* (Washington, DC: National Defense University Press, 1996).

13. On Khalkin Gol, see Chris Bellamy, *Absolute War: Soviet Russia in the Second World War* (New York: Alfred A. Knopf, 2007), pp. 83–84; Edward J. Drea, "Nomonhan: Japanese Soviet Tactical Combat 1939," Leavenworth Papers No. 2, Combat Studies Institute, Command and General Staff College, Ft. Leavenworth, 1981; Stuart D. Goldman, *Nomonhan, 1939: The Red Army's Victory That Shaped World War II* (Annapolis, MD: US Naval Institute Press, 2012).

14. For instance, see the recent work on the Battle of Prokhorovka in July 1943 (part of the larger battle of Kursk) where the Germans inflicted far higher

losses on the Soviets than they took themselves, contrary to what had been believed in the past. Despite this German tactical victory at Prokhorovka, the Red Army still won overall at Kursk. See George M. Nipe, *Blood, Steel and Myth: The II SS Panzer Korps and the Road to Prochorowka, July 1943* (Stamford, CT: RZM Publishing, 2011); Dennis E. Showalter, *Armor and Blood: The Battle of Kursk, Turning Point of World War II* (New York: Random House, 2013).

15. Christopher Donnelly, "The Soviet Soldier: Behavior, Performance, Effectiveness," in *Soviet Military Power*, ed. Erickson and Feuchtwanger, p. 125.

16. John Erickson, *The Road to Stalingrad: Stalin's War with Germany, Volume One* (New York: Harper and Row, 1975) esp. p. 26; and Miller, "The Development of Soviet Armor, 1926–1982," pp. 25–103.

17. Wardak, *The Voroshilov Lectures*, Vol. 1, pp. 83 and 264.

18. Ibid., p. 272.

19. Donnelly, *Red Banner*, p. 254; Garthoff, *How Russia Makes War*, pp. 272–274; Hemsley, "The Soviet Ground Forces," p. 48; HERO, *Studies in Soviet Combat Performance*, pp. 24, 41, 51, 72, 194; Miller, "The Development of Soviet Armor," pp. 260–263; Wardak, *The Voroshilov Lectures*, Vol. 1, pp. 171, 173–175, 219–220, 224, 228–229, 291, 297–298, 321.

20. Alan Clark, *Barbarossa: The Russian-German Conflict, 1941–1945*, Paperback ed. (New York: Quill, 1965), p. 123; Garthoff, *How Russia Makes War*, pp. 265–272.

21. Erickson et al., *Soviet Ground Forces*, p. 183; Garthoff, *How Russia Makes War*, pp. 253–262; Goldhamer, *The Soviet Soldier*, p. 115; Hemsley, "The Soviet Ground Forces," pp. 49, 55–60; Miller, "The Development of Soviet Armor," pp. 265, 463–464; Wardak, *The Voroshilov Lectures, Vol. 1*, pp. 226, 229, 291, 292–295, 317.

22. Cordesman and Wagner, *The Lessons of Modern War, Vol. III*, pp. 107–108; Erickson et al., *Soviet Ground Forces*, p. 183; HERO, pp. 8–13, 17, 24, 108, 133, 194.

23. Erickson et al., *Soviet Ground Forces*, p. 183.

24. Miller, "The Development of Soviet Armor," pp. 262–263.

25. Donnelly, *Red Banner*, p. 252; Garthoff, *How Russia Makes War*, pp. 89–90; Hemsley, "The Soviet Ground Forces," pp. 48, 55; HERO, *Studies in Soviet Combat Performance*, pp. 14, 29, 34–35, 60; Miller, "The Development of Soviet Armor," pp. 262–263; Wardak, *The Voroshilov Lectures*, Vol. 1, pp. 177, 272, 311.

26. Hemsley, "The Soviet Ground Forces," p. 48.

27. Donnelly, *Red Banner*, p. 76; Erickson, *The Road to Stalingrad*, p. 26; Hemsley, "The Soviet Ground Forces," p. 48, 55, 63; Miller, "The Development of Soviet Armor," pp. 25–103; Wardak, *The Voroshilov Lectures*, Vol. 1, pp. 272, 275–277, 309–310, 311.

28. Donnelly, *Red Banner*, p. 81; Erickson, *Soviet Military Power*, p. 18; Erickson et al., *Soviet Ground Forces*, p. 214; Hemsley, "The Soviet Ground Forces," pp. 48, 55.

29. Clark, *Barbarossa,* pp. 80, 257–472; Erickson, *The Road to Stalingrad,* pp. 101–472; John Erickson, *The Road to Berlin: Stalin's War with Germany,* Vol. 1I (London: Weidenfeld and Nicolson, 1983), entire; Stephen G. Fritz, *Ostkrieg: Hitler's War of Extermination in the East* (Lexington: University of Kentucky Press, 2011); HERO, *Studies in Soviet Combat Performance,* entire, esp. pp. 31, 109, 311, 275; Evan Mawdsley, *Thunder in the East: The Nazi-Soviet War 1941–1945* (London: Hodder Arnold, 2005).

30. Hemsley, "The Soviet Ground Forces," p. 48; Miller, "The Development of Soviet Armor," pp. 264–265.

31. Cordesman and Wagner, *The Lessons of Modern War, Vol. III,* pp. 38–50.

32. Erickson, "The Soviet Military System," in Erickson ed., *Soviet Military Power and Performance,* p. 33; Erickson et al., *Soviet Ground Forces,* pp. 16, 181, 217–218; Garthoff, *How Russia Makes War,* pp. 171–182; Hemsley, "The Soviet Ground Forces," pp. 48–50; Jonathan House, *Toward Combined Arms Warfare* (Fort Leavenworth, KS: CGSC, 1984), pp. 64–69, 99–103, 121–125, 142–146; Miller, "The Development of Soviet Armor," pp. 35–102, 270; Wardak, *The Voroshilov Lectures,* Vol. 1, pp. 82, 240–242; and author's interview with General Bernard Trainor, May 1994.

33. Erickson et al., *Soviet Ground Forces,* p. 16; Miller, "The Development of Soviet Armor," p. 105.

34. Clark, *Barbarossa,* entire, esp. p. 279; Erickson, *The Road to Stalingrad,* pp. 101–472; Erickson, *The Road to Berlin,* entire; HERO, *Studies in Soviet Combat Performance,* esp. pp. 29–29, 43.

35. HERO, *Studies in Soviet Combat Performance,* p. 27.

36. Cordesman and Wagner, *The Lessons of Modern War, Vol. III,* pp. 38–41, 45–94, 117, 124.

37. Wardak, *The Voroshilov Lectures,* Vol. 1, p. 262.

38. Erickson et al., *Soviet Ground Forces,* pp. 181–184, 186–193, 198; Wardak, *The Voroshilov Lectures,* Vol. 1, pp. 260, 262, 273, 278–279, 311, 316–339.

39. Clark, *Barbarossa,* p. 41; Cordesman and Wagner, *The Lessons of Modern War, Vol. III,* p. 211; Erickson, "The Soviet Military System," pp. 32–33; Hemsley, "The Soviet Ground Forces," p. 48; and author's interview with General Bernard Trainor, May 1994.

40. Donnelly, *Red Banner,* p. 217; Hemsley, "The Soviet Ground Forces," in Erickson ed., *Soviet Military Power and Performance*, pp. 48, 66–68. By contrast, traditional "pull" logistics systems require combat units to request specific supplies from their superior formations, and in many cases, send their own transport to collect them. While this system cuts down on waste, it is not terribly responsive to the demands of a fast-paced armored offensive.

41. Erickson, "The Soviet Military System," p. 34.

42. Canby, "The Alliance and Europe, Part 4," pp. 10–11.

43. Erickson, "The Soviet Military System," in Erickson ed., *Soviet Military Power and Performance*, p. 34; Erickson et al., *Soviet Ground Forces*, p. 35; Hemsley, "The Soviet Ground Forces," p. 68;

44. Cordesman and Wagner, *The Lessons of Modern War, Vol. III,* p. 209; Donnelly, *Red Banner,* p. 181; and author's interview with General Bernard Trainor, May 1994.

45. Cordesman and Wagner, *The Lessons of Modern War, Vol. III,* pp. 209–211; Erickson et al., *Soviet Ground Forces*, p. 127; Hemsley, "The Soviet Ground Forces," p. 68.

Chapter 3

1. There is a widely held misconception in the West that Iraq relied on Soviet doctrine and methods. This is entirely untrue. For more detail, see Kevin M. Woods, Williamson Murray, Elizabeth A. Nathan, Laila Sabara, and Ana M. Venegas, *Saddam's Generals: Perspectives of the Iran-Iraq War* (Washington, DC: Institute for Defense Analysis, 2011), esp. pp. 43–45.

2. For an Egyptian account of this, see Aboul-Enein, ed., *Reconstructing a Shattered Egyptian Army*, pp. 79, 97–98. For an account by a former Israeli military intelligence analyst, see Asher, *The Egyptian Strategy for the Yom Kippur War.*

3. Gregory R. Copley, *Defense and Foreign Affairs Handbook of Egypt, 1995* (London: International Media Corp., Ltd., 1995), p. 81; Lt. Colonel Joseph P. Englehardt, *Desert Shield and Desert Storm: A Chronology and Troop List for the 1990–1991 Persian Gulf Crisis* (Carlisle Barracks, PA: US Army War College Strategic Studies Institute, March 1991), p. 8.

4. Colonel Daniel M. Ferezan, "Memorandum for Commander, Third U.S. Army, Attn: G-3, APO NY, Subject: Project 5/Liaison Team Golf after Action Report," March 31, 1991, p. B-1. Col. Ferezan was one of the senior US liaison officers assigned to the Egyptian corps. This letter was obtained via a Freedom of Information Act request.

5. Ferezan, "Memorandum for Commander, Third U.S. Army," p. C-2; Brig. General Robert Scales, Jr., *Certain Victory* (Washington, DC: GPO, 1993), p. 222; Bruce W. Watson, Bruce George, Peter Tsouras, and B. L. Cyr, *Military Lessons of the Gulf War* (London: Greenhill Books, 1991), p. 106.

6. Rick Atkinson, *Crusade* (New York: Houghton Mifflin, 1993), p. 248.

7. Ferezan, "Memorandum for Commander, Third U.S. Army," pp. C-3-5; and author's interviews with US military officers, October–December 1996.

8. Englehardt, *Desert Shield and Desert Storm,* p. 8.

9. Author's interview with US military officer, November 1996.

10. Drew Middleton, "U.S. Aides say Egypt Lacks Ability to Handle Weapons," *The New York Times*, 21 February 1986, p. 8.

11. Author's interviews with US military officers November 1996 and US DoD personnel, July 1993.

12. See for example, Steve Rodan, "Report: Western Influence Enhances Egyptian AF Capability," *Defense News*, January 27–February 2, 1997, p. 9.

13. Author's interviews with US Department of Defense personnel and US military officers, January–March 1992, July 1993, October–December 1996, and February–March 1997.

14. Author's interviews with US DoD personnel, July 1993.

15. Author's interview with US military officer, November 1996.

16. Author's interview with US military, November 1996.

17. Author's interview with US DoD personnel, July 1993.

18. See, for instance, David Ottaway, "For Saudi Military, New Self-Confidence," *The Washington Post*, April 20, 1991, p. A14.

19. Ferezan, "Memorandum for Commander, Third U.S. Army," p. B-5.

20. Author's interviews with US DoD personnel and US military officers, January–March 1992, July 1993, October–December 1996, and February–March 1997.

21. Author's interviews with US DoD personnel, January–March 1992, July 1993. Also see Cordesman, *Jordanian Arms*, p. 52.

22. Author's interviews with US DoD personnel, January–March 1992, July 1993.

23. Author's interviews with US DoD personnel, January 1992.

24. Author's interview with US military officer familiar with the Egyptian military, February 1997.

25. Author's interviews with former Israeli military personnel, 1992–1994.

26. Col. D. Povkh, "Courage for Export: Interview with Lt. Col. Nikolai Kutyntsev," *Soviet Soldier*, No. 11 (November 1991), p. 65.

27. For his account of the action, see Brig. El-Edroos, *The Hashemite Arab Army*, p. 495.

28. Indeed, according to Charles Wakebridge, the Syrian Chief of Staff, General Mustafa Tlas, admitted to him in an interview that the Syrian General Staff was desperate to take the bridges, and these halts were entirely contrary to their desires. Charles Wakebridge, "The Syrian Side of the Hill," *Military Review*, Feb. 1976, p. 29.

29. Lt. Colonel Sergey Ivanovich Belzyudnyy, "Former Soviet Adviser Describes Experiences in Iraq: I Taught Saddam's Aces to Fly," (from *Komsomolskaya Pravda*, February 23, 1991), in JPRS-UMA-91-014, June 5, 1991, pp. 62–63.

30. Eliot A. Cohen, General Editor, *The Gulf War Air Power Survey, Volume II, Part II: Effects and Effectiveness*, hereafter referred to as GWAPS (Washington, DC: GPO, 1993), p. 122.

31. Mikhail Khodarenok, "Here's Why Assad's Army Can't Win the War in Syria," Gazeta.ru, September 6, 2016, translated and available in English at https://citeam.org/here-s-why-assad-s-army-can-t-win-the-war-in-syria/, downloaded on September 21, 2016.

Chapter 4

1. Roy E Appleman, *South to the Naktong, North to the Yalu* (Washington, DC: United States Army Center of Military History, 1998), pp. 381, 545; Allan R. Millett, *The War for Korea, 1950–1951: They Came from the North* (Lawrence: University of Kansas Press, 2010), pp. 29, 85; William J. Webb, *The Korean War: The Outbreak, 27 June–15 September 1950* (Washington, DC: US Army Center for Military History, 2012), pp. 7–9.

2. Kevin Mahoney, *Formidable Enemies: The North Korean and Chinese Soldier in the Korean War* (Novato, CA: Presidio, 2001), pp. 5, 11; Webb, *The Korean War,* pp. 3, 7.

3. Joel R. Campbell, "The Wrong War: The Soviets and the Korean War, 1945–1953," *International Social Science Review*, Vol. 88, No. 3 (2014), pp. 6–7.

4. Mahoney, *Formidable Enemies*, pp. 7–8; Millett, *The War for Korea, 1950–1951*, pp. 47–48; Kathryn Weathersby, "Soviet Aims in Korea and the Origins of the Korean War, 1945–1950: New Evidence from Russian Archives," Working Paper No. 8, Cold War International History Project, Woodrow Wilson International Center for Scholars, Washington, DC, November 1993, p. 30.

5. Samuel B. Griffith, *The Chinese People's Liberation Army* (New York: McGraw-Hill, 1967), p. 113; Mahoney, *Formidable Enemies*, p. 5; Millett, *The War for Korea, 1950–1951*, pp. 29, 48; Russell Spurr, *Enter the Dragon: China's Undeclared War against the US in Korea 1950–1951* (New York: Newmarket Press, 1988), pp. 13–14, 17–18; Richard W. Stewart, ed., *American Military History: Volume II, The United States Army in a Global Era, 1917–2003* (Washington, DC: The Center of Military History, 2005), p. 219.

6. Weathersby, "Soviet Aims in Korea," pp. 29–30.

7. Millett, *The War for Korea, 1950–1951*, pp. 29–37; Webb, *The Korean War*, p. 6.

8. On the shortcomings of the US Eighth Army in Japan, see Millett, *The War for Korea, 1950–1951*, pp. 78–84.

9. Millett, *The War for Korea, 1950–1951*, pp. 37–45.

10. For more extensive histories of the Korean War, I recommend Clay Blair, *The Forgotten War: America in Korea 1950–1953* (New York: Times Books, 1987); Bruce Cummings, *The Korean War: A History* (New York: The Modern Library, 2011); Millett, *The War for Korea, 1950–1951*; General Paik Sun Yup, ed., *From Pusan to Panmunjom* (McLean, VA: Brassey's, 1992).

11. Millett, *The War for Korea, 1950–1951*, p. 191.

12. Millett, *The War for Korea, 1950–1951*, pp. 190–197; Webb, *The Korean War,* pp. 12–17.

13. Millett, *The War for Korea, 1950–1951*, pp. 215–231; Webb, *The Korean War,* pp. 19, 22.

14. Blair, *The Forgotten War*, pp. 169–172, 214, 221–239, 281–295; Mahoney, *Formidable Enemies*, pp. 8–9, 45.

15. Millett, *The War for Korea, 1950–1951*, pp. 269–284; Stewart, ed., *American Military History: Volume II*, pp. 221–250.

16. On North Korean military effectiveness, see Blair, *The Forgotten War*, esp. pp. 102–369; Griffith, *The Chinese People's Liberation Army*; Paik, *From Pusan to Panmunjom*; General Matthew B. Ridgway, *The Korean War* (New York: Doubleday, 1967); Spurr, *Enter the Dragon*.

17. Millett, *The War for Korea, 1950–1951*, p. 108.

18. Mahoney, *Formidable Enemies*, pp. 53–55.

19. Millett, *The War for Korea, 1950–1951*, p. 190. See also Mahoney, *Formidable Enemies*, p. 46.

20. Blair, *The Forgotten War*, p. 102. See also Mahoney, *Formidable Enemies*, pp. 71–73.

21. Mahoney, *Formidable Enemies*, pp. 50, 87–90, 98.

22. Mahoney, *Formidable Enemies*, pp. 45–46, 71–74; Millett, *The War for Korea, 1950–1951*, pp. 89, 93–94, 135, 139, 218, 226, 255. Millet also notes problems with combined arms coordination, especially early in the war. For instance see pages 101, 107, and 138.

23. Mahoney, *Formidable Enemies*, p. 64.

24. Millett, *The War for Korea, 1950–1951*, p. 35.

25. Millett, *The War for Korea, 1950–1951*, see for instance, pp. 129–130, 140–143, 230.

26. Millett, *The War for Korea, 1950–1951*, pp. 36–37, 108–109, 151–153, 170–171; Paik, *From Pusan to Panmunjom*, p. 49.

27. This list of factors leading to North Korean defeat relies heavily on Blair, *The Forgotten War*, pp. 169–172; Millett, *The War for Korea, 1950–1951*, pp. 36–37, 108–109, 129–130, 140–143, 223–224, 230, 270–272; and Spurr, *Enter the Dragon*, pp. 20–22, 61–68.

28. Mitchell Bainwoll, "Cuba," in *Fighting Armies: Non-aligned Third World and Other Ground Armies, a Combat Assessment,* ed. Richard A. Gabriel (Westport, CT: Greenwood Press, 1983), pp. 228–230, 233; Defense Intelligence Agency (DIA), *Handbook of the Cuban Armed Forces*, DDB-2680-62-79, April 1979, pp. XIII; chapter 1 pp. 1, 4, 14–16; chapter 2, pp. 18–31, chapter 5, pp. 1, 11–12, 18–47, 49–65; Juan M. Del Aguila, "The Changing Character of Cuba's Armed Forces," in *The Cuban Military under Castro,* ed. Jaime Suchlicki (Miami, FL: Research Institute for Cuban Studies, University of Miami, 1989), pp. 27, 31; Leon Gouré, "Cuban Military Doctrine and Organization," in *The Cuban Military under Castro,* ed. Jaime Suchlicki (Miami, FL: Research Institute for Cuban Studies, University of Miami, 1989), pp. 66–69; Leon Gouré, "Soviet-Cuban Military Relations," in *The Cuban Military under Castro,* ed. Jaime Suchlicki (Miami, FL: Research Institute for Cuban Studies, University of Miami, 1989), pp. 165–182.

29. Edward George, *The Cuban Intervention in Angola, 1965–1991: From Che Guevara to Cuito Cuanavale* (London: Frank Cass, 2005), p. 74; Leopold Scholtz, *The SADF in the Border War 1966–1989* (Warwick, UK: Helion, 2013), p. 19.

30. Bainwoll, "Cuba," p. 231; Rafael Fermoselle, *The Evolution of the Cuban Military, 1492–1986* (Miami, FL: Ediciones Universal, 1987), pp. 399–402; George, *The Cuban Intervention in Angola, 1965–1991*, pp. 64–67, 115–117; Piero Gleijeses, "Moscow's Proxy? Cuba and Africa 1975–1988," *Journal of Cold War Studies,* Vol. 8, No. 4 (Fall 2006), p. 98; W. Martin James III, *A Political History of the Civil War in Angola, 1974–1990* (New Brunswick, NJ: Transaction, 1992), pp. 62–65; IISS, "Angola," *Strategic Survey, 1975* (London: IISS, 1975), p. 36; Scholtz, *The SADF in the Border War 196–1989*, p. 19; Ron Soodalter, "Over Where? Cuban Fighters in Angola's Civil War," *Military History Quarterly*, Vol. 28, No. 3 (Spring 2016), pp. 32–35; Daniel Spikes, *Angola and the Politics of Intervention* (Jefferson, NC: McFarland, 1993), pp. 147–203; Russ Stayanoff, "Third World Experience in Counterinsurgency: Cuba's Operation Carlotta, 1975," *Small Wars Journal,* available online at www.militaryhistoryonline.com/20thCentury/articles/cubansinafrica.aspx, downloaded on May 9, 2018.
31. George, *The Cuban Intervention in Angola, 1965–1991*, pp. 65, 74.
32. George, *The Cuban Intervention in Angola, 1965–1991*, p. 76.
33. George, *The Cuban Intervention in Angola, 1965–1991*, pp. 87–90; Peter Polack, *The Last Hot Battle of the Cold War: South Africa vs. Cuba in the Angolan Civil War* (Oxford: Casemate, 2013), p. 46.
34. George, *The Cuban Intervention in Angola, 1965–1991*, pp. 85–86.
35. Scholtz, *The SADF in the Border War 1966–1989*, p. 43.
36. William J. Durch, "The Cuban Military in Africa and the Middle East: From Algeria to Angola," *Studies in Comparative Communism*, Vol. 11, No. 1/2, Spring/Summer, 1978, pp. 67–68; Fermoselle, *The Evolution of the Cuban Military, 1492–1986*, pp. 402–404; George, *The Cuban Intervention in Angola, 1965–1991*, pp. 94–97; Ian Greig, *The Communist Challenge to Africa: An Analysis of Contemporary Soviet, Chinese and Cuban Policies* (Surrey, UK: Foreign Affairs, 1977), p. 231; James, *A Political History of the Civil War in Angola 1974–1990*, pp. 65–78; Spikes, *Angola and the Politics of Intervention*, pp. 212–307; Phyllis Greene Walker, "National Security," in *Cuba: A Country Study*, ed. James D. Rudolph (Washington, DC: GPO, 1985), p. 279.
37. George, *The Cuban Intervention in Angola, 1965–1991*, pp. 97–103; Scholtz, *The SADF in the Border War 1966–1989*, p. 19; Soodalter, "Over Where?," p. 35.
38. George, *The Cuban Intervention in Angola, 1965–1991*, pp. 106–115; Soodalter, "Over Where?," p. 35; Stayanoff, "Third World Experience in Counterinsurgency: Cuba's Operation Carlotta, 1975."
39. George, *The Cuban Intervention in Angola, 1965–1991*, pp. 106–110.
40. Fermoselle, *The Evolution of the Cuban Military, 1492–1896*, pp. 402–404; Greig, *The Communist Challenge to Africa,* p. 231; James, *A Political History of the Civil War in Angola 1974–1990,* pp. 65–78; Keith Somerville, *Foreign Military Intervention in Africa* (London: Printer Publishers, 1990), p. 99; Spikes, *Angola*

and the Politics of Intervention, pp. 212–307; Walker, *National Security,* p. 279; and author's interview with Jorge I. Domínguez, July 1995.

41. On the balance of forces, see Tom Cooper, *Wings over Ogaden: The Ethiopian-Somali War, 1978–1979* (Warwick, UK: Helion, 2015), online edition, available at www.acig.info/CMS/index.php?option=com_content&task=view&id=140&Itemid=0; Gebru Tareke, "The Ethiopia-Somalia War of 1977 Revisited," *The International Journal of African Historical Studies,* Vol. 33, No. 3 (2000), pp. 638–640; Gebru Tareke, *The Ethiopian Revolution: War in the Horn of Africa* (New Haven, CT: Yale University Press, 2009), pp. 186–190.

42. Tareke, *The Ethiopian Revolution,* p. 183.

43. Tareke, "The Ethiopia-Somalia War of 1977 Revisited," p. 639.

44. Patrick Gilkes, "Revolution and Military Strategy: The Ethiopian Army in the Ogaden and Eritrea, 1974–84," in *Proceedings of the Eleventh International Conference of Ethiopian Studies, Volume II,* ed. Bahru Zewde et al. (Addis Ababa, 1994), p. 723.

45. Tareke, "The Ethiopia-Somalia War of 1977 Revisited," p. 644; Tareke, *The Ethiopian Revolution,* p. 192.

46. Cooper, *Wings over Ogaden*; Gilkes, "Revolution and Military Strategy," p. 724; Tareke, "The Ethiopia-Somalia War of 1977 Revisited," pp. 646–647; Tareke, *The Ethiopian Revolution,* pp. 190–195.

47. Gilkes, "Revolution and Military Strategy," p. 725; Tareke, "The Ethiopia-Somalia War of 1977 Revisited," pp. 648–652; Tareke, *The Ethiopian Revolution,* pp. 195–200.

48. The first Cuban advisors arrived in Ethiopia in September. George, *The Cuban Intervention in Angola, 1965–1991,* pp. 132–133.

49. George, *The Cuban Intervention in Angola, 1965–1991,* pp. 132–133; Gilkes, "Revolution and Military Strategy," p. 726; Gleijeses, "Moscow's Proxy?" p. 98; Colin Legum ed., *Africa Contemporary Record, 1977–1978* [hereafter referred to as "ACR" with appropriate years] (New York: Africana, 1979), pp. B225–228; Colin Legum and Bill Lee, "Crisis in the Horn of Africa: International Dimensions of the Somali-Ethiopian Conflict," in *ACR, 1977–1978,* ed. Colin Legum (New York: Africana, 1979), pp. A44–45; William H. Lewis, "Ethiopia-Somalia (1977–78)," in *The Lessons of Recent Wars in the Third World,* Vol 1, ed. Robert Harkavy and Stephanie Neuman (Lexington, MA: Lexington Books, 1986), pp. 99–100, 110–112; Thomas Ofcansky, "National Security," in *Somalia: A Country Study,* ed. Helen Chapin Metz (Washington, DC: GPO, 1992), pp. 181–185; Tareke, "The Ethiopia-Somalia War of 1977 Revisited," p. 656; Tareke, *The Ethiopian Revolution,* pp. 121, 203–204; Nelson P. Valdés, "Cuban Foreign Policy in the Horn of Africa," *Cuban Studies,* Vol. 10, No. 1 (January 1980), pp. 54–58.

50. Col. Abdullahi Ahmed Jama, "The Horn of Africa Conflict," USAWC Military Studies Program Paper, US Army War College, March 9, 1989, p. 17; Tareke, "The Ethiopia-Somalia War of 1977 Revisited," p. 657.

51. Cooper, *Wings over Ogaden*; Somerville, *Foreign Military Intervention in Africa*, p. 136; Tareke, "The Ethiopia-Somalia War of 1977 Revisited," pp. 657–658; Tareke, *The Ethiopian Revolution*, pp. 205–208.

52. James E. Dougherty, *The Horn of Africa: A Map of Political-Strategic Conflict* (Cambridge, MA: Institute for Foreign Policy Analysis, 1982), pp. 34–35; IISS, "The Horn of Africa," *Strategic Study, 1978* (London: IISS, 1978), pp. 94–95; Legum, *ACR 1977–1978*, pp. B228–235, B377–378; Lewis, "Ethiopia-Somalia (1977–78)," pp. 112–114; Ofcansky, "National Security," in *Somalia: A Country Study*, ed., Metz pp. 185–186; Thomas P. Ofcansky, "National Security," in *Ethiopia: A Country Study*, ed. Thomas P. Ofcansky (Washington: GPO, 1991), pp. 297–314; Somerville, *Foreign Military Intervention in Africa*, p. 136; Tareke, *The Ethiopian Revolution*, p. 209; Valdés, "Cuban Foreign Policy in the Horn of Africa," pp. 58–61.

53. George, *The Cuban Intervention in Angola, 1965–1991*, pp. 115, 117.

54. George, *The Cuban Intervention in Angola, 1965–1991*, pp. 134–135; Helmoed-Römer Heitman, *War in Angola: The Final South African Phase* (Gibraltar: Ashanti Publishing Ltd., 1990), p. 16; Olga Nazario, "Cuba's Angola Operation," in *Cuban Internationalism in Sub-Saharan Africa*, ed. Sergio Díaz-Briquets (Pittsburgh, PA: Duquesne University Press, 1989), pp. 107–109, and fn. 14, p. 203; Scholtz, *The SADF in the Border War 1966–1989*, pp. 72–81; Soodalter, "Over Where?," p. 35.

55. George, *The Cuban Intervention in Angola, 1965–1991*, pp. 134–135, 164; Soodalter, "Over Where?," p. 36.

56. George, *The Cuban Intervention in Angola, 1965–1991*, p. 195.

57. Fred Bridgland, *The War for Africa: Twelve Months That Transformed a Continent* (Philadelphia: Casemate, 2017), pp. 43, 49; George, *The Cuban Intervention in Angola, 1965–1991*, pp. 196–198; Heitman, *War in Angola*, pp. 13–32; Daniel S. Papp, "The Angolan Civil War and Namibia: The Role of External Intervention," in *Making War and Waging Peace: Foreign Intervention in Africa*, ed. David R. Smock (Washington, DC: United States Institute of Peace Press, 1993), p. 180; Polack, *The Last Hot Battle of the Cold War*, pp. 23, 25; Peter Vanneman, "Soviet Foreign Policy for Angola/Namibia in the 1980s: A Strategy of Coercive Diplomacy," in *Disengagement from Southwest Africa: The Prospects for Peace in Angola and Namibia*, ed. Owen Ellison Kahn (New Brunswick, NJ: Transaction Books, 1990), p. 76.

58. George, *The Cuban Intervention in Angola, 1965–1991*, p. 200.

59. George, *The Cuban Intervention in Angola, 1965–1991*, pp. 203–204; Polack, *The Last Hot Battle of the Cold War*, p. 22.

60. George, *The Cuban Intervention in Angola, 1965–1991*, p. 203; Polack, *The Last Hot Battle of the Cold War*, pp. 22–23, 42, 87; Scholtz, *The SADF in the Border War 1966–1989*, p. 265.

61. Bridgland, *The War for Africa*, pp. 70–199; George, *The Cuban Intervention in Angola, 1965–1991*, pp. 204–209; Jeremy Harding, *The Fate of Africa: Trial*

by Fire (New York: Simon and Schuster, 1993), pp. 53–54; Heitman, *War in Angola*, pp. 32–108; Jeffrey Herbst, "The Angola-Namibia Accords: An Early Assessment," in Díaz-Briquets, pp. 145–146; Polack, *The Last Hot Battle of the Cold War*, pp. 91–103, 129–133; Scholtz, *The SADF in the Border War 1966–1989*, pp. 31, 266–277.

62. George, *The Cuban Intervention in Angola, 1965–1991*, pp. 207–211; Polack, *The Last Hot Battle of the Cold War*, pp. 22, 135–136.

63. Bridgland, *The War for Africa*, p. 455; George, *The Cuban Intervention in Angola, 1965–1991*, p. 215; Polack, *The Last Hot Battle of the Cold War*, pp. 38, 136; Scholtz, *The SADF in the Border War 1966–1989*, pp. 332–333.

64. George, *The Cuban Intervention in Angola, 1965–1991*, p. 215.

65. George, *The Cuban Intervention in Angola, 1965–1991*, pp. 216, 220; Scholtz, *The SADF in the Border War 1966–1989*, pp. 326–326, 339.

66. The South Africans had launched an initial attack on January 13, 1988, and while this had successfully driven off FAPLA's 21st Infantry Brigade, it took place before the Cubans took control of the battle or deployed their combat units, and the SADF was forced to give up the positions it had taken a few days later in any event. Bridgland, *The War for Africa*, pp. 317–341; George, *The Cuban Intervention in Angola, 1965–1991*, pp. 218–220; Polack, *The Last Hot Battle of the Cold War*, pp. 139–141; Scholtz, *The SADF in the Border War 1966–1989*, pp. 321–326.

67. Bridgland, *The War for Africa*, pp. 317–393; George, *The Cuban Intervention in Angola, 1965–1991*, pp. 223–225; Scholtz, *The SADF in the Border War 1966–1989,* p. 328.

68. George, *The Cuban Intervention in Angola, 1965–1991*, p. 224.

69. Raymond W. Copson, *Africa's Wars and Prospects for Peace* (Armonk, NY: M. E. Sharpe, 1994), p. 121; Harding, *The Fate of Africa,* pp. 55–57; George, *The Cuban Intervention in Angola, 1965–1991*, pp. 221–233; Heitman, *War in Angola*, pp. 118, 171, 190; Herbst, "The Angola-Namibia Accords," p. 146; IISS, *Strategic Survey, 1987–1988*, p. 194; James, *A Political History of the Civil War in Angola 1974–1990*, pp. 175–176, 231; Legum, *ACR, 1987–1988*, pp. B575–579; Nazario, "Cuba's Angola Operation," p. 111; Papp, "The Angolan Civil War and Namibia," pp. 181–183; Polack, *The Last Hot Battle of the Cold War*, pp. 142–150; Scholtz, *The SADF in the Border War 1966–1989*, pp. 325–358; Somerville, *Foreign Military Intervention in Africa*, pp. 99, 155; and author's interviews with Lt. General Bernard Trainor, May 1994.

70. George, *The Cuban Intervention in Angola, 1965–1991*, pp. 230, 236–237; Scholtz, *The SADF in the Border War 1966–1989*, pp. 371–372.

71. Bridgland, *The War for Africa*, pp. 406–417; Copson, *Africa's Wars and Prospects for Peace*, p. 121; George, *The Cuban Intervention in Angola, 1965–1991*, pp. 242–245; Harding, *The Fate of Africa,* p. 57; Heitman, *War in Angola*, pp. 199, 295–298; Herbst, "The Angola-Namibia Accords," p. 146; Papp, "The Angolan Civil War and Namibia," pp. 183–185; Scholtz, *The SADF*

in the Border War 1966–1989, pp. 377–381; and author's interviews with Lt. General Bernard Trainor, May, 1994.

72. For concurring and supporting views on Cuban tactical performance, see Bainwoll, "Cuba," p. 241; DIA, *Handbook of the Cuban Armed Forces*, ch. 5, p. 16; Sergio Diaz-Briquets, *Cuban Internationalism in Sub-Saharan Africa* (Pittsburgh, PA: Duquesne University Press, 1989), p. 4; Fermoselle, *The Evolution of the Cuban Military, 1492–1986*, pp. 7, 450; George, *The Cuban Intervention in Angola, 1965–1991*, esp. pp. 74–116, 201–245; Heitman, *War in Angola*, esp. pp. 71–78, 82–86, 197, 219–222, 231–233, 251, 261–267, 299–305; Lewis, "Ethiopia-Somalia (1977–78)," pp. 111–113; Ofcansky (Ethiopia), p. 313; Ofcansky (Somalia), p. 186; Polack, *The Last Hot Battle of the Cold War*, pp. 21–48, 76–77, 87–148; Scholtz, *The SADF in the Border War 1966–1989*, pp. 19, 268–381; Soodalter, "Over Where?," esp. pp. 35–36; Spikes, *Angola and the Politics of Intervention*, esp. pp. 240, 247, 260–271; and author's interviews with Lt. General Bernard Trainor, May 1994, and Jorge I. Domínguez, July 1995.

73. Fermoselle begins his landmark work on the history of the Cuban military by noting consistent patterns of behavior throughout Cuban military history, which he attributes to cultural factors. Thus he notes that a strong streak of ingenuity is considered a defining feature of Cuban culture, and that Cuban military forces have demonstrated this in combat time and again.

74. Bridgland, *The War for Africa*, p. 131; Heitman, *War in Angola*, esp. pp. 302–305; Lewis, "Ethiopia-Somalia (1977–78)," pp. 99–110; Spikes, *Angola and the Politics of Intervention*, pp. 260–307; and author's interviews with Lt. General Bernard Trainor, May 1994.

75. Heitman, *War in Angola*, p. 261.

76. Heitman, *War in Angola*, p. 197.

77. Tareke, "The Ethiopia-Somalia War of 1977 Revisited," p. 656.

78. On Castro's direction of these campaigns, see George, *The Cuban Intervention in Angola, 1965–1991*, pp. 211–216; Polack, *The Last Hot Battle of the Cold War*, pp. 37–45, 136; Scholtz, *The SADF in the Border War 1966–1989*, pp. 235–239, 326–333, 372.

79. Scholtz, *The SADF in the Border War 1966–1989*, p. 326.

80. Quote is from Heitman, *War in Angola*, p. 318. Also see Bridgland, *The War for Africa*, pp. 132–139; Dougherty, *The Horn of Africa:* p. 32; Fermoselle, *The Evolution of the Cuban Military, 1492–1986*, p. 407; George, *The Cuban Intervention in Angola, 1965–1991*, p. 225; Harding, *The Fate of Africa*, p. 24; Heitman, *War in Angola*, pp. 71, 79, 198, 310–320; James, *A Political History of the Civil War in Angola 1974–1990*, pp. 215–219, 232; Polack, *The Last Hot Battle of the Cold War*, pp. 39–40, 69, 143–144, 152, 161; Scholtz, *The SADF in the Border War 1966–1989*, pp. 163–164, 401–410; Somerville, *Foreign Military Intervention in Africa*, pp. 154–156.

81. Scholtz, *The SADF in the Border War 1966–1989*, p. 402.

82. Bridgland, *The War for Africa*, pp. 205–207; Polack, *The Last Hot Battle of the Cold War*, pp. 59–140; Scholtz, *The SADF in the Border War 1966–1989*, pp. 320, 408.

83. Bridgland, *The War for Africa*, pp. 131, 432–433; Dougherty, *The Horn of Africa*, p. 35; Harding, *The Fate of Africa,* p. 57; Heitman, *War in Angola*, pp. 143, 177, 196, 200, 211–212, 227, 250–252, 264–265, 279, 306, 310, 346; Valdés, *Cuban Foreign Policy in the Horn of Africa,* p. 61; and author's interviews with Lt. General Bernard Trainor, May 1994.

84. Heitman, *War in Angola*, p. 328.

85. Fermoselle, *The Evolution of the Cuban Military, 1492–1986*, pp. 10–11.

86. See for example, Bereket Habte Selassie, *Conflict and Intervention in the Horn of Africa* (New York: Monthly Review Press, 1980), p. 142.

87. Author's interviews with Lt. General Bernard Trainor, May 1994.

88. See for example Fermoselle, *The Evolution of the Cuban Military, 1492–1986*, pp. 401–402.

89. DIA, *Handbook of the Cuban Armed Forces*, ch. 2., pp. 30–35, ch. 4, p. 5.

90. Heitman, *War in Angola*, pp. 229 and 328; Scholtz, *The SADF in the Border War 1966–1989*, p. 410.

91. Jerry Asher with Eric Hammel, *Duel for the Golan* (New York: William Morris, 1987), p. 54; Fermoselle, *The Evolution of the Cuban Military, 1492–1986*, pp. 346, 397; J. M. Moreaux, "The Syrian Army," *Defence Update*, No. 79, March 1986, p. 42.

92. See for example Heitman, *War in Angola*, pp. 128, 209, 304.

93. Scholtz, *The SADF in the Border War 1966–1989*, p. 426.

94. Quoted in Isaac Saney, "African Stalingrad: The Cuban Revolution, Internationalism, and the End of Apartheid," *Latin American Perspectives*, Vol. 33, No. 5 (September 2006), p. 83.

95. Yaacov Ro'i and Dima P. Adamsky, "Conclusions," in *The Soviet Union and the June 1967 Six-Day War*, ed. Yaacov Ro'i and Boris Morozov (Stanford, CA: Stanford University Press, 2008), p. 275.

96. For concurring assessments, see Ro'i and Adamsky, "Conclusions," pp. 274–277; Norvell B. De Atkine, "Western Influence on Arab Militaries: Pounding Square Pegs into Round Holes." *Middle East Review of International Affairs*, Vol. 17, No. 1 (Spring 2013), p. 23.

97. Donnelly, *Red Banner*, pp. 29–43, 195, 211.

Chapter 5

1. Samuel Huntington, *The Soldier and the State: The Theory and Politics of Civil-Military Relations,* Vintage Paperback ed. (New York: Vintage Books, 1957), in particular, see pp. 19–25.

2. The term "praetorianism" was first coined by David Rapoport to refer to the involvement of the military in politics. David Rapoport,

"Praetorianism: Government without Consensus," unpublished dissertation (University of California, Berkeley, 1960); and Samuel P. Huntington, *Political Order in Changing Societies* (New Haven, CT: Yale University Press, 1968). Huntington's work is often considered the definitive statement of the phenomenon. However, there is an extensive body of literature on praetorianism, some of which predates Huntington's work. For a good, albeit brief, overview, see David C. Rapoport, "The Praetorian Army: Insecurity, Venality, and Impotence."

3. For the best discussion of *appropriate* civilian control of the military, see Eliot Cohen, *Supreme Command* (New York: Free Press, 2002).

4. J. C. Hurewitz, *Middle East Politics: The Military Dimension* (New York: Praeger, 1969), p. 7.

5. See for example, Owen, "The Role of the Army in Middle Eastern Politics," pp. 64–71.

6. On the effects of politicization of the military, see also Michael C. Desch, *Civilian Control of the Military: The Changing Security Environment* (Baltimore: Johns Hopkins University Press, 2001); Huntington, *The Soldier and the State*; Morris Janowitz, *The Professional Soldier* (New York: The Free Press, 1960); Rapoport, "The Praetorian Army: Insecurity, Venality, and/Impotence"; Talmadge, *The Dictator's Army*.

7. For a sample of the voluminous literature on military intervention in government, see Martin Edmonds, *Armed Services and Society* (Boulder, CO: Westview, 1990); Samuel E. Finer, *The Man on Horseback: The Role of the Military in Politics* (London: Pall Mall Press, 1962); Huntington, *Political Order in Changing Societies*; Amos Perlmutter, "The Praetorian State and the Praetorian Army," *Comparative Politics*, April 1969, 385; Amos Perlmutter and Valerie Plave Bennett, *The Political Influence of the Military: A Comparative Reader* (New Haven, CT: Yale University Press, 1980). For this phenomenon as it specifically applies to the Middle East, see for example, Eliezer Be'eri, *Army Officers in Arab Politics and Society*; Sidney Fisher, *The Military in the Middle East: Problems in Society and Government* (Columbus: Ohio State University Press, 1963); Majid Khadduri, "The Role of the Military in Middle Eastern Politics," *American Political Science Review*, No. 47, 1953, pp. 511–524; and Owen, "The Role of the Army in Middle Eastern Politics," pp. 63–81.

8. Be'eri, *Army Officers in Arab Politics and Society*, p. 4.

9. Be'eri, *Army Officers in Arab Politics and Society*, pp. 246–250.

10. On Iraqi military involvement in politics during this period see Kanaan Makiya (writing as Samir Al-Khalil), *Republic of Fear: The Politics of Modern Iraq* (Berkeley: University of California Press, 1989), pp. 21–27; Phebe Marr, *The Modern History of Iraq* (Boulder, CO: Westview, 1985), pp. 153–210; and Peter Sluggett and Marion Farouk Sluggett, *Iraq since 1958: From Revolution to Dictatorship* (London: KPI Ltd., 1987).

11. Derek Hopwood, *Syria, 1945–1986: Politics and Society* (London: Unwin Hyman, 1988), pp. 32–53.

12. On the impact of praetorianism on military performance, see Stanislav Andreski, "On the Peaceful Disposition of Military Dictatorships," *Journal of Strategic Studies*, Vol. 3, No. 3, December 1980, pp. 3–10; Huntington, *The Soldier and the State*; Janowitz, *The Professional Soldier*; and Rapoport, "The Praetorian Army."

13. David Rapoport was the first person to discuss this problem in any depth. See Rapoport, "The Praetorian Army." However, I may have been the first to fully develop the phenomenon in my doctoral thesis. See Pollack, "The Influence of Arab Culture on Arab Military Effectiveness," pp. 83–118. That said, the best known work on the subject is James T. Quinlivan, "Coup-Proofing: Its Practice and Consequences in the Middle East," pp. 131–165. Quinlivan's article drew on the work of my doctoral thesis—which he cites, and which we discussed when he was researching his own article.

14. Quinlivan, "Coup-Proofing," pp. 131–165. Jim's moniker is a great one and has caught on widely. However, I prefer to stick with "commissarism" both because of the reference back to its origin and for the parallelism with the term "praetorianism." It makes clear that this is another aspect of the wider problem of politicization rather than a stand-alone condition.

15. Amatzia Baram, "The Future of Ba'thist Iraq: Power Structure, Challenges, and Prospects," in *The Politics of Change in the Middle East,* ed. Robert Satloff (Boulder, CO: Westview, 1993), p. 36; Alasdair Drysdale, "The Syrian Armed Forces in National Politics: The Role of the Geographic and Ethnic Periphery," in *Soldiers, Peasants and Bureaucrats,* ed. Kolkowicz and Korbonski, pp. 52–62; Anthony Pascal, Michael Kennedy, and Steven Rosen, *Men and Arms in the Middle East: The Human Factor in Military Modernization,* RAND R-2460-NA, Santa Monica, June 1979, p. 41; and Martin Van Creveld, "The Human Dimension of War," in *The Lessons of Recent Wars in the Third World,* ed. Robert Harkavy and Stephanie Neuman, Vol. 2 (Lexington, MA: Lexington Books, 1987), p. 80.

16. Be'eri, *Army Officers in Arab Politics and Society,* p. 108.

17. Adeed Dawisha, "Saudi Arabia's Search for Security," in *Regional Security in the Middle East,* ed. Charles Tripp (London: IISS, 1984), p. 16; Thomas L. McNaugher, "Arms and Allies on the Arabian Peninsula, *Orbis*, Vol. 28, No. 3, Fall 1984, pp. 503–504; Peter Wilson and Douglas Graham, *Saudi Arabia: The Coming Storm* (Armonk, NY: M. E. Sharpe, 1994), p. 146.

18. Be'eri, *Army Officers in Arab Politics and Society,* p. 345; Dupuy, *Elusive Victory,* p. 378; Richard Gabriel, ed., *Antagonists in the Middle East,* pp. 29–35; James Lunt, *Hussein of Jordan* (London: MacMillan, 1989), pp. 29–50; Pascal, et al., *Men and Arms in the Middle East,* p. 41; Amos Perlmutter, *Egypt: The Praetorian State* (New Brunswick, NJ: Transaction, 1974), pp. 56–57.

19. Baram, p. 36; Hanna Batatu, "Political Power and Social Structure in Syria and Iraq," in *Arab Society: Continuity and Change,* ed. Samih K. Farsoun (London: Croom Helm, 1985), pp. 40–45; Fuad I, Khuri, "The Study of Civil-Military Relations in Modernizing Societies in the Middle East," p. 22; John S. Wagner, "Iraq: A Military Assessment," in *Fighting Armies: Antagonists in the Middle East,* ed. Richard Gabriel (Westport, CT: Greenwood Press, 1983), pp. 63–78.

20. Hanna Batatu, "Political Power and Social Structure in Syria and Iraq," in *Arab Society: Continuity and Change,* ed. Samih K. Farsoun (London: Croom Helm, 1985), pp. 37–40; Be'eri, *Army Officers in Arab Politics and Society,* p. 336; Cordesman, *The Arab-Israeli Military Balance and the Art of Operations,* pp. 45–46; Drysdale, "The Syrian Armed Forces in National Politics," p. 52, 69; Michael Eisenstadt, *Arming for Peace? Syria's Elusive Quest for Strategic Parity,* Policy Paper No. 31 (Washington, DC: The Washington Institute for Near East Policy, 1992), pp. 57–61; John Keegan, *World Armies* (London: MacMillan, 1979) p. 687; and Itamar Rabinovich, "Continuity and Change in the Ba'th Regime in Syria," in Rabinovich and Shaked eds., *From June to October* (New Brunswick: Transaction Books, 1978) esp. pp. 220–221.

21. For a concurring view, see Adrian Florea, "Spatial Rivalry and Coups against Dictators," *Security Studies,* published online at www.tandfonline.com/doi/abs/10.1080/09636412.2017.1360072, accessed on May 11, 2018: 1–26.

22. The considerable documentary and interview material gathered by the US military after the 2003 invasion of Iraq is particularly revealing in driving these points home. See Williamson Murray and Kevin M. Woods, *The Iran-Iraq War: A Military and Strategic History* (Cambridge: Cambridge University Press, 2014); Kevin M. Woods, *The Mother of All Battles: Saddam Hussein's Strategic Plan for the Persian Gulf War* (Annapolis, MD: US Naval Institute Press, 2008); Woods et. al., *Saddam's Generals.*

23. For the latest assessments of Kursk, see George M. Nipe, *Blood, Steel, and Myth*; Dennis E. Showalter, *Armor and Blood*; Valeriy Zamulin, "The Battle of Kursk: New Findings," *The Journal of Slavic Military Studies* Vol. 25 No. 3 (2012); Valeriy Zamulin, *Demolishing the Myth,* trans. and ed. Stuart Britton (Solihull, UK: Helion, 2011).

24. For a great description of how this worked in practice in a highly politicized military, see the lengthy interview with one of Saddam's military intelligence commanders in Woods et al., *Saddam's Generals,* pp. 87–110.

25. See for instance, Amatzia Baram, "Deterrence Lessons from Iraq: Rationality Is Not the Only Key to Containment," *Foreign Affairs,* Vol. 91, No. 4 (July/August 2012); Kevin M. Woods, David Palkki, and Mark Stout, eds., *The Saddam Tapes: The Inner Workings of a Tyrant's Regime 1978–2001* (Cambridge: Cambridge University Press, 2011); Woods et al., *Saddam's Generals,* esp. the interview with General Raad Hamdani, who repeatedly

challenged Saddam's strategic assessment of various military moves, pp. 29–86.

26. On morale and unit cohesion in the Red Army and the motivations of Soviet military personnel in World War II, see in particular, Glantz, *Colossus Reborn;* Catherine Merridale, *Ivan's War: Life and Death in the Red Army, 1939–1945* (New York: Metropolitan Books, 2006); Roger M. Reese, *Stalin's Reluctant Soldiers: A Social History of the Red Army, 1925–1941* (Lawrence: University of Kansas Press, 1996).

27. Lisa Anderson, correspondence with the author, April 25, 1994.

28. Manfred Halpern, *The Politics of Social Change in the Middle East and North Africa* (Princeton, NJ: Princeton University Press, 1963), pp. 256–257; Safran, *From War to War*, pp. 206–208; P. J. Vatikiotis, *The Egyptian Army in Politics* (Bloomington: Indiana University Press, 1961).

29. Be'eri, *Army Officers in Arab Politics and Society*; Fisher, *The Military in the Middle East,* pp. 254–255.

30. Theda Skocpol, *States and Social Revolutions: A Comparative Analysis of France, Russia and China* (New York: Cambridge University Press, 1979); Theda Skocpol, *Social Revolutions in the Modern World* (New York: Cambridge University Press, 1994).

31. Lawrence Kapp, "Military Officer Personnel Management: Key Concepts and Statutory Provisions," Congressional Research Service, Report 7-5700, R44496, May 10, 2016, p. 8.

32. William O. Staudenmaier, "Defense Planning in Iraq: An Alternative Perspective," in Stephanie Neuman, ed., *Defense Planning in Less-Industrialized States* (Lexington: Lexington Books, 1984), p. 54.

33. Clark, *Barbarossa: The Russian-German Conflict,* p. 34; Peter Whitewood, *The Red Army and the Great Terror: Stalin's Purge of the Soviet Military* (Lawrence: University of Kansas Press, 2015). Stephen McLaughlin notes that the same pattern held in the Soviet Navy. See Stephen McLaughlin, "USSR: The Voenno-Morskoi Flot SSR," in *On Seas Contested: The Seven Great Navies of the Second World War, ed.* Vincent P. O'Hara, W. David Dickson, and Richard Worth (Annapolis, MD: The Naval Institute Press, 2010), p. 254.

34. Florence Gaub, *Military Integration after Civil Wars: Multiethnic Armies, Identity, and Post-Conflict Reconstruction* (London: Routledge, 2011), p. 22.

35. In particular, see Paul Michael Bremner, "Soviet Troop Control: The Debate from 1963–1973," SM Thesis, Massachusetts Institute of Technology, 1984, p. 264; Donnelly, *Red Banner,* pp. 82–139; Erickson, *The Road to Berlin*; John Erickson et. al., *Soviet Ground Forces,* pp. 16–28; Forczyk, *Tank Warfare on the Eastern Front: Schwerpunkt,* esp. pp. 17, 34–36; David M. Glantz, *Stumbling Colossus: The Red Army on the Eve of World War* (Lawrence: University of Kansas Press, 1998), esp. pp. 33–40; Glantz, *Colossus Reborn,* esp. pp. 466–475.

36. On the comparative tactical effectiveness of German and Russian military formations, see Karl-Heinz Frieser *ed., Germany and the Second World War, Volume VIII: The Eastern Front 1943–1944, The War in the East and on the Neighbouring Fronts* (Oxford: Oxford University Press, 2017); C. J. Dick, *From Defeat to Victory: The Eastern Front, Summer 1944* (Lawrence: University of Kansas Press, 2016), esp. pp. 89–159.

37. Clark, *Barbarossa*, p. 20.

38. For some recent work on Hitler's politicization of the Wehrmacht and its impact on German fortunes, see Rolf-Dieter Müller, *Hitler's Wehrmacht, 1935–1945* (Lexington: University of Kentucky Press, 2016), esp. pp. 7–78, 155–198; Ben H. Shepherd, *Hitler's Soldiers: The German Army in the Third Reich* (New Haven, CT: Yale University Press, 2016), esp. pp. 3–21, 242–273, 376–396; Bernd Wegner, "Part VI: The War against the Soviet Union, 1942–1943," in *Germany and the Second World War, Volume VI: The Global War,* ed. Horst Boog, Werner Rahn, Reinhard Stumpf, and Bernd Wegner, trans. Ewald Osers, John Brownjohn, Patricia Crampton, and Louise Wilmot (Oxford: Oxford University Press, 2001), esp. pp. 1229–1230; Wolfram Wette, *The Wehrmacht: History, Myth, Reality*, trans. Deborah Lucas Schneider (Cambridge, MA: Harvard University Press 2006), esp. pp. 150–156.

39. James Dunkerley, "Central America: Collapse of the Military System," in *The Political Dilemmas of Military Regimes*, ed. Christopher Clapham and George Philip (London: Croom Helm, 1985), p. 196.

40. Dunkerley, "Central America," pp. 190–192.

41. Monica Duffy Toft, *Securing the Peace: The Durable Settlement of Civil Wars* (Princeton, NJ: Princeton University Press, 2010), p. 86.

42. Katherine Swift Gravino and David R. Segal, "The Empire Strikes Back: Military Professionalism in the South Atlantic War," in *The Regionalization of War*, ed. James Brown and William Snyder (New Brunswick, NJ: Transaction Books, 1990), p. 20.

43. Stephanie Cronin, *Armies and State-Building in the Middle East* (London: I. B. Tauris, 2014), esp. pp. 186–200; Steven R. Ward, *Immortal: A Military History of Iran and Its Armed Forces* (Washington, DC: Georgetown University Press, 2009), pp. 200–201, 208–210.

44. Murray and Woods, *The Iran-Iraq War*, p. 77.

45. William F. Hickman, *Ravaged and Reborn: The Iranian Army, 1982* (Washington, DC: The Brookings Institute, 1982), pp. 4–5.

46. Edgar O'Ballance, *The Gulf War* (London: Brassey's, 1988), p. 15.

47. O'Ballance, *The Gulf War*, p. 47.

48. Cronin, *Armies and State-Building in the Middle East*, pp. 133–137, 197–200.

49. Gregory F. Rose, "The Post-Revolutionary Purge of Iran's Armed Forces: A Revisionist Assessment," *Iranian Studies* Vol. 17, No. 2/3 (Spring-Summer 1984), pp. 153–194. Also see Ward, *Immortal*, pp. 228–230.

50. Murray and Woods, *The Iran-Iraq War*, pp. 68–75.

51. O'Ballance, *The Gulf War*, pp. 81–82.

52. Manfred Halpern, "The Army," in *Readings in Arab Middle Eastern Societies and Cultures*, ed. Abdulla M. Lutfiyya and Charles W. Churchill (The Hague: Mouton, 1970), pp. 431–432.

53. Rapoport, "The Praetorian Army," p. 258. See also his discussion of politicization of the Roman army and its impact on senior versus junior levels of command on pp. 257–258.

Chapter 6

1. On the praetorian politicization of the Egyptian armed forces, see Aboul-Enein, ed., *Reconstructing a Shattered Egyptian Army*, esp. pp. 6–9, 47.

2. Aboul-Enein, ed., *Reconstructing a Shattered Egyptian Army*, pp. 59–74.

3. Pollack, *Arabs at War*, p. 104.

4. Hassan El Badri, Taha El Magdoub, and Mohammed Dia El Din Zohdy, *The Ramadan War, 1973* (New York: Hippocrene, 1974), p. 18; Field Marshal Mohamed Abdel Ghani El-Gamasy, *The October War,* trans. Gilian Potter, Nadra Marcos, and Rosette Frances (Cairo: The American University in Cairo Press, 1993), pp. 155–157; Mohammed Heikal, "General Ismail and the War—Interview with Lt. General Ismail," *Journal of Palestine Studies*, Vol. 3, No. 2 (1974), pp. 217–219; The Insight Team of the London Sunday Times, *The Yom Kippur War* (New York: Doubleday, 1974), p. 224; Ibrahim Karawan, "Egypt's Defense Policy," in *Defense Planning in Less-Industrialized States,* ed. Stephanie Neuman (Lexington, MA: Lexington Books, 1984), p. 174; Lon O. Nordeen and David Nicole, *Phoenix over the Nile: A History of Egyptian Airpower, 1932–1994* (Washington, DC: Smithsonian Institution Press, 1996), pp. 257, 278; Lt. General Saad El-Shazli, *The Crossing of Suez* (San Francisco: American Mideast Research, 1980), pp. 17–47.

5. Shazli, *The Crossing of Suez*, p. 42

6. Chaim Herzog, *The Arab-Israeli Wars* (New York: Random House, 1982), pp. 34–35.

7. Baker, *Sadat and After,* p. 188; Dupuy, *Elusive Victory*, pp. 346–348; Heikal, "General Ismail and the War," pp. 217–219; The Insight Team of the London Sunday Times, *The Yom Kippur War,* p. 211; Edgar O'Ballance, *No Victor, No Vanquished: The Yom Kippur War* (London: Barrie and Jenkins, 1979), p. 157; Pollack, *Arabs at War*, p. 100.

8. Pollack, *Arabs at War*, pp. 106–107.

9. Quoted in The Insight Team of the London Sunday Times, *The Yom Kippur War,* p. 221.

10. Dupuy, *Elusive Victory*, pp. 488–489.

11. Author's interview with Major General Amnon Reshef, September 1996.

12. Avraham Adan, *On the Banks of the Suez,* 1991 ed. (Novato, CA: Presidio Press, 1991), p. 388. Both of these anecdotes are from Israeli communications intercepts at the time.

13. Pollack, *Arabs at War,* pp. 124–125.

14. Dupuy, *Elusive Victory,* pp. 550–556, 609; Insight Team, 188–189; Pollack, *Arabs at War,* p. 125; author's interview with Lt. General Binyamin Peled, IAF (Ret.), September 1996.

15. Lon Nordeen and David Nicolle, *Phoenix over the Nile: A History of Egyptian Air Power, 1932–1994* (Smithsonian Institution Press, Washington, D.C., 1996), p. 301.

16. Pollack, *Arabs at War,* p. 125.

Chapter 7

1. For a concurring assessment by the US government team that interviewed former Iraqi generals regarding their experiences in the Iran-Iraq War, see Woods et al., *Saddam's Generals,* starting with p. 7.

2. Author's interview with former Iraqi senior military officer, November 1998. Again, for concurring conclusions as well as the statements of other Iraqi generals who participated in the operation, see Woods et al., *Saddam's Generals,* including pp. 8–13; Murray and Woods, *The Iran-Iraq War,* pp. 95–98.

3. For more on this, see Woods et al., *Saddam's Generals,* including pp. 19–20.

4. Woods et al., *Saddam's Generals,* including pp. 190–195.

5. Wagner, "Iraq," p. 70.

6. For more detailed conversations about Saddam's depoliticization from Iraqi generals who lived through it, see Woods et al., *Saddam's Generals,* including pp. 12–15.

7. For some specific examples, see Woods et al., *Saddam's Generals,* including pp. 31, 33, 35–36, 50, 113.

8. Of course, there were limits to this. Saddam generally preferred to promote Sunni Arabs over Shi'ite Arabs or Kurds, and a competent officer with ties to Saddam invariably had a better chance than an equally competent officer without the same connections. See Batatu, "Political Power and Social Structure in Syria and Iraq," p. 40.

9. Murray and Woods, *The Iran-Iraq War,* p. 226.

10. Woods et al., *Saddam's Generals,* including p. 77.

11. Murray and Woods, *The Iran-Iraq War,* pp. 302–303.

12. There were considerable numbers of Egyptian military officers attached to the Iraqi armed forces as advisers in the latter part of the Iran-Iraq War, and the Egyptians claim that they taught the Iraqis to script their operations. The Iraqis insist they hit upon the same method without any input from the Egyptians. So far, there is no way of knowing who is right.

13. "Fourth Part of Saddam's al-Faw Meeting," in FBIS-NES-93-081, April 29, 1993, p. 30.

14. Woods et al., *Saddam's Generals*, pp. 102–109.

15. Army Component, United States Central Command (ARCENT), *Battlefield Reconstruction Study: The 100 Hour Ground War*, April 20, 1991, Declassified version, p. 30; Capt. Michael Bigelow, "The Faw Peninsula: A Battle Analysis," *Military Intelligence*, April–June 1991, p. 16; Cordesman and Wagner, *The Lessons of Modern War, Volume II*, p. 414; Lawrence Freedman and Efraim Karsh, *The Gulf Conflict, 1990–1991* (Princeton, NJ: Princeton University Press, 1993), p. 25; Michael R. Gordon and General Bernard E. Trainor, *The Generals' War: The Inside Story of the Conflict in the Gulf* (Boston: Little, Brown, 1995), p. 38; Eliot A. Cohen, General Editor, *The Gulf War Air Power Survey, Volume II, Part I: Operations*, hereafter referred to as GWAPS (Washington, DC: GPO, 1993), p. 198.

16. Ward, *Immortal*, 293.

17. This is what is described in Kevin M. Woods et al., *The Iraqi Perspectives Report: Saddan's Senior Leadership on Operation Iraqi Freedom from the Official U.S. Joint Forces Command Report* (Annapolis, MD: US Naval Institute Press, 2006), pp. 25–32, 39–64.

18. See for instance, Woods et al., *Saddam's Generals*, p. 73.

19. "Gen. Adnan Khairallah, 50, Dies; Iraqi Defense Chief and Adviser,' *The New York Times*, May 7, 1989; Daniel Williams, "Defector's Air Saddam's Family Affairs," *The Washington Post*, August 14, 1995.

20. "Stand-Off in the Gulf: Iraq's Defense Minister Replaced by Hero of the War against Iran," *The New York Times*, December 13, 1990.

21. Using comprehensive U-2 imagery of the entire theater, CIA photoanalysts counted 3,475 Iraqi tanks and 3,080 armored personnel carriers in the Kuwaiti Theater of Operations. They also determined that roughly one-third of those armored vehicles did not move or fight during the Coalition ground offensive. There were at least three common reasons that these vehicles did nothing during the ground war: they had been destroyed or immobilized by air strikes before the ground war began, they were inoperable because the Iraqis had largely stopped performing routine maintenance for fear of air strikes, or their crews fled either during the air campaign or the ground campaign. Based on accounts from Iraqi defectors and POWs, the distribution among these three problems appears about even, but it is difficult to know for sure. Consequently, the best we can say is that air strikes probably destroyed at least 600 Iraqi armored vehicles, and no more than about 1,800, although the right number is probably around 800–1,000. Central Intelligence Agency, *Operation Desert Storm: A Snapshot of the Battlefield* (Washington, DC: CIA, September 1993); *GWAPS, Vol. II, Part II: Effects and Effectiveness*, pp. 207–220.

22. Pollack, *Arabs at War*, pp. 246, 619 fn. 122.

23. ARCENT, *Battlefield Reconstruction Study,* p. 97.

24. CIA, *Snapshot of the Battlefield.*

25. Brig. Gen. Scales Jr., *Certain Victory,* p. 298.

26. Murray Hammick, "Iraqi Obstacles and Defensive Positions," *International Defense Review,* September 1991, p. 991.

27. For a superb, firsthand account of this process see Zacchea and Kemp, *The Ragged Edge.*

28. The canonical ratio is 1 security provider for every 50 civilians in a low-intensity conflict. See James T. Quinlivan, "Force Requirements in Stability Operations," *Parameters,* Winter 1995, pp. 56–69.

29. C. J. Chivers, "After Retreat, Iraqi Soldiers Fault Officers," *The New York Times,* July 1, 2014; Derek Harvey and Michael Pregent, "Who's to Blame for Iraq Crisis," CNN.com, June 12, 2014; Ned Parker, Isabel Coles, and Raheem Salman, "Special Report: How Mosul Fell—An Iraqi General Disputes Baghdad's Story," *Reuters,* October 14, 2014; David Zucchino, "Why Iraqi Army Can't Fight, Despite $25 Billion in U.S. Aid, Training," *Los Angeles Times,* November 3, 2014.

30. Michael Knights, "The Future of Iraq's Armed Forces," Al-Bayan Center for Planning and Studies, Baghdad, March 2016, p. 112.

31. Hamza Hendawi and Qassim Abdul-Zahra, "Humiliation at Rout Hits Iraqi Military Hard," Associated Press, June 18, 2014; Alissa J. Rubin and Michael R. Gordon, "Iraq's Military Seen as Unlikely to Turn the Tide," *New York Times,* June 22, 2014; Jessica Stern and J. M. Berger, *ISIS: The State of Terror* (New York: HarperCollins, 2015), p. 45; Zucchino, "Why Iraqi Army Can't Fight."

32. Hendawi and Abdul-Zahra, "Humiliation at Rout Hits Iraqi Military Hard."

33. Chivers, "After Retreat, Iraqi Soldiers Fault Officers;" International Institute for Strategic Studies, *The Military Balance, 2015* (London: Routledge, 2015), pp. 303–306; Parker et al. "Special Report"; Rubin and Gordon, "Iraq's Military Seen as Unlikely to Turn the Tide"; Stern and Berger, *ISIS,* p. 45; Zucchino, "Why Iraqi Army Can't Fight."

34. For accounts of the tenacious resistance of the Republican Guards at the 73 Easting, see ARCENT, *Battlefield Reconstruction Study,* pp. 117–121; Vince Crawley, "Ghost Troop's Battle at the 73 Easting," *Armor,* May–June 1991, pp. 7–12; Col. Gregory Fontenot, "Fright Night: Task Force 2/34 Armor," *Military Review,* January 1993, pp. 38–51; Michael J. Mazarr, Don M. Snider, and James A. Blackwell Jr., *Desert Storm* (Boulder, CO; Westview, 1993), p. 147; Jim Tice, "Coming Through: The Big Red Raid," *Army Times,* August 26, 1991, pp. 13–20; Steve Vogel, "A Swift Kick: 2nd ACR's Taming of the Guard," *Army Times,* August 5, 1991, pp. 28–61; Steve Vogel, "Metal Rain: 'Old Ironsides' and Iraqis Who Wouldn't Back Down," *Army Times,* September 16, 1991, p. 16; Steve Vogel, "The Tip of the Spear," *Army Times,* January 13, 1992, pp. 13–54; and US News and World Report,

Triumph without Victory (New York: Times Books, 1992), pp. 336–342, 351–370.

Chapter 8

1. Thomas R. Cantwell, "The Army of South Vietnam: A Military and Political History, 1950–1975," Doctoral Thesis, University of New South Wales, July 4, 1989, pp. 16–17. See also Nguyen Cao Ky, *How We Lost the Vietnam War*, First Scarborough Books ed. (New York: Stein and Day, 1978), pp. 125, 128–130.
2. Cantwell, "The Army of South Vietnam," esp. pp. 30–39, 101–124, 128–135, 141–150; Anthony James Joes, *The War for South Vietnam, 1954–1975*, Revised ed. (Westport, CT: Praeger, 2001), pp. 77, 86–87; Lewis Sorley, *A Better War: The Unexamined Victories and Final Tragedy of America's Last Years in Vietnam*, Paperback ed. (New York: Harcourt Brace, 1999), pp. 186, 265–266.
3. Joes, *The War for South Vietnam, 1954–1975*, pp. 73–86.
4. Cantwell, "The Army of South Vietnam," p. 39.
5. Cantwell, "The Army of South Vietnam," pp. 39, 62–63.
6. Cantwell, "The Army of South Vietnam," pp. 59–62; Joes, *The War for South Vietnam, 1954–1975*, p. 77.
7. Cantwell, "The Army of South Vietnam," pp. 124–145; Joes, *The War for South Vietnam, 1954–1975*, pp. 80–81.
8. Joes, *The War for South Vietnam, 1954–1975*, p. 82.
9. Joes, *The War for South Vietnam, 1954–1975*, pp. 81–93. Quote is on p. 93.
10. George J. Veith, *Black April: The Fall of South Vietnam 1973–75* (New York: Encounter Books, 2012), pp. 24–29.
11. Nguyen, *How We Lost the Vietnam War*, p. 105.
12. Cantwell, "The Army of South Vietnam," p. 39; Sorley, *A Better War*, p. 188.
13. Dale Andrade, *America's Last Vietnam Battle: Halting Hanoi's 1972 Easter Offensive* (Topeka: University Press of Kansas, 1995), p. 32.
14. Cantwell, "The Army of South Vietnam," p. 39.
15. Joes, *The War for South Vietnam, 1954–1975*, p. 91.
16. Andrade, *America's Last Vietnam Battle*, p. 31.
17. Cantwell, "The Army of South Vietnam," p. 130.
18. Allan E. Goodman, *An Institutional Profile of the South Vietnamese Officer Corps* (Santa Monica, CA: RAND, 1970), p. vi.
19. Cantwell, "The Army of South Vietnam," p. 131.
20. Cantwell, "The Army of South Vietnam," pp. 127–128.
21. Cantwell, "The Army of South Vietnam," pp. 130–131.
22. Andrew Wiest, *Vietnam's Forgotten Army: Heroism and Betrayal in the ARVN* (New York: New York University Press, 2008), p. 155.
23. Joes, *The War for South Vietnam, 1954–1975*, p. 89.
24. Cantwell, "The Army of South Vietnam," pp. 101, 130–133; Joes, *The War for South Vietnam, 1954–1975*, pp. 91–93; Nguyen, *How We Lost the Vietnam War*,

pp. 128, 151; James H. Willbanks, *Abandoning Vietnam: How America Left and South Vietnam Lost Its War* (Lawrence: University of Kansas Press, 2008), p. 5.

25. Andrade, *America's Last Vietnam Battle*, pp. 489–490.

26. Joes, *The War for South Vietnam, 1954–1975*, p. 99.

27. On the Tet Offensive, see Joes, *The War for South Vietnam, 1954–1975*, pp. 98–104; Stanley Karnow, *Vietnam: A History*, Revised and updated paperback ed. (New York: Penguin Books, 1991), pp. 536–565; Willbanks, *Abandoning Vietnam*, pp. 5–6.

28. Joes, *The War for South Vietnam, 1954–1975*, pp. 105–111; Karnow, *Vietnam*, pp. 569–612; Willbanks, *Abandoning Vietnam*, pp. 7–19; James H. Willbanks, *A Raid Too Far: Operation Lam Son 719 and Vietnamization in Laos* (College Station: Texas A&M Press, 2014), pp. 4–23.

29. Willbanks, *Abandoning Vietnam*, pp. 54–56.

30. The quote is from LTG Truong, the most successful and most respected of South Vietnam's generals. Quoted in Willbanks, *Abandoning Vietnam*, p. 55.

31. Willbanks, *Abandoning Vietnam*, p. 89.

32. Joes, *The War for South Vietnam, 1954–1975*, pp. 106–107; Karnow, *Vietnam*, pp. 606–608; Willbanks, *Abandoning Vietnam*, pp. 69–70.

33. Joes, *The War for South Vietnam, 1954–1975*, p. 106; Willbanks, *A Raid Too Far*, p. 21.

34. Willbanks, *A Raid Too Far*, p. 21; Willbanks, *Abandoning Vietnam*, pp. 79–80, 83–87.

35. Willbanks, *A Raid Too Far*, , p. 21.

36. Willbanks, *A Raid Too Far*, p. 23; Willbanks, *Abandoning Vietnam*, p. 88.

37. Willbanks, *Abandoning Vietnam*, p. 88.

38. Willbanks, *Abandoning Vietnam*, p. 88.

39. Quoted in Willbanks, *Abandoning Vietnam*, p. 89.

40. Joes, *The War for South Vietnam, 1954–1975*, p. 107; Karnow, *Vietnam*, p. 644; Willbanks, *A Raid Too Far*, pp. 27–35; Willbanks, *Abandoning Vietnam*, pp. 94–95.

41. Cantwell, "The Army of South Vietnam," p. 343; Joes, *The War for South Vietnam, 1954–1975*, p. 107; Willbanks, *A Raid Too Far*, pp. 40, 53–55, 60–63, 82–83, 103, 105, 121.

42. Andrade, *America's Last Vietnam Battle*, p. 2; Cantwell, "The Army of South Vietnam," p. 341.

43. Sorley, *A Better War*, pp. 257–258; Willbanks, *A Raid Too Far*, p. 55.

44. Willbanks, *A Raid Too Far*, pp. 52, 167

45. Karnow, *Vietnam*, p. 655; Wiest, *Vietnam's Forgotten Army*, p. 209.

46. Andrade, *America's Last Vietnam Battle*, p. 31.

47. Sorley, *A Better War*, pp. 257–258.

48. Andrade, *America's Last Vietnam Battle*, p. 35; Wiest, *Vietnam's Forgotten Army*, p. 211; Willbanks, *A Raid Too Far*, p. 55.

49. Wiest, *Vietnam's Forgotten Army*, p. 205; Willbanks, *A Raid Too Far*, pp. 87–90; Willbanks, *Abandoning Vietnam*, p. 106.

50. Willbanks, *A Raid Too Far*, pp. 117–132, 162–163.

51. Cantwell, "The Army of South Vietnam," p. 350; Joes, *The War for South Vietnam, 1954–1975*, p. 107; Sorley, *A Better War*, p. 260; Willbanks, *A Raid Too Far*, pp. 97–99, 103, 113, 137–139, 143–147, 163–169.

52. Cantwell, "The Army of South Vietnam," pp. 347, 352; "A Better War, But Good Enough?," *The Economist*, Democracy in America [blog] (October 13, 2009), available online at www.economist.com/node/20025327; Karnow, *Vietnam*, p. 645; Sorley, *A Better War*, pp. 257–258; Willbanks, *Abandoning Vietnam*, pp. 112–114; Willbanks, *A Raid Too Far*, pp. 164–167, 180.

53. Willbanks, *A Raid Too Far*, pp. 164–165.

54. Wiest, *Vietnam's Forgotten Army*, p. 227.

55. Willbanks, *A Raid Too Far*, p. 104. On Lam's many mistakes, see for instance, Willbanks, *A Raid Too Far*, pp. 105–107, 169. See also Andrade, *America's Last Vietnam Battle*, p. 2; Sorley, *A Better War*, p. 257.

56. Andrade, *America's Last Vietnam Battle*, pp. 19–27; Joes, *The War for South Vietnam, 1954–1975*, p. 108; Douglas Pike, *PAVN: People's Army of Vietnam*, Da Capo Paperback ed. (New York: Da Capo, 1986), p. 229.

57. Andrade, *America's Last Vietnam Battle*, p. 485; Phillip B. Davidson, *Vietnam at War: The History 1946–1975* (New York: Oxford University Press, 1988), pp. 595, 599–600, 609–612; Karnow, *Vietnam*, p. 618; Jeffrey Record, "Vietnam in Retrospect: Could We Have Won?," *Parameters*, Vol. 26, No. 4 (Winter 1996–1997), pp. 52–53; Military History Institute of Vietnam, *Victory in Vietnam: The Official History of the People's Army of Vietnam, 1954–1975*, trans. Merle Pribbenow (Lawrence: University of Kansas Press, 2002), pp. 237–252; Wiest, *Vietnam's Forgotten Army*, pp. 151–154; Willbanks, *Abandoning Vietnam*, pp. 56–58, 122–123.

58. Willbanks, *A Raid Too Far*, pp. 186–188.

59. Andrade, *America's Last Vietnam Battle*, pp. 23–24; Joes, *The War for South Vietnam, 1954–1975*, p. 108; Pike, *PAVN*, p. 229; G. H. Turley, *The Easter Offensive: Vietnam, 1972* (Novato, CA: Presidio, 1985, pp. 24, 270–271.

60. Andrade, *America's Last Vietnam Battle*, p. 484; Joes, *The War for South Vietnam, 1954–1975*, p. 108; Karnow, *Vietnam*, p. 657; Sorley, *A Better War*, p. 108; Turley, *The Easter Offensive*, p. 2; Willbanks, *Abandoning Vietnam*, pp. 125–126.

61. Karnow, *Vietnam*, p. 655; Turley, *The Easter Offensive*, pp. 270–271; Willbanks, *Abandoning Vietnam*, pp. 3, 128.

62. Andrade, *America's Last Vietnam Battle*, p. 25; Joes, *The War for South Vietnam, 1954–1975*, p. 108; Karnow, *Vietnam*, p. 655; Willbanks, *Abandoning Vietnam*, pp. 125–127

63. Sorley, *A Better War*, pp. 265–266; Willbanks, *A Raid Too Far*, pp. 178–180; Willbanks, *Abandoning Vietnam*, p. 116.

64. Joes, *The War for South Vietnam, 1954–1975*, p. 108; Willbanks, *Abandoning Vietnam*, p. 122, 280–281.

65. Andrade, *America's Last Vietnam Battle*, p. 35; Cantwell, "The Army of South Vietnam," pp. 356–360; Turley, *The Easter Offensive*, pp. 34–36; Willbanks, *Abandoning Vietnam*, p. 132.

66. Andrade, *America's Last Vietnam Battle*, p. 78; Turley, *The Easter Offensive*, pp. 59–60, 87–100, 105–108, 115, 128–129; Willbanks, *Abandoning Vietnam*, pp. 132–133.

67. Andrade, *America's Last Vietnam Battle*, pp. 207, 214.

68. Andrade, *America's Last Vietnam Battle*, pp. 222–250.

69. Andrade, *America's Last Vietnam Battle*, pp. 354–369; Willbanks, *Abandoning Vietnam*, pp. 135–138.

70. Andrade, *America's Last Vietnam Battle*, pp. 338, 351–352, 385–448; Joes, *The War for South Vietnam, 1954–1975*, p. 109; Karnow, *Vietnam*, p. 656; Willbanks, *Abandoning Vietnam*, pp. 137–139; James H. Willbanks, *The Battle of An Loc* (Bloomington: Indiana University Press, 2005).

71. Turley, *The Easter Offensive*, pp. 199–203, 217–218; Willbanks, *Abandoning Vietnam*, p. 135.

72. Andrade, *America's Last Vietnam Battle*, pp. 101–107; Turley, *The Easter Offensive*, pp. 217–222; Willbanks, *Abandoning Vietnam*, p. 142.

73. Joes, *The War for South Vietnam, 1954–1975*, p. 109; Turley, *The Easter Offensive*, p. 220–232, 248; Willbanks, *Abandoning Vietnam*, pp. 143–155.

74. Andrade, *America's Last Vietnam Battle*, pp. 253–256; Thomas P. McKenna, *Kontum: The Battle to Save South Vietnam* (Lexington: University of Kentucky Press, 2011); Willbanks, *Abandoning Vietnam*, p. 147.

75. Andrade, *America's Last Vietnam Battle*, pp. 288–292.

76. Andrade, *America's Last Vietnam Battle*, pp. 283–286.

77. Andrade, *America's Last Vietnam Battle*, pp. 265–266; Willbanks, *Abandoning Vietnam*, p. 147.

78. Andrade, *America's Last Vietnam Battle*, pp. 277–278; Karnow, *Vietnam*, p. 656; Willbanks, *Abandoning Vietnam*, p. 147.

79. Andrade, *America's Last Vietnam Battle*, pp. 266–267; Willbanks, *A Raid Too Far*, pp.196–197.

80. Andrade, *America's Last Vietnam Battle*, pp. 299–319, 329; Joes, *The War for South Vietnam, 1954–1975*, p. 110; Willbanks, *Abandoning Vietnam*, pp. 147–148.

81. Andrade, *America's Last Vietnam Battle*, pp. 179, 266–267; Joes, *The War for South Vietnam, 1954–1975*, p. 109; Willbanks, *Abandoning Vietnam*, pp. 148–150.

82. Cantwell, *Army of Vietnam*, pp. 370–371; Willbanks, *A Raid Too Far*, p. 197; Willbanks, *Abandoning Vietnam*, p. 152.

83. Phil Haun and Colin Jackson, "Breaker of Armies: Air Power in the Easter Offensive and the Myth of Linebacker I and II in the Vietnam War," *International Security*, Vol. 40, No. 3 (Winter 2015/16), p. 153.

84. Andrade, *America's Last Vietnam Battle*, p. 181.

85. On the importance of the US air campaign, see Andrade, *America's Last Vietnam Battle*, pp. 492–493; Matthew C. Brand, "Airpower and the 1972 Easter Offensive," Master's Thesis, US Army Command and General Staff College, Ft. Leavenworth, KS, 2007, esp. pp. 77–99; Haun and Jackson, "Breaker of Armies," pp. 139–178; Willbanks, *A Raid Too Far*, pp. 197–199; Willbanks, *Abandoning Vietnam*, pp. 158–159.

86. Quoted in Lewis Sorley, "The Real Afghan Lessons from Vietnam," *The Wall Street Journal,* Opinion, October 12, 2009. For arguments that the ARVN performance was the key to victory, see Joes, *The War for South Vietnam, 1954–1975*, pp. 110–111; Sorley, *A Better War,* p. 307.

87. For various examples of both, see Andrade, *America's Last Vietnam Battle*, pp. 135, 160, 271, 293, 294, 303; Karnow, *Vietnam*, p. 656; Turley, *The Easter Offensive*, pp. 53, 56, 58, 65, 80, 92, 133–134, 143–151, 237; Willbanks, *Abandoning Vietnam*, pp. 155–157.

88. Andrade, *America's Last Vietnam Battle*, p. 250.

89. Turley, *The Easter Offensive*, p. 134.

90. For examples of good combined arms integration by ARVN tactical formations, see Andrade, *America's Last Vietnam Battle*, pp. 95, 166–167, 181–185; Turley, *The Easter Offensive*, pp. 208–211, 230.

91. Willbanks, *Abandoning Vietnam*, p. 157.

92. For examples of ARVN maneuver, tactical counterattacks, and other aggressive tactical actions, see Andrade, *America's Last Vietnam Battle*, pp. 46–48, 68, 87, 92–93, 95–96, 166–167, 181–185, 187–197, 229, 272, 286, 292, 294, 302–303, 313, 317, 433, 454–455, 471; Turley, *The Easter Offensive*, pp. 250–261.

93. On the South Vietnamese Air Force, see Andrade, *America's Last Vietnam Battle*, pp. 69, 95, 268, 312; Turley, *The Easter Offensive*, pp. 163–164. 208.

94. Quoted in Andrade, *America's Last Vietnam Battle*, p. 69. See also Andrade, *America's Last Vietnam Battle*, p. 113, 67–69, 166–167; Turley, *The Easter Offensive*, p. 234.

95. For concurring opinions, see Sorley, *A Better War,* pp. 329–330, 333; Willbanks, *Abandoning Vietnam*, p. 158.

96. On Phu's leadership of the 1st ARVN Division, see Andrade, *America's Last Vietnam Battle*, p. 152.

97. On the critical role of American advisors in the Easter Offensive, see Karnow, *Vietnam*, p. 658; Turley, *The Easter Offensive*; Willbanks, *Abandoning Vietnam*, p. 159.

98. Andrade, *America's Last Vietnam Battle*, pp. 142–145, 147; Sorley, *A Better War,* pp. 329–330; Turley, *The Easter Offensive*, p. 265; Andrew Wiest, *Vietnam's Forgotten Army*, pp. 270–272; Willbanks, *A Raid Too Far*, p. 197.

99. Joes, *The War for South Vietnam, 1954–1975*, p. 136; Pike, *PAVN*, pp. 2, 229; Record, "Vietnam in Retrospect," p. 55; Veith, *Black April*, p. 46; Willbanks, *Abandoning Vietnam*, pp. 188–189, 208–209, 211–213, 232.

100. Davidson, *Vietnam at War*, pp. 596–597, 605–606; Joes, *The War for South Vietnam, 1954–1975*, p. 129; Nguyen, *How We Lost the Vietnam War*, p. 173; Veith, *Black April*, pp. 5–6.

101. Joes, *The War for South Vietnam, 1954–1975*, pp. 111, 129; Karnow, *Vietnam*, pp. 672–673; Veith, *Black April*, p. 117; Willbanks, *Abandoning Vietnam*, p. 201.

102. Karnow, *Vietnam*, p. 673; Veith, *Black April*, pp. 48, 56–58, 61–62.

103. Veith, *Black April*, p. 58.

104. Veith, *Black April*, pp. 77, 82, 96, 98, 143–145; Willbanks, *Abandoning Vietnam*, pp. 203–204.

105. Willbanks, *Abandoning Vietnam*, pp. 4, 196–197, 220.

106. Willbanks, *Abandoning Vietnam*, pp. 218, 285.

107. Cantwell, "The Army of South Vietnam," pp. 380–381; Joes, *The War for South Vietnam, 1954–1975*, pp. 130–131; Karnow, *Vietnam*, p. 675; Willbanks, *Abandoning Vietnam*, pp. 206–207.

108. Joes, *The War for South Vietnam, 1954–1975*, p. 136; Record, "Vietnam in Retrospect," p. 55; Veith, *Black April*, pp. 78–79; Willbanks, *Abandoning Vietnam*, pp. 4, 196–197, 220–222.

109. Willbanks, *Abandoning Vietnam*, pp. 222–227.

110. Willbanks, *Abandoning Vietnam*, pp. 224–229.

111. Joes, *The War for South Vietnam, 1954–1975*, p. 138; Veith, *Black April*, pp. 153–155; Willbanks, *Abandoning Vietnam*, pp. 227–235.

112. Joes, *The War for South Vietnam, 1954–975*, pp. 138–139; Veith, *Black April*, pp. 176–181; Willbanks, *Abandoning Vietnam*, pp. 235–236.

113. Joes, *The War for South Vietnam, 1954–1975*, pp. 139–141; Veith, *Black April*, pp. 179–181; Willbanks, *Abandoning Vietnam*, pp. 237–238.

114. Veith, *Black April*, pp. 181, 209; Willbanks, *Abandoning Vietnam*, pp. 239–245.

115. The quote is from Willbanks, *Abandoning Vietnam*, pp. 243–244. For the general points, see Willbanks, *Abandoning Vietnam*, pp. 241–245.

116. Veith, *Black April*, p. 234; Willbanks, *Abandoning Vietnam*, p. 245.

117. Joes, *The War for South Vietnam, 1954–1975*, pp. 142–143; Veith, *Black April*, pp. 264–305; Willbanks, *Abandoning Vietnam*, pp. 246–253.

118. Joes, *The War for South Vietnam, 1954–1975*, p. 143; Veith, *Black April*, pp. 346–347; Willbanks, *Abandoning Vietnam*, pp. 253–255.

119. Veith, *Black April*, pp. 436–459; Willbanks, *Abandoning Vietnam*, pp. 264–267.

120. Veith, *Black April*, pp. 466–467, 475.

121. Veith, *Black April*, pp. 466–496.

122. Veith, *Black April*, p. 495.

123. Veith, *Black April*, p. 340.

124. For examples of ARVN counterattacks during 1975, see Veith, *Black April*, pp. 96, 97, 158–162, 164, 247, 275, 276, 281, 294–296, 315, 402–404,

405–406, 412–413, 425, 444–447, 475–478, 484; Willbanks, *Abandoning Vietnam*, pp. 225, 226, 264–266.

125. Veith, *Black April*, pp. 444–447.

126. For their story, see Veith, *Black April*, pp. 390–392.

127. For other examples, see Veith, *Black April*, pp. 159, 215, 264–295, 304, 442–449.

128. Veith, *Black April*, pp. 405–406.

129. For instance, see Veith, *Black April*, pp. 73, 254–255.

130. Veith, *Black April*, p. 74.

131. For examples, see Veith, *Black April*, pp. 73, 162, 246–248, 256, 258, 294, 335, 337, 403, 442–444, 450.

132. Both quotes from Veith, *Black April*, pp. 356 and 371.

133. For examples, see Veith, *Black April*, pp. 164, 226, 228, 246, 248, 258, 276, 336–337, 343–344, 394, 405–406, 409, 416–417, 421, 443–451; Willbanks, *Abandoning Vietnam*, p. 266.

134. Veith, *Black April*, pp. 450–451; Willbanks, *Abandoning Vietnam*, p. 266.

135. Veith, *Black April*, p. 471.

136. For a concurring view and additional supporting evidence, see Veith, *Black April*, pp. 5–6, 73, 76, 93, 95, 96, 135–136, 147, 154, 241, 242, 256; and Wiest, *Vietnam's Forgotten Army*, pp. 268–269.

137. For additional evidence of ARVN formations fighting hard, see Veith, *Black April*, pp. 5, 73, 104, 108–109, 252, 253, 488–490.

138. For examples of RF/PF units standing tall, see Veith, *Black April*, pp. 107, 158, 244, 246, 403, 446, 487.

139. Quoted in Veith, *Black April*, p. 329.

140. Joes, *The War for South Vietnam, 1954–1975*, p. 142.

Chapter 9

1. C. L. Arceneaux, "Institutional Design, Military Rule and Regime Transition in Argentina (1976–1983): An Extension of the Remmer Thesis," *Bulletin of Latin American Research*, Vol. 6, No. 3 (1997), pp. 329–350; John F. Guilmartin Jr., "The South Atlantic War: Lessons and Analytical Guideposts—A Military Historian's Perspective," in *The Regionalization of War*, ed. James Brown and William Snyder (New Brunswick, NJ: Transaction Books, 1990), p. 60; Nora Kinzer Stewart, *Mates and Muchachos: Unit Cohesion in the Falklands/Malvinas War* (McLean, VA: Brassey's, 1991), pp. 44–45, 51–52; Paul W. Zagorski, "Civil-Military Relations and Argentine Democracy: The Armed Forces under the Menem Government," *Armed Forces and Society*, Vol. 20, No. 3 (Spring 1994), pp. 423–424.

2. Paul Eddy and Magnus Linklater, with Peter Gillman and the Sunday Times Insight Team, *The Falklands War* (London: Andre Deutsch, 1982), p. 61; Gravino and Segal, "The Empire Strikes Back," p. 20; Guilmartin, "The

South Atlantic War," p. 60; Juan Carlos Murguizur, "The South Atlantic Conflict—An Argentine Point of View," *International Defense Review*, February 1983, pp. 135–140.

3. Cordesman and Wagner, *The Lessons of Modern War, Vol. III*, p. 265; John Laffin, *Fight for the Falklands* (New York: St. Martin's Press, 1982), pp. 74–75.

4. Cordesman and Wagner, *The Lessons of Modern War, Vol. III*, p. 264; Gravino and Segal, "The Empire Strikes Back," p. 20.

5. Eddy et al., *The Falklands War*, pp. 15–22; Lawrence Freedman and Virginia Gamba-Stonehouse, *Signals of War: The Falklands Conflict of 1982* (London: Faber and Faber, 1990), pp. 103–116; Max Hastings and Simon Jenkins, *The Battle for the Falklands*, First Paperback ed. (New York: Norton, 1983), pp. 73–91; Martin Middlebrook, *The Fight for the "Malvinas": The Argentine Forces in the Falklands War* (London: Viking, 1989), pp. 16–34.

6. Freedman and Gamba-Stonehouse, *Signals of War*, p. 326; Hastings and Jenkins, *The Battle for the Falklands*, pp. 47–49; Rubén O. Moro, *The History of the South Atlantic Conflict: The War for the Malvinas*, trans. Michael Valuer (New York: Praeger, 1989), pp. 69, 81; Murguizur, "The South Atlantic Conflict," p. 136.

7. Cordesman and Wagner, *The Lessons of Modern War, Vol. III*, pp. 263–264; Freedman and Gamba-Stonehouse, *Signals of War*, p. 146; Middlebrook, *The Fight for the Malvinas*, p. 49; Moro, *The History of the South Atlantic Conflict*, p. 76; Murguizur, "The South Atlantic Conflict," p. 136.

8. Cordesman and Wagner, *The Lessons of Modern War, Vol. III*, pp. 261–262; Hastings and Jenkins, *The Battle for the Falklands*, pp. 179, 318; Laffin, *Fight for the Falklands*, pp. 43, 48, 57, 77; Middlebrook, *The Fight for the Malvinas*, pp. 63, 142. Please note that my figure for the British aircraft includes only the Harriers deployed to the Falklands and operating from the *Invincible* and *Hermes*. I have not included the half-dozen or so Vulcan bombers that conducted sporadic raids against Stanley airfield because their role in the fighting was negligible.

9. Cordesman and Wagner, *The Lessons of Modern War, Vol. III*, pp. 261, 312–313; Eddy et al., *The Falklands War*, pp. 105, 194; Freedman and Gamba-Stonehouse, *Signals of War*, p. 326; Hastings and Jenkins, *The Battle for the Falklands*, pp. 179, 318; Laffin, *Fight for the Falklands*, p. 57; Middlebrook, *The Fight for the Malvinas*, p. 64.

10. Cordesman and Wagner, *The Lessons of Modern War, Vol. III*, pp. 247–249; Gravino and Segal, "The Empire Strikes Back," p. 25; Hastings and Jenkins, *The Battle for the Falklands*, pp. 146–157; Middlebrook, *The Fight for the Malvinas*, pp. 84–103.

11. Cordesman and Wagner, *The Lessons of Modern War, Vol. III*, pp. 306–310; Hastings and Jenkins, *The Battle for the Falklands*, p. 207; Middlebrook, *The Fight for the Malvinas*, pp. 90–91.

12. Middlebrook, *The Fight for the Malvinas*, pp. 74–75.

13. Eddy et al., *The Falklands War*, pp. 200–208; Freedman and Gamba-Stonehouse, *Signals of War*, pp. 358–369; Gravino and Segal, "The Empire Strikes Back," p. 27; Hastings and Jenkins, *The Battle for the Falklands*, pp. 204–228; Laffin, *The Fight for the Falklands*, pp. 90–95; Middlebrook, *The Fight for the Malvinas*, pp. 151–175.

14. Freedman and Gamba-Stonehouse, *Signlas of War*, pp. 358, 363–364; Hastings and Jenkins, p. 323.

15. Patrick Bishop and John Witherow, *The Winter War* (London: Quartet Books, 1982), p. 92; Freedman and Gamba-Stonehouse, *Signals of War*, pp, 371–372; Hastings and Jenkins, *The Battle for the Falklands*, pp. 241; Middlebrook, *The Fight for the Malvinas*, pp. 178–179, 184, 197.

16. Max Arthur, *Above All Courage, The Falklands Front Line: First-Hand Accounts* (London: Sidgwick and Jackson, 1985), p. 144; Bishop and Witherow, *The Winter War*, pp. 92–94; Cordesman and Wagner, *The Lessons of Modern War, Vol. III*, pp. 255–256, 316; Eddy et al., *The Falklands War*, pp. 220–229; Hastings and Jenkins, *The Battle for the Falklands*, pp. 238–262; Middlebrook, *The Fight for the Malvinas*, pp. 182–197; Moro, *The History of the South Atlantic Conflict*, pp. 257–267; Julian Thompson, *No Picnic: 3 Commando Brigade in the South Atlantic, 1982*, Revised ed. (London: Leo Cooper, 1992).

17. Cordesman and Wagner, *The Lessons of Modern War, Vol. III*, pp. 256–258.

18. Cordesman and Wagner, *The Lessons of Modern War, Vol. III*, p. 258; Eddy et. al. pp. 243–244, 250–251; Freedman and Gamba-Stonehouse, *Signals of War*, pp. 385, 395–397; Hastings and Jenkins, *The Battle for the Falklands*, p. 285; Middlebrook, *The Fight for the Malvinas*, pp. 216, 220, 228, 244; Moro, *The History of the South Atlantic Conflict*, p. 308.

19. Arthur, *Above All Courage*, pp. 223–226; Cordesman and Wagner, *The Lessons of Modern War, Vol. III,*. 258; Freedman and Gamba-Stonehouse, *Signals of War*, p. 396; Middlebrook, *The Fight for the Malvinas*, pp. 232, 235–236; Moro, *The History of the South Atlantic Conflict*, pp. 306–307; Thompson, *No Picnic*, pp. 126–127

20. Bishop and Witherow, *The Winter War*, p. 125; Freedman and Gamba-Stonehouse, *Signals of War*, p. 396; Middlebrook, *The Fight for the Malvinas*, pp. 224, 237; Thompson, *No Picnic*, p. 133.

21. Freedman and Gamba-Stonehouse, *Signals of War*, p. 396; Middlebrook, pp. 241–243.

22. Moro, *The History of the South Atlantic Conflict*, p. 309.

23. Eddy et. al., p. 399; Hastings and Jenkins, *The Battle for the Falklands*, pp. 304–307; Middlebrook, *The Fight for the Malvinas*, pp. 263–267; Moro, *The History of the South Atlantic Conflict*, p. 310; Thompson, *No Picnic*, pp. 151- 152.

24. Middlebrook, *The Fight for the Malvinas*, p. 267.

25. Arthur, *Above All Courage*, p. 296; Cordesman and Wagner, *The Lessons of Modern War, Vol. III*, p. 259; Eddy et al., *The Falklands War*, p. 251; Freedman

and Gamba-Stonehouse, *Signals of War*, p. 398; Hastings and Jenkins, *The Battle for the Falklands*, pp. 301–302; Middlebrook, *The Fight for the Malvinas*, pp. 251–262, 284–286; Stewart, *Mates and Muchachos*, pp. 104–105, 108.

26. Cordesman and Wagner, *The Lessons of Modern War, Vol. III*, p. 267; Hastings and Jenkins, *The Battle for the Falklands*, p. 312; Middlebrook, *The Fight for the Malvinas*, pp. 282–286; Harlan K. Ullman, "Profound or Perfunctory: Observations on the South Atlantic Conflict," in *The Lessons of Recent Wars in the Third World, Volume I*, ed. Robert Harkavy and Stephanie Neuman (Lexington, MA: Lexington Books, 1986), p. 244.

27. Bishop and Witherow, *The Winter War*, p. 142; Cordesman and Wagner, *The Lessons of Modern War, Vol. III*, pp. 240–241, 264; Gravino and Segal, "The Empire Strikes Back," p. 19; Hastings and Jenkins, *The Battle for the Falklands*, pp. 177, 323; Middlebrook, *The Fight for the Malvinas*, pp. 49–51; Murguizur, "The South Atlantic Conflict," p. 136; Stewart, *Mates and Muchachos*, pp.130–131.

28. Bishop and Witherow, *The Winter War*, p. 142.

29. Eddy et al., *The Falklands War*, p. 382; Hastings and Jenkins, *The Battle for the Falklands*, p. 177.

30. Hastings and Jenkins, *The Battle for the Falklands*, p. 177.

31. Arthur, *Above All Courage*, p. 144; Cordesman and Wagner, *The Lessons of Modern War, Vol. III*, pp. 265–266; Gravino and Segal, "The Empire Strikes Back," p. 32; Hastings and Jenkins, *The Battle for the Falklands*, p. 295; Nora Kinzer Stewart, "A Case Study in Cohesion: South Atlantic Conflict, 1982," *Military Review*, April, 1989, p. 37; Stewart, *Mates and Muchachos*, p. 134.

32. Arthur, *Above All Courage*, p. 202; Bishop and Witherow, *The Winter War*, p. 27; Eddy et al., *The Falklands War*, pp. 254, 374; Gravino and Segal, "The Empire Strikes Back," p. 29; Hastings and Jenkins, *The Battle for the Falklands*, p. 262; Stewart, *Mates and Muchachos*, pp. 134–135.

33. Bishop and Witherow, *The Winter War*, p. 27; Stewart, "A Case Study in Cohesion," p. 36; Thompson, *No Picnic*, p. 143.

34. Thompson, *No Picnic*, p. 143.

35. Hastings and Jenkins, *The Battle for the Falklands*, p. 243; Middlebrook, *The Fight for the Malvinas*, pp. 184, 187–188, 192, 241; Moro, *The History of the South Atlantic Conflict*, p. 307.

36. Arthur, *Above All Courage*, pp. 154, 211; Freedman and Gamba-Stonehouse, *Signals of War*, pp. 375, 396–398; Hastings and Jenkins, *The Battle for the Falklands*, pp. 306–307; Middlebrook, *The Fight for the Malvinas*, pp. 184, 188–190, 241, 260, 264, 267; Moro, *The History of the South Atlantic Conflict*, pp. 263, 306; Thompson, *No Picnic*, p. 152.

37. See for example, Freedman and Gamba-Stonehouse, *Signals of War*, p. 398.

38. Arthur, *Above All Courage*, 237; Eddy et al., *The Falklands War*, pp. 372, 377–378, 380; Hastings and Jenkins, *The Battle for the Falklands*, pp. 177, 290; Middlebrook, *The Fight for the Malvinas*, p. 181; Thompson, *No Picnic*, pp. 111–113.

39. See for example, Arthur, *Above All Courage,* pp. 160, 191, 198–201, 251, 293–294; Bishop and Witherow, *The Winter War,* pp. 27, 92; Cordesman and Wagner, *The Lessons of Modern War, Vol. III,* p. 259; Eddy et al., *The Falklands War,* pp. 246, 250–251; Freedman and Gamba-Stonehouse, *Signals of War,* p. 373; Hastings and Jenkins, *The Battle for the Falklands,* pp. 294–296; 299; Laffin, *The Fight for the Falklands,* p. 104; Middlebrook, *The Fight for the Malvinas,* pp. 235, 255; Moro, *The History of the South Atlantic Conflict,* p. 311; Thompson, *No Picnic,* p. 112.

40. Arthur, *Above All Courage,* pp. 150, 198–201, 277; Eddy et al., *The Falklands War,* p. 374; Thompson, *No Picnic,* pp. 112, 128, 133.

41. Middlebrook, *The Fight For the Malvinas,* p. 234.

42. Bishop and Witherow, *The Winter War,* p. 129; Eddy et al., *The Falklands War,* p. 250; Freedman and Gamba-Stonehouse, *Signals of War,* p. 397; Thompson, *No Picnic,* pp. 77–80.

43. Bishop and Witherow, *The Winter War,* p. 125; Cordesman and Wagner, *The Lessons of Modern War, Vol. III,* pp. 265–266; Middlebrook, *The Fight for the Malvinas,* p. 237; Stewart, *Mates and Muchachos,* pp. 130–131; Thompson, *No Picnic,* p. 126.

44. Freedman and Gamba-Stonehouse, *Signals of War,* pp. 147–148.

45. Cordesman and Wagner, *The Lessons of Modern War, Vol. III,* p. 282; Eddy et al., *The Falklands War,* pp. 357–358, 395, 397; Freedman and Gamba-Stonehouse, *Signals of War,* pp.363- 364, 389; Hastings and Jenkins, *The Battle for the Falklands,* pp. 230, 324–325; Middlebrook, *The Fight for the Malvinas,* pp. 236, 244; Ullman, "Profound or Perfunctory," p. 250.

46. Michael Carver, *War since 1945* (London: Ashfield Press, 1990), p. 288.

47. Eddy et al., *The Falklands War,* p. 146; Hastings and Jenkins, *The Battle for the Falklands,* p. 322; Middlebrook, *The Fight for the Malvinas,* pp. 53, 55–56, 63.

48. Interestingly, even before the Israelis the Argentines were trained by the best in the world. One of the first AAF instructors after World War II was the legendary German Stuka pilot Hans-Ulrich Rudel.

49. Cordesman and Wagner, *The Lessons of Modern War, Vol. III,* p. 303; Eddy et al., *The Falklands War,* pp. 198, 207; Gravino and Segal, "The Empire Strikes Back," p. 27; Hastings and Jenkins, *The Battle for the Falklands,* pp. 115, 120; Laffin, *Fight for the Falklands,* pp. 92, 95; Ullman, "Profound or Perfunctory," p. 248; Dov Zakheim, "The South Atlantic: Evaluating the Lessons," in *The Regionalization of Warfare,* ed. James Brown and William P. Snyder (New Brunswick, NJ: Transaction Books, 1990), p. 39.

50. Hastings and Jenkins, *The Battle for the Falklands,* p. 205.

51. Cordesman and Wagner, *The Lessons of Modern War, Vol. III,* p. 238; Eddy et al., *The Falklands War,* p. 193.

52. Cordesman and Wagner, *The Lessons of Modern War, Vol. III,* p. 249; Eddy et al., *The Falklands War,* pp. 194–196; Hastings and Jenkins, *The Battle for the Falklands,* p. 48; Zackheim, "The South Atlantic," p. 39.

53. Cordesman and Wagner, *The Lessons of Modern War, Vol. III,* pp. 249, 302–303, 312, 336; Eddy et al., *The Falklands War,* p. 193; Middlebrook, *The Fight for the Malvinas,* pp. 87, 152.

54. Cordesman and Wagner, *The Lessons of Modern War, Vol. III,* p. 274; Eddy et al., *The Falklands War,* pp. 196, 199, 202–203; Hastings and Jenkins, *The Battle for the Falklands,* pp. 207–208; Middlebrook, *The Fight for the Malvinas,* p. 171.

55. Cordesman and Wagner, *The Lessons of Modern War, Vol. III,* p. 319; Eddy et al., *The Falklands War,* p. 202; Freedman and Gamba-Stonehouse, *Signals of War,* p. 360; Middlebrook, *The Fight for the Malvinas,* pp. 159, 286; Moro, *The History of the South Atlantic Conflict,* p. 227; Ullman, "Profound or Perfunctory," p. 243.

56. Eddy et al., *The Falklands War,* pp. 194–196; Hastings and Jenkins, *The Battle for the Falklands,* p. 207.

57. Arthur, *Above All Courage,* pp. 89–90; Cordesman and Wagner, *The Lessons of Modern War, Vol. III,* pp. 262–263, 309; Eddy et al., *The Falklands War,* p. 193; Hastings and Jenkins, *The Battle for the Falklands,* p. 207; Moro, p. 114.

58. Middlebrook, *The Fight for the Malvinas,* pp. 82–83, 90–91, 284–285; Murguizur, "The South Atlantic Conflict," p. 139.

59. Arthur, *Above All Courage,* pp. 89–90.

60. Cordesman and Wagner, *The Lessons of Modern War, Vol. III,* p. 318; Thompson, *No Picnic,* pp. 77–80.

61. Bishop and Witherow, *The Winter War,* p. 71; Cordesman and Wagner, *The Lessons of Modern War, Vol. III,* pp. 278–279, 320; Eddy et al., *The Falklands War,* p. 205; Freedman and Gamba-Stonehouse, *Signals of War,* pp. 233, 259, 289, 358, 361, 379; Middlebrook, *The Fight for the Malvinas,* pp. 122, 201; Moro, *The History of the South Atlantic Conflict,* pp. 252, 273.

62. Eddy et al., *The Falklands War,* pp. 205–208; Freedman and Gamba-Stonehouse, *Signlas of War,* p. 361; Middlebrook, *The Fight for the Malvinas,* pp. 123, 202; Moro, *The History of the South Atlantic Conflict,* pp. 274–276; Murguizur, "The South Atlantic Conflict," p. 138.

63. Bishop and Witherow, *The Winter War,* p. 82; Freedman and Gamba-Stonehouse, *Signals of War,* p. 361; Hastings and Jenkins, *The Battle for the Falklands,* p. 227; Middlebrook, *The Fight for the Malvinas,* pp. 164, 173–174.

64. Hastings and Jenkins, *The Battlke for the Falklands,* pp. 49, 322; Gravino and Segal, "The Empire Strikes Back," p. 23.

65. Bishop and Witherow, *The Winter War,* p. 71; Eddy et al., *The Falklands War,* pp. 122, 362, 380.

66. Freedman and Gamba-Stonehouse, *Signals of War,* p. 361.

67. Murguizur, "The South Atlantic Conflict," p. 138.

68. Middlebrook, *The Fight for the Malvinas,* pp. 65, 290; Murguizur, "The South Atlantic Conflict," p. 135.

69. Cordesman and Wagner, *The Lessons of Modern War, Vol. III,* pp. 265, 334; Eddy et al., *The Falklands War,* pp. 122, 125, 146; Hastings and Jenkins, *The*

Battle for the Falklands, pp. 286–287; Middlebrook, *The Fight for the Malvinas,* pp. 64, 142; Murguizur, "The South Atlantic Conflict," p. 136; Stewart, "A Case Study in Cohesion," p. 34.

70. Stewart, *Mates and Muchachos,* p. 74.
71. Freedman and Gamba-Stonehouse, *Signals of War,* p. 147; Middlebrook, *The Fight for the Malvinas,* p. 143.
72. Cordesman and Wagner, *The Lessons of Modern War, Vol. III,* pp. 265, 282, 328; Freedman and Gamba-Stonehouse, *Signals of War,* pp. 103, 144–145, 147, 359, 372; Hastings and Jenkins, *The Battle for the Falklands,* pp. 218, 322; Murguizur, "The South Atlantic Conflict," pp. 136, 138; Stewart, "A Case Study in Cohesion," p. 34; Ullman, "Profound or Perfunctory," p. 250.
73. Guilmartin, "The South Atlantic War," p. 62.
74. Middlebrook, *The Fight for the Malvinas,* p. 121; Moro, *The History of the South Atlantic Conflict,* p. 149. Please note that other sources claim that French technicians in Argentina performed this operation. However, Middlebrook convincingly argues (in part because he appears to have interviewed the technicians in question) that it was the Argentines themselves who married up the Exocets and the Super Etendards.
75. Bishop and Witherow, *The Winter War,* p. 18; Cordesman and Wagner, *The Lessons of Modern War, Vol. III,* p. 312; Middlebrook, *The Fight for the Malvinas,* p. 168.
76. Hastings and Jenkins, *The Battle for the Falklands,* p. 228.
77. The one possible exception to this rule is the case of Syria's invasion of Jordan in 1970 during Black September, when Defense Minister Hafiz al-Assad refused to commit the Syrian Air Force to the battle because he disagreed with the political leadership's decision to invade Jordan. This was a major factor in the Syrian defeat, ceding the skies to the Royal Jordanian Air Force, and may have doomed the invasion by itself.

Chapter 10

1. Paul M. Kennedy, *The Rise and Fall of the Great Powers: Economic Change and Military Conflict from 1500 to 2000* (New York: Random House, 1987).
2. Based on peacetime standards. It is reasonable to assume that in wartime these standards might be relaxed. CIA, *World Factbook* (Washington, DC: CIA, 1992).
3. Since the late 1950s, literacy rates in the Arab world have been sufficiently high that literacy has not been a major concern among the officer corps. However, to this day, illiterate enlisted personnel have been a constant problem for Arab armed forces. Consequently, many of the points raised here regarding the impact of illiteracy on military performance should, for the Arab world, be considered as affecting mainly the enlisted ranks.
4. Herbert Goldhamer, *The Soviet Soldier,* p. 323.

5. Zuyev with McConnell, *Fulcrum*, pp. 144–145.

6. See in particular, Alex Inkeles and David H. Smith, *Becoming Modern: Individual Change in Six Developing Societies* (Cambridge, MA.: Harvard University Press, 1974), esp. pp. 314–315. Also see David E. Apter, *The Politics of Modernization*, in which Apter notes dramatic differences in initiative and passivity among various West African tribes.

7. While the sources on this are vast, some of the best on this particular topic include David French, *Raising Churchill's Army: The British Army and the War against Germany 1919–1945* (Oxford: Oxford University Press, 2000); Russell A. Hart, *Clash of Arms: How the Allies Won in Normandy* (Norman: University of Oklahoma Press, 2001); Jonathan House, *Toward Combined Arms*; and the various essays in Allan Millet and Williamson Murray, eds., *Military Effectiveness*, 3 Vols. (Boston: Allen and Unwin, 1988).

Chapter 11

1. Charles Issawi, *An Economic History of the Middle East and North Africa* (New York: Columbia University Press, 1982), p. 54.

2. Issawi, *An Economic History of the Middle East and North Africa*, p. 233.

3. Pollack, *Arabs at War*, pp. 447–448.

4. Pollack, *Arabs at War*, p. 454.

5. Ze'ev Schiff and Ehud Ya'ari, *Israel's Lebanon War*, ed. and trans. Ina Friedman (New York: Simon and Schuster, 1984).

6. Pollack, *Arabs at War*, p. 525.

7. Pollack, *Arabs at War*, p. 525.

8. Pollack, *Arabs at War*, p. 523.

9. Pollack, *Arabs at War*, pp. 532–533.

10. Pollack, *Arabs at War*, pp. 533–534.

11. Quoted in Anthony H. Cordesman and Abraham R. Wagner, *The Lessons of Modern War: Volume I, The Arab-Israeli Conflicts, 1973–1989* (Boulder, CO: Westview, 1990), p. 197.

12. Benjamin S. Lambeth, *Moscow's Lessons from the 1982 Lebanon Air War*, RAND Report R-3000-AF (Santa Monica, CA: RAND, September 1984), p. 31.

13. Quoted in Patrick Seale, *Asad of Syria* (London: I. B. Tauris, 1988), p. 381.

14. Author's interview with MG Amir Drori, IDF (Ret), September 1996. There is some confusion as to how the Syrian T-72s were destroyed in this clash. However, in September 1996, Maj. General Amir Drori, IDF (Ret), the overall commander of the Israeli invasion, confirmed to me that the majority of the T-72s were destroyed by TOW ATGMs, and a minority by Israeli tanks.

15. Pollack, *Arabs at War*, p. 540.

16. For other insightful perspectives, see Cordesman and Wagner, *The Lessons of Modern War, Vol. I,* pp. 151–152; Col. Trevor N. Dupuy and Paul Martell, *Flawed Victory: The Arab-Israeli Conflict and the 1982 War in Lebanon* (Fairfax,

VA: Hero Books, 1983), pp. 218–226; Richard Gabriel, *Operation Peace for Galilee* (New York: Hill and Wang, 1984), p. 119.

17. Author's interview with MG Amir Drori, IDF (Ret), September 1996.
18. Herzog, *The Arab-Israeli Wars*, p. 357.
19. Author's interview with senior IDF officer, September 1996.
20. Cordesman, *Jordanian Arms*, p.77.
21. See Pollack, *Arabs at War*, pp. 457–523.

Chapter 12

1. On Qadhafi's various motives for coveting the Aouzou Strip and intervening in Chad, see Colin Legum, "Libya's Intervention in Chad," in *Crisis and Conflicts in the Middle East*, ed. Colin Legum (New York: Holmes and Meier, 1981), p. 53; Mary Jane Deeb, *Libya's Foreign Policy in North Africa* (Boulder, CO: Westview, 1990), p. 132; John Wright, *Libya, Chad and the Central Sahara* (Totowa, NJ: Barnes and Noble, 1987), p. 144. René Lemarchand notes that Qadhafi also had reason to fear Libyan dissidents operating from Chad and the large Israeli presence there in the early 1970s. René Lemarchand, "The Case of Chad," in *The Green and The Black: Qadhafi's Policies in Africa*, ed. René Lemarchand (Bloomington, IN: Indiana University Press, 1988). pp. 109–110.
2. Virginia Thompson and Richard Adloff, *Conflict in Chad* (Berkeley: University of California Press, 1981), pp. 55, 120–123; Wright, *Libya, Chad and the Central Sahara*, p. 129.
3. Pollack, *Arabs at War*, p. 379.
4. Pollack, *Arabs at War*, pp. 380–381.
5. Author's interview with US government official, September 1995.
6. Pollack, *Arabs at War*, pp. 386–388; interviews with US government officials, September 1995.
7. James Brooke, "Modern Arms a Key Factor in Chadian Gains," *New York Times*, April 2, 1987, p. A8; William J. Foltz, "Libya's Military Power," in *The Green and the Black*, ed. Lemarchand, p. 65; Franziska James, "Habré's Hour of Glory," *Africa Report*, September–October 1987, p. 21; Colin Legum, *Africa Contemporary Record, 1986–87* (New York: Africana 1988), p. B190; author's interviews with US government officials, September 1995.
8. Pollack, *Arabs at War*, p. 393.
9. Author's interview with Lt. General Bernard E. Trainor, May, 1994.
10. Pollack, *Arabs at War*, pp. 394–395.
11. Pollack, *Arabs at War*, p. 396.
12. Pollack, *Arabs at War*, pp. 395–397.
13. Pollack, *Arabs at War*, p. 397.
14. Anthony Cordesman, *After the Storm: The Changing Military Balance in the Middle East* (Boulder, CO: Westview, 1993), p. 145; Jean R. Tartter, "National

Security," in *Libya: A Country Study*, ed. Helen Chapin Metz (Washington, DC: GPO, 1989), p. 262.

15. Foltz, "Libya's Military Power," p. 58.

16. Cordesman, *After the Storm*, p. 146.

17. Author's interviews with US government officials, September 1995.

Chapter 13

1. Patrick C. Coe, *The Dragon Strikes: China and the Korean War: June–December 1950* (Novato, CA: Presidio, 2000), p. ix.

2. Mahoney, *Formidable Enemies,* p. 32.

3. Coe, *The Dragon Strikes*, pp. 419–420.

4. Spurr, *Enter the Dragon*, p. 19.

5. Defense Intelligence Agency, *The Chinese Armed Forces Today: The US Defense Intelligence Agency Handbook of China's Army, Navy and Air Force* (Englewood Cliffs, NJ: Prentice-Hall, 1979), p. 13.

6. Lt. Col. Roy E. Appleman, *Disaster in Korea: The Chinese Confront MacArthur* (College Station: Texas A&M University Press, 1989), pp. 12, 19, 44–45; Clay Blair, *The Forgotten War*, p. 391; Coe, *The Dragon Strikes*, p. 233; Edwin P. Hoyt, *The Day the Chinese Attacked: Korea 1950*, Paperback ed. (New York: Paragon House, 1993), pp. 93, 119, 146, 169; Spurr, *Enter The Dragon,* pp. 79-80, 118, 167–168, 268

7. Appleman provides the following breakdown in experience levels for Chinese military personnel in November 1950: 15 percent were Communist veterans of World War II or before, 25 percent were Communist veterans of the Chinese Civil War, 30 percent were former Nationalist soldiers, and 30 percent were young men inducted since 1948. Appleman, *Disaster in Korea,* p. 352.

8. Allen S. Whiting, *China Crosses the Yalu* (New York: MacMillan, 1960), p. 122.

9. Appleman, *Disaster in Korea,* pp. 17–18, 44–45; Coe, *The Dragon Strikes,* pp. 161, 418; Griffith, *The Chinese People's Liberation Army*, p. 131; Hoyt, *The Day the Chinese Attacked,* p. 100; Spurr, *Enter the Dragon,* pp. 118–119, 170; Whiting, *China Crosses the Yalu,* p. 124.

10. Coe, *The Dragon Strikes*, pp. ix–x, 402–404; Griffith, *The Chinese People's Liberation Army*, pp. 127, 142, 147; Hoyt, *The Day the Chinese Attacked,* pp. 127–134; Ridgway, *The Korean War*, pp. 45–52; Spurr, *Enter the Dragon,* pp. 158–159.

11. Coe, *The Dragon Strikes*, p. 144.

12. Appleman, *Disaster in Korea,* pp. 20–21; Coe, *The Dragon Strikes*, pp. 156–190; Griffith, *The Chinese People's Liberation Army*, pp. 127–128, 132–133; Hoyt, *The Day the Chinese Attacked,* pp. 88–98; Millett, *The War for Korea, 1950–1951,*

pp. 301–305; Paik Sun Yup, *From Pusan to Panmunjom*, pp. 85–97; Ridgway, *The Korean War,* pp. 54–56; Spurr, *Enter the Dragon,* p. 136, 139–151;

13. Coe, *The Dragon Strikes,* pp. 232–236; Hoyt, *The Day the Chinese Attacked,* pp. 108–112; Peng Dehuai, *Memoirs of a Chinese Marshal: The Autobiographical Notes of Peng Dehuai (1898–1974),* trans. Zheng Longpu (Beijing: Foreign Languages Press, 1984), pp. 475–476.

14. Coe, *The Dragon Strikes,* p. 233; Griffith, *The Chinese People's Liberation Army,* p. 138; Spurr, *Enter the Dragon,* pp. 118–119.

15. Millett, *The War for Korea, 1950–1951,* p. 335.

16. Blair, *The Forgotten War,* pp. 429–440; Ridgway, *The Korean War,* pp. 60–61.

17. Coe, *The Dragon Strikes,* pp. 93, 429, 434–435; Mahoney, *Formidable Enemies,* pp. 66–67, 73–82.

18. For concurring assessments that the Chinese rarely conducted human wave attacks and actually employed highly sophisticated infantry tactics, see Appleman, *Disaster in Korea,* p. 353; S. L. A. Marshall, *Infantry Operations and Weapons Usage in Korea,* 1988 Edition (London: Greenhill Books, 1988), p. 5; Gerald Segal, *Defending China* (New York: Oxford University Press, 1985), pp. 101, 147.

19. Appleman, *Disaster in Korea,* pp. 17, 79, 80–84, 98, 159, 162, 168–169; Blair, *The Forgotten War,* pp. 375–975, esp. p. 382; Coe, *The Dragon Strikes,* pp. 433–436; DIA, *The Chinese Armed Forces Today,* pp. 29, 37; Griffith, *The Chinese People's Liberation Army,* pp. 131, 142–144, 169; Hoyt, pp. 94, 103–104, 146; Mahoney, *Formidable Enemies,* pp. 53–62, 73–82; S. L. A. Marshall, *The River and the Gauntlet* (New York: William Morrow and Co., 1953), pp. 34, 60, 65, 73, 144, 201–204, 243, 266; Paik, *From Pusan to Panmunjom*, pp. 85–91, 92, 100; Ridgway, *The Korean War,* pp. 52–56, 71, 82, 89, 106, 172; Spurr, *Enter the Dragon,* pp. 137–139; 155, 224, 288.

20. Appleman, *Disaster in Korea,* pp. 98, 117, 159; Hoyt, *The Day the Chinese Attacked,* p. 110; Spurr, *Enter the Dragon,* p. 288.

21. Appleman, *Disaster in Korea,* pp.54–203, 220–324, 397; Blair, *The Forgotten War,* pp. 440–521, 534–545; Griffith, *The Chinese People's Liberation Army,* pp. 141–146; Hoyt, *The Day the Chinese Attacked,* pp. 127–166; Millett, *The War for Korea, 1950–1951,* pp. 336–357; Paik, *From Pusan to Panmunjom,* pp. 105–109; Peng, *Memoirs of a Chinese Marshal,* pp. 475–476; Ridgway, *The Korean War,* pp. 64–82; Spurr, *Enter the Dragon,* pp. 167–219, 270–277.

22. Appleman, *Disaster in Korea,* pp. 300–304, 311, 351–354, 364; Blair, *The Forgotten War,* pp. 545–556; Coe, *The Dragon Strikes,* pp. 378–380, 390–394, 436–437; Hoyt, *The Day the Chinese Attacked,* p. 167; Mahoney, *Formidable Enemies,* pp. 47–48; Millett, *The War for Korea, 1950–1951,* esp. pp. 339–340, 356–357; Ridgway, *The Korean War,* p. 73; Segal, *Defending China,* pp. 101–102; Spurr, *Enter the Dragon,* pp. 220–251, 270.

23. Blair, *The Forgotten War,* pp. 592–630; Griffith, *The Chinese People's Liberation Army,* pp. 151–152; Hoyt, *The Day the Chinese Attacked,* pp. 169–187;

Millett, *The War for Korea, 1950–1951*, pp. 383–390; Paik, *From Pusan to Panmunjom*, pp. 115–121; Ridgway, *The Korean War,* pp. 93–102; Spurr, *Enter the Dragon,* pp. 251–266, 278–300.

24. Hoyt, *The Day the Chinese Attacked,* p. 195; Paik, *From Pusan to Panmunjom,* p. 121; Peng, *Memoirs of a Chinese Marshal,* p. 478; Spurr, *Enter the Dragon,* pp. 300–305.

25. Blair, *The Forgotten War,* pp. 633–712; Millett, *The War for Korea, 1950–1951,* pp. 398–411; Ridgway, *The Korean War,* pp. 106–119; Segal, *Defending China,* p. 103; Spurr, *Enter the Dragon,* pp. 124–125.

26. Blair, *The Forgotten War,* pp. 715–855; Griffith, *The Chinese People's Liberation Army,* pp. 162–165; Hoyt, *The Day the Chinese Attacked,* pp. 203–205; Millett, *The War for Korea, 1950–1951,* pp. 417–420, 426–435, 441–452; Paik, *From Pusan to Panmunjom,* pp. 144–156; Ridgway, *The Korean War,* pp. 171–175; Segal, *Defending China,* p. 102.

27. Peng, *Memoirs of a Chinese Marshal,* p. 482.

28. Blair, *The Forgotten War,* pp. 855–975; Griffith, *The Chinese People's Liberation Army,* pp. 169–171; Hoyt, *The Day the Chinese Attacked,* pp. 210–211; Ellis Joffe, *The Chinese Army after Mao* (London: Weideneld and Nicolson, 1987), p. 5; Ridgway, *The Korean War,* pp. 179–224; Segal, *Defending China,* pp. 103–104; Spurr, *Enter the Dragon,* p. 267.

29. Chinese pilots began training on Soviet jets in 1950 and began taking delivery of MiG-15s in early 1951, before the real opening of the Soviet arsenal to China. Robert Jackson, *Air War over Korea* (New York: Charles Scribner's Sons, 1973), pp. 54–84.

30. Appleman, *Disaster in Korea,* pp. 362–363; James E. Dornan Jr and Nigel de Lee, *The Chinese War Machine* (London: Salamander, 1979), pp. 126–127; Robert Futrell, *The United States Air Force in Korea, 1950–1953* (New York: Duell, Sloan and Pearce, 1961), pp. 651–655; Griffith, *The Chinese People's Liberation Army,* pp. 166–168; Jackson, *Air War over Korea,* pp. 54–63.

31. Jackson, *Air War over Korea,* pp. 84–117.

32. Coe, *The Dragon Strikes,* p. 144; Hoyt, *The Day the Chinese Attacked,* p. 202; Millett, *The War for Korea, 1950–1951,* pp. 306–308.

33. Griffith, *The Chinese People's Liberation Army,* p. 177; Jackson, *Air War over Korea,* pp. 117–153.

34. Douglas Dildy and Warren Thompson, *F-86 Sabre vs MiG-15: Korea 1950–53* (Oxford: Osprey, 2013).

35. Blair, *The Forgotten War,* p. 975; Hoyt, *The Day the Chinese Attacked,* p. 313.

36. General Ridgway had nothing but praise for his Chinese opposites, see Griffith, *The Chinese People's Liberation Army,* p. 171. Also see Spurr, *Enter the Dragon,* p. 4.

37. Millett, *The War for Korea, 1950–1951,* p. 336.

38. Appleman, *Disaster in Korea,* pp. XIII, 28, 133–134, 202; King C. Chen, "China's War against Vietnam, 1979: A Military Analysis," *The Journal of East Asian Affairs* 3(1) (Spring/Summer 1983), pp. 249–250; Griffith, *The*

Chinese People's Liberation Army, pp. 129, 134, 142, 148, 171; Hoyt, *The Day the Chinese Attacked,* pp. 138, 166; Major Sita Ram Johri, *Chinese Invasion of NEFA* (Lucknow: Himalaya Publications, 1968), pp. 44, 80; Marshall, *The River and the Gauntlet*, p. 70; Spurr, *Enter the Dragon,* pp. 81, 191–219, 252.

39. Coe, *The Dragon Strikes*, p. 82; Mahoney, *Formidable Enemies*, pp. 36–37.

40. Mahoney, *Formidable Enemies*, p. 36.

41. Coe, *The Dragon Strikes*, p. 425.

42. Coe, *The Dragon Strikes*, p. 93; Millett, *The War for Korea, 1950–1951,* pp. 300–301, 355–357.

43. Hoyt, *The Day the Chinese Attacked,* p. 96.

44. Appleman, *Disaster in Korea,* pp. 162, 154–211; DIA, *The Chinese Armed Forces Today,* pp. 30–31, 66; Major Jer Donald Get, "Lessons Learned in Vietnam: PLA," *Military Review* 67 (July 1987), p. 22; Griffith, *The Chinese People's Liberation Army*, p. 132; Hoyt, *The Day the Chinese Attacked,* pp. 110, 138; Joffe, *The Chinese Army after Mao,* p. 95; Johri, *Chinese Invasion of NEFA*, p. 173; Mahoney, *Formidable Enemies*, pp. 62–63; Marshall, *The River and the Gauntlet*, p. 85.

45. Appleman, *Disaster in Korea,* pp. 68–159; Blair, *The Forgotten War*, pp. 375–975; Chen, "China's War against Vietnam, 1979," pp. 249–250; DIA, *The Chinese Armed Forces Today,* pp. 30–31, 37, 160; Dornan and de Lee, *The Chinese War Machine,* p. 31; Griffith, *The Chinese People's Liberation Army*, pp. 131, 169; Hoyt, *The Day the Chinese Attacked,* pp. 126, 150; Johri, *Chinese Invasion of NEFA*, pp. 44, 80, 88, 110–114, 130, 141, 162; Marshall, *The River and the Gauntlet*, pp. 60, 73, 144, 164, 201–203, 330; Peng, p. 475; Spurr, *Enter the Dragon,* pp. 179, 224.

46. See Appleman, *Disaster in Korea,* p. 152.

47. Appleman, *Disaster in Korea,* pp. 80–81, 135–137, 179; DIA, *The Chinese Armed Forces Today,* p. 37; Hoyt, *The Day the Chinese Attacked,* p. 104; Johri, *Chinese Invasion of NEFA*, p. 164; Ridgway, *The Korean War,* p. 54; Spurr, *Enter the Dragon,* pp. 137, 289.

48. Shu Guang Zhang, *Mao's Military Romanticism: China and the Korean War, 1950–1953* (Lawrence: University of Kansas Press, 1995), pp. 76–77. Also see Coe, *The Dragon Strikes*, pp. 78, 82.

49. Appleman, *Disaster in Korea,* pp. XIII, 98, 134; Blair, *The Forgotten War*, pp. 375–975, esp. p. 382; Chen, "China's War against Vietnam, 1979," p. 249; DIA, *The Chinese Armed Forces Today,* p. 37; Griffith, *The Chinese People's Liberation Army*, pp. 143–144; Hoyt, *The Day the Chinese Attacked,* pp. 142, 146, 149, 160; Jencks, p. 810; Johri, *Chinese Invasion of NEFA*, p. 68, 80–87; Marshall, *The River and the Gauntlet*, pp. 105–193, 330; S. L. A. Marshall, *Infantry Operations,* p. 128; Paik, *From Pusan to Panmunjom*, pp. 85–91; Segal, *Defending China,* pp. 147, 219; Spurr, *Enter the Dragon,* pp. 81, 137, 288.

50. After the Battle of Susangerd in 1981, the Iraqis also learned this tactic and attempted to employ it frequently afterward. The difference between the

Iraqis and the Chinese, however, was that the Chinese consistently made it work and the Iraqis rarely did.

51. Appleman, *Disaster in Korea,* 241–243, 252–255, 246–283; DIA, *The Chinese Armed Forces Today,* p. 29; Griffith, *The Chinese People's Liberation Army,* p. 169; Hoyt, *The Day the Chinese Attacked,* p. 159; Mahoney, *Formidable Enemies,* pp. 87–106; Marshall, *The River and the Gauntlet,* pp. 27, 304–342; Marshall, *Infantry Operations,* p. 130; Paik, *From Pusan to Panmunjom,* pp. 176–177.

52. Griffith, *The Chinese People's Liberation Army,* p. 130; Spurr, *Enter the Dragon,* p. 119.

53. See in particular Chen, "China's War against Vietnam, 1979," pp. 246–256; Spurr, *Enter the Dragon,* 260–313.

54. Appleman, *Disaster in Korea,* p. 127; Marshall, *The River and the Gauntlet,* pp. 233, 258; Marshall, *Infantry Operations,* p. 72.

55. Appleman, *Disaster in Korea,* pp. 118, 173, 178, 185; DIA, *The Chinese Armed Forces Today,* p. 35; Griffith, *The Chinese People's Liberation Army,* p. 169; Marshall, *The River and the Gauntlet,* pp. 141–142, 149, 159; Ridgway, *The Korean War,* p. 218.

56. Hoyt, *The Day the Chinese Attacked,* p. 174.

57. Spurr, *Enter the Dragon,* p. 170.

58. Griffith, *The Chinese People's Liberation Army,* p. 158; Jackson, *Air War over Korea,* pp. 8–283; Johri, *Chinese Invasion of NEFA,* pp. 112–114.

59. Michael Peck, "Cold War Battle in the Sky: F-86 Saber vs. MiG-15," *The National Interest* online, May 18, 2015, available at http://nationalinterest.org/feature/cold-war-battle-the-sky-f-86-saber-vs-mig-15-12909, accessed November 28, 2017.

60. Anthony Cordesman, *The Iraq War: Strategy, Tactics, and Military Lessons* (Westport, CT: Praeger, 2003), pp. 15–16; Kenneth M. Pollack, *The Threatening Storm* (New York: Random House, 2002), p. 158.

Chapter 14

1. On these incidents, see Pollack, *Arabs at War,* pp. 368–375, 412–422.

2. Sorley, *A Better War,* pp. 259–260.

3. Andrade, *America's Last Vietnam Battle,* p. 66.

4. Lt. Colonel Natanel Lorch, *The Edge of the Sword: Israel's War of Independence, 1947–1949* (New York: Putnam, 1961), p. 351.

5. Pollack, *Arabs at War,* pp. 110–111.

6. Pollack, *Arabs at War,* p. 168.

Chapter 15

1. Wayne E. Lee, *Waging War: Conflict, Culture, and Innovation in World History* (Oxford: Oxford University Press, 2016).

2. Charles Tilly, *The Formation of National States in Western Europe* (Princeton, NJ: Princeton University Press, 1975).

3. John A. Lynn, "The Evolution of Army Style in the Modern West, 800–2000," *The International History Review*, Vol. 18, No. 3 (August 1996), p. 510.

4. Lee, *Waging War*, pp. 99–110.

5. Stephen D. Biddle, *Military Power: Explaining Victory and Defeat in Modern Battle* (Princeton, NJ: Princeton University Press, 2004).

6. On the dramatic decline of the British Army's military effectiveness and its roots in a persistent approach to warfare that was highly effective in the eighteenth and nineteenth centuries but become entirely ineffective in the twentieth, see for instance Shelford Bidwell and Dominick Graham, *Fire-Power: British Army Weapons and Theories of War. 1904–1945* (London: George Allen and Unwin, 1982); Brian Bond, *British Military Policy between the Two World Wars* (New York: Oxford University Press, 1980); French, *Raising Churchill's Army*; Hart, *Clash of Arms*; Charles Messenger, *For Love of Regiment: A History of British Infantry, Volume Two, 1915–1994* (London: Leo Cooper, 1996); Timothy Harrison Place, *Military Training in the British Army, 1940–1944: From Dunkirk to D-Day* (London: Frank Cass, 2000).

7. Raymond Aron, *The Imperial Republic: The United States and the World, 1945–1973* (Washington, DC: University Press of America, 1974), p. 99.

8. On organizational culture, see Edgar H. Schein, *Organizational Culture and Leadership*, Third ed. (San Francisco: John Wiley and Sons, 2004).

Chapter 16

1. In formulating this definition, I have drawn on the discussions of culture in Raymond Cohen, *Culture and Conflict in Egyptian-Israeli Relations* (Bloomington: Indiana University Press, 1990); Clifford Geertz, *The Interpretation of Cultures* (New York: Basic Books, 1973); Sania Hamady, *The Temperament and Character of the Arabs* (New York: Twayne, 1960); Mansour Khalid, "The Sociocultural Determinants of Arab Diplomacy," in *Arab and American Cultures*, ed. George N. Atiyeh (Washington, DC: American Enterprise Institute for Public Policy Research, 1977); Clyde Kluckohn, "Culture and Behavior," in *Handbook of Social Psychology*, ed. Gardner Lindzey (Cambridge, MA: Addison Wesley, 1954); Robert A. LeVine, "Properties of Culture: An Ethnographic View," in *Culture Theory: Essays on Mind, Self, and Emotion,* ed. Richard A. Schweder and Robert A. LeVine (New York: Cambridge University Press, 1984); Robert P. Pearson and Leon E. Clark, *Through Middle Eastern Eyes* (New York: Cite Books, 1993), p. 19; Patrick Porter, *Military Orientalism: Eastern War through Western Eyes* (New York: Columbia University Press, 2009), p. 15; Maxime Rodinson, *The Arabs*, trans. Arthur Goldhammer (Chicago: University of Chicago Press, 1981); Joseph Rothschild, "Culture and War," in *The Lessons of Recent Wars in the Third World, Vol. 2*, ed. Robert Harkavy and Stephanie Neuman (Lexington, MA: Lexington Books, 1987); Philip Carl Salzman, *Culture and*

Conflict in the Middle East (Amherst, NY: Humanity Books, 2008), p. 10; and William H. Sewell Jr., "The Concept(s) of Culture," in *Beyond the Cultural Turn: New Directions in the Study of Society and Culture,* ed. Victoria E. Bonnell and Lynn Hunt (Berkeley: University of California Press, 1999), pp. 39 and 44.

2. See Harry C, Triandis, "Foreword," in *Culture, Leadership, and Organizations: The GLOBE Study of 62 Societies,* ed. Robert J. House, Paul Hanges, Mansour Javidan, Peter W. Dorfman, and Vipin Gupta (Thousand Oaks, CA: Sage, 2004), p. xv.

3. For an outstanding discussion of the impact of geography, topography, climate, and history on the development of culture, specifically in the Middle East, see Gary S. Gregg, *The Middle East: A Cultural Psychology* (New York: Oxford University Press, 2005), pp. 50–77, 351–354. On the general point that culture develops in response to the situation of the society, Elizabeth Fernea has an eloquent passage on the topic. See Elizabeth Warnock Fernea, "Childhood in the Muslim Middle East," in *Children in the Muslim Middle East,* ed. Elizabeth Warnock Fernea (Austin: University of Texas Press, 1995), p. 11.

4. Quoted in Kenneth W. Terhune, "From National Character to National Behavior: A Reformulation," *Journal of Conflict Resolution*, Vol. 14, No. 2 (June 1970), p. 222. Emphasis in original.

5. Gary S. Gregg, *Culture and Identity in a Muslim Society* (Oxford: Oxford University Press, 2007), pp. 292–293; Yasuko Minoura, "A Sensitive Period for the Incorporation of a Cultural Meaning System," *Ethos*, Vol. 20, No. 3 (1992), pp. 304–339.

6. Tarek Heggy, *The Arab Cocoon: Progress and Modernity in Arab Societies* (London: Valentine Mitchell, 2010), p. 50; Sewell, "The Concept(s) of Culture," pp. 54–55.

7. Issa J. Boullata, "Challenges to Arab Cultural Authenticity," in *The Next Arab Decade: Alternative Futures*, ed. Hisham Sharabi (Boulder, CO: Westview, 1988), p. 148.

8. Edward J. Drea, *Japan's Imperial Army: Its Rise and Fall, 1853–1945* (Lawrence: University of Kansas Press, 2009), esp. pp. 17–19, 158, 212, 240–249, 257–258.

9. Andrea B. Rugh, *Family in Contemporary Egypt* (Syracuse, NY: Syracuse University Press, 1984), p. 33. Emphasis in original.

10. Marwan Dwairy, *Counseling and Psychotherapy with Arabs and Muslims: A Culturally Sensitive Approach* (New York: Teacher's College Press, 2006), p. ix.

11. Gregg, *The Middle East,* p. 91.

12. Alexander Abdennur notes that psychological studies have consistently found differences in value prioritization, cognitive approaches, and learning methods between Arabs and Westerners (and other cultures). As an example, he describes his own study of Canadian versus Arab (Lebanese) students.

See Alexander Abdennur, *The Arab Mind: An Ontology of Abstraction and Concreteness* (Ottawa, Canada: Kogna, 2008), pp. 45–47. See also Dwairy, *Counseling and Psychotherapy with Arabs and Muslims*, p. 26.

13. Marwan Dwairy, *Cross-Cultural Counseling: The Arab-Palestinian Case* (Binghamton, NY: Haworth Press, 1998), pp. 33–34. See also Gregg, *Culture and Identity in a Muslim Society*, p. 283.

14. Tony Pfaff, "Development and Reform of the Iraqi Police Forces" (Carlisle, PA: US Army War College, January 2008), p. 30.

15. Sewell, "The Concept(s) of Culture," p. 53.

16. See in particular the discussion in Gregg, *Culture and Identity in a Muslim Society*, pp. 19–36.

17. Sewell, "The Concept(s) of Culture," pp. 55–57.

18. Halim Barakat, *The Arab World: Society, Culture, and State* (Berkeley: University of California Press, 1993), p. 42.

19. Hamady, *The Temperament and Character of the Arabs*, p. 23.

20. Please note that simply by pursuing the topic of Arab culture I will be dealing with what are, inevitably, stereotypes; I view this as unavoidable. Without question, all Arabs, as individuals, act differently from one another, and the notion of culture is least useful in understanding the behavior of individuals. No scholarly work regarding culture can claim to accurately predict the behavior of individuals in specific circumstances. Nevertheless, I accept the notion that culturally regular behavior does exist and that it is an important influence on the behavior of both individuals and groups, and that as such, it is too important an element of human behavior to be ignored.

21. Gregg, *The Middle East*, p. 6. Emphasis in the original.

22. Yehoshofat Harkabi, "Basic Factors in the Arab Collapse during the Six-Day War," *Orbis*, Fall 1967.

23. Robert J. House, Paul Hanges, Mansour Javidan, Peter W. Dorfman, and Vipin Gupta, eds., *Culture, Leadership, and Organizations: The GLOBE Study of 62 Societies* (Thousand Oaks, CA: Sage, 2004), p. 77. Hereafter referred to simply as "GLOBE." The GLOBE Research Program was a 10-year project that surveyed 17,000 managers in 62 different countries.

24. GLOBE, p. 276.

25. For concurring views of the essential similarity of Arab culture across this region, see Alexander Abdennur, *The Arab Mind*, pp. ix, 6; Ahmed Al Soufi, "Cultural Differences between Arabs and Danes: The Intracultural Diversity's Effect on Intercultural Negotiations," Unpublished master's thesis, Aarhus University, Denmark, 2005, pp. 33–36; Roy R. Anderson, Robert F. Seibert, and Jon G. Wagner, *Politics and Change in the Middle East* (Englewood Cliffs, NJ: Prentice Hall, 1990), p. 18; Barakat, *The Arab World*, p. 12; Michael N. Barnett, *Dialogues in Arab Politics: Negotiations in Regional Order* (New York: Columbia University Press, 1998), see for instance. pp. 8, 31–32; Dwairy, *Counseling and Psychotherapy with Arabs and*

Muslims, pp. 12–15; Ellen Feghali, "Arab Cultural Communication Patterns," *International Journal of Intercultural Relations,* Vol. 21, No. 3 (1997), pp. 346–350; Ernest Gellner, *Muslim Society* (Cambridge: Cambridge University Press, 1981), p. 80; Gregg, *The Middle East,* pp. 4–6, 334–338, 359; Leila Shukry El-Hamamsy, "The Assertion of Egyptian Identity," in *Arab Society in Transition: A Reader,* ed. Saad Eddin Ibrahim and Nicholas S. Hopkins. (Malta: Interprint [Malta] Ltd., 1977), pp. 72–73 Hammoudi looks at culture and how it sustains authoritarianism in Morocco, but explicitly says that he is merely using Morocco as an example for the entire Arab world. Abdellah Hammoudi, *Master and Disciple: The Cultural Foundations of Moroccan Authoritarianism* (Chicago: University of Chicago Press, 1997), p. 3; Heggy, *The Arab Cocoon,* p. 40; Michael Hudson, "The Integration Puzzle in Arab Regional Politics," in *The Arab Future: Critical Issues,* ed. Michael C. Hudson (Washington, DC: Center for Contemporary Arab Studies, Georgetown University, 1979), p. 82; Charles Lindholm, *The Islamic Middle East,* Revised ed. (Oxford: Blackwell Publishing, 2002), p. 6; Fuad M. Moughrabi, "The Arab Basic Personality: A Critical Survey of the Literature," *International Journal of Middle East Studies,* 1978, p. 111; Pearson and Clark, *Through Middle Eastern Eyes,* pp. 18–19; Rodinson, *The Arabs,* pp. 1–12, 130–131; the passages from El-Sayyid Yassin in Halim Barakat, "Beyond the Always and the Never: A Critique of Social Psychological Interpretations of Arab Society and Culture," in *Theory, Politics and the Arab World: Critical Responses,* ed. Hisham Sharabi (New York: Routledge, 1990), pp. 140–141; and Constantine Zurayk, according to Hani A. Faris, "Constantine Zurayk: Advocate of Rationalism in Modern Arab Thought," in *Arab Civilization: Challenges and Responses,* ed. George N. Atiyeh and Ibrahim M. Oweiss (Albany: SUNY Press, 1988), p. 10.

26. United Nations Development Programme, The Arab Human Development Reports, 2002–2016, available online at www.arab-hdr.org, accessed March 1, 2017. Henceforth, I will refer to each report as "AHDR" and the year of its publication.

27. As just one example, see Ramadan A. Ahmed and Uwe P. Gielen eds., *Psychology in the Arab Countries* (Cairo: Menoufia University Press, 1998). Ahmed and Gielen provide a comprehensive overview of psychology—both the practice and the subject matter—across the Arab world based on the uncontested recognition that the psychology of Arabs is both different from that of other societies, *and* effectively the same across the Arab world.

28. Gregg, *The Middle East,* pp. 6 and 77.

29. Salzman, *Culture and Conflict in the Middle East,* p. 15.

30. For authors making the same point in prior decades, see Barakat, *The Arab World,* p. 21; Hamady, pp. 17–18; Abdallah Laroui, "Sands and Dreams," in *Arab and American Cultures,* ed. Atiyeh, p. 8.

31. Barakat, *The Arab World,* pp. XI-13, and 42; and Barakat, "Beyond the Always and the Never," pp. 140–141.

32. For example, see Barakat, *The Arab World*, p. 42; and Halim Barakat, "Arab Society: Prospects for Political Transformation," in Hudson, *The Arab Future*, pp. 65–66.

33. Andersen et al., *Politics and Change in the Middle East,* p. 12.

34. On similarities and differences between the Bedouin subculture and the dominant Arab culture see Abdennur, *The Arab Mind*, pp. 23–24; Barakat, *The Arab World*, pp. 52–53; Daniel Bates and Amal Rassam, *Peoples and Cultures of the Middle East* (Englewood Cliffs, NJ: Prentice Hall, 1983), pp. 107–128; Morroe Berger, *The Arab World Today* (New York: Anchor, 1962), pp. 46–66; Dale F. Eickelman, *The Middle East: An Anthropological Approach* (Englewood Cliffs, NJ: Prentice Hall, 1981), pp. 63–83; Hamady, *The Temperament and Character of the Arabs*, esp. pp. 97–106; Henry Rosenfeld, "The Social Composition of the Military in the Process of State Formation in the Arabian Desert," *Journal of the Royal Anthropological Institute*, Vol. 95, 1965, pp. 75–86 and 174–194; Ali Wardi, *Understanding Iraq: Society, Culture, and Personality*, trans Fuad Baali (Lewiston, NY: The Edwin Mellen Press, 2008), esp. pp. 3–41, 60–66, 82–85.

35. Clifford Geertz, *Islam Observed* (Chicago: University of Chicago Press, 1971). On this point, the reader should not be confused as to the impact of the Arab-Islamic conquest of Morocco, which was unquestionably enormous. Moroccan culture changed dramatically as a result of this event. However, this change was wrought by a combination of the new religion—Islam—and the new culture—Arabism—that were simultaneously imposed on the existing society. The Arab conquerors forcibly reshaped the societies they conquered. While in many ways, this reshaping was done in the name of Islam, because Islam, especially at that point in time, was a reflection of Arab culture, the changes were primarily in accord with Arab culture.

36. For example, see Geertz, *Islam Observed*, as well as Salzman, *Culture and Conflict in the Middle East*, pp. 137–160; C.A.O. Van Nieuwenhuijze, *Sociology of the Middle East* (Leiden: E. J. Brill, 1971), pp. 25–27;

37. For a good, if simplistic, overview of divergences between the actual practices of Saudi Arabia, Iran, and other Middle Eastern states and the dictates of classical Islam, see chapter 2, "The Foundations of Islam," and chapter 11, "The Islamic Revival and the Islamic Republic," in Andersen et al, *Politics and Change in the Middle East.*

38. Rugh, *Family in Contemporary Egypt*, p. 6.

39. Porter, *Military Orientalism,* p. 67.

40. Dwairy, *Counseling and Psychotherapy with Arabs and Muslims*, p. x.

41. For two massive studies demonstrating these recurrences (but also noting the unique differences), see Geert Hofstede, *Culture's Consequences*, Second ed. (Thousand Oaks, CA: Sage, 2001) and GLOBE.

42. Gregg, *The Middle East*, p. 98; Rugh, *Family in Contemporary Egypt*, p. 275.

43. Gregg, *The Middle East*, p. 107.

44. Michael Herzfeld, "Honour and Shame: Problems in the Comparative Analysis of Moral Systems," *Man*, Vol. 15, No. 2 (June 1980), pp. 339–351.

Chapter 17

1. Gregg, *The Middle East*, pp. 87, 341–356; Hammoudi, *Master and Disciple*, esp. pp. ix–xi, 4; Tarik Sabry, *Arab Cultural Studies: Mapping the Field* (London: I. B. Tauris, 2012), p. 8.
2. See for example, Raymond Ibrahim, "Studying the Islamic Way of War," National Review Online, September 11, 2008, available at www .nationalreview.com/article/225611/studying-islamic-way-war-raymond-ibrahim, accessed April 15, 2017; Robert Harkavy, "The Lessons of Recent Wars: Toward Comparative Analysis," in *The Lessons of Recent Wars in the Third World*, Vol. 2, ed. Robert Harkavy and Stephanie Neuman (Lexington, MA: Lexington Books, 1987). p. 17.
3. On arguments that Arab fatalism is paralyzing, see Halim Barakat, "Socioeconomic, Cultural and Personality Forces Determining Development in Arab Society," in *Arab Society in Transition: A Reader,* ed. Saad Eddin Ibrahim and Nicholas S. Hopkins (Malta: Interprint [Malta] Ltd., 1977), p. 679; Hamady, *The Temperament and Character of the Arabs*, pp. 184–190; Heggy, *The Arab Cocoon*, p. 99; Pervez Hoodbhoy, *Islam and Science* (London: Zed Books, 1991), pp. 50–51; and David Pryce-Jones, *The Closed Circle: An Interpretation of the Arabs* (New York: Harper Perennial, 1989), pp. 34–35.
4. On arguments that Arab fatalism has no impact on Arab work habits or other behavior see Evelyn A. Early, "Fertility and Fate: Medical Practices among *Baladi* Women of Cairo," in *Everyday Life in the Muslim Middle East,* ed. Donna Lee Bowen and Evelyn A. Early (Bloomington: Indiana University, 1993), pp. 102–108; Gregg, *The Middle East*, pp. 31–33; Halpern, *The Politics of Social Change in the Middle Eats and North Africa*, pp. 90–91; Abdullah M. Lutfiyya, *Baytin: A Jordanian Village* (The Hague: Mouton and Co., 1966), pp. 44–46; Levon H. Melikian, "The Modal Personality of Saudi College Students: A Study in National Character," in *Psychological Dimensions of Near Eastern Studies*, ed. L. Carl Brown and Norman Itzkowitz (Princeton, NJ: The Darwin Press, 1977), p. 172; and John Waterbury, "Islam and Hajj Ibrahim's World," in *Everyday Life in the Muslim Middle East,* ed. Donna Lee Bowen and Evelyn A. Early (Bloomington: Indiana University, 1993), pp. 178–180.
5. Quote is from Berger, *The Arab World Today*, p. 33. Also on this point, see Hamed Ammar, *Growing Up in an Egyptian Village: Silwa, Province of Aswan* (New York: Octagon Books, 1973), p. 132; Barakat, "Beyond the Always and the Never," p. 146; Barakat, *The Arab World*, p. 201; Cohen, *Culture and Conflict in Egyptian-Israeli Relations*, p. 22; Hamady, *The Temperament and Character of the Arabs*, p. 28; Fatima Mernissi, *Islam and Democracy*, trans. Mary Jo Lakeland (Reading, MA: Addison Wesley, 1992), pp. 104–113; and Van Nieuwenhuijze, *Sociology of the Middle East*, p. 381.

6. Afif I. Tannous, "Group Behavior in the Village Community of Lebanon," in *Readings in Arab Middle Eastern Studies and Cultures*, ed. Abdulla M. Lutfiyya and Charles W. Churchill (The Hague: Mouton, 1970), p. 100.

7. Barakat, *The Arab World*, p. 24.

8. Cohen, *Culture and Conflict in Egyptian-Israeli Relations*, p. 46.

9. Ammar, *Growing up in an Egyptian Village,* p. 48. See also Maxime Rodinson, *The Arabs*, trans. Arthur Goldhammer (Chicago: University of Chicago Press, 1981), p. 166.

10. Levon H. Melikian, "Authoritarianism and Its Correlates in the Egyptian Culture and in the United States," *Journal of Social Issues*, 1959, pp. 60–61.

11. Sana Al-Khayyat, *Honor and Shame: Women in Modern Iraq* (London: Saqi Books, 1990). For additional support for this trait, see Barakat, *The Arab World*, pp. 202–205; Berger, *The Arab World Today*, p. 136; Hamady, *The Temperament and Character of the Arabs*, p. 34.

12. Barakat, *The Arab World*, pp. 105–106; Sahair El-Calamawy, "The Impact of Tradition on the Development of Modern Arabic Literature," in *Arab and American Cultures*, ed. George N. Atiyeh (Washington, DC: American Enterprise Institute for Public Policy Research, 1977), p. 47; Hamady, *The Temperament and Character of the Arabs,* pp. 38–92, and 152–153; Dawisha, "Saudi Arabia's Search for Security," p. 258; Pryce-Jones, *The Closed Circle,* pp. 35–44; and Rodinson, *The Arabs*, pp. 164–165.

13. Heggy, *The Arab Cocoon*, p. 97.

14. Jacques Berque, *The Arabs* (New York: Praeger, 1965), p. 241.

15. El-Hamamsy, "The Assertion of Egyptian Identity," pp. 71–72.

16. Abdulla H. Lutfiyya, "Islam and Village Culture," in *Readings in Arab Middle Eastern Societies and Cultures*, ed. Abdulla M. Lutfiyya and Charles W. Churchill (The Hague: Mouton, 1970), p. 53.

17. Lutfiyya, *Baytin*, p. 49.

18. In addition to the specific citations below, see also Dwairy, *Counseling and Psychotherapy with Arabs and Muslims*, pp. 73–75; Heggy, *The Arab Cocoon*, p. 40.

19. Heggy, *The Arab Cocoon*, p. 97.

20. Barakat, "Beyond the Always and the Never," pp. 152–153.

21. In Cohen, *Culture and Conflict in Egyptian-Israeli Relations*, p. 22.

22. Hisham Sharabi, *Neopatriarchy: A Theory of Distorted Change in Arab Society* (Oxford: Oxford University Press, 1988), p. 47.

23. Berque, *The Arabs*, p. 32; Gellner, *Muslim Society,* p. 24.

24. Lutfiyya, *Baytin*, p. 49.

25. In Mounah Khouri, "Criticism and the Heritage: Adonis as Advocate of a New Arab Culture," in *Arab Civilization: Challenges and Responses,* ed. George N. Atiyeh and Ibrahim M. Oweiss (Albany, NY: SUNY Press, 1988), p. 188.

26. Ammar, *Growing up in an Egyptian Village,* p. 205. Further evidence of formal and informal codes proscribing innovation can be found in Manfred Halpern, "Four Contrasting Repertories of Human Relations in Islam," in *Psychological*

Dimensions of Near Eastern Studies, ed. L. Carl Brown and Norman Itzkowitz (Princeton, NJ: The Darwin Press, 1977), p. 60.

27. Pascal et al., *Men and Arms in the Middle East*, p. 27.

28. Levon H. Melikian, "The Modal Personality of Saudi College Students: A Study in National Character," in *Psychological Dimensions of Near Eastern Studies*, ed. L. Carl Brown and Norman Itzkowitz (Princeton, NJ: The Darwin Press, 1977), p. 170.

29. Joshua Mitchell, *Tocqueville in Arabia: Dilemmas in a Democratic Age* (Chicago: University of Chicago Press, 2013), p. 45.

30. Edward Said, *Orientalism* (New York: Vintage, 1979). pp. 74–77. Quote is from p. 77.

31. Rugh, *Family in Contemporary Egypt*, p. 280.

32. Mernissi, *Islam and Democracy*, pp. 95 and 96.

33. Bassam Tibi, *Islam and the Cultural Accommodation of Social Change*, trans. Clare Krojzl (Boulder, CO: Westview, 1991), p. 55. Also see Ajami, *The Arab Predicament*, p. 103.

34. Lutfiyya, "Islam and Village Culture," p. 53.

35. In Cohen, *Culture and Conflict in Egyptian-Israeli Relations*, p. 22.

36. Barakat, *The Arab World*, 106.

37. Saad Eddin Ibrahim and Nicholas S. Hopkins, "Introduction to Part II: Family and Sex Roles in Transition," in Ibrahim and Hopkins, *Arab Society in Transition*, p.84. For additional support on the suppression of creativity and innovation, see Berger, *The Arab World Today*, pp. 120–121, 156–158; Halpern, *Politics of Social Change in the Middle East and North Africa*, p. 33; Hamady, *The Temperament and Character of the Arabs*, pp. 152–153; Laroui, "Sands and Dreams," p. 50; Mernissi, *Islam and Democracy*, pp. 90–95; Gerald D. Miller, "Classroom 19: A Study in Behavior in a Classroom of a Moroccan Primary School," *Psychological Dimensions of Near Eastern Studies*, ed. L. Carl Brown and Norman Itzkowitz (Princeton, NJ: The Darwin Press, 1977), esp. p. 151; Moughrabi, "The Arab Basic Personality," p. 107; Pryce-Jones, *The Closed Circle*, pp. 40, 382–388; Wilson and Graham, *Saudi Arabia: The Coming Storm*, p. 16. Also see Monte Palmer, Abdelrahman Al-Hegelan, Mohammed Bushara Abdelrahman, Ali Leila, and El Sayeed Yassin, "Bureaucratic Innovation and Economic Development in the Middle East: A Study of Egypt, Saudi Arabia, and the Sudan," *Journal of Asian and African Studies*, Vol. 14, No. 1, 1989, pp. 14–24.

38. Dwairy, *Cross-Cultural Counseling*, pp. 74–75. The emphasis is mine.

39. Bates and Rassam, *Peoples and Cultures of the Middle East*, pp. 197–198.

40. Bates and Rassam, *Peoples and Cultures of the Middle East*, p. 198.

41. Donna Lee Bowen and Evelyn A. Early, "Generations and Life Passages: Introduction," in *Everyday Life in the Muslim Middle East*, ed. Bowen and Early, p. 14. See also Derek Hopwood, *Egypt: Politics and Society, 1945–1990*, 3rd ed. (London: Harper Collins Academic, 1991), chap 17.

42. Suad Joseph, "Anthropology of the Future: Arab Youth and the State of State," in *Anthropology of the Middle East and North Africa: Into the New Millennium*, ed. Sherine Hafez and Susan Slymovics (Bloomington: Indiana University Press, 2013), p. 118.

43. Barakat, *The Arab World*, p. 23; Hamady, *The Temperament and Character of the Arabs*, pp. 28–34; Rodinson, *The Arabs*, pp. 149–166.

44. Barakat, *The Arab World*, p. 23. For additional evidence of the persistent strength of the extended, patriarchal family in Arab society, see Ammar, *Growing up in an Egyptian Village*, pp. 44–70; Leonard Binder, "Egypt: The Integrative Revolution," in *Political Culture and Political Development*, ed. Lucian W. Pye and Sidney Verba (Princeton, NJ: Princeton University Press, 1965), p. 409; Dwairy, *Cross-Cultural Counseling*, pp. 22–29; Samih K. Farsoun and Lisa Hajjar, "The Contemporary Sociology of the Middle East: An Assessment, in Sharabi, *Theory, Politics, and the Arab World*, p. 176; George H. Gardner, "The Arab Middle East: Some Background Interpretations," *The Journal of Social Issues*, Vol. 20, No. 3, 1959, pp. 24–25; Rodinson, *The Arabs*, p. 149; Hisham Sharabi in collaboration with Mukhtar Ani, "Impact of Class and Culture on Social Behavior: The Feudal-Bourgeois Family in Arab Society, in *Psychological Dimensions of Near Eastern Studies*, ed. Brown and Itzkowitz, esp. pp. 242–248; Sharabi, *Neopatriarchy*, esp. pp. 29–31; Afif I. Tannous, "Group Behavior in the Village Community of Lebanon," *American Journal of Sociology* 48 (2) (September 1942), pp. 100–104.

45. Barakat, *The Arab World*, p. 23. For concurring opinions, see for example, Binder, "Egypt," p. 409; Abdelwahab Bouhdiba, *Sexuality in Islam* (London: Routledge & Kegan Paul, 1985); Gardner, *The Arab Middle East*, pp. 24–25; Gregg, *The Middle East*, pp. 218–219; Gregg, *Culture and Identity in a Muslim Society*, p. 306; Sharabi, "Impact of Class and Culture on Social Behavior," p. 243; Sharabi, *Neopatriarchy*, esp. pp. 7–20; and Unni Wikan, *Life among the Poor in Cairo*, trans. Ann Henning (London: Tavistock Publications, 1980), p. 65.

46. Ilse Lichtenstadter, "An Arab-Egyptian Family," in Abdulla Lutfiyya and Churchill eds., *Readings in Arab Middle Eastern Societies and Cultures*, p. 607.

47. Abdulla Lutfiyya, "The Family," in Lufiyya and Churchill eds., *Readings in Arab Middle Eastern Societies and Cultures*, pp. 518–519.

48. See for instance, Pascal Menoret, *Joyriding in Riyadh: Oil, Urbanism, and Road Revolt* (New York: Cambridge University Press, 2014), p. 183.

49. Van Nieuwenhuijze, *Sociology of the Middle East*, pp. 385–386. See also, Barakat, "Between the Always and the Never," p. 146; Hamady, *The Temperament and Character of the Arabs*, p. 32; Lichtenstadter, "An Arab-Egyptian Family," p. 607; Rugh, *Family in Contemporary Egypt*, p. 71.

50. Ammar, *Growing up in an Egyptian Village*, p. 50.

51. Pegrouhi Najarian, "Adjustment in the Family and Patterns of Family Living," *Journal of Social Issues*, Vol. 15, No. 3, 1959, pp. 35–36.

52. Ammar, *Growing up in an Egyptian Village,* pp. 52 and 127; Barakat, "Socioeconomic, Cultural and Personality Forces Determining Development in Arab Society," p. 680; Binder, "Egypt," p. 409; Cohen, *Culture and Conflict in Egyptian-Israeli Relations,* p. 27; Gardner, *The Arab Middle East,* p. 39; and Wikan, *Life among the Poor in Cairo,* p. 65.

53. Perhaps the most powerful statement of the influence of Arab family patterns on all other organizations and institutions in the Arab world is Hisham Sharabi's *Neopatriarchy,* see especially, pp. 7–47. See also Hammoudi, *Master and Disciple,* pp. 81–97; Rugh, *Family in Contemporary Egypt,* pp. 43–45.

54. Hamady, *The Temperament and Character of Arabs,* p. 88. See also Fernea, "Childhood in the Muslim Middle East," p. 11; Hammoudi, *Master and Disciple,* pp. 81–97; Rugh, *Family in Contemporary Egypt,* pp. 43–45.

55. Jamil E. Jreisat, "Bureaucracy and Development in Jordan," *Journal of Asian and African Studies,* Vol. 24, Nos. 1–2, 1989, p. 100.

56. Barakat, *The Arab World,* p. 23. For additional support for this argument, see Cohen, *Culture and Conflict in Egyptian-Israeli Relations,* p. 27.

57. Rugh, *Family in Contemporary Egypt,* p. 44.

58. Gregg, *Culture and Identity in a Muslim Society,* p. 312; Hammoudi, *Master and Disciple,* esp. pp. vii–xi.

59. Gregg, *Culture and Identity in a Muslim Society,* p. 37. Emphasis in original.

60. See for instance, Al Soufi, "Cultural Differences between Arabs and Danes," pp. 59–60.

61. Dwairy, *Counseling and Psychotherapy with Arabs and Muslims,* pp. 6–12; Gregg, *The Middle East,* p. 103; Heggy, *The Arab Cocoon,* p. 40.

62. Cohen, *Culture and Conflict in Egyptian-Israeli Relations,* p. 22.

63. Cohen, *Culture and Conflict in Egyptian-Israeli Relations,* p. 28.

64. Gregg, *The Middle East,* pp. 244–245. Quote is from Gregg, *The Middle East,* p. 245. Emphasis in original.

65. Dwairy, *Cross-Cultural Counseling,* p. 29. See also Berque, *The Arabs,* pp. 103.

66. Al Soufi, "Cultural Differences between Arabs and Danes," pp. 42, 51; Dwairy, *Counseling and Psychotherapy with Arabs and Muslims,* pp. 13, 26; Fernea, "Childhood in the Muslim Middle East," pp. 10–11; Gregg, *The Middle East,* pp. 30, 90–113, 217; Lila Abu-Lughod, *Veiled Sentiments: Honor and Poetry in a Bedouin Society* (Berkeley: University of California Press, 1986); Mitchell, *Tocqueville in Arabia,* pp. 45–50.

67. Gregg, *The Middle East,* p. 28. See also p. 91.

68. Rodinson, *The Arabs,* p. 165.

69. Salzman, *Culture and Conflict in the Middle East,* p. 105. Also see Judith Williams, *The Youth of Haouch el Harimi, A Lebanese Village* (Cambridge, MA: Harvard University Press, 1968), pp. 39–40.

70. Hamady, *The Temperament and Character of the Arabs,* p. 35.

71. Ammar, *Growing Up in an Egyptian Village,* p. 230.

72. Quoted in Miller, "Classroom 19," p. 151. For additional support for the importance of honor and shame as motivating forces in Arab society, see Richard T. Antoun, *Arab Village: A Social Structural Study of a TransJordanian Peasant Community* (Bloomington,: Indiana University Press, 1972), p. 97; Barakat, *The Arab World*, pp. 105–106, and 202; Berque, *The Arabs*, p. 32; Cohen, *Culture and Conflict in Egyptian-Israeli Relations*, pp. 23–24; Hamady, *The Temperament and Character of the Arabs*, pp. 34–35; Lutfiyya, *Baytin*, p. 17; Phebe Marr, "The Iraqi Village: Prospects for Change," in Lutfiyya and Churchill eds., *Reading in Arab Middle Eastern Societies and Cultures*, p. 335; Pryce-Jones, *The Closed Circle*, pp. 35–40; Sharabi, "Impact of Class and Culture on Social behavior," p. 247; and Hisham Sharabi, "The Scholarly Point of View: Politics, Perspective, Paradigm," in *Theory, Politics and the Arab World*, ed. Sharabi, p. 100.
73. Rugh, *Family in Contemporary Egypt*, p. 284.
74. Dwairy, *Counseling and Psychotherapy with Arabs and Muslims*, p. 13. See also Fernea, "Childhood in the Muslim Middle East," p. 11; Heggy, *The Arab Cocoon*, pp. 101–102.
75. Barakat, *The Arab World*, p. 24; Hamady, *The Temperament and Character of the Arabs*, pp. 34–35; and Wikan, *Life Amoing the Poor in Cairo*, p. 123.
76. Sharabi, "Impact of Class and Culture on Social Behavior," p. 249.
77. Hamady, *The Temperament and Character of the Arabs*, p. 34.
78. Lichtenstadter, "An Arab-Egyptian Family," p. 607.
79. Barakat, "Beyond the Always and the Never," pp. 144–146, Barakat, *The Arab World*, pp. 23–24; Lichtenstadter, "An Arab-Egyptian Family," p. 607; Sharabi, "Impact of Class and Culture on Social Behavior," p. 249.
80. Barakat, "Beyond the Always and the Never," pp. 152–153.
81. Pascal et al., *Men and Arms in the Middle East*, p. 27.
82. Pascal et al., *Men and Arms in the Middle East*, p. 34.
83. On this point the sources are voluminous, but see in particular, Dwairy, *Counseling and Psychotherapy with Arabs and Muslims*; Rugh, *Family in Contemporary Egypt*; Salzman, *Culture and Conflict in the Middle East*, pp. 11–13, 16, 31–32, 52–53, 66–100.
84. Al Soufi, "Cultural Differences between Arabs and Danes," p. 37.
85. Dwairy, *Counseling and Psychotherapy with Arabs and Muslims*, p. 3.
86. Dwairy, *Counseling and Psychotherapy with Arabs and Muslims*, p. 10.
87. Rugh, *Family in Contemporary Egypt*, p. 34.
88. Rugh, *Family in Contemporary Egypt*, pp. 32–33, 283.
89. Abdennur, *The Arab Mind*, p. 25.
90. Barakat, *The Arab World*, p. 62. Also see Barakat, *The Arab World*, pp. 63, 201; Berger, *The Arab World Today*, p. 83; Hamady, *The Temperament and Character of the Arabs*, p. 28; Hamamsy, *The Assertion of Egyptian Identity*, pp. 71–72; Al-Khayyat, *Honour and Shame*, p. 11; Nawal el-Messiri Nadim, "Family Relationships in a 'Harah' in Cairo," in Hopkins and Ibrahim eds., *Arab Society*, p. 111; Rodinson, *The Arabs*, p. 151.

91. Melikian, "The Modal Personality of Saudi College Students," pp. 170–171. For additional support for the extension of loyalties beyond kin, see Ammar, *Growing up in an Egyptian Village*, p. 73; Barakat, *The Arab World*, pp. 24, 57, 63; Eickelman, *The Middle East*, pp. 76, 110–116; Gellner, *Muslim Society*, p. 69; Hamady, *The Temperament and Character of the Arabs*, p. 28; Van Nieuwenhuijze, *Sociology of the Middle East*, p. 388.

92. Van Nieuwenhuijze, *Sociology of the Middle East*, p. 390.

93. Eickelman, *The Middle East*, pp. 37, 110–116; Gregg, *The Middle East*, pp. 66–67.

94. Eickelman, *The Middle East*, p. 76.

95. Hamady, *The Temperament and Character of the Arabs*, p. 56. See also Mitchell, *Tocqueville in Arabia*, p. 4.

96. Lufiyya, *Baytin*, p. 177.

97. El-Hamamsy, *The Assertion of Egyptian Identity*, p. 71–72.

98. Melikian, "The Modal Personality of Saudi College Students," pp. 170–171. See also Ammar, *Growing up in an Egyptian Village*, p. 47, 73; Barakat, *The Arab World*, pp. 24, 98–100; Cohen, *Culture and Conflict in Egyptian-Israeli Relations*, p. 23; Eickelman, *The Middle East*, pp. 110–116; Gardner, *The Arab Middle East*, pp. 24–25; El-Hamamsy, *The Assertion of Egyptian Identity*, p. 75; Hamady, *The Temperament and Character of the Arabs*, p. 29; Stephen H. Longrigg and Frank Stoakes,"The Social Pattern," in Lutfiyya and Churchill eds., *Readings in Arab Middle Eastern Societies and Cultures*, p. 67; Sharabi, *Neopatriarchy*, p. 28.

99. Abdennur, *The Arab Mind:*, p. 25; Gregg, *The Middle East*, pp. 54–55, 66–67; Rugh, *Family in Contemporary Egypt*, pp. 38–40.

100. See for example, Barakat, *The Arab World*, p. 25; Berger, *The Arab World Today*, p. 144; Hamady, *The Temperament and Character of the Arabs*, p. 62; Pryce-Jones, *The Closed Circle*, p. 41; Wikan, *Life among the Poor in Cairo*, p. 123.

101. Feghali, "Arab Cultural Communication Patterns," esp. p. 358.

102. Hamady, *The Temperament and Character of the Arabs*, pp. 71–72.

103. Pryce-Jones, *The Closed Circle*, p. 41.

104. Pascal et al., *Men and Arms in the Middle East*, p. 27.

105. Hamady, *The Temperament and Character of the Arabs*, pp. 45–46; Harkabi, *Basic Factors in the Arab Collapse During the Six Day War*, pp. 687–688.

106. Barakat, *The Arab World*, p. 25.

107. Salzman, *Culture and Conflict in the Middle East*, p. 120.

108. Salzman, *Culture and Conflict in the Middle East*, pp. 121–125.

109. Rugh, *Family in Contemporary Egypt*, p. 282.

110. Hamady, *The Temperament and Character of the Arabs*, pp. 36–37.

111. Cohen, *Culture and Conflict in Egyptian-Israeli Relations*, p. 23.

112. Sharabi, "Impact of Class and Culture on Social Behavior," p. 249.

113. Wikan, *Life among the Poor in Cairo*, p. 49. See also p. 123.

114. Melikian, "The Modal Personality of Saudi College Students," p. 172. See also, Ammar, *Growing up in an Egyptian Village,* p. 230; Berger, *The Arab World Today,* p. 144, Binder, "Egypt," p. 411; Hamady, *The Temperament and Character of the Arabs,* pp. 100–101; Sharabi, "Impact of Class and Culture on Social Behavior," pp. 249, 255.

115. Barakat, *The Arab World,* p. 106.

116. Cited in Pryce-Jones, *The Closed Circle,* p. 44. See also Ajami, *The Arab Predicament,* p. 49; Barakat, *The Arab World,* p. 25: Cohen, *Culture and Conflict in Egyptian-Israeli Relations,* p. 24; Michael Gilsenan, "Lying, Honor, and Contradiction," in *Everyday Life in the Muslim Middle East,* ed. Bowen and Early, pp. 157–158; Hamady, *The Temperament and Character of the Arabs,* pp. 34–37; Wikan, *Life among the Poor in Cairo,* p. 123.

117. Heggy, *The Arab Cocoon,* pp. 49, 132–134.

118. Hamady, *The Temperament and Character of the Arabs,* p. 209.

119. Bernard Lewis, *The Arabs in History*, Revised ed. (New York: Harper, 1966), p. 141.

120. Lewis, *The Arabs in History,* p. 142. See also, Dwairy, *Counseling and Psychotherapy with Arabs and Muslims,* pp. 18–19.

121. Lewis, *The Arabs in History,* p. 142.

122. Quoted in AHDR 2003, p. 35.

123. Berger, *The Arab World Today,* p. 159. For concurring views, see Ajami, *The Arab Predicament,* p. 186; Barakat, "Beyond the Always and the Never," p. 144; Barakat, *The Arab World,* p. 275; Gellner, *Muslim Society,* pp. 124–125; and Rodinson, *The Arabs,* p. 168.

124. Halpern, *The Politics of Social Change in the Middle East*, p. 355.

125. Hamady, *The Temperament and Character of the Arabs,* pp. 209–211.

126. Jreisat, *Bureaucracy and Development in Jordan,* p. 100.

127. Abdennur, *The Arab Mind*, pp, 84–87, 267.

128. Abdennur, *The Arab Mind*, p. 53.

129. Abdennur, *The Arab Mind*, p. 83.

130. Heggy, *The Arab Cocoon,* pp. 136–137.

131. Pascal et al., *Men and Arms in the Middle East,* p. 27.

132. AHDR, 2003, p. 123.

133. Rodinson, *The Arabs,* p. 164.

134. El-Hamamsy, *The Assertion of Egyptian Identity,* pp. 71–73.

135. Gregg, *The Middle East,* pp. 216–239, 264–266. The quote is from p. 257.

136. Khalid, "The Socio-cultural Determinants of Arab Diplomacy," p. 127.

137. In Cohen, *Culture and Conflict in Egyptian-Israeli Relations,* p. 22.

138. Ammar, *Growing Up in an Egyptian Village*; Antoun, *Arab Village*; Lutfiyya, *Baytin*; and Marr, "The Iraqi Village, Prospects for Change."

139. Nadim, "Family Relationships in a 'Harah' in Cairo"; Wikan, *Life among the Poor in Cairo.*

140. John Bagot Glubb, *The Story of the Arab Legion* (New York: Da Capo, 1976), p. 253.

141. Barakat, *The Arab World*, p. 53; P. A. Kluck, "The Society and Its Environment," in Richard F. Nyrop, *Saudi Arabia: A Country Study*, Fourth ed. (Washington, DC: Government Printing Office, 1984), p. 125; Pascal et al., *Men and Arms in the Middle East,* pp. VIII, 27; Pryce-Jones, *The Closed Circle,* p. 268; Mohamed Rabie, "The Future of Education in the Arab World," in *The Arab Future,* ed. Hudson, pp. 23–27; also see Milton Viorst, *Sandcastles: The Arabs in Search of the Modern World* (New York: Alfred A. Knopf, 1994), p. 246.

142. John Gulick, "Two Streams into One," in Lutfiyya and Churchill eds., *Readings in Arab Middle Eastern Societies and Cultures,* p. 342.

143. Gellner, *Muslim Society,* p. 88. Dana Adams Schmidt found the same sentiments in the Yemen. Dana Adams Schmidt, *Yemen: The Unknown War* (London: The Bodly Head, 1968), p. 71.

144. Abdennur, *The Arab Mind*, p. 24. See also Hamady, *The Temperament and Character of the Arabs,* pp. 147 and 38.

145. Berger, *The Arab World Today,* p. 405.

146. Fahim I. Qubain, *Education and Science in the Arab World* (Baltimore, MD: Johns Hopkins University Press, 1966), p. 25.

147. Gregg, *The Middle East*, p. 81

148. Hopwood, *Egypt*, p. 139.

149. E. A. Kinch, "Labour Problems in the Early Days of the Industry," in Lutfiyya and Churchill eds., *Readings in Arab Middle Eastern Societies and Cultures,* p. 358. Emphasis in original.

150. Donna Lee Bowen and Evelyn A. Early, "Home, Community and Work: Introduction," in *Everyday Life in the Muslim Middle East,* ed. Bowen and Early, p. 126.

151. See as just one example, the World Bank, *Middle East and North Africa Region Economic Developments and Prospects, 2007: Job Creation in an Era of High Growth.* Washington, DC: The World Bank, 2007, p. 40. However, World Bank reports on the Arab world generally and Arab states specifically have repeatedly made this point for decades.

152. Hoodbhoy, *Islam and Science,* p. 50.

153. Albert Hourani, *A History of the Arab Peoples* (Cambridge, MA: Belknap Press, 1991), p. 391.

154. Heggy, *The Arab Cocoon*, p. 83.

155. Unni Wikan, *Tomorrow, God Willing: Self-Made Destinies in Cairo* (Chicago: University of Chicago Press, 1996), p. 164.

156. Hoodbhoy, *Islam and Science,* pp. 124–126; Pascal et al., *Men and Arms in the Middle East,* 23–25.

157. Faris, *Constantine Zurayk,* p. 13.

158. Joseph G. Jabbra, "Bureaucracy and Development in the Arab World," *Journal of Asian and African Studies*, Vol. 24, Nos. 1–2, 1989, p. 4.

159. Rabie, *The Future of Education in the Arab World*, p. 23.

160. Pascal et al., *Men and Arms in the Middle East*, pp. 23–24. See also Hopwood, *Egypt*, p. 141; Hopwood, *Syria*, p. 125; Wilson and Graham, *Saudi Arabia: The Coming Storm*, p. 28; and P. J. Vatikiotis, *Politics and the Military in Jordan* (London: Frank Cass, 1967), p. 25.

161. Marcus Noland and Howard Pack, *The Arab Economies in a Changing World* (Washington, DC: Peterson Institute for International Economics, 2007), esp. p. 94.

162. Zahlan, *Science Policy in the Arab World*, p. 31.

163. Zahlan, *Science Policy in the Arab World*, p. 28. For concurring views, see Pascal et al., *Men and Arms in the Middle East*, pp. 28–34; Sharabi, *Neopatriarchy*, p. 81; and Michael J. Simpson, "The Prospects of Technological Growth in Arab Societies: An Analysis of the Potential for Progress toward Technological Autonomy in the Arab World, 1985–1995," in Sharabi, *The Next Arab Decade*, pp. 132–133.

164. Noland and Pack, *The Arab Economies in a Changing World*, pp. 178–79.

165. AHDR 2003, p. 71.

166. AHDR 2003, p. 78.

167. AHDR 2003, 71.

168. Calvert W. Jones, *Bedouins into Bourgeois: Remaking Citizens for Globalization* (Cambridge: Cambridge University Press, 2017).

Chapter 18

1. Leonard Wong, Thomas A. Kolditz, Raymond A. Millen, and Terrence M. Potter, *Why They Fight: Combat Motivation in the Iraq War* (Carlisle Barracks, PA: Strategic Studies Institute, US Army War College, 2003), p. 8.

2. Lt. Gen. Gus Pagonis with Jeffrey L. Cruikshank, *Moving Mountains: Lessons in Leadership and Logistics from the Gulf War* (Cambridge, MA: Harvard Business School Press, 1992), p. 101.

3. David McDonald, a former student of mine at Georgetown, has proposed an interesting idea that may explain part or all of the mystery around Arab logistics and engineering: the oil industry. Both Iraq and Libya (and to a lesser extent Egypt) have extensive oil industries, which required tremendous logistical operations across vast deserts and a certain amount of engineering ability, although much of that has been typically performed by foreign oil firms. It may be that all three were able to extrapolate from this experience to the military equivalents. Of course, Syria also had a modest oil industry before the descent into civil war in 2012. Again, this explanation may be spot on, and the mystery that needs explaining is why the Syrians didn't benefit the way that the Iraqis, Libyans, and Egyptians did.

4. "Total Military Personnel of the U.S. Army for Fiscal Years 2016 and 2018, by Rank," Statista, Available at www.statista.com/statistics/239383/ total-military-personnel-of-the-us-army-by-grade/, accessed December 16, 2017.

Chapter 19

1. Palmer et al., *Bureaucratic Innovation and Economic Development in the Middle East,* pp. 19–24.
2. Berque, *The Arabs*, p. 30; Cohen, *Culture and Conflict in Egyptian- Israeli Relations*, p. 27; Hamady, *The Temperament and Character of the Arabs,* pp. 111–113; Samir Mutawi, *Jordan in the 1967 War* (Cambridge: Cambridge University Press, 1987), p. 1; Pascal et al., *Men and Arms in the Middle East,* p. 35; Hisham Sharabi, *Government and Politics of the Middle East* (Princeton, NJ: Van Nostrand, 1962), ch. 1; Wardi, *Understanding Iraq*, pp. 60–66.
3. Organization for Economic Co-operation and Development, "Progress in Public Management in the Middle East and North Africa," OECD, 2010.
4. AHDR, 2003, esp. pp. 113–131.
5. AHDR, 2003, p. 35.
6. GLOBE, esp. pp. 654–668.
7. GLOBE, pp. 74–78.
8. For a sample of this work, see Abbas J. Ali, "Decision-Making Style, Individualism, and Attitudes toward Risk of Arab Executives," *International Studies of Management and Organization*, Vol. 23, No. 3 (1993), pp. 53–73; Hanan AlMazrouei and Richard J. Pech, "Working in the UAE: Expatriate Management Experiences," *Journal of Islamic Accounting and Business Research*, Vol. 6, No. 1 (2015), pp. 74–79; Ali Al-Kubaisy, "A Model in the Administrative Development of Arab Gulf Countries." *The Arab Gulf* 17, No. 2 (1985), pp. 29–48; Al Soufi, "Cultural Differences between Arabs and Danes;" Syed Aziz Anwar and Mohammad Naim Chaker, "Globalization of Corporate America and Its Implications for Management Styles in an Arabian Cultural Context," *International Journal of Management,* Vol. 20, No. 1 (March 2003), pp. 44–45, 52; M. K. Badawy, "Styles of Middle Eastern Managers," *California Management Review*, Vol. 22, No. 2 (Spring 1980), p. 51; Colin Butler, "Leadership in a Multicultural Arab Organization," *Leadership and Organization Development Journal*, Vol. 30, No. 2 (2009), pp. 139–151; Samer S. Shehata, *Shop Floor Culture and Politics in Egypt* (Albany: SUNY Press, 2009), R. S. Zaharna, Ed.D, "Bridging Cultural Differences: American Public Relations Practices and Arab Communications Patterns," *Public Relations Review*, Vol. 21 (1995), pp. 241–255.
9. Shehata, *Shop Floor Culture and Politics in Egypt*, p. 3.
10. AHDR 2003, p. 137.
11. AHDR 2003, p. 138.

12. The World Bank, *Middle East and North Africa Region Economic Developments and Prospects, 2007*, p. 91.

13. International Labour Office, "Global Employment Trends Brief," January 2007, p. 4.

14. Nimrod Raphaeli, "Unemployment in the Middle East—Causes and Consequences," MEMRI, February 11, 2006.

15. Delwin A. Roy, "Saudi Arabian Education: Development Policy," *Middle Eastern Studies*, Vol. 28, No. 3 (July 1992), p. 478.

16. See for instance, Ali, "Decision-Making Style, Individualism, and Attitudes toward Risk of Arab Executives," pp. 53–73; AlMazrouei and Pech, "Working in the UAE," pp. 74–79; Anwar and Chaker, "Globalization of Corporate America and Its Implications for Management Styles in an Arabian Cultural Context," pp. 43–55; GLOBE, esp. pp. 539–540, 548–549; Heggy, *The Arab Cocoon*, p. 139; Shehata, *Shop Floor Culture and Politics in Egypt*, entire.

17. Shehata, *Shop Floor Culture and Politics in Egypt*, p. 154.

18. Shehata, *Shop Floor Culture and Politics in Egypt*, p. 131.

19. Ali, "Decision-Making Style, Individualism, and Attitudes toward Risk of Arab Executives," p. 55.

20. Culturally, they found this incredibly difficult. Pfaff, "Development and Reform of the Iraqi Police Forces," pp. 9–12.

21. GLOBE, pp. 539–540, 548–549.

22. Badawy, "Styles of Middle Eastern Managers," p. 57; Shehata, *Shop Floor Culture and Politics in Egypt*, entire but esp. pp. 54–55.

23. GLOBE, p. 707.

24. GLOBE, pp. 268–276.

25. Shehata, *Shop Floor Culture and Politics in Egypt*, p. 155.

26. Badawy, "Styles of Middle Eastern Managers," pp. 52–56.

27. R. S. Zaharna, Ed.D, "Bridging Cultural Differences: American Public Relations Practices and Arab Communications Patterns," *Public Relations Review*, Vol. 21 (1995), pp. 241–255.

28. Shehata, *Shop Floor Culture and Politics in Egypt*, p. 155.

29. GLOBE, p. 7.

30. GLOBE, p. 14.

31. GLOBE, p; 7.

32. Anwar and Chaker, "Globalization of Corporate America and Its Implications for Management Styles in an Arabian Cultural Context," pp. 46–47.

33. Pfaff, "Development and Reform of the Iraqi Police Forces," p. VII. Also see pp. 12–14.

34. GLOBE, pp. 695–697.

35. The Kingdom of Saudi Arabia, "Vision 2030, " Released April 2016, available at http://vision2030.gov.sa/en, accessed May 11, 2018. See also Heggy, *The Arab Cocoon*, pp. 78–96.

Chapter 20

1. AHDR 2003, pp. 3–6.
2. AHDR 2002, pp. 52–55; Gabriella Gonzalez, Lynn A. Karoly, Louay Constant, Hanine Salem, and Charles A. Goldman, "Facing Human Capital Challenges of the 21st Century: Education and Labor Market Initiatives in Lebanon, Oman, Qatar, and the United Arab Emirates," Santa Monica, CA: The RAND Corporation, 2008, esp. pp. 2–3, 50–55; Farrukh Iqbal, *Sustaining Gains in Poverty Reduction and Human Development in the Middle East and North Africa* (Washington, DC: The World Bank, 2006), pp. 33–46; Noland and Pack, *The Arab Economies in a Changing World*, p. 70; The World Bank, *The Road Not Traveled: Education Reform in the Middle East and Africa*, MENA Development Report (Washington, DC: The World Bank, 2008), pp. 9–17, 296.
3. George T. Abed and Hamid R. Davoodi, "Challenges of Growth and Globalization in the Middle East and North Africa." International Monetary Fund, 2003, available at www.imf.org/external/pubs/ft/med/2003/eng/abed.htm, accessed May 11, 2018.
4. AHDR 2002, p. 53.
5. AHDR 2002, p. 54; "Regional Fact Sheet: Education in the Arab States," UNESCO, January 2013, available at www.google.com/url?sa=t&rct=j&q=&esrc=s&source=web&cd=8&ved=0ahUKEwjH4tKowb_ZAhWIwFMKHbYAA2gQFgh_MAc&url=https%3A%2F%2Fen.unesco.org%2F2Fgem-report%2Fsites%2Fgem-report%2Ffiles%2F219170e.pdf&usg=AOvVaw22I-Ynf-7EqafgVRymVRMb, accessed February 24, 2018.
6. Iqbal, *Sustaining Gains in Poverty Reduction and Human Development in the Middle East and North Africa*, pp. 44–45.
7. AHDR 2003, p. 55.
8. For the results of these studies see AHDR 2003, pp. 55–56; and Trends in International Mathematics and Science Study, 2003, Chapter 1: International Student Achievement in Math, available online at http://isc.bc.edu/PDF/t03_download/T03_M_Chap1.pdf, accessed May 28, 2007; and Trends in International Mathematics and Science Study, 2003, Chapter 1: International Student Achievement in Science, available online at http://isc.bc.edu/PDF/t03_download/T03_S_Chap1.pdf, downloaded May 28, 2007.
9. The World Bank, *The Road Not Traveled*, p. 19.
10. AHDR 2003, p. 4.
11. Gonzalez et al., "Facing Human Capital Challenges of the 21st Century," pp. 50–51.
12. The World Bank, *The Road Not Traveled*, p. xvi.
13. Roy, "Saudi Arabian Education," p. 485. For concurring views, see AHDR 2003, esp. pp. 3, 51–56; Ahmed Galal, "The Paradox of Education and Unemployment in Egypt," The Egyptian Center for Economic Studies, March

2002, pp. 2–4; Heggy, *The Arab Cocoon*, p. 102; Noland and Pack, *The Arab Economies in a Changing World*, p. 37; Roy, "Saudi Arabian Education," pp. 480, 483–484, 489, 506.

14. Gregg, *The Middle East*, p. 45. Also see p. 351.
15. Barakat, *The Arab World*, p. 118; Gregg, *The Middle East*, pp. 292–293; Minoura, "A Sensitive Period for the Incorporation of a Cultural Meaning System," pp. 304–339.
16. AHDR 2003, p. 51.
17. Gregg, *The Middle East*, p. 214.
18. Dwairy, *Counseling and Psychotherapy with Arabs and Muslims*, p. 53.
19. Barakat, "Beyond the Always and the Never," p. 144. Also see Ammar, *Growing Up in an Egyptian Village*, p. 127; Hamady, *The Temperament and Character of the Arabs*, p. 70; Lutfiyya, "The Family," pp. 518–519.
20. Barakat, "Socioeconomic, Cultural and Personality Forces Determining Development in Arab Society," p. 680.
21. Gregg, *The Middle East*, p. 212. On this point, see also Ammar, *Growing up in an Egyptian Village,* pp. 50, 52, 127; Barakat, *The Arab World*, p. 23; Barakat, "Between the Always and the Never," p. 146; Barakat, "Socioeconomic, Cultural and Personality Forces Determining Development in Arab Society," p. 113; Berque, *The Arabs*, pp. 103; Binder, "Egypt," p. 409; Judy Brink, "Changing Child-Rearing Patterns in an Egyptian Village," in *Children in the Muslim Middle East,* ed. Elizabeth Fernea (Austin: University of Texas Press, 1995), p. 86; Cohen, *Culture and Conflict in Egyptian-Israeli Relations*, p. 27; Dwairy, *Counseling and Psychotherapy with Arabs and Muslims*, esp. pp. 25, 53–56; Fernea, "Childhood in the Muslim Middle East," pp. 7–8; Gardner, "The Arab Middle East," pp. 24–25, 39; Gregg, *The Middle East*, pp. 154, 193, 212–215, 220–225, 235–236; Hamady, *The Temperament and Character of the Arabs,* p. 32; Ibrahim and Hopkins, *Arab Society in Transition,* pp. 83–84; Lichtenstadter, "An Arab-Egyptian Family," pp. 35–36; Pascal et. al., *Men and Arms in the Middle East*, p. 27; Sharabi, "Impact of Class and Culture on Social Behavior," p. 243; Sharabi, *Neopatriarchy*, pp. 7–20, 44–47; Van Nieuwenhuijze, *Sociology of the Middle East*, pp. 385–386; Karen Walker, "Teachers and Teacher World-Views," *International Education Journal*, Vol. 5, No. 3 (2004), esp. pp. 436–437; Wikan, *Life among the Poor in Cairo*, p. 65; Wikan, *Tomorrow, God Willing*, pp. 148–150.
22. Ammar, *Growing up in an Egyptian Village,* p. 231.
23. Cohen, *Culture and Conflict in Egyptian-Israeli Relations*, p. 22.
24. Ibid.
25. In Cohen, *Culture and Conflict in Egyptian-Israeli Relations*, p. 22. See also Ammar, *Growing up in an Egyptian Village,* pp. 48, 132; Barakat, "Between the Always and the Never," p. 146; Barakat, *The Arab World*, pp. 106, 201–205; Berger, *The Arab World Today,* p. 136; Cohen, p. 22; Dwairy, *Cross-Cultural Counseling*, pp. 60–70; Hamady, *The Temperament and Character of the Arabs,*

pp. 28, 34; Ibrahim and Hopkins, *Arab Society in Transition,* pp. 83–84; Khouri, "Criticism and the Heritage," p. 188; Lutfiyya, *Baytin,* p. 49; Mernissi, *Islam and Democracy,* pp. 104–113; Van Nieuwenhuijze, *Sociology of the Middle East,* p. 381; Sharabi, *Neopatriarchy,* p. 47; Tannous, "Group Behavior in the Village Community of Lebanon," p. 100.

26. Dwairy, *Cross-Cultural Counseling,* p. 60.

27. Dwairy, *Cross-Cultural Counseling,* p. 70. Emphasis in original.

28. Ibrahim and Hopkins, *Arab Society in Transition,* p. 83–84.

29. Walker, "Teachers and Teacher World-Views," p. 437.

30. In particular, see Gilsenan, "Lying, Honor, and Contradiction," pp. 157–159.

31. Barakat, *The Arab World,* p. 23.

32. Sharabi, "Impact of Class and Culture on Social Behavior," p. 249.

33. Hamady, *The Temperament and Character of the Arabs,* p. 38. Also on this point, see Barakat, *The Arab World,* p. 53; Berger, *The Arab World Today,* p. 405; Bowen and Early, "Home, Community and Work," p. 126; Gulick, "Two Streams into One," p. 342; Hamady, *The Temperament and Character of the Arabs,* p. 147; Hopwood, *Syria, 1945–1986,* p. 125; Jabbra, "Bureaucracy and Development in the Arab World," p. 4; Kinch, "Labour Problems in the Early Days of the Industry," p. 358; Kluck, "The Society and its Environment," p. 125; Pascal et al., *Men and Arms in the Middle East,* pp. VIII, 27; Pryce-Jones, *The Closed Circle,* p. 268; Rabie, "The Future of Education in the Arab World," pp. 23–27.

34. See Barakat, "Beyond the Always and the Never Was," p. 143.

35. Sharabi, "Impact of Class and Culture on Social Behavior," p. 250.

36. Ibrahim and Hopkins, eds., *Arab Society in Transition,* p. 84.

37. Sharabi, "Impact of Class and Culture on Social Behavior," p. 251.

38. Sharabi, "Impact of Class and Culture on Social Behavior," p. 251.

39. Al-Khayyat, *Honor and Shame,* p. 53. See also, Barakat, *The Arab World,* pp. 105–106; Miller, "Classroom 19," p. 151.

40. Dwairy, *Cross-Cultural Counseling,* pp. 70–71.

41. Gregg, *The Middle East,* p. 242; Miller, "Classroom 19," esp. pp. 152–153; Tibi, *Islam and the Cultural Accommodation of Social Change,* p. 103.

42. AHDR 2003, pp. 53–54; Alan Richards and John Waterbury, *A Political Economy of the Middle East,* Third Edition (Boulder, CO: Westview, 2008), p. 122. See also, Miller, "Classroom 19," p. 144.

43. Miller, "Classroom 19," p. 144.

44. Gregg, *The Middle East,* p. 240.

45. Hoodbhoy, *Islam and Science,* pp. 38–39.

46. Berque, *The Arabs,* p. 30; Susan Dorsky and Thomas B. Stevenson, "Childhood and Education in Highland North Yemen," in *Children in the Muslim Middle East,* Elizabeth Warnock Fernea (Austin: University of Texas Press, 1995), p. 317; Gregg, *The Middle East,* p. 241.

47. Eickelman, *The Middle East,* pp. 238–240; Hoodbhoy, *Islam and Science,* pp. 55–65, 123–124.

48. Binder, *Egypt,* p. 413.

49. On this point generally, see Gregg, *The Middle East,* pp. 237–238, 272; Walker, "Teachers and Teacher World-Views," pp. 435–437.

50. Miller, "Classroom 19," p. 142.

51. Gregg, *The Middle East,* p. 242.

52. Heggy, *The Arab Cocoon,* p. 4

53. Hoodbhoy, *Islam and Science,* pp. 39, 55.

54. Qubain, *Education and Science in the Arab World,* p. 10.

55. AHDR, 2003, p. 53; Jerine B. Bird, "Revolution for Children in Saudi Arabia," in *Children in the Muslim Middle East,* ed. Elizabeth Warnock Fernea (Austin: University of Texas Press, 1995), p. 279; Dwairy, *Cross-Cultural Counseling,* pp. 37–39; Pascal et al., *Men and Arms in the Middle East,* p. 23; Rugh, *Family in Contemporary Egypt,* p. 25; Walker, "Teachers and Teacher World-Views," p. 436; Reeva S. Simon, *Iraq between the Two World Wars: The Creation and Implementation of a Nationalist Ideology* (New York: Columbia University Press, 1986), p. 79; Joseph Szyliowicz, *Education and Modernization in the Middle East* (Ithaca, NY: Cornell University Press, 1973), p. 183.

56. Dwairy, *Counseling and Psychotherapy with Arabs and Muslims,* p. 26.

57. Hopwood, *Syria, 1945--1986,* p. 116.

58. Hopwood, *Egypt,* pp. 138–139.

59. AHDR 2003, p. 54. See also, Ammar, *Growing up in an Egyptian Village,* p. 204, fn. 2.

60. Lisa Anderson, "Arab Democracy: Dismal Prospects," *World Policy Journal,* Vol. 18, No. 3 (Fall 2001), pp. 53–61; Berger, *The Arab World Today,* p. 119; Hamady, *The Temperament and Character of the Arabs,* p. 211; Hoodbhoy, *Islam and Science,* p. 39; David Lamb, *The Arabs,* Paperback ed. (New York: Vintage Books, 1988), p. 4; Mernissi, *Islam and Democracy,* p. 78; Pascal et al., *Men and Arms in the Middle East,* pp. 23, 25, 34; Qubain, *Education and Science in the Arab World,* p. 10; Sharabi, "Impact of Class and Culture on Social Behavior," p. 251; Sharabi, *Neopatriarchy,* pp. 85–96; Szyliowicz, *Education and Modernization in the Middle East,* pp. 183, 195–197, 274, 289, 306; Tibi, *Islam and the Cultural Accomodation of Social Change,* pp. 110–112; Viorst, *Sandcastles,* p. 358.

61. Rabie, "The Future of Education in the Arab World," p. 25. Rabie claims this description applies to a universal stage of educational development. However, he makes it clear that he is really describing the Arab educational system, and he makes no effort to demonstrate that this description applies to any other system. Indeed, his work focuses completely on the Arab world and makes no comparison with other societies, and his analysis and conclusions are narrowly focused on the Arab educational experience.

62. Roderic D. Matthews and Matta Akrawi, *Education in Arab Countries of the Near East* (Washington, DC: American Council on Education, 1949), pp. 157, 169–170; Hoodbhoy, *Islam and Science,* p. 55; Miller, "Classroom 19,"

pp. 142–150; Pascal et al., *Men and Arms in the Middle East,* p. 23; Sharabi, *Neopatriarchy*, p. 85; Tibi, *Islam and the Cultural Accomodation of Social Change,* p. 103.

63. Miller, "Classroom 19," p. 146.

64. Rabie, "The Future of Education in the Arab World," p. 24.

65. Pascal et al., *Men and Arms in the Middle East,* p. 43.

66. AHDR 2003, p. 53.

67. Hamady, *The Temperament and Character of the Arabs,* p. 211; Hoodbhoy, *Islam and Science,* pp. 33–43; Miller, "Classroom 19," p. 144; Pascal et al., *Men and Arms in the Middle East,* p. 27; Viorst, *Sandcastles*, p. 358.

68. Szyliowicz, *Education and Modernization in the Middle East*, p. 273.

69. In Faris, "Constantine Zurayk," p. 27. See also Hoodbhoy, *Islam and Science,* p. 43.

70. Pascal et al., *Men and Arms in the Middle East,* p. 27.

71. Miller, "Classroom 19," p. 152.

72. Viorst, *Sandcastles,* p. 358.

73. Dwairy, Marwan *Cross-Cultural Counseling,* p. 36.

74. Hoodbhoy, *Islam and Science,* pp. 33–48, 124; Matthews and Akrawi, *Education in Arab Countries of the Near East,* p. 170; Qubain, *Education and Science in the Arab World,* p. 134; Szyliowicz, *Education and Modernization in the Middle East,* pp. 39, 290.

75. Tibi, *Islam and the Cultural Accomodation of Social Change,* p. 114.

76. Tibi, *Islam and the Cultural Accomodation of Social Change,* p. 110. See also Hoodbhoy, *Islam and Science,* p. 48.

77. Hopwood, *Syria*, p. 127.

78. Qubain, *Education and Science in the Arab World,* p. 239. Also see his description of the teaching of science in Syria, pp. 447–448.

79. Qubain, *Education and Science in the Arab World,* p. 239.

80. Qubain, *Education and Science in the Arab World,* p. 19.

81. Matthews and Akrawi, *Education in Arab Countires of the Near East,* p. 549; Szyliowicz, *Education and Modernization in the Middle East*, p. 313.

82. Szyliowicz, *Education and Modernization in the Middle East*, pp. 307–308.

83. Wilson and Graham, *Saudi Arabia*, p. 257.

84. Hopwood, *Syria*, p. 122.

85. Roy, "Saudi Arabian Education," p. 493.

86. AHDR 2003, p. 71.

87. The World Bank, *The Road Not Traveled*, p. 21. See also p. 184.

88. Rugh, *Family in Contemporary Egypt*, p. 26.

89. Roy, "Saudi Arabian Education," pp. 486–487.

90. AHDR 2003, pp. 71–73; Roy, "Saudi Arabian Education," pp. 477–478; Rugh, *Family in Contemporary Egypt*, pp. 25–26.

91. See for example, Szyliowicz, *Education and Modernization in the Middle East,* p. 315.

92. Szyliowicz, *Education and Modernization in the Middle East*, pp. 269–270.

93. Louay Constant and Vazha Nadareishvili with Hanine Salem, "A Survey of Qatari Secondary School Seniors," The RAND Corporation, 2008, p. 13.

94. The World Bank, *The Road Not Traveled*, p. 223.

95. Sharabi, *Neopatriarchy*, p. 81.

96. Trends in International Mathematics and Science Study, National Center for Education Statistics, Various years, available at https://nces.ed.gov/timss/, accessed February 4, 2018.

97. Saneya Abdel Wahab Saleh, "The Brain Drain in Egypt," *Cairo Papers in Social Science,* Vol. 2, Monograph 5, May 1979, p. 33.

98. Saleh, "The Brain Drain in Egypt," p. 35.

99. Saleh, "The Brain Drain in Egypt," pp. 96–99.

100. Matthews and Akrawi, *Education in Arab Countries of the Near East,* p. 157.

101. Matthews and Akrawi, *Education in Arab Countries of the Near East,* pp. 169–170.

102. Matthews and Akrawi, *Education in Arab Countries of the Near East,* p. 170.

103. Matthews and Akrawi, *Education in Arab Countries of the Near East,* p. 361.

104. Matthews and Akrawi, *Education in Arab Countries of the Near East,* p. 439.

105. Szyliowicz, *Education and Modernization in the Middle East*, pp. 195–196.

106. Szyliowicz, *Education and Modernization in the Middle East*, p. 197.

107. Szyliowicz, *Education and Modernization in the Middle East*, p. 274.

108. Szyliowicz, *Education and Modernization in the Middle East*, p. 289.

109. AHDR 2003, p. 53.

110. AHDR 2003, p. 54.

111. AHDR 2003, p. 168.

112. Ammar, *Growing up in an Egyptian Village,* p. 204, fn. 2.

113. Mitchell, *Tocqueville in Arabia*, p. 79. On Qatar's educational reforms and their limited impact, see Gonzalez et al., "Facing Human Capital Challenges of the 21st Century," esp. pp. 31–34.

114. On the RAND study of education in Qatar, see in particular Catherine H. Augustine and Cathy Krop, "Aligning Post-Secondary Educational Choices to Societal Needs: A New Scholarship System for Qatar," The RAND Corporation, 2008; Constant and Nadareishvili with Salem, "A Survey of Qatari Secondary School Seniors," The RAND Corporation, 2008; Gonzalez et al., "Facing Human Capital Challenges of the 21st Century"; Cathleen Stasz, Eric R. Eide, and Francisco Martorell, "Post-Secondary Education in Qatar: Employer Demand, Student Choice, and Options for Policy," The RAND Corporation, 2008; Gail L. Zellman, Gery W. Ryan, Rita Karam, et al., "Implementation of the K-12 Education Reform in Qatar's Schools," The RAND Corporation, 2008.

Chapter 21

1. El Badri et al., *The Ramadan War,* pp. 17–90; Cordesman, *After the Storm,* p. 268; Roy K. Flint, Peter W. Kozumplik, and Thomas J. Waraksa, *The West Point Military History Series: The Arab-Israeli Wars, The Chinese Civil War, and*

the *Korean War* (Wayne, NJ: Avery, 1982), pp. 16, 23; Mohammed Heikal, "An Interview with Lt. General Ahmed Ismail," *Journal of Palestine Studies,* Vol. 3, No. 2., p. 217; Chaim Herzog, *The War of Atonement* (London: Weidenfeld and Nicolson, 1975), pp. 34–35, 74; The Insight Team of the London Sunday Times, *The Yom Kippur War* [hereafter referred to as "Insight Team"], p. 224; Edward N. Luttwak and Daniel Horowitz, *The Israeli Army, 1948–1973* (Cambridge, MA: Abt Books, 1983), pp. 283–284; National Training Center (NTC), *The Iraqi Army: Organization and Tactics,* NTC Handbook 100–91, January 3, 1991, p. 42; Donald Neff, *Warriors against Israel* (Brattleboro, VT: Amana Books, 1988), p. 125; O'Ballance, *No Victor, No Vanquished,* p. 27; General D. K. Palit, *Return to Sinai: The Arab Offensive, October 1973* (Dehra Dun: Palit and Palit, 1974), p. 40; Stephen C. Pelletiere, *The Iran-Iraq War: Chaos in a Vacuum* (New York: Praeger, 1992), p. 147; Ariel Sharon with David Chanoff, *Warrior: The Autobiography of Ariel Sharon* (New York: Simon and Schuster, 1989), p. 263; Ehud Yonay, *No Margin for Error: The Making of the Israeli Air Force* (New York: Pantheon, 1993), p. 314; Rechavam Zeevy, "The Military Lessons of the Sinai Campaign," in *The Suez-Sinai Crisis 1956: Retrospective and Reappraisal,* ed. Selwyn I. Tröen and Moshe Shemesh (London: Frank Cass, 1990), p. 70; and author's interviews with US military and former Israeli military personnel, 1992–1994.

2. See for example, Frank Aker, *October 1973: The Arab-Israeli War* (Hamden, CT: Archon Books, 1985), p. 51; Gordon and Trainor, *The Generals' War,* p. 104; Hammel, *Six Days in June,* p. 143; Herzog, *War of Atonement,* p. 128; O'Ballance, *The Third Arab-Israeli War,* p. 90; Safran, *From War to War,* p. 95.

3. Quoted in Insight Team, p. 134.

4. Cohen, *The Gulf War Air Power Survey, Volume II, Part I* [hereafter referred to as GWAPS], p. 76. The quote is from a US Navy SPEAR document on the Iraqi air force.

5. Herzog, *War of Atonement,* p. 147.

6. Aker, *October 1973,* p. 110; Anthony Cordesman, *After the Storm: The Changing Military Balance in the Middle East,* (Boulder, CO: Westview, 1993), p. 268; Cordesman and Wagner, *The Lessons of Modern War, Vol. I,* pp. 351–353; Moshe Dayan, *Diary of the Suez Campaign* (New York: Harper and Row, 1965), p. 35; Insight Team, p. 341; Drew Middleton, "US Aides Say Egypt Lacks Ability to Handle Weapons," *New York Times,* February 21, 1986, p. 8; Tzvi Ofer ed., *The Iraqi Army in the Yom Kippur War,* trans. "Hatzav" (Tel Aviv: Ma'arachot, 1986), p. 96; Author's interviews with US DoD personnel, March 1992 and July 1993.

7. Lt. General Saad El Shazli, *The Crossing of the Suez,* p. 47.

8. Cohen, *Israel's Best Defense,* pp. 465–472; Cordesman and Wagner, *The Lessons of Modern War: Volume I,* pp. 144, 197–203; Hirsh Goodman and W. Seth Carus, *The Future Battlefield and the Arab-Israeli Conflict* (New Brunswick, NJ: Transaction Books, 1990), p. 26; Gordon and Trainor, *The Generals' War,* p. 104; *GWAPS, Volume II, Part I: Operations,* p. 76; *GWAPS, Vol II, Part*

II: Effects and Effectiveness, p. 122; Lambeth, *Moscow's Lessons from the 1982 Lebanon Air War*, esp. pp. 7–11; Seale, *Asad of Syria*, p. 381; Francis Tusa, "Lebanon 1982: Israeli Hubris or Syrian Strength?," *Armed Forces*, Vol. 6, No. 9, September 1987, pp. 418–419; Yonay, *No Margin for Error*, p. 358.

9. Luttwak and Horowitz, *The Israeli Army*, p. 288.

10. Author's interview with Lt. Gen. Bernard Trainor, June 1994.

11. Adan, *On the Banks of the Suez*, pp. 63–64; Herzog, *The War of Atonement*, pp. 34–35; O'Ballance, *No Victor, No Vanquished*, p. 27; Shazli, *The Crossing of Suez*, p. 42.

12. See for example, Cordesman and Wagner, *The Lessons of Modern War, Vol. I*, pp. 54–55, 187; Cordesman and Wagner, *The Lessons of Modern War, Volume II*, p. 60; *GWAPS, Volume II, Part I: Operations*, p. 76; Herzog, *The Arab-Israeli Wars*, p. 145; Palit, *Return to Sinai*, p. 40; and author's interviews with US DoD personnel, March 1992 and July 1993.

13. Cordesman and Wagner, *The Arab-Israeli Conflicts*, pp. 86, 200; O'Ballance, *No Victor, No Vanquished*, p. 287; O'Ballance, *The Gulf War*, p. 44; Edgar O'Ballance, *The Electronic War in the Middle East, 1968–1970* (London: Faber and Faber Ltd., 1974), p. 79; and author's interviews with US military, US DoD, and former Israeli military personnel, 1992–1994.

14. Author's interviews with US military personnel, Washington, DC, April and July 1997; author's interview with US military personnel, Cairo, Egypt, October 1997.

15. Author's interviews with US military personnel, Cairo, Egypt, October 1997.

16. Author's interviews with former Israeli military personnel, 1992–1994.

17. Aker, *October 1973*, p. 51; Belzyudnyy, "I Taught Saddam's Aces to Fly," pp. 62–63; Anthony Cordesman, "Defense Planning in Saudi Arabia," in Stephanie G. Neuman, *Defense-Planning in Less-Industrialized States* (Lexington, MA: Lexington Books, 1984), p. 68, fn. 5; Cordesman and Wagner, *The Arab-Israeli Conflicts*, p. 352; Cordesman and Wagner, *The Lessons of Modern War, Vol. II*, p. 83; Herzog, *War of Atonement*, pp. 34–37, 74–76; Ephraim Kam, "Gulf War Lessons Learned by Egypt," Paper prepared for the Center for National Security Studies, Los Alamos National Laboratory, Los Alamos, New Mexico, March 1992, pp. 16–17; Author's interviews with US DoD officials, March 1992 and July 1993 and US military personnel, May 1993.

18. Author's interviews with US military personnel in Iraq, 2003–2011. See also Zacchea and Kemp, *The Ragged Edge*.

19. Michael N. Barnett, *Confronting the Costs of War: Military Power, State, and Society in Egypt and Israel* (Princeton, NJ: Princeton University Press, 1992), pp. 123–125; Belzyudnyy, "Former Soviet Adviser Describes Experiences in Iraq," p. 62; Cordesman and Wagner, *The Arab-Israeli Conflicts*, p. 97; Cordesman and Wagner, *The Lessons of Modern War, Vol. II*, pp. 153, 355–356;

The Economist, "Iraq's Army: The Lessons from the War with Iran," January 12, 1991, p. 36; Eytan and Levran, *The Middle East Military Balance,* p. 184; Flint et al., *The West Point Military Series,* p. 16; El-Gamasy, *The October War,* pp. 155–157; Heikal interview with Isma'il, p. 223; Mohamed Heikal, *The Road to Ramadan* (New York: Ballantine Books, 1975), pp. 33–35; Heller, *State- and Regime-Maintenance and Military Incompetence in Iraq,* p. 46; Herzog, *The War of Atonement,* p. 14; Keegan, *World Armies,* p. 196; Korn, *Stalemate,* p. 91; O'Ballance, *No Victor, No Vanquished,* p. 26; Palit, *Return to Sinai,* p. 83; Pelletiere, *The Iran-Iraq War,* p. 105; Scales, *Certain Victory,* p. 117; Simon Shamir, "Arab Military Lessons from the October War," in *Military Aspects of the Arab-Israeli Conflict,* ed. Louis Williams (Tel Aviv: University Publishing Projects, 1975), p. 173; Shazli, *The Crossing of Suez,* pp. 21, 47–49; Staudenmaier, "Defense Planning in Iraq," p. 54; author's interviews with US DoD officials, March 1992 and July 1993.

20. Armstrong, "Egypt," p. 173; Barnett, *Confronting the Costs of War,* pp. 123–125; Flint et al., *The West Point Military Series,* p. 16; Gamasy, *The October War,* pp. 155–157; Heikal interview with Isma'il, p. 223; Heikal, *The Road to Ramadan,* pp. 33–35; Herzog, *The War of Atonement,* p. 14; Keegan, *World Armies,* p. 196; Korn, *Stalemate,* p. 91; O'Ballance, *No Victor, No Vanquished,* pp. 26; Palit, *Return to Sinai,* p. 83; Shamir, "Arab Military Lessons from the October War," p. 173; Shazli, *The Crossing of Suez,* pp. 21, 47–49.

21. Author's interview with US military officer, Cairo, Egypt, October 1997.

22. Dupuy, *Elusive Victory,* pp. 532–534; Herzog, *The Arab-Israeli Wars,* pp. 303–304; O'Ballance, *No Victor, No Vanquished,* pp. 317–318; Ofer, ed., *The Iraqi Army in the Yom Kippur War,* pp. 128–165.

23. A far smaller number of Iraqi manuals were from other sources, mostly Soviet. For example, the Iraqis copied the Soviet manuals for the operation of Soviet-weapons systems (an obvious necessity) as well as a number of other technical subjects. In addition, the Iraqis seemed to employ Soviet manuals in a few areas where they undoubtedly found the British doctrine very skimpy because of differences in Soviet and British military styles. For example, Soviet-derived material predominates in Iraqi tactical manuals on ground-based air defenses and chemical warfare. Finally, in a few places in other manuals Soviet influences are apparent. For example, several Iraqi manuals reflect the Soviet obsession with precisely defined unit frontages, while a small number of other manuals (mostly British-based texts) have a page or two at the end that briefly note the Soviet approach to the same kind of operation.

24. The manuals I was able to examine were *Manual: Artillery in Battle,* 96-4-20 (Baghdad: Training and Technical Affairs, 1977); *Manual: Hunting Tanks* (Baghdad: Training Bureau, Combat Development Directorate, December 1983); *Firing Methods from Tanks* (Baghdad: Ministry of Defense, Training Department, Armor Division, 1990); *Conduct of Fire for Armor Subunits: Platoon/Company* (Baghdad: Army Chief of Staff,

Training Office, Armor Directorate, January 1988); *General Official Handbook Number 759, Handbook: Handling Enemy Defenses for Dirt Covers* (Earthen Berms] (Army Chief of Staff Training Command, Directorate of Combat Development, May 1986); *Guide to the Use of the Armored Branch in All Phases of Combat*, 576-1-8 (Baghdad: Training Office, Armor Directorate, May 1984); *Volume 1, The Art of War; Manual: Battle Group Tactics* (revised) (Baghdad: Office of the Army Chief of Staff, Training Bureau, Combat Development Directorate, October 1987); *Combined Staff Course, Chapter One, Indexation of Infantry Lectures*, Published by the Iraqi Staff College (Baghdad: 1979); *Volume Three, All Categories: Combat Area Defenses and Fortifications* (Baghdad: The Training Department, Combat Development Administration, June 1987); *Appendix K to the Manual, "The Infantry Battalion Battle"—Revisions Relating to the Combat Employment of Infantry Battalions in Light of the Infantry Battalion (Provisional) of 1987* (Baghdad: Army Chief of Staff, Training Office, Combat Development Directorate, April 1988); *Fixing T-72 Breakdowns during Battle* (Iraq: Republican Guard 9th Armored Brigade, 56th Tank Battalion); *Experimental Manual No. 62, Defense against Modern Attack Helicopters*, Second ed. (Baghdad: Army Hqs, Directorate of Training, Department of Combat Readiness, January 1987); *Poisoning by Biological and Chemical Agents in the Field: Protective Measures and Treatment* (Baghdad: Ministry of Defense, Combat Development Directorate of the Training Bureau, June 1989); *Guidelines for Specialized Tank Fire* (Baghdad: Ministry of Defense, Training Office, Armor Directorate, October 1990); *Manual: Tactical Use of Flame and Smoke in Corps Offensive and Defensive Operations* (Baghdad: Army Chief of Staff, Chemical Corps Directorate, December 1981); Standard Operating Procedures for an Iraqi Republican Guard Infantry Brigade (Baghdad: 1986); *Notebook: Training Course for Warrant Officers, Procedures and Maintenance for T-55 Tank* (Tank Battalion 77); *Official Notebook No. 58, Notebook Number 12, Basic Training Examinations and Distance Estimates for the Infantry Divisions*, Fifth ed. (Baghdad: Army Central Command, Training Circuit, Infantry Administration, November 1983); *Manual: Concepts of Defense in Mountainous Areas against a Conventional Enemy* (Iraq: Training Bureau, Combat Development Directorate, May 1984).

25. *General Official Handbook number 759, Handbook: Handling Enemy Defenses for Dirt Covers* [Earthen Berms], Army Chief of Staff Training Command, Directorate of Combat Development, May 1986, pp. 37, 40.
26. *General Official Handbook number 759*, pp. 24–25.
27. *Handling Enemy Defenses for Dirt Covers* (Earthen Berms], p. 39.
28. *Combined Staff Course, Chapter One, Indexation of Infantry Lectures*, Published by the Iraqi Staff College (Baghdad: 1979), pp. 73–74.
29. *Manual: Overcoming Enemy Earthworks Defenses*, p. 17.
30. *Manual: Overcoming Enemy Earthworks Defenses*, p. 18.

Chapter 22

1. Uri Bar-Joseph, *The Best of Enemies: Israel and Transjordan in the War of 1948* (London: Frank Cass, 1987), p. 57; Be'eri, *Army Officers in Arab Politics and Society*, pp. 343–344; Dupuy, *Elusive Victory*, p. 16; Brigadier Syed Ali El-Edroos, *The Hashemite Arab Army*, p. 250; John Bagot Glubb, *The Changing Scenes of Life: An Autobiography* (London: Quartet Books, 1983), pp. 121–128; Vatikiotis, *Politics and the Military in Jordan*, pp. 73–75.

2. Bregman, *Israel's Wars*, pp. 24–25; Morris, *1948: The First Arab-Israeli War* (New Haven, CT: Yale University Press, 2008), pp. 205, 208–209; Dupuy, *Elusive Victory*, pp. 43–44; Edgar O'Ballance, *The Arab-Israeli War, 1948* (London: Faber and Faber Ltd., 1956), pp. 70–74.

3. Bregman, *Israel's Wars*, p. 24.

4. O'Ballance, *The Arab-Israeli War*, pp. 98–99.

5. Bar-Joseph, *The Best of Enemies*, pp. 4–56; Lorch, *The Edge of the Sword*, pp. 142–144; Morris, *1948*, pp. 189–194, 210–211.

6. Bar-Joseph, *The Best of Enemies*, p. 15. See also Dupuy, *Elusive Victory*, p. 29; Glubb, *The Story of the Arab Legion*, p. 141.

7. Morris, *1948*, pp. 180–198.

8. Morris questions whether Tal acted on his own initiative, noting that the capture of the Etzioni Bloc was a clear strategic requirement of Glubb's plan. While I agree with the latter, it does not invalidate the notion that Tal took it on himself to launch the attack. At the time, as Morris himself notes, Jordanian plans were still evolving and there is no evidence that Glubb's plans had been finalized or that he had given orders for them to be executed. The relevant section is Morris, *1948*, pp. 168–169.

9. Morris, *1948*, pp. 168–171; Pollack, *Arabs at War*, pp. 272–273.

10. Dupuy, *Elusive Victory*, pp. 62–63; El-Edroos, *The Hashemite Arab Army*, pp. 254–256; Herzog, *The Arab-Israeli Wars*, pp. 59–60; Lorch, *The Edge of the Sword*, pp. 179–180.

11. Radar Hill was the former site of a British radar station, hence the name. It dominated the Tel Aviv-Jerusalem road several miles west of Jerusalem.

12. Dupuy, *Elusive Victory*, pp. 63–64; El-Edroos, *The Hashemite Arab Army*, p. 257; Herzog, *The Arab-Israeli Wars*, pp. 63–65; Samuel M. Katz, *Fire and Steel: Israel's 7th Armored Brigade* (New York: Pocket Books, 1996), pp. 31–32, 35; Lorch, *The Edge of the Sword*, pp. 189–191; O'Ballance, *The Arab-Israeli War*, p. 106.

13. Dupuy, *Elusive Victory*, pp. 75–77; El-Edroos, *The Hashemite Arab Army*, pp. 258–259; Herzog, *The Arab-Israeli Wars*, p. 75; Lorch, *The Edge of the Sword*, pp. 249–251, 289–290.

14. Lorch, *The Edge of the Sword*, p. 290.

15. For a concurring opinion, see Morris, *1948*, p. 207.

16. As only one example, see the account in Herzog, *The Arab-Israeli Wars*, p. 83.

17. El-Edroos, *The Hashemite Arab Army*, p. 312.

18. Dupuy, *Elusive Victory*, p. 627. For British and Israeli authors with concurring views, see for example General Uzi Narkiss, *The Liberation of Jerusalem: The Battle of 1967* (London: Valentine Mitchell, 1987), p. 52; Safran, *From War to War*, p. 233; Brigadier Peter Young, *The Israeli Campaign, 1967* (London: William Kimber, 1967), pp. 50–51.

19. Be'eri, *Army Officers in Arab Politics and Society*, p. 345; Matthews and Akrawi, *Education in Arab Countries of the Near East*, pp. 299–321; Robert B. Satloff, *Troubles on the East Bank* (New York: Praeger, 1986), p. 63. On the more progressive teaching of the British schools, see Hoodbhoy, *Islam and Science*, pp. 39, 125.

20. Again, the key sources on this are Gregg, *Culture and Identity in a Muslim Society*, pp. 292–293; and Minoura, "A Sensitive Period for the Incorporation of a Cultural Meaning System," pp. 304–339.

21. Mohamaed Awad, "Living Conditions of Nomadic, Semi-nomadic and Settled Tribal Groups," in *Readings in Arab Middle Eastern Studies and Cultures*, ed. Abdulla M. Lutfiyya and Charles W. Churchill (The Hague: Mouton, 1970), pp. 140–141; Barakat, *The Arab World*, pp. 52–53; Berger, *The Arab World Today*, pp. 46–49; Eickelman, *The Middle East*, pp. 67–71; Hamady, *The Temperament and Character of the Arabs*, pp. 93, 97, 104–106, 199; Lewis, *The Arabs in History*, p. 29; Mutawi, *Jordan in the 1967 War*, p. 42.

22. Bregman, *Israel's Wars*, pp. 25–26.

23. Be'eri, *Army Officers in Arab Politics and Society*, p. 344; Pollack, *Arabs at War*, pp. 284–288; 293–294.

24. Pollack, *Arabs at War*, pp. 299–357.

25. Safran, *From War to War*, p. 233.

26. Hanna Batatu, "Some Observations on the Social Roots of Syria's Ruling Military Groups and the Causes for Its Dominance," *Middle East Journal*, Vol. 35, No. 3, Summer 1981, p. 332; Eisenstadt, *Arming for Peace?*, p. 29, Gabriel, *Operation Peace for Galilee*, p. 119; Moreaux, "The Syrian Army," pp. 26, 30; Mark Urban, "Fire in the Galilee, Part 2: Syria," *Armed Forces*, May 1986, p. 209.

27. Anthony Cordesman, *The Arab-Israeli Military Balance and the Art of Operations* (Lanham, MD: University Press, 1987), pp. 118–119; Eisenstadt, *Arming for Peace?*, p. 29; Gabriel, *Operation Peace for Galilee*, p. 119; Moreaux, "The Syrian Army," pp. 26, 30; Urban, "Fire in the Galilee," p. 209.

28. Cordesman and Wagner, *The Lessons of Modern War: Volume I*, pp. 109, 118, 277–278; Cordesman, *The Arab-Israeli Military Balance and the Art of Operations*, p. 45; Eisenstadt, *Arming for Peace?*, pp. 24–25, 28, 98–99.

29. Gabriel, *Operation Peace for Galilee*, p. 119.

Chapter 23

1. Leon Barkho, "Saddam Says Iraqi Army Ready to Fight Israel," *The Associated Press*, November 10, 2000; GlobalSecurity, "Hammurabi Division (Armored), available online at www.globalsecurity.org/military/world/iraq/

hammurabi.htm, downloaded July 13, 2002; David Zeev Harris, "Iraq Moves Troops West," *Jerusalem Post Radio*, October 12, 2000, available online at http://wander.co.il/samples/, downloaded July 13, 2002; "Hussein Kamel on Army Strength, Saddam Fedayeen," *al-Watan al-'Arabi*, in FBIS-NES, November 27, 1995, p. 33; "Israeli Chief of Staff Warns of 'Regional Deterioration': Arafat Plane 'Smuggling Arms,'" *BBC Summary of World Broadcasts*, November 9, 2000; Radio Free Europe/Radio Liberty, "Iraqi Armored Units in Western Iraq Withdrawing," *Iraq Report*, Volume 3, No. 36 (November 3, 2000).

2. Daniel Byman, "Understanding Proto-insurgencies," *Journal of Strategic Studies*, Vol. 31, No. 2 (April 2008), p. 166; Bruce Hoffman, "The Modern Terrorist Mindset," in *Terrorism and Counterterrorism: Understanding the New Security Environment*, ed. Russell D. Howard and Reid L. Sawyer (Gilford, CT: McGraw-Hill 2002), p. 84.

3. Augustus Richard Norton, *Hezbollah: A Short History* (Princeton, NJ: Princeton University Press, 2009), p. 33.

4. Daniel Byman, *A High Price: The Triumphs and Failures of Israeli Counterterrorism* (New York: Oxford, 2011), pp. 209–265, esp. 212–215.

5. Dilip Hiro, *Lebanon: Fire and Embers* (New York: St. Martin's Press, 1992), pp. 129–133; Riad Kaj, "Rival Amal, Hezbollah Militias Fight in West Beirut," UPI, April 17, 1990.

6. Byman, *A High Price*, p. 225; Ahmad Nizar Hamzeh, *In the Path of Hizbullah* (New York: Syracuse University Press, 2004), pp. 71–72; Norton, *Hezbollah*, pp. 69–94.

7. Byman, *A High Price*, p. 225.

8. Byman, *A High Price*, pp. 212–213, 225.

9. Byman, *A High Price*, p. 213. Also see Amal Saad-Ghorayeb, *Hizbu'llah: Politics and Religion* (Sterling, VA: Pluto Press, 2002), p. 14.

10. Byman, *A High Price*, p. 225.

11. Nicholas Blanford, *Warriors of God: Inside Hezbollah's Thirty-Year Struggle against Israel* (New York: Random House, 2011), p. 145; Byman, *A High Price*, p. 228.

12. Byman, *A High Price*, p. 240.

13. Stephen Biddle and Jeffrey A. Friedman, "The 2006 Lebanon Campaign and the Future of Warfare: Implications for Army and Defense Policy," The Strategic Studies Institute, the US Army War College, September 2008, p. 30.

14. William M. Arkin, *Divining Victory: Airpower in the 2006 Israel-Hezbollah War* (Maxwell Air Force Base, AL: Air University Press, 2007), p. 25; Andrew Exum, "Hizballah at War: A Military Assessment," Washington, DC: Washington Institute for Near East Policy, 2006, p. 5; David E. Johnson, "Hard Fighting: Israel in Lebanon and Gaza," RAND, 2011, p. 46.

15. Biddle and Friedman, "The 2006 Lebanon Campaign and the Future of Warfare," p. 33.

16. Arkin, *Divining Victory*, p. 53; Lazar Berman, "Beyond the Basics: Looking Beyond the Conventional Wisdom Surrounding the IDF Campaigns against Hizbullah and Hamas," SmallWarsJournal.com, April 28, 2011, pp. 10–11; Byman, *A High Price*, pp. 249–258; Exum, "Hizballah at War," p. 10; Johnson, "Hard Fighting," pp. 39–44, 56, 71–73, 81–88; Avi Kober, "The Israel Defense Forces in the Second Lebanon War: Why the Poor Performance?," *The Journal of Strategic Studies*, Vol. 31, No. 1 (February 2008), pp. 14–16, 22; David Makovsky and Jeffrey White, "Lessons and Implications of the Israel-Hizballah War: A Preliminary Assessment," Washington, DC: Washington Institute for Near East Policy, 2006, pp. 42–45, 52–55.

17. Arkin, *Divining Victory*, p. 136; Byman, *A High Price*, pp. 248–249; Kober, "The Israel Defense Forces in the Second Lebanon War," p. 16.

18. Arkin, *Divining Victory*, pp. 25–27, 49; Byman, *A High Price*, p. 248; Exum, "Hizballah at War," pp. 3–4; Johnson, "Hard Fighting," pp. 45–49.

19. Exum, "Hizballah at War," p. 9; Makovsky and White, "Lessons and Implications of the Israel-Hizballah War," pp. 38, 49.

20. Blanford, *Warriors of God*, p. 131; Johnson, "Hard Fighting," p. 50.

21. Johnson, "Hard Fighting," pp. xviii, 119; Makovsky and White, "Lessons and Implications of the Israel-Hizballah War," p. 38.

22. Biddle and Friedman, "The 2006 Lebanon Campaign and the Future of Warfare," pp. 35–38; Exum, "Hizballah at War," pp. 9–10; Makovsky and White, "Lessons and Implications of the Israel-Hizballah War," pp. 45–49.

23. Exum, "Hizballah at War," p. 7.

24. Biddle and Friedman, "The 2006 Lebanon Campaign and the Future of Warfare," pp. 42, 258.

25. Blanford, *Warriors of God*, pp. 348–349; Iver Gabrielsen, "The Evolution of Hezbollah's Strategy and Military Performance, 1982–2006," *Small Wars & Insurgencies*, Vol. 25, No. 2 (2014), p. 273; Makovsky and White, "Lessons and Implications of the Israel-Hizballah War," p. 46.

26. Blanford, *Warriors of God*, pp. 342–345; Gabrielsen, "The Evolution of Hezbollah's Strategy and Military Performance, 1982–2006," pp. 273–274; Johnson, "Hard Fighting," pp. 52–54; Magnus Ranstorp, "The Hizballah Training Camps of Lebanon," in *The Making of a Terrorist: Recruitment, Training, and Root Causes, Vol. 2*, ed. James Forest (Westport: Praeger Security International, 2006), p. 256.

27. Arkin, *Divining Victory*, p. 50; Biddle and Friedman, "The 2006 Lebanon Campaign and the Future of Warfare," p. 59; Makovsky and White, "Lessons and Implications of the Israel-Hizballah War," p. 48.

28. Arkin, *Divining Victory*, p. 25; Biddle and Friedman, "The 2006 Lebanon Campaign and the Future of Warfare," p. 39; Exum, "Hizballah at War," p. 5; Yiftah S. Shapir, "Hezbollah as an Army," *Strategic Assessment*, Vol. 19, No. 4 (January 2017), p. 74.

29. Biddle and Friedman, "The 2006 Lebanon Campaign and the Future of Warfare," pp. 39–40; Exum, "Hizballah at War," p. 10; Makovsky and White, "Lessons and Implications of the Israel-Hizballah War," p. 39.

30. Biddle and Friedman, "The 2006 Lebanon Campaign and the Future of Warfare," p. 76.

31. Biddle and Friedman, "The 2006 Lebanon Campaign and the Future of Warfare," pp. 39–41, 60, 69–72; Byman, *A High Price,* p. 258; Gabrielsen, "The Evolution of Hezbollah's Strategy and Military Performance, 1982–2006," p. 274.

32. Biddle and Friedman, "The 2006 Lebanon Campaign and the Future of Warfare," p. 71.

33. Biddle and Friedman, "The 2006 Lebanon Campaign and the Future of Warfare," p. xiv.

34. Anne Barnard and Hwaida Saad, "Hezbollah Aids Syrian Military in a Key Battle," *New York Times*, May 20, 2013; Nicholas Blanford, "The Battle for Qusayr: How the Syrian Regime and Hizb Allah Tipped the Balance," CTC Sentinel, Vol. 6, No. 8 (August 2013), p. 22; Nicholas Blanford, "Slow Drip Offensive Underway in Qalamoun," *Daily Star*, October 25, 2013; Alex Simon and Mohammed Rabie, "Cross Border Sectarian Showdown: The Battle for Qalamoun," Syria Direct, November 26, 2013; David Hirst, "Hezbollah Uses Its Military Power in a Contradictory Manner," *The Daily Star*, October 23, 2012; Marisa Sullivan, "Hezbollah in Syria," Middle East Security Report 19, Institute for the Study of War, April 2014, pp. 11–14.

35. Loveday Morris, "In Syria, Hezbollah Forces Appear Ready to Attack Rebels in City of Aleppo," *Washington Post*, June 2, 2013.

36. Benedetta Berti, "The Syrian Civil War and Its Consequences for Hezbollah," Foreign Policy Research Institute, December 2015; International Crisis Group, "Hizbollah's Syria Conundrum," Report No. 175, March 14, 2017, p. 4, fn. 7, available at www.crisisgroup.org/middle-east-north-africa/eastern-mediterranean/lebanon/175-hizbollah-s-syria-conundrum, accessed May 15, 2017.

37. Jeffrey White, "Hizb Allah at War in Syria: Forces, Operations, Effects and Implications," *The CTC Sentinel*, Vol. 7, No. 1 (January 2014), pp. 15–16; Sullivan, "Hezbollah in Syria," p. 23.

38. Colin P. Clarke and Chad C. Serena, "Hezbollah Is Winning the War in Syria," National Interest Online, January 29, 2017, available at http://nationalinterest.org/feature/hezbollah-winning-the-war-syria-19229?page=show, accessed May 14, 2017.

39. Blanford, "The Battle for Qusayr," p. 19; Sullivan, "Hezbollah in Syria," p. 26.

40. Blanford, "The Battle for Qusayr," p. 18.

41. Blanford, "The Battle for Qusayr," p. 19.

42. Blanford, "The Battle for Qusayr," p. 19.

43. White, "Hizb Allah at War in Syria," p. 16.

44. White, "Hizb Allah at War in Syria," p. 15.

45. International Crisis Group, "Hizbollah's Syria Conundrum," p. 16; Tom Perry, Laila Bassam, Suleiman Al-Khalidi, and Tom Miles, "Hezbollah, Other Shi'ite Allies Helped Assad Win in Aleppo," *Reuters*, December 14, 2016.

46. Sullivan, "Hezbollah in Syria," p. 17.

47. Blanford, *Warriors of God*, pp. 103–122.

48. Michael Eisenstadt and Kendall Bianchi, "The Ties That Bind: Families, Clans, and Hizballah's Military Effectiveness," The Washington Institute for Near East Policy, forthcoming, p. 2.

49. Eisenstadt and Bianchi, "The Ties That Bind," p. 5.

50. Sullivan, "Hezbollah in Syria," pp. 14–15.

51. Marc R. DeVore and Armin B. Stähli, "Explaining Hezbollah's Effectiveness: Internal and External Determinants of the Rise of Violent Non-state Actors," *Terrorism and Political Violence*, Vol. 27, No. 2 (2015), p. 344.

52. DeVore and Stähli, "Explaining Hezbollah's Effectiveness," pp. 332–345.

53. DeVore and Stähli, "Explaining Hezbollah's Effectiveness," p. 332.

54. Nicholas Blanford, "Hezbollah Lowers Fighting Age as It Takes on Islamic State," *The Christian Science Monitor*, August 18, 2014; Blanford, "The Battle for Qusayr," p. 18; Byman, *A High Price*, pp. 224–225.

55. Shapir, "Hezbollah as an Army," p. 70.

56. DeVore and Stähli, "Explaining Hezbollah's Effectiveness," pp. 342–343. The quote is from 343.

57. Arkin, *Divining Victory*, p. 25; Exum, "Hizballah at War," pp, 5, 10–14; Johnson, "Hard Fighting," p. 47. But not too cellular; see Biddle and Friedman, "The 2006 Lebanon Campaign and the Future of Warfare," p. 59.

58. Shapir, "Hezbollah as an Army," pp. 71–75.

59. International Crisis Group, "Hizbollah's Syria Conundrum," p. 16.

60. For some support for the idea, see AHDR 2003, pp. 172–173; Nikki R. Keddie, *Modern Iran: Roots and Results of Revolution*, Revised and Updated ed. (New Haven, CT: Yale University Press, 2003), pp. 9–20. Please note that Syria's Alawi population is not a good surrogate since their religion is a very distinct offshoot of Shi'ism, reflecting similarly different cultural predilections.

61. Daniel Byman, *Al Qaeda, The Islamic State, and the Global Jihadist Movement: What Everyone Needs to Know* (Oxford: Oxford University Press, 2015), pp. 119, 165–167; Peter R. Mansoor, *Surge: My Journey with General David Petraeus and the Remaking of the Iraq War* (New Haven, CT: Yale University Press, 2013), esp. pp. 34–90, 120–176; Kenneth M. Pollack, "The Fall and Rise and Fall of Iraq," Middle East Memo No. 29, The Saban Center for Middle East Policy at the Brookings Institution, August 2013, available at www.brookings.edu/wp-content/uploads/2016/06/Pollack_Iraq.pdf, accessed May 19, 2017, pp. 7–13.

62. Byman, *Al Qaeda, The Islamic State, and the Global Jihadist Movement*, pp. 165–167; International Crisis Group, "Syria's Metastasizing Conflicts," Middle East Report No. 143, June 27, 2013, available at www.crisisgroup.org/~/media/Files/Middle%20East%20North%20Africa/Iraq%20Syria%20Lebanon/Syria/143-syrias-metastasising-conflicts.pdf, accessed November 14, 2016; Charles Lister, "Profiling the Islamic State," Analysis Paper No. 13, Brookings Doha Center, November 2014, pp. 4–36, available at www.brookings.edu/~/media/Research/Files/Reports/2014/11/profiling%20islamic%20state%20lister/en_web_lister.pdf, accessed November 14, 2016.

63. Pollack, "The Fall and Rise and Fall of Iraq," pp. 13–19; Kenneth M. Pollack, "Reading Machiavelli in Baghdad," *The National Interest*, No. 122 (November/December 2012), pp. 8–20.

64. Jennifer Cafarella, "ISIS Advances in Deir ez-Zour," Institute for the Study of War, July 5, 2014, available online at http://iswresearch.blogspot.com/2014/07/isis-advances-in-deir-ez-zour.html, accessed May 20, 2017; Eyal Zisser, "The Islamic State Kingdom in Syria," in *The Islamic State: How Viable Is It?*, ed. Yoram Schweitzer and Omer Einav (Tel Aviv: Institute for National Security Studies, 2016), pp. 125–126.

65. On the Da'ish assault force, see Jessica Lewis, "The Terrorist Army Marching on Baghdad," *The Wall Street Journal*, June 12, 2014. On the actual size of Iraqi forces in Mosul, see Hendawi and Abdul-Zahra, "Humiliation at Rout Hits Iraqi Military Hard"; Parker, Coles, and Salman, "Special Report." Parket et al. note that the two Army divisions that should have had 24,000 troops had only about 10,000 in Mosul, while Hendawi and Abdul-Zahra note there was an equal number of federal police present—both in theory and in actuality.

66. IISS, *The Military Balance, 2015*, pp. 303–306; Scott Jasper and Scott Moreland, "The Islamic State Is a Hybrid Threat: Why Does That Matter?," smallwarsjournal.com, December 2, 2014, available online at http://smallwarsjournal.com/jrnl/art/the-islamic-state-is-a-hybrid-threat-why-does-that-matter, accessed May 11, 2018.

67. IISS, *The Military Balance, 2015*, pp. 303–306.

68. Jasper and Scott Moreland, "The Islamic State Is a Hybrid Threat," pp. 5–6.

69. Jessica D. Lewis, "The Islamic State: A Counter-Strategy for a Counter-State," Institute for the Study of War, July 2014, p. 17.

70. Michael Knights and Alexandre Mello, "The Cult of the Offensive: The Islamic State on Defense," *CTC Sentinel* 8, No. 4 (April 2015): p. 5, available at www.ctc.usma.edu/posts/the-cult-of-the-offensive-the-islamic-state-on-defense, accessed May 17, 2017. See also IISS, *The Military Balance, 2015*, pp. 303–306; Michael M. Gunter and Nahro Zagros, "Why Can't We Defeat ISIS?," *Hurst*, 17 October 2014, available at www.hurstpublishers.com/cant-defeat-isis/, accessed May 20, 2017.

71. Christoph Reuter, "Secret Files Reveal the Structure of the Islamic State," *Der Spiegel*, April 18, 2015.

72. See for instance, Valerie Szybala, "The Islamic State of Iraq and Al-Sham and the 'Cleansing' of Deir Ez-Zour," Institute for the Study of War, May 14, 2014.

73. Alaa Al-Lami, "ISIS' Fighting Doctrine: Sorting Fact from Fiction," Al-Akhbar English, October 31, 2014, pp. 4–5, available online at http://english.al-akhbar.com/node/22280, accessed May 20, 2017; Gabi Siboni, "The Military Power of the Islamic State," in *The Islamic State: How Viable Is It?*, ed. Yoram Schweitzer and Omer Einav (Tel Aviv: Institute for National Security Studies, 2016), p. 66.

74. The following is based on the author's extensive interviews and conversations with US, Coalition, Iraqi, and Kurdish military personnel in Baghdad, Erbil, Kuwait, Amman, Washington, and Tampa, as well as Al-Lami, "ISIS' Fighting Doctrine"; Siboni, "The Military Power of the Islamic State," pp. 66–69.

75. Margaret Coker, "How Islamic State's Win in Ramadi Reveals New Weapons, Tactical Sophistication and Prowess," *The Wall Street Journal*, May 25, 2015.

76. Siboni, "The Military Power of the Islamic State," p. 69.

77. Siboni, "The Military Power of the Islamic State," pp. 66–67.

78. Hillel Frisch, "The ISIS Challenge in Syria," *Mideast Security and Policy Studies* No. 118 (May 2016), *Begin-Sadat Center for Strategic Studies,* pp. 23. See also, Knights and Mello, "The Cult of the Offensive," p. 3.

79. Knights and Mello, "The Cult of the Offensive," p. 1.

80. William Booth and Aaso Ameen Shwan, "Islamic State Tunnels below Mosul Are Hidden and Deadly Danger," *Washington Post*, November 5, 2016; Michael R. Gordon, "Iraqi Forces Prepare Next U.S.-Backed Attack on ISIS, with Mosul on Horizon," *New York Times*, November 30, 2015.

81. Daveed Gartenstein-Ross, "The Islamic State's Anbar Offensive and Abu Umar Al-Shishani," warontherocks.com, October 9, 2014, available online at https://warontherocks.com/2014/10/the-islamic-states-anbar-offensive-and-abu-umar-al-shishani/, accessed May 20, 2017; Knights and Mello, "The Cult of the Offensive," p. 5.

82. Byman, *Al Qaeda, The Islamic State, and the Global Jihadist Movement*, pp. 174–175.

83. Amos Yadlin, "The Islamic State Challenge: How Severe Is It?," in *The Islamic State: How Viable Is It?*, ed. Schweitzer and Eina, pp. 276–277.

84. Siboni, "The Military Power of the Islamic State," p. 65.

85. Siboni, "The Military Power of the Islamic State," p. 69.

86. Barak Barfi, "The Military Doctrine of the Islamic State and the Limits of Ba'athist Influence," *CTC Sentinel* 9, No. 211 (February 19, 2016), p. 18, available online at www.ctc.usma.edu/posts/

the-military-doctrine-of-the-islamic-state-and-the-limits-of-baathist-influence, accessed May 20, 2017; Byman, *Al Qaeda, The Islamic State, and the Global Jihadist Movement*, p. 174.

87. Barfi, "The Military Doctrine of the Islamic State," pp. 18–19.

88. Hamza Hendawi, "IS Top Command Dominated by Ex-officers in Saddam's Army," Associated Press, August 8, 2015.

89. Isabel Coles and Ned Parker, "Special Report: How Saddam's Men Help Islamic State Rule," Reuters, December 11, 2015; Hendawi, "IS Top Command Dominated by Ex-officers in Saddam's Army"; Ben Hubbard and Eric Schmitt, "Military Skill and Terrorist Technique Fuel Success of ISIS," *New York Times*, August 27, 2014; Liz Sly, "The Hidden Hand behind the Islamic State Militants? Saddam Hussein's," *Washington Post*, April 4, 2015.

90. Byman, *Al Qaeda, The Islamic State, and the Global Jihadist Movement*, pp. 165, 174–175; Hendawi, "IS Top Command Dominated by Ex-officers in Saddam's Army."

91. Aaron Bazin, "Defeating ISIS and Their Complex Way of War," *Small Wars Journal*, Vol. 10, No. 9 (September 2014); IISS, *The Military Balance*, pp. 303–306; Siboni, "The Military Power of the Islamic State," pp. 68–69.

92. Knights and Mello, "The Cult of the Offensive," p. 3.

93. Yadlin, "The Islamic State Challenge," p. 277.

94. Daveed Gartenstein-Ross, "How Many Fighters Does the Islamic State Really Have?," warontherocks.com, February 9, 2015, available at https://warontherocks.com/2015/02/how-many-fighters-does-the-islamic-state-really-have/, accessed May 20, 2017.

95. See the discussion in Gregg, *The Middle East*, pp. 38–39.

96. Byman, *Al Qaeda, The Islamic State, and the Global Jihadist Movement*, p. 173; Charles Lister, *The Islamic State: A Brief Introduction* (Washington, DC: Brookings Institution Press, 2015), p. 26.

97. Siboni, "The Military Power of the Islamic State," p. 68.

98. al-Lami, "ISIS' Fighting Doctrine," p. 4.

99. Inevitably, reports have surfaced that Tarkhan himself is not the brilliant military commander, and instead it is his brother Tamaz. Either way, they are both Chechens from Georgia. Kyle Orton, "Profiles of Islamic State Leaders," The Henry Jackson Society, 2016, p. 44.

100. Gartenstein-Ross, "The Islamic State's Anbar Offensive and Abu Umar Al-Shishani"; Daveed Gartenstein-Ross, "The Fight Goes on in Anbar: ISIL vs. the World," warontherocks.com, October 15, 2014, available online at https://warontherocks.com/2014/10/the-fight-goes-on-in-anbar-isil-vs-the-world/, accessed May 20, 2017; Orton, "Profiles of Islamic State Leaders," pp. 38–44; Sirwan Kajjo, "A Portrait of Omar al-Shishani: The Northern Commander in Syria of the Islamic State of Iraq and Syria," Militant Leadership Monitor, Vol. 5, No. 1 (January 2014), pp. 3–5.

101. Michael Weiss and Katie Zavadski, "Vladimir Putin's Newest Export: Terrorists," *The Daily Beast*, January 4, 2017, available online at www.thedailybeast.com/articles/2017/01/04/vladimir-putin-s-newest-export-terrorists.html, accessed May 20, 2017; "ISIS: US-trained Tajik Special Forces Chief Gulmurod Khalimov Becomes ISIS 'War Minister,'" *The International Business Times*, September 6, 2016, www.ibtimes.co.uk/isis-us-trained-tajik-special-forces-chief-gulmurod-khalimov-becomes-isis-war-minister-1579966, accessed May 20, 2017.

102. Norvell B. De Atkine, "The Arab as Insurgent," *American Diplomacy* (September 2009), available at www.unc.edu/depts/diplomat/item/2009/0709/comm/deatkine_insurgent.html, accessed November 12, 2017.

103. De Atkine, "The Arab as Insurgent."

104. Eisenstadt and Bianchi, "The Ties That Bind," p. 2.

Conclusion

1. For instance, see AHDR 2003, p. 47; Gregg, *The Middle East*, esp. pp. 342–356; Gregg, *Culture and Identity in a Muslim Society*, pp. 37, 312; Hammoudi, *Master and Disciple*, esp. pp. vii–xi.

2. Gregg, *The Middle East*, pp. 87, 341–356; Hammoudi, *Master and Disciple*, esp. pp. ix–xi; Rugh, *Family in Contemporary Egypt*, p. 45; Sabry, *Arab Cultural Studies*, p. 8.

3. For instance, see Rugh, *Family in Contemporary Egypt*, p. 41.

4. Hammoudi, *Master and Disciple*, pp. 46–68.

5. For a discussion of this, see Gregg, *The Middle East*, pp. 341–356.

6. Quoted in Michael Kaplan, "Cultural Ergonomics: An Evolving Focus for Military Human Factors," in *Handbook of Military Psychology*, ed. Reuven Gal and A. David Mangelsdorff (New York, John Wiley and Sons, 1991), p. 159.

7. Some recent work on the interaction of economic development and political regimes has also touched on the impact of culture, although they have typically argued for the primacy of economic development over politics and culture, or the primacy of politics in driving both culture and economic development. I would argue that all three interact endlessly and equally along with a variety of other factors such as geography, resource endowments, and historical contingency. See, for instance, Douglass C. North, John J. Wallis, and Barry R. Weingast, *Violence and Social Orders: A Conceptual Framework for Interpreting Recorded Human History* (Cambridge: Cambridge University Press, 2009); and Daron Acemoglu and James A. Robinson, *Why Nations Fail: The Origins of Power, Prosperity, and Poverty* (New York, Crown, 2012).

8. For an insightful work entirely on this problem, see Gal Luft, *Beer, Bacon and Bullets: The Cultural Factor in Coalition Warfare from Gallipoli to Iraq* (New York: Booksurge, 2009).

9. Pascal et al., *Men and Arms in the Middle East*.

10. On the sources and course of change in the Arab world, see in particular Asef Bayat, *Life as Politics: How Ordinary People Change the Middle East*, Second ed. (Palo Alto, CA: Stanford University Press, 2013); Marc Lynch, *The Arab Uprising: The Unfinished Revolutions of the New Middle East* (New York: PublicAffairs, 2013); Menoret, *Joyriding in Riyadh*; Kenneth M. Pollack, *A Path out of the Desert: A Grand Strategy for America in the Middle East* (New York: Random House, 2008), esp. pp 67–195; Kenneth M. Pollack et al., *The Arab Awakening: America and the Transformation of the Middle East* (Washington, DC: The Brookings Institution, 2012), esp. pp. 1–212.

11. Gregg, *The Middle East*, pp. 239–242.

12. Gregg, *The Middle East*, p. 239.

13. See, for instance, Brink, "Child-Rearing Patterns in an Egyptian Village," p. 85.

SELECTED BIBLIOGRAPHY

Abdennur, Alexander. *The Arab Mind: An Ontology of Abstraction and Concreteness.* Ottawa, Canada: Kogna, 2008.

Abir, Mordechai. "Saudi Security and Military Endeavor." *Jerusalem Quarterly* 33 (Fall 1984): 79–94.

Aboul-Enein, Yousef H., ed. *Reconstructing a Shattered Egyptian Army: War Minister Gen. Mohamed Fawzi's Memoirs, 1967–1971.* Annapolis, MD: US Naval Institute Press, 2014.

Abu-Lughod, Lila. *Veiled Sentiments: Honor and Poetry in a Bedouin Society.* Berkeley: University of California Press, 1986.

Abu-Lughod, Lila. "Writing against Culture." In *Recapturing Anthropology: Working in the Present:* 137–162, ed. Richard G. Fox. Santa Fe, NM: School of American Research Press, 1991.

Adan, Avraham ("Bren.") *On the Banks of the Suez.* San Francisco: Presidio, 1980.

Ahmed, Ramadan A. and Uwe P. Gielen, eds. *Psychology in the Arab Countries.* Cairo, Egypt: Menoufia University Press, 1998.

Ajami, Fouad. *The Arab Predicament.* Cambridge: Cambridge University Press, 1985.

Aker, Frank. *October 1973: The Arab-Israeli War.* New York: Archon, 1985.

Al Farsy, Fouad A. "Cultural Stereotyping and Foreign Policy." *Journal of Arab-American Affairs* 31 (Winter 1989/1990): 1–10.

Al-Khayyat, Sana. *Honor and Shame: Women in Modern Iraq.* London: Saqi Books, 1990.

Al Soufi, Ahmed. H. *Cultural Differences between Arabs and Danes: The Intracultural Diversity's Effect on Intercultural Negotiations.* Unpublished master's thesis. Aarhus University, Denmark, 2005.

Ali, Abbas J. "Decision-Making Style, Individualism, and Attitudes toward Risk of Arab Executives." *International Studies of Management and Organization* 23(3) (1993): 53–73.

AlMazrouei, Hanan and Richard J. Pech. "Working in the UAE: Expatriate Manatement Experiences." *Journal of Islamic Accounting and Business Research* 6(1) (2015): 73–93.

Ammar, Hamed. *Growing Up in an Egyptian Village: Silwa Province of Aswan.* Second US ed., New York: Octagon Books, 1973.

Andersen, Roy R., Robert F. Seibert, and Jon G. Wagner. *Politics and Change in the Middle East.* Third ed., Englewood Cliffs, NJ: Prentice Hall, 1990.

Andrade, Dale. *America's Last Vietnam Battle: Halting Hanoi's 1972 Easter Offensive.* Topeka: University Press of Kansas, 1995.

Andress, Carter with Malcolm McConnell. *Victory Undone: The Defeat of al-Qaeda in Iraq and Its Resurgence as ISIS.* Washington, DC: Regnery, 2014.

Antal, Major John F. "The Iraqi Army Forged in the Other Gulf War." *Military Review* LXXI (2) (February 1991): 63-64.

Antoun, Richard T. *Arab Village: A Social Structural Study of a Transjordan Peasant Community.* Bloomington: University of Indiana Press, 1972.

Antoun, Richard T. and Donald Qutaert, eds. *Syria: Society, Culture, and Polity.* Albany: SUNY Press, 1991.

Anwar, Syed Aziz and Mohammad Naim Chaker. "Globalization of Corporate America and Its Implications for Management Styles in an Arabian Cultural Context." *International Journal of Management* 20(1) (March 2003): 43–55.

Appleman, Roy E. *South to the Naktong, North to the Yalu.* Washington, DC: United States Army Center of Military History, 1998.

Appleman, Lt. Col. Roy E. *Disaster in Korea: The Chinese Confront MacArthur.* College Station: Texas A&M University Press, 1989.

Apter, David E. *The Politics of Modernization.* Chicago: University of Chicago Press, 1965.

Arkin, William M. *Divining Victory: Airpower in the 2006 Israel-Hezbollah War.* Maxwell Air Force Base, AL: Air University Press, 2007.

Arlinghaus, Bruce and Pauline H. Baker, eds. *African Armies: Evolution and Capabilities.* Boulder, CO: Westview, 1986.

Armstrong, G. P. "Egypt: A Combat Assessment." In *Fighting Armies: Antagonists in the Middle East* 148-175, ed. Richard Gabriel. Westport, CT: Greenwood Press, 1983.

Armstrong, Lt. Col. Richard. *Battlefield Innovations: Red Army War Experiences, 1941–1945.* J. F. Kennedy School of Government, 1992. Master's Thesis

Arthur, Max. *Above All, Courage.* London: Sidgwick and Jackson, 1985.

Asher, Lt. Colonel Daniel. "The Syrian Invasion of Lebanon—Military Moves as a Political Tool." Ma'arachot. 255 (June 1977): 2-9.

Asher, Brigadier General Dani, ed. *Inside Israel's Northern Command: The Yom Kippur War on the Syrian Border.* Lexington: University Press of Kentucky, 2014.

Asher, Brigadier General Dani. *The Egyptian Strategy for the Yom Kippur War.* Translated by Moshe Tlamim. Jefferson, NC: McFarland and Co., 2009.

Asher, Jerry with Eric Hammel. *Duel for the Golan.* New York: William Morrow, 1987.

Ashkar, Riad. "The Syrian and Egyptian Campaigns." *Journal of Palestine Studies* 3(2) (1974): 15–33.

Ashkar, Riad and Haytham al-Ayyubi. "The Middle East Conflict: The Military Dimension—Interviews with Riad Ashkar and Haytham al-Ayyubi." *Journal of Palestine Studies* 4(4) (1975): 3–25.

Atiyeh, George N., ed. *Arab and American Cultures.* Washington, DC: American Enterprise Institute for Public Policy Research, 1977.

Atiyeh, George N. and Ibrahim M. Oweiss, eds. *Arab Civilization: Challenges and Responses.* Albany: SUNY Press, 1988.

Atkeson, Major General Edward B. "Iraq's Arsenal: Tool of Ambition." 41 *Army* (March 1991): 22–30.

Atkinson, Rick. *Crusade.* New York: Houghton Mifflin, 1993.

Augustine, Catherine H. and Cathy Crop. "Aligning Post-Secondary Educational Choices to Societal Needs: A New Scholarship System for Qatar." Santa Monica, CA: RAND, 2008.

Ayubi, Nazih N. "Bureaucracy and Development in Egypt Today." *Journal of Asian and African Studies* 24(1–2) (1989): 62–78.

Badawy, M. K, "Styles of Middle Eastern Managers." *California Management Review* 22(2) Spring 1980): 51–58.

Badolato, E. V. "A Clash of Cultures: The Expulsion of Soviet Military Advisors from Egypt." *US Naval War College Review* 37 (March–April 1984): 69–81.

Badri, Hassan El, Taha El Magdoub, and Mohammed Dia El Din Zohdy. *The Ramadan War, 1973.* New York: Hippocrene, 1974.

Baker, Raymond. *Sadat and After: Struggles for Egypt's Political Soul.* Cambridge, MA: Harvard University Press, 1990.

Ball, Desmond. *The Intelligence War in the Gulf.* Canberra, Australia: Strategic Studies Centre, Australian National University, 1991.

Bandmann, Yonah. "The Egyptian Armed Forces during the Kadesh Campaign." In *The Suez-Sinai Crisis 1956: Retrospective and Reappraisal* 74–99, ed. Selwyn I. Troën and Moshe Shemesh. London: Frank Cass, 1989.

Banuazizi, Ali. "Iranian National Character: A Critique of Some Western Perspectives." In *Psychological Dimensions of Near Eastern Studies,* 210–240, ed. L. Carl Brown and Norman Itzkowitz, Princeton, NJ: Darwin Press, 1973.

Banuazizi, Ali. "Social-Psychological Approaches to Political Development." In *Understanding Political Development* 281–316, ed. Myron Weiner and Samuel P. Huntington. Boston: Little, Brown and Co., 1987.

Bar-Joseph, Uri. *The Best of Enemies: Israel and Transjordan in the War of 1948.* London: Frank Cass, 1987.

Barakat, Halim. *Six Days.* First English ed., Translated by Bassam Frangieh and Scott McGehee. Washington, DC: Three Continents Press, 1990.

Barakat, Halim. *The Arab World: Society, Culture and State.* Berkeley: University of California Press, 1993.

Baram, Amatzia and Barry Rubin, eds. *Iraq's Road to War.* New York: St. Martin's Press, 1993.

Baram, Amatzia. "Deterrence Lessons from Iraq: Rationality Is Not the Only Key to Containment." *Foreign Affairs* 91(4) (July/August 2012): 76–90.

Barclay, C. N. "Learning the Hard Way: Lessons from the October War." *Army* 24 (March 1974): 25–9.

Barkawi, Tarak and Keith Stanski, eds. *Orientalism and War.* New York: Columbia University Press, 2012.

Barnett, Michael N. and Jack S. Levy. "Domestic Sources of Alliances and Alignments: The Case of Egypt, 1962–1973." *International Organization* 45(3) (Summer 1991): 369–395.

Barnett, Michael N. *Confronting the Costs of War: Military Power, State, and Society in Egypt and Israel.* Princeton, NJ: Princeton University Press, 1993.

Barnett, Michael N. *Dialogues in Arab Politics: Negotiations in Regional Order.* New York: Columbia University Press, 1998.

Bates, Daniel G. and Amal Rassam. *Peoples and Cultures of the Middle East.* Englewood Cliffs, NJ: Prentice-Hall, 1983.

Baxter, William P. *Soviet Airland Battle Tactics.* Novato, CA: Presidio, 1986.

Bay, Austin and James F. Dunnigan. *From Shield to Storm.* New York: Morrow, 1992.

Bayat, Asef. *Life as Politics: How Ordinary People Change the Middle East.* Second ed. Palo Alto, CA: Stanford University Press, 2013.

Be'eri, Eliezer. *Army Officers in Arab Politics and Society.* New York: Praeger, 1970.

Bearman, Jonathan. *Qadhafi's Libya.* London: Zed Books, 1986.

Beit-Hallahami, B. "Some Psychosocial and Cultural Factors in the Arab-Israeli Conflict: A Review of the Literature." *Journal of Conflict Resolution* 16(2) (1972): 269–280.

Bell, J. Bowyer. "National Character and Military Strategy: The Egyptian Experience, October 1973." *Parameters* 5(14) (Spring 1975 1975): 6–17.

Bellamy, Christopher. *Expert Witness: A Defence Correspondent's Gulf War 1990–91.* London: Brassey's, 1993.

Bellamy, Chris. *Absolute War: Soviet Russia in the Second World War.* New York: Alfred A. Knopf, 2007.

Bellows, Thomas J. "Proxy War in Indochina." *Asian Affairs* (September-October 1979): 13–30.

Bender, Gerald. "Angola, the Cubans and American Anxieties." *Foreign Policy* 31 (Summer 1978): 3–30.

Berger, Morroe. *The Arab World Today*. Paperback ed., New York: Anchor, 1962.

Bergquist, Maj. Ronald E. *The Role of Airpower in the Iran-Iraq War*. Alabama: Air University Press, 1988.

Berman, Lazar. "Beyond the Basics: Looking beyond the Conventional Wisdom Surrounding the IDF Campaigns against Hizbullah and Hamas." SmallWarsJournal.com, April 28, 2011.

Berque, Jacques. *The Arabs*. New York: Praeger, 1965.

Berque, Jacques. *Arab Rebirth: Pain and Ecstasy*. Translated by Quintin Hoare. London: Al Saqi Books, 1983.

Beufre, General d'Armee Andre. *The Suez Expedition, 1956*. Translated by Richard Barry. New York: Praeger, 1969.

Bezlyudnyy, Lt. Col. Sergey. "Former Soviet Advisor Describes Experiences in Iraq: 'I Taught Saddam's Aces to Fly.'" JPRS-UMA-91-0145 (June 5, 1991).

Biddle, Stephen D. *Military Power: Explaining Victory and Defeat in Modern Battle*. Princeton, NJ: Princeton University Press, 2004.

Biddle, Stephen and Jeffrey A. Friedman. "The 2006 Lebanon Campaign and the Future of Warfare: Implications for Army and Defense Policy." The Strategic Studies Institute, the US Army War College, September 2008.

Bigelow, Captain Michael E. "The Faw Peninsula: A Battle Analysis." *Military Intelligence* (April–June 1991): 13-18.

Bishop, Patrick and John Witherow. *The Winter War*. London: Quartet Books, 1982.

Bishop, Patrick. "Egyptians Overcome Determined Defence." *Daily Telegraph*, February 26, 1991.

Black, Jeremy. *War and the Cultural Turn*. London: Polity Books, 2012.

Blackwell, Major James. *Thunder in the Desert*. New York: Bantam, 1991.

Blackwell, Major James and William J. Taylor. "The Ground War in the Gulf." *Survival* 33 (May/June 1991): 230–245.

Blackwell, James. "Georgia Punch: 24th Mech Puts the Squeeze on Iraq." *Army Times* (December 2, 1991): 312–314.

Blair, Arthur H. *At War in the Gulf*. College Station: Texas A&M Press, 1992.

Blair, Clay. *The Forgotten War: America in Korea 1950–1953*. New York: Times Books, 1987.

Blanford, Nicholas. *Warriors of God: Inside Hezbollah's Thirty-Year Struggle against Israel*. New York: Random House, 2011.

Blocksome, Patricia. "Internal Security Forces: Their Capability, Legitimacy and Effect on Internal Violence." Arthur D. Simons Center for Interagency Cooperation, Fort Leavenworth, Kansas, IAS-002, April 2013.

Bloomfield, Lincoln P., Jr.,. "Saudi Arabia's Security Problems in the 1980s." In *Defense Planning in Less-Industrialized States* 95–111, ed. Stephanie Neuman. Lexington, MA: Lexington Books, 1984.

Bonnell, Victoria E. and Lynn Hunt, eds. *Beyond the Cultural Turn: New Directions in the Study of Society and Culture.* Berkeley: University of California Press, 1999.

Bowen, Donna Lee and Evelyn A. Early, eds. *Everyday Life in the Middle East.* Bloomington: University of Indiana Press, 1993.

Brand, Matthew C. "Airpower and the 1972 Easter Offensive." Master's Thesis, US Army Command and General Staff College, Ft. Leavenworth, KS, 2007.

Bregman, Ahron. *Israel's Wars: A History since 1947.* 2010 ed. London: Routledge, 2010.

Bremner, Paul Michael. "Soviet Troop Control: The Debate from 1963–1973." Master of Science Thesis, Massachusetts Institute of Technology, 1984.

Bridgland, Fred. *The War for Africa: Twelve Months That Transformed a Continent.* Philadelphia, PA: Casemate, 2017.

Brink, Judy H. "Child-Rearing Patterns in an Egyptian Village." In *Children in the Muslim Middle East* 84–92, ed. Elizabeth Warnock Fernea. Austin: University of Texas Press, 1995.

Brodsky, C. W. S. "India and Pakistan: A Combat Assessment." In *Fighting Armies: Non-aligned, Third World, and Other Ground Armies*_3-27, ed. Richard Gabriel. Westport, CT: Greenwood Press, 1983.

Brooke, James. "Libyan Jets Bomb Chadian Units." *New York Times*, March 31, 1987, A8.

Brooke, James. "Modern Arms a Key Factor in Chadian Gains." *New York Times*, April 2, 1987, A8.

Brooke, James. "Chadians Describe Victory in Desert." *New York Times*, August 14, 1987, A1, A5.

Brooke, James. "Chad Reports New Libyan Attack." *New York Times*, August 15. 1987, A3–A4.

Brower, Kenneth. "The Yom Kippur War." *Military Review* 54 (March 1974): 25–26.

Brown, L. Carl and Norman Itzkowitz, eds. *Psychological Dimensions of Near Eastern Studies.* Princeton, NJ: The Darwin Press, 1977.

Brown, James and William P. Snyder, eds. *The Regionalization of Warfare.* New Brunswick, NJ: Transaction Books, 1990.

Bulloch, John and Harvey Morris. *The Gulf War.* London: Methuen, 1989.

Buri, J. "The Nature of Humankind, Authoritarianism and Self-Esteem." *Journal of Psychology and Christianity* 29(7) (1988): 32–38.

Butler, Colin. "Leadership in a Multicultural Arab Organisation." *Leadership & Organization Development Journal* 30(2) (2009): 139–151.

Byman, Daniel. *A High Price: The Triumphs and Failures of Israeli Counterterrorism.* New York: Oxford, 2011.

Byman, Daniel. *Al Qaeda, The Islamic State, and the Global Jihadist Movement: What Everyone Needs to Know.* Oxford: Oxford University Press, 2015.

Campbell, Joel R. "The Wrong War: The Soviets and the Korean War, 1945–1953." *International Social Science Review* 88 (3) (2014): 1–29.

Campbell, Kirk S. "Civil-Military Relations and Political Liberalization: A Comparative Study of the Military's Corporateness and Political Values in Egypt, Syria, Turkey and Pakistan." PhD Thesis, George Washington University, January 31, 2009.

Cantwell, Thomas R. "The Army of South Vietnam: A Military and Political History, 1950–1975." Doctoral Thesis, University of New South Wales, July 4, 1989.

Carus, W. Seth. "The Bekaa Valley Campaign." *Washington Quarterly* (September ' 1982): 34-41.

Carus, W. Seth. "Defense Planning in Iraq." In *Defense Planning in Less-Industrialized States* 29–52. ed. Stephanie Neuman. Lexington, MA: Lexington Books, 1984.

Carus, W. Seth. "Military Lessons of the 1982 Israel-Syria Conflict." In *The Lessons of Recent Wars in the Third World* 261–280, Volume 1, ed. Robert Harkavy and Stephanie Neuman. Lexington, MA: Lexington Books, 1986.

Carus, W. Seth and Hirsh Goodman. *The Future Battlefield and the Arab-Israeli Conflict*. New Brunswick, NJ: Transaction Books, 1990.

Carus, Seth. "How Vulnerable Is Iraq's Military?" Washington, DC: Washington Institute for Near East Policy Research, 1990.

Carver, Michael. *War since 1945*. London: Weidenfield and Nicholson, 1980.

Castillon, Lt. Colonel Michel L. "Low-Intensity Conflict in the 1980s: The French Experience." *Military Review* (January 1986): 68–77.

"Chad: The Battle of Ouadi Doum." *The Economist*, March 28 1987, 38.

"Chad's Toyota War." *The Economist*, September 12 1987, 43–44.

Chen, King C. "China's War against Vietnam, 1979: A Military Analysis." *The Journal of East Asian Affairs* 3(1) (Spring/ Summer 1983): 233–263.

Churchill, Randolph S. and Winston S. Churchill. *The Six Day War*. London: Heinemann, 1967.

Cigar, Norman. "Iraq's Strategic Mindset and the Gulf War." *Journal of Strategic Studies* (March 1992): 1–29.

Clapham, Christopher and George Philip, eds. *The Political Dilemmas of Military Regimes*. London: Croom Helm, 1985.

Clark, Alan. *Barbarossa: The Russian-German Conflict, 1941–1945*. Paperback ed., New York: Quill, 1965.

Coe, Patrick C. *The Dragon Strikes: China and the Korean War: June–December 1950*. Novato, CA: Presidio, 2000.

Cohen, Eliot. "Distant Battles." In *The Lessons of Recent Wars in the Third World*, 7–32, Volume 2, ed. Robert Harkavy and Stephanie Neuman. Lexington, MA: Lexington Books, 1987.

Cohen, Stephen. *The Indian Army*. 2nd ed., New Delhi: Oxford University Press, 1990.

Cohen, Raymond. *Culture and Conflict in Egyptian-Israeli Relations*. Bloomington: University of Indiana Press, 1990.

Cohen, Col. Eliezer. *Israel's Best Defense: The First Full Story of the Israeli Air Force.* Translated by Jonathan Cordis. New York: Orion, 1993.

Constant, Louay and Vazha Nadareishvili with Hanine Salem. "A Survey of Qatari Secondary School Seniors." Santa Monica, CA: The RAND Corporation, 2008.

Cooley, John K. *Libyan Sandstorm.* New York: Holt, Rinehart and Winston, 1981.

Copson, Raymond W. *Africa's Wars and Prospects for Peace.* Armonk, New York: M.E. Sharpe, 1994.

Cordesman, Anthony. *Jordanian Arms and the Middle East Balance.* Washington, DC: Middle East Institute, 1983.

Cordesman, Anthony. "Defense Planning in Saudi Arabia." In *Defense Planning in Less-Industrialized States* 67–94, ed. Stephanie Neuman. Lexington, MA: Lexington Books, 1984.

Cordesman, Anthony. *The Arab Israeli Military Balance and the Art of Operations.* Lanham, MD: University Free Press, 1987.

Cordesman, Anthony. *Western Strategic Interests in Saudi Arabia.* London: Croom Helm, 1987.

Cordesman, Anthony. *The Gulf and the West: Strategic Relations and Military Realities.* Boulder, CO: Westview, 1988.

Cordesman, Anthony and Abraham Wagner. *The Lessons of Modern War, Vol. 1: The Arab-Israeli Wars, 1973–1989.* New York: Westview, 1990.

Cordesman, Anthony and Abraham Wagner. *The Lessons of Modern War, Vol. 2: The Iran-Iraq War.* Boulder, CO: Westview, 1990.

Cordesman, Anthony and Abraham Wagner. *The Lessons of Modern War, Vol. 3: The Afghan and Falkland Islands Wars.* Boulder, CO: Westview, 1990.

Cordesman, Anthony. *After the Storm: The Changing Military Balance in the Middle East.* Boulder, CO: Westview, 1993.

Cordesman, Anthony. *The Iraq War: Strategy, Tactics, and Military Lessons.* Westport, CT: Praeger, 2003.

Craft, Douglas W. *An Operational Analysis of the Persian Gulf War.* Carlisle, PA: Strategic Studies Institute, US Army War College, 1992.

Crawley, Vince. "Ghost Troop's Battle at the 73 Easting." *Armor* (May–June 1991): 7–12__.

Cronin, Stephanie. *Armies and State-Building in the Middle East.* London: I.B. Tauris, 2014.

Danis, Aaron. "Iraqi Army Operations and Doctrine." *Military Intelligence* (April–June 1991): 6–12.

Davidson, Phillip B. *Vietnam at War: The History 1946–1975.* New York: Oxford University Press, 1988.

Davis, M. Thomas. *40 Km into Lebanon.* Washington, DC: National Defense University Press, 1987.

Dawisha, Adeed. "Saudi Arabia's Search for Security." In *Regional Security in the Middle East* 1–27, ed. Charles Tripp. London: IISS, 1984.

Day, Arthur R. *East Bank/West Bank*. New York: Council on Foreign Relations, 1986.

Dayan, Moshe. *Diary of the Sinai Campaign*. New York: Harper and Row, 1965.

Dayan, Moshe. *The Story of My Life*. New York: William Morrow, 1976.

De Atkine, Norvell B. "Why Arabs Lose Wars." *Middle East Quarterly* 6(4) (December 1999): 7–27.

De Atkine, Norvell B. "Western Influence on Arab Militaries: Pounding Square Pegs into Round Holes." *Middle East Review of International Affairs* 17(1) (Spring 2013): 18–31.

De Atkine, Norvell B. "The Arab as Insurgent." *American Diplomacy* (September 2009), available at http://www.unc.edu/depts/diplomat/item/2009/0709/comm/deatkine_insurgent.html, accessed on November 12, 2017.

De La Billiere, General Sir Peter. *Storm Command: A Personal Account of the Gulf War*. Dubai, UAE: Motivate, 1992.

Deeb, Marius. *The Lebanese Civil War*. New York: Praeger, 1980.

Defense, US Department of. *Conduct of the Persian Gulf War: Final Report to Congress, April 1992*. Washington, DC: GPO, 1992.

Desch, Michael C. "Culture Clash: Assessing the Importance of Ideas in Security Studies." *International Security* 23(1) (Summer, 1998): 141–170.

DeVore, Marc R. and Armin B. Stähli. "Explaining Hezbollah's Effectiveness: Internal and External Determinants of the Rise of Violent Non-state Actors." *Terrorism and Political Violence* 27(2) (2015): 331–357.

DeVos, George and Lola Romanucci-Ross, eds. *Ethnic Identity: Cultural Continuities and Change*. University of Chicago ed., Chicago: University of Chicago Press, 1982.

DIA. *Handbook on the Cuban Armed Forces*, DDB-2680-62-79. Washington, DC: DIA, 1979.

DIA. *The Chinese Armed Forces Today: The US Defense Intelligence Agency Handbook of China's Army, Navy and Air Force*. Englewood Cliffs, NJ: Prentice-Hall, 1979.

Díaz-Briquets, Sergio, ed. *Cuban Internationalism in Sub-Saharan Africa*. Pittsburgh, PA: Duquesne University Press, 1989.

Dodd, Peter C. "Family Honor and the Forces of Change in Arab Society." *International Journal of Middle East Studies* 4 (1973): 40–54.

Dominguez, Jorge. *Cuba: Order and Revolution*. Cambridge, MA: Belknap Press, 1978.

Dominguez, Jorge I. "The Cuban Operation in Angola: Costs and Benefits for the Armed Forces." *Cuban Studies* 8(1) (January 1978): 10–20.

Domínguez, Jorge I. "The Cuban Armed Forces, the Party and Society in Wartime and during Rectification (1986–1988)." *The Journal of Communist Studies* 5(4) (December 1989): 45–62.

Donnelly, Christopher. *Red Banner: The Soviet Military System in Peace and War*. Alexandria, VA: Jane's, 1988.

Dornan, James E., Jr. and Nigel de Lee. *The Chinese War Machine*. London: Salamander, 1979.

Dougherty, James E. *The Horn of Africa: A Map of Political-Strategic Conflict*. Cambridge, MA: Institute for Foreign Policy Analysis, 1982.

Drea, Edward J. "Nomonhan: Japanese Soviet Tactical Combat 1939." Leavenworth Papers No. 2, Combat Studies Institute, Command and General Staff College, Ft. Leavenworth, 1981.

Duncan, Col. Andrew. "The Military Threat to Israel." In *Regional Security in the Middle East* 98–107, ed. Charles Tripp. London: IISS, 1984.

Dunn, Major James A. "Lessons from the Third World." *Military Review* (February 1990): 55-63.

Dunnigan, James and Austin Bay. *From Shield to Storm*. New York: Morrow, 1992.

Dupuy, Col. Trevor. *Elusive Victory*. New York: Harper and Row, 1978.

Dupuy, Col. Trevor and Paul Martell. *Flawed Victory*. Washington, DC: Hero, 1985.

Durch, William J. "The Cuban Military in Angola and the Middle East: From Algeria to Angola." *Studies in Comparative Communism* 11(1/2) (Spring/Summer 1978): 34–74.

Dwairy, Marwan. *Cross-Cultural Counseling: The Arab-Palestinian Case*. Binghamton, NY: Haworth Press, 1998.

Dwairy, Marwan. *Counseling and Psychotherapy with Arabs and Muslims: A Culturally Sensitive Approach*. New York: Teacher's College Press, 2006.

Eaker, Ira C. "The Fourth Arab-Israeli War." *Strategic Review* 2(1) (1974): 18–25.

Eddy, Paul, Magnus Linlaeter, Peter Gillman, and The Sunday Times Insight Team, eds. *The Falklands War*. London: Andre Deutsch Ltd., 1982.

Edmonds, Martin. *Armed Services and Society*. Boulder, CO: Westview, 1988.

Eickelman, Dale F. *The Middle East: An Anthropological Approach*. Englewood Cliffs, NJ: Prentice Hall, 1981.

Eilts, Hermann Frederick. "Commentary: Defense Planning in Egypt." In *Defense Planning in Less-Industrialized States* 167–193, ed. Stephanie Neuman. Lexington, MA: Lexington Books, 1984.

Eisenstadt, Michael. *Arming for Peace? Syria's Elusive Quest for "Strategic Parity."*. Washington, DC: The Washington Institute for Near East Policy, 1992.

Eisenstadt, Michael. "The Iraqi Armed Forces, Two Years On." *Jane's Intelligence Digest* (March 1993): 121–127.

Eisentadt, Michael. *The Sword of the Arabs: Iraq's Strategic Weapons*. Washington DC: Washington Institute for Near East Policy, 1990.

Eisenstadt, Michael and Kendall Bianchi. "The Ties That Bind: Families, Clans, and Hizballah's Military Effectiveness." The Washington Institute for Near East Policy, forthcoming.

El Edroos, S.A. *The Hashemite Arab Army, 1908–1979*. Amman: Amman Publishing Committee, 1980.

El-Gamasy, Mohamed Abdel Ghani. *The October War: Memoirs of Field Marshal El-Gamasy of Egypt.* Translated by Gillian Potter, Nadra Morcos, Rosette Frances. Cairo, Egypt: American University in Cairo Press, 1993.

Eldar, Colonel, Lt. Colonel (Res) Nahum, and Lt. Col (res) Tzvi. "Combat against the Egyptian Commandos during the Yom Kippur War." *Ma'arachot* (November–December 1992): 20–25.

Emery, Fred. "North Korean Pilots in Egypt MIGs Open Fire on Israelis." *The Times*, October 19, 1973, 12.

Englehardt, Lt. Col. Joseph. "Desert Shield and Desert Storm: A Chronology and Troop List for the 1990–1991 Persian Gulf Crisis." Carlisle, PA: US Army War College, 1991.

Erickson, John and E. J. Feuchtwanger, eds. *Soviet Military Power and Performance.* New York: Archon Books, 1979.

Erickson, John, Lynn Hansen, and William Schneider, eds. *Soviet Ground Forces.* Boulder, CO: Westview, 1986.

Exum, Andrew. "Hizballah at War: A Military Assessment." Washington, DC: Washington Institute for Near East Policy, 2006.

Eytan, Zeev and Aharon Levran. *The Middle East Military Balance 1986.* ed. Jaffee Center for Strategic Studies. Boulder, CO: Westview, 1986.

Eytan, Zeev and Aharon Levran. *The Middle East Military Balance 1987–88.* ed. Jaffee Center for Strategic Studies. Boulder, CO: Westview, 1988.

Ezov, Amiram. *Crossing Suez*, 1973. Translated by Zvi Hazanov. Tel Aviv: ContentoNow, 2016.

Fahad, A. H. "In Defense of Saudi Arabia: Why Has Such a Rich State Had Such a Weak Military." *Washington Post*, February 12, 1991.

Falk, Pamela. "Cuba in Africa." *Foreign Affairs* 65(5) (Summer 1987): 1077–1096.

Farah, Tawfic E. "Political Culture and Development in a Rentier State: The Case of Kuwait." *Journal of Asian and African Studies* 24(1–2) (1989): 106-113.

Farer, Tom. *War Clouds on the Horn of Africa: The Widening Storm.* New York: The Carnegie Endowment, 1979.

Farsoun, Sami K., ed. *Arab Society: Continuity and Change.* London: Croom Helm, 1985.

Feghali, Ellen. "Arab Cultural Communication Patterns." *International Journal of Intercultural Relations* 21(3) (1997): 345–378.

Fermoselle, Rafael. *The Evolution of the Cuban Military: 1492–1986.* Miami, FL: Ediciones Universal, 1987.

Fernea, Elizabeth Warnock, ed. *Children in the Muslim Middle East.* Austin: University of Texas Press, 1995.

Fergany, Nader, Farida Bennani, et al. *The Arab Human Development Report 2003.* United Nations Development Programme and the Arab Fund for Economic and Social Development: New York: United Nations, 2003.

Finer, Samuel. *The Man on Horseback.* London: Pall Mall Press, 1962.

Fisher, Sidney. *The Military in the Middle East: Problems in Society and Government.* Columbus: Ohio State University Press, 1963.

Fisk, Robert. *Pity the Nation: The Abduction of Lebanon.* New York: Atheneum, 1990.

Fontenot, Col. Gregory. "Fright Night: Task Force 2/34 Armor." *Military Review* (January 1993): 38–52.

Forczyk, Robert. *Tank Warfare on the Eastern Front, 1941–1942: Schwerpunkt.* Barnsley, UK: Pen and Sword, 2013.

Forczyk, Robert. *Tank Warfare on the Eastern Front, 1943–1945: Red Steamroller.* Barnsley, UK: Pen and Sword, 2016.

Freedman, Lawrence and Virginia Gamba-Stonehouse. *Signals of War: The Falkland Islands Conflict of 1982.* London: Faber and Faber, 1990.

Freedman, Lawrence and Efraim Karsh. *The Gulf Conflict 1990–1991.* Princeton, NJ: Princeton University Press, 1992.

Friedman, Norman. *Desert Victory.* Annapolis, MD: Naval Institute Press, 1991.

Fuldheim, Dorothy. *Where Were the Arabs.* Cleveland: World, 1967.

Fuller, Graham. *The Center of the Universe: The Geopolitics of Iran.* Boulder, CO: Westview, 1991.

Fullick, Roy and Geoffrey Powell. *Suez: The Double War.* London: Hamish Hamilton, 1979.

Gabriel, Richard, ed. *Fighting Armies: Antagonists in the Middle East.* Westport, CT: Greenwood Press, 1983.

Gabriel, Richard, ed. *Fighting Armies: Non-aligned, Third World, and Other Ground Armies.* Westport, CT: Greenwood Press, 1983.

Gabriel, Richard. "Lessons of War: The IDF in Lebanon." *Military Review* 64 (8) (Aug 1984): 47–65.

Gabriel, Richard. *Operation Peace for Galilee.* New York: Hill and Wang, 1984.

Gabrielsen, Iver. "The Evolution of Hezbollah's Strategy and Military Performance, 1982–2006." *Small Wars & Insurgencies* 25(2) (2014): 257–283.

Gal, Reuven and A. David Mangelsdorff eds. *Handbook of Military Psychology.* New York, John Wiley and Sons, 1991.

Ganz, A. Harding. "Abu Ageila—Two Battles, Part I: 1956." *Armor* (May–June 1974).

Ganz, A Harding. "Abu Ageila—Two Battles, Part II: 1967." *Armor* (July–August 1974).

Gardner, George H. "The Arab Middle East: Some Background Interpretations." *Journal of Social Issues* 15(3) (1959): 20–27.

Garthoff, Raymond L. *How Russia Makes War: Soviet Military Doctrine.* London: George Allen and Unwin, 1954.

Gause, III, F. Gregory. "Saudi Arabia: Desert Storm and After." In *The Middle East after Iraq's Invasion of Kuwait* 209–216, ed. Robert O. Freedman. Gainesville: University Press of Florida, 1993.

Gavshon, Arthur. *Crisis in Africa: Battleground of East and West.* New York: Penguin, 1981.

Gawrych, George. "Egyptian High Command in the 1973 War." *Armed Forces and Society* 13 (Summer 1987): 535–559.

Gawrych, George W. *Key to the Sinai: The Battles for Abu Agheila in the 1956 and 1967 Arab-Israeli Wars.* Fort Leavenworth, KS: Command and General Staff College, 1990.

Gawrych, George W. "The Egyptian Military Defeat of 1967." *Journal of Contemporary History* 26 (1991): 277–305.

Geertz, Clifford. *Islam Observed.* Chicago: University of Chicago Press, 1971.

Geertz, Clifford. *The Interpretation of Cultures.* New York: Basic Books, 1973.

Gellner, Ernest. *Muslim Society.* Cambridge: Cambridge University Press, 1981.

George, Edward. *The Cuban Intervention in Angola, 1965–1991: From Che Guevara to Cuito Cuanavale.* London: Frank Cass, 2005.

Get, Major Jer Donald. "Lessons Learned in Vietnam: PLA." *Military Review* LXVII (July 1987): 20–28.

Gilkes, Patrick. "Revolution and Military Strategy: The Ethiopian Army in the Ogaden and Eritrea, 1974–84." In *Proceedings of the Eleventh International Conference of Ethiopian Studies, Volume II* 721–726, ed. Bahru Zewde et. al., Addis Ababa, 1994.

Glantz, David M. *Stumbling Colossus: The Red Army on the Eve of World War.* Lawrence: University of Kansas Press, 1998.

Glantz, David M. *Colossus Reborn: The Red Army at War, 1941–1943.* Lawrence: University of Kansas Press, 2005.

Glassman, Jon D. *Arms for the Arabs: The Soviet Union and War in the Middle East.* Baltimore: Johns Hopkins University Press, 1975.

Gleijeses, Piero. "Moscow's Proxy? Cuba and Africa 1975–1988." *Journal of Cold War Studies* 8(4) (Fall 2006): 98–146.

Gleijeses, Piero. *Conflicting Missions: Havana, Washington, and Africa, 1959–1976.* Chapel Hill: University of North Carolina Press, 2002.

Glubb, John Bagot. *The Story of the Arab Legion.* New York: Da Capo, 1976.

Glubb, Sir John Bagot. *The Changing Scenes of Life: An Autobiography.* London: Quartet Books, 1983.

Goldhamer, Herbert. *The Soviet Soldier: Soviet Military Management at the Troop Level.* New York: Crane, Russak, 1975.

Goldman, Stuart D. *Nomonhan, 1939: The Red Army's Victory That Shaped World War II.* Annapolis, MD: US Naval Institute Press, 2012.

Gonzalez, Emilio. "Development of the Cuban Army." *Military Review* LXI (April 1981): 56–64.

Gonzalez, Gabriella, Lynn A. Karoly, Louay Constant, Hanine Salem, and Charles A. Goldman. "Facing Human Capital Challenges of the 21st: Education and Labor Market Initiatives in Lebanon, Oman, Qatar, and the United Arab Emirates." Santa Monica, CA: The RAND Corporation, 2008.

Grau, Lester W. trans. and ed. *The Bear Went Over the Mountain: Soviet Combat Tactics in Afghanistan.* Washington, DC: National Defense University Press, 1996.

Gravino, Katherine Swift and David R. Segal. "The Empire Strikes Back: Military Professionalism in the South Atlantic War." In *The Regionalization of Warfare* 17–36 ed. James Brown and William P. Snyder. New Brunswick, NJ: Transaction Books, 1990.

Gregg, Gary S. *The Middle East: A Cultural Psychology*. New York: Oxford University Press, 2005.

Gregg, Gary S. *Culture and Identity in a Muslim Society*. Oxford: Oxford University Press, 2007.

Greenhous, Brereton. "The Israeli Experience." In *Case Studies in the Development of Close Air Support*, 513–524, ed. Benjamin F. Cooling. Washington, DC: Office of Air Force History, 1990.

Greenhouse, Steven. "Chad Says Troops Are Razing Base Captured in Libya." *New York Times*, September 7, 1987, A1, A3.

Greig, Ian. *The Communist Challenge to Africa*. Surrey, UK: The Foreign Affairs Publishing Co., 1978.

Griffith, Samuel B. *The Chinese People's Liberation Army*. New York: McGraw-Hill, 1967.

Guilmartin, John F. Jr. "The South Atlantic War: Lessons and Analytical Guideposts—A Military Historian's Perspective." In *The Regionalization of Warfare*, 55–78, ed. James Brown and William P. Snyder. New Brunswick: Transaction Books, 1990.

GWAPS. *Gulf War Air Power Survey, Volume I, Part 1: Planning*. Washington, DC: GPO, 1993.

GWAPS. *Gulf War Air Power Survey, Volume II, Part 1: Operations*. Washington, DC: GPO, 1993.

GWAPS. *Gulf War Air Power Survey, Volume II, Part 2: Effects and Effectiveness*. Washington, DC: GPO, 1993.

Halion, Richard. *Storm over Iraq*. Washington, DC: Smithsonian Institution Press, 1992.

Halpern, Manfred. *The Politics of Social Change in the Middle East and North Africa*. First Princeton Paperback ed., Princeton, NJ: Princeton University Press, 1965.

Hamady, Dr. Sania. *The Temperament and Character of the Arabs*. New York: Twayne, 1960.

Hammel, Eric. *Six Days in June*. New York: Scribners, 1992.

Hammoudi, Abdellah. *Master and Disciple: The Cultural Foundations of Moroccan Authoritarianism*. Chicago: University of Chicago Press, 1997.

Hamzeh, Ahmad Nizar. *In the Path of Hizbullah*. New York: Syracuse University Press, 2004.

Harding, Jeremy. *The Fate of Africa: Trial by Fire*. New York: Simon and Schuster, 1993.

Harel, Amos and Avi Issacharoff. *34 Days: Israel, Hezbollah, and the War in Lebanon*. New York: Palgrave Macmillan, 2008.

Harkabi, Yehoshofat. "Basic Factors in the Arab Collapse during the Six Day War." *Orbis* 11 (Fall 1967): 677–691.

Harkavy, Robert. "The Lessons of Recent Wars in the Third World: Toward Comparative Analysis." In *The Lessons of Recent Wars in the Third World*, ed. Robert Harkavy and Stephanie Neuman. 1. Lexington, Ma: Lexington Books, 1986.

Harkavy, Robert. "Lessons Learned, Insights Gained, Issues Raised: Summary and Agenda for Further Research." In *The Lessons of Recent Wars in the Third World* 315–321, Vol. 2, ed. Robert Harkavy and Stephanie Neuman. Lexington, MA: Lexington Books, 1987.

Harrison, Richard W. *The Russian Way of War: Operational Art, 1904–1940*. Lawrence: University of Kansas Press, 2001.

Hastings, Max and Simon Jenkins. *Battle for the Falklands*. New York: Norton, 1983.

Haun, Phil and Colin Jackson. "Breaker of Armies: Air Power in the Easter Offensive and the Myth of Linebacker I and II in the Vietnam War." *International Security* 40 (3) (Winter 2015/2016): 139–178.

Hazen, William E and Mohammed Mughisuddin. *Middle Eastern Subcultures*. Lexington, MA: Lexington Books, 1975.

Heggy, Tarek. *The Arab Cocoon: Progress and Modernity in Arab Societies*. London: Valentine Mitchell, 2010.

Heikal, Mohammed. *The Road to Ramadan*. Paperback ed., New York: Ballantine Books, 1975.

Heikal, Mohammed. *The Sphinx and the Commissar*. New York: Harper and Row, 1978.

Heitman, Heloed-Röemer. *War in Angola: The Final South African Phase*. Gibraltar: Ashanti, 1990.

Heller, Mark. "Politics and the Military In Iraq and Jordan, 1920–1958." *Armed Forces and Society* 4(1) (November 1977): 75–99.

Heller, Mark. "Israeli and Syrian Military Concepts in Light of the Lebanon War." *IDF Journal* 16 (Winter 1989): 42–46, 95.

Hemphill, Paul P. J. "The Formation of the Iraqi Army, 1921–1933." In *The Integration of Modern Iraq* 88–110. ed. Abbas Kelidar. New York: St. Martin's, 1979.

Henderson, George. "Qaddafy's Waterloo." *Africa Report* 32 (5) (September–October 1987): 24–28.

HERO (Historical Evaluation and Research Organization). *Studies on Soviet Combat Performance*. McLean, VA: NOVA Publications, 1977.

HERO (Historical Evaluations and Research Organization). *A Historical Analysis of the Effectiveness of Tactical Air Operations Against, and in Support of Armored Forces*. McLean, VA: NOVA Publications, 1980.

Herzfeld, Michael. "Honour and Shame: Problems in the Comparative Analysis of Moral Systems." *Man* 15 (2 June 1980): 339–351.

Herzog, Chaim. *The War of Atonement*. London: Weidenfeld and Nicolson, 1975.

Herzog, Chaim. *The Arab-Israeli Wars*. New York: Random House, 1982.

Hickman, William F. "Ravaged and Reborn: The Iranian Army, 1982." Washington, DC: The Brookings Institution, 1982.

Hilsman, Roger. *George Bush vs. Saddam Hussein.* Novato, California: Lyford Books, 1992.

Hinnebusch, Raymond A. "Bureaucracy and Development in Syria: The Case of Agriculture." *Journal of Asian and African Studies* 24(1–2) 1989): 79–93.

Hiro, Dilip. *Desert Shield to Desert Storm: The Second Gulf War.* New York: Routledge, 1992.

Hiro, Dilip. *Lebanon: Fire and Embers, A History of the Lebanese Civil War.* New York: St. Martin's, 1992.

Hoodbhoy, Pervez. *Islam and Science.* London: Zed Books, 1991.

Hooker, Richard D., Jr., ed. *Maneuver Warfare: An Anthology.* Novato, CA: Presidio, 1993.

Hopwood, Derek. *Syria, 1945–1986: Politics and Society.* London: Unwin Hyman, 1988.

Hopwood, Derek. *Egypt: Politics and Society 1945–90.* London: Harper Collins, 1991.

Hotz, Robert. "Egypt Plans Modernized Air Arm." *Aviation Week and Space Technology* 102 (26) (June 30, 1975): 12–13.

Hourani, Albert. *A History of the Arab Peoples.* Cambridge, MA: Belknap Press, 1991.

House, Capt. Jonathan M. *Toward Combined Arms Warfare: A Survey of 20th Century Tactics, Doctrine, and Organization.* Fort Leavenworth, KS: US Command and General Staff College, 1984.

House, Robert J., Paul Hanges, Mansour Javidan, Peter W. Dorfman, and Vipin Gupta eds. *Culture, Leadership, and Organizations: The GLOBE Study of 62 Societies.* Thousand Oaks, CA: Sage, 2004.

Hoyt, Edwin P. *The Day the Chinese Attacked: Korea, 1950.* Paperback ed., New York: Paragon, 1993.

Hudson, Michael C., ed. *The Arab Future: Critical Issues.* Washington, DC: Center for Contemporary Arab Studies, Georgetown University, 1979.

Huntington, Samuel. *The Soldier and the State.* Cambridge, MA: Harvard University Press, 1957.

Hurewitz, J. C. *Middle East Politics: The Military Dimension.* New York: Praeger, 1969.

Ibrahim, Saad Eddin and Nicholas S. Hopkins, eds. *Arab Society in Transition: A Reader.* Malta: Interprint (Malta) Ltd., 1977.

IISS. "The Middle East War." In *The Strategic Survey* 16–55. London: IISS, 1973.

IISS. "Angola." In *Strategic Survey, 1975,* at ___, ed. IISS. London: IISS, 1975.

IISS. "Angola." In *Strategic Survey, 1976,* at _____, ed. IISS. London: IISS, 1976.

IISS. "The Horn of Africa." In *Strategic Survey, 1978, at* _____. London: IISS, 1978.

IISS. "The War in Angola Heats Up." In *Strategic Survey, 1985–1986,* at _____, ed. IISS. London: IISS, 1986.

IISS. "Southern Africa: Conflict and Disruption." In *Strategic Survey, 1986–1987,* at _ ___, ed. IISS. London: IISS, 1987.

IISS. "Chad: Libya on the Run." In *Strategic Survey, 1986–1987.* London: IISS, 1987.

IISS. "Escalating Conflict in Angola." In *Strategic Survey, 1987–1988*, at 193–196, ed. IISS. London: IISS, 1988.

IISS. "Chad: Libya Heading North." In *Strategic Survey, 1987–1988*. London: IISS, 1988.

Inkeles, Alex and Daniel Levinson. "National Character: The Study of Modal Personality and Socio-Cultural Systems." In *Handbook of Social Psychology* 418–506, ed. Gardner Lindzey and Elliot Aronson. Reading, PA: Addison, Wesley, 1969.

Inkeles, Alex and David H. Smith. *Becoming Modern*. Cambridge, MA: Harvard University Press, 1974.

Insight Team, of The London Sunday Times. *The Yom Kippur War*. New York: Doubleday, 1974.

"Iraq's Army: The Lessons from the War with Iran." *The Economist*, January 12, 1991.

Ismail, Lt. General Ahmad. "General Ismail and the War—Interview with Lt. Gen Ismail." *Journal of Palestine Studies* 3(2) (1974): 210–226.

Issawi, Charles. *An Economic History of the Middle East*. London: Methuen, 1982.

Jabbra, Joseph G. "Bureaucracy and Development in the Arab World." *Journal of Asian and African Studies* 24 (1–2) 1989): 1–11.

Jackson, Robert. *Air War over Korea*. New York: Charles Scribner's Sons, 1973.

Jama, Col. Abdullahi Ahmed. "The Horn of Africa Conflict." USAWC Military Studies Program Paper. US Army War College, March 9, 1989.

James, Franziska. "Habré's Hour of Glory." *Africa Report* 32 (5) (September–October 1987): 20–24.

James, W. Martin, III. *A Political History of the Civil War in Angola 1974–1990*. New Brunswick, NJ: Transaction Books, 1992.

Janowitz, Morris. *The Professional Soldier*. New York: Free Press, 1960.

Janowitz, Morris. "Comparative Analysis of Middle Eastern Military Institutions." In *Military Conflict: Essays in the Institutional Analysis of War and Peace* 303–333, ed. Morris Janowitz. Beverly Hills, CA: Sage, 1975.

Jasper, Scott and Scott Moreland. "The Islamic State Is a Hybrid Threat: Why Does That Matter?" *Small Wars Journal*. December 2, 2014. Available online at http://smallwarsjournal.com/jrnl/art/the-islamic-state-is-a-hybrid-threat-why- does-that-matter, accessed on May 20, 2017.

Jencks, Harlan. "China's Punitive War in Vietnam: A Military Assessment." *Asian Survey* 19 (August 5, 1979): 801–815.

Jencks, Harlan. "Lessons of a Lesson: China-Vietnam 1979." In *The Lessons of Recent Wars in the Third World* 148–153, ed. Robert Harkavy and Stephanie Neuman. Lexington, MA: Lexington Books, 1986.

Joarder, Safiuddin. *Syria under the French Mandate, The Early Phase: 1920–1927*. Dacca: The Asiatic Society of Bangladesh, 1977.

Joes, Anthony James. *The War for South Vietnam, 1954–1975*. Revised Ed. Westport, CT: Praeger, 2001.

Joffe, Ellis. *The Chinese Army after Mao*. London: Weidenfeld and Nicolson, 1987.

Johnson, David E. "Hard Fighting: Israel in Lebanon and Gaza." Santa Monica, CA: RAND, 2011.

Johri, Major Sita Ram. *Chinese Invasion of NEFA*. Lucknow: Himalaya Publications, 1968.

Jones, Calvert W. *Bedouins into Bourgeois: Remaking Citizens for Globalization*. Cambridge: Cambridge University Press, 2017.

Joseph, Suad. "Anthropology of the Future: Arab Youth and the State of State." In *Anthropology of the Middle East and North Africa: Into the New Millennium* 105–124, ed. Sherine Hafez and Susan Slymovics. Bloomington: Indiana University Press, 2013.

Jreisat, Jamil E. "Bureaucracy and Development in Jordan." *Journal of Asian and African Studies* 24 (1–2) (1989): 94–105.

Jupa, Richard and James Dingeman. "The Republican Guards: Loyal, Aggressive, Able." *Army* 41 (3) (March 1991): 54–62.

Kahalani, Avigdor. *The Heights of Courage: A Tank Leader's War on the Golan*. New York: Praeger, 1992.

Kam, Ephraim. *Gulf War Lessons Learned by Egypt*. Center for National Security Studies at Los Alamos, 1992.

Kamiya, Maj. Jason J. *A History of the 24th Mechanized Infantry Division Combat Team during Operation Desert Storm*. Fort Stewart, GA: US Department of the Army—Hqs, 24th Mechanized Division, 1992.

Kamrava, Mehran. "Military Professionalization and Civil-Military Relations in the Middle East." *Political Science Quarterly* 115 (1) (Spring 2000): 67–92.

Kaplan, Robert B. "Cultural Thought Patterns in Inter-Cultural Education." *Language Learning* 16(1–2) (1966): 1–20.

Karawan, Ibrahim A. "Egypt's Defense Policy." In *Defense Planning in Less-Industrialized States* 147–179, ed. Stephanie Neuman. Lexington, Ma: Lexington Books, 1984.

Karnow, Stanley. *Vietnam: A History*. Revised and updated paperback ed. New York: Penguin Books, 1991.

Karsh, Efraim. "The Iran-Iraq War: A Military Analysis." London: IISS, 1987.

Karsh, Efraim and Inari Rautsi. *Saddam Hussein: A Political Biography*. New York: The Free Press, 1991.

Karsh, Efraim. *Gulf War Lessons: The Case of Iraq*. Center for National Security Studies, 1992.

Karsh, Efraim. *Gulf War Lessons: Syria*. Center for National Security Studies, 1992.

Kavic, Lorne J. *India's Quest for Security: Defense Policies 1947–1965*. Berkeley: University of California Press, 1967.

Keegan, John. *World Armies*. First ed., London: MacMillan, 1979.

Khadduri, Majid. "The Role of the Military in Middle Eastern Politics." *American Political Science Review* 47 (1953): 511–524.

Khaled, HRH General Bin Sultan. *Desert Warrior: A Personal View of the Gulf War by the Joint Forces Commander*. New York: Harper Collins, 1995.

Kindsvatter, Lt. Col. Peter S. "VII Corps in the Gulf War." *Military Review* 72 (1) (February 1992): 2–16.

King, Diane E. "The Personal Is Patrilineal: *Namus* as Sovereignty." *Identities* 15(3) (2008): 317–342.

Klein, Yitzhak. "A Theory of Strategic Culture." *Comparative Strategy* 10 (1991): 3–23.

Kluckohn, Clyde. "Culture and Behavior." In *Handbook of Social Psychology* 921–976, ed. Gardner Lindzey. Cambridge, MA: Addison-Wesley, 1954.

Knights, Michael. "The Future of Iraq's Armed Forces." Al-Bayan Center for Planning and Studies, Baghdad, March 2016.

Kober, Avi. "The Israel Defense Forces in the Second Lebanon War: Why the Poor Performance?" *The Journal of Strategic Studies* 31(1) (February 2008): 3–40.

Kolkowicsz, Roman and Andrej Korbonski, eds. *Soldiers, Peasants and Bureaucrats: Civil-Military Relations in Communist and Modernizing Societies.* London: George Allen and Unwin, 1982.

Korn, David A. *Stalemate: The War of Attrition and Great Power Diplomacy in the Middle East, 1967–1970.* Boulder, CO: Westview Press, 1992.

Kraft, Scott. "Suddenly Nation Is United: Chad's Civil War Turns into a Battle with Libya." *Los Angeles Times*, March 9, 1987, A1.

Kraft, Scott. "Chad Victory over Libyans a Major Setback for Kadafi." *Los Angeles Times*, March 25, 1987, A1.

Krivosheev, Colonel-General G.F. *Soviet Casualties and Combat Losses in the Twentieth Century.* London: Greenhill Books, 1997.

Kupchan, Charles A. *The Persian Gulf and the West: Dilemmas of Security.* Boston: Allen and Unwin, 1987.

Kyle, Keith. *Suez.* New York: St. Martin's, 1991.

Laffin, John. *Fight for the Falklands!* New York: St. Martin's Press, 1982.

Laffin, John. *War of Desperation.* London: Osprey, 1985.

Lamb, David. *The Arabs.* New York: Vintage, 1987.

Lambeth, Benjamin S. *Moscow's Lessons from the 1982 Lebanon War.* RAND Corp, 1984. R-3000-AF.

Lane, Ruth. "Political Culture: Residual Category or General Theory?" *Comparative Political Studies* 25(3) (October 1992): 362–387.

Laron, Guy. *The Six-Day War: The Breaking of the Middle East.* New Haven, CT: Yale University Press, 2017.

Laroui, Abdallah. *The Crisis of the Arab Intellectual.* Trans. Diarmid Cammell. Berkeley: University of California Press, 1976.

Lee, Wayne E. *Waging War: Conflict, Culture, and Innovation in World History.* Oxford: Oxford University Press, 2016.

Legum, Colin and Bill Lee. "Crisis in the Horn of Africa: International Dimensions of the Somali-Ethiopian Conflict." In *Africa Contemporary Record,* 1977–1978, at A33–A46, ed. Colin Legum. New York: Africana, 1979.

Legum, Colin, ed. *Africa Contemporary Record, 1977–1978.* New York: Africana, 1979.

Legum, Colin, ed. *Africa Contemporary Record, 1985–1986*. New York: Africana, 1987.

Legum, Colin, ed. *Africa Contemporary Record, 1986–1987*. New York: Africana 1988.

Legum, Colin, ed. *Africa Contemporary Record, 1987–1988*. New York: Africana, 1989.

Lemarchand, René, ed. *The Green and The Black: Qadhafi's Policies in Africa*. Bloomington, IN: Indiana University Press, 1988.

Lerner, Daniel and Richard D. Robinson. "Swords and Ploughshares: The Turkish Army as a Modernizing Force." *World Politics* 13 (1960): 117–148.

Lerner, Daniel. *The Passing of Traditional Society: Modernizing the Middle East*. First paperback ed., London: The Free Press of Glencoe, 1964.

LeVine, Robert A. "Properties of Culture: An Ethnographic View." In *Culture Theory: Essays on Mind, Self, and Emotion* 67–87, ed. Richard A. Schweder and Robert A. LeVine. New York: Cambridge University Press, 1984.

Lewis, Bernard. *The Arabs in History*. London: Hutchinson, 1950.

Lewis, Bernard. *The Political Language of Islam*. Chicago: University of Chicago Press, 1988.

Lewis, Jessica D. "The Islamic State: A Counter-Strategy for a Counter-State." Institute for the Study of War, July 2014.

Lewis, Paul. "Libyans Said to Begin Retreating from Last Major Foothold in Chad." *New York Times*, March 26, 1987, A1 & A5.

Lewis, William H. "The Ethiopian-Somali War, 1977–1978." In *The Lessons of Recent Wars in the Third World* 99–116, ed. Robert Harkavy and Stephanie Neuman. Lexington, MA: Lexington Books, 1986.

Lewis, William H. "War in the Western Sahara." In *The Lessons of Recent Wars in the Third World* 117–137, ed. Robert Harkavy and Stephanie Neuman. Lexington, MA: Lexington Books, 1986.

Lindholm, Charles. *The Islamic Middle East*. Revised ed. Oxford: Blackwell, 2002.

Lister, Charles. "Dynamic Stalemate: Surveying Syria's Military Landscape." *Brookings Doha Center* (May 2014).

Lister, Charles. *The Islamic State: A Brief Introduction*. Washington, DC: Brookings Institution Press, 2015.

Lorch, Lt. Col. Natanel. *The Edge of the Sword: Israel's War of Independence, 1947–1949*. New York: Putnam, 1961.

Lord, Carnes. "American Strategic Culture." *Comparative Strategy* 5(3) (1985): 269–293.

Lorell, Mark A. *Airpower in Peripheral Conflict: The French Experience in Africa*. RAND Corp., 1989. R-3660-AF.

Love, Kennett. *Suez: The Twice-Fought War*. New York: McGraw Hill, 1969.

Luft, Gal. *Beer, Bacon and Bullets: The Cultural Factor in Coalition Warfare from Gallipoli to Iraq*. New York: Booksurge, 2009.

Lunt, James. *Hussein of Jordan*. London: MacMillan, 1989.

Lutfiyya, Abdullah. *Baytin: A Jordanian Village*. The Hague: Mouton and Co., 1966.

Lutfiyya, Abdulla M. and Charles W. Churchill, eds. *Readings in Arab Middle Eastern Societies and Cultures*. The Hague: Mouton and Co., 1970.

Luttwak, Edward and Dan Horowitz. *The Israeli Army*. New York: Harper and Row, 1975.

Luttwak, Edward. "Cubans in Arabia? Or, The Meaning of Strategy." *Commentary* 68(6) (December 1979): 6–66.

Ma'oz, Moshe and Avner Yaniv, eds. *Syria under Assad: Domestic Constraints and Regional Risks*. New York: St. Martin's Press, 1986.

MacCoun, Robert, Elizabeth Kier, and Aaron Belkin. "Does Social Cohesion Determine Motivation in Combat? An Old Question with an Old Answer." *Armed Forces and Society* 32(4) (July 2006): 646–654.

MacLeod, Robert B. "The Arab Middle East: Some Psychological Problems." *Journal of Social Issues* 15(3) (1959): 69–75.

Mahoney, Kevin. *Formidable Enemies: The North Korean and Chinese Soldier in the Korean War*. Novato, CA: Presidio, 2001.

Makiya, Kanaan. *Republic of Fear: The Politics of Modern Iraq*. Berkeley: University of California Press, 1989.

Makovsky, David and Jeffrey White. "Lessons and Implications of the Israel-Hizballah War: A Preliminary Assessment." Washington, DC: Washington Institute for Near East Policy, 2006.

al-Marashi, Ibrahim and Sammy Salama. *Iraq's Armed Forces: An Analytical History*. New York, Routledge, 2008.

Marr, Phebe. *The Modern History of Iraq*. Boulder, CO: Westview, 1985.

Marshall, S. L. A. *The River and the Gauntlet*. New York: William Morrow and Co., 1953.

Marshall, S. L. A. "Egypt's Two-Week Military Myth." *The New Leader* (November 12, 1973): 11.

Marshall, S. L. A. "Tank Warrior in the Golan." *Military Review* 56 (January 1976): 3–12.

Marshall, S. L. A. *Infantry Operations and Weapons Usage in Korea*. 1988 Greenhill ed., London: Greenhill Books, 1988.

Mason, R. A. "The Air War in the Gulf." *Survival* 33(3) (May/June 1991): 211–229.

Matthews, Roderic D. and Matta Akrawi. *Education in Arab Countries of the Near East*. Washington, DC: American Council on Education, 1949.

Mayall, James. "The Battle for the Horn of Africa." *World Today* 34 (9) (September 1978): 336–345.

Mazarr, Michael J., Don M. Snider, and James A. Blackwell Jr. *Desert Storm: The Gulf War and What We Learned*. Boulder, CO: Westview Press, 1993.

McIntire, Katherine. "Speed Bumps: The 82nd Airborne's Shaky Line in the Sand." *Army Times* (October 21, 1991).

McLaurin, R. D. *Military Operations in the Gulf War: The Battle of Korramshahr*. US Army Human Engineering Lab, 1982.

McNaugher, Thomas L. "Arms and Allies on the Arabian Peninsula." *Orbis* 28(3) (Fall 1984): 489–526.

Melikian, L. "Authoritarianism and Its Correlates in the Egyptian Culture and the United States." *Journal of Social Issues* 15(3) (1959): 58–69.

Menoret, Pascal. *Joyriding in Riyadh: Oil, Urbanism, and Road Revolt.* New York: Cambridge University Press, 2014.

Mernissi, Fatima. *Islam and Democracy.* trans. Mary Jo Lakeland. Reading, MA: Addison-Wesley, 1992.

Mesa-Lago, Carmela. *The Economy of Socialist Cuba.* Albuquerque: University of New Mexico Press, 1981.

Metz, Helen Chapin. *Iraq: A Country Study.* Washington, DC: Library of Congress, 1990.

Metz, Helen Chapin. *Jordan: A Country Study.* Washington, DC: Library of Congress, 1991.

Middlebrook, Martin. *Operation Corporate: The Falklands War, 1982.* London: Viking, 1985.

Middlebrook, Martin. *The Fight for the "Malvinas:" The Argentine Forces in the Falklands War.* London: Viking, 1989.

Middlebrook, Martin. *Argentine Fight for the Falklands.* Barnsley, UK: Pen and Sword, 2012).

Middleton, Drew. "US Aides Say Egypt Lacks Ability to Handle Weapons." *New York Times*, February 21, 1986, 8.

Military History Institute of Vietnam. *Victory in Vietnam: The Official History of the People's Army of Vietnam, 1954–1975.* trans. Merle Pribbenow. Lawrence: University of Kansas Press, 2002.

Miller, Benjamin. "The Development of Soviet Armor." Unpublished PhD dissertation, Cornell University, 1984.

Millett, Allan R. *The War for Korea, 1950–1951: They Came from the North.* Lawrence: University of Kansas Press, 2010.

Ministry of Defence, Israel. *The Six Day's War.* Tel Aviv, Israel: Israel Press Ltd, 1967.

Mitchell, Joshua. *Tocqueville in Arabia: Dilemmas in a Democratic Age.* Chicago: University of Chicago Press, 2013.

Moodie, Michael. "Six Months of Conflict." *The Washington Quarterly* 5 (4) (Autumn 1982): 25–33.

Moore, Molly. *A Woman at War: Storming Kuwait with the US Marines.* New York: Charles Scribner's Sons, 1993.

Moreaux, J. M. "The Syrian Army." *Defense Update* (69) (March 1986): 26–31, 42–43.

Moreaux, J. M. "The Syrian Army." *Defence Update* (73) (July 1986): 35–40.

Moro, Rubén O. *The History of the South Atlantic Conflict: The War for the Malvinas.* New York: Praeger, 1989.

Moskin, J. Robert. *Among Lions: The Definitive Account of the 1967 Battle for Jerusalem.* New York: Arbor House, 1982.

Moughrabi, Fouad M. "The Arab Basic Personality: A Critical Survey of the Literature." *International Journal of Middle East Studies* 9 (1978): 99–112.

Müller, Rolf-Dieter. *Hitler's Wehrmacht, 1935–1945*. Lexington: University of Kentucky Press, 2016.

Murguizur, Juan Carlos. "The South Atlantic Conflict—An Argentine Point of View." *International Defense Review* 16 (2) (Feb 1983): 135–136.

Murray, Williamson. "Does Military Culture Matter?" In *American the Vulnerable: Our Military Problems and How to Fix Them* 134–151, ed. John Lehman and Harvey Sicherman. Philadelphia: FPRI, 2002.

Murray, Williamson and Kevin M. Woods. *The Iran-Iraq War: A Military and Strategic History.* Cambridge: Cambridge University Press, 2014.

Mutawi, Samir. *Jordan in the 1967 War.* Cambridge: Cambridge University Press, 1987.

Najarian, Pergrouhi. "Adjustment in the Family and Patterns of Family Living." *Journal of Social Issues* 15(3) (1959): 28–44.

Narkiss, Uzi. *The Liberation of Jerusalem.* London: Valentine Mitchell, 1983.

Naylor, Sean D. "Flight of Eagles: 101st Airborne Division's Raids into Iraq." *Army Times* (July 22, 1991): 8–12, 15.

Neff, Donald. *Warriors against Israel.* Brattleboro, VT: Amana Books, 1988.

Nelson, S. S. "Cultural Differences a Factor in Saudi Deployment." *Air Force Times* (September 10, 1990).

Neuberger, Benyamin. *Involvement, Invasion and Withdrawal: Qadhdhafi's Libya and Chad, 1969–1981.* Vol. 83. Occasional Papers of the Shiloah Center for Middle Eastern and African Studies, Tel Aviv: Shiloah Center for Middle Eastern and African Studies, Tel Aviv University, 1982.

Nguyen Cao Ky. *Twenty Years and Twenty Days.* New York: Stein & Day, 1976.

Niblock, Tim. *State, Society and Economy in Saudi Arabia.* London: Croom Helms, 1982.

Niddrie, David. "Angola: The Siege of Cuito Cuanavale." *Africa Confidential* 29(3) (February 5, 1988): 1–3.

Nieuwenhuize, C. A. O. Van. *Sociology of the Middle East.* Leiden: E. J. Brill, 1971.

Nordeen, Lon and David Nicolle. *Phoenix Over the Nile: A History of Egyptian Air Power, 1932-1994.* Smithsonian Institution Press, Washington, D.C., 1996.

NTC. *The Iraqi Army: Organization and Tactics.* Fort Irwin, California: National Training Center, 1991.

Nyrop, Richard F., ed. *Syria: A Country Study.* Foreign Area Studies. Washington, DC: GPO, 1978.

Nyrop, Richard F., ed. *Saudi Arabia: A Country Study.* Fourth ed., Washington, DC: Government Printing Office, 1984.

O'Ballance, Edgar. *The Arab Israeli War, 1948.* London: Faber and Faber, 1956.

O'Ballance, Edgar. *War in the Yemen.* Hamden, CT: Archon Books, 1971.

O'Ballance, Edgar. *The Third Arab-Israeli War.* Hamden, CT: Archon, 1972.

O'Ballance, Edgar. *Arab Guerilla Power 1967–1972.* Hamden, CT: Archon, 1973.

O'Ballance, Edgar. *The Kurdish Revolt, 1961–1970.* Hamden, CT: Archon Books, 1973.

O'Ballance, Edgar. *The Electronic War in the Middle East: 1968–1970*. London: Faber and Faber, 1974.

O'Ballance, Edgar. *No Victor, No Vanquished: The Yom Kippur War*. San Rafael, CA: Presidio, 1978.

O'Ballance, Edgar. *The Gulf War*. London: Brassey's, 1988.

Ofcansky, Thomas P. "National Security." In *Ethiopia: A Country Study* 235–290, ed. Thomas P. Ofcansky and LaVerle Berry. Washington, DC: GPO, 1991.

Ofcansky, Thomas P. "National Security." In *Somalia: A Country Study* 179–226, ed. Helen Chapin Metz. Washington, DC: GPO, 1992.

Ofer, Tzvi, ed. *The Iraqi Army in the Yom Kippur War*. Maarakhot Forum for Military Studies. Tel Aviv: Maarakhot, 1986.

Oren, Michael B. *Six Days of War: June 1967 and the Making of the Modern Middle East*. Oxford: Oxford University Press, 2002.

Ottaway, David. "For Saudi Military, New Self-Confidence." *The Washington Post*, April 20, 1991, A14.

Owen, Roger. "The Role of the Army in Middle Eastern Politics—A Critique of Existing Analyses." *Review of Middle East Studies* 3 (1978): 64–71.

Palit, Gen. D. *The Lightning Campaign: The Indo-Pakistani War, 1971*. Salisbury, UK: Compton Press, 1972.

Palit, D. K. *Return to Sinai: The Arab Offensive, October 1973*. New Delhi: Palit and Palit, 1974.

Palmer, Michael A. *Guardians of the Gulf*. New York: The Free Press, 1992.

Palmer, Monte, Abdelrahman Al-Hegelan, Al-Sayeed Yassin, and Ali Leila. "Bureaucratic Innovation and Economic Development in the Middle East." *Journal of Asian and African Studies* 24 (1–2) (January–April 1989): 12–27.

Papp, Daniel S. "The Soviet Union and Cuba in Ethiopia." *Current History* 76 (March 1979): 110–114, 129–130.

Papp, Daniel S. "The Angolan Civil War and Namibia: The Role of External Intervention." In *Making War and Waging Peace: Foreign Intervention in Africa* 161–196, ed. David R. Smock. Washington, DC: United States Institute of Peace Press, 1993.

Pardew, James W. Jr. "The Iraqi Army's Defeat in Kuwait." *Parameters* 21 (Winter 1991–92): 17–23.

Pascal, Anthony, Michael Kennedy, Steven Rosen, and Et. Al. *Men and Arms in the Middle East*. Rand Corporation, 1979. R-2460-NA.

Pascal, Anthony. *Are Third World Armies Third Rate? Human Capital and Organizational Impediments to Military Effectiveness*. RAND Corporation, 1980.

Pearson, Robert P. and Leon E. Clark. *Through Middle Eastern Eyes*. New York: Cite Books, 1993.

Peng, Dehuai. *Memoirs of a Chinese Marshal: The Autobiographical notes of Peng Dehuai (1898–1974)*. Beijing: Foreign Languages Press, 1984.

Perlmutter, Amos. *Egypt: The Praetorian State*. New Brunswick, NJ: Transaction Books, 1974.

Perlmutter, Amos and Valerie Plave Bennett. *The Political Influence of the Military: A Comparative Reader.* New Haven, CT: Yale University Press, 1980.

Peterson, J. E. "Guerilla Warfare and Ideological Confrontation in the Arabian Peninsula: The Rebellion in Dhofar." *World Affairs* 139 (Spring 1977): 278–295.

Peterson, J. E. *Defending Arabia.* New York: St. Martin's Press, 1986.

Peterson, J. E. "The GCC States after the Iran-Iraq War." *Journal of Arab-American Affairs* (26) (Fall 1988): 96–106.

Petran, Tabitha. *Syria.* New York: Praeger, 1972.

Pike, Douglas. *PAVN: People's Army of Vietnam.* Da Capo Paperback ed., New York: Da Capo, 1986.

Pimlott, John and Stephen Badsey, eds. *The Gulf War Assessed.* London: Arms and Armour Press, 1992.

Pfaff, Tony. "Development and Reform of the Iraqi Police Forces." Carlisle, PA: US Army War College, January 2008.

Polack, Peter. *The Last Hot Battle of the Cold War: South Africa vs. Cuba in the Angolan Civil War.* Oxford: Casemate, 2013.

Pollack, Kenneth M. *Arabs at War: Military Effectiveness, 1948–1991.* Lincoln: University of Nebraska Press, 2002.

Porter, Patrick. *Military Orientalism: Eastern War through Western Eyes.* New York: Columbia University Press, 2009.

Prothro, E. Terry. *Child Rearing in the Lebanon.* Cambridge: Cambridge University Press, 1961.

Pye, Lucian and S. Verba. *Political Culture and Political Development.* Princeton, NJ: Princeton University Press, 1965.

Qubain, Fahim I. *Education and Science in the Arab World.* Baltimore: The Johns Hopkins Press, 1966.

Quinlivan, James T. "Coup-Proofing: Its Practice and Consequences in the Middle East." *International Security* 24(2) (Fall 1999): 131–165.

Rabin, Yitzahk. *The Rabin Memoirs.* London: Weidenfeld and Nicolson, 1979.

Rabinovich, Itamar and Haim Shaked, eds. *From June to October.* New Brunswick, NJ: Transaction Books, 1978.

Rabinovich, Itamar. "The Limits of Military Power: Syria's Role." In *Lebanon in Crisis* 55–74, ed. P. Edward Haley and Lewis W. Snider. Syracuse, NY: Syracuse University Press, 1979.

Rabinovich, Itamar. *The War for Lebanon: 1970–1985.* Second ed. Ithaca, NY: Cornell University Press, 1985.

Rabinovich, Abraham. *The Battle for Jerusalem.* Philadelphia: The Jewish Publication Society, 1987.

Rahmy, Ali Abdel Rahman. *The Egyptian Policy in the Arab World: Intervention in Yemen, 1962–1967.* Washington, DC: University Press of America, 1983.

Ranstorp, Magnus. "The Hizballah Training Camps of Lebanon." In *The Making of a Terrorist: Recruitment, Training, and Root Causes, Vol. 2,* ed. James Forest. Westport, CT: Praeger Security International, 2006): 243–262.

Record, Jeffrey. "The October War: Burying the Blitzkrieg." *Military Review* 56 (4) (1976): 19–21.

Record, Jeffrey. *Hollow Victory: A Contrary View of the Gulf War.* Washington, DC: Brassey's, 1993.

Record, Jeffrey. "Vietnam in Retrospect: Could We Have Won?" *Parameters* 26(4) (Winter 1996–1997): pp. 51–65.

Reese, Roger R. *The Soviet Military Experience.* London: Routledge, 2000.

Ridgway, General Matthew B. *The Korean War.* New York: Doubleday, 1967.

Robbins, Carla Anne. *The Cuban Threat.* New York: McGraw Hill, 1983.

Rodinson, Maxime. *The Arabs.* trans. Arthur Goldhammer. Chicago: University of Chicago Press, 1981.

Ro'I, Yaacov and Boris Morozov eds. *The Soviet Union and the June 1967 Six-Day War.* Stanford, CA: Stanford University Press, 2008.

Rose, Gregory F. "The Post-Revolutionary Purge of Iran's Armed Forces: A Revisionist Assessment." *Iranian Studies* 17 (2/3) (Spring–Summer 1984): 153–194.

Rose, Leo. "Conflict in the Himalayas." *Military Review* 43 (February 1963): 3–15.

Rosen, Laurence. "Expecting the Unexpected: Cultural Components of Arab Governance." *Annals of the American Academy of Political and Social Science* 603 (Law, Society, and Democracy: Comparative Perspectives, January 2006): 163–178.

Rosen, Stephen Peter. "Brown Soldiers, White Officers." *The Washington Quarterly* (Spring 1982).

Rosen, Stephen Peter. *Societies and Military Power: The Indian Army in Comparative Perspective.* Ithaca, NY: Cornell University Press, 1996.

Rosen, Stephen Peter. *War and Human Nature.* Princeton, NJ: Princeton University Press, 2005.

Rothschild, Joseph. "Culture and War." In *The Lessons of Recent Wars in the Third World*, Vol. 2, 53–72, ed. Robert Harkavy and Stephanie Neuman. Lexington, MA: Lexington Books, 1987.

Rugh, Andrea B. *Family in Contemporary Egypt.* Syracuse, NY: Syracuse University Press, 1984.

Sabry, Tarik. *Arab Cultural Studies: Mapping the Field.* London: I. B. Tauris, 2012.

Safran, Nadav. *From War to War.* New York: Pegasus, 1969.

Safran, Nadav. *Saudi Arabia: Ceaseless Quest for Security.* Paperback ed., Ithaca, NY: Cornell University Press, 1988.

Said, Edward. *Orientalism.* New York: Vintage, 1979.

Sakal, Major General Emanuel, IDF (Ret). *Soldier in the Sinai: A General's Account of the Yom Kippur War.* Lexington: University Press of Kentucky, 2014.

Salzman, Philip Carl. *Culture and Conflict in the Middle East.* Amherst, NY: Humanity Books, 2008.

Saleh, Saneya Abdel Wahab. "The Brain Drain in Egypt." *Cairo Papers in Social Science* 2 (Monograph 5 1979): 136 pages.

Saney, Isaac. "African Stalingrad: The Cuban Revolution, Internationalism, and the End of Apartheid." *Latin American Perspectives* 33((5) (September 2006): 81–117.

Sanchez, Nestor D. and Jay Mallin Sr. "The Military and Transition in Cuba." *International Research 2000 Inc.*, 1995.

Satloff, Robert. *Troubles on the East Bank*. New York: Praeger, 1986.

Satloff, Robert. *The Politics of Change in the Middle East*. Boulder, CO: Westview, 1993.

Scales, Brigadier General Robert H. *Certain Victory*. Washington, DC: Office of the Chief of Staff of the US Army, 1993.

Schanzer, Jonathan. *Al-Qaeda's Armies*. Washington, DC: The Washington Institute for Near East Policy, 2005.

Schein, Edgar H. *Organizational Culture and Leadership*. Third ed. San Francisco: John Wiley and Sons, 2004.

Schiff, Ze'ev and Ehud Ya'ari. *Israel's Lebanon War*. New York: Simon and Schuster, 1984.

Schiff, Ze'ev. *A History of the Israeli Army*. New York: MacMillan, 1985.

Schmidt, Dana Adam. *Yemen: The Unknown War*. London: The Bodley Head, 1968.

Scholtz, Leopold. *The SADF in the Border War 1966–1989*. Warwick, UK: Helion, 2013.

Schwarzkopf, Gen. Norman and Peter Petre. *It Doesn't Take a Hero*. New York: Bantam, 1992.

Schweitzer, Yoram and Omer Einav, eds. *The Islamic State: How Viable Is It?* Tel Aviv: Institute for National Security Studies, 2016.

Scicchitano, J. Paul. "Eye of the Tiger: Stalking Iraqi Prey with the Tiger Brigade." *Army Times* (June 10, 1991): 13–61.

Sciolino, Elaine. "Chad Takes Another Key Libya Base." *NY Times*, 28 March 1987, A3.

Seale, Patrick. *The Struggle for Syria: A Study of Post-War Arab Politics, 1945–1958*. 1986 ed., London: I. B. Tauris, 1986.

Seale, Patrick. *Asad of Syria: The Struggle for the Middle East*. London: I. B. Tauris, 1988.

Segal, Gerald. *Defending China*. New York: Oxford University Press, 1985.

Segal, David. "The Iran-Iraq War: A Military Analysis." *Foreign Affairs* 66 (5) (Summer 1988): 950–958.

Selassie, Bereket Habte. *Conflict and Intervention in the Horn of Africa*. New York: Monthly Review Press, 1980.

Sella, Amnon. *Soviet Political and Military Conduct in the Middle East*. New York: St. Martin's Press, 1981.

Sewell, William H. Jr. "The Concept(s) of Culture.' In *Beyond the Cultural Turn: New Directions in the Study of Society and Culture* 35–61, ed. Victoria E. Bonnell and Lynn Hunt. Berkeley: University of California Press, 1999:

Shamir, Shimon. "Arab Military Lessons from the October War." In *Military Aspects of the Arab-Israeli Conflict* 172–178, ed. Louis Williams (Tel Aviv: University Publishing Projects, 1975).

Shapir, Yiftah S. "Hezbollah as an Army." *Strategic Assessment* 19(4) (January 2017): 67–78.

Sharabi, Hisham. *Neopatriarchy: A Theory of Distorted Change in Arab Society*. Oxford: Oxford University Press, 1988.

Sharabi, Hisham, ed. *The Next Arab Decade: Alternative Futures*. Boulder, CO: Westview, 1988.

Sharabi, Hisham, ed. *Theory, Politics and the Arab World*. New York: Routledge, 1990.

Sharon, Ariel with David Chanoff. *Warrior: The Autobiography of Ariel Sharon*. New York: Simon and Schuster, 1989.

Shazli, Lt. General Sa'ad Din. "How the Egyptians Crossed the Canal—Interview with Lt. General Shazli." *Journal of Palestine Studies* 3(2) 1974): 163–168.

Shazli, Lt. General Saad El. *The Crossing of Suez*. San Francisco: American Mideast Research, 1980.

Shehata, Samer S. *Shop Floor Culture and Politics in Egypt*. Albany: SUNY Press, 2009.

Shemesh, Haim. *Soviet-Iraqi Relations 1968–1988*. Boulder, CO: Lynn Rienner, 1992.

Shepherd, Ben H. *Hitler's Soldiers: The German Army in the Third Reich*. New Haven, CT: Yale University Press, 2016.

Shouby, Eli. "The Influence of the Arabic Language on the Psychology of Arabs." *The Middle East Journal* 5(3) (Summer 1951): 284–302.

Sienkiewicz. "Some Military Lessons of the War in Lebanon: June 1982." In *The Regionalization of Warfare* 85–95, ed. James Brown and William P. Snyder. New Brunswick: Transaction Books, 1990.

Simon, Reeva S. *Iraq between the Two World Wars*. New York: Columbia University Press, 1986.

Sinai, Anne and Allen Pollack. *The Syrian Arab Republic: A Handbook. The Middle East Confrontation States*. New York: American Academic Association for Peace in the Middle East, 1976.

Sinai, Anne and Allen Pollack. *The Hashemite Kingdom of Jordan and the West Bank: A Handbook*. New York: American Academic Association for Peace in the Middle East, 1977.

Sluglett, Marion Farouk. "Contemporary Iraq: Some Recent Writings Reconsidered." *Review of Middle East Studies* 3 (1978): 82–104.

Sluglett, Peter and Marion Farouk-Sluglett. *Iraq since 1958: From Revolution to Dictatorship*. London: KPI Ltd., 1987.

Smiley, David with Peter Kemp. *Arabian Assignment*. London: Leo Cooper, 1975.

Smyth, Phillip. "The Shiite Jihad in Syria and Its Regional Effects." The Washington Institute for Near East Policy, Policy Focus 138, 2015.

Somerville, Keith. *Foreign Military Intervention in Africa*. London: Pinter, 1990.

Soodalter, Ron. "Over Where? Cuban Fighters in Angola's Civil War." *Military History Quarterly* 28(3) (Spring 2016): 28–37.

Sorley, Lewis. *A Better War: The Unexamined Victories and Final Tragedy of America's Last Years in Vietnam*. Paperback ed., New York: Harcourt Brace, 1999.

Spikes, Daniel. *Angola and the Politics of Intervention*. Jefferson, NC: McFarland, 1993.

Spurr, Russell. *Enter the Dragon: China's Undeclared War against the US in Korea 1950–1951*. New York: Newmarket Press, 1988.

Stanhope, Henry. "Text-Book Invaders Dither towards Disaster." *The Times*, October 26, 1973.

Stanhope, Henry. "A Bitter Lesson for the Arabs." *The Times*, October 22, 1973, 20.

Stapleton, Timothy J. *A Military History of Africa: Volume 3, The Era of Inependence: From the Congo Crisis to Africa's World War (ca. 1963–)*. Santa Barbara, CA: Praeger, 2013.

Staudenmaier, William O. "A Strategic Analysis of the Gulf War." Carlisle Barracks, PA: Strategic Studies Institute, US Army War College, 1982.

Staudenmaier, William O. "Defense Planning in Iraq: An Alternative Perspective." In *Defense Planning in Less-Industrialized States* 53–66, ed. Stephanie Neuman. Lexington, MA: Lexington Books, 1984.

Staudenmaier, William O. "The Iran-Iraq War." In *The Lessons of Recent Wars in the Third World* 211–231, ed. Robert Harkavy and Stephanie Neuman. Lexington, MA: Lexington Books, 1986.

Stayanoff, Russ. "Third World Experience in Counterinsurgency: Cuba's Operation Carlotta, 1975." *Small Wars Journal* (May 2008): available online at www.militaryhistoryonline.com/20thCentury/articles/cubansinafrica.aspx, downloaded on May 9, 2018.

Steele, Dennis. "Down in the Sand: The First Brushes." *Army* 41 (3) (March 1991): 33–38.

Steenkamp, William. *South Africa's Border War 1966–1989*. United Kingdom: 2014.

Stern, Jessica and J. M. Berger. *ISIS: The State of Terror*. New York: HarperCollins, 2015.

Stewart, Nora Kinzer. "A Case Study in Cohesion: The South Atlantic Conflict 1982." *Military Review* LXIX (February 1989): 31–40.

Stewart, Nora Kinzer. *Mates and Muchachos: Unit Cohesion in the Falklands/Malvinas War*. McLean, VA: Brassey's, 1991.

Sturgill, Claude C. *The Military History of the Third World since 1945*. Westport, CT: Greenwood Press, 1994.

Subrahmanyam, K. "Commentary: Evolution of Defense Planning in India." In *Defense Planning in Less-Industrialized States*, ed. Stephanie Neuman. Lexington, MA: Lexington Books, 1984.

Suchlicki, Jaime, ed. *The Cuban Military under Castro*. Miami, FL: Research Institute for Cuban Studies, University of Miami, 1989.

Suleiman, Michael. "National Stereotypes as Weapons in the Arab-Israeli Conflict." *The Journal of Palestine Studies* 3(3) (1974): 109–121.

Sullivan, Marisa. "Hezbollah in Syria." Middle East Security Report 19, Institute for the Study of War, April 2014.

Sweet, Louise, ed. *People's and Cultures of the Middle East: An Anthropological Reader.* New York: Natural History Press, 1970.

"Syria and Egypt: Against Iraq." *The Economist,* January 5, 1991,

Szyliowicz, Joseph. *The Contemporary MidEast: Tradition and Innovation.* New York: Random House, 1965.

Szyliowicz, Joseph. *Education and Modernization in the Middle East.* Ithaca, NY: Cornell University Press, 1973.

Tahtinen, Dale R. "The Evolution of the Military in Middle East Societies." In *The Military and Security in the Third World: Domestic and International Impacts,* ed. Sheldon W. Simon. Boulder, CO: Westview, 1978.

Talmadge, Caitlin. *The Dictator's Army: Battlefield Effectiveness in Authoritarian Regimes.* Ithaca, NY: Cornell University Press, 2015.

Tarbush, Mohammed A. *The Role of the Military in Politics: A Case Study of Iraq to 1941.* London: Kegan Paul International, 1982.

Tareke, Gebru. "The Ethiopia-Somalia War of 1977 Revisited." *The International Journal of African Historical Studies.* 33 (3) (2000): 635–667.

Tareke, Gebru. *The Ethiopian Revolution: War in the Horn of Africa.* New Haven, CT: Yale University Press, 2009.

Tartter, Jean E. "National Security." In *Libya: A Country Study* 237–292, ed. Helen Chapin Metz. Washington, DC: GPO, 1989.

Tartter, Jean R. "National Security." In *Chad: A Country Study* 172–208, ed. Thomas Collelo. Washington, DC: GPO, 1990.

Taylor, Thomas. *Lightning in the Storm: The 101st Air Assault Division in the Gulf War.* New York: Hippocrene, 1994.

Terhune, K. W. "From National Character to National Behavior: A Reformulation." *Journal of Conflict Resolution* 14(2) (1970): 203–263.

Teveth, Shabtai. *The Tanks of Tammuz.* New York: Viking Press, 1968.

"The Royal Jordanian Air Force: The Arab Professionals." *Air International* 9 (3) (September 1975): 111–117.

Thompson, Brigadier Julian. *No Picnic, 3 Commando Brigade in the South Atlantic: 1982.* Revised ed., London: Leo Cooper, 1992.

Tibi, Bassam. *Islam and the Cultural Accommodation of Social Change.* Boulder, CO: Westview, 1991.

Tice, Jim. "Coming Through: The Big Red Raid." *Army Times* (August 26, 1991): 12, 16, 18, 20.

Tow, William T. "Chinese Strategic Thought: Evolution toward Reality." *Asian Affairs* 7 (4) (March–April 1980): 248–269.

Trainor, Bernard. "Chad's Anti-Libya Offensive: Surprising Successes." *New York Times,* January 12, 1987, A3.

Trainor, Bernard. "Victories Shore Up Chadians." *New York Times,* January 18, 1987, A14.

Trainor, Bernard. "France and US Aiding Chadians with Intelligence to Rout Libyans." *New York Times,* April 3, 1987, A1 & A5.

Trainor, Bernard. "Desert Tactics of Chadians: Like Old West." *New York Times*, April 5, 1987, A4.

Trainor, Bernard. "In the Desert, Chad Exhibits Spoils of War." *New York Times*, April 13, 1987, A1 & A12.

Trainor, Lt. Gen. Bernard. "Iraqi Offensive: Victory Goes Beyond Battlefield." *New York Times*, April 20, 1988.

Trainor, Lt. Gen. Bernard and Michael R. Gordon. *The Generals' War.* Boston: Little, Brown, 1995.

Tretiak, Daniel. "China's Vietnam War and Its Consequences." *China Quarterly* 80 (December 1979): 740–767.

Tripp, Charles. "The Iran-Iraq War and the Iraqi State." In *Iraq: Power and Society* 91–116, ed. Derek Hopwood, Habib Ishow, and Thomas Koszinowski. Reading, UK: Ithaca Press, 1993.

Turley, G. H. *The Easter Offensive: Vietnam, 1972.* Novato, CA: Presidio, 1985.

Turner, Arthur Campbell. "Nationalism and Religion: Iran and Iraq at War." In *The Regionalization of Warfare*, 144–163, ed. James Brown and William P. Snyder. New Brunswick, NJ: Transaction Books, 1990.

Tusa, Francis. "Lebanon 1982: Israeli Hubris or Syrian Strength?" *Armed Forces* 6(9) (September 1987): 415–419.

Ullman, Harlan K. "Profound or Perfunctory: Observations on the South Atlantic Conflict." In *The Lessons of Recent Wars in the Third World* 239–259. ed. Robert Harkavy and Stephanie Neuman. Lexington, MA: Lexington Books, 1986.

Urban, Mark. "Fire in the Galilee, Part 2: Syria." *Armed Forces* 5(5) (May 1986): 208–213.

Urban, Mark. "Fire in the Galilee, Part 3: A Future Conflict." *Armed Forces* 5(6), June 1986).

US News and World Report. *Triumph without Victory.* New York: Times Books, 1992.

Valdés, Nelson P. "Cuban Foreign Policy in the Horn of Africa." *Cuban Studies* 10(1) 1980): 63–75.

Valenta, Jiri. "The Soviet-Cuban Intervention in Angola 1975." *Studies in Comparative Communism* 11(1/2) (Spring/Summer 1978): 3–33.

Van Creveld, Martin. "The Human Dimension of War." In *The Lessons of Recent Wars in the Third World*, 73–90, Vol. 2, ed. Robert Harkavy and Stephanie Neuman. Lexington, MA: Lexington Books, 1987.

Van Dam, Nikolaos. *The Struggle for Power in Syria: Sectarianism, Regionalism and Tribalism in Politics, 1961–1978.* New York: St. Martin's Press, 1979.

Vanneman, Peter. "Soviet Foreign Policy for Angola/Namibia in the 1980s: A Strategy of Coercive Diplomacy." In *Disengagement from Southwest Africa: The Prospects for Peace in Angola and Namibia* 69–96, ed. Owen Ellison Kahn. New Brunswick, NJ: Transaction Books, 1990.

Various, ed. *The Seventh Day: Soldier's Talk about the Six Day War.* London: Andre Deutsch, 1970.

Vatikiotis, P. J. *Politics and the Military in Jordan.* London: Frank Cass, 1967.

Vatikiotis, P. J. *The Egyptian Army in Politics.* Bloomington: Indiana University Press, 1961.

Vatikiotis, P. J. *The History of Modern Egypt.* Fourth ed., Baltimore: Johns Hopkins University, 1991.

Veith, George J. *Black April: The Fall of South Vietnam 1973–75.* New York: Encounter Books, 2012.

Viksne, Lt. Col. J. "The Yom Kippur War in Retrospect, Part II—Technology." *Army Journal* (Australia) (324), May 1976): 33–35.

Viorst, Milton. "Iraq at War." *Foreign Affairs* 65 (2) (Winter 1986–1987): 349–365.

Viorst, Milton. *Sandcastles: The Arabs in Search of the Modern World.* New York: Alfred A. Knopf, 1994.

Vogel, Steve. "A Swift Kick: 2nd ACR's Taming of the Guard." *Army Times* (August 5, 1991): 10–18, 28–30.

Vogel, Steve. "Metal Rain: 'Old Ironsides' and the Iraqis Who Wouldn't Back Down." *Army Times* (September 16, 1991): 8–22, 61.

Vogel, Steve. "The Tip of the Spear." *Army Times* (January 13, 1992): 8–16, 54.

Von Pivka, Otto. *Armies of the Middle East.* New York: Mayflower, 1979.

Wagner, John S. "Iraq: A Combat Assessment." In *Fighting Armies: Antagonists in the Middle East*, 63–84, ed. Richard Gabriel. Westport, CT.: Greenwood Press, 1983.

Wakebridge, Charles. "The Egyptian Staff Solution." *Military Review* 55 (March 1975): 3–11.

Wakebridge, Charles. "The Syrian Side of the Hill." *Military Review* 56 (February 1976): 20–30.

Wald, Emanuel. *The Wald Report: The Decline of Israeli National Security since 1967.* Boulder, CO: Westview Press, 1987.

Walker, Phyllis Greene. "National Security." In *Cuba: A Country Study* 225–291, ed. James D. Rudolph. Washington, DC: GPO, 1987.

Ward, Steven R. *Immortal: A Military History of Iran and Its Armed Forces.* Washington, DC: Georgetown University Press, 2009.

Wardak, Col. Ghulam Dastagir (compilation and transcription). *The Voroshilov Lectures: Materials from the Soviet General Staff Academy.* Vol. 1. Washington, DC: National Defense University Press, 1989.

Wardi, Ali. *Understanding Iraq: Society, Culture, and Personality.* trans. Fuad Baali. Lewiston, NY: The Edwin Mellen Press, 2008.

Watson, Bruce W. et al. *The Military Lessons of the Gulf War.* London: Greenhill Books, 1991.

Weathersby, Kathryn. " 'Should We Fear This?' Stalin and the Danger of War with America." Working Paper No. 8, Cold War International History Project, Woodrow Wilson International Center for Scholars, Washington, DC, November 1993.

Weathersby, Kathryn. "Soviet Aims in Korea and the Origins of the Korean War, 1945–1950: New Evidence from Russian Archives." Working Paper No. 39, Cold War International History Project, Woodrow Wilson International Center for Scholars, Washington, DC, July 2002.

Webb, William J. *The Korean War: The Outbreak, 27 June–15 September 1950.* Washington, DC: US Army Center for Military History, 2012.

Wegner, Bernd. "Part VI: The War against the Soviet Union, 1942–1943." In *Germany and the Second World War, Volume VI: The Global War* 843–1216, ed. Horst Boog, Werner Rahn, Reinhard Stumpf, and Bernd Wegner, trans. Ewald Osers, John Brownjohn, Patricia Crampton, and Louise Wilmot. Oxford: Oxford University Press, 2001.

Weinberger, Naomi. *Syrian Intervention in Lebanon.* New York: Oxford University Press, 1986.

Weller, Jack. "Infantry and the October War." *Army* 24 (August 1974): 21–26.

Whetten, Lawrence L. "The Military Dimension." In *Lebanon in Crisis* 75–90, ed. P. Edward Haley and Lewis W. Snider. Syracuse, NY: Syracuse University Press, 1979.

White, Jeffrey. "Hizb Allah at War in Syria: Forces, Operations, Effects and Implications." Combating Terrorism Center, United States Military Academy, January 15, 2014, available online at https://www.ctc.usma.edu/posts/hizb-allah-at-war-in-syria-forces-operations-effects-and-implications, accessed May 22, 2016.

Whitewood, Peter. *The Red Army and the Great Terror: Stalin's Purge of the Soviet Military.* Lawrence: University of Kansas Press, 2015.

Whiting, Allen S. *China Crosses the Yalu.* New York: MacMillan, 1960.

Wiest, Andrew. *Vietnam's Forgotten Army: Heroism and Betrayal in the ARVN.* New York: New York University Press, 2008.

Wikan, Unni. *Life among the Poor of Cairo.* trans. Ann Henning. London: Tavistock Publications, 1980.

Wikan, Unni. *Tomorrow, God Willing: Self-Made Destinies in Cairo.* Chicago: University of Chicago Press, 1996.

Wildavsky, A. "Choosing Preferences by Constructing Institutions: A Cultural Theory of Preference Formation." *American Political Science Review* 81 (1) (March 1987): 3–22.

Willbanks, James H. *The Battle of An Loc.* Bloomington: Indiana University Press, 2005.

Willbanks, James H. *Abandoning Vietnam: How America Left and South Vietnam Lost Its War.* Lawrence: University of Kansas Press, 2008.

Willbanks, James H. *A Raid Too Far: Operation Lam Son 719 and Vietnamization in Laos.* College Station: Texas A&M Press, 2014.

Williams, Judith. *The Youth of Haouch el Harimi, A Lebanese Village.* Cambridge, MA: Harvard University Press, 1968.

Williams, Louis, ed. *Military Aspects of the Arab-Israeli Conflict*. Tel Aviv: University Publishers, 1975.

Wilson, George C. "Libyan Sailors, Aviatos Reportedly Unskilled." *Washington Post*, January 9, 1986, 24.

Wilson, Peter W. and Douglas F. Graham. *Saudi Arabia: The Coming Storm*. Armonk, NY: M.E. Sharpe, 1994.

Wilson, Stephen. "For a Socio-historical Approach to the Study of Western Military Culture." *Armed Forces and Society* 6 (4) (Summer 1980): 527–552.

Witty, David. "A Regular Army in Counterinsurgency Operations: Egypt in North Yemen, 1962–1967." *The Journal of Military History*. 65(2) (April 2001): 401–439.

Wong, Leonard, Thomas A. Kolditz, Raymond A. Millen, and Terrence M. Potter. *Why They Fight: Combat Motivation in the Iraq War*. Carlisle Barracks, PA: Strategic Studies Institute, US Army War College, 2003.

Woods, Kevin M. *The Iraqi Perspectives Report: Saddan's Senior Leadership on Operation Iraqi Freedom from the Official U.S. Joint Forces Command Report*. Annapolis, MD: US Naval Institute Press, 2006.

Woods, Kevin M. *The Mother of All Battles: Saddam Hussein's Strategic Plan for the Persian Gulf War*. Annapolis, MD: US Naval Institute Press, 2008.

Woods, Kevin M., Williamson Murray, Elizabeth A. Nathan, Laila Sabara, and Ana M. Venegas. *Saddam's Generals: Perspectives of the Iran-Iraq War*. Washington, DC: Institute for Defense Analysis, 2011.

Woods, Kevin M., David Palkki, and Mark Stout, eds. *The Saddam Tapes: The Inner Workings of a Tyrant's Regime 1978–2001*. Cambridge: Cambridge University Press, 2011.

Woodward, Bob. *The Commanders*. New York: Simon and Schuster, 1991.

Wright, John. *Libya, Chad and the Central Sahara*. Totowa, NJ: Barnes and Noble Books, 1989.

Wunderle, William D. "Through the Lens of Cultural Awareness: A Primer for US Armed Forces Deploying to Arab and Middle Eastern Countries." Fort Leavenworth, KS: Combat Studies Institute Press, 2006.

Yonay, Ehud. *No Margin for Error: The Making of the Israeli Air Force*. New York: Pantheon Books, 1993.

Young, Brigadier Peter. *The Israeli Campaign, 1967*. London: William Kimber, 1967.

Yup, General Paik Sun. *From Pusan to Panmunjom*. McLean, VA: Brassey's, 1992.

Zabhi, Sepehr. *The Iranian Military in Revolution and War*. London: Routledge, 1988.

Zacchea, Michael and Ted Kemp. *The Ragged Edge: A U.S. Marine's Account of Leading the Iraqi Army Fifth Battalion*. Chicago: Chicago Review Press, 2017.

Zackheim, Dov. "The South Atlantic: Evaluating the Lessons." In *The Regionalization of Warfare*, 37–54, ed. James Brown and William P. Snyder. New Brunswick, NJ: Transaction Books, 1990.

Zaharna, R. S. "Bridging Cultural Differences: American Public Relations Practices and Arab Communications Patterns." *Public Relations Review* 21 (1995): 241–255.

Zahlan, A. B. *Science and Science Policy in the Arab World.* New York: St. Martin's Press, 1980.

Zaloga, Steven J. *Red Thrust: Attack on the Central Front, Soviet Tactics and Capabilities in the 1990s.* Novato, CA: Presidio, 1989.

INDEX

Andrade, Dale, 334
Angola
    air forces' roles during fighting in,
        95–97, 99–102, 334
    Cabinda province in, 84, 86
    Castro's "Western Offensive" in, 96
    counterinsurgency phase of conflict
        (late 1970s) in, 91
    Cuban military operations (1975-
        88) in, 77–78, 84–87, 90–101,
        298, 333–36
    Cuito Cuanavale offensive (1987-88)
        in, 92–96, 99, 102, 336
    maps of, 85, 93
    Namibia conflict and, 91–92
    Portugal's withdrawal from, 84
    South African military operations
        (1975-88) in, 77–78, 85
    Soviet military aid and advisers to,
        92, 94, 100
    Soviet military doctrine and, 99
    tank warfare in, 95–96
    Zaire's involvement in, 84, 86–87
Ani, Muktar, 421
Antoun, Richard, 389
Aouzou Strip (Chad)
    Chadian-Libyan War (1986-87) and,
        287, 291–94, 305
    Libya intervention (1978) and, 277
    Libya's claims to, 276–77
    Libya's intervention in Chad (1983-86)
        and, 282–83
    Libya's intervention in Chad (1980-81)
        in, 279, 281
    Libya's military morale
        regarding, 36, 41
    uranium and, 276
Arab culture
    ambivalence toward manual labor
        and technical work in, 389–93,
        401–2, 421
    Arab military effectiveness and,
        19–20, 41, 133, 343, 368, 370,

        394–405, 437–38, 450, 471,
        473–75, 509, 511–13, 515, 518
    atomization of knowledge and, 386–
        88, 397, 427–28
    broad similarities within different
        countries within, 362–64
    business organizations and, 406–14
    centralization of authority and, 375–
        77, 406–8, 410–13, 434, 513
    conformity and, 371–74, 394, 396,
        416, 419–20, 422, 424, 428,
        433–35, 513
    deference to authority in, 378–80,
        395, 397, 406–7, 410–11, 419,
        422, 424–25, 514, 518
    educational institutions and, 390–91,
        393, 402, 406, 415–38, 450–51
    evolving nature of, 365–66, 371,
        519–20, 522
    family socialization and, 418–19
    fatalism and, 370
    folk theories and, 369
    globalization and, 520
    government agencies and, 406–7, 413
    group loyalty and, 358–59, 381–84,
        400–401, 412, 416, 419–20,
        488, 491–92, 514
    honesty and, 358–59
    honor and shame in, 379–80, 384–
        86, 395, 419, 421
    imperialism's impact on, 368–69, 514
    Islam and, 364–65, 391
    kinship networks and, 382–83,
        400–401, 420
    manipulation of information and,
        384–86, 395, 406, 411–12, 419
    military training and, 439, 449–50
    modern technology's impact on,
        366, 519
    national subcultures and, 362
    neighborhoods as units of, 382
    patriarchal family norms and, 375–
        77, 380, 383, 413, 520

personal courage and, 388–89,
401, 506
psychoanalytical perspectives on, 358
regional subcultures in, 363
societal concepts of time and, 245
stereotypes and, 363, 416, 574n20
tradition valued in, 372
urban settlements as dominant unit
of, 364, 382
worker productivity and, 409–10
Arab educational institutions
atomization of knowledge in,
423, 427–28
autocratic governments in the Arab
world and, 435–37
conformity and, 416, 419–20, 422,
424, 428, 433–35
deference to authority and, 419,
422, 424–25
the family and, 418–23, 436
group loyalty and, 416, 420
qualitative *versus* quantitative
considerations in, 417–18
Quranic schools and, 423–24, 435
rote learning and, 421–29, 432–37
shame as educational tool in, 421
societal academic performance levels
and, 417–18
technical education and, 428–32
universities and, 431, 434
white-collar professions valorized in,
421, 431
Arab Human Development Reports (*ADHR*,
2002-16)
on atomization of knowledge in the
Arab world, 388
economic deficiencies in Arab world
chronicled in, 414, 477
economic reforms advocated by,
412–13, 515
educational problems discussed in,
408, 414, 417–18, 425–27,
430, 434–35

on patriarchal family norms in Arab
world, 419
scientific and technological
deficiencies outlined in, 393
on worker productivity levels, 409
Arab-Israeli War of 1967. *See*
Six-Day War
Arab Legion. *See* Jordanian
Armed Forces
Arab military effectiveness
air forces and, 26, 28–29, 40, 43, 61,
70, 171–73, 229, 263, 273, 338,
397–98, 401, 403, 442, 511
Arab culture and, 19–20, 41, 133,
343, 368, 370, 394–405, 437–
38, 450, 471, 473–75, 509, 511–
13, 515, 518
chain of command as a variable in
determining levels of, 403–5
combined arms operations and, 254–
55, 397, 403, 511
cowardice explanations and,
40–41, 43
definition of Arab world and, 23, 362
economic underdevelopment and,
19–20, 41, 233–35, 247, 272–75,
329–31, 334, 338–39, 343, 401,
403–5, 451, 511–13, 515
foreign intervention in military
conflicts and, 29
information and intelligence
management problems and,
27–28, 40, 42, 61, 70, 138, 142,
145, 169–72, 226, 229, 273,
338–39, 395–96, 398, 403, 468,
511, 513
internal security demands and,
38, 118
Iran-Iraq War (1980s) and, 19, 30–32,
74, 118, 144–48, 150–51, 171–
72, 226–28, 333
Iraq's Kurdish campaigns (1960s)
and, 30

Arab military effectiveness (*Cont.*)

strategic leadership record in,
294–95, 298
Sudan and, 281
tactical leadership record in, 285–86,
295–96, 298, 307–8, 338
Tibesti region and, 32, 276, 281–82,
287–88, 291–93, 296, 301, 303
Toubou ethnic group in, 276–79, 285,
288, 300
unit cohesion in, 296
US aid to, 281, 285, 297
weapons handling and, 333
Chechnya conflict, 51, 506
Chernyakhovsky, Ivan, 125
Chile, 205–7, 220
China
air force in, 318–20, 326–27, 329, 338
bravery among soldiers of, 324, 330
combat engineering performance
of, 336
comissarism and, 321–22, 395
economic development and education
levels in, 309–10, 325, 328–32
infantry deployment tactics and, 313–
15, 317–18, 327
Korean War (1950-53) and, 81, 309–
30, 336, 567n7
literacy rates in, 332
mass conscription army in, 309–10
military armament problems in, 312
military intelligence and, 328
military logistics record in, 313, 316–
18, 325–26, 328, 336
military training in, 316, 327
Mongol invasions of, 353
Soviet military aid to,
318–19, 324–25
strategic leadership record in,
320–22, 327
tactical leadership record in, 322–24,
327–30, 338
weapons handling abilities in, 309,
324–25, 333

Chongchon River (Korea), 313, 320
Chuikov, Vasily, 124
Churchill, Winston, 516
Cintra Frías, Leopoldo
("Polo"), 94–95
Circassians, 113
Clausewitz, Carl von, 473
Coe, Patrick, 309, 321
Cohen, Raymond, 378, 385, 420
Colás, Víctor Schueg, 87
Colborne, John, 349–50
comissarism. See under politicization of
militaries
Confederate States of America, 351
Cordesman, Anthony, 270, 306
Cronin, Stephanie, 127
Cuba
air force of, 84, 95–102, 334, 338
Angola operations (1975-88) of,
77–78, 84–87, 90–101,
298, 333–36
combat engineering performance
of, 335–36
combined arms operations and, 97
comissarism in, 228, 395
economic development levels
in, 331–32
Ethiopia military operations (1978)
by, 77, 87–91, 97–98, 100,
102, 336
literacy rates in, 332
military logistics and,
100–101, 334–36
Soviet military aid and, 84
Soviet military doctrine and, 21, 77,
84, 99, 102–3, 298
strategic leadership successes
of, 228–29
tactical leadership record of, 338
unit cohesion and, 100
weapons handling and, 333–34
Cuito Cuanavale campaign (Angola,
1987-88), 92, 94–102, 336

culture's role in warfare
  contested and contradictory elements
      of culture and, 359
  cultural adaptation and, 347–48, 351,
      355–57, 365–66
  definitions of culture and,
      355–56, 360
  dominant cultures *versus* subcultures
      and, 359–60, 363
  interpersonal behavior within
      hierarchies and, 361–62, 380–81
  militaries' organizational cultures
      and, 352, 354
  Mongols and, 347–48, 353–54
  national cultures and, 352, 354
  nineteenth-century European wars
      and, 348–50
  organization of military forces
      and, 344–45
  Roman Empire and, 353–54
  Sparta and, 346–47
  stereotypes and, 361
  technology and, 344–45,
      347–48, 350–51
Cunene (Angola), 92, 96, 98
Czechoslovakia, 47, 62

Da'ish
  air strikes against, 500, 513, 517
  "blitzkrieg" (2014) by, 494–97, 504
  combined arms operations and, 499
  defensive engagements by, 499–501
  foreign fighters in, 505–6, 509
  former Iraqi staff officers among
      leaders of, 31, 502–4
  group loyalty and, 506–7
  Hashd ash-Shaabi militias' fight
      against, 478
  Iran and, 494
  Iraq conquests (2013-15) of, 31,
      494–97, 499
  Iraqi civil war (2014-17) and,
      59, 477–78

Iraqi military failures against, 30,
      168–69, 171–72, 494–96, 501,
      504, 517
Iraq's disaffected Sunni population
      and, 494, 498
military failures of, 497, 499
military morale among, 36, 41,
      501–2, 506
personal courage and, 506
politicization of Iraqi military and,
      168–69, 226, 229, 495, 497
psychological warfare and,
      497–99, 507–8
Al Qa'ida and, 492, 495, 504
reconnaissance successes of, 500
record of strategic successes of,
      495–509
recruitment strategies of, 508–9
size of, 494, 502–5, 508
suicide bombings and,
      498–501, 506
Syria conquests (2012-15) of, 31, 477,
      494–95, 497, 500–501
Syrian civil war (2012-) and, 59,
      492, 503
unorthodox hierarchy of, 504–5, 508
US-led international campaign
      (2014-2017) against, 36, 493–
      94, 498–500, 504, 512–13, 517
Damascus (Syria), 486–87, 489, 494
Danang (Vietnam), 198–99, 204
Dao, Le Minh, 200, 203
Dat, Le Duc, 188, 193
Dayan, Moshe, 251
Dayr Ayub (Israel), 459
Dayr az-Zawr (Syria), 494, 497
DeAtkine, Norvell, 506–7
Deby, Idris, 286
Deganyahs (Israel), 249, 251–52, 255
DeVore, Marc, 489–90
Dhofar Rebellion (Oman,1962-76),
      59, 478
Diem, Ngo Dinh, 175–77

military information management
in, 223–24
morale issues among Argentine forces
in, 214–15, 226
naval forces' role in, 207–8, 212,
221, 223–25
politicization of Argentine military
and, 174, 205, 217–18, 226, 228
strategic leadership among Argentine
forces in, 217–20, 227
tactical leadership among Argentine
forces in, 215–17
unit cohesion in, 215
weapons handling problems among
Argentine forces in, 215
Fallujah (Iraq), 36, 41, 478, 493, 497
Faya-Largeau (Chad)
Chadian-Libyan War (1986-87), 289,
294, 299, 305
Libyan intervention (1978) and, 277
Libyan intervention (1979)
and, 277–78
Libyan intervention in Chad (1980-
81) and, 279–80
Libya's intervention in Chad (1983-
86) and, 282–83
Faysal II (king of Iraq), 110
Force Armée Nationale
Tchadien (FANT)
Chadian-Libyan War (1986-87) and,
287–93, 297, 300–302, 306
Libya's intervention in Chad
(1983-86), 282–84
military equipment issues and, 285
military logistics issues and, 286
Forces Armée du Nord (FAN, Chad),
279–81, 299, 306
Forczyk, Robert, 50
France
Chad aided by, 277, 281, 283,
285–87, 289, 293, 297, 299,
306, 336
Falklands War (1982) and, 225

military training in Syria and,
61, 246
Napoleonic Wars and, 349–50
Persian Gulf War and, 162
Sinai-Suez War (1956) and, 39
Franks, Fred, 163
Frederick the Great (emperor of
Prussia), 349
Freud, Sigmund, 355
Friedman, Jeffrey, 484–85
Front for the Liberation of the Enclave of
Cabinda (FLEC), 84, 86
Futah ar-Rawi, Iyad, 149, 152

Galal, Ahmed, 418
Galilee
Israeli War of Independence (1948)
and, 249, 251–53, 255
Six-Day War and, 10, 12, 15
Gamaat Islami insurgency (Egypt), 478
al-Gamasy, 'Abd al-Ghani, 131–33, 141
Gaza, 4, 335
Gazelle helicopters (Syria), 260,
266, 270
Geertz, Clifford, 364
Gellner, Ernest, 372, 390
Gemayel, Bashir, 257
General Belgrano (Argentine cruiser), 207
Genghis Khan, 348
Georgia, 51
Germany
Battle of Kursk (1943) and, 116
comissarism in Nazi Germany and,
115, 125
World War I and, 344
World War II and, 51–54, 115–16,
124–25, 242, 347
al-Ghanimi, Uthman, 170
Giai, Vu Van, 187, 189–91, 193
Gibbs, H.A.R., 387
Global Leadership and Organizational
Behavior Effectiveness (GLOBE)
study, 408, 410–12

Glubb, John Bagot
    Arab Legion training and, 453–54,
        463, 465–66
    ceasefire to Israeli War of
        Independence and, 462
    concerns regarding casualties in
        Israeli War of Independence
        and, 454
    Jerusalem battles and, 456–58
    Latrun battles (1948) and, 459–61
    on personal courage in Arab
        culture, 389
Golan
    Israeli invasion of Lebanon (1982)
        and, 257–58, 267
    Israeli War of Independence (1948)
        and, 252
    map of, 14
    October War (1973) and, 37, 40, 72–
        74, 339, 440
    Six-Day War and, 14–17, 32, 41
Goose Green (Falklands Islands), 210–
    12, 215, 217–19, 223
Göring, Hermann, 125
Gorou, Ahmed, 286, 289, 292
Goukouni Oueddei
    Chadian-Libyan War (1986-87) and,
        287–88, 294, 300
    Government d'Union Nationale de
        Transition (GUNT) and, 277
    Habré and, 276
    Libya intervention in Chad (1978)
        and, 276
    Libya intervention in Chad (1979)
        and, 277–78
    Libya's intervention in Chad (1980-
        81) and, 279–81
    Libya's intervention in Chad (1983-
        86) and, 281–83
    Qadhafi and, 276, 279, 281, 288
    Tibesti region controlled (1978) by, 276
    Toubou ethnic group and, 276–77
    Volcan Army and, 277

Government d'Union Nationale de
    Transition (GUNT, Chad)
    Chadian-Libyan War (1986-87) and,
        286–89, 294, 296, 301–3, 512
    establishment (1979) of, 277
    Libyan intervention in Chad
        (1983-86), 282–84
    Libya's intervention in Chad (1980-
        81) and, 279–81
Graham, Douglas, 430
Great Britain
    Afghanistan conflict (1980s)
        and, 54–55
    air force in, 208, 211–13,
        217–18, 221–22
    Egyptian military training and, 58,
        61–62, 246, 463
    Falklands War (1982) and, 206–25
    Israeli War of Independence (1948)
        and, 454, 457, 460–64
    Jordan military training and, 29
    military training in Iraq and, 58,
        118, 447–49, 463
    Napoleonic Wars and, 349–51
    naval forces in, 207–8, 212,
        221, 223–24
    Persian Gulf War (1991) and,
        162, 165
    Sinai-Suez War (1956) and, 39
    World War I and, 351
    World War II and, 242
Gregg, Gary, 358, 360, 362–63, 366–67,
    377–79, 389, 418–19, 424–25,
    505, 520
Griffith, Ronald, 163
Gulf War. See Persian Gulf War
Gulick, John, 390

Habré, Hissène
    Chadian-Libyan War (1986-87) and,
        287–90, 293–94, 297, 305
    declaration of presidency (1982)
        of, 282

Hopkins, Nicholas, 374, 420, 422
Hopwood, Derek, 425, 429–30
Horowitz, Daniel, 441
Hourani, Albert, 391
Houthi ethnic group (Yemen), 32, 36, 38, 59, 477, 507
Hue (Vietnam), 191, 198, 201
Hung, Le Van, 188–90, 193, 203
Hurewitz, J.C., 109
Husayn, Saddam. *See* Saddam Husayn
Husayn 'Ali, Salim, 149
Hussein (king of Jordan), 3, 7, 466, 468
Hussein, Mahmud, 47

Ibn Khaldun, 488
Ibrahim, Saad Eddin, 374, 420, 422
ijtihad (independent reasoning), 491
Indonesia, 364
Inkeles, Alex, 242
Iran. *See also* Iran-Iraq War
  air force in, 74
  comissarism in, 113, 126–27
  Da'ish and, 494
  Green Revolt (2009) in, 520
  Hizballah and, 478–79, 481, 483, 488–90
  Islamic fundamentalism and, 365
  Persian ethnic majority in, 489
  revolution (1979) in, 127
  Shi'ism as dominant sect in, 489
  Syrian Civil War (2012-) and, 485–86
Iran-Iraq War (1980-88)
  air forces' role in, 74, 144–45, 151, 202
  Al-Faw Peninsula fighting (1986) in, 151–52
  Arab states' aid to Iraq during, 149
  arms embargo on Iran and, 473
  cease-fire (1988) in, 157
  chemical weapons used by Iraq during, 149, 154, 172, 472
  Egypt and, 549n12
  Iranian military and, 126–27, 489

Iran's oil industry targeted in, 151
Iraqi unit cohesion problems in, 32, 400
Iraq's combat engineering successes in, 335
Iraq's military failures (1980-1986) in, 144–47, 150, 171–72, 333–34, 441, 444–45, 496, 512
Iraq's military logistics record and, 34, 333–34, 337
Iraq's military successes (1986-88) in, 31, 144–47, 150–54, 170, 172, 229, 245, 445, 447, 449, 452, 472–75, 503, 507, 512
  maps from, 146, 148, 155
  Soviet military doctrine and, 59
  US aid to Iraq during, 149, 154, 157, 170, 172, 473
Iraq. *See also* Iran-Iraq War
  air defenses in, 159
  air force in, 3, 74–75, 144–45, 150–51, 159, 202, 333, 401, 441
  Al Qa'ida in, 477, 492, 495, 503–4
  Arab Spring (2011) and, 520
  Ba'th Party in, 122, 144
  British military training and doctrine in, 58, 118, 447–49, 463
  campaigns against Iranian-backed militias (2000s) in, 165
  civil war (2005-2009) in, 59, 503–4
  civil war (2014-17) in, 59
  combat engineering record in, 335
  comissarism in, 112–13, 144, 167–68
  conformity emphasized in village life of, 422
  coups (1950s and 1960s) in, 110, 115
  courage among the soldiers in, 401
  Da'ish's conquests in, 30, 168–69, 171–72, 494–96, 501, 504, 517
  economic development levels in, 235, 238, 309–10, 332
  educational system in, 390, 392, 429, 432, 434

al-Masri, Abu Jandal, 506
Matthews, Roderic, 432–33, 435
McDonald, David, 586n3
Melikian, Levon, 371, 373, 378,
    382–83, 386
Mello, Alex, 497, 500, 504
Menendez, Mario
    Battle for Port Stanley and,
        211–13, 218–20
    command and control scheme
        of, 218–19
    East Falklands command of, 208,
        210–11, 223
    logistical problems and, 225
    politicization of Argentina military
        and, 217–18
    strategic leadership problems of, 228
Mernissi, Fatima, 374
Middlebrook, Martin, 221
military training in the Arab world
    Arab culture and, 439, 449–50
    Arab military effectiveness and,
        37–40, 43, 72, 245–46,
        440–51, 518
    atomization of knowledge and
        overspecialization in, 441–42
    conformity and, 445–49, 473–74
    deference to authority and, 442–44
    rote memorization and, 439–40,
        442–44, 473
Miller, Gerald, 423–26
Millett, Allen, 80, 82, 320
Mishmar HaYarden (Israel),
    252–55, 273
Mitchell, Joshua, 373, 436–37
Mitla Pass (Egypt), 8–9
Mitterrand, Francois, 283, 285, 287
Model, Walter, 229
Mongols, 347–48, 353–54
Morocco
    Arab Spring (2011) and, 520
    educational system in, 419, 423–27
    internal security concerns in, 118

Islam and, 364, 576n35
    societal academic performance in,
        417, 431
Mosul (Iraq)
    Da'ish control of, 168, 494, 496,
        500–501
    Da'ish surrender of, 36
    Iraqi military performance against
        Da'ish at, 170, 172, 339, 496
Mount Harriet (Falklands Islands),
    211–12, 215–16
Moynihan, Daniel Patrick, 520
Mubarak, Husni, 63, 67, 71
Mujahidin (Afghan fighting force),
    50–51, 54–55
Muslim Brotherhood (Syria), 478

Naguib, Mohamed, 122
Najaf (Iraq), 148
Najarian, Pergrouhi, 376
Najdi tribes (Saudi Arabia), 113
Namibia, 91–92
Napoleon Bonaparte, 30, 349–50
Narkiss,Uzi, 10
Nasser, 'Abd al-
    anti-Communism of, 62
    comissarism and, 113
    Egyptian educational system and,
        392, 436
    Free Officers' coup (1952) and, 2
    Pan-Arabism and, 276
    professionalization of Egyptian
        military and, 130–31, 142, 169
    Republican Guard created by, 119
    Six-Day War (1967) and, 3, 36
    Soviet military doctrine and, 62
National Front for the Liberation
    of Angola (FNLA), 84,
    86–87, 100
National Union for the Total
    Independence of Angola
    (UNITA), 84, 86–87,
    91–92, 94–96

People's Armed Forces of Liberation of
    Angola (FAPLA)
  counterinsurgency and, 91–92
  Cuban aid to, 84–85
  Cuban coordination with, 86–87, 94–
    95, 98, 100
  Cuito Cuanavale campaign
    (1987-88), 92–96
  South African Air Force and, 99
  unit cohesions problems and, 92, 100
People's Army of Vietnam (PAVN,
    North Vietnamese Army)
  Cambodia campaign (1970)
    and, 180–81
  Chinese and Soviet aid to, 185, 194
  Laos campaign (1971) and, 183–85
  South Vietnam's fall (1975) and,
    194–200, 204
    Easter Offensive (1972)
      and, 187–94
Persian Gulf War (1990-91)
  air forces and, 66, 75, 333, 441
  Arab military effectiveness and, 19,
    28, 159–65, 172
  Egypt and, 19, 59, 63–71, 366, 517
  Iraqi desertions during, 41, 66–67
  Iraqi military and, 28, 31, 36, 41, 59,
    65–67, 75, 159–64, 170, 172,
    300, 333, 366, 401, 440–41,
    474, 476, 516, 529n4, 550n21
  Iraq's Scud missile attacks and, 159
  Joint Forces Command-North (JFC-
    N) and, 64–65, 67
  Kuwaiti Theater of Operations and,
    159–61, 529n4, 550n21
  maps from, 64, 160
  morale factors and, 36, 41
  Soviet military doctrine and, 59, 74–75
  Syria and, 65
  tank warfare and, 161
  United States and, 28, 65–67, 75,
    159–65, 333

weapons handling problems as factor
  in, 28–29
Pfaff, Tony, 410, 412
Phalange militia (Lebanon), 478
phalanx effectiveness, 346–47
Phouc Long (Vietnam), 197–98
Phu, Pham Van, 197–99
Pleiku (Vietnam), 197, 199
Polisario insurgency (Western
  Sahara), 478
politicization of militaries
  Arab military effectiveness and, 39,
    41, 107–23, 127–31, 168–69,
    171–73, 226–27, 229–30, 339,
    343, 395, 403–5, 413, 450, 495,
    510, 512, 514
  Argentina and, 174, 205, 217–18,
    226, 228, 395
  centralization of authority and,
    114, 122
  China and, 321
  comissarism and, 108, 110, 112–16,
    120, 122–23, 125–27, 129–
    30, 144, 175, 177, 228, 321,
    510, 544n14
  corruption and, 110, 176–77
  coups and, 109–10, 121
  definition of politicization and, 107
  Egypt and, 113, 115, 119, 122, 130–
    31, 168, 226–27, 229
  falsification of information as problem
    with, 116, 172
  Iran and, 113, 126–27
  Iraq and, 112–13, 115, 121–23, 167–
    68, 226–27, 229, 495, 497, 503
  Jordan and, 113
  in Latin America, 125–26
  Libya and, 112, 115, 284
  loyalty valued over competence in,
    111, 114–15, 121, 177, 229
  morale impacted by, 111, 116, 121,
    128, 172

South Africa. *See also* South African
    Defense Force (SADF)
  air force in, 99
  Angola conflict (1975-88) and, 77–78,
    85–87, 91–92, 94–100, 102,
    298, 336
  Namibia occupied by, 91–92
  Zulu warriors in, 233
South African Defense Force (SADF)
  Castro's "Western Offensive" and, 96
  Cuban air forces' engagement in
    Angola and, 99
  Cuban military's successes
    against, 97–98
  Cuito Cuanavale campaign (1987-88)
    and, 94–96, 336
  Israeli military doctrine and, 86, 101
  Namibia conflict and, 91–92
  Operation SAVANNAH (invasion of
    Angola) and, 85
  Tumpo bridgehead and, 95
  UNITA's coordination with,
    86–87, 92
South Korea. *See* Republic of Korea
South Vietnam
  Catholic minority population's
    disproportionate power in, 175
  combat engineering record of, 336
  comissarism in, 175, 177, 395
  corruption in, 176–77
  coup against Diem (1963) in, 176
  economic development levels
    in, 331–32
  fall (1975) of, 194–200, 204
  internal security concerns in, 176–77
  literacy rates in, 332
  military logistics record of,
    333–34, 336–37
  palace guardism in, 177, 203
  politicization of the military in, 175–
    76, 178, 182–84, 193, 201, 203,
    226, 228
  praetorianism in, 176–77

US efforts to combat corruption in,
    177, 182, 186
  US training of military forces
    in, 179–80
  "Vietnamization" policy and,
    178–80, 194
South Vietnamese Air Force (VNAF),
    202, 338
South West African People's
    Organisation (SWAPO), 91–92
Soviet military doctrine
  Afghanistan conflict (1980s) and,
    50–51, 54–55
  air forces and, 50, 55, 62, 74–75
  Angola conflict and, 99
  Arab military effectiveness and, 19–
    20, 41, 47–48, 56–63, 71–76,
    339, 343, 450, 518
  battlefield air interdiction (BAI)
    and, 55
  close-air support (CAS) and, 55, 99
  combined arms operations
    emphasized in, 54, 84, 103
  command and control structure
    and, 48–52
  Cuba and, 21, 77, 84, 99,
    102–3, 298
  Egypt, 58–59, 61–63, 71–73,
    102–3, 518
  fast operational tempo (OPTEMPO)
    emphasized in, 53
  ground-controlled intercept (GCI)
    and, 50, 62, 74–75, 99, 430–31
  improvisation emphasized in,
    49–51, 103
  intelligence gathering and, 52–53
  Iran-Iraq War (1980s) and, 59
  Iraq and, 58–59, 74–75, 444
  Israeli invasion of Lebanon (1982)
    and, 60
  Israeli War of Independence (1948)
    and, 59
  logistics and, 55–56

North Korea and, 21, 77–78, 81, 83–
84, 102–3, 228–29
October War (1973) and, 58–61,
63, 71–74
offensive initiative emphasized in,
52–53, 84
operational level and, 48, 103
Persian Gulf War (1990-91) and,
59, 74–75
schwerpunkt (decisive point of the
front), 53–54
Sinai-Suez Conflict (1956) and, 58–59
Six-Day War (1967) and, 59–62
Somali military and, 88–90
Syria and, 14, 34, 60–62, 72–74,
102–3, 261, 267, 518
training systems and, 49
World War II and, 50–55, 102–3, 124
Yemen and, 59–60
Soviet Union
Central Asian soldiers in, 238–39
comissarism and, 108, 115, 117
Stalin's purges of military leaders in,
115, 123–24
Sparta, 346–47
Spurr, Russell, 309
Stähli, Armin, 489–90
Stalin, Joseph
Battle of the Kursk (1943) and, 116
depoliticization of Soviet military
during World War II by, 117
Husayn's admiration of, 143–44
Korean War and, 228
purges of military leaders (1930s) by,
115, 123–24
Stewart, Nora Kinzer, 224
Sudan, 110, 281, 407, 419
Suez Canal. *See also* Sinai-Suez
Conflict (1956)
maps of campaigns at, 135, 137, 139
October War (1973) and, 131–35,
137–41, 229, 335
Six-Day War and, 8–9

Sultan Yaqub (Lebanon), 266
Sunnism, doctrine of, 489
Sun Tzu, 516
Al Suofi, Ahmed, 381
Sweden, 234–35, 238, 331, 351
Syria
air defenses of, 258, 261–63, 268
air force in, 3, 7, 40, 61, 113, 249,
253, 260, 262–63, 266–69, 273,
333, 398, 401, 441
Alawi sect in, 113, 121, 485, 492
Arab Spring uprising (2011) and, 121,
492, 520
Ba'th Party in, 122–23
Black September campaign (1970-71)
and, 60
civil war (2012-) in, 59–60, 75–76,
366, 477, 485–87, 492, 503
combined arms operations in military
of, 254–55
comissarism and, 113
commando units of, 258–61, 264,
266, 268–73, 469–72, 475,
487, 507
corruption in the military of, 34
coups (1950s and 1960s) in, 110, 115
economic development levels in, 235,
247–48, 273–74, 331–32, 334
educational system in, 425, 429–30,
433, 436
French military training in, 61, 246
increasing professionalization of army
(1970s) in, 119
internal security concerns in, 118
Israeli invasion of Lebanon (1982)
and, 29–30, 32–33, 40–41, 60,
247, 256–73, 333–34, 336, 441,
452, 469–72, 475–76, 487, 507
Israeli War of Independence (1948)
and, 34, 39, 60, 247–55, 272–73,
334, 336, 400
Lebanon invasion (1976) by, 34,
257, 476